SOURCES OF
THE AMERICAN
SOCIAL TRADITION

SOURCES OF THE AMERICAN SOCIAL TRADITION

EDITED BY

David J. Rothman

&

Sheila M. Rothman

Basic Books, Inc., Publishers New York

Permission to reprint the lyrics from the following song is gratefully acknowledged.

"It Had To Be You" by Isham Jones and Gus Kahn. © 1924 Jerome H. Remick & Company. Copyright renewed. All Rights Reserved. Used by permission of Warner Bros. Music.

Library of Congress Cataloging in Publication Data

Rothman, David J   comp.
  Sources of the American social tradition,

  Bibliography: p.
  1.   United States—Social conditions—Addresses,
essays, lectures.   I.   Rothman, Sheila M., joint comp.
II.   Title.
HN57.R574   309.1'73   74-78474
ISBN 0-465-08083-9

To Matthew
to help him understand that history
is more than the story of great persons

CONTENTS

The Making of Modern America, 1865–1920

Our Times, 1920 to the Present

Illustrations

PREFACE

OVER THE PAST several years, teaching and research in American history have undergone a fundamental change. To an unprecedented degree, the discipline has moved from a primary focus on political, diplomatic, and military history to a broader interest in social history. Heretofore, elections, treaties and wars, politicians, ambassadors, and generals tended to dominate the writing and teaching of American history. Now such concerns as social order, social mobility, and ethnicity, the roles of anonymous Americans, women, and immigrants are of major interest. In a sense, the scene has shifted from Washington and the state capitals to the local communities, from legislative halls to families and factories. From all indications, this change is not a passing fancy. Social history has already revised our understanding of the past in such novel and important ways that it is not likely again to be neglected.

It is the aim of this book to bring before students in American history the issues, the questions and answers, that are at the heart of this new perspective. That the book takes the form of a collection of sources reflects several important considerations.

We are well aware of the fact that "documents" have a rather low reputation as teaching tools in history classrooms. But that reputation, we are convinced, is undeserved. Or to put this another way, it reflects the fact that in the past "documents" almost always were political or diplomatic documents. Hence, as a rule, students had already read in texts or in other books about the same document that they then saw in a collection. The Fourteen Points, for example, of Woodrow Wilson were already familiar to them; to read the document itself served only as the occasion to review or to memorize them. Moreover, these types of documents are generally dry and static. To read the legislation we know as the Missouri Compromise tells little about why and how the Compromise was enacted.

Documents in American social history are of a very different quality. First, they are often intrinsically interesting, supplying vivid examples of how persons lived, say, on the frontier, or how they adjusted to life in new immigrant ghettos. Second, and even more important, they enable the students to form ideas of their own, to analyze by themselves the process of change over time. In essence, the sources make the students active, not passive, inviting them to react to materials, not to memorize them.

To these ends, the sources in this book do not approach American history in scattered, hit-or-miss fashion. Rather, we have organized the materials around institutions and around themes that are central to the American experience. The Introduction that follows will present in more detail the intellectual bases for this kind of focus. It suffices to note here that in each chapter, five or six selections will explore in detail the same subject. In this way, students will have the opportunity to put the pieces of the story together, to reach a synthesis of their own. Our hope is that these materials will move the student outward, into the field of American history—that they will open up, not close off, inquiry. Just as the law school case book uses several cases to create an awareness of a general theme, so each of these chapters uses several documents to create an awareness of the crucial elements in the development of American society. We have not attempted to be "complete" in our coverage. We assume that a text or related readings will be used alongside this book. But we have, to facilitate the use of this volume, arranged the materials in chronological fashion; each of the chapters here should fit neatly into the normal sequence of discussion in the American history survey course or in the American social history course. For purposes of clarity and readability, we have modernized spelling and punctuation and have omitted ellipses when we made excerpts from lengthy documents. At no point have we altered the meaning of the original material; our goal throughout has been to make these documents accessible and interesting to the student. At the same time, we have selected for analysis the institution, be it the family or the church or the factory or the department store, at a moment in time when it illuminates a broader trend in American society, or it is itself of such crucial significance as to warrant close attention.

In our own use of these sources in classrooms here and abroad, we have found that they excite and stimulate students. Either in classroom discussions or in smaller section meetings, the sources have encouraged and enabled students to reach for interesting and important themes in the story of America's past. We trust that other teachers will find these selections as useful as we have.

SHEILA M. ROTHMAN
DAVID J. ROTHMAN

New York City

INTRODUCTION

MOST OF US share an instinctive curiosity about the ways that Americans before us lived their lives. We wonder how our predecessors organized their households, how they dressed and ate, how they conducted their friendships, courtships, and marriages, how they reared and educated their children, how they amused themselves, and how they earned their livings. What was it really like for frontier settlers to inhabit the wilderness, for immigrants to walk paved streets in strange cities? What was it like to be an ordinary American at different times in our past? These are simple questions, but they exert a powerful appeal to our imagination.

Despite the inherently interesting character of these inquiries, historians have been notably reluctant to pursue them. Until very recently, the craft of history has focused almost exclusively on great events and exceptional personalities. Presidential elections, diplomatic maneuvers, military contests, Congressional politics—these subjects have dominated, almost monopolized, the writing and teaching of history. This choice is not difficult to understand. History is the story of change, the account of how a society moves from one point in its development to another. In order to pursue this theme, historians have traditionally focused on the top, on the obviously important decision makers, and then looked down to the rest of society for implications of their actions. As a result, the story of the American Revolution becomes essentially a chronicle of the activities and ideas of political elites here and in England; the coming of the Civil War is understood first and foremost in terms of national party structure and leadership. American history becomes the story of George Washington and John Adams, Abraham Lincoln and Stephan Douglas. The lives of ordinary Americans, by comparison, seem unimportant and irrelevant.

Since the most scholarly and professional historians did not bother to satisfy our curiosity about anonymous Americans, the amateurs did. Eager to bring this important information to light, these amateur historians all too often were content to present a haphazard collection of quaint stories. This is how colonial women dressed, this is how their children played, this is what they ate. They reported on charming old customs and offered a string of curiosities. In many ways, our forefathers became our "most unforgettable characters." But this kind of approach, unfortunately, gave us little understanding of why earlier styles of life differed so dramatically from our own. Even more important, it made no effort to link its catalogue of customs to the problem of historical change. In these pages, too, ordinary Americans seemed irrelevant to the major events in our past.

Over the past several years, a growing number of historians have attempted to break out of this mold, to inform us about the bottom as well as the top layers of society and, at the same time, to show us how crucial their contributions have been to historical change. The goals of this new social history are twofold. First, it insists that to understand change one must look beyond the role of the elite, beyond the activities of leaders in business and politics. No shift, for example, was more important to America's history than the change from an agrarian to an industrial economy, from a nation of small farms to one of large factories. It will not do, insist social historians, to analyze this phenomenon exclusively in terms of the robber barons or entrepreneurs who organized the first factories, railroads, and oil combines. Rather, one must look also to the workers who operated the machines or extracted the mineral resources from the ground. Why were they willing to take on these tasks? Where did they come from—native farms or European villages? How did they adjust to the new rhythm of industrial work? How did they struggle with their lot? Did their struggles advance or retard industrial progress? Only by answering these questions can the full story of change be mapped and understood.

Second, social history is determined to expand its focus to encompass all levels of society. Traditional studies of political or economic elites invariably isolated their materials—the realm of politics seems to have little to do with the realm of business. In a sense, these historians constructed a "political man," one who held office or bargained for power in the caucus rooms as if politics were all he knew and all he was—as if the politician was not a member of an ethnic group, an economic class, or a church. The goal of social history is to bring these several considerations together, to integrate rather than to particularize.

To this end, social history focuses on the institutions of society, the organizations that crucially influence and shape individual behavior, that to a large degree determine the way people act and think. Institutions in this sense are the organizations that take individual pieces and shape them into a common mold. Whether it be the school, the family, the church, or the factory, the institution trains its members in common styles of behavior. Social history is not as concerned with the psychological or biological variations among people as it is with the ways that they learn to act together. If biography is mainly interested in the special attributes and contributions of one person, social history is concerned with the special qualities and attributes of the group. The group can be those in school together, those on the assembly line together, or those sitting around the dining-room table together. From this perspective, society is made up of a collection of institutions; the task of social history is to analyze how each of them influences individual behavior and how they operate together to give a unity to people's lives and experiences.

Think for a moment of the impact of institutions on our own lives; it immediately becomes apparent how important institutions must have been to the lives of our predecessors. Think of how much of our ordinary behavior reflects lessons we have learned within the family. Or think of the school, not its instruction in reading or writing, but its transmission of a code of behavior, the rules that will guide us in public conduct. The church, too, is an institution of major importance— it carefully and insistently defines acceptable and unacceptable styles of action. The factory is no less an institution; it instructs workers and managers alike in right and wrong behavior, establishing not only work habits but life habits as well. Hence, if one is to understand the way that people behaved in the past, the best starting point is to examine the institutions that dominated their lives.

Once social history accepts institutions as its cast of characters, many important issues immediately present themselves. In any given era, which institutions exerted the most crucial influences? The hierarchy visible today would offer little guide to the past. We might not list the church as one of the most important institutions now, but surely we could not omit it from an analysis of seventeenth-century society. Once we have a sense of the hierarchy of institutions for a period in our past, we can alert ourselves to the emergence of new institutions, and try to understand the causes and implications of such changes. When did the school begin to rival the family in importance? What difference did it make to the family that the factory became the central workplace, giving out its own special messages? This focus on institutions permits us to analyze the degree of agreement and disagreement among the institutions, offering us a broad view of the entire society.

In fact, this institutional focus allows us to understand better the problems of social order and disorder in American society. A tight bond among citizens is forged when they all follow the rules set down and established for them by institutions. If everyone plays the game by the same rules, the stability of the society is promoted. Common expectations and common practices become preeminent. Hence, an institutional focus in social history allows us to observe the ways by which American society has attempted to achieve consensus among its members. This approach also illuminates the sources of discontent and disorder; conflict is no less central to the story of American history than is consensus. When different institutions transmit fundamentally opposing messages, we have located a source of tension that can reveal both the particular points of conflict and the more general issue of social cohesion. When a religious institution tells its members to give alms to the poor and tries to moderate the thrust for profits by instilling a sense of obligation to others, and at the same time marketplace institutions urge people to be thrifty in order to invest and to make as handsome a profit as possible, we have a dynamic that surely will be relevant to political factionalism, economic conflict, and religious dissension. This example comes right out of early Massachusetts history, as we shall see when we read the will of a Puritan merchant, Robert Keayne.

Ultimately, social history is concerned with such things as the nature of courtship patterns, education, and church going, not simply because they are intrinsically interesting, but because of the light they shed on the larger questions of social order and social change. The details are both revelatory and significant. The selections that follow reflect this judgment. The documents are interesting in themselves, and therefore one's curiosity about life on the frontier or life in a factory will be satisfied. But the larger implications of these bits of information should emerge as well. The materials are organized by institutions, and they are designed to illuminate the workings of the major institutions that have shaped American society. From the Puritan church in the colonial period, to the factory and plantation in the antebellum period, to the department store and immigrant ghetto in the late nineteenth century, to the family in the 1920s, and to the relief office in the 1930s, down to the black ghetto and counterculture commune of our own day, the history of America's institutions may inspire an ongoing fascination with the nature and substance of American social history.

American Colonial Society, 1607–1800

THE PROPER PLANTATION

THE PURITAN CHURCH

THE COLONIAL FAMILY

THE REVOLUTIONARY CROWD

INTRODUCTION

THE FIRST English settlers in the New World confidently expected to transplant their own particular institutions intact into their new environment. The adventurers in Virginia in 1607 wished to establish trading enterprises resembling those that had succeeded so well in other parts of the world, especially Ireland and India. Puritan newcomers to Massachusetts, while determined to improve on some English practices, also anticipated duplicating many of the political and social arrangements that were typical of England in the seventeenth century. But in fact no simple transfer of institutions took place. Time and again, New World conditions modified European customs. The wilderness did not prove to be hospitable soil for Old World programs.

American social history in the colonial period is in many ways the story of traditional European institutions undergoing change, of surprising and unanticipated results from the most carefully calculated plans. This theme emerges vividly in the experience of the Virginia settlement. The Virginia Company had a very clear idea of how it would profit from New World wealth: the *proper plantation*, a fortified trading post, would enable the company men to skim off the riches of the wilderness. But reality did not follow expectation. An outpost quickly became a colony; a military organization became a complex society. And with that story, American social history properly begins.

The Puritans also carried across the ocean an elaborate design for the new commonwealth, but invariably the New World experience upset their plans. Their goal was nothing less than to show their Anglican brethren the error of their religious ways. But here the *Puritan church* had to confront a series of unexpected challenges. In the end, this church was one of the most important institutions in the community, influencing the behavior of members and nonmembers alike. To understand the nature of public order in Massachusetts, one must analyze the workings of the church. For all its power, this institution was a hybrid whose exact shape and structure came as a surprise to its originators.

Another institution of major significance in ordering seventeenth- and eighteenth-century American communities was the *family*. But again, the organization of the family in the New World differed in many ways from its European counterpart. The family's role in main-

3

taining public order expanded, perhaps because many other institutions existed here in only a rudimentary state. To understand the stability of American colonial society, as well as the ways by which New World conditions altered European institutions, the changes in family organization demand close scrutiny.

Finally, the structure of American society emerges vividly in the crisis of the Revolution. This was a time of testing, a period when traditional lines of authority were severed and new ones were established. No institution presented a more dramatic challenge to everyday political life than the *Revolutionary crowd*. The ways it functioned and the ways citizens understood its role reveal just how different American society was from European society by the outbreak of the Revolution.

Chapter I

The Proper Plantation

THE INITIAL SETTLEMENT of the English at Jamestown, Virginia, in 1607, was anything but a glorious adventure. The first encounter with the New World was brutal and debilitating; the mortality rate among the arrivals was high, and those who survived lived dangerously close to savagery. The English were unprepared for what they found and were hard put to deal with it. Their intention had been to reap an easy and quick profit from the resources of the New World. They planned to mine the wealth of America, not to establish a permanent rural society. But their grandoise expectations were soon disappointed. As they tried to adjust they moved, unthinkingly but steadily, to a new design. By 1624, after incredible hardships and disappointments, and to many people's genuine surprise, there was actually an ongoing agricultural settlement in Virginia.

The organizing spirit of the Jamestown enterprise was the Virginia Company, a joint-stock company chartered by the Crown with exclusive rights to the land and minerals of the territory. The capital for the venture came from selling shares to the public; the Crown, while encouraging the enterprise, was unwilling to fund it. Instead, Englishmen eager to accumulate a profit, anxious to see their flag fly over New World territory, or determined to spread the gospel of Christ to the heathens in foreign parts bought the company shares. Here was an enterprise that would bring wealth to its investors, glory to England, and Christianity to the Indians.

The Virginia Company set out to accomplish these goals by establishing a *proper plantation*, that is, a fortified trading post. All comers to Virginia were employees of the Virginia Company and were obliged to labor in its behalf in return for a share of the profits. From this trading post the company workers were to venture forth into the wilderness and gather in the riches of the new land. Remembering how the Spanish explorers had first discovered temples of gold in Mexico and Peru and then enslaved a well-organized band of natives to work the mines, the company hoped to repeat the experience and reap similar rewards. The natives in Virginia would show them to the gold and, where necessary, dig it up.

In the spirit of this plan, the Englishmen decided to make their base at Jamestown. It was a swampy area, with land hardly fit for cultivation. But it was well situated on a river, and therefore easy to defend and ideal for making trading trips into the interior. Obviously, no member of the Virginia Company in 1607 intended to transplant English society here. On the contrary, this was to be a quasi-military adventure. Living on the edge of the New World, they would exploit it.

Unhappily for the company, there were no temples of gold in Virginia, nor any tractable Indian tribes ready to make up labor gangs. And there was no obvious commodity that could be loaded onto ships and sold profitably in England. As a result, the company found it impossible to reap a return on its investment. Moreover, having anticipated immediate wealth and regular commerce between Jamestown and London, the company had made few preparations for self-sustaining agricultural activities. Soon the band at Jamestown was facing the most elementary problems of survival. In 1609, when the company treasury in London was low and supply boats were late in coming, the Virginia adventurers suffered starvation, to the point where instances of cannibalism occurred. Clearly the organization at Jamestown was floundering badly.

Under the pressure of these circumstances, the company changed tactics. Recognizing that the only thing of value the company owned in the New World was the land itself, it began urging English settlers to emigrate. In 1618, for the first time, the company tried to attract families, not adventurers, to the colony. To this end they held out the promise of land ownership, a comparatively rare condition among lower-class Englishmen. Their hope, in return, was to make a profit from the land taxes. A kind of company store, which would sell provisions to the settlers, would also prosper. In this way the company transformed Virginia from a trading post into a colony. Its goal changed from exploitation to settlement. In one sense, the company did succeed; settlers came and the colony started to grow. But the company could not make its profit. Taxes had to be kept very low or else Englishmen could not make the trip to the New World. As subsistence farmers began to raise their own commodities, they had less and less occasion to buy provisions from the company store. And there was still no crop raised in Virginia that could bring handsome profits in England; although some farmers experimented with growing tobacco, no one as yet was very enthusiastic about the crop. By 1624, the company was bankrupt and the Crown took over control of the colony. But if one enterprise was dead another had been born. The colony in Virginia was well rooted and would continue to expand. American society had begun to develop.

I

The several motives of Englishmen in supporting the colonization of the New World emerge clearly in this pamphlet advertising the glories of Virginia. Since the venture had the approval, but not the financial backing, of the Crown, the joint-stock company had to raise money by selling shares to the general public; in pursuing this goal, it tried to appeal to the widest audience. Thus, this tract plays skillfully upon the patriotism of the English, on their Christianity, and on their desire, as investors, for a good profit. In all, the response to this well-drawn argument was generous. And even when the infant colony suffered setbacks, investors continued to put up funds.

NOVA BRITANNIA, 1609

The country itself is large and great assuredly, though as yet, no exact discovery can be made of all. It is also commendable and hopeful every way, the air and climate most sweet and wholesome, and very agreeable to our nature. It is inhabited with wild and savage people, that live and lie up and down in troupes like herds of deer in a forest; they have no law but nature, their apparel, skins of beasts, but most go naked; the better sort have houses, but poor ones; they have no arts nor sciences, yet they live under superior command such as it is; they are generally very loving and gentle, and do entertain and relieve our people with great kindness; the land yieldeth naturally for the sustenance of man, abundance of fish, infinite store of deer, and hares, with many fruits and roots.

There are valleys and plains streaming with sweet springs, there are hills and mountains making a sensible proffer of hidden treasure, never yet searched; the land is full of minerals, plenty of woods; the soil is strong and sends out naturally fruitful vines running upon trees, and shrubs: it yields also resin, turpentine, pitch and tar, sassafras, mulberry trees and silkworms, many skins and rich furs, many sweet woods, and costly dyes; plenty of sturgeon, timber for shipping. But of this that I have said, if bare nature be so amiable in its naked kind, what may be hope, when art and nature both shall join and strive together, to give best content to man and beast? As now in handling the several parts propounded, I shall show in order as they lie.

For the first how it may tend to advance the kingdom of God, by reducing savage people from their blind superstition to the light of religion, when some object, we seek nothing less than the cause of God, being led on by our own private ends, and secondly how we can warrant

Originally entitled "Nova Britannia, Offering Most Excellent Fruits by Planting in Virginia" (London, 1609). Reprinted in *Tracts and Other Papers Relating Principally to the Colonies in North America*, ed. Peter Force (Washington, D.C., 1836–1844), vol. I, pp. 11–17.

a supplantation of those Indians, or an invasion into their right and possessions.

But we must beware that under this pretense that bitter root of greedy gain be not so settled in our hearts, if it fall not out presently to our expectation, we slink away with discontent, and draw our purses from the charge. What must be our direction then, no more but this: if thou do once approve the work, lay thy hand to it cheerfully, and withdraw it not till task be done, for here lies the poison of all good attempts; when as men without hauling and pulling will not be drawn to performance, for by this others are discouraged, the action lies undone, and the first experience is lost. But are we to look for no gain in the adventures? Yes, undoubtedly, there is assured hope of gain but look it be not chief in your thoughts; God that has said by Solomon— Cast thy bread upon the waters, and after many days thou shalt find it—He will give the blessing. And as for supplanting the savages, we have no such intent: Our intrusion into their possessions shall tend to their great good, and no way to their hurt, unless as unbridled beasts, they procure it to themselves. We purpose to proclaim and make it known to them all, by some public interpretation, that our coming hither is to plant ourselves in their country; yet not to supplant and root them out, but to bring them from their base condition to a far better: First, in regard of God the Creator, and of Jesus Christ their Redeemer, if they will believe in Him. And secondly, in respect of earthly blessing, whereof they have now no comfortable use, but in beastly brutish manner, with promise to defend them against all public and private enemies.

We require nothing at their hands, but a quiet residence to us and ours, that by our own labor and toil, we may work this good unto them and recompense our own adventures, costs, and travels in the end; wherein, they shall be most friendly welcome to join their labors with ours, and shall enjoy equal privileges with us, in whatsoever good success, time or means may bring to pass. To which purpose, we may verily believe that God has reserved in this last age of the world, an infinite number of those lost and scattered sheep, to be won and recovered by our means.

But for my second point propounded, the honor of our King, by enlarging his kingdoms, to prove how this may tend to that, no argument of mine can make it so manifest, as the same is clear in itself.

And upon good warrant I speak it here in private, what by these new discoveries into the Western parts, and our hopeful settling in chief places of the East, with our former known trades in other parts of the world, I do not doubt (by the help of God) but I may live to see the days (if merchants have their due encouragement) that the wisdom, Majesty, and Honor of our King shall be spread and enlarged to the ends of the world, our navigations mightily increased, and his Majesty's customs more than trebled.

And as for the general sort that shall go to be planters, be they never so poor, so they be honest, and take pains, the place will make them rich; all kinds of artificers we must first employ, to make it fit all necessaries, for comfort and use of the colony, and for such as are of no trades (if they be industrious) they shall have there employment enough for there is a world of means to set many thousands awork, partly in such things as I mentioned before, and many other profitable works, for no man must live idle there.

And by this employment, we may happily stop the course of those irregular youths of no religion, that daily run from us to Rome and Rhemes for exhibition, which after a little hammering and training there by Parson and his imps, they become pliable for the impression of any villainy whatsoever, as appears by their positions and practices at home and abroad.

And hereby our mariners shall not lie idle, nor our owners sell their ships for want of freight: you know how many good ships are daily sold, and made away to foreign nations; how many men for want of employment, betake themselves to Tunis, Spain, and Florence, and to serve in courses not warrantable, which would better beseem, our own walls and borders to be spread with such branches, than their native country.

The thing to make this plantation is money, to be raised among the adventurers, [stockholders] wherein the sooner and more deeply men engage themselves, their charge will be the shorter, and their gain the greater.

First you shall understand that his Majesty has granted us an enlargement of our charter, with many ample privileges, wherein we have knights and gentlemen of good place, named for the King's Council of Virginia to govern us. As also every planter and adventurer shall be inserted in the patent by name. This ground being laid, we purpose presently to make supply of men, women, and children (so many as we can) to make the plantation. We call those planters that go in their persons to dwell there and those adventurers that adventure their money and go not in person, and both do make the members of one colony. We do account twelve pound ten shillings to be a single share adventured. Every ordinary man or woman, if they will go and dwell there, and every child above ten years that shall be carried thither to remain, shall be allowed for each of their persons a single share, as if they had adventured twelve pound ten shillings in money. Every extraordinary man, as divines, governors, ministers of state and justice, gentlemen, physicians, and such as be men of worth for special services, are all to go as planters, and to execute their several functions in the colony, and are to be maintained at the common charge, and are to receive their dividend (as others do) at seven years end, and they are to be agreed with all before they go, and to be rated by the council, according to the value of their persons, which shall be set down and registered in a book, that it may always appear what people have gone to the plantation, at what time they went, and how their persons were valued. And likewise, if any that go to be planters will lay down money to the treasurer, it shall be also registered and their shares enlarged accordingly, be it for more or less. All charges of settling and maintaining the plantation and of making supplies shall be born in a joint stock of the adventurers for seven years; we supply from here at our own charge all necessary food and apparel, for fortifying and building of houses in a joint stock, so they are also to return from thence the increase and fruits of their labors, for the use and advancement of the same joint stock, till the end of seven years; at which time we purpose (God willing) to make a division by commissioners appointed, of all the lands granted unto us by his Majesty, to every of the colony, according to each man's several adventure, agreeing with our register book, which we doubt not will be for every share of twelve pound ten shillings, five hundred acres at least. And as for the value and little worth now of those grounds in Virginia, we know that in England within these thirty or forty years, the yearly rent of those grounds (in many places) were not worth five shillings, that now go for forty or more.

II

The anticipation among the company leaders that the 1607 expedition would quickly and easily skim off the wealth of the New World is apparent in this list of those first participating in the venture. The occupations of these men, as well as the absence in the list of women and children, make clear that it was to be a trading company operation, not the start of a colony. The second document— a call for new recruits—composed in 1609, represents something of a shift in company thinking. They were now beginning to think more in terms of self-sufficiency among the adventurers. Still, it is clear that trade and not settlement was uppermost in their minds.

THE VIRGINIA COMPANY LIST OF ADVENTURERS, 1607

The names of them that were the first planters, were these following.*

Counselors
Mr. Edward Maria Wingfield
Capt. Bartholomew Gosnoll
Capt. John Smyth
Capt. John Rat[c]liffe
Capt. John Martin
Capt. George Kendall

Gentlemen
Thomas Sands
John Robinson
Ustis Clovill
Kellam Throgmorton
Nathaniel Powell

Robert Behethland
Jeremy Alicock
Thomas Studley
Richard Crofts
Nicholas Houlgrace
Thomas Webbe
John Waler
William Tankard
Francis Snarsbrough
Edward Brookes
Richard Dixon
John Martin
George Martin
Anthony Gosnold

* With diverse others to the number of 105.
In *Narratives of Early Virginia, 1606–1625,* ed. Lyon Gardiner Tyler (New York, 1907), pp. 125–26.

Thomas Wotton
Thomas Gore
Francis Midwinter

Carpenters
William Laxon
Edward Pising
Tho. Emry
Rob. Small

Anas Todkill
John Capper

Gentlemen
Mr. Robert Hunt, *Preacher*
Mr. George Percie
Anthony Gosnoll
Capt. Gabriell Archer
Robert Ford
William Bruster
Dru Pickhouse
John Brookes

James Read, *Blacksmith*
Jonas Profit, *Sailor*
Tho. Couper, *Barber*
John Herd, *Bricklayer*

William Garret, *Bricklayer*
Edward Brinto, *Mason*
William Love, *Tailor*
Nic. Skot, *Drummer*

Laborers
John Laydon
William Cassen
George Cassen
Tho. Cassen
William Rods
William White
Ould Edward
Henry Tavin
George Golding
John Dods
William Johnson
Will. Unger

Will. Wilkinson, *Surgeon*

Boys
Samuell Collier
Nat. Pecock
James Brumfield
Rich. Mutton

THE CALL FOR NEW RECRUITS, 1609

To render a more particular satisfaction and account of our care, in providing to attend the *Right Honourable the Lord de la Warr*, in this concluded and present supply, men of most use and necessity to the *Foundation* of a *Commonwealth*; and to avoid both the scandal and peril of accepting idle and wicked persons; such as shame or fear compels into this action; and such as are the weeds and rankness of

In *The Genesis of the United States*, ed. Alexander Brown (New York, 1890), vol. 1, pp. 352–53.

this land; who being the surfeit of an able, healthy, and composed body must need be the poison of one so tender, feeble, and as yet unformed: and to divulge and declare to all men what kind of persons, as well for their religion and conversations, as faculties, arts, and trades, we propose to accept of—we have thought it convenient to pronounce that for the first provision, we will receive no man that cannot bring or render some good testimony of his religion to God, and civil manners and behavior to his neighbor, with whom he hath lived; and for the second, we have set down in a table annexed, the proportion and number we will entertain in every necessary art, upon proof and assurance, that every man shall be able to perform that which he doth undertake, whereby such as are requisite to us may have knowledge and preparation, to offer themselves, and we shall be ready to give honest entertainment and content, and to recompense with extraordinary reward every fit and industrious person, respectively *to his pains and quality.*

The table of such as are required to *this plantation.*

4.	*Honest and learned Ministers*	4.	*Brickmakers*
2.	*Surgeons*	2.	*Tile-makers*
2.	*Druggists*	10.	*Fishermen*
10.	*Iron men for the Furnace and Hammer*	6.	*Fowlers*
2.	*Armorers*	4.	*Sturgeon dressers and preservers of Caviar*
2.	*Gun-founders*	2.	*Salt-makers*
6.	*Blacksmiths*	6.	*Coopers*
10.	*Sawyers*	2.	*Collar-makers for draught*
6.	*Carpenters*	2.	*Plowwrights*
6.	*Shipwrights*	4.	*Rope-makers*
6.	*Gardeners*	6.	*Vine-dressers*
4.	*Turners*	2.	*Press-makers*

2.	Joiners	2.	Silk-dressers
2.	Soap-ash men	2.	Pearl Drillers
4.	Pitch Boilers	2.	Bakers
2.	Mineral men	2.	Brewers
2.	Planters of Sugarcane	2.	Colliers

III

The daily routine of life in Virginia under company rule was a military one. The men, as employees of the company, did not own any of their own property. Rather, they were housed, fed, and clothed by the company and were expected to obey its every rule. The company's head in Virginia was an officer in charge of the ranks, enjoying vast powers. Below are the rules governing the residents of the Virginia colony in 1610–1611—and they demonstrate with remarkable clarity how far from a rural society the proper plantation was.

ARTICLES, LAWS, AND ORDERS FOR VIRGINIA, 1611

Whereas his Majesty like himself a most zealous Prince hath in his own realms a principal care of true religion and reverence to God, and hath always strictly commanded his generals and governors, with all his forces wheresoever, to let their ways be like his ends, for the glory of God.

And foreasmuch as no good service can be performed, or were well managed, where military discipline is not observed, and military discipline cannot be kept where the rules or chief parts thereof be not certainly set down and generally known, I do now publish them to all persons in the colony, that they may as well take knowledge of the laws themselves, as of the penalty and punishment, which without partiality shall be inflicted upon the breakers of the same.

First, since we owe our highest and supreme duty, our greatest, and all our allegiance to Him from whom all power and authority is derived, we must alone expect our success from Him who is only the blesser of all good attempts, the King of kings. I do strictly command and charge all captains and officers to have a care that the Almighty God be duly and daily served, and that they call upon their people to hear sermons, as that also they diligently frequent morning and evening prayer themselves by their own example and daily life, and duty herein, encouraging others thereunto, and that such, who shall often and will-

Originally entitled "Articles, Laws, and Orders . . . for the Colony in Virginia" (London, 1611). Reprinted in *Tracts and Other Papers Relating Principally to the Colonies in North America* (Washington, D.C., 1836–1844), vol. 3, pp. 9–13, 56–62.

fully absent themselves, be duly punished according to the martial law in that case provided.

That no man speak impiously or maliciously against the holy and blessed Trinity, God the Son, and God the Holy Ghost, or against the known Articles of the Christian faith, upon pain of death.

No man shall use any traitorous words against his Majesty's person, or royal authority upon pain of death.

No man shall speak any word, or do any act, which may tend to the derision of God's holy word upon pain of death.

Every man and woman duly twice a day upon the first tolling of the bell shall upon the working days repair unto the Church, to hear divine service upon pain of losing his or her day's allowance for the first omission, for the second to be whipped, and for the third to be condemned to the galleys for six months. Likewise no man or woman shall dare to violate or break the Sabbath by any gaming, or private abroad, or at home, but duly sanctify and observe the same, both himself and his family, by preparing themselves at home with private prayer, that they may be the better filled for the public.

No manner of person whatsoever shall dare to detract, slander, calumniate, or utter unseemly and unfitting speeches, either against his Majesty or against the committees, assistants unto the counsel, or against the zealous endeavors, and intentions of the whole body of adventurers for this pious and Christian plantation.

No manner of person whatsoever, contrary to the word of God, shall detract, slander, calumniate, murmur, mutiny, resist, disobey, or neglect the commandments, either of the Lord Governor and Captain General, the Lieutenant General, the Marshall, the counsel or any authorized captain, commander, or public officer, upon pain for the first time so offending to be whipped three several times, and upon his knees to acknowledge his offense, for the second time so offending to be condemned to the galley for three years; and for the third time so offending to be punished with death.

No man shall rifle or despoil, by force or violence, take away anything from any Indian coming to trade, or otherwise, upon pain of death.

There shall no captain, master, mariner, sailor, or anyone else of what quality or condition soever, belonging to any ship or ships, at this time remaining, or which shall hereafter arrive within this our river, bargain, buy, truck, or trade with any one member in this colony, man, woman, or child for any tool or instrument of iron, steel, or what else.

Instructions of the Marshall for the Better Enabling of a Private Soldier to the Executing of His Duty in This Present Colony

June 22, 1611.

It is requisite that he who will enter into this function of a soldier, that he dedicate himself wholly for the planting and establishing of true religion, the honor of his Prince, the safety of his country, and to learn the art which he professes, which is in this place to hold war and the service requisite to the subsisting of a colony. There be many men of mean descent, who have this way attained to great dignity, credit, and honor.

Having thus dedicated himself with a constant resolution, he ought to be diligent, careful, vigilant, and obedient, and principally to have the fear of God and his honor in greatest esteem.

He must be careful to serve God privately and publicly; for all professions are there unto tied, that carry hope with them to prosper, and none more highly than the soldier, for he is ever in the mouth of death, and certainly he that is thus religiously armed, fights more confidently and with greater courage.

He must not set his mind overgreedily upon his belly and continual feeding, but rest himself contented with such provisions as may be conveniently provided, by his own labor purchase, or his means reach unto; above all things he must eschew that detestable vice of drunkenness.

He must be true-hearted to his captain and obey him and the rest of the officers of the camp, town, or fort with great respect, for by the very oath which he takes he does bind himself and promises to serve his Prince, and obey his officers: for the true order of war is fitly resembled to true religion ordained of God, which binds the soldier to observe justice, loyalty, faith, constance, patience, silence, and, above all, obedience, through the which is easily obtained the perfection in arms.

He shall continue at his work until the drum beats and that his captain, his officer, or overseers of the work, gives order unto a cessation for the time, and for the same purpose attends to lead him in, whom he shall orderly and comely follow into the camp, town, or fort, by his said captain, officer, or overseer him meeting, to be conducted unto the church to hear divine service, after which he may repay to his house or lodging to prepare for his dinner, and to repose him until the drum shall call him forth again in the afternoon, when so (as before) he shall accompany his chief officer unto the field, or where else the work lies, and there to follow his easy task until again the drum beats to return home; at which time according as in the forenoon, he shall follow his chief officer unto the church to hear divine service and after dispose of himself as he shall best please, and as his own business shall require.

IV

By 1618, the company realized that its original goals could not be fulfilled and they therefore moved to encourage permanent settlement. They instituted a headright system, guaranteeing fifty acres of land to any Englishman who paid his own way over to the New World, and an additional fifty acres for every person he brought with him. They also tried to make conditions as attractive as possible, to enhance the likelihood of settlement. Among other things, they founded a House of Burgesses, so that traditional English political practices would take hold here. As the letter from the company to Virginia's officials makes clear, a vitally important shift had occurred in the relationship between the company and its constituents. In 1609–1610, when exploitation of Virginia's wealth had been the primary goal, military discipline was encouraged. Now that settlement was the goal, no concession was too great to make conditions more attractive for would-be emigrants. For the first time, women and marriage play a role in the story.

LETTER TO THE GOVERNOR IN VIRGINIA, 1622

There come now over in this ship, and are immediately to follow in some others many hundreds of people, to whom as we here think ourselves bound to give the best encouragement for their going, there is no way left to increase the plantation, but by abundance of private undertakers; so we think you obliged to give all possible furtherance and assistance, for the good entertaining and well settling of them, that they may both thrive and prosper and others by their welfare be drawn after them. This is the way that we conceive most effectual for the engaging of this state, and securing of Virginia, for in the multitude of people is the strength of a kingdom. The allotting out of the settling of private persons, we leave unto your wisdom and judgment; not doubt-

Originally entitled "Letter to the Governor and Council in Virginia," August 12, 1622, by the Treasurer and Council for the Virginia Company. In *Records of the Virginia Company of London*, ed. S. M. Kingsbury (Washington, D.C., 1933), vol. 3, pp. 492–94.

ing but you will find out some course as shall give content to reasonable minds; not suffering any to plant or set down anywhere but with so sufficient a number of able men and well provided, as may, not in their own, but in your judgments (who shall be therefore accountable), defend themselves from any assaults of the Indians. In which regard, as also for their better civil government, we think it fit that the houses and buildings be so contrived together as may make if not handsome towns yet compact and orderly villages; that this is the most proper and successful manner of proceeding in new plantations.

We send you in this ship one widow and eleven maids for wives for the people in Virginia: there hath been especial care had in the choice of them; for there hath not any one of them been received but upon good commendations. We pray you all therefore in general to take them into your care; and more especially we recommend that at their first landing they may be housed, lodged, and provided for of diet till they be married; for such was the haste of sending them away, as that straightened with time we had no means to put provisions aboard. And in case they cannot be presently married we desire they may be put to several households that have wives till they can be provided of husbands. There are nearly fifty more which are shortly to come, are sent by certain worthy gentlemen, who taking into their consideration that the plantation can never flourish till families be planted, and the respect of wives and children fix the people on the soil. Therefore have given this fair beginning: for the reimbursing of whose charges it is ordered that every man that marries them give 120 weight of the best leaf tobacco for each of them, and in case any of them die, that proportion must be advanced to it upon those that survive. That marriage be free according to the law of nature, yet would we not have these maids deceived and married to servants, but only to such free men or tenants as have means to maintain them. We pray you therefore to be fathers to them in this business, not enforcing them to marry against their wills; neither send we them to be servants, save in case of extremity, for we would have their condition so much bettered as multitudes may be allured thereby to come unto you. And you may assure such men as marry those women that the first servants sent over by the company shall be consigned to them; it being our intent to preserve families, and to prefer married men before single persons.

V

The persistent inability of the company to return a profit to its investors bred bad feeling among its more influential investors. In the early 1620s, investigating committees went over to Virginia to discover who was to blame for the poor financial condition. Charges promoted countercharges, and company officials busily defended themselves. In 1622, there occurred the proverbial straw that broke the company's back: an Indian massacre of many of its settlers. An

uproar immediately broke out. Why had the company been unable
to prevent this or to protect itself? Officials, in the document below,
tried to respond, but they were clearly on the defensive. (Compare
the tone of this reply to that of the 1609 document, Nova Britannia.)
Within two years, the company was bankrupt and disbanded; but
the settlers in Virginia remained, and the colony's roots were firmly
established.

THE STATE OF THE COLONY IN VIRGINIA, 1622

That all men may see the impartial ingenuity of this discourse, we freely
confess, that the country is not so good, as the natives are bad, whose
barbarous selves need more cultivation then the ground itself, being
more overspread with incivility and treachery, than that with briars.
For the land, being tilled and used well by us, deceive not our expectation but rather exceeded it far, being so thankful as to return a hundred
for one. But the savages, though never a nation used so kindly upon
so small desert, have instead of that harvest which our pains merited,
returned nothing but briars and thorns, pricking even to death many
of their benefactors. Yet doubt we not, but that as all wickedness is
crafty to undo itself, so these also have more wounded themselves than
us, God Almighty making way for severity there, where a fair gentleness
would not take place. The occasion whereof thus I relate from thence.

The last May there came a letter from Sir Francis Wiat Governor
in Virginia, which did advertise that when in November last he arrived
in Virginia and entered upon his government, he found the country
settled in a peace (as all men there thought), sure and unviolable, not
only because it was solemnly ratified and sworn, but as being advantageous to both parts; to the savages as the weaker, under which they
were safely sheltered and defended; to us, as being the easiest way
then thought to pursue and advance our projects of buildings, plantings,
and effecting their conversion by peaceable and fair means. And such
was the conceit of firm peace and amity as that there was seldom or
never a sword worn, by which assurance of security. The plantations of
particular adventurers and planters were placed scatteringly and
stragglingly as a choice vein of rich ground invited them, and the further
from neighbors held the better. The houses generally set open to the
savages, who were always friendly entertained at the tables of the
English, and commonly lodged in their bedchambers. The old planters
(as they thought now come to reap the benefit of their long travels)
placed with wonderful content upon their private lands, and their
familiarity with the natives, seeming to open a fair gate for their conversion to Christianity.

The country being in this estate, an occasion was ministered of
sending to Opachankano, the King of these savages, about the middle
of March last, what time the messenger returned back with these words

Originally entitled "A Declaration of the State of the Colonie and Affairs in
Virginia" (London, 1622). Reprinted in *Records of the Virginia Company of
London* (Washington, D.C., 1933), vol. 3, pp. 549–51, 555–57.

from him, that he held the peace concluded so firm as the sky should sooner fall than it dissolve. Yea, such was the treacherous dissimulation of that people who then had contrived our destruction, that even two days before the massacre, some of our men were guided through the woods by them in safety. Yea, they borrowed our own boats to convey themselves across the river (on the banks of both sides whereof all our plantations were) to consult of the devilish murder that ensued, and of our utter extirpation, which God of His mercy (by the means of themselves converted to Christianity) prevented. And as well on the Friday morning (the fatal day) the twenty-second of March, as also in the evening, as on other days before, they came unarmed into our houses, without bows or arrows, or other weapons, with deer, turkey, fish, fur, and other provisions to sell and trade with us for glass, beads, and other trifles. Yet in some places, they sat down at breakfast with our people at their tables, whom immediately with their own tools and weapons either laid down, or standing in their houses, they basely and barbarously murdered, not sparing either age or sex, man, woman, or child, so sudden in their cruel execution that few or none discerned the weapon or blow that brought them to destruction. In which manner they also slew many of our people then at their several work and husbandries in the fields, and without their houses, some in planting corn and tobacco, some in gardening, some in making brick, building, sawing, and other kinds of husbandry, they well knowing in what places and quarters each of our men were, in regard of their daily familiarity and resort to us for trading and other negotiations, which the more willingly was by us continued and cherished for the desire we had of effecting that great masterpiece of works, their conversion. And by this means that fatal Friday morning, there fell under the bloody and barbarous hands of that perfidious and inhuman people, contrary to all laws of God and men, of nature and nations, three hundred forty seven men, women, and children, most by their own weapons. And not being content with taking away life alone, they fell after again upon the dead, making as well as they could, a fresh murder, defacing, dragging, and mangling the dead carcasses into many pieces, and carrying some parts away in derision, with base and brutish triumph. That the slaughter had been universal, if God had not put it into the heart of an Indian belonging to one Perry to disclose it, who living in the house of one Pace, was urged by another Indian his brother (who came the night before and lay with him) to kill Pace. Telling further that by such an hour in the morning a number would come from different places to finish the execution, who failed not at the time, Perry's Indian rose out of his bed and revealed it to Pace, that used him as a son. And thus the rest of the colony that had warning given them by this means was saved. Such was (God be thanked for it) the good fruit of an infidel converted to Christianity. For though three hundred and more of ours died by many of these pagan infidels, yet thousands of ours were saved by the means of one of them alone which was made a Christian. Blessed be God forever, whose mercy endureth forever.

Thus have you seen the particulars of this massacre, wherein treachery and cruelty have done their worst to us, or rather to themselves; for whose understanding is so shallow, as not to perceive that this must needs be for the good of the plantation after, and the loss of this blood to make the body more healthful, as by these reasons may be manifest.

First, because betraying innocence never rests unpunished.

Secondly, because our hands, which before were tied with gentleness and fair usage, are now set at liberty by the treacherous violence of the savages, not untying the knot, but cutting it. So that we, who hitherto have had possession of no more ground than their waste, and our purchase at a valuable consideration to their own contentment gained, may now, by right of war and law of nations, invade the country, and destroy them who sought to destroy us. Whereby we shall enjoy their cultivated places, possessing the fruits of others' labors. Now their cleared grounds in all their villages (which are situated in the fruitfulest places of the land) shall be inhabited by us, whereas heretofore the grubbing of woods was the greatest labor.

Thirdly, because those commodities which the Indians enjoyed as much or rather more than we, shall now also be entirely possessed by us. The deer and other beasts will be in safety, and infinitely increase, which heretofore not only in the general huntings of the King, but by each particular Indian were destroyed at all times of the year, without any difference of male, dame, or young.

There will be also a great increase of wild turkeys, and other weighty fowl, for the Indians never put difference of destroying the hen, but kill them whether in season or not, whether in breeding time, or sitting on their eggs, or having new hatched, it is all one to them.

Fourthly, because the way of conquering them is much more easy than of civilizing them by fair means, for they are a rude, barbarous, and naked people, scattered in small companies, which are helps to victory, but hindrance to civility. Besides that, a conquest may be of many, and at once; but civility is in particular and slow, the effect of long time, and great industry. Moreover, victory of them may be gained many ways: by force, by surprise, by famine in burning their corn, by destroying and burning their boats, canoes, and houses, by breaking their fishing wares, by assailing them in their huntings, whereby they get the greatest part of their sustenance in winter, by pursuing and chasing them with our horses and bloodhounds to draw after them, and mastiffs to tear them.

Chapter 2

The Puritan Church

IN 1630, under the direction of John Winthrop, the Puritans established their commonwealth in the New World. This was no ordinary settlement, nor did it seek ordinary goals. The Puritans wished to establish a community where they could worship in their own particular manner. But they had not left England to undertake the rigors of the wilderness for that alone; they also sought to improve their financial condition. Nevertheless, economic motives were not at the heart of the movement. Rather, their ultimate purpose in this venture was, in Winthrop's words, to found "a city upon a hill," to establish a godly commonwealth, and thereby to set an example for mankind in general —and the English in particular—of how to conduct themselves in this world. Their venture was nothing less than utopian. Massachusetts was to mark a new divide in the history of mankind. In this setting religious truths, as well as social and political ones, would emerge. Church organization would follow God's word and by its success promote emulation. Social relationships among Christians would achieve a new quality, with men treating one another as brothers. This was a mission into the wilderness—inspired by the hope of sparking a general reform.

No institution had greater significance in this grandoise plan than the Congregational church. This church differed in several doctrinal ways from its Anglican counterpart in England. First, no church hierarchy ruled over the individual churches. The authority of these hierarchical bodies, Puritans believed, was an unfortunate outgrowth of papal practices and had no place in proper church structure. Secondly, the Congregational church simplified ritual. The elaborate practices of Catholic churches that had corrupted Protestant procedures had to be eliminated. Finally, church membership was to become more exclusive, in order to bring about a closer correspondence between the invisible church (that heavenly church made up only of the truly saved) and the visible church (the church on earth). Before gaining membership and receiving the sacraments, one had to experience, and describe fully

21

to the congregation, saving grace, that moment of illumination wherein one felt the full majesty of God.

These beliefs reflected something even more fundamental in Puritanism: the covenant theology. Catholicism, they believed, had become far too mechanical a religion, and contemporary Anglicanism lacked any mystery of God. Puritans were determined to realize God as omnipotent without robbing human initiative of all meaning. Hence, according to covenant theology, if men did right, they probably were among the elect, the chosen of God. But there was no predicting with full confidence the workings of the Divine. The tree was known by its fruits; good works were a likely sign of salvation. Nevertheless, no one could be absolutely certain that he was in fact among the chosen of God. Consequently, there was a necessary tension about one's life. Deeply religious Puritans, like Michael Wadsworth, vacillated between moments of confidence and those of acute self-doubt and self-denigration.

The secular functions of the church were almost as significant as its religious ones. The responsibility for maintaining the good order of the community and the proper behavior of its members rested in large part with the church. Each Christian had to assume responsibility for the moral well-being of his neighbor. If, to a modern eye, such a doctrine violated the right of privacy and encouraged snooping, to the seventeenth-century Puritan, mutual responsibility was an obvious and vital part of Christian brotherhood. Thus, offenders against society faced not only sanctions from a civil court, but from the church as well. The judges fined and whipped, the church censured, admonished, and expeled. The line between political and religious crimes was drawn only faintly. To attack the doctrines of the church was to attack the stability of society, and hence both secular and religious institutions responded quickly and punitively. Roger Williams and Anne Hutchinson felt the arm of both church and state for departing from theological doctrines, and their fates are only famous examples of an ongoing discipline.

In the first generation of settlement, 1630 to 1660, the church came close to fulfilling its grandiose expectations, exerting unprecedented influence over men's attitudes and actions. The deviations that did occur were taken so seriously that they testify to the institution's strength. The prosecution of Robert Keayne for selling his nails at too high a price reflected the power of church and state over all aspects of its members' lives. But the hegemony of the church did not stand up well to conditions in the New World. Throughout the seventeenth century its discipline gradually weakened. To be sure, the principles of church authority were slow to change. Men still judged themselves by the rigorous standards of the first generation. But, in fact, citizens were steadily abandoning the ideal of establishing the city on a hill for the more mundane pleasures of life in a growing town.

I

No document better exemplifies the spirit behind the Puritan migration to the New World than John Winthrop's A Modell of Christian Charity. *Delivered as a sermon on board the* Arbella *as the band of Puritans were making their way across the Atlantic,* The Modell *expressed in eloquent and moving terms the hopes and fears of the mission. Winthrop himself, about to become the first governor of the Massachusetts Bay Colony, personified the curious Puritan blend of someone eager for worldly success yet equally concerned with otherworld salvation. He effectively summarized the goals of the first American Puritans.*

A MODELL OF CHRISTIAN CHARITY, 1630

JOHN WINTHROP

Written on Board the Arbella, *on the Atlantic Ocean*

God almighty in His most holy and wise providence hath so disposed of the condition of mankind, as in all times some must be rich, some poor, some high and eminent in power and dignity, others mean and in subjection.

Reason: First, to hold conformity with the rest of His works, being delighted to show forth the glory of His wisdom in the variety and difference of the creatures and the glory of His power, in ordering all these differences for the preservation and good of the whole.

Reason: Secondly, that He might have the more occasion to manifest the work of His spirit. First, upon the wicked in moderating and restraining them, so that the rich and mighty should not eat up the poor, nor the poor and despised rise up against their superiors and shake off their yoke. Secondly, in the regenerate in exercising His graces in them, as in the great ones, their love, mercy, gentleness, temperance, etc., in the poor and inferior sort, their faith, patience, obedience, etc.

Reason: Thirdly, that every man might have need of other, and from hence they might be all knit more nearly together in the bond of brotherly affection. From hence it appears plainly that no man is made more honorable than another, or more wealthy, etc., out of any particular and singular respect to himself, but for the glory of his creator and the common good of the creature, man.

Thus stands the cause between God and us. We are entered into covenant with Him for this work, we have taken out a commission, the Lord hath given us leave to draw our own articles, we have professed to enterprise these actions upon these and these ends, we have hereupon besought Him of favor and blessing. Now if the Lord shall please

In *The American Puritans*, ed. Perry Miller (New York, 1956), pp. 79–83.

to hear us, and bring us in peace to the place we desire, then hath He ratified this covenant and sealed our commission, [and] will expect a strict performance of the articles contained in it, but if we shall neglect the observations of these articles which are the ends we have propounded, and dissembling with our God, shall fall to embrace this present world and prosecute our carnal intentions seeking great things for ourselves and our posterity, the Lord will surely break out in wrath against us, be revenged of such a perjured people, and make us know the price of the breach of such a covenant.

Now the only way to avoid this shipwreck and to provide for our posterity is to follow the counsel of Micah, to do justly, to love mercy, to walk humbly with our God. For this end we must be knit together in this work as one man, we must entertain each other in brotherly affection, we must be willing to abridge ourselves of our superfluities for the supply of others' necessities, we must uphold a familiar commerce together in all meekness, gentleness, patience, and liberality, we must delight in each other, make others' conditions our own, rejoice together, mourn together, labor and suffer together, always having before our eyes our commission and community in the work, our community as members of the same body. So shall we keep the unity of the spirit in the bond of peace. The Lord will be our God and delight to dwell among us as His own people, and will command a blessing upon us in all our ways, so that we shall see much more of His wisdom, power, goodness, and truth than formerly we have been acquainted with. We shall find that the God of Israel is among us, when ten of us shall be able to resist a thousand of our enemies, when He shall make us a praise and glory, that men shall say of succeeding plantations, the Lord make it like that of New England. For we must consider that we shall be as a city upon a hill, the eyes of all people are upon us. So that if we shall deal falsely with our God in this work we have undertaken and so cause Him to withdraw His present help from us, we shall be made a story and a byword through the world, we shall open the mouths of enemies to speak evil of the ways of God and all professors for God's sake, we shall shame the faces of many of God's worthy servants, and cause their prayers to be turned into curses upon us till we be consumed out of the good land whither we are going. And to shut up this discourse with that exhortation of Moses, that faithful servant of the Lord in His last farewell to Israel, Deut. 30., Beloved, there is now set before us life and good, death and evil, in that we are commanded this day to love the Lord our God, and to love one another, to walk in His ways and to keep His commandments and His ordinance, and His laws, and the articles of our covenant with Him that we may live and be multiplied, and that the Lord our God may bless us in the land whither we go to possess it. But if our hearts shall turn away so that we will not obey, but shall be seduced and worship other Gods, our pleasures, our profits, and serve them, it is propounded unto us this day we shall surely perish out of the good land whither we pass over this vast sea to possess it. Therefore let us choose life, that we, and our seed, may live, and by obeying His voice, and cleaving to Him, for He is our life, and our prosperity.

II

The Cambridge Platform of 1648 defined the essentials of Puritan church organization. At the request of the General Court, the governing body of the Massachusetts Bay Colony, a Synod, made up of ministers and laymen, gathered at Cambridge, first in 1646, and then again in 1647 and 1648. These meetings hammered out the form that church government was to take in the new colony, an issue that was of pressing importance to the Puritan mission. The 1648 session was the most productive. It started in a curiously symbolic way. A snake (the personification of the devil) crept into the pulpit at the opening sermon, and an elder, "a man of great faith," killed it immediately. Thereafter, all seemed to go well. The Platform has been called "one of the greatest creations of the founding fathers," and its principles remained foremost in Bay Colony churches throughout the colonial period.

THE CAMBRIDGE PLATFORM, 1648

Of the Form of Church Government; and That It Is One, Immutable, and Prescribed in the Word

Ecclesiastical Polity, or Church Government or Discipline, is nothing else but that form and order that is to be observed in the Church of Christ upon Earth, both for the constitution of it and all the administrations that therein are to be performed.

Of the Nature of the Catholic Church in General, and in Special of a Particular Visible Church

The Catholic Church is the whole company of those that are elected, redeemed, and in time effectually called from the state of sin and death, unto a state of grace and salvation in Jesus Christ.

This Church is either triumphant or militant. Triumphant, the number of them who are glorified in Heaven: Militant, the number of them who are conflicting with their enemies upon Earth.

Of the Officers of the Church, and Especially of Pastors and Teachers

A Church being a company of people combined together by covenant for the worship of God, it appeareth thereby, there may be the essence and being of a church without any officers.

Nevertheless, though officers be not absolutely necessary to the simple being of churches, when they be called, yet ordinarily to their

In *American Christianity*, ed. Robert T. Handy and Lefferts A. Loetschen (New York, 1960), vol. 1, pp. 129–40.

calling they are, and to their well-being; and therefore the Lord Jesus, out of His tender compassion, hath appointed and ordained officers, which He would not have done, if they had not been useful and needful for the Church.

Of Elders, (who are also in Scripture called Bishops) some attend chiefly to the ministry of the word, as the Pastors and Teachers; others attend especially unto rule, who are therefore called Ruling Elders.

The Office of Pastor and Teacher appears to be distinct. The Pastors special work is to attend to exhortation, and therein to administer a word of wisdom. The Teacher is to attend to doctrine, and therein to administer a word of knowledge.

Of the Election of Church Officers

A Church being free, cannot become subject to any, but by a free election; yet when such a people do choose any to be over them in the Lord, then do they become subject, and most willingly submit to their Ministry in the Lord, whom they have so chosen.

And if the Church have power to choose their officers and ministers, then in case of manifest unworthiness and delinquency, they have power also to depose them: For, to open and shut, to choose and refuse, to constitute in office, and remove from office, are acts belonging to the same power.

Of the Admission of Members into the Church

The Doors of the Churches of Christ upon Earth do not by God's appointment stand so wide open, that all sorts of people, good or bad, may freely enter therein at their pleasure, but such as are admitted thereto, as members, ought to be examined and tried first, whether they be fit and meet to be received into church society, or not. The officers are charged with the keeping of the Doors of the Church. Twelve angels are set at the Gates of the Temple, lest such as were ceremonially unclean should enter thereinto.

The things which are requisite to be found in all church members are repentance from sin, and faith in Jesus Christ.

The weakest measure of faith is to be accepted in those that desire to be admitted into the Church, because weak Christians, if sincere, have the substance of that faith, repentance, and holiness which is required in church members; and such have most need of the ordinances for their confirmation and growth in grace.

Of Church Members, Their Removal from One Church to Another, and of Recommendation and Dismission

Church members may not remove or depart from the Church, and so one from another as they please, nor without just and weighty cause, but ought to live and dwell together, forasmuch as they are commanded not to forsake the assembling of themselves together.

It is therefore the duty of church members in such times and places where counsel may be had, to consult with the Church whereof they are members about their removal, that accordingly they having their approbation, may be encouraged, or otherwise desist. They who are joined with consent, should not depart without consent, except forced thereunto.

Order requires that a member thus removing have letters testimonial, and of dismission from the Church whereof he yet is, unto the Church whereunto he desireth to be joined, lest the Church should be deluded; that the Church may receive him in faith, and not be corrupted by receiving deceivers, and false brethren. Until the person dismissed be received into another Church, he ceaseth not by his letters of dismission, to be a member of the Church whereof he was. The Church cannot make a member no member, but by excommunication.

Of Excommunication, and Other Censures

The censures of the Church are appointed by Christ for the preventing, removing, and healing of offences in the Church; for the reclaiming and gaining of offending brethren, for the deterring others from the like offences.

In dealing with an offender, great care is to be taken that we be neither over strict or rigorous, nor too indulgent or remiss; our proceeding herein ought to be with a spirit of meekness, considering ourselves, lest we also be tempted; and that the best of us have need of much forgiveness from the Lord. On some have compassion, others save with fear.

Excommunication being a spiritual punishment, it doth not prejudice the excommunicate in, nor deprive him of his civil rights, and therefore toucheth not princes, nor other magistrates in point of their civil dignity or authority.

Of the Civil Magistrates Power in Matters Ecclesiastical

It is lawful, profitable, and necessary for Christians to gather themselves together into church estate, and therein to exercise all the ordinances of Christ, according unto the word, although the consent of the magistrate could not be had thereunto; because the Apostles and Christians in their time did frequently thus practise, when the magistrates all of them being Jewish or pagan, and most persecuting enemies, would give no countenance or consent to such matters.

Church government stands in no opposition to civil government of commonwealths, nor any way intrencheth upon the authority of civil magistrates in their jurisdiction.

It is not in the power of magistrates to compel their subjects to become church members, and to partake at the Lord's table.

As it is unlawful for church officers to meddle with the sword of the magistrate, so it is unlawful for the magistrate to meddle with the work proper to church officers.

Idolatry, blasphemy, heresy, venting corrupt and pernicious opinions that destroy the foundation, open contempt of the word preached, profanation of the Lord's day, disturbing the peaceable administration and exercise of the worship and holy things of God, and the like, are to be restrained and punished by civil authority.

If any Church one or more, shall grow schismatical, rending itself from the communion of other Churches, or shall walk incorrigibly or obstinately in any corrupt way of their own, contrary to the rule of the word; in such a case, the magistrate is to put forth his coercive power, as the matter shall require.

III

The day-to-day discipline exercised by the Puritan church emerges vividly in the records of the First Church at Dorchester, an outlying section of Boston. The authority of the church extended first and foremost to members; they could be flogged for religious offenses, and excommunicated for major sins. Members' lives were closely watched by fellow congregants; hence the colonists believed that the more the church policed a community, the more well-ordered it would be. The church also had some authority over nonmembers. As many as one-half of the settlers in Massachusetts probably remained outside the church. But attendance at services was compulsory for everybody, and neither the church nor the state would tolerate attacks on doctrine.

RECORDS OF THE DORCHESTER CHURCH, 1659–1779

The thirteenth of September 1659 it was declared unto the church and commended unto them from the general court to have a public day of thanksgiving to be observed by all the churches within this jurisdiction:

In *Records of the First Church at Dorchester in New England*, 1636–1734 (Boston, 1891), pp. 32–33, 45–46, 50–51, 58, 70, 75–76, 83, 87.

In humble and thankful acknowledging [of] the mercy of God to New England in the continuation of our peace and for the gracious return of our prayers put up unto Him in the wet spring by giving His people a joint consent to withstand and suppress the blasphemers of His truth and gospel and the day appointed is to be the eighth day of October 1659.

The fifth day of November 1659 it was purposed by our teacher unto the church from some of the-elders hereabouts whether it were not convenient that the churches (as many of them as could) should jointly set apart a day of humiliation on the behalf of our native country to which this church did consent.

The Twenty-fifth of January 1660

The day above said, report was made by Mr. Mather unto the congregation, of a sad accident that was fallen out at Hartford, namely of a young man named Abraham Warner, about the age of twenty years (who being left of God and prevailed with by Satan) drowned himself in the water, leaving behind him in his brother's pocket a writing to his father wherein he does advise his father to look to the ways and walkings of the children and families.

The Thirteenth of March 1660

This day Mr. Mather after the evening exercise desired to speak a word or two unto the church the substance thereof was this:

First he desired the church and the members of it to take notice: that children of such as are members of the church are to be looked at as members also though as yet they have not been received to the Lord's Supper.

Secondly his exhortation was unto the brethren and sisters of the church that they would mind it and make conscience of performing that duty of watchfulness and exhortation unto such children as their age and capacity did require or would admit of.

Thirdly his exhortation was unto such children of the church that they would so look at themselves as to expect the benefit and privilege of church watchfulness and that they would so carry themselves as such as must give an account in case of defect according as their age or capacity would permit.

The Twelfth of December 1664

The day above said, after the evening exercise the church was asked to stay, the reason was (as the elder did declare) because there were several young men in the town who would be willing to join to the church if they might have their confession taken in private by writing and declared publicly to the church, they standing forth and owning what was declared, and their engaging themselves in the covenant; upon this there was some debate and some did declare themselves willing that it should be so practiced but one or two of the brethren declared themselves to the contrary. In conclusion the matter was left to a further consideration.

The Second of February 1665

The day above said, it was also proposed to the church the second time whether they would be willing that men as well as women should be received into the church by the private relation being taken in writing and publicly read before the church: after some agitation the conclusion and vote of the church was that it should be left to the elders, namely that they might hear their relations in private and if their voice were so low in private that Mr. Mather could not hear them so as to write it from their mouths, then the party might write it himself and present it to the elders. But if they judged any man able to make a public relation by his own mouth, they should endeavor to persuade him so to do.

The Thirtieth of July 1666

The day above said, the elders made report to the church of some offense that lay upon Mrs. Clark, the wife of Captain Thomas Clark of Boston, about her reproachful and slanderous tongue against the honored governor Mr. Richard Bellengham, and other lying expression against the general court, and for absenting herself from the public ordinances and other miscarriages for which the church thought meet to call her before them to give satisfaction therein; but she not appearing, the church did forbear further proceeding till another time to see if she would personally appear to make answer thereunto.

The Fourteenth of August 1666

The day above said, Mrs. Clark, the wife of Captain Thomas Clark of Boston, was called before the church (she being yet a member of this church) for some offense committed for slanderous and lying expressions of her tongue; but she, manifesting no repentance for the same, was solemnly admonished before the church.

This being sacrament day, Robert Spur was called forth before the church to make his acknowledgment of the offense which he lay under in giving entertainment in his house of loose and vain persons, especially Joseph Belcher, his frequent coming to his daughter contrary to the admonition of the court which was greatly to the offense of the said Belcher's nearest relations and divers others.

Dorchester's Covenant for Reformation

The Fourth of March 1677

Upon serious search into our own hearts and ways in this day of divine rebuke, finding ourselves guilty of many heinous violations of our holy covenant by omissions of duty and commissions of iniquity, we do judge and condemn ourselves of the same, and do jointly and severally renew our said holy covenant with God and one with another.

First, to reform our own hearts, by endeavoring to recover the spirit like and power of Godliness with our first love, faith, zeal, and integrity.

Secondly, to reform our families, engaging ourselves to a conscientious care to set up and maintain the worship of God in them and to walk in our houses with perfect hearts in a faithful discharge of all domestic duties: educating, instructing, and charging our children and our households to keep the ways of the Lord: restraining them, as much as us, from all evil and especially the sins of the times and watching over them in the Lord.

Thirdly, to reform (according to our place and power) the general growing evil of this time; as pride appearing in gaudy apparel or otherwise and profanenesses, and profanation of God's holy Sabbath, taking God's holy name in vain, all irreverence in the ordinances and worship of God, disobedience to superiors, in family, town, church, or commonwealth, drunkenness, idleness, vain company keeping, unrighteous dealing between man and man, lasciviousness, uncleanliness, false speaking, slandering, coveting, with all other violations of God's holy law.

Fourthly, to reform our church to lay aside all envy, wrath, evil, surmises, jealousies, disrespect of persons, undue designings, sidings, contentions, and whatever is contrary to sound love and charity; to own and obey them that are over us in the Lord. To uphold, maintain, encourage, cleave to, and stand by a godly, able, painful, faithful, powerful ministry in this church and congregation; and to our power to encourage, cleave to, and stand by one another, in times of prosecution, to labor to recover the vigorous, studious, and impartial administration of discipline, to uphold the due administration of all God's holy ordinances, to be very serious and solemn in our preparations unto and attendance upon God in all divine worship and sabbaths, fasts, sacraments, that we may obtain the saving good of them.

Fifthly, to reform our defects and neglects of duty toward the children of the covenant, humbly and from our hearts acknowledging and bewailing our sin herein, beseeching and waiting upon God in our Lord Jesus for pardon and healing by His name.

Unto the performance of these things, we do, in the name of our Lord Jesus Christ, engage ourselves unto God, taking this holy covenant by a renewed act of confederation upon ourselves solemnly, with full purpose of heart in the strength of Christ to stand to it in all the parts of it.

June 6, 1671

John Merrifield (though not in full communion) was called forth before the church to answer for his sin of drunkenness and also for contempt and slighting the power of Christ in his church in not appearing formerly, though often called upon and sent unto: but he made some excuse for his drunkenness in that being not well at Boston, he took a little strong water, and coming out in the air distempered him, and for the other offense he did acknowledge his fault therein.

December 19, 1678

Church met again and Samuel Rigbe was called forth again, and he gave so much satisfaction that his censure of admonition was ordered to be respected for a while, and this on his good demeanor: if it did appear for some time then the censure [is] to be taken off. The same time Robert Spursen was called on to give satisfaction but he was not up to full satisfaction; therefore it was voted that he should be admonished. Also Nathan Wiett, John Spur, Daniel Ellen, and Joshua George, for their contempt of and neglecting and refusing to come to give an account of their knowledge to the elders or church, were therefore voted to be excommunicated.

August 28, 1679

Samuel Blake, the son of William Blake, now of the church at Melton, was called before the church to make confession of his sin of fornication before marriage; with time he did own the fact and made some kind of acknowledgment, but his voice was so low that scarcely any heard the little which he spoke except a few which stood close by him.

September 2, 1679

Samuel Rigbe was excommunicated for those sins for which he was formerly admonished and for contempt in not appearing before the church, being called thereunto.

IV

Although it is not likely that many other Puritans felt the anguish of their existence with as keen and acute a sensibility as Michael Wigglesworth, his attitudes and beliefs reflect one major strand in Puritanism. A minister in the Bay Colony, Wigglesworth wrote the widely read Day of Doom; *this account of the judgment day went through five editions between 1662 and 1701. His diary, parts of which are reprinted below, conveys the religious tension that he experienced. Even if personal, psychological explanations account for some of Wigglesworth's feelings, one must remember that he was still a man of his times.*

THE DIARY OF MICHAEL WIGGLESWORTH, 1653

March 1653

Mr. Mitchel preached twice today and we saw His glory. Now woe is me! That I cannot see Christ's glory, I never find my heart more carnal and my eyes more blind that I cannot behold and feel a present excellency in Christ, than when His glory is displayed before me. My love to Christ is gone and all saviour of His sweetness in a manner so

In *The Diary of Michael Wigglesworth, 1653–1657* (New York, 1946), pp. 10–18, 23–31, 46–49, 52–55.

that I may with trembling fear the vileness of my own heart, when Christ is most to be seen. Vain thoughts break in upon me. My soul can't get over a disconsolate, troubled, devoted frame. Ah Lord let me see thy face that will fill up all my emptiness and the dissatisfaction I find in the creature. I wait and oh, that I could long for thy salvation.

O wretch that I am, my iniquity, like clay and fetters, holds me down that the good I would do I can't; the evil I would not do, that do I. Nay I feel my heart apt secretly to give way to my vain thoughts in holy duties, and glued as it were to my sensuality or love to the creature full of hope since and can't get over sinking and disquietments of spirit; and as for pride, why it overcomes me in holiest duties where there should be most abasement.

March the Twenty-third

I came to New Haven, I preached my first sermon at Pequit. Much difficulty I found in my journey, my back and breast almost shaked in pieces with riding. In my pain and anguish I lift up my heart and voice to the Lord my God, and He helped me through the difficulty, giving me so much strength as enabled me to bear it. We were lost the first day and rode above an hour within evening. God brought us to a house where we had a guide to our desired place. Near Pequit we were lost and passed through craggy, dangerous ways; yet God kept us and all [that] belonged to us and brought us safe, notwithstanding the rumors of the Indian plots.

This Sabbath I found much enlargement in private duties, yet pride thereupon prevailing, which I desired to resist and loath myself for. I find vain thoughts and vile heart ready to give them lodging, slow to see and feel any evil in them. And there is also a carnal heart that cannot savor the things of God, but whorishly departs from Him. What impressions and tastes of Himself God leaves at present are soon gone. This makes me exceedingly afraid of myself and my own spirit of whoredoms. These things open a gap to unbelief; I am ashamed to lift up mine eyes to heaven and call God my gracious father, my only portion, seeing I deal so unworthily with Him. Ah wretched backsliding heart! What evil hast thou found in God that thy love and affection to Him are so quickly cooled? I abhor myself before the Lord for my shameless pride, especially now when God is abasing me. I am ashamed of my apostatizing heart of unbelief in departing from the living God, to whom in my distress I am ever crying, arise and save me.

April 17, 18, 19

I was somewhat dejected with some fears in the forenoon and was not yet clear of them in the evening of the Sabbath, having heard Mr. Davenport preach how and what a winter Christians indeed might go through both in respect of grace and comfort. My daily decays [loss] of love to God and saviour of the things of God, this profane, loose heart that is weary of watchful attending upon God in holy duties fills me with fears of my own estate. Chewing upon such cogitations I thought that if God would not save me at last, yet there was something that pleased me in this, that my Lord should have glory in my damnation.

On the sixth day which was the next day after the fast, God let me see the prevalency of a multitude of abominable sins in me. As 1: Weariness of God's service, in which is great unbelief, though God has said 'tis not a vain thing to seek Him; great unthankfulness for such a gracious opportunity which the damned would prize at a high rate. Great slothfulness that cannot away with taking pains in constant seeking God by spiritual worship. 2: Peevishness and impatience, though God were patient and bore long my dullness, nay averseness to learn of Him, now groundless anger makes me give place to the Devil so that my spot is not the spot of God's children. 3: Affirming that for truth which I doubt or am not certain of; now who is the father of lies? 4: Want of natural affection to my father, in desiring the continuance of his life which God ranks among those sins whereto men were given up of God to a reprobate mind. Lord why hast thou caused me to err from thy ways, or hardened my heart from thy fear? 5: Want of honoring my mother, yea, slighting of her speech; now the eye that despises his mother, the ravens of the valley shall peck it out and the young ravens shall eat it. Lord, I can't stand before thee because of these abominations. Against thee I have committed them, not obeying thy holy rules though thou didst redeem me for thy self to thy service. Nay, sixthly, I find again whorish desertions of my heart from God to the creature. It pleased God to make me earnest in prayer both that evening and the next morning for pardon of them for Jesus' sake and for power against them according to God's covenant to redeem me from all iniquity.

April 27

On the fourth day at lecture I found my vile heart apt to be weary beforehand of the feared length of the public ordinances. And I feel my spirit so leavened with sensuality that I cannot but be hankering in my thoughts after creature comforts as of meat and drink when I should be holy intent to God's worship in religious services, especially if they put me by the other. I took time to look into the evil of this also and much I did see. Now the good Lord looks down at last and hears the groaning of his poor prisoner, and comes and saves me from the tyranny of these enemies of his.

June 26

Tuesday was a private fast. I was very deadhearted in the beginning of the day [and] the night before. In public it pleased the Lord to pour upon me some measure of affection, but now woe is me! How incurable is my wound that while I am confessing and shaming myself before God for my pride and sensuality and security, even then pride of God's gifts (good affections) arise. No marvel then He blasts my endeavors and makes the college and country about me fare the worse for my sake. Though He punish my barrenness with public drought; though He say of this poor society: I have shown such and such favour to one of you, and lo! He loathes me, cares not for me, robs me of my glory, and all this for my love; I'll show you no more mercy, my spirit shall strive with no more of you.

July 9

Saturday at night I was importuned to go preach at Roxbury because the elders were both ill. I did so, and preached out of the same text I had done at Concord, the Lord assisting me more than formerly when I preached the same.

Wednesday

I feel such distractions in holy duties, such deadness of heart at lecture, such pride in divine assistance and in my own notions, even then when I have been taught to have no confidence in the flesh, a pang of worldly desires amidst hearing the word, that I am ashamed to lift up my face to heaven. Father forgive or else I perish. Oh hide not thy face, which is my life, from me.

But above all, my vileness breaks forth again while I am hearing the word. An atheistic irreverent frame seizes upon me; and while God is bidding me see His glory I cannot see it; vile and unworthy conceptions concerning God come into my mind. I cannot desire heaven because 'tis a place where I shall see and wonder at and acknowledge the glory of God forever. But I rather desire a heaven where I might be doing for God than only thinking and gazing on His excellency. Blind mind! Carnal heart! I am afraid, ashamed, heavy laden under such cursed frames of heart as ever and anon beset me. My soul groans, my body faints, Lord, while I pray and cry for pardon and redemption.

V

In the first years of settlement, the Puritan community attempted to regulate all aspects of life. The city on the hill would point the way not only in church organization but in economic conduct as well. To this end, the General Court set price and wage regulations. Profit was allowed, but no usury. If a shortage of goods reflected God's judgment (for example, a shipwreck or a drought), a higher price for the item was allowable. But if a merchant's greed caused the price rise, then the court would act. The most famous instance of a Puritan merchant running afoul of these regulations was Robert Keayne's imbroglio over the price of nails. His accusers claimed he charged an excessive price; Keayne consistently maintained his innocence. The court fined him, and the church admonished him— and Keayne never forgot the incident. His last will and testament gave him the opportunity to reargue the case, to protest his unfair treatment. The intensity of his feelings, as well as the norms of the community, emerge clearly in this document. By 1660, the state could no longer maintain economic control. A shortage of goods and of labor bred conditions that outstripped regulation. But for a moment the commonwealth had tried to enforce a broad kind of Christian brotherhood.

THE APOLOGIA OF ROBERT KEAYNE, 1653

THE LAST WILL AND TESTAMENT OF ME, ROBERT KEAYNE,
ALL OF IT WRITTEN WITH MY OWN HANDS AND BEGAN BY
ME, MO: 6: 1: 1653, COMMONY CALLED AUGUST

I, Robert Keayne, citizen and merchant tailor of London by freedom and by the good providence of God now dwelling at Boston in New England in America, being at this time through the great goodness of my God both in health of body and of able and sufficient memory, do therefore now in my health make, ordain, and declare this to be my last will and testament and to stand and to be as effectual as if I had made it in my sickness or in the day or hour of my death, which is in manner and form following.

Thanks to a Merciful God: His Declaration of Faith

First and before all things, I commend and commit my precious soul into the hands of Almighty God, who not only as a loving creator hath given it unto me when He might have made me a brute beast, but also as a most loving father and merciful saviour hath redeemed it with the precious blood of His own dear son and my sweet Jesus from that gulf of misery and ruin that I by original sin and actual transgressions had plunged it into.

I do further desire from my heart to renounce all confidence or expectation of merit or desert in any of the best duties or services that ever I have, shall, or can be able to perform, acknowledging that all my righteousness, sanctification, and close walking with God, if it were or had been a thousand times more exact that ever let I attained to, is all polluted and corrupt and falls short of commending me to God in point of my justification or helping forward my redemption or salvation.

It may be some on the other side may marvel (especially some who have been acquainted with some expressions or purposes of mine in former wills) that I should give away so much of my estate in private legacies and to private uses which might better have been spared and to give little or nothing to any public use for the general good of the country and commonwealth [except] what I have appropriated to our own town of Boston.

To answer this doubt or objection I must acknowledge that it hath been in my full purpose and resolution ever since God hath given me any comfortable estate to do good withal, not only before I came into New England but often since, to study and endeavor both in my life and at my death to do what I could do to help on any public, profitable, and general good here. . . . My thoughts and intents have been about the castle for public defense, the college and schools for learning, the setting up of a bridewell or workhouse for prisoners, malefactors, and

In *The Apologia of Robert Keayne*, ed. Bernard Bailyn (New York, 1964),
pp. 1–2, 48, 52–53, 59–60.

some sort of poor people, stubborn, idle, and undutiful youth, as children and servants, to have been kept at work in either for correction or to get their living, and some other things that I need not mention. In which things, though I could not have done so much as I desired, yet so much I should have done as might have proved an example and encouragement to others of greater estates and willing minds to have done more and to have helped to carry them on to more perfection. For I have held it a great degree of unthankfulness to God that when He hath bestowed many blessings and a large or comfortable outward estate upon a man that he should leave all to his wife and children to advance them only by making them great and rich in the world or to bestow it upon some friends or kindred that it maybe hath no great need of it and to dispose none or very little of it to public charitable or good works such as may tend to His glory and the good of others in way of a thankful acknowledgment to Him for so great favors.

But the truth is that unkindness and ill requital of my former love, both in Old England and here which I have taken to promote the good of this place has been answered by divers [various people] here with unchristian, uncharitable, and unjust reproaches and slanders since I came hither, as if men had the liberty of their tongues to reproach any that were not beneficial to them. [These attacks came] together with that deep and sharp censure that was laid upon me in the country and carried on with so much bitterness and indignation of some, contrary both to law or any foregoing precedent if I mistake not, and, I am sure, contrary or beyond the quality and desert of the complaints that came against me, which indeed were rather shadows of offense, out of a desire of revenge. Yet by some it was carried on with such violence and pretended zeal as if they had had some of the greatest sins in the world to censure. . . . Had it been in their power or could they have carried it they would not have corrected or reformed but utterly have ruined myself and all that I had, as if no punishment had been sufficient to expiate my offense [of] selling a good bridle for 2 s. that now worse are sold without offense for 3 s., 6 d. nails for 7 d., and 8 d. nails for 10 d. per hundred, which since and to this day are frequently sold by many for a great deal more. And so [it was] in all other things proportionably, as selling gold buttons for two shilling nine pence a dozen that cost above 2 in London and yet were never paid for by them that complained.

These were the great matters in which I had offended, when myself have often seen and heard offenses, complaints, and crimes of a high nature against God and men, such as filthy uncleanness, fornications, drunkenness, fearful oaths, quarreling, mutinies, sabbath breakings, thefts, forgeries, and such like, which hath passed with fines or censures so small or easy as hath not been worth the naming or regarding. These [things] I cannot think upon but with sad thoughts of inequality of such proceedings, which hath been the very cause of tying up my heart and hands from doing such general and public good acts as in my heart I both desired and intended.

I did submit to the censure, I paid the fine to the uttermost, which is not nor hath been done by many (nor so earnestly required as mine was) though for certain and not supposed offenses of far higher nature, which I can make good not by hearsay only but in my own knowledge,

yea offenses of the same kind. [My own offense] was so greatly aggra-
vated and with such indignation pursued by some, as if no censure could
be too great or too severe, as if I had not been worthy to have lived
upon the earth. [Such offenses] are not only now common almost in
every shop and warehouse but even then and ever since with a higher
measure of excess, yea even by some of them that were most zealous and
had their hands and tongues deepest in my censure. [At that time] they
were buyers, [but since then] they are turned sellers and peddling
merchants themselves, so that they are become no offenses now nor
worthy questioning nor taking notice of in others.

The oppression lay justly and truly on the buyer's hand rather than
on the seller; but then the country was all buyers and few sellers, though
it would not be seen on that side then. For if the lion will say the lamb
is a fox, it must be so, the lamb must be content to leave it. But now
the country hath got better experience in merchandise, and they have
soundly paid for their experience since, so that it is now and was many
years ago become a common proverb amongst most buyers that knew
those times that my goods and prices were cheap pennyworths in comparison of what hath been taken since and especially [in comparison
with] the prices of these times. Yet I have borne this patiently and without disturbance or troubling the Court with any petitions for remission
or abatement of the fine, though I have been advised by many friends,
yea and some of the same Court, so to do, as if they would be willing to
embrace such an occasion to undo what was then done in a hurry and
in displeasure, or at least would lessen or mitigate it in a great measure.
But I have not been persuaded to it because the more innocently that
I suffer, the more patiently have I borne it, leaving my cause therein
to the Lord.

I did not then nor dare not now go about to justify all my actions.
I know God is righteous and doth all upon just grounds, though men
may mistake in their grounds and proceedings, counsel have erred and
courts may err and a faction may be too hard and outvote the better or
more discerning part. I know the errors of my life. The failings in my
trade and otherwise have been many. Therefore from God [the censure]
was most just. Though it had been much more severe I dare not so open
my mouth against it, nor never did as I remember, [except to] justify
Him. Yet I dare not say nor did I ever think (as far as I can call to
mind) that the censure was just and righteous from men. Was the price
of a bridle, not for taking but only asking, 2 s. for [what] cost here
20 d. such a heinous sin? [Such bridles] have since been commonly sold
and still are for 2 s. 6 d. and 3 s. or more, though worse in kind. Was
it such a heinous sin to sell two or three dozen of great gold buttons for
2 s. 10 d. per dozen that cost 2 s. 2 d. ready money in London, bought
at the best hand, as I showed to many by my invoice (though I could
not find it at the instant when the Court desired to see it) and since
was confirmed by special testimony from London? The buttons [were
not even] paid for when the complaint was made, nor I think not yet;
neither did the complaint come from him that bought and owed them
nor with his knowledge or consent, as he hath since affirmed, but merely
from the spleen and envy of another, whom it did nothing concern. Was
this so great an offense? Indeed, that it might be made so, some out of

their ignorance would needs say they were copper and not worth 9 d. per dozen. But these were weak grounds to pass heavy censures upon.

Yea, and our own church, when they called all those complaints over again that was laid to my charge (as it was meet they should) to see how far there was equity in them and how far I was guilty of all those clamors and rumors that then I lay under, they heard my defense equally and patiently, and after all their exquisite search into them and attention to what others could allege or prove against me, they found no cause but only to give me an admonition. Less they could not do without some offense, considering what had passed in Court before against me. Now if the church had seen or apprehended or could have proved that I had been so justly guilty as others imagined, they could have done no less than to have excommunicated and cast me out of their society and fellowship as an unworthy member.

Chapter 3

The Colonial Family

EIGHTEENTH-CENTURY Americans made the family the most vital institution in the perpetuation of social ideas and the preservation of social order. They endowed the family with so many responsibilities that the lines between it and the community were blurred. In a society where many other institutions were in a rudimentary state or were altogether missing, the family performed innumerable tasks. It was, of course, the place where children were reared and nurtured. But it was also a school, teaching its members how to read and write and offering vocational training, through the system of apprenticeship, to outsiders as well as to its own children. Rather than enter a classroom to learn the skills of a trade, a child in the colonial period went to live with his master, learning the necessary arts directly from him. The family was also a center of employment, using the labor of the household and supplementary labor as necessary. Typically, everybody working on the family farm lived in the homestead. Additionally, the family was in charge of the relief of the aged and care of the young. In the absence of hospitals and almshouses, neighbors cared for neighbors, taking in disabled or decrepit people, and feeding, clothing, and caring for them. Then, too, the family was something of a church—with all the various members of the household coming together several times a day for periods of worship. In essence, the colonial household was not an insular, self-serving institution, dedicated only to the welfare of its own kin; it was a public institution, taking into its midst servants, hapless neighbors, and community children.

The family in this period was somewhat larger than its modern counterpart. Not only were more outsiders boarding with it, but there were more children per family, and the households might hold more distant relatives. Extended families—parents, grandparents, and children living under one roof—were by no means uncommon in the colonies. Modified extended families also existed—clusters of families living one next to the other, not under one roof, but not really separated.

Then too, nuclear families—just the parents and children—could be found, particularly in western areas where sons had gone off to look for new and fertile land. Just about every variant of these types existed, testimony to the great variety of conditions under which colonial families organized themselves.

Social expectations of the colonial family were well defined. The family was to be authoritarian, duplicating within its walls the hierarchical structure of the society outside. The father's power, like that of the colonial governor, was supposed to be unlimited. He ruled his offspring, his wife, and the servants or apprentices who lived with him with a firm hand. Ministers counseled him to wear his authority lightly, to rely upon the love and affection of those around him to win obedience. But they left no doubt that when all else failed, his rule must be paramount. The maxim of Solomon, that he who spares the rod invariably spoils the child, was quoted again and again in well-read pamphlets on child care. The parent had to inculcate obedience in the child, and failure would breed a disruptive, lawless citizen.

Did the colonial family, in fact, live up to this charge? Was the authority of the father so complete? Did he invariably control his children and his wife with a firm hand? Or did conditions in the New World operate to undermine his influence? Did a democratization occur within the household? Some of the conditions in the New World may well have worked to lessen parental authority. Clearly, there was an abundance of land, so that sons in America, unlike their counterparts in England, did not have to stand at the beck and call of their fathers, hoping to get a piece of land through inheritance. Instead, they could pick up stakes, move westward, and set up households of their own. So, too, a shortage of labor gave unusual economic opportunities to the lower classes. Unlike England, where too many laborers competed for too few jobs, unskilled workers were in demand. The master who worked his apprentice too hard might find that his servant had run away, confident that he could find employment elsewhere.

Nevertheless, strong pressures operated to buttress parental discipline. The norms upholding the father's authority may well have offset the effects of land wealth and labor shortages. Furthermore the primitive conditions facing the westward migrant—new soil to be broken and houses to be built—may have intensified reliance on his own family, strengthening mutual interdependence rather than weakening it.

The materials below illuminate the workings and relative strengths of these historical forces. The history of the family does not easily lend itself to fixed and sure conclusions. But the field is both inherently interesting and of major importance to understanding the development of American society.

I

Advice-to-parents books have a long tradition in this country. In every generation there are tracts setting down the norms that parents ought to follow—Dr. Spock is only the latest in a long line of authors. On the whole, these volumes are well worth scrutinizing. They do not, it is true, tell us very much in firsthand fashion about the reality of family life; statements of ideals do not present family life as it was lived. Nevertheless, the advice books reveal in dramatic fashion the goals that a society sets for the family, thereby inform- ing us directly of hopes and fears for social order and stability. Moreover, it is not unreasonable to expect some correspondence between ideals and practices. At least we can know the standards by which families judged themselves, and moreover, we can know what themes to look for as we read in individual diaries and letters about family habits. Furthermore, it is important to note who the authors of the tracts were. In the seventeenth century, clergymen composed them; later, as we shall see, it was doctors and psy- chiatrists. The sermon below, delivered by Congregational min- ister Benjamin Wadsworth in 1712, is a typical statement of the colonial view of the family, a view that includes the relationships between husbands and wives, children and parents, and servants and masters.

A WELL-ORDERED FAMILY, 1712

BENJAMIN WADSWORTH

DOCTRINE

Christians should endeavor to please and glorify God, in whatever capacity or relation they sustain.

Under this doctrine, my design is (by God's help) to say something about *relative duties*, particularly in *families*. I shall therefore endeavor to speak as briefly and plainly as I can about: (1) *family prayer*; (2) *the duties of husbands and wives*; (3) *the duties of parents and children*; (4) *the duties of masters and servants*.

About Family Prayer

Family prayer is a duty. A family should pray to God for family mercies which are needed, and praise Him for family benefits which are enjoyed. *The neglect of family prayer* expose one to God's displeasure.

To answer some objections too apt to be made against this duty.

In *A Well-Ordered Family*, 2nd edition, by Benjamin Wadsworth (Boston, 1719), pp. 4–5, 22–59, 99–121.

Objection: I am so busy and taken up with much business, that I have no time to pray with my family.

Answer: It is a shame that you should make this objection. Have you time to eat, drink, sleep, to follow your outward affairs, and yet you can spare no time to pray in? Can you find time to receive God's mercies, and none to pray for them, or to give thanks for them? Possibly you spend as much or more time than what is needed for family prayer at this tavern in idleness, in needless chatting or diversion.

If you cannot find time to serve God, do not think that He will find time to save you.

Your honest, lawful business will not suffer for your taking time for family prayer. You should *pray* as well as work for your daily bread. In all your ways acknowledge Him (that is; God) and He shall direct your paths.

About the Duties of Husbands and Wives

Concerning the duties of this relation we may assert a few things. *It is their duty to dwell together with one another.* Surely they should dwell together; if one house cannot hold them, surely they are not affected to each other as they should be. They should have a very great and tender love and affection to one another. This is plainly commanded by God. This duty of love is mutual; it should be performed by each, to each of them. When, therefore, they quarrel or disagree, then they do the Devil's work; he is pleased at it, glad of it. But such contention provokes God; it dishonors Him; it is a vile example before inferiors in the family; it tends to prevent family prayer.

As to outward things. If the one is sick, troubled or distressed, the other should manifest care, tenderness, pity, and compassion, and afford all possible relief and succor. They should likewise unite their prudent counsels and endeavors, comfortably to maintain themselves and the family under their joint care.

Husband and wife should be patient one toward another. If both are truly pious, yet neither of them is perfectly holy, in such cases a patient, forgiving, forbearing spirit is very needful. You, therefore, that are husbands and wives, do not aggravate every error or mistake, every wrong or hasty word, every wry step as though it were a willfuly designed intolerable crime; for this would soon break all to pieces: but

rather put the best construction on things, and bear with and forgive one another's failings.

The husband's government ought to be gentle and easy, and the wife's obedience ready and cheerful. The husband is called the head of the woman. It belongs to the head to rule and govern. Wives are part of the house and family, and ought to be under the husband's government. Yet his government should not be with rigor, haughtiness, harshness, severity, but with the greatest love, gentleness, kindness, tenderness that may be. Though he governs her, he must not treat her as a servant, but as his own flesh; he must love her as himself.

Those husbands are much to blame who do not carry it lovingly and kindly to their wives. O man, if your wife is not so young, beautiful, healthy, well-tempered, and qualified as you would wish; if she did not bring a large estate to you, or cannot do so much for you, as some other women have done for their husbands; yet she is your wife, and the great God commands you to love her, not be bitter, but kind to her. What can be more plain and expressive than that?

Those wives are much to blame who do not carry it lovingly and obediently to their own husbands. O woman, if your husband is not as young, beautiful, healthy, so well-tempered, and qualified as you could wish; if he has not such abilities, riches, honors, as some others have; yet he is your husband, and the great God commands you to love, honor, and obey him. Yea, though possibly you have greater abilities of mind than he has, was of some high birth, and he of a more common birth, or did bring more estate, yet since he is your husband, God has made him your head, and set him above you, and made it your duty to love and revere him.

Parents should act wisely and prudently in the matching of their children. They should endeavor that they may marry someone who is most proper for them, most likely to bring blessings to them.

About the Duties of Parents and Children

They should love their children, and carefully provide for their outward supply and comfort while unable to provide for themselves. As soon as the mother perceives herself with child, she should be careful not to do anything injurious to herself or to the child God has formed in her. Mothers also, if they are able, should suckle their children; and yet through sloth or niceness neglect to suckle them, it seems very criminal and blameworthy.

Yet by way of caution I might say, let wisdom and prudence sway, more than fond or indulgent fancy, in feeding and clothing your children. Too much niceness and delicateness in these things is not good; it tends not to make them healthy in their bodies, nor serviceable and useful in their generation, but rather the contrary.

Parents should bring up their children to be diligent in some lawful business. It is true, time for lawful recreation now and then is not altogether to be denied them. Yet for them to do little or nothing else but play in the streets, especially when almost able to earn their living, is a great sin and shame. They should by no means be brought up in idleness, or merely to learn fashions, ceremonious compliments, and to dress after the newest mode. Such folly as this ruins many children. Boys and girls should be brought up diligently in such business as they are capable of, and as is proper for them. Christians are bid to be not slothful in business. And if Christians should be thus diligent in business, surely they should be brought up to it while young. Train up a child in the way wherein he should go.

Parents should teach their children good manners. A civil, respectful, courteous behavior is comely and commendable; those who will not put suitable marks of respect and honor on others, especially on superiors, or those in authority, do not imitate the commendable examples of the godly recorded in Scripture.

Parents should instruct their children in the only true religion taught in the Scriptures. You should bring them up in the nurture and admonition of the Lord. You should also teach them to be sober, chaste, and temperate, to be just to all and bountiful to the poor as they have opportunity and ability.

Parents should govern their children well; restrain, reprove, correct them as there is occasion. A Christian householder should rule well his own house. Children should not be left to themselves, to a loose end to do as they please, but should be under tutors and governors, not being fit to govern themselves. Children being bid to obey their parents in all things plainly implies that parents should give suitable precepts to and maintain a wise government over their children, so carry it, as their children may both fear and love them. You should reprove them for their faults. He that spares the rod, hates his son. Yet on the other hand, a father should pity his children. You should by no means carry it ill to them, you should not frown, be harsh, morose, faulting, and blaming them when they do not deserve it, but do behave themselves well. Again, you should never be cruel or barbarous in your corrections; and if milder ones will reform them, more severe ones should never be used. You should not suffer your children needlessly to frequent taverns nor to be abroad unseasonable on nights, lest they are drawn into numberless hazards and mischiefs thereby.

About the Duties of Children to Their Parents

Children should love their parents. If children duly consider, they will find they have abundant cause to love their parents, they are very vile if they neglect it.

Children should fear their parents. Children should fear both, fear to offend, grieve, disobey, or displease either of them. The great God of Heaven bids children fear their parents; if therefore they fear them not, they rebel against God.

Children should patiently bear and grow better by the needful corrections their parents give them. O child, if you are not bettered by the correction of parents, you are in danger of being terribly destroyed. Children should be faithful and obedient to their parents. What their parents give them they should be thankful for, but they should not take what is their parents' without their knowledge and good liking. When children are disobedient to parents, God is often provoked to leave them to those sins which bring them to great shame and misery in this world.

Alas, children, if you once become disobedient to parents, you do not know what vile abominations God may leave you to fall into. When persons have been brought to die at the gallows for their crimes, how often have they confessed that disobedience to parents led them to those crimes?

Children should be very willing and ready to support and maintain their indigent parents. If our parents are poor, aged, weak, sickly, and not able to maintain themselves, we are bound in duty and conscience to do what we can to provide for them, nourish, support, and comfort them.

About the Duties of Masters to Their Servants

Masters should suitably provide for the bodily support and comfort of their servants. Servants are part of their household. Masters should keep their servants diligently employed. Indeed, they should allow them sufficient time to eat, drink, sleep; on proper occassions some short space for relaxation and diversion may be very advisable. To be sure, servants should be allowed time for prayer and Bible reading. But though time should be allowed for these things, yet we may say, in general, servants should be kept diligently employed. Do not let your servants be idle; oversee them carefully.

About the Duty of Servants to Their Masters

Servants should fear their masters. Servants should honor their masters. Servants should obey their masters, be diligent and faithful in their service and to their interest. The word of God is very plain and expressive for this. You that are servants, take your Bibles, frequently read these plain commands of the great God, that out of obedience to His supreme indisputable authority you may be moved and quickened, conscientiously to obey your masters, and to be faithful to their interest. And you that are masters, if your servants are disobedient or unfaithful to you, then read to them these plain commands of the great God, endeavoring to impress upon their consciences a sense of God's authority and their own duty.

II

By their very nature, diaries are highly idiosyncratic and personal records. To generalize from any one such source is a highly dubious affair—indeed, any one diary may reflect the precise character of the individual more than any overriding truth about a society. But diaries can convey much about the temper of a time; and in the case of the family, if we are to have any intimate picture of its functioning, we must examine and study them. One of the most famous and interesting diaries of the period comes from Samuel

Sewall, a noted figure in Boston, an officeholder and leader of the community. At the age of forty Sewall found himself a widower, and set about courting a woman in similar circumstance, Mrs. Winthrop. It was not a successful courtship; but his record of the abortive romance illustrates the quality of personal and family relationships in late seventeenth-century Boston.

THE DIARY OF SAMUEL SEWALL, 1720

September 30 [1720]

Mr. Colman's lecture. Daughter Sewall acquaints Madam Winthrop that if she pleased to be within at 3 P.M., I would wait on her. She answered she would be at home.

October 1. Saturday

I dine at Mr. Stoddard's; from thence I went to Madam Winthrop's just at 3. Spake to her, saying my loving wife died so soon and suddenly, 'twas hardly convenient for me to think of marrying again; however, I came to this resolution, that I would not make my court to any person without first consulting with her. Had a pleasant discourse about 7 (seven) single persons sitting in the foreseat September 29, *viz.* Madam Rebecca Dudley, Katherine Winthrop, Bridget Usher, Deliverance Legg, Rebecca Lloyd, Lydia Colman, Elizabeth Bellingham. She propounded one and another for me; but none would do; said Mrs. Lloyd was about her age.

October 3.

Waited on Madam Winthrop again; 'twas a little while before she came in. Her daughter Noyes being there alone with me, I said I hoped my waiting on her mother would not be disagreeable to her. She answered she should not be against that that might be for her comfort. I saluted her, and told her I perceived I must shortly wish her a good time (her mother had told me she was with child and within a month or two of her time). At last Madam Winthrop came too. After a considerable time I went up to her and said if it might not be inconvenient, I desired to speak with her. She assented. Then I ushered in discourse from the names in the foreseat; at last I prayed that Katherine [Mrs. Winthrop] might be the person assigned for me. She instantly took it up in the way of denial, as if she had catched at an opportunity to do it, saying she could not do it before she was asked. Said that was her mind unless she should change it, which she believed she should not; could not leave her children. I expressed my sorrow that she should do it so speedily, prayed her consideration, and asked her when I should wait on her again. [I] took leave.

In *The American Puritans*, ed. Perry Miller (New York, 1956), pp. 244–47, 251–53.

October 6th.

A little after 6 P.M. I went to Madam Winthrop's. She was not within. After a while Dr. Noyes came in with his mother, and quickly after his wife came in; they sat talking, I think, till eight o'clock. I said I feared I might be some interruption to their business; Dr. Noyes replied pleasantly he feared they might be an interruption to me, and went away. Madam seemed to harp upon the same string. Must take care of her children; could not leave that house and neighborhood where she had dwelt so long. I told her she might do her children as much or more good by bestowing what she laid out in housekeeping, upon them. Said her son would be of age the 7th of August. I said it might be inconvenient for her to dwell with her daughter-in-law, who must be mistress of the house.

October 21. Friday

My son the minister came to me by appointment and we prayed one for another in the old chamber, more especially respecting my courtship. About 6 o'clock I go to Madam Winthrop's. She received me courteously. I asked when our proceedings should be made public; she said they were like to be no more public than they were already. Offered me no wine that I remember. I rose up at 11 o'clock to come away, saying I would put on my coat; she offered not to help me. I prayed her that Juno might light me home; she opened the shutter and said 'twas pretty light abroad, Juno was weary and gone to bed. So I came home by starlight as well as I could.

November 4th. Friday

Went again about 7 o'clock; found there Mr. John Walley and his wife; sat discoursing pleasantly. I showed them Isaac Moses's [an Indian] writing. Madam W. served comfits to us. After a while a table was spread, and supper was set. I urged Mr. Walley to crave a blessing; but he put it upon me. About 9 they went away. I asked Madam what fashioned necklace I should present her with; she said, "None at all." I asked her whereabout we left off last time, mentioned what I had offered to give her, asked her what she would give me; she said she could not change her condition, she had said so from the beginning, could not be so far from her children. If she held in that mind, I must go home and bewail my rashness in making more haste than good speed.

Monday, November 7th

My son prayed in the old chamber. Our time had been taken up by Son and Daughter Cooper's visit, so that I only read the 130th and 143rd Psalm. 'Twas on the account of my courtship. I went to Madam Winthrop; found her rocking her little Katee in the cradle. I excused my coming so late (near eight). She set me an armed chair and cushion; and so the cradle was between her armed chair and mine. Gave her the remnant of my almonds; she did not eat of them as before, but laid them away; I said I came to inquire whether she had altered her mind since Friday, or remained of the same mind still. She said, "Thereabouts."

I told her I loved her, and was so fond as to think that she loved me. She said [she] had a great respect for me. I told her I had made her an offer without asking any advice; she had so many to advise with that 'twas a hindrance. The fire was come to one short brand besides the block, which brand was set up in end; at last it fell to pieces, and no recruit was made. She gave me a glass of wine. I think I repeated again that I would go home and bewail my rashness in making more haste than good speed. I would endeavor to contain myself, and not go on to solicit her to do that which she could not consent to. Took leave of her. As came down the steps she bid me have a care. Treated me courteously. Told her she had entered the 4th year of her widowhood. I had given her the *News-Letter* before. I did not bid her draw off her glove as sometime I had done. Her dress was not so clean as sometime it had been.

Midweek, November 9th

Dine at Brother Stoddard's; were so kind as to inquire of me if they should invite Madam Winthrop; I answered, "No."

III

Until the introduction of demographic techniques into the study of history, a host of myths about the nature of the colonial family flourished. Everyone assumed that colonial families were composed of very large numbers, including six or more children living with their parents, grandparents, and assorted relatives all under one roof. These were extended families, ostensibly characteristic of a preindustrial society. With the advent of more sophisticated techniques, the picture underwent drastic change. Analyzing hundreds of documents, of which the one below is an example, counting the actual size of the families and the numbers of relatives in the household, demographers came out with a different finding. The colonial family was often composed of only one generation, and it was frequently a good deal smaller in size than had been believed.

The following document is the record taken in 1688 of the inhabitants of Bristol, Rhode Island. Even a quick glance at the information reveals many basic characteristics of family size. Clearly, before we can understand very much about what went on inside the family, we must know about who was in the family.

CENSUS OF BRISTOL, 1688

Feb. 11. All the Families in New Bristol and Children and Servants

	WIFE	CHILDREN	SERVANTS
Mr. Saffin	I	0	8
G. Lewis	I	6	0
G. Martin	I	6	0
G. Penfield	I	5	0

	WIFE	CHILDREN	SERVANTS
Jeremiah Finny	1	1	0
Joshua Finney	1	0	0
Robert Dutch	1	3	0
Solomon G.	1	3	1
Robert Taft	1	5	0
Nathaniel Bosworth	1	2	0
Tommy and Edward (grandchildren)		2	0
Bellamy Bosworth	1	2	0
Benjamin Fenner	1	2 (grown)	0
——— Bowman	1	2	0
David Cary	1	1	0
John Cary	1	7	0
Nicholas Mead	1	6	0
Hugh Woodbury	1	5	0
Anthony Fry	1	7	0
Capt. Sam Woodbry	1	2	2
Eliaship Adams	0	0	0
Nathaniel Paine	1	4	2
John Rogers	1	3	1
William Hedge	1	3	0
Widow Wally	0	1	0
Nathaniel Reynolds	1	8	0
Jeremy Osborn	1	1	1
Major Wally	1	5	4
Stephen Bucklin	1	2	1
John Walkley	1	5	2
Jabez Howland	1	4	2
Simon Davis	1	1	1
William Brutton	1	2	0
Thomas Blesgo	1	0	2
Joseph Sardy	1	3	0
Sam Smith	1	2	0
Sam Cobbett	1	0	0
Watching Atherton	1	4	0
Capt. Nathaniel Byfield	1	2	10
			1 Black
John Wilson	1	3	0
Capt. Benjamin Church	1	6	3
Timothy Ingraham	1	0	0
Capt. Nathan Hayman	1	6	2
Capt. Timothy Clark	1	5	2
William Hoar	1	3	3
Joseph Bastor	1	1	0
Ben Ingle	1	0	0
James Burrough	1	3	1
Smithmason [Anon.]	1	5	0
Dan Langdon	1	7	0
Thomas Doggett	1	2	2
Sam Gallop	1	1	0
Edmund Ranger	1	4	0
James Buzzell	1	1	0
John Gladwin	1	7	0
Peter Papillion	1	4	0
G. White younger	1	1	3
Thomas Walker	1	2	1

	WIFE	CHILDREN	SERVANTS
John Smith	1	3	0
Uzal Wardel	1	6	0
Jabez Goram	1	4	0
G. Denis	1	3	0
G. White	1	4	0
G. Corpe	1	3	0
G. Brown	0	3	0
Pumpmaker [Anon.]	1	2	0
William Throop	1	5	0
His son-in-law	1	1	1
Joseph Landen	1	0	0
G. Row	1	10	0
G. Hampden	1	4	0

       70 families 421 souls
Jacob Mason 1 more
Zachary Cary 1 more
      423

In *Early Rehoboth*, ed. Richard Bowen (Rehoboth, Mass., 1945), pp. 74–76.

IV

*Like the family, the school in colonial society was very much concerned
with the proper moral upbringing of children. Indeed, the task of
schooling, even more clearly in the seventeenth and eighteenth
centuries than now, was self-consciously aimed at preparing children for their moral and public roles. Schoolmasters were perceived
as parents, a definition that gave them wide authority over the
children in their charge, including the responsibility for ensuring
their understanding and compliance with the religious and secular
standards of the society. Hence, when it came to teaching the skills
of reading, teachers delighted in using lessons that would not only
improve reading skills but behavior as well. The selection below
comes from* The New England Primer, *the most popular reading
book for children. It takes little imagination to sense what schooling
must have been like—and what family life must have been like—if
these were the kind of sentences that students poured over.*

THE NEW ENGLAND PRIMER, 1727

*Now the child being entered in his letters and spelling, let him learn
these, and such like sentences by heart, whereby he will be both instructed in his duty, and encouraged in his learning.*

In *The New England Primer* (1727). Reprint edition, ed. Paul L. Ford (New
York, 1897), pp. 69–72, 78–80.

THE DUTIFUL CHILD'S PROMISES

I   will fear GOD, and honor the KING.
     I will honor my father and mother.
I   will obey my superiors.
I   will submit to my elders.
I   will love my friends.
I   will hate no man.
I   will forgive my enemies, and pray to God for them.
I   will as much as in me lies keep all God's Holy Commandments.
I   will learn my catechism.
I   will keep the Lord's day holy.
I   will reverence God's sanctuary,
     For our GOD is a consuming fire.

AN ALPHABET OF LESSONS FOR YOUTH

A   wise son makes a glad father, but a foolish son
     is the heaviness of his mother.
B   etter is a little with the fear of the
     Lord, than great treasure and trouble therewith.
C   ome unto CHRIST all ye that labor
     and are heavy laden, and He will give you rest.
D   o not the abominable thing which I hate,
     saith the Lord.
E   xcept a man be born again, he cannot
     see the Kingdom of God.
F   oolishness is bound up in the heart of
     a child, but the rod of correction
     shall drive it far from him.
G   rieve not the Holy Spirit.
H   oliness becomes God's house forever.
I   t is good for me to draw near unto God.
K   eep thy heart with all diligence, for
     out of it are the issues of life.
L   iars shall have their part in the lake
     which burns with fire and brimstone.

M any are the afflictions of the
righteous, but the Lord delivers them
out of them all.

N ow is the accepted time, now is the day of salvation.

O ut of the abundance of the heart the mouth speaketh.

P ray to thy Father which is in secret and thy Father
which sees in secret shall reward thee openly.

R emember thy Creator in the days of thy youth.

S alvation belongeth to the Lord.

T rust in God at all times ye people,
pour out your hearts before him.

U pon the wicked God shall rain a horrible
tempest.

W oe to the wicked, it shall be ill with him,
for the reward of his hands shall be given him.

eX ort one another daily while it is called today,
lest any of you be hardened through the deceitfulness
of sin.

Y oung men ye have overcome the wicked one.

Z eal hath consumed me, because thy enemies
have forgotten the words of God.

DUTY OF CHILDREN TOWARD THEIR PARENTS

God hath commanded saying, honor thy father and mother, and
who curseth father or mother, let him die the death.

Children obey your parents in the Lord for this is right.

Honor thy father and mother (which is the first Commandment
with promise).

That it may be well with thee, and that thou may live long on the
Earth.

Children, obey your parents in all things, for that is well pleasing
unto the Lord.

My son, help thy father in his age, and grieve him not as long as he
lives.

And if his understanding fails, have patience with him, and despise
him not when thou art in thy full strength.

Who curseth his father or his mother, his lamp shall be out in
obscure darkness.

VERSES

I in the Burying Place may see
Graves shorter there than I;
From Death's Arrest no age is free,
Young children too may die;
My God, may such an awful Sight,
Awakening be to me!
Oh! that by early Grace I might
For Death prepared be.

AGAIN

First in the Morning when thou dost awake,
To God for his Grace thy Petition make,
Some Heavenly Petition use daily to say,
That the God of heaven may bless thee alway.

V

The stake of the society in the good order of the family is dramatically apparent in the nature of court actions and decisions. The line between a moral offense and an illegal act was not finely drawn in eighteenth-century Massachusetts. To the contrary, the very idea of such a division would have provoked surprise and disapproval from eighteenth-century public officials. In many ways, the court saw itself as acting to strengthen the family's rule—it was as outrageous to disobey one's parent as to disobey a magistrate. The courts, like the schools, devoted an extraordinary amount of attention to enforcing not just a law-abiding life style, but a moral life style as well. The case records below, taken from the Massachusetts court at the end of the seventeenth century, convey the quality of this attention.

RECORDS OF THE SUFFOLK COUNTY COURT, 1671–1680

Division of Lorine Estate

Upon the motion of the administrator of the estate of Thomas Lorine, late of Hull, for a division of said estate, the court orders that the widow have her thirds for her life, the eldest son a double portion and the rest of the children equal portions according to law.

Bragg Sentenced

Peter Bragg, presented by the selectmen of this town for abiding in this town without their leave and having a wife in England. The court sentenced him to depart for England with the first opportunity, on penalty of twenty pounds according to law.

Johnson and Moore Sentenced

Abigail Johnson Senior and Naomi Moore [were] convicted for giving entertainment to persons drinking in their houses at unseasonable times of the night. The court sentenced them to give in twenty pounds bond apiece for the good behavior and pay fees of court. Standing committed till the sentence be performed.

Stiles Presented

Robert Stiles being presented for an idle person, the court admonished him and so dismissed him.

In *Collections*, part 1, 1671–1680, Publications of the Colonial Society of Massachusetts (Boston, 1933), vol. 29, pp. 119, 148, 255, 257, 302, 336, 442–443.

Adams Fined Five Pounds

Jonathan Adams of Medfield being presented for absenting himself from the public worship of God on the sabbath days, he owned in court that he worshipped God but did not frequent the public assembly. The court having considered of his offense sentenced him to pay five pounds in money fine to the county and fees of court.

Robinson's Sentence

James Robinson presented for using wicked expressions, the court disenables the said Robinson from crying anything as a public cryer and, upon his first attempt so to do that, he shall be forthwith apprehended by the Constable of Boston and be whipped with fifteen stripes severely laid on and to pay fee of court.

Scott Sentenced

Sarah Scott presented for reviling and striking her mother. Upon due hearing of the case, the court sentenced her to stand upon a block or stool two foot high in the marketplace in Boston upon a Thursday immediately after lecture with an inscription upon her breast in a fair character for undutiful, abusive, and reviling speeches and carriages to her natural mother and to give bond for her good behavior till the next court of this county, ten pounds herself and five pounds apiece, and to pay fee of court; said Sarah Scott as principal in ten pounds and Nathan Greenwood and Thomas Bill as sureties in five pounds apiece acknowledged themselves respectively bound to the treasury of Suffolk on condition that the said Sarah Scott should be of good behavior till the next court of this county and should then appear.

Smith's Sentence

Joseph Smith bound over to this court to answer for his being found by the watch in the house of Abigail King in Boston amongst others at an unreasonable time of the night, where they had been drinking, of which he was convicted in court. The court having considered of his offense herein and his night walking sentenced him to be sent to the house of correction or to pay twenty shillings in money.

Buckminster Sentenced

Sarah Buckminster, widow, being sent for to appear before the court to answer for her committing of fornication and having a bastard child. She owned in court that her husband had been dead about three years and that she had a child of about six weeks old. The court sentenced her to be whipped with ten stripes and ordered the selectmen of Boston to dispose of her into some good family where she may be under government.

Bedwell's Sentence

Mary Bedwell bound over to answer for her keeping company and being too familiar with Walter Hickson, of which she was convicted in court. The court sentenced her to sit in the stocks two hours and to be whipped with fifteen stripes or to pay forty shillings in money as a fine to the county and fees of court standing committed until the sentence be performed and if at any time hereafter she be taken in company of the said Walter Hickson without other company to be forthwith apprehended by the Constable and to be whipped with ten stripes.

Thorn Fined Five Pounds

Mary Thorn bound over to this court to answer for her selling strong beer and ale without license, she owned in court that she did sell strong beer upon a trading day. The court sentenced her to pay five pounds in money as a fine to the county according to law and fees of court standing committed until she performed this sentence.

Wheeler and Peirce Admonished

Elizabeth Wheeler and Joanna Peirce being summoned to appear before the court to answer for their disorderly carriage in the house of Thomas Watts, being married women and found sitting in other men's laps with their arms about their necks. The court upon their acknowledgement of their fault and promise to avoid such offenses for time to come admonished them, ordered them to pay fees of court, and so discharged them.

Chapter 4

The Revolutionary Crowd

THE YEARS 1763 to 1776 were especially turbulent ones for the American colonists. The period that culminated in the outbreak of the American Revolution witnessed an unprecedented number of riots and disorders. In fact, outbreaks were so numerous that the issue of public disorder inevitably became linked with the Revolution itself. To some contemporaries, as well as to later historians, the origins of the Revolution rested with the internal dissension among the colonists. The issue of home rule (the colonists versus the British) became tied to the issue of who should rule at home (the colonists versus the colonists).

There can be no doubt that there was widespread disorder. Immediately following the passage of the Stamp Act riots broke out in Boston, New York, and Newport. Mob actions forced stamp-tax collectors to resign; the homes and furniture of these representatives of British officialdom were put to fire; and in one case, at least, the crowds ran free for several days without the slightest check from public officials. The great moments in the story of the coming of the Revolution were often violent moments; the Tea Act and the Boston Massacre certainly belong to this tradition. Moreover, other incidents of violence broke out during these same years. In North Carolina frontiersmen protested conditions by taking up arms; and although the militia put down the uprising without firing a shot, force—not legal process—ruled the day. In Westchester, New York tenants of the large estates along the Hudson participated in rent strikes; again, it was the militia and not the courts that settled the issue in favor of the landowners.

It is not surprising that historians attempting to understand the roots of the American Revolution have focused on these riots. Many of them contend that the British efforts to tax the colonists or to extend the power of British administrators were necessary—and not especially harmful—acts, which were altogether within the rights of Parliament. And yet the colonists greeted every measure with frantic protests. Why was it that Americans so violently fought the stamp tax

when their rate of taxation was so low? Why did they see in every British act a menace to their liberty? The answer seemed to rest with the tumult at home. According to this interpretation, they were fighting the British because of internal differences. Fundamental class divisions separated the colonists—upper-class property holders in New York, Massachusetts, and Virginia, be they merchants or planters, had very different interests than the lower-class artisans and the propertyless. The riots reflected these differences, and in a sense the British were trapped in the middle. Tumult from below turned against the British, and hence the Revolution.

But social historians consider this explanation inadequate in many respects, and the image of a class-divided, class-warring society in the colonies appears inaccurate. The economic differences among the citizens seem much less striking than their basic similarities. The spread of property throughout colonial society was by no means equal; in fact, increasing differences did emerge, especially in the cities. Yes, there were some large merchants and planters. But an image of the property-less versus the propertied hardly does justice to the vast numbers of citizen freeholders who owned their tools and land, and gave a middle-class character to the social structure.

The materials that follow focus on the famous riots of the Revolutionary era and offer insights into the basic quality of colonial society. As you read them, question whether these riots seem at root to be moments when the unpropertied attacked the propertied. Or do they point to something quite different: an alliance of the propertied and unpropertied, a harmony of interests, or perhaps even a control of the crowd by the propertied? Does the crowd's behavior seem focused and specific, aimed directly at British actions, or do the mobs seem more free floating in character, expressing a general hostility that those in power might well wish to control? The answers to these questions will illuminate not only the basic nature of American society on the eve of the Revolution but will also offer insights into the origins of the Revolution itself.

I

*The first of the great riots in the pre-Revolutionary period took place in
protest against the Stamp Act. This was the first time the colonists
in number and in concert had so vigorously protested an act of
Parliament. Understandably, interest in the riots ran high, both
at home and abroad. Not only the colonists but British officials
as well wondered what these outbursts meant for the future of the
imperial links. Cadwallader Colden, New York's lieutenant governor,
wrote to his superiors in England a full account of the New York
Stamp Act riot, trying to place the events in the context of the
colony's social composition. His description helps to clarify the
nature of the relationship between public riots and social harmony
in the Revolutionary era.*

AN ACCOUNT OF THE STAMP ACT RIOT, 1765

C A D W A L L A D E R   C O L D E N

*State of the Province of New York
(Sent to the Secretary of State and Board of Trade.)*

The people of New York are properly distinguished in different
ranks.

1. The proprietors of the large tracts of land, who include within their
    claims from one hundred thousand of acres to above one million
    of acres under one grant.
2. The gentlemen of the law make the second class in which properly
    are included both the bench and the bar. Both of them act on the
    same principles and are of the most distinguished rank in the policy
    of the province.
3. The merchants make the third class. Many of them have rose sud-
    denly from the lowest rank of the people to considerable fortunes,
    and chiefly by illicit trade in the last war. They abhor every limita-
    tions of trade and duty on it, and therefore gladly go into every
    measure whereby they hope to have trade free.
4. In the last rank may be placed the farmers and mechanics [artisans].
    Though the farmers hold their lands in fee simple, they are as to
    condition of life in no way superior to the common farmers in
    England; and the mechanics such only as are necessary in domestic
    life. This last rank comprehends the bulk of the people, and in them
    consists the strength of the province. They are the most useful and
    the most moral, but always made the dupes of the former; and often
    are ignorantly made their tools for the worst purposes.

The gentlemen of the law, both the judges and principal practi-
tioners at the bar, are either owners, heirs, or strongly connected in

Originally entitled "The Account of the Lieutenant Governor of New York,
Cadwallader Colden, of the Stamp Act Riot, Sent to the Secretary of State and
the Board of Trade in England." In *Collections of the New York Historical
Society for the Year 1877* (New York, 1878), vol. 2, pp. 68–71, 74–77.

family interest with the proprietors. In general, all the lawyers unite in promoting contention, prolonging suits, and increasing the expense of obtaining justice. Every artifice and chicanery in the law has been so much connived at, or rather encouraged, that honest men who are not of affluent fortunes are deterred from defending their rights or seeking justice.

People in general complain of these things and lament the state of justice, but yet the power of the lawyers is such that every man is afraid of offending them and is deterred from making any public opposition to their power and the daily increase of it.

The gentlemen of the law some years since entered into an association with intention, among other things, to assume the direction of government by the influence they had in the assembly, gained by their family connections and by the profession of the law, whereby they are unavoidably in the secrets of many families—many court their friendship, and all dread their hatred. By these means, though few of them are members, they rule the House of Assembly in all matters of importance. The greatest number of the assembly, being common farmers who know little either of men or things, are easily deluded and seduced.

By this association, united in interest and family connections with the proprietors of the great tracts of land, a domination of lawyers was formed in this province which for some years past has been too strong for the executive powers of government. A domination founded on the same principles and carried on by the same wicked artifices that the domination of priests formerly was in the times of ignorance in the papish countries. Every man's character who dares to discover his sentiments in opposition to theirs is loaded with infamy by every falsehood which malice can invent, and thereby exposed to the brutal rage of the mob. Nothing is too wicked for them to attempt which serves their purposes—the press is to them what the pulpit was in times of popery.

When the king's order in his private council of the twenty-sixth of July arrived in September last, it revived all the rage of the profession

of the law and, taking advantage of the spirit of sedition which was raised in all the colonies against the act of Parliament for laying a stamp duty in the colonies, they turned the rage of the mob against the person of the lieutenant governor, after all other methods which their malice had invented for that purpose had failed.

In the night of the first of November, a great mob came up to the fort gate with two images carried on a scaffold: one representing their gray-haired governor, the other the devil whispering him in the ear. After continuing thus at the gate, with all the insulting ribaldry that malice could invent, they broke open the lieutenant governor's coach house which was without the walls of the fort, carried his chariot round the streets of the town in triumph with the images, returned a second time to the fort gate, and, in an open place near the fort, finished their insult with all the indignities that the malice of their leaders could invent. Their view certainly was to provoke the garrison, then placed on the ramparts, to some act which might be called a commencement of hostilities, in which case it cannot be said what was further intended. Being disappointed in this, the mob expended their rage by destroying everything they found in the house of Major James of the Royal Artillery, for which no reason can be assigned other than his putting the fort in a proper state of defense as his duty in his department required of him.

While the lieutenant governor was in the country as usual during the heat of summer, he received a letter from General Gage informing him that the public papers were crammed with treason. The minds of the people [were] disturbed, excited, and encouraged to revolt against the government to subvert the constitution and trample on the laws.

When the lieutenant governor came to town he found the general had ordered Major James to carry in such artillery and military stores as he thought necessary for the defense of the fort; and two companies of artillery having opportunely arrived at that time from England, they had likewise been ordered into the fort to strengthen the garrison. Mr. James is certainly a benevolent, humane man and had distinguished himself on several occasions in the late war. No objection could be made to him, but his daring to put the king's fort in a state of defense, against the sovereign lords—the people, as they styled themselves—for which offense they resolved to make him an example of their displeasure.

Before these additional defenses were made and while the garrison consisted only of forty-four privates and two subaltern officers, the fort could not have been defended against a hundred resolute men, in which case the governor must have submitted to every shameful condition which the insolence of the leaders of the mob should think proper to impose upon him. They certainly had this in view while the fort remained in its defenseless state. But after it was put in that state of offense as well as defense, in which it was put after the first of November by the engineers of the army, the style of the leaders of the mob was changed from threatening to deprecating, and they only wanted some color [reason] for desisting from their designs to save their credit with the deluded people. It became evident that the fort could not be carried by assault and that in the attempt the town would be exposed to desolation. In the state the fort then was, it was the opinion of the

gentlemen of the army that one regiment in the city would have been sufficient to have subdued the seditious spirit which then prevailed.

The authors of the sedition place their security in the number of offenders and that no jury in the colonies will convict any of them. Were it possible that these men could succeed in their hope of independence of a British Parliament, many judicious persons think (though they dare not declare what they think) we shall become a most unhappy people, the obligation of oaths daringly profaned, and every bond of society dissolved. The liberty and property of individuals will become subject to the avarice and ambition of wicked men who have art enough to keep the colony in perpetual factions by deluding an ignorant mob, and the colonies must become thereby useless to Great Britain.

II

It is surprising how quickly the colonists integrated the fact of political riots into an overview of the nature of the relationship between the mother country and the colony. After all, to the colonists, who were raised in the English tradition, the rule of the mob was hardly a phenomenon that should cheer or please them. And yet, the post-1765 riots did not spark fundamental and grave fears for the safety of social order. Instead, the more prevalent response was to urge caution, while at the same time to defend the legitimacy of the riot. One of the most notable examples of this spirit appeared in the writings of John Dickinson. Soon after the Stamp Act was passed, he addressed the following argument to his countrymen.

LETTER FROM A FARMER IN PENNSYLVANIA, 1768

JOHN DICKINSON

My dear Countrymen,

Could you look into my heart you would instantly perceive a zealous attachment to your interests, and a lively resentment of every insult and injury offered to you, to be the motives that have engaged me to address you.

I am no further concerned in anything affecting *American*, than any one of you; and when liberty leaves it, I can quit it much more conveniently than most of you. But while Divine Providence, that gave men existence in a land of freedom, permits my head to think, my lips to speak, and my hand to move, I shall so highly and gratefully value the blessing received as to take care that my silence and inactivity shall not give my implied assent to any act, degrading my brethren and myself from the birthright, wherewith heaven itself *"hath made us free."*

Sorry I am to learn that there are some few persons who shake their heads with solemn motion, and pretend to wonder, what can be the meaning of these letters. *"Great Britain,"* they say, *"is too powerful to contend with; she is determined to oppress us; it is in vain to speak of right on one side, when there is power on the other; when we are strong enough to resist we shall attempt it; but now we are not strong enough, and therefore we had better be quiet, and if we should get into riots and tumults about the late act, it will only draw down heavier displeasure upon us."*

Are these men ignorant that usurpations, which might have been successfully opposed at first, acquire strength by continuance, and thus become irresistible? Do they condemn the conduct of these colonies, concerning the *Stamp Act?* Or have they forgot its successful issue? Should the colonies at that time, instead of acting as they did, have trusted for relief to the fortuitous events of futurity? If it is needless *"to speak of rights"* now, it was as needless then. If the behavior of the colonies was prudent and glorious then, and successful too, it will be equally prudent and glorious to act in the same manner now, if our rights *are* equally invaded, and may be as successful.

As to *"riots and tumults,"* the gentlemen who are so apprehensive

In *Letters from a Farmer in Pennsylvania,* by John Dickinson (1768). Reprint edition (New York, 1962), pp. 15–20.

of them are much mistaken if they think that grievances cannot be redressed without such assistance.

I will now tell the gentlemen what is "the meaning of these letters." The meaning of them is to convince the people of these colonies that they are at this moment exposed to the most imminent dangers, and to persuade them immediately, vigorously, and unanimously, to exert themselves in the most firm, but most peaceable, manner, for obtaining relief.

The cause of *liberty* is a cause of too much dignity to be sullied by turbulence and tumult. It ought to be maintained in a manner suitable to her nature. Those who engage in it should breathe a sedate yet fervent spirit, animating them to actions of prudence, justice, modesty, bravery, humanity, and magnanimity.

I hope, my dear countrymen, that you will, in every colony, be upon your guard against those who may at any time endeavor to stir you up, under pretenses of patriotism, to any measures disrespectful to our Sovereign, and our mother country. Hot, rash, disorderly proceedings injure the reputation of the people as to wisdom, valor, and virtue, without procuring them the least benefit. I pray God that he may be pleased to inspire you and your posterity, to the latest ages, with a spirit of which I have an idea, that I find a difficulty to express. To express it in the best manner I can, I mean a spirit that shall so guide you that it will be impossible to determine whether an *American's* character is most distinguishable for his loyalty to his Sovereign, his duty to his mother country, his love of freedom, or his affection for his native soil.

Every government at some time or other falls into wrong measures. These may proceed from mistake or passion. But every such measure does not dissolve the obligation between the governors and the governed. The mistake may be corrected; the passion may subside. It is the duty of the governed to endeavor to rectify the mistake, and to appease the passion. They have not at first any other right, than to represent their grievances, and to pray for redress, unless an emergency is so pressing as not to allow time for receiving an answer to their applications, which rarely happens. If their applications are disregarded, then that kind of *opposition* becomes justifiable which can be made without breaking the laws or disturbing the public peace. This conflicts in the *prevention of the oppressors reaping advantage from their oppressions*, and not in their punishment. For experience may teach them what reason did not; and harsh methods cannot be proper until milder ones have failed.

If at length it becomes *undoubted* that an inveterate resolution is formed to annihilate the liberties of the governed, the *English* history affords frequent examples of resistance by force. What particular circumstances will in any future case justify such resistance can never be ascertained till they happen. Perhaps it may be allowable to say generally that it never can be justifiable until the people are *fully convinced* that any further submission will be destructive to their happiness.

When the appeal is made to the sword, highly probable is it that the punishment will exceed the offense; and the calamities attending on war outweigh those preceding it. These considerations of justice and prudence will always have great influence with good and wise men.

We cannot act with too much caution in our disputes. Anger produces anger; and differences, that might be accommodated by kind and respectful behavior, may, by imprudence, be enlarged to an incurable rage. In quarrels between countries, as well as in those between individuals, when they have risen to a certain height, the first cause of dissension is no longer remembered, the minds of the parties being wholly engaged in recollecting and resenting the mutual expressions of their dislike. When feuds have reached that fatal point, all considerations of reason and equity vanish; and a blind fury governs, or rather confounds all things. A people no longer regards their interest, but the gratification of their wrath.

The constitutional modes of obtaining relief are those which I wish to see pursued on the present occasion; that is, by petitions of our assemblies, or where they are not permitted to meet, of the people, to the powers that can afford us relief.

We have an excellent Prince, in whose good dispositions toward us we may confide. We have a generous, sensible, and humane nation, to whom we may apply. They may be deceived. They may, by artful men, be provoked to anger against us. I cannot believe they will be cruel and unjust; or that their anger will be implacable. Let us behave like dutiful children who have received unmerited blows from a beloved parent. Let us complain to our parent; but let our complaints speak at the same time the language of affliction and veneration.

If, however, it shall happen, by an unfortunate course of affairs, that our applications to his Majesty and the Parliament for redress, prove ineffectual, let us then take *another step*, by withholding from *Great Britain* all the advantages she has been used to receive from us. Then let us try, if our ingenuity, industry, and frugality will not give weight to our remonstrances. Let us all be united with one spirit, in one cause. Let us invent—let us work—let us save—let us, continually, keep up our claim, and incessantly repeat our complaints—but, above all, let us implore the protection of that infinitely good and gracious being, "by whom kings reign, and princes decree justice."

Nil desperandum.

Nothing is to be despaired of.
                                        A Farmer

III

Few of the colonial riots inspired as many charges and countercharges as the Boston Massacre. For some observers it represented nothing more than an instance of the riffraff of the city, particularly its sailors, needlessly provoking the British soldier; for others, it was the very culmination of their worst fears—British soldiers, quartered in Boston against the wishes of the colonists, had murdered in senseless fashion a well-ordered, albeit protesting,

*crowd. Below are two reports on the event. They offer the reader
the opportunity to play historical detective. Which of the reports
seems the more genuine and accurate? More important, the two
accounts reveal just how far apart the views of the colonists were
from those of the British officials.*

CAPTAIN PRESTON'S ACCOUNT OF THE BOSTON MASSACRE, 1770

THOMAS PRESTON

It is [a] matter of too great notoriety to need any proofs that the
arrival of his Majesty's troops in Boston was extremely obnoxious to
its inhabitants. They have ever used all means in their power to weaken
the regiments, and to bring them into contempt by promoting and
aiding desertions. On the arrival of the sixthy-fourth and sixty-fifth
their ardor seemingly began to abate; it being too expensive to buy off
so many, and attempts of that kind rendered too dangerous from the
numbers. But the same spirit revived immediately on its being known
that those regiments were ordered for Halifax, and has ever since their
departure been breaking out with greater violence after their embarka-
tion. One of their justices, most thoroughly acquainted with the people
and their intentions, openly and publicly in the hearing of great
numbers of people and from the seat of justice, declared "that the
soldiers must now take care of themselves, *nor trust too much their
arms*, for they were but a handful; that the inhabitants carried weapons
concealed under their clothes, and would destroy them in a moment,
if they pleased." This, considering the malicious temper of the people,
was an alarming circumstance to the soldiery. Since which several disputes have happened between the townspeople and the soldiers of both
regiments, the former being encouraged thereto by the countenance of
even some of the magistrates, and by the protection of all the party
against government. In general such disputes have been kept too secret
from the officers. On the second of March, two of the twenty-ninth going
through one Gray's ropewalk, the ropemakers insultingly asked them if
they would empty a vault [outhouse]. This had the desired effect
by provoking the soldiers, and from words they went to blows. Both
parties suffered in this affray, and finally the soldiers retired to their
quarters. The insolence as well as utter hatred of the inhabitants to the
troops increased daily, insomuch that Monday and Tuesday, the fifth
and sixth instant, were privately agreed on for a general engagement,
in consequence of which several of the militia came from the country
armed to join their friends, menacing to destroy any who should oppose
them. This plan has since been discovered.

On Monday night about 8 o'clock two soldiers were attacked and
beaten. But the party of the townspeople in order to carry matters to
the utmost length, broke into two meetinghouses and rang the alarm
bells, which I supposed was for fire as usual, but was soon undeceived.

In *English Historical Documents*, vol. 9, *American Colonial Documents to
1776*, ed. Merrill Jensen (London, 1964), pp. 750–53.

About 9 some of the guard came to and informed me the town inhabitants were assembling to attack the troops, and that the bells were ringing as the signal for that purpose and not for fire, and the beacon intended to be fired to bring in the distant people of the country. This, as I was captain of the day, occasioned my repairing immediately to the main guard. In my way there I saw the people in great commotion, and heard them use the most cruel and horrid threats against the troops. In a few minutes after I reached the guard, about one hundred people passed it and went toward the customhouse where the King's money is lodged. They immediately surrounded the sentry posted there, and with clubs and other weapons threatened to execute their vengeance on him. I was soon informed by a townsman their intention was to carry off the soldier from his post and probably murder him.

This I feared might be a prelude to their plundering the King's chest. I immediately sent a noncommissioned officer and twelve men to protect the sentry and the King's money, and very soon followed myself to prevent, if possible, all disorder, fearing lest the officer and soldiers, by the insults and provocations of the rioters, should be thrown off their guard and commit some rash act. They soon rushed through the people, and by charging their bayonets in half-circles, kept them at a little distance. Nay, so far was I from intending the death of any person that I suffered the troops to go to the spot where the unhappy affair took place without any loading in their pieces; nor did I ever give orders for loading them. This remiss conduct in me perhaps merits censure; yet it is evidence, resulting from the nature of things, which is the best and surest that can be offered, that my intention was not to act offensively, but the contrary part, and that not without compulsion. The mob still increased and were more outrageous, striking their clubs or budgeons one against another, and calling out, come on you rascals, you bloody backs, you lobster scoundrels, fire if you dare, God damn you, fire and be damned, we know you dare not, and much more such language was used. At this time I was between the soldiers and the mob, parleying with, and endeavoring all in my power to persuade them to retire peaceably, but to no purpose. They advanced to the points of the bayonets, struck some of them. On which some well behaved persons asked me if the guns were charged. I replied yes. They then asked me if I intended to order the men to fire. I answered no, by no means, observing to them that I was advanced before the muzzles of the men's pieces, and must fall a sacrifice if they fired; that the soldiers were upon the half cock and charged bayonets, and my giving the word fire under those circumstances would prove me to be no officer. While I was thus speaking, one of the soldiers having received a severe blow with a stick, stepped a little on one side and instantly fired, on which turning to and asking him why he fired without orders, I was struck with a club on my arm, which for some time deprived me of the use of it, which blow had it been placed on my head, most probably would have destroyed me. On this a general attack was made on the men by a great number of heavy clubs and snowballs being thrown at them, by which all our lives were in imminent danger, some persons at the same time from behind calling out, damn your bloods—why don't you fire. Instantly three or four of the soldiers fired, one after another, and directly after three more in the same confusion and hurry. The mob then ran away, except three unhappy men who instantly expired, one more is since dead, three others are dangerously, and four slightly wounded. The whole of this melancholy affair was transacted in almost twenty minutes. On my asking the soldiers why they fired without orders, they said they heard the word fire and supposed it came from me. This might be the case as many of the mob called out fire, fire, but I assured the men that I gave no such order; that my words were, don't fire, stop your firing. In short, it was scarcely possible for the soldiers to know who said fire, or don't fire, or stop your firing.

A Council was immediately called, on the breaking up of which three justices met and issued a warrant to apprehend me and eight soldiers. On hearing of this procedure I instantly went to the sheriff and surrendered myself, though for the space of four hours I had it in my power to have made my escape, which I most undoubtedly should have attempted and could easily executed, had I been the least conscious of any guilt. Five or six more are to swear I gave the word to fire. So bitter and inveterate are many of the malcontents here that they are industriously using every method to fish out evidence to prove it was a concerted scheme to murder the inhabitants. Others are infusing the utmost malice and revenge into the minds of the people who are to be my jurors by false publications, votes of towns, and all other artifices. That so from a settled rancor against the officers and troops in general, the suddenness of my trial after the affair while the people's minds are all greatly inflamed, I am, though perfectly innocent under most unhappy circumstances, having nothing in reason to expect but the loss of life in a very ignominious manner, without the interposition of his Majesty's royal goodness.

THE HORRID MASSACRE IN BOSTON, 1770

PERPETRATED IN THE EVENING OF THE FIFTH DAY OF MARCH 1770, BY SOLDIERS OF THE TWENTY-NINTH REGIMENT, WHICH WITH THE FOURTEENTH REGIMENT WERE THEN QUARTERED THERE; WITH SOME OBSERVATIONS ON THE STATE OF THINGS PRIOR TO THAT CATASTROPHE. GATHERED AND PRINTED BY THE TOWN OF BOSTON, 1770.

It may be a proper introduction to this narrative briefly to represent the state of things for some time previous to the said massacre; and this seems necessary in order to the forming a just idea of the causes of it.

At the end of the late war, in which this province bore so distinguished a part, a happy union subsisted between Great Britain and the colonies. This was unfortunately interrupted by the Stamp Act; but it was in some measure restored by the repeal of it. It was again

In *A Short Narrative of the Horrid Massacre in Boston* (Boston, 1770). Reprint edition (New York, 1849), pp. 13–19, 21–22, 28–30.

interrupted by other acts of Parliament for taxing America; and by the appointment of a Board of Commissioners, in pursuance of an act, which by the face of it was made for the relief and encouragement of commerce, but which in its operation, it was apprehended, would have, and it has in fact had, a contrary effect. By the said act the said Commissioners were "to be resident in some convenient part of his Majesty's dominions in America." This must be understood to be in some part convenient for the whole. Judging by the act, it may seem this town was intended to be favored, by the Commissioners being appointed to reside here; and that the consequence of that residence would be relief and encouragement of commerce; but the reverse has been the constant and uniform effect of it; so that the commerce of the town, from the embarrassments in which it has been lately involved, is greatly reduced.

The residence of the Commissioners here has been detrimental, not only to the commerce, but to the political interest of the town and province; and not only so, but we can trace from it the causes of the late horrid massacre. Soon after their arrival here in November 1767, instead of confining themselves to the proper business of their office, they became partisans of Governor Bernard in his political schemes; and had the weakness and temerity to infringe upon one of the most essential rights of the house of commons of this province—that of giving their votes with freedom, and not being accountable therefore but to their constituents. One of the members of that house, Captain Timothy Folgier, having voted in some affair contrary to the mind of said Commissioners, was for so doing dismissed from the office he held under them.

These proceedings of theirs, the difficulty of access to them on office business, and a supercilious behavior, rendered them disgustful to people in general, who in consequence thereof treated them with neglect. This probably stimulated them to resent it; and to make their resentment felt, they and their coadjutor, Governor Bernard, made such representations to his Majesty's ministers as they thought best calculated to bring the displeasure of the nation upon the town and province; and in order that those representations might have the more weight, they are said to have contrived and executed plans for exciting disturbances and tumults, which otherwise would probably never have existed; and, when excited, to have transmitted to the ministry the most exaggerated accounts of them.

Unfortunately for us, they have been to successful in their said representations, which, in conjunction with Governor Bernard's, have occasioned his Majesty's faithful subjects of this town and province to be treated as enemies and rebels, by an invasion of the town by sea and land. While the town was surrounded by a considerable number of his Majesty's ships of war, two regiments landed and took possession of it; and to support these, two other regiments arrived some time after from Ireland; one of which landed at Castle Island, and the other in the town.

Thus were we, in aggravation of our other embarrassments, embarrassed with troops, forced upon us contrary to our inclination, contrary to the very letter of the Bill of Rights, in which it is declared that the raising or keeping of a standing army within the kingdom in time of peace, unless it be with the consent of Parliament, is against law, and without the desire of the civil magistrates, to aid whom was the pretense for sending the troops hither; who were quartered in the town in direct violation of an act of Parliament for quartering troops in America.

As they were the procuring cause of troops being sent hither, they must therefore be the remote and blameable cause of all the disturbances and bloodshed that have taken place in consequence of that measure.

We shall next attend to the conduct of the troops, and to some circumstances relative to them.

The challenging [of] the inhabitants by sentinels posted in all parts of the town before the lodgings of officers, which (for about six months, while it lasted), occasioned many quarrels and uneasiness.

Captain Wilson, of the fifty-ninth, exciting the Negroes of the town to take away their masters' lives and property, and repair to the army for protection, which was fully proved against him. The attack of a party of soldiers on some of the magistrates of the town—the repeated rescues of soldiers from peace officers—the firing of a loaded musket in a public street, to the endangering a great number of peaceable inhabitants—the frequent wounding of persons by their bayonets and cutlasses, and the numerous instances of bad behavior in the soldiery, made us early sensible that the troops were not sent here for any benefit to the town or province, and that we had no good to expect from such conservators of the peace.

It was not expected, however, that such an outrage and massacre, as happened here on the evening of the fifth instant, would have been perpetrated. There were then killed and wounded, by a discharge of musketry, eleven of his Majesty's subjects, viz.:

> Mr. Samuel Gray, killed on the spot by a ball entering his head.
> Crispus Attucks, a mulatto, killed on the spot, two balls entering his breast.
> Mr. James Caldwell, killed on the spot, by two balls entering his back.
> Mr. Samuel Maverick, a youth of seventeen years of age, mortally wounded; he died the next morning.
> Mr. Patrick Carr mortally wounded; he died the fourteenth instant.
> Christopher Monk and John Clark, youths about seventeen years of age, dangerously wounded. It is apprehended they will die.
> Mr. Edward Payne, merchant, standing at his door; wounded.
> Messrs. John Green, Robert Patterson, and David Parker; all dangerously wounded.

The actors in this dreadful tragedy were a party of soldiers commanded by Captain Preston of the twenty-ninth regiment. This party, including the Captain, consisted of eight, who are all committed to jail.

What gave occasion to the melancholy event of that evening seems to have been this. A difference having happened near Mr. Gray's ropewalk, between a soldier and a man belonging to it, the soldier challenged the ropemakers to a boxing match. The challenge was accepted by one of them, and the soldier worsted. He ran to the barrack in the neighborhood, and returned with several of his companions. The fray was renewed, and the soldiers were driven off. This happened several times till at length a considerable body of soldiers was collected, and they also were driven off, the ropemakers having been joined by their brethren of the contiguous ropewalks. By this time Mr. Gray being alarmed interposed, and with the assistance of some gentlemen prevented any further disturbance. To satisfy the soldiers and punish the man who had been the occasion of the first difference, and as an example to the rest, he turned him out of his service; and waited on Colonel Dalrymple, the commanding officer of the troops, and with him concerted measures for preventing further mischief. Though this affair ended thus, it made a strong impression on the minds of the soldiers in general, who thought the honor of the regiment concerned to revenge those repeated repulses. For this purpose they seem to have formed a combination to commit some outrage upon the inhabitants of the town indiscriminately; and this was to be done on the evening of the fifth instant or soon after.

Samuel Drowne [a witness] declares that, about nine o'clock of the evening of the fifth of March current, standing at his own door in Cornhill, he saw about fourteen or fifteen soldiers of the twenty-ninth regiment, who came from Murray's barracks, armed with naked cutlasses, swords, etc., and came upon the inhabitants of the town, then standing or walking in Cornhill, and abused some, and violently assaulted others as they met them; most of them were without so much as a stick in their hand to defend themselves, as he very clearly could discern, it being moonlight, and himself being one of the assaulted persons. All or most of the said soldiers he saw go into King Street (some of them through Royal Exchange Lane), and there followed them, and soon discovered them to be quarreling and fighting with the people whom they saw there, which he thinks were not more than a dozen, when the soldiers came first, armed as aforesaid. Of those dozen people, the most of them were gentlemen, standing together a little below the Town House, upon the Exchange. At the appearance of those soldiers so armed, the most of the twelve persons went off, some of them being first assaulted.

The violent proceedings of this party, and their going into King Street "quarreling and fighting with the people whom they saw there" (mentioned in Mr. Drowne's deposition), was immediately introductory to the grand catastrophe.

These assailants, who issued from Murray's barracks (so-called), after attacking and wounding divers persons in Cornhill, as abovementioned, being armed, proceeded (most of them) up the Royal Exchange Lane into King Street; where, making a short stop, and after assaulting and driving away the few they met there, they brandished their arms and cried out, "Where are the boogers! Where are the cowards!" At this time there were very few persons in the street beside themselves. This party in proceeding from Exchange Lane into King Street, must pass the sentry posted at the westerly corner of the Custom House, which butts on that lane and fronts on that street. This is needful to be mentioned, as near that spot and in that street the bloody tragedy was acted, and the street actors in it were stationed: their station being but a few feet from the front side of the said Custom House. The outrageous behavior and the threats of the said party occasioned the ringing of the meetinghouse bell near the head of King Street, which bell ringing quick, as for fire, it presently brought out a number of the inhabitants, who being soon sensible of the occasion of it, were naturally led to King Street, where the said party had made a stop but a little while before, and where their stopping had drawn together a number of boys, round the sentry at the Custom House. Whether the boys mistook the sentry for one of the said party, and thence took occasion to differ with him, or whether he first affronted them, which is affirmed in several depositions—however that may be, there was much foul language between them, and some of them, in consequence of his pushing at them with his bayonet, threw snowballs at him, which occasioned him to knock hastily at the door of the Custom House. From hence two persons thereupon proceeded immediately to the mainguard which was posted opposite to the State House, at a small distance, near the head of the said street. The officer on guard was Captain Preston, who with seven or eight soldiers, with firearms and charged bayonets, issued from the guardhouse, and in great haste posted himself and his soldiers in front of the Custom House, near the corner aforesaid. In passing to this station the soldiers pushed several persons with their bayonets, driving through the people in so rough a manner that it appeared they intended to create a disturbance. This occasioned some snowballs to be thrown at them, which seems to have been the only provocation that was given. Mr. Knox (between whom and Captain Preston there was some conversation on the spot) declares that while he was talking with Captain Preston, the soldiers of his detachment had attacked the people with their bayonets; and that there was not the least provocation given to Captain Preston or his party; the backs of the people being toward them when the people were attacked. He also declares that Captain Preston seemed to be in great haste and much agitated, and that, according to his opinion, there were not then present in King Street above seventy or eighty persons at the extent.

The said party was formed into a half circle; and within a short time after they had been posted at the Custom House, began to fire upon the people.

Captain Preston is said to have ordered them to fire, and to have repeated that order. One gun was fired first; then others in succession, and with deliberation, till ten or a dozen guns were fired; or till that number of discharges were made from the guns that were fired. By which means eleven persons were killed or wounded, as above represented.

IV

One result of the Boston Massacre was to inspire a commemorative meeting and oration every year on March fifteenth. The second speech in this series was made by Joseph Warren, and he, like others, used this occasion to consider British-American problems. His speech offers a good opportunity to evaluate the political implications of mob violence. Compare Warren's views with those in Dickinson's tract. Mob action clearly has become a more legitimate form of political action. There is little indication here of the community being at odds with itself. Rather, to a remarkable degree, Warren's rhetoric points to a confident acceptance of the risks inherent in such violent tactics.

BOSTON MASSACRE ORATION, 1772

JOSEPH WARREN

The ruinous consequences of standing armies to free communities may be seen in the histories of Syracuse, Rome, and many other once flourishing states; some of which have now scarce a name! Their baneful influence is most suddenly felt when they are placed in populous cities; for, by a corruption of morals, the public happiness is immediately affected! And that this is one of the effects of quartering troops in a populous city, is a truth, to which many a mourning parent, many a lost despairing child in this metropolis must bear a very melancholy testimony. Soldiers are also taught to consider arms as the only arbiters by which every dispute is to be decided between contending states; they are instructed implicitly to obey their commanders, without enquiring into the justice of the cause they are engaged to support; hence it is that they are ever to be dreaded as the ready engines of tyranny and oppression. And it is too observable that they are prone to introduce the same mode of decision in the disputes of individuals, and from thence have often arisen great animosities between them and the inhabitants, who, while in a naked, defenseless state, are frequently insulted and abused by an armed soldiery. And this will be more especially the case when the troops are informed that the intention of their being stationed in any city is to overawe the inhabitants. That this was the avowed design of stationing an armed force in this town is sufficiently known; and we, my fellow citizens, have seen, we have felt the tragical effects! *The fatal fifth of March 1770, can never be forgotten.* The horrors of *that dreadful night* are but too deeply impressed on our hearts. Language is too feeble to paint the emotion of our souls, when our streets were stained with the blood of our brethren— when our ears were wounded by the groans of the dying, and our eyes were tormented with the sight of the mangled bodies of the dead.

The immediate actors in the tragedy of that night were surrendered to justice. It is not mine to say how far they were guilty. They have been tried by the country and *acquitted* of murder! And they are not to be again arraigned at an earthly bar; but, surely the men who have promiscuously scattered death amid the innocent inhabitants of a populous city ought to see well to it that they be prepared to stand at

In *English Historical Documents*, vol. 9, *American Colonial Documents to 1776*, ed. Merrill Jensen (London, 1964), pp. 755–59.

the bar of an omniscient judge! And all who contrived or encouraged the stationing troops in this place have reasons of eternal importance to reflect with deep contrition on their base designs, and humbly to repent of their impious machinations.

The infatuation which hath seemed, for a number of years, to prevail in the British councils, with regard to us, is truly astonishing! What can be proposed by the repeated attacks made upon our freedom, I really cannot surmise; even leaving justice and humanity out of question. I do not know one single advantage which can arise to the British nation from our being enslaved. I know not of any gains which can be wrung from us by oppression which they may not obtain from us by our own consent in the smooth channel of commerce. We wish the wealth and prosperity of Britain; we contribute largely to both. Does what we contribute loose all its value because it is done voluntarily?

If we complain, our complaints are treated with contempt; if we assert our rights, that assertion is deemed insolence; if we humbly offer to submit the matter to the impartial decision of reason, the *sword* is judged the most proper argument to silence our murmurs! But this cannot long be the case. Surely the British nation will not suffer the reputation of their justice and their honor to be thus sported away by a capricious ministry; no, they will in a short time open their eyes to their true interest. They nourish in their own breasts a noble love of liberty; they hold her dear, and they know that all who have once possessed her charms had rather die than suffer her to be torn from their embraces.

You have, my friends and countrymen, frustrated the designs of your enemies by your unanimity and fortitude. It was your union and determined spirit which expelled those troops who polluted your streets with innocent blood. You have appointed this anniversary as a standard memorial of the *bloody consequences of placing an armed force in a populous city*, and of your deliverance from the dangers which then seemed to hang over your heads; and I am confident that you never will betray the least want of spirit when called upon to guard your freedom. None but they who set a just value upon the blessings of liberty are worthy to enjoy her. Your illustrious fathers were her zealous votaries. When the blasting frowns of tyranny drove her from public view they clasped her in their arms; they brought her safe over the rough ocean and fixed her seat in this then dreary wilderness; they nursed her infant age with the most tender care; for her sake they patiently bore the severest hardships; for her support they underwent the most rugged toils, in her defense they boldly encountered the most alarming dangers; neither the ravenous beasts that ranged the woods for prey, nor the more furious savages of the wilderness could damp ardor! While with one hand they broke the stubborn glebe, with the other they grasped their weapons, ever ready to protect her from danger. No sacrifice, not even their own blood, was esteemed too rich a libation for her altar!

And as they left you this glorious legacy, they have undoubtedly transmitted to you some portion of their noble spirit, to inspire you with virtue to merit her, and courage to preserve her. You surely cannot, with such examples before your eyes, as every page of the history of this country affords, suffer your liberties to be ravished from you by lawless force, or cajoled away by flattery and fraud. If you, with united zeal and fortitude, oppose the torrent of oppression; if you feel the true fire of patriotism burning in your breasts; if you, from your souls, despise the most gaudy dress that slavery can wear; if you really prefer the lonely cottage (while blessed with liberty) to gilded palaces surrounded with the ensigns of slavery, you may have the fullest assurance that tyranny, with her whole accursed train, will hide their hideous heads in confusion, shame, and despair. If you perform your part, you must have the strongest confidence that the same Almighty Being who protected your pious and venerable forefathers—who enabled them to turn a barren wilderness into a fruitful field, who so often made bare his arm for their salvation, will still be mindful of you, their offspring.

May this Almighty Being graciously preside in all our councils. May He direct us to such measures as He Himself shall approve, and be pleased to bless. May we ever be a people favored of God. May our land be a land of liberty, the seat of virtue, the asylum of the oppressed, a name and a praise in the whole earth, until the last shock of time shall bury the empires of the world in one common undistinguished ruin!

V

To those American colonists who opposed the break with the mother country—Tories—the mob actions represented all that was irrational and mistaken about the move to independence. For the Tories, but not for the Revolutionaries, the unleashing of the mob was to be condemned not only for precipitating the war with England, but for promising to keep this country in turmoil for decades to come. In fact, the differing views on mob action most dramatically separated the Loyalist from the Revolutionary. The Tory analysis presented by Peter Oliver will help the reader to form his own judgments on the impulse and character of mob action in the Revolutionary era.

ORIGIN AND PROGRESS OF THE AMERICAN REBELLION, 1781

PETER OLIVER

Tarring and Feathering

About this time was invented the art of tarring and feathering; and the invention was reserved for the genius of New England. The town of Salem, about twenty miles from Boston, hath the honor of

In *Origin and Progress of the American Rebellion*, by Peter Oliver, ed. Douglas Adair and John Schutz (San Marino, Calif., 1963), pp. 93-96, 98, 100-105, 118-21.

this invention, as well as that of witchcraft in the year 1692, when many innocent persons suffered death by judicial processes.

The following is the recipe for an effectual operation. "First, strip a person naked, then heat the tar until it is thin, and pour it upon the naked flesh, or rub it over with a tar brush. After which, sprinkle decently upon the tar, while it is yet warm, as many feathers as will stick to it. Then hold a lighted candle to the feathers, and try to set it all on fire; if it will burn, so much the better.

I know no other origin of this modern punishment by the rabble of their state criminals than this; namely, that the first book that New England children are taught to read in is called *The New England Primer*. In the front of it is depicted the Pope, stuck around with darts. This is the only clue I can find to lead me to the origin of this invention. In order to keep in memory the soldiers firing on the night of the fifth of March, they instituted an anniversary oration, upon what they called the Massacre. This kept the minds of the rabble in constant irritation, and thus was the fire of contention fed with constant fuel, until the town of Boston was evacuated of the filth of sedition in 1775.

1772

In the winter of this year, the ruling powers seized upon a custom-house officer for execution. They stripped him, tarred, feathered, and haltered him, carried him to the gallows, and whipped him with great barbarity in the presence of thousands, some of them members of the general court. Like the Negro drivers in the West Indies, if you grumbled at so wholesome a discipline, you had iniquity added to transgression, and lash succeeded lash; and there was but one way of escaping, which was to feign yourself dead if you were not already so; for in that case you would be left to yourself to come to life again as well as you could, they being afraid of such dead men lest they themselves should die after them, sooner or later. One customhouse officer they left so for dead, but some persons of humanity stepped into his relief and saved him.

The plague which spread through the great part of Massachusetts, and had overspread the town of Boston was of the confluent sort. It was so contagious that the infection was caught by the neighboring colonies. Rhode Island, some years before in a most riotous manner had rifled the houses and hunted after the lives of several gentlemen who were obnoxious by their attachment to government. In this year, the mob burnt his Majesty's schooner *Gaspee* on the Narragansset Shore, about twenty miles from Newport. This made some noise in England; from a misrepresentation of facts, a commission was sent over, empowering the Governor of Rhode Island, the Chief Justices of Massachusetts, New York, and New Jersies, and the Judge of the Vice Admiralty Court of Massachusetts, to inquire into the facts. The people of that colony were so closely connected, and so disaffected from the nature of their government to British legislation that it was perfectly futile to make an inquiry, and the matter ended without any other effect from the commission than an encouragement to those colonists to play the same game again upon the first opportunity.

Boston Tea Party

Thus things went on until 1773, when the design of the Parliament was announced of sending over the East India Company's tea. The decks were now cleared for an engagement, and all hands were ready. The teas at last arrived in the latter end of autumn, and now committee men and mob men were buzzing about in swarms, like bees, with every one their sting. They applied first to the consignees to compel them to ship the teas back again. The mob collected with their great men in front. They attacked the stores and dwelling houses of the consignees, but they found them too firm to flinch from their duty; the mob insisted that the teas should be sent to England. At last, the rage of the mob, urged on by the smugglers and the heads of the faction, was increased to such a height that the consignees were obliged to fly for protection to the Castle, as the King's ship in the harbor, which was ordered to give them protection, refused it to them. There was no authority to defend any man from injury.

The faction did what was right in their own eyes; they accordingly planned their maneuver and procured some of the inhabitants of the neighboring towns to assist them. The mob had, partly, Indian dresses procured for them, and that the action they were about to perpetrate might be sanctified in a peculiar manner, Adams, Hancock, and the leaders of the faction assembled the rabble in the largest dissenting meetinghouse in the town, where they had frequently assembled to pronounce their annual orations upon their massacre, and to perpetrate their most atrocious acts of treason and rebellion, thus, literally, "turning the house of God into a den of thieves."

Thus assembled on December fourteenth, they whiled away the

time in speechmaking, hissing, and clapping, cursing and swearing until it grew near to darkness; and then the signal was given to act their deeds of darkness. They crowded down to the wharves where the tea ships lay and began to unload. They then burst the chests of tea, when many persons filled their bags and their pockets with it, and made a teapot of the harbor of Boston with the remainder; and it required a large teapot for several hundred chests of tea to be poured into at one time. Had they have been prudent enough to have poured it into fresh water instead of salt water, they and their wives, their children, and their little ones might have regaled upon it, at free cost, for twelve months, but now the fish had the whole regale to themselves. Whether it suited the constitution of a fish is not said; but it is said that some of the inhabitants of Boston would not eat of fish caught in their harbor because they had drank of the East India tea.

After the destruction of the tea, the Massachusetts faction found they had past the Rubicon; it was now neck or nothing. They therefore went upon committees of correspondence and drew up what they called a solemn league and covenant, whereto everyone was to subscribe, not to import from England nor to deal with any that did, and to renounce all connection with those who sold English goods. This was a truly infernal scheme; it was setting the nearest relations and most intimate friends at irreconcilable variance, and it had that most accursed effect of raising a most unnatural enmity between parents and children and husbands and wives.

The dissenting hierarchy lent their aid to sanctify the treason and I knew a clergyman of some note in a country town who went to the meetinghouse where the inhabitants usually assembled upon their civil affairs and took his seat at the communion table, and in the plentitude of priestly power declared to the assembly then convened on the solemn league and covenant that whoever would not subscribe to it was not fit to approach that table to commemorate the death and sufferings of the savior of mankind. This was truly making a league with the Devil and a covenant with hell.

Thus, tarring and feathering, solemn leagues and covenants, and riots reigned uncontrolled. The liberty of the press was restrained by the very men who, for years past, had been halloowing for liberty herself; those printers, who were inclined to support government, were threatened and greatly discouraged. So that the people were deprived of the means of information and the faction had engrossed the press, which now groaned with all the falsities that seditious brains could invent, which were crammed down the credulity of the vulgar.

Lexington and Concord

In the spring of 1775, the war began to redden. General Gage having intelligence that a quantity of warlike stores were collected at Concord, about twenty miles from Boston, judged it most prudent to seize them. Accordingly, just about midnight of the eighteenth of April, he privately dispatched about eight hundred men for that purpose, they executed part of their orders, but to no important effect. This party was attacked by a number who had previous notice of their march. Much stress has been laid upon who fired the first gun. This was immaterial, for as the civil government had been resolved by the Suffolk resolves, the military power had a right to suppress all hostile appearances. But in the present case, the commanding officer ordered the armed rabble to disperse, upon which some of the armed rabble returned an answer from their loaded muskets. The King's troops then returned the fire, the alarm spread, and ten or twelve thousand men, some say more, flanked them and kept in the rear at turns. The battle continued for the whole day. After this first corps had fought, on their return, for many miles, they had expended most of their ammunition, and must have submitted as prisoners had not Lord Percy met them with a fresh brigade, with two pieces of artillery. This fortunate circumstance saved them from total ruin. When united, they still fought, but the cannon checked the progress of the rebels, who kept at a greater distance and chiefly fired from houses and from behind hedges, trees, and stone walls. As the King's troops approached their headquarters, the battle thickened upon them, for every town which they passed through increased the numbers of their enemies, so that they had not less than ten or twelve thousand to combat with in the course of the day.

After the battle of Lexington, there was a general uproar through the neighboring colonies, the echo of which soon extended throughout the continent. Adams, with his rabble rout and his clergy sounding the trumpet of rebellion to inspire them, had blown the bellows so long that the iron was quite hot enough to be hammered. The news of the battle flew with rapidity; one post met another to tell the doleful tale of the King's troops burning houses and putting to death the inhabitants of towns. Industry never labored harder than the faction did in propagating the most atrocious falsehoods to inspirit the people to the grossest acts of violence, and they had a great advantage in doing it by engrossing the tale almost to themselves, and by suppressing the true state of facts. At last, indeed, General Gage, by great assiduity, found means to undeceive those who had preserved any coolness of temper. As for the *qui vult decipi decipiatur* [those who wish to be deceived, let them be deceived], he there could make no impression; thus the rupture could not be closed.

SUGGESTIONS FOR
FURTHER READING

The history of the *Proper Plantation* in Virginia and subsequent developments in the colony are traced in Wesley F. Craven, *The Southern Colonies in the 17th Century, 1607–1689* (Baton Rouge, 1949), and his *White, Red and Black* (Princeton, 1972). An older, but fascinating account of Virginia's social history is to be found in Philip A. Bruce, *The Institutional History of Virginia* (two volumes, New York, 1910).

A brief and readable introduction to *Puritanism* can be found in Edmund Morgan, *The Puritan Dilemma: The Story of John Winthrop* (Boston, 1958). On the decline of the authority of the Puritan Church see Darrett Rutman, *Winthrop's Boston* (Chapel Hill, 1965). An interesting, if erratic, analysis of a major crisis in the Puritan community is Emery Battis's biography of Anne Hutchinson, *Saints and Sectaries* (New Brunswick, N.J., 1962). Indispensable for understanding the Puritan mentality is Perry Miller's *Errand into the Wilderness* (Cambridge, Mass., 1956).

For an intimate picture of the *Colonial Family*, see John Demos, *A Little Commonwealth* (New York, 1970). The ideas that underlay the colonial family are explored in detail by Edmund Morgan's *The Puritan Family* (Boston, 1944). A demographic analysis that relates land ownership to family authority is Philip Grevin, *Four Generations* (Ithaca, New York, 1970).

The actions and motivating ideas of the *Revolutionary Crowd* are explored in Edmund Morgan and Helen Morgan, *The Stamp Act Crisis* (rev. ed., New York, 1963), and in Pauline Maier, *From Resistance to Revolution* (New York, 1972). The ideology of American Revolutionaries, particularly their fears about a British conspiracy against their liberties, is traced superbly by Bernard Bailyn in *The Ideological Origins of American Revolution* (Cambridge, Mass., 1967).

The first representations of the Indians of the New World were highly ideal-
ized. Just as the land seemed to be one of milk and honey (see the description in *Nova Britannia*, p. 7), so the Indians seemed to resemble classical
Greek figures. The drawings of John White, a member of one of the
first expeditions to Virginia, popularized this image: Note how orderly the
village arrangement is and how symmetrical the designs are. Surely, no
would-be member of the Virginia Company would have to fear such a tribe.
*Watercolor of John White, 1591, reproduced from the collection of the Library
of Congress.*

By 1624 a far more devil-like image of the Virginia Indians
had become popular. Now the scenes were not of peaceable
villages but of Indians attacking and being attacked by the
English. The engravings that accompanied a 1624 history of
John Smith's expedition tried to justify the use of force against
the Indians (as did the 1622 account of the Indian massacre,
see p. 18). The natives tied and bound Smith, then danced
their primitive dance around him; it is John Smith's rifle versus
the Indians' bows and arrows. In essence, force had to be met
with force. *Engraving of Robert Vaughan, from John Smith,
Generall Historie, 1624, reproduced from the collection of the
Library of Congress.*

Nothing better illustrates the legitimacy of colonial mob actions than this engraving by Paul Revere of the Boston Massacre. Just as the colonists placed all the blame for the uprising on the British troops, (see *The Horrid Massacre in Boston*, p. 68), so did Revere. The colonists claimed that Captain Preston, with cool calculation, ordered the troops to fire, and Revere has sketched him standing behind his troops, not in front as he insisted; it is not the Custom's House that he is defending but Butcher's Hall. The victims of the fire are all well-dressed Bostonians, not the sailors or youngsters who were actually there. And there is even a gun being fired from the Custom's House itself, another indication of how the British, in calculated fashion, murdered the colonists. Here was a picture sure to inflame colonial sentiments. *Paul Revere, The Boston Massacre, reproduced courtesy of the New-York Historical Society, New York City.*

As one looks at this photograph of the Lowell Mills, it is not difficult to imagine just how different factory work was from agricultural work. The architecture seems to echo the discipline of the machine: ordered, regularized, monotonous. Window follows upon window, row follows upon row. Keep this image in mind when reading the *Lowell Offering* column occasioned by two girls' suicide (p. 98). *Lowell Mills on the Merrimack River, Detroit Publishing Company, 1908, reproduced from the collection of the Library of Congress.*

TO BE SOLD on board the Ship *Bance-Island*, on tuesday the 6th of *May* next, at *Ashley-Ferry*; a choice cargo of about 250 fine healthy NEGROES, just arrived from the Windward & Rice Coast. —The utmost care has already been taken, and shall be continued, to keep them free from the least danger of being infected with the SMALL-POX, no boat having been on board, and all other communication with people from *Charles-Town* prevented.

Austin, Laurens, & Appleby.

N. B. Full one Half of the above Negroes have had the SMALL-POX in their own Country.

This eighteenth-century poster advertising the forthcoming sale of newly arrived Africans tries to assure would-be buyers of the slaves' physical health. Clearly, it was not a concern for the welfare of the blacks that led the ship's captain to keep them isolated from an epidemic of small-pox; rather, with an eye to profits, he was trying to protect his cargo from disease. Just how significant this dynamic was in the history of slavery is very much in debate (see the Bennet Barrow records, pp. 105). Did the profitability of slave labor place a significant floor on the level of treatment slaves would receive? *Reproduced from the collection of the Library of Congress.*

The isolation of frontier settlers is grimly apparent in this photograph of a Dakota settler. The image of loneliness, of men and women striving to eke out a living against the elements, is all too clear in this setting. Yet one must remember that this family would immediately come to the aid of any neighbor in trouble. Caroline Kirkland might well jibe at neighbor's reliance upon neighbor (see p. 144). But families such as this had little else they could count on in time of crisis. *Dakota Home, 1885, reproduced from the collection of the Library of Congress.*

The order and discipline that the first common schools sought to inculcate is expressed vividly in this lithograph of the children's routine in a New York school. The children march in unison, their arms upraised together. The teacher has all the characteristics of a drill sergeant. And note the clock in the middle of the back wall. Bell-ringing punctuality here, as in the Cheshire schools (see p. 177), was a prime virtue. *First Infant School in Green Street, New York City, lithograph by Imbert after a drawing by A. Robertson, 1828. Reproduced courtesy of the New-York Historical Society, New York City.*

This illustration seems to represent a major state occasion—one in which a major Congressional speech is about to be delivered, for example. But in fact, this is a lithograph of the American Art Union's annual drawing for its lottery prize. Clearly, the Art Union patrons thought of themselves as fulfilling a significant and worthy patriotic duty; they were promoting works of culture to demonstrate American superiority in the arts. Since the lottery scheme was at the heart of the enterprise, (see the American Art Union *Bulletin*, 1849, p. 194), it deserved this kind of celebration. *Lithograph of the American Art Union, Distribution of Prizes, 1847, reproduced courtesy of the New-York Historical Society, New York City.*

Illustrations of the American Anti-Slavery Almanac for 1840.

"Our Peculiar Domestic Institutions."

Northern Hospitality—New-York nine months law. [The Slave steps out of the Slave State, and his chains fall. A Free State, with another chain, stands ready to re-enslave him.]

Burning of McIntosh at St. Louis, in April, 1836.

Showing how slavery improves the condition of the female sex.

The Negro Pew, or "Free" Seats for black Christians.

Mayor of New-York refusing a Carman's license to a colored Man.

Servility of the Northern States in arresting and returning fugitive Slaves.

Selling a Mother from her Child.

Hunting Slaves with dogs and guns. A Slave drowned by the dogs.

"Poor things, 'they can't take care of themselves.' "

Mothers with young Children at work in the field.

A Woman chained to a Girl, and a Man in irons at work in the field.

Branding Slaves.

Cutting up a Slave in Kentucky.

Paid.   Unpaid.

One of the several techniques used by abolitionist societies to stimulate Northern opposition to slavery was to print and circulate posters portraying the grossest abuses of the system. These societies, in fact, were among the first to use lithographs for organized political ends, and they were proud of it (see Angelina Grimké's comments, p. 225). The images of women being whipped or separated from their children, and of men being branded or hanged, were to dominate people's view of slavery. *Illustrations of the American Anti-Slavery Almanac for 1840, reproduced from the collection of the Library of Congress.*

The New Nation, 1800–1865

THE FACTORY

THE PLANTATION

THE FRONTIER COMMUNITY

THE COMMON SCHOOL

THE AMERICAN ART UNION

ABOLITIONIST SOCIETIES

INTRODUCTION

IN THE DECADES following the Revolution, each of the new nation's three major regions followed a very particular course of development. And in each instance the special character of the region emerged in the rise and spread of one special institution. In the Northeast the first factories sprang up; in the South the plantation took hold; and in the Western territories a new type of frontier community appeared. Certainly similarities did remain among the sections. Small subsistence farms were found throughout the republic, and occasional factories did appear in the South. Nevertheless, the distinctive nature of regional developments is most apparent in these decades, and the differences emerge most clearly in analysis of these three typical institutions.

The first textile mills were organized in New England in the 1820s. Newly created corporations, with sizable aggregates of capital and employing hundreds of laborers, took the nation on its first steps toward industrial development. New kinds of work arrangements and new life styles took hold, demanding adjustment and readjustment on the part of workers. Nowhere was this development more advanced than at Lowell, Massachusetts. The industrial enterprise there became in many ways the test case for industrialism. Americans were understandably nervous about the rise and spread of factories. With images of the horrors of the English mill towns in their minds, citizens honestly questioned the price paid for industry. Would the Lowell experience recapitulate that of Manchester—would factories pauperize and demoralize once honest and independent citizens? Would American laborers even undertake factory work? After all, unlike in England, no group of hungry, landless, and unemployed men roamed the city and the countryside here. Hence, the Lowell enterprise was watched and examined very closely by a wide range of observers. Only slightly exaggerated was the claim that as Lowell went, so would go the course of industrial development in the United States.

No less unusual or important was the character of the plantation. Without question, this institution gave the antebellum South its special character, although subsistence farmers remained in the region, and the number of large-sized plantations was small. For blacks, the slave experience was identical with the plantation experience; and it was the planters who, to an extraordinary degree, dominated the political, economic, and social life of the South. If we are to understand the history of the South in these years, and the experience of both blacks and whites, the nature of this very peculiar institution must be examined in detail.

In the West, frontier communities represented a new departure. Here were communities made up of families on the move, settlers coming together before there were churches, courts, or other institutions common to the older Eastern communities. And there was also a notable paucity of goods and services. Tools were in short supply and so was labor—and yet somehow the community would have to keep order and allow citizens to go about the process of dividing and cultivating virgin soil. The solutions were unpredictable and often ingenious, and highlight the issue of social stability in antebellum America.

Given all these new developments, it is not surprising that Americans in the antebellum period were especially concerned with the problems of social order. Indeed, one cannot begin to understand the nature of educational or cultural developments without a sensitivity to this issue. The Jacksonian period, for example, was a time when various "reforms" occurred. Most notable among them were new ways of caring for the insane and the poor, new ways of punishing the criminal, and, not coincidentally, new ways of educating the populace. The rise of the common school, the spread of free public education in the new republic, exemplifies these movements. The question of why common schools should have developed in these years brings us directly to the issue of how American society as a whole came to grips with these crucial and in many ways frightening changes. Indeed, these same concerns had a vital influence on the development of American culture. The character of artistic production is as reflective of this concern as the school. And the founding of one of the most novel institutions to spread artistic production through the country, the American Art Union, clarifies the dimensions of this story.

Finally, a focus on the nature of the abolitionist societies unites these several themes. The outbreak of the Civil War represented the culmination of both national and regional developments in the years 1800–1860. And one of the very best routes to understanding the causes of this conflict is through the abolitionist efforts. What was the basis of their critique of the South? How did the citizenry respond to it? How was their message spread? An understanding of these issues will clarify the origins of the most important conflict of nineteenth-century America.

Chapter 5

The Factory

PROBABLY no institution in pre–Civil War America more radically transformed the life styles of those who came under its influence than the factory. Its routine and organization demanded a sharp and dramatic break with traditional rural habits. The first workers who moved from the farm to the factory had to adjust to a new discipline of time and motion, to new relationships among fellow workers and employers. And yet, as dramatic as the shift was, the introduction of the factory into the United States, unlike its introduction into England, was accomplished relatively peaceably and efficiently. Americans took to the machine extraordinarily well.

Two basic measurements highlight the nature of the change that the factory brought to the nation's economy. In 1829, Americans produced 102,000 tons of bituminous coal; by 1859, the figure had leaped to 6,013,000. In 1820, Americans manufactured 54,000 tons of pig iron; by 1859, the amount had swelled to 821,000. These figures point not only to an economic revolution but also to a social one. How did an essentially agrarian nation transform itself into an industrial one? And why did the change proceed smoothly and effectively, with a minimum of protest and a maximum of inventiveness? Indeed, Americans in the 1820s were acutely aware of the blight and misery that factory life had brought to such English cities as Manchester. Whatever benefits they could imagine resulting from industrial production were more than balanced by a nagging fear that the machine would pauperize and demoralize a large number of citizens. Yet they apparently overcame these deep and genuine concerns to accept the factory system. Legislators were eager to incorporate the ventures, and entrepreneurs were prepared to invest in them. And last, but by no means least important, a labor force was ready to enter the mills and work the machines. Rather than attack the power looms of the first textile factories, as some of their counterparts in England had done, American workers, in the

words of one contemporary, "hail with satisfaction all mechanical improvements."

To understand the special nature of this response, the selections that follow focus on one of the first manufacturing enterprises in this country, the Lowell textile mills. In 1822, a group of Boston businessmen established a number of mills at Lowell, some twenty-five miles from Boston. The enterprise grew quickly, so that by 1840 210,000 workers were producing enormous quantities of cotton and woolen goods. But Lowell's importance transcended the size of its factories and their output. Lowell was, in essence, the test case for American industrialism, the experiment that would resolve whether factories here could avoid replicating the English horrors. Accordingly, observers devoted an enormous amount of attention to conditions there. Foreign visitors invariably made Lowell one of their first stops, while state legislators and clergymen frequently visited the site to take its moral temperature.

The founders of Lowell were themselves acutely conscious of the model character of their enterprise. They very self-consciously set out to demonstrate that the factory need not destroy the virtue of the worker or the integrity of the society. In fact, this sense of Lowell as a national experiment coincided with one of the investors' most basic economic concerns. The mills, after all, had to attract a labor force—this at a time when no ready pool of labor was easily available. The agricultural character of the nation's economy meant that nearly all available hands were already occupied on the farm. The solution advanced by the Lowell Associates to this problem was to recruit to their mills the one group that was marginal to the economic life of the farm: the younger daughters of not very well-off New England farmers. But this was not an easy group to attract. Fathers had to be persuaded that the experience would not be ruinous, that their daughters could still marry after leaving the factory, that the girls would not be compromised in any way. So, in a sense, the larger problem of persuading Americans to accept the factory became at Lowell the very specific issue of convincing fathers to let their children come to the mills.

The Lowell system, with its elaborate boardinghouse arrangements, moral policing, and elaborate rules and regulations, was an effort to solve this problem, and it was effective. The success of the Lowell venture went far in proving both the feasibility and desirability of industrial production in the United States.

I

One of the most complete accounts of the Lowell system was written by Henry Miles, a local Protestant clergyman. That as a minister he felt compelled to report on this economic enterprise points to the significance of the moral issues that Lowell posed. That he was prepared to defend the propriety and effectiveness of its arrangements points to the diligence with which the owners sought to assure the nation in general and the parents in particular of the value of their enterprise. Clearly Miles was not an altogether impartial observer; he undoubtedly mingled more with the owners than with the workers. Still, his account may be considered an accurate rendition of the basic organization at Lowell, and it helped assure many of his fellow citizens of the essential legitimacy of factory life.

LOWELL, AS IT WAS AND AS IT IS, 1845

HENRY A. MILES

Lowell has been highly commended by some, as a model community, for its good order, industry, and general freedom from vice. It has been strongly condemned, by others, as a hotbed of corruption, tainting the whole land. We all, in New England, have an interest in knowing what are the exact facts of the case. We are destined to be a great manufacturing people. The influences that go forth from Lowell will go forth from many other manufacturing villages and cities. If these influences are pernicious, we have a great calamity impending over us. Rather than endure it, we should prefer to have every factory destroyed.

If, on the other hand, a system has been introduced, carefully provided with checks and safeguards, and strong moral and conservative influences, it is our duty to see that this system be faithfully carried

In *Lowell, As It Was and As It Is,* by Henry A. Miles (Boston, 1845), pp. 62–63, 66–67, 100–103, 128–35, 140–47.

out, so as to prevent the disastrous results which have developed themselves in the manufacturing towns of other countries. Hence the topics
assume the importance of the highest moral questions. The author
writes after a nine years' residence in this city, during which he has
closely observed the working of the factory system, and has gathered
a great amount of statistical facts which have a bearing upon this subject. He believes himself to be unaffected by any partisan views, as he
stands wholly aside from the sphere of any interested motives.

A Lowell Boardinghouse

Each of the long blocks of boardinghouses is divided into six or
eight tenements, and are generally three stories high. These tenements
are finished off in a style much above the common farmhouses of the
country, and more nearly resemble the abodes of respectable mechanics
in rural villages. These are constantly kept clean, the buildings well
painted, and the premises thoroughly whitewashed every spring, at the
corporation's expense.

As one important feature in the management of these houses, it
deserves to be named that male operatives and female operatives do
not board in the same tenement; and the following regulations, printed
by one of the companies, and given to each keeper of their houses, are
here subjoined, as a simple statement of the rules generally observed
by all the corporations.

> Regulations to be observed by persons occupying the boardinghouses
> belonging to the Merrimack Manufacturing Company.
> They must not board any persons not employed by the company,
> unless by special permission.
> No disorderly or improper conduct must be allowed in the houses.
> The doors must be closed at ten o'clock in the evening.
> Those who keep the houses, when required, must give an account
> of the number, names, and employment of their boarders; also with
> regard to their general conduct, and whether they are in the habit of
> attending public worship.
> The buildings, both inside and out, and the yards about them, must
> be kept clean, and in good order.

The hours of taking meals in these houses are uniform throughout
all the corporations in the city. The time allowed for each meal is thirty
minutes for breakfast, when that meal is taken after beginning work; for
dinner, thirty minutes.

The food that is furnished in these houses is of a substantial and
wholesome kind, is neatly served, and in sufficient abundance. Operatives are under no compulsion to board in one tenement rather than
another. And then, as to the character of these boardinghouse keepers
themselves, on no point is the superintendent more particular than on
this. Applications for these situations are very numerous. The rents of
the company's houses are purposely low, averaging only from one-third
to one-half of what similar houses rent for in the city. There is no intention on the part of the corporation to make any revenue from these
houses. They are a great source of annual expense. But the advantages
of supervision are more than an equivalent for this.

The influence which this system of boardinghouses has exerted upon the good order and good morals of the place, has been vast and beneficent. To a very great degree the future condition of Lowell is dependent upon a faithful adhesion to this system.

The following table shows the average hours per day of running the mills, throughout the year, on all the corporations in Lowell:

Hours of Labor

	H.	M.		H.	M.
January	11	24	July	12	45
February	12	00	August	12	45
March	11	52	September	12	23
April	13	31	October	12	10
May	12	45	November	11	56
June	12	45	December	11	24

In addition to the above, it should be stated that lamps are never lighted on Saturday evening, and that four holidays are allowed in the year, viz. Fast Day, Fourth of July, Thanksgiving Day, and Christmas Day.

The average daily time of running the mills is twelve hours and ten minutes. Arguments are not needed to prove that toil, if it be continued for this length of time, each day, month after month, and year after year, is excessive, and too much for the tender frames of young women to bear. No one can more sincerely desire than the writer of this book, that they had more leisure time for mental improvement and social enjoyment. It must be remembered, however, that their work is comparatively light. All the hard processes, not conducted by men, are performed by machines, the movements of which female operatives are required merely to oversee and adjust.

Moral Police of the Corporations

The productiveness of these works depends upon one primary and indispensable condition—the existence of an industrious, sober, orderly, and moral class of operatives. Without this, the mills in Lowell would be worthless. Profits would be absorbed by cases of irregularity, carelessness, and neglect; while the existence of any great moral exposure in Lowell would cut off the supply of help from the virtuous homesteads of the country. Public morals and private interests, identical in all places, are here seen to be linked together in an indissoluble connection. Accordingly, the sagacity of self-interest, as well as more disinterested considerations, has led to the adoption of a strict system of moral police.

The female operatives in Lowell do not work, on an average, more than four and a half years in the factories. They then return to their homes, and their places are taken by their sisters, or by other female friends from their neighborhood.

To obtain this constant importation of female hands from the country, it is necessary to secure *the moral protection of their characters while they are resident in Lowell.* This, therefore, is the chief object of that moral police.

No persons are employed on the corporations who are addicted to intemperance, or who are known to be guilty of any immoralities of conduct. As the parent of all other vices, intemperance is most carefully excluded.

In respect to discharged operatives, there is a system observed. Any person wishing to leave a mill is at liberty to do so, at any time, after giving a fortnight's notice. The operative so leaving, if of good character, and having worked a year, is entitled, as a matter of right, to an honorable discharge.

That form is as follows:

> Mr. or Miss _____ _____, has been employed by the _____ Manufacturing Company, in a _____ room, _____ years _____ months, and is honorably discharged.
>
> _____ _____, *Superintendent.*
>
> LOWELL, _____ _____

This discharge is a letter of recommendation to any other mill in the city, and not without its influence in procuring employment in any other mill in New England. Those dishonorable have another treatment. The names of all persons dismissed for bad conduct, or who leave the mill irregularly, are also entered in a book, and these names are sent to all the counting rooms of the city. *Such persons obtain no more employment throughout the city.*

Any description of the moral care, studied by the corporations, would be defective if it omitted a reference to the overseers. Every room in every mill has its first and second overseer. At his small desk, near the door, where he can see all who go out or come in, the overseer may generally be found, and he is held responsible for the good order, and attention to business, of the operatives of that room. Hence, this is a post of much importance. It is for this reason that peculiar care is exercised in their appointment. The overseers are almost universally married men, with families; and as a body, numbering about one hundred and eighty in all, are among the most permanent residents, and most trustworthy and valuable citizens of the place. The guiding and salutary influence which they exert over the operatives is one of the most essential parts of the moral machinery of the mills.

It may not be out of place to present here the regulations, which are observed alike on all the corporations, which are given to the operatives when they are first employed, and are posted up conspicuously in all the mills. They are as follows:

> *Regulations to be observed by all persons employed by the Manufacturing Company, in the factories.*

> Every overseer is required to be punctual himself, and to see that those employed under him are so.

> The overseers may, at their discretion, grant leave of absence to those employed under them, when there are sufficient spare hands in the room to supply their place; but when there are not sufficient spare hands, they are not allowed to grant leave of absence unless in cases of absolute necessity.

> All persons are required to observe the regulations of the room in which they are employed. They are not allowed to be absent from their

work without the consent of their overseer, except in case of sickness, and then they are required to send him word of the cause of their absence.

All persons are required to board in one of the boardinghouses belonging to the company, and conform to the regulations of the house in which they board.

All persons are required to be constant in attendance on public worship, at one of the regular places of worship in this place.

Persons who do not comply with the above regulations will not be employed by the company.

Persons entering the employment of the company are considered as engaging to work one year.

All persons intending to leave the employment of the company are required to give notice of the same to their overseer, at least two weeks previous to the time of leaving.

Anyone who shall take from the mills, or the yard, any yarn, cloth, or other article belonging to the company will be considered guilty of *stealing*—and prosecuted accordingly.

The above regulations are considered part of the contract with all persons entering the employment of the _____ Manufacturing Company. All persons who shall have complied with them, on leaving the employment of the company, shall be entitled to an honorable discharge, which will serve as a recommendation to any of the factories in Lowell. No one who shall not have complied with them will be entitled to such a discharge.

_____ _____, Agent.

II

The novelty of Lowell emerges vividly in this description by a visiting Englishman, William Scorseby. He made an earnest attempt to discern the root differences between Lowell and its English counterparts. Why was it that Lowell seemed so much less grim, physically and morally, than English mill towns? His answers are but the beginning of a resolution of this issue. They do, however, point the way to a better understanding of the dynamics responsible for the special origins of industrialism in the United States.

AMERICAN FACTORIES AND THEIR FEMALE OPERATIVES, 1845

WILLIAM SCORSEBY

On entering Lowell, a stranger is naturally struck with the contrast presented by that place to an English manufacturing town. Here, in Bradford [England], every building is of stone, or brick, solid, sub-

In *American Factories . . . and Their Female Operatives*, by William Scorseby (Boston: 1845), pp. 11–15, 78–79, 92–95.

stantial, with little of the freshness that might be looked for in so rapidly an increasing town: there, in Lowell, though the mills and boardinghouses are generally of brick, the chief part of the other buildings, houses, hotels, and even churches, are of wood, and nearly the whole as fresh looking as if built within a year. Here, with us, everything, externally, is discolored with smoke; buildings, streets, and causeways alike bearing a sooty covering; the mud of the streets in color and consistency like blackish gray paint, and the air of heaven darkened as by a dense cloud: there, nothing is discolored, neither houses nor mills nor trees—the red brick factories and boardinghouses, and the other edifices of wood painted in light colors, look as fresh as if just finished. Then the trees and plants which, with us, soon become dingy after their foliage bursts out, there, in Lowell, were fresh and flourishing. Hence, as to Lowell, large as it has grown, it is yet rural in its appearance, and, notwithstanding its being a city of factories, is yet fresh and cleanly.

Soon after arriving we were joined by a gentleman, Mr. ——— Lawrence, a principal in a large woolen factory, who had been expecting us—and we had also the assistance of the manager of the cotton mills of one of the principal corporations.

We proceeded, without further delay, to one of the factories, that we might see the factory workers as they came out to their dinners. Several hundreds of young women, but not any children, issued from the mills, altogether very orderly in their manner, and very respectable in their appearance. They were neatly dressed, and clean in their persons; many with their hair nicely arranged. There was not the slightest appearance of boldness or vulgarity; on the contrary, a very becoming propriety and respectability of manner, approaching, with some, to genteel.

When I see the levity of behavior of some of our mill girls as they come out from their work into the street, I cannot but wish that I could show them how their sisters in America conduct themselves, at least the many hundreds whom I saw at Lowell, under the same circumstances. And let me tell you what I consider to be the fact—that no such thing is ever to be seen among the young women of Lowell as *rudeness*, and very rarely indeed, I believe, anything like levity or immodesty of behavior in the streets.

The position in which a majority of these young women are placed—as strangers from the country, separated from their natural protectors and left almost entirely to their own discretion and moral self-dependence—is one singularly exposed to risk and temptation. Nor, under ordinary influences, would their being congregated in such considerable numbers together in their sleeping rooms and boardinghouses, by any means tend to their greater security.

But from all the information I could obtain, tested by all available means, and received with all reasonable caution, I have been led to infer that their character and moral conduct are unusually high.

While the case of Lowell will afford us some leading and important suggestions [for British adoption] that case, it will be easily perceived, has its peculiarities; such peculiarities, therefore, must prevent what is done there becoming in all respects a model for us.

One great and striking difference, in the present positions of England and America, is found in the history and rise of our respective manufacturing establishments. In England, for the most part, they consist of enlargements of old, and successions of new manufactories, within a previously existing manufacturing town. But in America, the manufactories consist altogether of new, or at least of very modern erections; and these are not unfrequently planted, as in the case of Lowell, not as grafts upon the stock of a town venerable in age, but as the original occupants of the ground, and as the stock on which the town itself is grafted.

Hence the American manufacturing towns possess, in many cases, the advantage of a peculiar unity of construction—each part, like the mass of machinery in a factory, having an essential relation to, or connection with, the whole. There is no previously existing idle and profligate population to inoculate with its viciousness the incoming country females; nor is there already there any unhappily pauperized population to depress with its burdensomeness the enterprise of the manufacturers. They have not, as with us it commonly happens, to contend with preexisting difficulties; but have, or in most cases may have, a clear and unembarrassed field for their manufacturing enterprises—a field wherein they can build on a plan to their liking, adopt the best models, introduce the most perfect and efficient machinery, and then order the principal contingencies, requisite for carrying on their works, on some commodious general plan.

Again, find we a want of analogy in the two countries in several other circumstances, more or less peculiar to the manufactories of the United States, such as, in the high prices they obtain, through their protective tariff and other causes, for their manufactured goods consumed at home; in the ample wages which, from the general scarcity of laborers, the operatives may demand, and which the remuneration in high prices enables the manufacturer to pay; in the cheapness of their board and lodging, yielding more clear gain and saving to the prudent operatives; and in the superior and more independent class of persons who, by reason of these latter advantages, are induced to engage in the business of the factories.

III

For all the satisfaction that outsiders took in the progress of the Lowell experiment, the women themselves decidedly did not have an easy time of it. The balance sheet was mixed. The excitement of leaving the confines of the homestead, of accumulating some funds that might go into a dowry, and of being on their own was offset by the experience of coming under a stranger's authority, by the long hours and tedious work, by the exacting routine, and by the women's sense that their work was menial and their status something less than that of respectable women. The redeeming element undoubtedly was that their stay was temporary. For most of them, work at Lowell was a brief interlude, less than four years, between family responsibilities. Lucy Larcom's memoir of what it was like to be a Lowell woman offers the reader a glimpse into the personal nature of the experience.

A NEW ENGLAND GIRLHOOD, 1889

LUCY LARCOM

I went to my first day's work in the mill with a light heart. The novelty of it made it seem easy, and it really was not hard, just to change the bobbins on the spinning-frames every three-quarters of an hour or so, with half a dozen other little girls who were doing the same thing.

And for a little while it was only a new amusement; I liked it better than going to school and "making believe." And there was a great deal of play mixed with it. We were not occupied more than half the time. The intervals were spent frolicking around among the spinning-frames, teasing and talking to the older girls, or entertaining ourselves with games and stories in a corner.

I never cared much for machinery. The buzzing and hissing and whizzing of pulleys and rollers and spindles and flyers around me often grew tiresome. But in a room below us we were sometimes allowed to peer in through a sort of blind door at the great waterwheel that carried the works of the whole mill. It was so huge that we could only watch a few of its spokes at a time, moving with a slow, measured strength

In *A New England Girlhood*, by Lucy Larcom (Boston, 1889), pp. 153–55, 175.

through the darkness that shut it in. It impressed me with something of the awe which comes to us in thinking of the great Power which keeps the mechanism of the universe in motion.

There were compensations for being shut in to daily toil so early. The mill itself had its lessons for us. But it was not, and could not be, the right sort of life for a child, and we were happy in the knowledge that, at the longest, our employment was only to be temporary.

I learned to do a spinner's work, and I obtained permission to tend some frames that stood directly in front of the river windows, with only them and the wall behind me, extending half the length of the mill, and one young woman beside me, at the farther end of the row. She was a sober, mature person, who scarcely thought it worth her while to speak often to a child like me; and I was, when with strangers, rather a re-served girl; so I kept myself occupied with the river, my work, and my thoughts.

The printed regulations forbade us to bring books into the mill. Some of the girls could not believe that the Bible was meant to be counted among forbidden books. The overseer, caring more for law than gospel, confiscated all he found. He had his desk full of Bibles. It sounded oddly to hear him say to the most religious girl in the room, when he took hers away, "I did think you had more conscience than to bring that book here." It was a rigid code of morality under which we lived. Nobody complained of it, however, and we were doubtless better off for its strictness, in the end.

My grandfather came to see my mother once at about this time and visited the mills. When he had entered our room, and looked around for a moment, he took off his hat and made a low bow to the girls, first toward the right, and then toward the left. But we had never seen anybody bow to a room full of mill girls in that polite way, and someone afterward asked him why he did so. He looked a little surprised at the question, but answered promptly and with dignity, "I always take off my hat to ladies."

His courtesy was genuine. Still, we did not call ourselves ladies. We did not forget that we were working-girls, wearing coarse aprons suitable to our work, and that there was some danger of our becoming drudges. I know that sometimes the confinement of the mill became very wearisome to me. In the sweet June weather I would lean far out of the window and try not to hear the unceasing clash of sound inside. Looking away to the hills, my whole stifled being would cry out,

Oh, that I had wings!

Still I was there from choice, and

The prison unto which we doom ourselves,
No prison is.

And I was every day making discoveries about life, and about myself. I loved quietness. The noise of machinery was particularly distasteful to me. I discovered, too, that I could so accustom myself to the noise that it became like a silence to me. And I defied the machinery to make me its slave. Its incessant discords could not drown the music of my thoughts if I would let them fly high enough. Even the long hours, the early rising, and the regularity enforced by the clang of the bell were good discipline for one who was naturally inclined to dally and to dream, and who loved her own personal liberty with a willful rebellion against control. Perhaps I could have brought myself into the limitations of order and method in no other way.

IV

As part of the effort to make Lowell a model community, the mill owners not only supported a library and encouraged its use, but also sponsored a newspaper. The Lowell Offering was often cited as evidence of the uplifting character of the Lowell enterprise. As one would expect, most of its pages were filled with inconsequential and badly written stories and sentimental poetry. But occasionally something more genuine appeared in its pages. The suicides of two Lowell workers occasioned one such response.

THE LOWELL OFFERING, 1845

The Suicide

Within a few weeks the papers of the day have announced the deaths of two young female operatives, by their own hands—one in Lowell, the other in an adjacent manufacturing town. With the simple announcement these papers have left the affair to their readers. And how have the community received this intelligence? Apparently with much indifference; but where we hear an expression of opinion it is one of horror. The human being who has dared, herself, to wrench away the barrier which separated her from the Giver of her life, and who will judge her for this rash act, is spoken of as a reckless contemner of His laws, both natural and revealed.

In the first instance, were the causes mental or physical which led to the deed? We believe in this, and indeed in all cases, that both operated upon the individual. Morbid dejection and wounded sensibility have, in these instances, produced that insanity which prompted suicide. Is it not an appropriate question to ask here whether or not there was anything in their mode of life which tended to this dreadful result?

We have been accused of representing unfairly the relative advantages and disadvantages of factory life. We are thought to give the former too great prominence, and the latter too little, in the pictures we have drawn. Are we guilty?

We have not thought it necessary to state, or rather to constantly reiterate, that our life was a toilsome one—for we supposed that would be universally understood, after we had stated how many hours in a

In *The Lowell Offering*, July 1845, p. 154.

day we tended our machines. We have not thought a constant repetition of the fact necessary, that our life was one of confinement, when it was known that we work in one spot of one room. We have not thought it necessary to enlarge upon the fact that there was ignorance and folly among a large population of young females, away from their homes, and indiscriminately collected from all quarters. But, are the operatives here as happy as females in the prime of life, in the constant intercourse of society, in the enjoyment of all necessaries, and many comforts—with money at their own command, and the means of gratifying their peculiar tastes in dress, etc.—are they as happy as they would be, with all this, in some other situations? We sometimes fear they are not.

And was there anything, we ask again, in the situation of these young women which influenced them to this melancholy act? In factory labor it is sometimes an advantage, but also sometimes the contrary, that the mind is sometimes thrown back upon itself—it is forced to depend upon its own resources, for a large proportion of the time of the operative. Excepting by sight, the females hold but little companionship with each other. This is why the young girls rush so furiously together when they are set at liberty. But, when a young woman is naturally of a morbid tone of mind, or when afflictions have created such a state, that employment which forces thoughts back upon an unceasing reminiscence of its own misery, is not the right one.

Last summer, a young woman of this city, who was weary of her monotonous life but saw no hope of redemption, opened her heart to a benevolent lady. "And now," said she, as she concluded her tale of grievances, "what shall I do?" The lady was appalled by a misery for which there was no relief. She could give her kind and soothing words, but these would have no permanent power to reconcile her to her lot. "I can tell you of nothing," she replied, "but *to throw yourself into the canal.*"

There is something better than this—and we are glad so noble a spirit is manifested by our operatives, for there *is* something noble in their general cheerfulness and contentment. "They also serve who only stand and wait." They serve, even more acceptably, who labor patiently and wait.

V

Beginning in the 1840s, and increasing steadily thereafter, a crucial change occurred in Lowell. Where the first factory girls had been recruited exclusively from New England farms, their successors came from the growing numbers of Irish immigrants. The Irish, fleeing from the drastic effects of the potato famine, emigrated to Boston in sizable numbers. One result of this immigration was the creation for the first time of a surplus labor pool in the Northeast. These immigrants, unattached to the farm, were desperate for work, and ready for hire. The mill owners responded predictably—with

*the success of the Lowell experiment assured, and the availability
of labor no longer at issue, they dropped the paternalistic mode of
management. In short order, Lowell became less of a model and
more of a modern textile town. Wages dropped, hours increased,
and the women protested. But the protests had little impact. The
Massachusetts legislature did conduct an inquiry into the Lowell
factories in 1845, but they found little to criticize. The factory
owners were now more or less free to conduct their business in
whatever way they wished. There would be few successful challenges to management's authority for the next several generations.*

MASSACHUSETTS INVESTIGATION OF LABOR CONDITIONS, 1845

The Special Committee to which was referred sundry petitions relating
to the hours of labor, submit the following report:

The first petition which was referred to your committee came from
the city of Lowell, and was signed by Mr. John Quincy Adams Thayer,
and eight hundred and fifty others, "peaceable, industrious, hard-working
men and women of Lowell." The petitioners declare that they are confined "from thirteen to fourteen hours per day in unhealthy apartments,"
and are thereby "hastening through pain, disease, and privation down
to a premature grave." They therefore ask the Legislature "to pass a law
providing that ten hours shall constitute a day's work," and that no
corporation or private citizen "shall be allowed, except in cases of
emergency, to employ one set of hands more than ten hours per day."

On the thirteenth of February, the Committee held a session to hear
the petitioners from the city of Lowell.

The first petitioner who testified was Eliza R. Hemmingway. She
had worked two years and nine months in the Lowell Factories; two
years in the Middlesex; and nine months in the Hamilton Corporations.
Her employment is weaving—works by the piece. Her wages average
from sixteen to twenty-three dollars a month exclusive of board. She
complained of the hours for labor being too many, and the time for
meals too limited. In the summer season, the work is commenced at
five o'clock A.M., and continued till seven o'clock P.M., with half an hour
for breakfast and three-quarters of an hour for dinner. The air in the
room she considered not to be wholesome. About one hundred and thirty
females, eleven men, and twelve children (between the ages of eleven
and fourteen) work in the room with her. The children work but nine
months out of twelve. The other three months they must attend school.

Most of the girls are from the country, who work in the Lowell Mills.
The average time which they remain there is about three years.

There is always a large number of girls at the gate wishing to get in
before the bell rings. On the Middlesex Corporation one-fourth part of
the females go into the mill before they are obliged to. They do this to

In *Investigation of Labor Conditions*, Massachusetts House Document, No. 50,
March 1845. Reprinted in *A Documentary History of American Industrial
Society,* ed. John R. Commons et al. (New York, 1910), vol. 8, pp. 133–51.

make more wages. A large number come to Lowell to make money to aid their parents who are poor. She knew of many cases where married women came to Lowell and worked in the mills to assist their husbands to pay for their farms. The moral character of the operatives is good.

Miss Sarah G. Bagley said she had worked in the Lowell Mills eight years and a half. She is a weaver and works by the piece. She worked in the mills three years before her health began to fail. She is a native of New Hampshire. Last year she was out of the mill a third of the time. She thinks the health of the operatives is not so good as the health of females who do housework. The chief evil, so far as health is concerned, is the shortness of time allowed for meals. The next evil is the length of time employed—not giving them time to cultivate their minds. She spoke of the high moral and intellectual character of the girls. That many were engaged as teachers in the Sunday schools. That many attended the lectures of the Lowell Institute.

Mr. Gilman Gale, a member of the city council, and who keeps a provision store, testified that the short time allowed for meals he thought the greatest evil. He spoke highly of the character of the operatives and of the agents; also of the boardinghouses and the public schools. He had two children in the mills who enjoyed good health.

Mr. Herman Abbott had worked in the Lawrence Corporation thirteen years. Never heard much complaint among the girls about the long hours, never heard the subject spoken of in the mills. Does not think it would be satisfactory to the girls to work only ten hours, if their wages were to be reduced in proportion. Forty-two girls work in the room with him. The girls often get back to the gate before the bell rings.

Mr. John Quincy Adams Thayer has lived in Lowell four years, "works at physical labor in the summer season, and mental labor in the winter." Has worked in the big machine shop twenty-four months, off and on; never worked in a cotton or woolen mill; thinks that the mechanics in the machine shop are not so healthy as in other shops; nor so intelligent as the other classes in Lowell. He drafted the petition. Has heard many complain of the long hours.

On Saturday the first of March, a portion of the Committee went to Lowell to examine the mills, and to observe the general appearance of the operatives therein employed. They first proceeded to the Merrimack Cotton Mills, in which are employed usually 1,200 females and 300 males. They were permitted to visit every part of the works and to make whatever inquiries they pleased of the persons employed. They found every apartment neat and clean, and the girls, so far as personal appearance went, healthy and robust, as girls are in our country towns.

The Committee also visited the Massachusetts and Boott Mills, both of which manufacture cotton goods. The same spirit of thrift and cleanliness, of personal comfort and contentment, prevailed there. The rooms are large and well lighted, the temperature comfortable, and in most of the windowsills were numerous shrubs and plants. These were the pets of the factory girls, and they were to the Committee convincing evidence of the elevated moral tone and refined taste of the operatives. Not only is the interior of the mills kept in the best order, but great regard has been paid by many of the agents to the arrangement of the enclosed grounds. In short, everything in and about the mills, and the boardinghouses appeared, to have for its end, health and comfort. The same remark would apply to the city generally. Your Committee returned fully satisfied that the order, decorum, and general appearance of things in and about the mills could not be improved by any suggestion of theirs, or by any act of the Legislature.

We have come to the conclusion unanimously that legislation is not necessary at the present time, and for the following reasons:

1. That a law limiting the hours of labor, if enacted at all, should be of a general nature. That it should apply to individuals or copartnerships as well as to corporations.

2. Your Committee believes that the factory system, as it is called, is not more injurious to health than other kinds of indoor labor. That a law which would compel all of the factories in Massachusetts to run their machinery but ten hours out of the twenty-four, while those in Maine, New Hampshire, Rhode Island, and other states in the Union were not restricted at all, the effect would be to close the gate of every mill in the State.

3. It would be impossible to legislate to restrict the hours of labor, without affecting very materially the question of wages; and that is a matter which experience has taught us can be much better regulated by the parties themselves than by the Legislature. Labor in Massachusetts is a very different commodity from what it is in foreign countries. Here labor is on an equality with capital, and indeed controls it, and so it ever will be while free education and free constitutions exist. Labor is intelligent enough to make its own bargains, and look out for its own interests without any interference from us.

4. The Committee does not wish to be understood as conveying the impression that there are no abuses in the present system of labor; we think there are abuses; we think that many improvements may be made, and we believe will be made, by which labor will not be so severely tasked as it now is. We think that it would be better if the hours for labor were less, if more time was allowed for meals, if more attention was paid to ventilation and pure air in our manufactories, and workshops, and many other matters. We acknowledge all this, but we say, the remedy is not with us. We look for it in the progressive improvement in art and science, in a higher appreciation of man's destiny, in a less love for money, and a more ardent love for social happiness and intellectual superiority. Your Committee, therefore, while they agree with the petitioners in their desire to lessen the burdens imposed upon labor, differ only as to the means by which these burdens are sought to be removed.

Chapter 6

The Plantation

ALTHOUGH the number of plantations in the antebellum South was not very great, this institution exerted the most profound effect on the lives of both whites and blacks. The plantation determined both the structure of the region's economy and its social organization.

Planters were the minority of a minority. On the eve of the Civil War, when the plantation system was at its height, only some 383,600 families in the entire South owned slaves; and fully one-third of this group only owned one slave. Just 10,658 planters owned over fifty slaves, and a bare 2,292 men owned over one hundred slaves. Altogether, as of 1860 there were probably somewhat less than 4,000 great planters in the South.

Yet it was this group that in the first instance fastened the cotton crop onto the region. In 1820, the Southern states produced 732,000 bales of cotton; by 1840, it was producing some one million bales, and by 1860, an incredible 4,300,000 bales! Not surprisingly, the growth of slavery proceeded apace with the cotton crop. In 1820, there were a little over 1,500,000 slaves in the South. By 1860, the number stood at 4,440,000. For blacks, the plantation was the common experience. Less than 5 percent of all blacks lived on farms where there were less than two slaves; 25 percent of blacks lived on plantations with over fifty slaves. Therefore, if one is to understand the South in the antebellum era, one must look first not to the small family farms which raised crops for subsistence but to the plantations, where slaves in large numbers spent their day planting and harvesting cotton.

Given the size of the region and the vagaries of human nature, a wide variety of styles characterized plantation management. Some units, particularly in the deep South, were probably more determined than others to maximize at all costs the size of the crop. A few especially decent and humanitarian owners devoted more attention to the welfare of their slaves. But one generalization can characterize all plantations: they were economic units designed to produce the cotton crop for a profit. The plantation, at heart, was a factory that turned out raw fibers, not at all unlike those factories in the North that turned the raw fibers into cloth. That the plantation also ordered the relationship between the races is clear. But it was the economic goals of the institution that dictated the behavior of owners and determined the fate of their slaves.

Plantations were, it must be noted, profitable ventures. Planters could ordinarily count on making returns from cotton production that were just about as great as those available to factory owners. To be sure, returns in Virginia, where the land was more exhausted, did not equal those in the Mississippi delta. But on the average, the plantation returned a rather handsome 10 percent profit.

The implications of this fact must be borne in mind as one examines the enormous amount of documentary material that survives from the plantation era. As one reads the planters' records, their correspondence with overseers, the accounts of escaped slaves, or travelers' reports, one must constantly keep the economic realities prominently in mind. Did the planters actually correspond to the image of a cultivated gentleman taking his leisure on a well-appointed veranda? Just how central to his daily routine were the ledger books? What degree of protection did these economic considerations provide for the blacks? Did their productivity in the cotton fields at once insure their continued exploitation by the planters while it set a minimum to the kind of treatment that they would receive? Was the black slave too valuable a commodity to allow owners to overwork or underfeed or excessively punish him? Finally, how did the plantation organize itself to fulfill both economic and social functions? It was at once a factory and a community. It was also a prison. The sources that follow touch on these many facets of the plantation, and permit an assessment of the impact of this institution on the South.

I

The plantation records of Bennet H. Barrow (1811–1854) are remarkably complete. They include not only his diary but also a record of punishments meted out to slaves, the number of slave births and deaths, and the rules and regulations in effect on his plantation. Barrow was typical of his class. He raised cotton on a large scale in Louisiana all the while carrying out the "right" activities, even holding office at the county level, but not above it. There is no reason to think him an especially harsh or particularly benevolent owner. In all, his materials offer an excellent starting point for re-creating a picture of antebellum plantation life.

THE DIARY OF BENNET H. BARROW, 1836–1845

RULES OF HIGHLAND PLANTATION[*]

No Negro shall leave the place at any time without my permission, or in my absence that of the driver, the driver in that case being responsible for the cause of such absence, which ought never to be omitted to be enquired into.

The driver should never leave the plantation, unless on business of the plantation.

No Negro shall be allowed to marry out of the plantation.

No Negro shall be allowed to sell anything without my express permission. The very security of the plantation requires that a general and uniform control over the people of it should be exercised. Who are to protect the plantation from the intrusions of ill-designed persons when everybody is abroad? Who can tell the moment when a plantation might be threatened with destruction from fire—could the flames be arrested if the Negroes are scattered throughout the neighborhood, seeking their amusement. Are these not duties of great importance, and in which every Negro himself is deeply interested. To render this part of the rule justly applicable, however, it would be necessary that such a settled arrangement should exist on the plantation as to make it unnecessary for a Negro to leave it—or to have a good plea for doing so. You must therefore make him as comfortably at home at possible, affording him what is essentially necessary for his happiness—you must provide for him yourself and by that means create in him a habit of perfect dependence on you. Allow it once to be understood by a Negro that he is to provide for himself, and you that moment give him an undeniable claim on you for a portion of his time to make this provision, and should you from necessity, or any other cause, encroach upon his time—disappointment and discontent are seriously felt. If I employ a laborer to perform a certain quantum of work per day and I agree to pay him a certain amount for the performance of said work when he has accomplished it, I of course have no further claim on him for his time or services—but how different is it with a slave. Who can calculate the exact profit or expense of a slave one year with another. If I furnish my Negro with every necessary of life, without the least care on his part—if I support him in sickness, however long it may be, and pay all his expenses, though he does nothing—if I maintain him in his old age, when he is incapable of rendering either himself or myself any service, am I not entitled to an exclusive right to his time? Good feelings and a sense of propriety would always prevent unnecessary employment on the Sabbath, and policy would check any exaction of excessive labor in common.

* The "Rules" were copied in the Diary on May 1, 1838.
In *Plantation Life in the Florida Parishes of Louisiana, 1836–1846, as Reflected in the Diary of Bennet H. Barrow*, ed. Edwin A. Davis (New York, 1943), pp. 126–36, 406–10, 427–37. Reprinted by permission of the publisher, Columbia University Press.

I never give a Negro a pass to go from home without he first states particularly where he wishes to go, and assigns a cause for his desiring to be absent. If he offers a good reason, I never refuse. Some think that after a Negro has done his work it is an act of oppression to confine him to the plantation, when he might be strolling about the neighborhood for his amusement and recreation—this is certainly a mistaken humanity. Habit is everything. The Negro who is accustomed to remain constantly at home is just as satisfied with the society on the plantation as that which he would find elsewhere, and the very restrictions laid upon him being equally imposed on others, he does not feel them, for society is kept at home for them. No rule that I have stated is of more importance than that relating to Negroes marrying out of the plantation. It seems to me, from what observations I have made, it is utterly impossible to have any method or regularity when the men and women are permitted to take wives and husbands indiscriminately off the plantation. Negroes are very much disposed to pursue a course of this kind, and without being able to assign a good reason, though the motive can be readily perceived, and is a strong one with them, but one that tends not in the least to the benefit of the master, or their ultimate good. The inconveniences that at once strike one as arising out of such a practice are these:

1. In allowing the men to marry out of the plantation, you give them an uncontrollable right to be frequently absent.

2. Wherever their wives live, there they consider their homes, consequently they are indifferent to the interest of the plantation to which they actually belong.

3. It creates a feeling of independence, from being, of right, out of the control of the masters for a time.

4. They are repeatedly exposed to temptation from meeting and associating with Negroes from different directions, and with various habits and vices.

5. Where there are several women on a plantation, they may have husbands from different plantations belonging to different persons. These men possess different habits, are accustomed to different treatment, and have different privileges, so your plantation everyday becomes a rendezvous of a medley of characters. When your Negroes

are at work, and the driver engaged, they either take possession of houses their wives live [in]—and go to sleep or stroll about in perfect idleness—feeling themselves accessible to everything.

6.   When a man and his wife belong to different persons, they are liable to be separated from each other, as well as their children, either by caprice of either of the parties, or when there is a sale of property— this keeps up an unsettled state of things, and gives rise to repeated new connections. For to adopt rules merely because they are good in themselves and not to pursue a plan which would make them applicable, would be fallacious. I prefer giving them money of Christmas to their making anything, thereby creating an interest with you and yours. I furnish my Negroes regularly with their full share of allowance weekly: four pounds and five pounds of meat to everything that goes in the field; two pounds over four years; one and a half between fifteen months and four years old; clear good meat. I give them clothes twice a year: two suits, one pair shoes for winter; every third year a blanket—"single Negro—two." I supply them with tobacco. If a Negro is suffered to sell anything he chooses without any inquiry being made, a spirit of trafficking at once is created to carry this on, both means and time are necessary, neither of which is he of right possessed. A Negro would not be content to sell only what he raises or makes or either corn (should he be permitted) or poultry, or the like, but he would sell a part of his allowance also, and would be tempted to commit robberies to obtain things to sell. Besides, he would never go through his work carefully, particularly when other engagements more interesting and pleasing are constantly passing through his mind, but would be apt to slight his work. That the general conduct of master has a very considerable influence on the character and habits of his slave, will be readily admitted. When a master is uniform in his own habits and conduct, his slaves know his wishes, and what they are to expect if they act in opposition to, or conformity with them, therefore, the more order and contentment exist.

A plantation might be considered as a piece of machinery, to operate successfully, all of its parts should be uniform and exact, and the impelling force regular and steady; and the master, if he pretended at all to attend to his business, should be their impelling force. If a master exhibits no extraordinary interest in the proceedings on his plantation, it is hardly to be expected that any other feelings but apathy could exist with his Negroes, and it would be unreasonable for him to expect attention and exaction from those who have no other interest than to avoid the displeasure of their master. In the different departments on the plantation as much distinction and separation are kept up as possible with a view to create responsibility. The driver has a directed charge of everything, but there are subordinate persons who take the more immediate care of the different departments. For instance, I make one person answerable for my stock, horses, cattle, hogs, etc. Another the plantation utensils, etc. One the sick, one the poultry. Another providing for and taking care of the children whose parents are in the field, etc. As good a plan as could be adopted, to establish security and good order on the plantation is that of constituting a watch at night, consisting of two or more men. They are answerable of all trespasses commited during their watch, unless they produce the offender or give immediate alarm. When the protection of a plantation is left to the

Negroes generally, you at once perceive the truth of the maxim that what is everyone's business, is no one's business. But when a regular watch is established, each in turn performs his tour of duty, so that the most careless is at times made to be observant and watchful. The very act of organizing a watch bespeaks a care and attention on the part of a master which has the due influence on the Negro.

Most of the above rules (in fact with the exception of the last) I have adopted since 1833. And with success—get your Negroes once disciplined and planting is a pleasure—a H[ell] without it. Never have an overseer. Every Negro to come up Sunday after their allowance clean and head well combed—it gives pride to everyone, the fact of master feeling proud of them, when clean etc.

Never allow any man to talk to your Negroes, nothing more injurious.

Slave Births: 1836–1839

MOTHER	CHILD	DATE OF BIRTH	COMMENTS
Margaret	Orange	February 1, 1836	
Cealy	Jane Bello	April 22, 1836	
Candis	Isaac	August 1, 1836	
Sidney		July 10, 1836	Born dead.
Maria	Kitty	July 10, 1836	
Harriet	Ned	November 20, 1836	
Patty		December 19, 1836	Died.
Leah	Adeline	March 6, 1837	
Margaret	Edmond	September 21, 1837	Died.
Mary	Rose	January 9, 1838	
Sidney	Robert	February 21, 1838	
Edny		June 7, 1838	[Died].
Fanny		July 4, 1838	Died.
Jane		September 29, 1838	Died.
Candis		October 12, 1838	Died.
Maria	Horace	November 30, 1838	
Harriet	Sally	December 2, 1838	
Leah		December 10, 1838	Died.

Slave Deaths: 1836–1839

NAME	DATE	AGE	COMMENTS
Old Rheuben	1836	60 years	
Old Betty	1836	65 years	Found dead. Crippled five years.
Billy	1836		Died of worms six hours after taken.
Nelly	1837	26 years	Died twenty-four hours after I saw her. Received some injury. In the family way.
Easter	1837	50 years	Died of pleurisy, drinking, etc. Relapse, died very suddenly. Great loss.
William	1837	3 years	Died suddenly. Worms.
Hanover	1837	6 years	Died of worms, suddenly.
Edny's child	1838	1 week	Died of lockjaw, June 13.
Candis' child	1838	1 week	Died of lockjaw, October 19.

NAME	DATE	AGE	COMMENTS
Harriet's Ned	1838		Died suddenly, December 1.
Fanny's child		4 months	Died from carelessness.
Jane's child			Died from disease of mother.
Leah's child	1838	1 week	December 17.

INVENTORY OF THE ESTATE OF BENNET H. BARROW

Succession of Bennet H.　　　　　　　　*State of Louisiana*
Barrow, deceased　　　　　　　　*Parish of West Feliciana*

Be it remembered that on this the fourteenth day of June in the year of our Lord one thousand eight hundred and fifty-four, I, Bertrand Haralson, Recorder in and for said parish attended this day, at the late residence of Bennet H. Barrow, deceased, for the purpose of making an inventory and appraisement of all the property, real and personal, rights and credits, belonging to Bennet H. Barrow, deceased.

TO WIT

A certain tract of land, with all the buildings and improvements thereon, known as the home place containing about fourteen hundred arpents, which said lands and improvements were valued and appraised at the sum of forty-two thousand dollars.

[Slave Evaluations]

Stephen, aged 6 years, valued at two hundred and 50 dollars	250.00
Rodem, aged 5 years, valued at two hundred dollars	200.00
Jack, aged 51 years, valued at eight hundred dollars	800.00
Eliza, aged 44 years, valued at five hundred dollars	500.00
Bazil, aged 20 years, valued at six hundred dollars	600.00
Little Cato, aged 37 years, valued at six hundred dollars	600.00
Hetty, aged 36 years, valued at five hundred dollars	500.00
Amos, an infant, valued at fifty dollars	50.00
Temps, aged 43 years, valued at fifty dollars	50.00
Lindy, aged 23 years, valued at seven hundred dollars	700.00
Virginia, aged 2 years, valued at one hundred and fifty dollars	150.00
Sidney, aged 39 years, valued at six hundred and fifty dollars	650.00
Aggy, aged 20 years, valued at seven hundred and fifty dollars	750.00
Angelle, an infant, valued at fifty dollars	50.00
Cynthis, aged 13 years, valued at four hundred dollars	400.00
Suckey, aged 9 years, valued at three hundred dollars	300.00
Spencer, aged 7 years, valued at three hundred dollars	300.00
Dave, aged 46 years, valued at seven hundred dollars	700.00
Little Jim, aged 24 years, valued at nine hundred dollars	900.00
Maria, aged 19 years, valued at six hundred dollars	600.00
Old Jimmy, aged 59 years, valued at five hundred dollars	500.00
Nat, aged 28 years, valued at eight hundred and fifty dollars	850.00
Levy, aged 39 years, valued at four hundred and fifty dollars	450.00
Grace, aged 29 years, valued at six hundred dollars	600.00
Phil, aged 75 years, valued at one hundred dollars	100.00
Esther, aged 25 years, valued at seven hundred and fifty dollars	750.00
Rilla, aged 3 years, valued at two hundred dollars	200.00

Marshall, aged 9 years, valued at two hundred and fifty dollars	250.00
Ada, aged 23 years, valued at seven hundred and fifty dollars	750.00
Desery, aged 4 years, valued at one hundred and fifty dollars	150.00
Treson, an infant, valued at one hundred dollars	100.00
Louisa, aged 19 years, valued at six hundred and fifty dollars	650.00
Angy, aged 15 years, valued at six hundred and fifty dollars	650.00
Edny, aged 49 years, valued at three hundred dollars	300.00
Lizzy, aged 23 years, valued at six hundred and fifty dollars	650.00
Arie, aged 14 years, valued at five hundred dollars	500.00
Little Phil, aged 26 years, valued at nine hundred and fifty dollars	950.00

Misconduct and Punishments: 1840–1841

Darcas		Left the field today without the consent of the driver. Pretending to be sick.
Anica		Filthiness, in the milk and butter. Her and Darcas alike. December 10, 1840 improved very much.
Peter		Told me several lies Christmas. Drunkard, etc.
Candis		Saw Dennis while runaway.
Jenney		Saw Dennis while runaway.
Patience		Not trashing cotton well. Leaving yellow locks in it, etc.
Julia		Not trashing cotton well.
Bet	X*	Not trashing cotton well.
Luckey	X	Not trashing cotton well.
O. Hannah	X	Not trashing cotton well.
F. Jerry		For going to town with very dirty clothes and keeping himself so, "generally."
Patty		Inattention to work and herself.
Lavenia		Inattention to work and herself.
Mary		For scaring son, Bat. "Stories, etc."
L. Hannah		For taking rails and breaking good ones.
Margaret		With Hannah, but taking none but pieces.
O. Hannah	X	Not trashing cotton enough. Found the gin stopped everytime I've been down at the gin place.
Bet	X	Not trashing cotton enough.
Harriet		Not trashing cotton enough, and dirty clothes.
F. Jerry	X	Up too late and out of his house.
Jerry	X	Up too late and out of his house.
Bet	X	Up after 10 o'clock.
Ben		Up after 10 o'clock.
Wash		Carelessness with his plough, horses, gear, etc.
Dave L.		Neglect in hauling cotton repeatedly.
Wash		Neglect of his horses.
Randall		Up too late, sleeping in chair, etc.
Luce		Neglect of child. Its foot burnt.
Jim		Inattention to work, moving seed, and impudence to driver.
Lize	X	Inattention to work.
Levi	X	Carelessness with his oxen and talking to the workman. Neglect of business.
Bet	XX	Careless in dropping seed, disowning it, etc.
Anica		Meanness to the sick, and hiding from me, etc.
Dennis		Severity to his mules.

* X signifies whipping.

Wade		For lying, and out of his house.
Fanney		Hoeing too careless, and mad.
Oney		Sore back horse.
Oney		Carelessness, ploughing, etc.
Isreal		Impudence to the driver.
Oney	X	Neglect in planting peas, etc.
Julia	X	Neglect in planting peas, etc.
Patience		Bad conduct, impudence to driver, and neglected work.
Patience	X	Did not go in the field till breakfast "late" and told the driver "Alfred" she was sick and had been to the house for a dose of oil, and told me the same, found she had not been and she acknowledged the lie, but told Margaret she would give her some cloth if she would get the earache and tell Patty she had been here after oil, etc. And told me a dozen lies while questioning her. Gave her a very severe whipping.
Maria		For not reporting herself when sick. Remained in the quarter 3 days without my knowledge.
Patty		And all the house ones for general bad conduct. Can't let a peach get ripe, etc.
Jane		The meanest Negro living. Filth in cooking. Saw me coming to the house at 1:20; left the kitchen, etc. Of[f] near two days, foiled her having anything to do with anyone, and chained at nights.
O. Fill	X	Not reporting the plough hands for injuring the cotton, covering up bottom limbs, etc.
Demps		Sound beating with my stick. Impudence of manner.
Atean	X	Covering up cotton limbs with ploughs.
Isreal	X	Covering up cotton limbs with ploughs.

Diary

September 1

Clear, warm—picking above, best picking this year—three sick; gave every cotton picker a light whipping for picking trashy cotton.

2 Clear, wind north—and quite cool—sudden change—hands averaged higher yesterday than they have this year—163—upward of twenty bales out—ten bales behind last year and thirty bales behind 1836—difference in the season.

3 Clear, quite cold. Picking cotton gins place—good picking—started all my gins—don't like the appearance of my crop: most ragged looking crop I ever had, bent and broke down—two sick—three lame, etc.

4 Clear, wind east—cool, picking home (above) since dinner.

5 Cloudy, wind east—best picking today I've had this year—went to Ruffins with family—and went in the swamp killing alligators—after dinner went driving. Started two large bucks in Wades field—stood on the road between Roberts and Ruffins —one came through—Sidney Flower took first shot standing—neither of his *shots* were fatal—ran to me. Missed first fire, second wounded him very badly—ran short distance and stopped, nearly falling.

6 Few clouds, cool mornings. Took Joseph Bell, Fanny Bell, and Grey Luzbourough colts of Lucillas up to train—also Pressure

and Dick Haile—a strong string—O. Jacob cut the end of his right forefinger nearly off—two others slightly cut—with broad ax—average 170 pound cotton yesterday—appearance of rain tonight—sprinkle.

7 Few clouds—wind east—fine picking, averaged 183 yesterday—cotton forty bales out last night—thirty bales behind last year at this time; went down to see John Joor, his cotton has suffered very much for want of rain.

8 Cloudy, warm—hand generally did not pick as well yesterday as day before—fine picking, highest yesterday and this year 260. Atean, small boy Owens, the best boy I ever saw.

9 Clear, pleasant; hands picked finely yesterday; averaged 209.

10 Clear, very cool morning—upward of fifty bales out, thirty odd gined, picking gins, fine picking.

11 Clear, cool morning. Four first rate cotton pickers sick hands picked well yesterday. Atean 300, Dave L. 310, highest this year—sent to town after my bagging and rope, waiting for it three weeks past—knocked the blind teeth out of my gray Luzbourough colt. Little Independence.

12 Clear, cool mornings—five sick, picking above—twenty bales out at gins, pressing home—the best cotton and best picking in upper new corn land cotton I ever saw.

13 Clear, cool morning—weighed cotton in the field—five sick, augue and fever.

14 Cloudy, warm—most of the hands picked well yesterday, highest 325—will have picked off of the new corn land above (fifty acres) twenty-five bales, at least fifty bales to pick—averaged yesterday 209—twenty-five bales pressed last night.

15 Cloudy, *sprinkling* of rain—hands picked higher yesterday than they have done this year—averaged 226—Owens boy thirteen years old picked 200—best boy I ever saw. Very light sprinkle rain this evening.

16 Stormy looking day, great deal of rain last night and still raining—wind from the east. Hands picked well yesterday, highest average this year 234½.

17 Dark and Cloudy—wind south—pressing gins and home—women spinning, men and trash gang trashing cotton and raising house.

18 Cloudy, damp morning—some rain at noon. Picking cotton since breakfast—went driving with James Leak, Dr. Desmont, and Sidney Flower. Started two fawns in my field, ran some time, dogs quit them.

19 Clear pleasant morning—sixty-two bales pressed last night—cotton bend down very much from wind on Sunday—between ninety and one hundred bales out in November—went hunting in my field, started three deer. Killed a young buck—several joined me afterward—went driving on the swamp—started a deer, dogs ran off—in coming out of the drive started a bear. Only one dog—he became too much frightened to do anything.

20 Clear, pleasant—picking P. Rice bottom—hands pick well considering the storm—several sick.

21 Very foggy morning—commenced hauling cotton this morning
—first shipment—bales will average 470 pounds upward of
100 out in November. 115 of 400. This time last year had out
125—25 behind last year, owing to the season—cotton more
backward in opening—at first picking—never had cotton picked
more trashy than yesterday. And today by dinner—some few
picked badly—five sick and two children.

22 Considerable rain before breakfast, appearance of a bad day—
pressing—four sick—caught Darcas with dirt in cotton bag
last night, weighed fifteen pounds—Tom Beauf picked badly
yesterday morning. Whipped him, few cuts—left the field some
time in the evening without his cotton and have not seen him
since—he is in the habit of doing so yearly, except last year.
Heavy rains during the day, women spinning—trashing cotton,
men and children—Tom B. showed himself—"sick"—cotton
picked since the storm looks very bad—cotton market opened
this year at 13 and 13¾ cents—bagging and cordage 20 and
24 and 8½ and 9 cents—pork from sixteen to twenty-four dollars a barrel—Never commence hauling cotton that it did not
rain—worked the ford at Little Creek in the gins field.

23 Clear, very cool, wind from the north—nine degrees colder
than yesterday morning—intend most of the hands to dry and
trash cotton today. Frank Kish, Henry, and Isreal pressed bales
today, one dollar each—killed a wild cow this morning, as fat
as could well be.

24 Clear, quite cold—P. Dohertys gin house burnt down on Friday
night last. Light enough at my scaffold yard to read names and
figures on the slate—and at least five miles—Mr. Tisdale our
trainer came down from Kentucky yesterday—had my cart
wheels tired yesterday at Ruffins.

25 Clear, cool—went to town—hauled forty-nine bales to Ratliffs
Landing yesterday—twelve to town today—sixty-one in all—
went driving yesterday. Killed two fawns—and one young buck
in my gins field with the most singular horns I ever heard of or
saw—very fat—several sick, most this year.

26 Clear, pleasant weather. Shipped today eighty bales cotton, very
fine—six or seven lying up—picked badly for two days past—
cotton selling fourteen cents.

27 Clear, pleasant—went hunting in the swamp in company of
Dr. Desmont, J. Leake, M. Courtney, W. H. Barrow, Pat Doherty,
R. D. Percey, L. Flower, and Mr. Pain from Isle of Madeira—
a large wine importer—very large—killed three deer, lost Mr.
Pain, stayed until after dark firing guns, etc., the old gentleman
found the briar and came up to Ruffins well scratched and
bloody—he refused to call Leake by his name—having lost a
cargo of wine, vessel springing a *leak.*

28 Cloudy, cool wind from the north—John Joor sent a hand up
to exchange with me, yesterday, his hands pick very badly—
Dennis and Tom Beauf ran off on Wednesday—Dennis came in
yesterday morning after I went hunting. "Sick"—left the sick
house this morning—if I can see either of them and have a gun

at the time will let them have the contents of it—Dennis returned to the sick house at dinner.

29 Foggy morning—warm day. A. G. Barrow, Dr. Walker, and William Munson stayed with me last night, went hunting today. Munson missed—Emily went to Woodville yesterday—hands picked better yesterday than they have done since the storm— averaged 200. Tom B. went to picking, cotton this morning— didn't bring his cotton to be weighed—came to me after I went to bed.

30 Clear, pleasant weather—upward of 130 bales out.

II

By reputation, the cruelest of the plantations were those of the absentee owners, where the management of affairs was exclusively in the hands of an overseer. Even during the antebellum period, Southerners insisted that overseers did not represent the system, while abolitionists argued to the contrary that they exemplified it. The correspondence here between an overseer (John Evans) and an owner (George Jones) offers another vantage point from which to evaluate plantation conditions. Here, too, the relationship between economic needs and the fate of the slave emerges vividly, as does the subtle but not unimportant community pressures that could limit plantation autocracy.

THE CORRESPONDENCE OF GEORGE JONES, 1852–1855

John Evans to George Noble Jones

[CHEMOONIE, April 2, 1852]

Mr. Jones, Sir,

I wrote you on the twentieth of March and directed my letter to Newport, R. I. I will inform you that I am getting on finely now with my business. I finished planting cotton today at nine o'clock. Now the crop is all planted. I have cleared up and ditched a nice pond and planted it in rice. I will be ready to go to ploughing and hoeing corn about the sixth of this month. The first cotton that I planted is coming up fine.

I have sheared the sheep and altered the lambs but have not spayed any shoats yet but will next week if it is a good time. The team is a little thin but will now get fat. Minder had billious colic and I could

In *Florida Plantation Records from the Papers of George Noble Jones*, ed. U. B. Phillips and J. D. Glunt (St. Louis, 1927), pp. 98, 110–12, 123–24, 150–53. Reprinted by permission of the Missouri Historical Society, St. Louis, Missouri.

not cure her and I was fearful that she would get worse so I sent for Dr. Randolph and he came one time to see her and she has since recovered. Randolph said that inflammation had taken place was the cause of my not curing her. He said my prescription was right, the rest of the black people are all well except Juner [Juno] and Little Joe. They eat dirt and are bloated up. I think that I have got Joe broken off from eating dirt now and I think I will have Juner curred by another week.

You directed me to send you all of the names of the Negroes on Chemoonie in familes which I will do in my next letter which will be on the fifteenth of this [month]. Jim asked me to let him have Martha for a wife so I have gave them leave to marry. Both of them are very smart and I think they are well matched. Also Lafayette Renty asked for leave to marry Lear, I also gave them leave. Rose, Renty's other wife, says that she don't want to live with Renty on the account of his having so many children and they were always quarreling so I let them seperate. Lear says she is willing to help Renty take care of his children. I will send the load of cotton to Newport on the eighth of this month.

I believe I have written you all of the news from Chemoonie.

John Evans to George Noble Jones

CHEMOONIE, F[L]A. June 15, 1852

Mr. George Jones,

I am glad to hear that your family is all well. I have been enjoying fine health until lately. I am now sick but not confined, I am able to attend to my business.

The black people have not been so well of late either. You will see in the copy of the journal who has been sick. There has been a heap of wet weather in F[l]a. of late which was the cause of the sickness on Chemoonie. I think I notice that most every large plantation in this settlement has got the measles, except your plantations. I am very fearful that they will get here for they are at Billingsleys, close by. I don't allow one of the young hands to leave the plantation, not even to visit El Desteno [a neighboring plantation].

I have the best prospect for a corn crop that I ever have had since I have been managing for you. The cotton crop is not good, it is the smallest cotton that I ever have had for the time of year. I do not like the cotton crop on Chemoonie, there have been too many of those heavy washing rains on this place of late years. The washing rains have carried off a heap of the soil and the soil will have to be replaced by manuring pretty heavily before there can be large crops of cotton made on Chemoonie again.

John Evans to George Noble Jones

Leon Co. F[l]a, Sept. 9, 1854

Mr. George Jones,

Sir, after my best respects to you and family I will state to you that I am well, also the black people with the exception of two light cases of fever on the plantation which will be well by tomorrow.

I am getting on very well with my business and have caught the two boys that ran off and gave them a light flogging and put them to work. The cause of Esau's and Little Dick's running away was this. Jacob and England and Nathan had made a plot to leave if I should attempt to flog them for picking cotton and persuaded those two boys into it. So I gave Jacob and England and Nathan a flogging apiece. They acknowledge they had done wrong so I let them off lightly.

This is the driest and hottest weather in Florida that I have ever experienced. The cotton crop looks bad.

My object in writing to you is principally this—it is not a great while before my term will be up with you. So I think it is always best for both parties to know in due time what we will do another year. I am poor and expect to follow overseeing a few more years, and I think it is to my interest always to know in due time what I am going to do another year, so if we don't agree to live together why it will give us both a chance to look around. We both are pretty well acquainted with each other now and I like the way you have your business managed and I am satisfied to do business for you another year or four more years. I will just leave this with you. I will make this proposition—if you will furnish me plenty of such provisions as the plantation affords, give me six hundred dollars, and allow me the same privileges you have always been giving me, I will live with you four more years if you want me, and you may put just as many hands here as you are a mind to. If you will give me this I never shall ask you to raise my wages anymore. I have been overseeing now eleven years and I think I ought to have as good wages as some of the rest of the overseers in Florida that don't manage any more hands than I do. I have been living with you now eight years nearly, and I can say more than most of the Florida overseers, that I never have had a cross word with my employer. Not flattering of you, I can say with a clear conscience that I have been studying your interest for the last eight years. Please answer this letter soon, and whether you hire me or not you may depend upon my attending to your business promptly until the last hour that I stay with you.

And another thing I forgot to mention is this. Should I take a notion to marry you must give me leave to get a wife. I don't know that I shall ever marry but I merely mention this so we will know what to depend upon. I would not think of getting a wife without your consent. I think if I had a wife I could get along better. I would have someone to help nurse the sick women and so forth.

John Evans to George Noble Jones

Chemoonie Florida, Oct. 18, 1854

Mr. George Jones,

Mr. Moxley called on me last week to go to El Desteno and see him whip one of the mill boys, Aberdeen. He said that he went to flog or put Aberdeen's sister in jail and she ran and he caught her and Aberdeen took an ax to him but did not use it, the driver kept him from it. I went down and saw Mr. Moxley give him a genteel flogging which I think he deserved. Aberdeen acknowledged that he did take the ax to Mr. Moxley. There were four of the women run away from him and went to Tallahassee and got in jail which cost Moxley about thirteen dollars to get them out and lawyer Davis examined them and reported about town that they were badly whipped, which is not so. I examined their backs myself and I did not see anything that was cruel about them. Also Mr. Blocker and Demilly examined them in jail, so they told me. They say that they were not cruelly flogged. This man Davis is a sort of a queer fellow, so people tell me about town. The cause of those women going to Tallahassee is this—this Negro Tom Blackledge that has Dealier for a wife on El Desteno coaxed them off. This man Davis has Tom hired, and the women went to Tom's house and the jailer heard that they were there and he went and got them and put them in jail. I don't think that Mr. Moxley treats the Negroes on El Desteno cruelly when they don't deserve it. You know that the Negroes on El Desteno have not been at work for the last four years so Moxley has to be pretty strict on them to get anything out of them. I think Moxley is a good planter and would treat the Negroes well if they would behave themselves. There is but one thing I see in Mr. Moxley's management that I don't like and it is this, I think when he flogs he puts it on in too large doses. I think moderate floggings the best. Whenever I see that I have convinced a Negro I always turn him loose. I always punish according to the crime, if it is a large one I give him a genteel flogging with a strap, about seventy-five lashes I think is a good whipping. When picking cotton I never put on more than twenty stripes and very frequently not more than ten or fifteen. I find I get along with this as well as if I was to give them larger whippings. I think if the mill hands was kept steadily at work it would add to the quarters at El Desteno. Mr. Moxley says that the mill hands don't get to work before an hour be sun [after sunrise] some mornings, and Negroes is this disposition, if they see Negroes around them idling why they want to do so too. I merely write this because I think it is my duty when I see anything going on wrong in Florida on your plantations. When you come out you can see for yourself. I think Mr. Moxley is the right kind of man for El Desteno, except the large floggings. Mr. Moxley says if there is not an alteration at El Desteno he won't stay another year. I told him not to get disheartened for he would find you to be the right kind of a man.

George Noble Jones to W. G. M. Davis

El Desteno, Jefferson County, Florida,
January 22, 1855

Dear Sir,

Messrs. Anderson and Houston did me the favor to investigate the conduct of my overseer, Mr. Moxley, in relation to the four women who fled to your house. I regret you could not have been present.

It has always been a source of great anxiety to me to protect my Negroes from unnecessary punishment. I pay the highest wages in hopes of obtaining good overseers. (On large plantations where more than a hundred Negroes are together, it seems necessary to observe a stricter discipline than with a smaller number might be sufficient. That my Negroes have not been seriously injured by the punishment they have received may perhaps be evidenced in their general appearance and in their natural increase which in the last year has been over 10 percent; in a gang of 120, there having been but three deaths of infants and fourteen births and no instance of miscarriage. I should be pleased at any time to see you at my plantation and show you every part of it.)

With many thanks for the interest you have shown in my people I remain etc.

John Evans to George Noble Jones

[Chemoonie, January 10, 1856]

Mr. Jones,

Sir, as we disagreed the other day at your house about the business of the plantation, you appeared to be so much dissatisfied with my management of your business you will not perhaps be much surprised when I inform you that I have come to the conclusion to quit your employment, for you will doubtless recollect perfectly well the fact of my having always told you that I would live with no man who was not satisfied with the manner in which I manage his business. I have always endeavored to do you justice and although I say it no man has ever labored more faithfully for another than I have for you. Your Negroes behave badly behind my back and then run to you and you appear to believe what they say. From circumstances that have happened I am led to believe that I run great risks of my life in the case of Jacob. When I mentioned it to you that my life had been threatened by him you seemed to pay no attention to it whatever. I have always been accustomed to having my friends to see me and the indulgence of it never for a moment caused me to neglect the business committed to my charge and now when I am married and might naturally expect the friends of my wife and self to visit us in a reasonable manner your expression about this matter the other day at your house was enough to let me know that you did not want my friends to come and see me. Taking all these circumstances into due consideration I think I am but acting right when I seek to dissolve the connection that has existed between us for nine years, and in doing so I wish you to believe that I am moved by no unfriendly feelings whatever but solely by a regard for my own interest. You will be pleased to come over early in the morning and let us settle and get your keys. You owe me a little on the taxes I paid for you in 1855.

III

Northern travelers through the South often recorded their impressions of plantation life. Their comments did not always add up to a consistent picture, partly because tourists are not systematic observers, and partly because each visitor brought to the scene his

own particular biases and those of his region and class. But this
very problem makes these reports all the more valuable today. They
not only add to our knowledge about plantation conditions but also
illuminate the preconceptions through which Northerners viewed
the phenomenon. Nehemiah Adams, a New England minister, spent
three months in the South in 1853. The following year he published
A Southside View of Slavery.

A SOUTHSIDE VIEW OF SLAVERY, 1860

NEHEMIAH ADAMS

FAVORABLE APPEARANCES IN SOUTHERN SOCIETY AND IN SLAVERY

Good Order

The streets of Southern cities and towns immediately struck me as being remarkably quiet in the evening and at night.

"What is the cause of so much quiet?" I said to a friend.

"Our colored people are mostly at home. After eight o'clock they cannot be abroad without a written pass, which they must show on being challenged, or go to the guard house. The master must pay fifty cents for a release. White policemen in cities, and in town patrols of white citizens, walk the streets at night."

Here I received my first impression of intereference with the personal liberty of the colored people. The white servants, if there be any, the boys, the apprentices, the few Irish, have liberty; the colored men are under restraint.

From the numbers in the streets, though not great, you would not suspect that the blacks are restricted at night; yet I do not remember one instance of rudeness or unsuitable behavior among them in any place. Around the drinking saloons there were white men and boys whose appearance and behavior reminded me of "liberty and pursuit of happiness" in similar places at the North; but there were no colored men there; the slaves are generally free as to street brawls and open drunkenness. I called to mind a place at the North whose streets every evening, and especially on sabbath evenings, are a nuisance. If that place could enforce a law forbidding certain youths to be in the streets after a certain hour without a pass from their employers, it would do much to raise them to an equality in good manners with their more respectable colored fellowmen at the South.

There have been mournful cases in which the murderer of a Negro has escaped deserved punishments; but it was not because it was a Negro that was killed. The murderers of white people have as frequently obtained impunity.

The laws allow the master great extent in chastising a slave, as a

In *A Southside View of Slavery*, by Nehemiah Adams (Boston, 1860), pp. 24–25, 41, 44, 47–49.

protection to himself and to secure subordination. Here room is given for brutal acts; barbarous modes of inflicting pain, resulting in death, are employed; but it is increasingly the case that vengeance overtakes and punishes such transgressors.

Prevention of Crime

Prevention of crime among the lower class of society is one striking feature of slavery. Day and night every one of them is amenable to a master. If ill disposed, he has his own policeman in his owner. Thus three million of the laboring class of our population are in a condition most favorable to preservation from crimes against society.

A prosecuting officer, who has six or eight counties in his district, told me that during eight years of service, he had made out about two thousand bills of indictment, of which not more than twelve were against colored people. It must follow of necessity that a large amount of crime is prevented by the personal relation of the colored man to a white citizen. It would be a benefit to some of our immigrants at the North, and to society, if government could thus prevent or reach disturbances of the peace through masters, overseers, or guardians. But we cannot rival in our police measures the beneficial system of the South in its distributive agencies to prevent burglaries and arson.

A physician, relating his experience in his rides at night, said that in solitary places the sudden appearance of a white man generally excited some apprehension with regard to personal safety, but the sight of a black man was always cheering, and made him feel safe. Husbands and fathers feel secure on leaving home for several days, even where their houses are surrounded by Negro cabins.

Absence of Mobs

One consequence of the disposal of the colored people as to individual control is the absence of mobs. That fearful element in society, an irresponsible and low class, is diminished at the South. Street brawls and conflicts between two races of laboring people, or the ignorant and more excitable portions of different religious denominations, are mostly unknown within the bounds of slavery.

When the remains of Mr. Calhoun were brought to Charleston, a gentleman from a free state in the procession said to a Southern gentleman, "Where is your underswell?" referring to the motley crowd of men and boys of all nations which gather in most of our large places on public occasions. He was surprised to learn that those respectable, well-dressed, well-behaved colored men and boys on the sidewalks were a substitute for that class of population which he had elsewhere been accustomed to see with repugnant feelings on public occasions.

Absence of Pauperism

Pauperism is prevented by slavery. This idea is absurd, no doubt, in the apprehension of many at the North, who think that slaves are, as a matter of course, paupers. Nothing can be more untrue.

Every slave has an inalienable claim in law upon his owner for support for the whole of life. He cannot be thrust into an almshouse, he cannot become a vagrant, he cannot beg his living, he cannot be wholly neglected when he is old and decrepit.

I saw a white-headed Negro at the door of his cabin on a gentleman's estate, who had done no work for ten years. He enjoys all the privileges of the plantation, garden, and orchard; is clothed and fed as carefully as though he were useful. On asking him his age, he said he thought he "must be nigh a hundred."

Thus the pauper establishment of the free states, the burden and care of immigrants, are almost entirely obviated at the South by the colored population. In laboring for the present and future welfare of immigrants, we are subjected to evils of which we are ashamed to complain, but from which the South is enviably free. To have a neighborhood of a certain description of foreigners about your dwellings; to see a horde of them get possession of a respectable dwelling in a court, and thus force the residents, as they always do, to flee, it being impossible to live with comfort in close connection with them; to have all the senses assailed from their opened doors; to have your sabbath utterly destroyed, is not so agreeable as the presence of a respectable colored population, every individual of which is under the responsible oversight of a master or mistress who restrains and governs him, and has a reputation to maintain in his respectable appearance and comfort, and keeps him from being a burden on the community.

The following case, that came to my knowledge, offers a good illustration of the views which many slaves take of their dependent condition. A colored woman with her children lived in a separate cabin belonging to her master, washing clothes for families in that place. She paid her master a percentage of her earnings, and had laid up more than enough to buy her freedom and that of her children. Why, as she might be made free, does she not use it rather?

She says that if she were to buy her freedom, she would have no one to take care of her for the rest of her life. Now her master is responsible for her support.

REVOLTING FEATURES OF SLAVERY

Homes of the Slaves

The homes of the slaves is a topic of deep interest, bearing in a vital manner upon the system. It can hardly be said in general that slaves have regularly constituted homes. Husbands and wives, in a large proportion of cases, belong to different masters, and reside on separate plantations, the husband sometimes walking several miles, night and morning, to and from his family, and many of them returning home only on Saturday afternoon. In cities, also, husbands and wives most commonly belong to different families. Laboring apart, and having their meals apart, the binds of domestic life are few and weak. A slave, his wife, and their children, around that charmed center, a family table, with its influences of love, instruction, discipline, humble as they necessarily would be, yet such as God had given them, are too seldom seen. To encourage and protect their homes generally would be in effect to put an end to slavery as it is.

It was remarked to me by an eminent and venerable physician at the South that maternal attachments in slave mothers are singularly short-lived. Their pain and grief at the sale of their children, their jealousy, their self-sacrificing efforts for them, are peculiar, but they are easily supplanted.

Everyone can see not only the probability but the cause of this limited parental affection. From the first moment of maternal solicitude, the idea of property on the part of the owner in the offspring is connected with the maternal instinct. It grows side by side with it, becomes a neutralizing element, prevents the inviolable links of natural affection from reaching deep into the heart. We need no slave auctions or separations of families to make us feel the inherent, awful nature of the present system of slavery.

The same day that my friend made his remark to me, I had an accidental confirmation of it in the conversation of an intelligent landlord, who was telling me of the recent lamentable death of an old slave mother who had nursed him and all his brothers and sisters. His mother said to the dying woman, "How do you feel about leaving your children?" for she had several who were still young. "O missis," she said, "you will take care of them; I don't mind them. I don't want to leave you, missis, and your Charley and Ann. What will they do without me, little dears?" Slavery had loosened the natural attachments of this woman to her offspring, and those attachments had sought and found objects to grow upon in the children of another. There must be something essentially wrong in a system which thus interferes with the nature which God has made.

I was in a large colored sabbath school. The superintendent at the close gave the scholars a kind word of exhortation to this effect: "Now, children, I want to repeat what I have said to you so often; you must all try to be good children, wherever you are, remembering that you are never out of God's sight. If you love and obey Him, if your are good children at home, what a comfort you will be to your" (I expected the words *fathers* and *mothers*) "masters and mistresses." I felt as when I have heard the earth fall upon a stranger's coffin; it was all correct, all kind; but the inability to use those names, the perfect naturalness with which other names came in to fill the place of *father* and *mother*, brought to my heart the truth: the slaves generally have no homes. Separated as they necessarily are under the present system, the relations of husbands and wives are not so inviolable as they otherwise would be. Marriage among the slaves is not a civil contract; it is formed and continues by permission of the masters; it has no binding force, except as moral principle preserves it; and it is subject, of course, to the changes of fortune on the part of the owners. This is the theory; but humane and benevolent hearts in every community combine to modify its operation; yet there are cases of hardship over which they are compelled to weep, and very many of them do weep as we should in their places; still the system remains, and now and then asserts its awful power.

Yet the cases of violent separation of husband and wife are not so many as the voluntary and criminal separations by the parties themselves. This, after all, is the chief evil connected with the looseness of domestic ties in slavery. Conjugal love among the slaves is not invariably the poetical thing which amateurs of slaves sometimes picture it; for there are probably no more happy conjugal unions among the slaves than among the whites.

IV

*The few accounts of plantation life written by blacks appear in the
narratives of those who escaped slavery or were emancipated. These
volumes, however, were invariably published in the North with
the help of abolitionists, so that one cannot be sure whether the
former slave is telling his audience what it wants to hear or
whether he is accurately reporting his experiences. Then, too,
these slaves may have been atypical, the victims of more brutal
treatment, hence their escape, or more benevolent treatment, hence
their emancipation. Nevertheless, many of these reports have a
ring of authenticity. A close textual analysis may help to reveal
the effects of the system upon the slaves. The account below was
written by Jacob Stroyer, an emancipated slave who spent his youth
on a large plantation in South Carolina. Eventually, Stroyer became a minister in the African Episcopal Church in Salem,
Massachusetts.*

MY LIFE IN THE SOUTH, 1885

JACOB STROYER

Father

Father had a surname, Stroyer, which he could not use in public,
as the surname Stroyer would be against the law; he was known only by
the name of William Singleton, because that was his master's name. So
the title Stroyer was forbidden him, and could be used only by his
children after the emancipation of the slaves.

There were two reasons given by the slaveholders why they did not
allow a slave to use his own name, but rather that of the master. The
first was that if he ran away, he would not be so easily detected by using
his own name as if he used that of his master instead. The second was
that to allow him to use his own name would be sharing an honor which
was due only to his master, and that would be too much for a Negro,
said they, who was nothing more than a servant. So it was held as a
crime for the slave to be caught using his own name, which would
expose him to severe punishment.

Mother

Mother's name was Chloe. She belonged to Colonel M. R. Singleton
too; she was a field hand, and never was sold, but her parents were once.

The family from which mother came, the most of them had trades
of some kind; some were carpenters, some blacksmiths, some house
servants, and others were made drivers over the other Negroes.

In *My Life in the South*, by Jacob Stroyer (Salem, Mass., 1885), pp. 19–23.

Most of them had trades of some kind; but she had to take her chance in the field with those who had to weather the storm. But my readers are not to think that those having trades were free from punishment, for they were not; some of them had more troubles than the field hands. At times the overseer, who was a white man, would go to the shop of the blacksmith or carpenter, and would pick a quarrel with him, so as to get an opportunity to punish him. He would say to the Negro, "Oh, ye think yourself as good as ye master, ye————." Of course he knew what the overseer was after, so he was afraid to speak; the overseer, hearing no answer, would turn to him and cry out, "Ye so big ye can't speak to me, ye————," and then the conflict would begin, and he would give that man such a punishment as would disable him for two or three months. The merciless overseer would say to him, "Ye think because ye have a trade ye are as good as ye master, ye————; but I will show ye that ye are nothing but a nigger."

I did not go to the sand-hill, or summer seat, my allotted time, but stopped on the plantation with father, as I said that he used to take care of horses and mules. I was around with him in the barnyard when but a very small boy; of course that gave me an early relish for the occupation of hostler, and I soon made known my preference to Colonel Singleton, who was a sportsman and had fine horses. And, although I was too small to work, the Colonel granted my request; hence I was allowed to be numbered among those who took care of the fine horses, and learned to ride. But I soon found that my new occupation demanded a little more than I cared for.

It was not long after I had entered my new work before they put me upon the back of a horse which threw me to the ground almost as soon as I reached his back. It hurt me a little, but that was not the worst of it, for when I got up there was a man standing near with a switch in hand, and he immediately began to beat me. Although I was a very bad boy, this was the first time I had been whipped by anyone except father and mother, so I cried out in a tone of voice as if I would say, this is the first and last whipping you will give me when father gets hold of you.

When I got away from him I ran to father with all my might, but soon found my expectation blasted, as father very coolly said to me, "Go back to your work and be a good boy, for I cannot do anything for you." But that did not satisfy me, so on I went to mother with my complaint and she came out to the man who whipped me; he was a groom, a white man whom master hired to train his horses, as he was a man of that trade. Mother and he began to talk, then he took a whip and started for her, and she ran from him, talking all the time. I ran back and forth between mother and him until he stopped beating her. After the fight between the groom and mother, he took me back to the stable yard and gave me a severe flogging. And although mother failed to help me at first, still I had faith that when he took me back to the stable yard, and commenced whipping me, that she would come and stop him, but I looked in vain, for she did not come.

Then the idea first came to me that I, with my dear father and mother and the rest of my fellow Negroes, was doomed to cruel treatment through life, and was defenseless. But when I found that father and mother could not save me from punishment, as they themselves had to submit to the same treatment, I concluded to appeal to the sympathy of the groom, who seemed to have had full control over me; but my pitiful cries never touched his sympathy, for things seemed to grow worse rather than better; so I made up my mind to stem the storm the best I could.

One day, about two weeks after Boney Young and mother had the conflict, he called me to him, as though he was in his pleasantest mood; he was singing. I ran to him as if to say by action, I will do anything you bid me willingly. When I got him he said, "Go and bring me a switch, sir." I answered "Yes, sir," and off I went and brought him one; then he said, "Come in here, sir;" I answered, "Yes, sir;" and I went into a horse's stall, but while I was going in a thousand thoughts passed through my mind as to what he wanted me to go into the stall for, but when I got in I soon learned, for he gave me a first-class flogging.

That evening when I went home to father and mother, I said to them, "Mr. Young is whipping me too much now; I shall not stand it, I shall fight him." Father said to me, "You must not do that, because if you do he will say that your mother and I advised you to do it, and it will make it hard for your mother and me, as well as for yourself. You must do as I told you, my son; do your work the best you can, and do not say anything." I said to father, "But I don't know what I have done that he should whip me; he does not tell me what wrong I have done, he simply calls me to him and whips me when he gets ready." Father said, "I can do nothing more than pray to the Lord to hasten the time when these things shall be done away; that is all I can do." When mother stripped me and looked at the wounds that were upon me, she burst into tears, and said, "If he were not so small I would not mind it so much; this will break his constitution; I am going to master about it, because I know he will not allow Mr. Young to treat this child so."

And I thought to myself that had mother gone to master about it, it would have helped me some, for he and she grew up together and he thought a great deal of her. But father said to mother, "You better not go to master, for while he might stop the child from being treated badly, Mr. Young may revenge himself through the overseer, for you know that they are very friendly to each other." So said father to mother, "You would gain nothing in the end; the best thing for us to do is to pray much over it, for I believe that the time will come when this boy with the rest of the children will be free, though we may not live to see it."

V

The most famous, and deadly, slave rebellion in the South was led by Nat Turner in Virginia. Before the revolt was crushed, fifty-seven white planters, women, and children had been killed. The incident gained notoriety from the dimensions of the deed, and also from

the document, The Confessions of Nat Turner, *published in 1832
by Thomas Gray, a white Virginian who talked with Turner in his
cell before Turner's trial. It is difficult to know how accurately
Gray recounted Turner's story. He certainly did make stylistic
changes, and possibly he put some of his own sentiments and fears
into Turner's mouth. Still, the* Confessions *is worth close scrutiny.
It was widely read in the South and helped to increase whites'
fear and repression of blacks. Moreover, it offers some insights into
Turner's intellectual and emotional character. Ultimately, the*
Confessions *not only casts light on the nature of slave life, but
may also help to explain why there were not more slave revolts
in the South.*

THE CONFESSIONS OF NAT TURNER, 1832

Agreeable to his own appointment, on the evening he was committed to prison, with permission of the jailer, I visited Nat on Tuesday the first of November, when, without being questioned at all, he commenced his narrative in the following words:
Sir,

You have asked me to give a history of the motives which induced me to undertake the late insurrection, as you call it. To do so I must go back to the days of my infancy, and even before I was born. I was thirty-one years of age the second of October last, and born the property of Benjamin Turner, of this county. In my childhood a circumstance occurred which made an indelible impression on my mind, and laid the groundwork of that enthusiasm which has terminated so fatally to many both white and black, and for which I am about to atone at the gallows. It is here necessary to relate this circumstance—trifling as it may seem, it was the commencement of that belief which has grown with time, and even now, sir, in this dungeon, helpless and forsaken as I am, I cannot divest myself of. Being at play with other children, when three or four years old, I was telling them something, which my mother overhearing, said it had happened before I was born. I stuck to my story, however, and related some things which went in her opinion to confirm it. Others being called on were greatly astonished, knowing that these things had happened, and caused them to say in my hearing, I surely would be a prophet, as the Lord had shown me things that had happened before my birth. And my father and mother strengthened me in this my first impression, saying in my presence, I was intended for some great purpose, which they had always thought from certain marks on my head and breast.

My grandmother, who was very religious, and to whom I was much attached—my master, who belonged to the church, and other religious persons who visited the house, and whom I often saw at prayers, noticing the singularity of my manners, I suppose, and my uncommon

In *The Confessions of Nat Turner . . . as Fully and Voluntarily Made to Thomas R. Gray* (Richmond, Va., 1832). Reprint edition (New York: 1964), pp. 5–17.

intelligence for a child, remarked I had too much sense to be raised—
and if I was, I would never be of any service to any one—as a slave.
The manner in which I learned to read and write, not only had great
influence on my own mind, as I acquired it with the most perfect
ease, so much so that I have no recollection whatever of learning the
alphabet—but to the astonishment of the family, one day, when a
book was shown me to keep me from crying, I began spelling the names
of different objects—this was a source of wonder to all in the neighborhood, particularly the blacks—and this learning was constantly improved
at all opportunities. When I got large enough to go to work, while
employed, I was reflecting on many things that would present themselves to my imagination. I was not addicted to stealing in my youth,
nor have never been. Yet such was the confidence of the Negroes in the
neighborhood, even at this early period of my life, in my superior
judgment, that they would often carry me with them when they were
going on any roguery, to plan for them. Growing up among them, with
this confidence in my superior judgment, and when this, in their
opinions, was perfected by divine inspiration, from the circumstances
already alluded to in my infancy, and which belief was ever afterward
zealously inculcated by the austerity of my life and manners, which
became the subject of remark by white and black. By this time, having
arrived to man's estate, and hearing the Scriptures commented on at
meetings, I was struck with that particular passage which says: "Seek
ye the kingdom of Heaven and all things shall be added unto you." I
reflected much on this passage, and prayed daily for light on this subject.
As I was praying one day at my plough, the spirit spoke to me, saying
"Seek ye the kingdom of Heaven and all things shall be added unto you."
Question—What do you mean by the Spirit. *Answer*—The Spirit that
spoke to the prophets in former days—and I was greatly astonished,
and for two years prayed continually, whenever my duty would permit
—and then again I had the same revelation, which fully confirmed me
in the impression that I was ordained for some great purpose in the
hands of the Almighty. Several years rolled round, in which many
events occurred to strengthen me in this my belief. At this time I
reverted in my mind to the remarks made of me in my childhood, and
the things that had been shown me. And as it had been said of me in
my childhood by those whom I had been taught to pray, both white
and black, and in whom I had the greatest confidence, that I had too
much sense to be raised, and if I was I would never be of any use to
anyone as a slave. Now finding I had arrived to man's estate, and was
a slave, and these revelations being made known to me, I began to
direct my attention to this great object, to fulfill the purpose for which,
by this time, I felt assured I was intended. Knowing the influence I
had obtained over the minds of my fellow servants, (not by the means
of conjuring and such like tricks—for to them I always spoke of such
things with contempt) but by the communion of the Spirit whose revelations I often communicated to them, and they believed and said my
wisdom came from God.

And on the twelfth of May 1828, I heard a loud noise in the
heavens, and the Spirit instantly appeared to me and said the Serpent
was loosened, and Christ had laid down the yoke he had borne for the

sins of men, and that I should take it on and fight against the Serpent, for the time was fast approaching, when the first should be last and the last should be first. *Question*—Do you not find yourself mistaken now? *Answer*—Was not Christ crucified? And by signs in the heavens that it would make known to me when I should commence the great work— and until the first sign appeared, I should conceal it from the knowledge of men—and on the appearance of the sign (the eclipse of the sun last February), I should arise and prepare myself, and slay my enemies with their own weapons. And immediately on the sign appearing in the heavens, the seal was removed from my lips, and I communicated the great work laid out for me to do, to four in whom I had the greatest confidence (Henry, Hark, Nelson, and Sam). It was intended by us to have begun the work of death on the fourth of July last. Many were the plans formed and rejected by us, and it affected my mind to such a degree that I fell sick, and the time passed without our coming to any determination how to commence—still forming new schemes and reject- ing them when the sign appeared again, which determined me not to wait longer.

Since the commencement of 1830, I had been living with Mr. Joseph Travis, who was to me a kind master, and placed the greatest confidence in me; in fact, I had no cause to complain of his treatment to me. On Saturday evening, the twentieth of August, it was agreed between Henry, Hark, and myself to prepare a dinner the next day for the men we expected, and then to concert a plan, as we had not yet determined on any. Hark on the following morning brought a pig, and Henry brandy, and being joined by Sam, Nelson, Will, and Jack, they prepared in the woods a dinner, where, about three o'clock, I joined them. *Question*—Why were you so backward in joining them? *Answer*—The same reason that had caused me not to mix with them for years before.

I saluted them on coming up, and asked Will how came he there; he answered his life was worth no more than others, and his liberty as dear to him. I asked him if he thought to obtain it? He said he would, or lose his life. This was enough to put him in full confidence. Jack, I knew, was only a tool in the hands of Hark. It was quickly agreed we should commence at home (Mr. J. Travis') on that night, and until we had armed and equipped ourselves, and gathered sufficient force, neither age nor sex was to be spared (which was invariably adhered to). We remained at the feast until about two hours in the night, when we went to the house and found Austin; they all went to the cider press and drank, except myself. On returning to the house, Hark went to the door with an ax, for the purpose of breaking it open, as we knew we were strong enough to murder the family, if they were awakened by the noise; but reflecting that it might create an alarm in the neighbor- hood, we determined to enter the house secretly, and murder them while sleeping. Hark got a ladder and set it against the chimney, on which I ascended, and hoisting a window, entered and came down stairs, unbarred the door, and removed the guns from their places. It was then observed that I must spill the first blood. On which armed with a hatchet, and accompanied by Will, I entered my master's chamber; it being dark, I could not give a death blow, the hatchet glanced from his head, he sprang from the bed and called his wife, it was his last word. Will laid him dead, with a blow of his ax, and Mrs. Travis shared the same fate, as she lay in bed. The murder of this family, five in number, was the work of a moment, not one of them awoke; there was a little infant sleeping in a cradle, that was forgotten, until we had left the house and gone some distance, when Henry and Will returned and killed it. We got here four guns that would shoot, and several old muskets, with a pound or two of powder. We remained some time at the barn, where we paraded; I formed them in a line as soldiers, and after carrying them through all the maneuvers I was master of, marched them off to Mr. Salathul Francis', about six hundred yards distant. Sam and Will went to the door and knocked. Mr. Francis asked who was there, Sam replied it was him, and he had a letter for him, on which he got up and came to the door; they immediately seized him, and dragging him out a little from the door, he was dispatched by repeated blows on the head; there was no other white person in the family. We started from there for Mrs. Reese's, maintaining the most perfect silence on our march, where finding the door unlocked, we entered, and murdered Mrs. Reese in her bed, while sleeping; her son awoke, but it was only to sleep the sleep of death, he had only time to say who is that, and he was no more. From Mrs. Reese's we went to Mrs. Turner's, a mile distant, which we reached about sunrise on Monday morning. Henry, Austin, and Sam went to the still, where, finding Mr. Peebles, Austin shot him, and the rest of us went to the house; as we approached, the family discovered us, and shut the door. Vain hope! Will, with one stroke of his ax, opened it, and we entered and found Mrs. Turner and Mrs Newsome in the middle of a room almost frightened to death. Will immediately killed Mrs. Turner, with one blow of his ax. I took Mrs. Newsome by the hand, and with the sword I had when I was apprehended, I struck her several blows over the head, but not being able to kill her, as the sword was dull. Will turning around and discovering it, dispatched her also. A general destruction of property and search for money and ammunition always succeeded the murders. By this time my company amounted to fifteen, and nine men mounted, who started for Mrs. Whitehead's (the other six were to go through a byway to Mr. Bryant's and rejoin us at Mrs. Whitehead's), as we approached the house we discovered Mr. Richard Whitehead standing in the cotton patch, near the lane fence; we called him over into the lane, and Will, the executioner, was near at hand with his fatal ax, to send him to an untimely grave. As we pushed on to the house, I discovered someone running round the garden, and thinking it was some of the white family, I pursued them, but finding it was a servant girl belonging to the house, I returned to commence the work of death, but they whom I left had not been idle; all the family were already murdered, but Mrs. Whitehead and her daughter Margaret. As I came round to the door I saw Will pulling Mrs. Whitehead out of the house, and at the step he nearly severed her head from her body, with his broad ax. Miss Margaret, when I discovered her had concealed herself in the corner, formed by the projection of the cellar cap from the house; on my approach she fled, but was soon overtaken, and after repeated blows with a sword, I killed her by a blow on the head with a fence rail. By this time, the six who had gone by Mr. Bryant's rejoined us, and informed me they had done the work of death assigned them. We again divided, part going to Mr. Richard Porter's, and from thence to Nathaniel Francis', the others to Mr. Howell Harris', and Mr. T. Doyle's. On my reaching Mr. Porter's, he had escaped with his family. I understood there that the alarm had already spread.

I proceeded to Mr. Levi Waller's, two or three miles distant. I took my station in the rear, and as it was my object to carry terror and devastation wherever we went, I placed fifteen or twenty of the best armed and most to be relied on in front, who generally approached the houses as fast as their horses could run; this was for two purposes, to prevent their escape and strike terror to the inhabitants—on this account I never got to the houses, after leaving Mrs. Whitehead's, until the murders were committed, except in one case. I sometimes got in sight in time to see the work of death completed, viewed the mangled bodies as they lay, in silent satisfaction, and immediately started in quest of other victims. Having murdered Mrs. Waller and ten children, we started for Mr. William Williams'—having killed him and two little boys that were there; while engaged in this, Mrs. Williams fled and got some distance from the house, but she was pursued, overtaken, and compelled to get up behind one of the company, who brought her back, and after showing her the mangled body of her lifeless husband, she was told to get down and lay by his side, where she was shot dead. I then started for Mr. Jacob Wililams', where the family were murdered. Here we found a young man named Drury, who had come on business with Mr. Wililams. He was pursued, overtaken, and shot. Mrs. Vaughan's was the next place we visited—and after murdering the family here, I determined on starting for Jerusalem. Our number amounted now to fifty or sixty, all mounted and armed with guns, axes, swords, and clubs. On reaching Mr. James W. Parker's gate, immediately on the road leading to Jerusalem, and about three miles distant, it was proposed to me to call there, but I objected, as I knew he was gone to Jerusalem, and my object was to reach there as soon as possible; but some of the men having relations at Mr. Parker's it was agreed that they might call and get his people. I remained at the gate on the road, with seven or eight; the others going across the field to the house, about half a mile off. After waiting some time for them, I became impatient, and started to the house for them, and on our return we were met by a party of white men, who had pursued our blood-stained track and who had fired on those at the gate and dispersed them, which I knew nothing of, not having been at that time rejoined by any of them. Immediately on discovering the whites, I ordered my men to halt and form, as they appeared to be alarmed. The white men, eighteen in number, approached us in about one hundred yards, when one of them fired.

I then ordered my men to fire and rush on them; the few remaining stood their ground until we approached within fifty yards, when they fired and retreated. We pursued and overtook some of them who we thought we left dead; after pursuing them about two hundred yards, and rising a little hill, I discovered they were met by another party, and had halted, and were reloading their guns, thinking that those who retreated first, and the party who fired on us at fifty or sixty yards distant, had all only fallen back to meet others with ammunition. As

I saw them reloading their guns, and more coming up than I saw at first, and several of my bravest men being wounded, the others became panic struck and squandered over the field; the white men pursued and fired on us several times. Hark had his horse shot under him, and I caught another for him as it was running by me; five or six of my men were wounded, but none left on the field; finding myself defeated here I instantly determined to go through a private way, and cross the Nottoway River at the Cypress Bridge, three miles below Jerusalem, and attack that place in the rear, as I expected they would look for me on the other road, and I had a great desire to get there to procure arms and ammunition. After going a short distance in this private way, accompanied by about twenty men, I overtook two or three who told me the others were dispersed in every direction. After trying in vain to collect a sufficient force to proceed to Jerusalem, I determined to return, as I was sure they would make back to their old neighborhood, where they would rejoin me, make new recruits, and come down again. On my way back, I called at Mrs. Thomas's, Mrs. Spencer's, and several other places. The white families having fled, we found no more victims to gratify our thirst for blood, we stopped at Major Ridley's quarter for the night, and being joined by four of his men, with the recruits made since my defeat, we mustered now about forty strong. After placing out sentinels, I laid down to sleep, but was quickly roused by a great racket. Starting up, I found some mounted, and others in great confusion; one of the sentinels having given the alarm that we were about to be attacked, I ordered some to ride round and reconnoiter, and on their return the others being more alarmed, not knowing who they were, fled in different ways, so that I was reduced to about twenty again; with this I determined to attempt to recruit, and proceed on to rally in the neighborhood I had left. Dr. Blunt's was the nearest house, which we reached just before day; on riding up the yard, Hark fired a gun. We expected Dr. Blunt and his family were at Major Ridley's, as I knew there was a company of men there; the gun was fired to ascertain if any of the family were at home; we were immediately fired upon and retreated leaving several of my men. I do not know what became of them, as I never saw them afterward. Pursuing our course back, and coming in sight of Captain Harris's, where we had been the day before, we discovered a party of white men at the house, on which all deserted me but two (Jacob and Nat), we concealed ourselves in the woods until near night, when I sent them in search of Henry, Sam, Nelson, and Hark, and directed them to rally all they could at the place we had had our dinner the Sunday before, where they would find me, and I accordingly returned there as soon as it was dark, and remained until Wednesday evening, when discovering white men riding around the place as though they were looking for someone, and none of my men joining me, I concluded Jacob and Nat had been taken, and compelled to betray me. On this I gave up all hope for the present; and on Thursday night, after having supplied myself with provisions from Mr. Travis's, I scratched a hole under a pile of fence rails in a field, where I concealed myself for six weeks, never leaving my hiding place but for a few minutes in the dead of night to get water, which was very near; thinking by this time I could venture out, I began to go about in the night and eavesdrop the houses in the neighborhood; pursuing this course for about a fortnight and gathering little or no intelligence, afraid of speaking to any human being, and returning every morning to my cave before the dawn of day. I know not how long I might have led this life, if accident had not betrayed me, a dog in the neighborhood passing by my hiding place one night while I was out was attracted by some meat I had in my cave, and crawled in and stole it, and was coming out just as I returned. A few nights after, two Negroes having started to go hunting with the same dog, and passed that way, the dog came again to the place, and having just gone out to walk about, discovered me and barked, on which, thinking myself discovered, I spoke to them to beg concealment. On making myself known, they fled from me. Knowing then they would betray me, I immediately left my hiding place, and was pursued almost incessantly until I was taken a fortnight afterward by Mr. Benjamin Phipps, in a little hole I had dug out with my sword, for the purpose of concealment, under the top of a fallen tree. On Mr. Phipps discovering the place of my concealment, he cocked his gun and aimed at me. I requested him not to shoot, and I would give up, upon which he demanded my sword. I delivered it to him, and he brought me to prison. During the time I was pursued, I had many hair breadth escapes, which your time will not permit you to relate. I am here loaded with chains, and willing to suffer the fate that awaits me.

I here proceeded to make some inquiries of him, after assuring him of the certain death that awaited him, and that concealment would only bring destruction on the innocent as well as guilty, of his own color, if he knew of any extensive or concerted plan. His answer was, I do not. When I questioned him as to the insurrection in North Carolina happening about the same time, he denied any knowledge of it.

Chapter 7

The Frontier Community

TO A WIDE RANGE of observers, from European visitors to professional historians, the institution that has exerted the greatest influence on the American character and culture is the frontier. These communities, claimed their most famous historian, Frederick Jackson Turner, established the essential characteristics of American individualism and democratic politics. Pioneers, living on the edge of settlement in a day-to-day encounter with the wilderness, abandoned traditional European habits and adopted uniquely American ones. "This expansion westward," declared Turner, "with its new opportunities, its continuous touch with simplicity of primitive society, furnish the forces dominating the American character. The true point of view in the history of this nation is not the Atlantic coast, it is the Great West."

Neither Turner nor his many followers ever defined the frontier itself very specifically. At some times they seemed to be analyzing a demographic phenomenon; that is, the impact on the community of living in a sparsely settled region. At other times they seemed to be describing a process, how men and women adjusted to wilderness conditions. Nor were they very precise about the period of time during which the frontier flourished—ostensibly its impact on American society was continuous throughout the whole nineteenth century. And they were never very exact about which regions they were analyzing; presumably the experience of the Ohio Valley settlers was duplicated by those in the Mississippi region, and then on the Great Plains, and finally in the Far West. Yet for all the vagueness of the writing, the Turner camp had a compelling breadth of vision. They brought together in a grand design a series of very particular and local developments.

While the spaciousness of this interpretation remains very appealing, one might well wish to question the basic thrust of the argument. That the wilderness or population scarcity influenced both the personality of the settlers and the organization of their communities seems indisputable. What is at issue is the exact nature of that in-

fluence. Did frontier conditions actually stimulate individualism? Or, to the contrary, were Western settlers even more community minded and community dependent than their Eastern counterparts? Did primitive conditions encourage men to go their own way? Should we retain our image of frontiersmen as Daniel Boone types, each with a rifle in hand, striking out further westward as soon as he saw smoke on the horizon? Or were they so reliant on each other as to remind us of seventeenth-century Puritans, knit together in tightly bound communities?

The selections that follow address themselves directly to this question. They are concerned first with the very nature of migration, the way people traveled in early nineteenth-century America. An incredible amount of movement went on during these decades. In 1790, the eastern seaboard states (including Kentucky and Tennessee) accounted for 100 percent of the nation's population. By 1860, only 55 percent of the country resided there. Put another way, some seven million people took up residence in the Midwest, in a territory stretching from Ohio to Wisconsin. How was this shift in population accomplished? Why did settlers move from region to region? Some contemporary accounts of this phenomenon claimed that there was more poetry and fantasy to this movement than there was hard-headed economic calculation. How valid does such an interpretation seem today?

Once on the frontier, how did the settlers arrange their lives? Clearly, they lacked all the customary institutions that functioned in the East—they were without courts or schools or churches or jails. Did they attempt to re-create these familiar institutions or to construct new ones? Did they attempt to copy older forms and in so doing create, albeit unintentionally, some new arrangements? Did these pioneers diligently try to make it on their own, or were they far more comfortable invoking a spirit of cooperation and mutual dependence than we have previously realized?

I

Travelers' accounts of life in the West had a special attraction to Americans in the early nineteenth century, who were eager to read of the customs and manners of their pioneer countrymen. One of the

*most popular narratives was written by Timothy Flint, a clergyman
sent out by the Missionary Society of Connecticut to distribute
Bibles and religious tracts and to preach in and around the Mississippi Valley. Although Flint does more than his share of moraliz-
ing, he vividly portrays both the motives of frontiersmen and the
nature of the communities they organized.*

RECOLLECTIONS, 1826

TIMOTHY FLINT

The people in the Atlantic states have not yet recovered from the horror
inspired by the term "backwoodsman." When I first visited this country,
I had my full share. I heard a thousand stories of gougings and robberies
and shooting down with the rifle. I have travelled in these regions thousands of miles under all circumstances of exposure and danger. I never
have carried the slightest weapon of defense. I scarcely remember to
have experienced anything that resembled insult, or to have felt myself
in danger from the people.

When we look round these immense regions, and consider that I
have been in settlements three hundred miles from any court of justice,
the wonder is that so few outrages and murders occur. It is true there
are gamblers and gougers and outlaws; but there are fewer of them,
than from the nature of things, we ought to expect. The backwoodsman
of the West, as I have seen him, is generally an amiable and virtuous
man. His general motive for coming here is to be a freeholder, to have
plenty of rich land, and to be able to settle his children about him. It
is a most virtuous motive. I fully believe that nine in ten of the emigrants
have come here with no other motive. You find, in truth, that he has
vices and barbarisms peculiar to his situation. His manners are rough.
He wears, it may be, a long beard. He has a great quantity of bear or
deer skins wrought into his household establishment, his furniture,
and dress. He carries a knife, or a dirk, in his bosom, and when in the
woods has a rifle on his back, and a pack of dogs at his heels. An
Atlantic stranger, transferred directly from one of our cities to his door,
would recoil from an encounter with him. But remember that his rifle
and his dogs are among his chief means of support and profit. Remember that all his first days here were passed in dread of the savages.
Enter his door, and tell him you are benighted, and wish the shelter of
his cabin for the night. The welcome is indeed seemingly ungracious.
But this apparent ungraciousness is the harbinger of every kindness
that he can bestow, and every comfort that his cabin can afford. Good
coffee, corn bread and butter, venison, pork, wild and tame fowls are set
before you. You are shown to the best bed which the house can offer.
When this kind of hospitality has been afforded you as long as you
choose to stay, and when you depart, and speak about your bill, you are
most commonly told with some slight mark of resentment that they do

In *Recollections of the Last Ten Years*, by Timothy Flint (Boston, 1826),
pp. 74–75, 170–73, 178–83, 198–201, 232–35, 240–43.

not keep tavern. The people here are not yet a reading people. Few good books are brought into the country. The people are too busy, too much occupied in making farms and speculations, to think of literature.

America inherits a taste for puffing. The people are idolaters to the "golden calves." Some favorite man, fashion, or opinion sweep everything before them. This region is the paradise of puffers.

I have been amused in reading puffing advertisements in the newspapers. A little subscription school, in which half the pupils are abecedarians, is a college. The misfortune is that these vile pretensions finally induce the people to believe that there is a "royal road" to learning.

Town making introduces another species of puffing. Art and ingenuity have been exhausted in devising new ways of alluring purchasers to take lots and build in the new town. There are the fine rivers, the healthy hills, the mineral springs, the clear running water, the valuable forests, the fine steamboat navigation, the vast country adjacent, the central position, the admirable soil, and last of all the cheerful and undoubting predictions of what the town must one day be. I have read more than a hundred advertisements of this sort. Then the legislature must be tampered with in order to make the town either the metropolis, or at least the seat of justice.

A coarse caricature of this abomination of town making appeared in the St. Louis papers. The name was "Ne plus ultra." The streets were laid out a mile in width; the squares were to be sections, each containing six hundred and forty acres. The mall was a vast standing forest. In the center of this modern Babylon, roads were to cross each other in a meridional line at right angles.

In truth, while traveling on the prairies of the Illinois and Missouri, and observing such immense tracts of rich soil, remarking the beautiful simplicity of the limits of farms, introduced by our government, in causing the land to be all surveyed in exact squares, and thus destroying here the barbarous prescription, which has in the settled countries laid out the lands in ugly farms, and bounded them by zigzag lines—seeing the guardian genius, Liberty, hovering over the country—measuring the progress of the future, only by the analogy of the past—it will be difficult for the imagination to assign limits to the future growth and prosperity of the country.

I shall have occasion to remark upon the moving or migratory character of the western people generally. Though they have generally good houses, they might almost as well, like the Tartars, dwell in tents. Everything shifts under your eye. The present occupants sell, pack up, depart. Strangers replace them. Before they have gained the confidence of their neighbors, they hear of a better place, pack up, and follow their precursors.

I have spoken of the movable part of the community, and unfortunately for the Western country, it constitutes too great a proportion of the whole community. The general inclination here is too much like that of the Tartars. Next to hunting, Indian wars, and the wonderful exuberance of Kentucky, the favorite topic is new countries. They talk of them. They are attached to the associations connected with such conversations. They have a fatal effect upon their exertions. They only make such improvements as they can leave without reluctance

and without loss. I have everywhere noted the operation of this impediment in the way of those permanent and noble improvements which grow out of a love for that appropriated spot where we were born, and where we expect to die. There is a fund of virtuous habits, arising out of these permanent establishments, which give to our patriotism "a local habitation and a name." But neither do I at all believe the perverse representation of these same moving people, who have no affection for one spot more than another, and whose home is in the wild woods, or the boundless prairies, or wherever their dogs, their cattle, and their servants are about them. They lose, no doubt, some of the noble prejudices which are transmitted with durable mansions through successive generations. But they, in their turn, have virtues that are called into exercise by the peculiarities of their case and character, which are equally unknown. But whatever may be the effect of the stationary or the moving life upon the parties respectively, there can be no doubt about the result of this spirit upon the face of the country. Durable houses of brick or of stone, which are peculiarly called for, on account of the scarcity of timber, fences of hedge and ditch, barns and granaries of the more durable kind, the establishment of the coarser manufactories so necessary in a country like this, the planting of artificial forests, which on the wide prairies would be so beautiful and useful, all that accumulation of labor, industry, taste, and wealth that unite to beautify a family residence, to be transmitted as a proud and useful memento of the family—these improvements, which seem to be so naturally called for on these fertile plains, will not become general for many years. Scarcely has a family fixed itself, and enclosed a plantation with the universal fence, reared a suitable number of log buildings, in short, achieved the first rough improvements, that appertain to the most absolute necessity, than the assembled family about the winter fire begin to talk about the prevailing theme—some country that has become the rage, as a point of immigration. They offer their farm for sale, and move away.

The inducements to emigration arise, as most of our actions do, from mixed motives. There is more of the material of poetry than we imagine, diffused through all the classes of the community. And upon this part of the character it is that the disposition to emigration operates, and brings in aid the influence of its imperceptible but magic power. Very few, except the Germans, emigrate simply to find better and cheaper lands. The notion of new and more beautiful woods and streams, of a milder climate, deer, fish, fowl, game, and all those delightful images of enjoyment that so readily associate with the idea of the wild and boundless license of new regions; all that restless hope of finding in a new country, and in new views and combinations of things, something that we crave but have not.

I am ready to believe, from my own experience, and from what I have seen in the case of others, that this influence of imagination has no inconsiderable agency in producing emigration. Indeed, the saturnine and illiterate emigrant may not be conscious that such motives had any agency in fixing him in his purpose. They arrive, after long and diversified, but generally painful journeys, painful, especially if they have young and helpless members in their families, in the region for which they started. The first difficulty, and it is not a small one, is, among an infinite variety of choices, where to fix. The speculator, the surveyor, the different circles all propose different places, and each vaunts the exclusive excellence of his choice. If the emigrant is a reader, he betakes himself to the papers, and in the infinity of advertisements, his uncertainty is increased.

After the long uncertainty of choice is finally fixed—which is not till after the expenses and the lapse of a year—a few weeks' familiar acquaintance with the scene dispels the charms and the illusions of the imagination. The earth, the water, and the wood of these distant lands are found to be the same well-known realities of his own country. Hunting, though the game be plenty, is a laborious and unproductive business, and everything visionary and unreal gradually gives way to truth and reality.

In my view, after all the evils of the condition of an immigrant are considered, there is a great balance of real and actual advantages in his favor. There is much in that real and genuine American independence which is possessed by an industrious and frugal planter in a great degree. Any person, able and disposed to labor, is forever freed from the apprehension of poverty; and let philosophers in their bitter irony pronounce as many eulogies as they may on poverty, it is a bitter evil, and all its fruits are bitter. We need not travel these wilds in order to understand what a blessing it is to be freed forever from the apprehension of this evil. Even here there are sick, and there is little sympathy; no poor laws, no resource but in the charity of a people not remarkable for their feeling.

Thence it results that there are the more inducements to form families, and those ties, which are the cause, that while one is sick the rest are bound for his nursing and sustenance. A father can settle his children about him. A vigorous and active young man needs but two years of personal labor to have a farm ready for the support of a small family. There is less need of labor for actual support. The soil is free from stones, loose and mellow, and needs no manure, and it is very abundant in the productions natural to it, the principal of which are corn, fruits, and wheat. The calculation is commonly made that two days in a week contribute as much to support here, as the whole week at the North. The objection commonly made is that this ease of subsistence fosters idleness. But it is equally true that this depends entirely on the person, and a man of good principles and habits will find useful and happy employment for all that time which the wants of actual subsistence do not require.

One of the first things that a man, who is capable of learning anything in this country, learns is the folly of selecting his associates according to their country, or of having his friends and companions of the same country with himself. He sees good and bad, promiscuously, from all countries, and soon learns to try and weigh men by their character, and not by the place of birth. During the ten years of my acquaintance with the country, I have discovered these feelings lessening in every place. The time will come and is rapidly approaching when all local partialities will be merged in the pride of being a citizen of our great and free country, a country which is destined shortly to make a most distinguished figure among the nations.

II

Travel guides meticulously set down the best routes for westward migrants to follow, the equipment to bring, and the ways to organize the trip. These guides, not especially vital for migrants into the Midwest, were of crucial significance for those who took the long and difficult journey across the Great Plains. One typical set of instructions was issued by Randolph Marcy, an army captain who led such expeditions. The model company moving westward may have had more in common with Puritans crossing the Atlantic than with Daniel Boone types moving westward.

THE PRAIRIE TRAVELER, 1861

RANDOLPH MARCY

From Fort Leavenworth to Santa Fé, by the Way of the Upper Ferry of the Kansas River and the Cimarron

(Wood, water, and grass are found at all points where the absence of them is not stated.)

MILES FROM FORT LEAVENWORTH TO
2.88   Salt Creek.
9.59   Stranger's Creek.
13.54   "   "

In *The Prairie Traveller: A Handbook for Overland Expeditions*, by Randolph Marcy (New York, 1861), pp. 22–25, 276–79.

9.60   Grasshopper Creek.

4.54   Soldier's Creek.

2.45   Upper Ferry, Kansas River.

7.41   Pottawatomie Settlement.

3.89   White Wakarussi Creek.

7.78   "   "

0.73   Road from Independence. No place to encamp.

7.97   Elm Creek. Water generally.

8.06   Diamond Spring.

15.46   Lost Spring. No wood.

9.25   Mud Creek. Water uncertain; no wood.

7.76   Cottonwood Creek.

6.16   Water Holes. Water generally; no wood.

12.44   Big Turkey Creek. No water.

7.83   Little Turkey Creek. Water uncertain; no wood.

18.19   Little Arkansas River.

10.60   Owl Creek. Water generally in holes above and below crossing.

6.39   Little Cow Creek. Water only occasionally.

2.93   Big Cow Creek. Water holes, ten miles (estimated). Water uncertain; no wood.

18.24   Bend of the Arkansas.

16.35   Pawnee Rock. Teams sometimes camp near here, and drive stock to the Arkansas to water. No wood.

5.28   Ash Creek. Water above and below crossing, uncertain.

6.65   Pawnee Fork. Best grass some distance above crossing.

      From Pawnee Fork to the lower crossing of the Arkansas, a distance of ninety-eight and one half miles, convenient camping places can be found along the Arkansas; the most prominent localities are therefore only mentioned. A supply of fuel should be laid in at Pawnee Fork to last till you pass Fort Mann, though it may be obtained, but inconveniently, from the *opposite* side of the Arkansas. Dry Route branches off at three and one half miles (estimated). It is said to be a good one, but deficient in water and without wood.

11.43   Coon Creek.

10.05   Fort Mann.

25.34   Lower Crossing of the Arkansas. A supply of wood should be got from this vicinity to last till you reach Cedar Creek.

15.68   Water hole. Water uncertain; no wood.

30.02   Two water holes. Water uncertain; no wood.

14.14   Lower Cimarron Springs. No wood.

20.00   Pools of Water. Water uncertain; no wood.

19.02   Middle Springs of the Cimarron. No wood.

12.93   Little Crossing of the Cimarron. No wood.

14.10   Upper Cimarron Springs. No wood. Pools of water, seven miles (estimated). No wood.

19.05   Cold Spring. A tree here and there in the vicinity. Pools of water, eleven miles (estimated). Water uncertain; no wood.

16.13   Cedar Creek. M'Nees' Creek, ten miles (estimated). Water indifferent and uncertain; scant pasture; no wood.

21.99   Cottonwood Creek. No water.

15.17   Rabbit Ear Creek. Ten miles (estimated), springs. Round Mound, eight miles (estimated). No water; no wood; no camping place. Rock Creek, ten miles (estimated). Grazing scant; no wood.

26.40   Whetstone Creek. Spring; no wood. Water, etc., to the left of the road.

14.13   Point of Rocks. Water and grass *up the canyon*, just after crossing the *point;* scattering shrub cedars on the neighboring heights.

16.62   Sandy Arroyo. Water uncertain; no wood. Grazing above the crossing; willows.

10.05   Rio Ocaté. Wood one third of a mile to right of road; grass in the canyon. Pond of water, thirteen and one half miles (estimated). No wood.

19.65   Wagon Mound.

21.62   Canyon del Lobo. Rio Moro, three and one half miles (estimated).

18.00   Las Vegas. Forage purchasable.

13.05   Tacolote. Forage purchasable. No grass to speak of.

14.00   San Miguel. Forage purchasable; no grass.

21.81   Ruins of Pecos. Grazing very scant. Water uncertain; no grass.

13.41   Stone Corral. No grass.

10.80   Santa Fé. Forage purchasable; no grazing.

Organization of Companies

After a particular route has been selected to make the journey across the plains, and the requisite number have arrived at the eastern terminus, their first business should be to organize themselves into a company and elect a commander. The company should be of sufficient magnitude to herd and guard animals, and for protection against Indians.

From fifty to seventy men, properly armed and equipped, will be enough for these purposes, and any greater number only makes the movements of the party more cumbersome and tardy.

In the selection of a captain, good judgment, integrity of purpose, and practical experience are the essential requisites, and these are indispensable to the harmony and consolidation of the association. His duty should be to direct the order of march, the time of starting and halting, to select the camps, detail and give orders to guards, and, indeed, to control and superintend all the movements of the company.

An obligation should then be drawn up and signed by all the members of the association, wherein each one should bind himself to abide in all cases by the orders and decisions of the captain, and to aid him by every means in his power in the execution of his duties; and they should also obligate themselves to aid each other, so as to make the individual interest of each member the common concern of the whole company. To insure this, a fund should be raised for the purchase of extra animals to supply the places of those which may give out or die on the road; and if the wagon or team of a particular member should fail and have to be abandoned, the company should obligate themselves to transport his luggage, and the captain should see that he has his share of transportation equal with any other member. Thus it will be made the interest of every member of the company to watch over and protect the property of others as well as his own.

In case of failure on the part of anyone to comply with the obligations imposed by the articles of agreement after they have been duly executed, the company should of course have the power to punish the delinquent member, and, if necessary, to exclude him from all the benefits of the association.

The advantages of an association such as I have mentioned are manifestly numerous. The animals can be herded together and guarded by the different members of the company in rotation, thereby securing to all the opportunities of sleep and rest. Besides, this is the only way to resist depredations of the Indians, and to prevent their stampeding and driving off animals; and much more efficiency is secured in every respect, especially in crossing streams, repairing roads, etc., etc.

When a captain has once been chosen, he should be sustained in all his decisions unless he commits some manifest outrage, when a majority of the company can always remove him, and put a more competent man in his place.

III

Migrants generally moved westward in successive steps, going in a typical sequence from western New York to Ohio, and then on to Michigan. In this way, they gradually accommodated themselves to frontier life. Occasionally, however, a family moved in one leap from settled Eastern communities to frontier communities, and the shock of displacement made them sensitive observers of the unique qualities of their new environment. One such person was Caroline Kirkland. Her memoir, A New Home, Who'll Follow? *reflects Eastern prejudices, and thereby points to much that was especially characteristic of frontier settlements.*

A NEW HOME, WHO'LL FOLLOW? 1839

CAROLINE S. KIRKLAND

When my husband purchased two hundred acres of wild land and drew with a piece of chalk on the barroom table the plan of a village, I little thought I was destined to make myself famous by handing down to posterity a faithful record of the advancing fortunes of that favored spot.

"The madness of the people" in those days of golden dreams took

In *A New Home, Who'll Follow?*, by Caroline S. Kirkland [pseud.] (n.p., 1839), pp. 8–9, 67–69, 82–83, 88–91, 111, 114–15.

more commonly the form of city building; but there were a few who contented themselves with planning villages on the banks of streams which never could be expected to bear navies, but which might yet be turned to account in the more homely way of grinding or sawing— operations which must necessarily be performed somewhere for the well-being of those very cities. It is of one of these humble attempts that it is my lot to speak, and I make my confession at the outset, warning any fashionable reader who may have taken up my book that I intend to be "decidedly low."

It did not require a very long residence in Michigan to convince me that it is unwise to attempt to stem directly the current of society, even in the wilderness, but I have since learned many ways of *wearing round* which give me the opportunity of living very much after my own fashion, without offending, very seriously, anybody's prejudices.

No settlers are so uncomfortable as those who, coming with abundant means as they suppose to be comfortable, set out with a determination to live as they have been accustomed to live. They soon find that there are places where the "almighty dollar" is almost power-less; or rather, that powerful as it is, it meets with its conqueror in the jealous pride of those whose services must be had in order to live at all.

It would be in vain to pretend that this state of society can ever be agreeable to those who have been accustomed to the more rational arrangements of the older world. The social character of the meals, in particular, is quite destroyed, by the constant presence of strangers, whose manners, habits of thinking, and social connections are quite different from your own, and often exceedingly repugnant to your taste. Granting the correctness of the opinion which may be read in their countenances that they are "as good as you are," I must insist that a greasy cookmaid, or a redolent stableboy can never be, to my thinking, an agreeable table companion—putting pride, that most terrific bug-bear of the woods, out of the question.

Some of my dear theorizing friends in the civilized world had dis-suaded me most earnestly from bringing a maid with me.

"She would always be discontented and anxious to return; and you'll find plenty of good farmer's daughters ready to live with you for the sake of earning a little money."

Good souls! how little did they know of Michigan! I have since that day seen the interior of many a wretched dwelling, with almost literally nothing in it but a bed, a chest, and a table; children ragged to the last degree, and potatoes the only fare; but never yet saw I one where the daughter was willing to own herself obliged to live out at service. She would "hire out" long enough to buy some article of dress perhaps, money to pay the doctor, or for some such special reason; but never as a regular calling, or with an acknowledgment of inferior station.

This state of things appalled me at first; but I have learned a better philosophy since. I find no difficulty now in getting such aid as I require, and but little in retaining it as long as I wish, though there is always a desire of making an occasional display of independence. Since living with one for wages is considered by common consent a favor, I take it as a favor; and, this point once conceded, all goes well. Perhaps I have been peculiarly fortunate; but certainly with one or two exceptions, I

have little or nothing to complain of on this essential point of domestic comfort.

To be sure, I had one damsel who crammed herself almost to suffocation with sweatmeats and other things which she esteemed very nice; and ate up her own pies and cake, to the exclusion of those for whom they were intended; who would put her head in at a door with, "*Miss* Clavers, did you hollar? I thought I *heered* a yell."

And another who was highly offended because room was not made for her at table with guests from the city, and that her company was not requested for tea visits. And this latter highborn damsel sent in from the kitchen a circumstantial account *in writing,* of the instances wherein she considered herself aggrieved; well written it was, too, and expressed with much naïveté, and abundant respect. I answered it in the way which "turneth away wrath." Yet it was not long before this fiery spirit was aroused again, and I was forced to part with my country belle.

I took especial care to be impartial in my own visiting habits, determined at all sacrifice to live down the impression that I felt *above* my neighbors. In fact, however we may justify certain exclusive habits in populous places, they are strikingly and confessedly ridiculous in the wilderness. What can be more absurd than a feeling of proud distinction, where a stray spark of fire, a sudden illness, or a day's contretemps may throw you entirely upon the kindness of your humblest neighbor? If I treat Mrs. Timson with neglect today can I with any face borrow her broom tomorrow? And what would become of me if, in revenge for my declining her invitation to tea this afternoon, she should decline coming to do my washing on Monday?

"Mother wants your sifter," said Miss Ianthe Howard, a young lady of six years' standing, attired in a tattered calico, thickened with dirt; her unkempt locks straggling from under that hideous substitute for a bonnet, so universal in the western country, a dirty cotton handkerchief, which is used, *ad nauseam,* for all sorts of purposes.

"Mother wants your sifter, and she says she guesses you can let her have some sugar and tea, 'cause you've got plenty."

This excellent reason, " 'cause you've got plenty," is conclusive as to sharing with your neighbors. Whoever comes into Michigan with nothing, will be sure to better his condition; but woe to him that brings with him anything like an appearance of abundance, whether of money or mere household conveniences. To have them, and not be willing to share them in some sort with the whole community, is an unpardonable crime. You must lend your best horse to *qui que ce soit*, to go ten miles over hill and marsh, in the darkest night, for a doctor; or your team to travel twenty after a "gal;" your wheelbarrows, your shovels, your utensils of all sorts, belong, not to yourself, but to the public, who do not think it necessary even to *ask* a loan, but take it for granted. The two saddles and bridles of Montacute spend most of their time travelling from house to house a-manback; and I have actually known a stray martingale to be traced to four dwellings two miles apart, having been lent from one to another, without a word to the original proprietor, who sat waiting, not very patiently, to commence a journey.

Then within doors, an inventory of your plenishing of all sorts would scarcely more than include the articles which you are solicited to lend. Not only are all kitchen utensils as much your neighbors as your own, but bedsteads, beds, blankets, sheets travel from house to house, a pleasant and effectual mode of securing the perpetuity of certain efflorescent peculiarities of the skin, for which Michigan is becoming almost as famous as the land " 'twixt Maidenkirk and John o' Groat's." Sieves, smoothing irons, and churns run about as if they had legs; one brass kettle is enough for a whole neighborhood; and I could point to a cradle which has rocked half the babies in Montacute. For my own part, I have lent my broom, my thread, my tape, my spoons, my cat, my thimble, my scissors, my shawl, my shoes; and have been asked for my combs and brushes: and my husband, for his shaving apparatus and his pantaloons.

Many English families reside in our vicinity, some of them well calculated to make their way anywhere; close, penurious, grasping, and indefatigable; denying themselves all but the necessaries of life, in order to add to their lands, and make the most of their crops; and somewhat apt in bargaining to overreach even the wary pumpkin-eaters, their neighbors: others to whom all these things seem so foreign and so unsuitable that one cannot but wonder that the vagaries of fortune should have sent them into so uncongenial an atmosphere. The class last mentioned generally live retired, and show little inclination to mingle with their rustic neighbors; and, of course, they become at once the objects of suspicion and dislike. The principle of "let-a-be for let-a-be" holds not with us. Whoever exhibits any desire for privacy is set down as "proud," or something worse; no matter how inoffensive, or even how benevolent he may be; and of all places in the world in which to live on the shady side of public opinion, an American backwoods settlement is the very worst, as many of these unfortunately mistaken emigrants have been made to feel.

The better classes of English settlers seem to have left their own country with high-wrought notions of the unbounded freedom to be enjoyed in this; and it is with feelings of angry surprise that they learn after a short residence here that this very universal freedom abridges

their own liberty to do as they please in their individual capacity; that
the absolute democracy which prevails in country places imposes as
heavy restraints upon one's freewill in some particulars, as do the
overbearing pride and haughty distinctions of the old world in others;
and after one has changed one's whole plan of life, and crossed the
wide ocean to find a Utopia, the waking to reality is attended with feelings of no slight bitterness. In some instances within my knowledge
these feelings of disappointment have been so severe as to neutralize
all that was good in American life, and to produce a degree of sour
discontent which increased every real evil and went far toward alienating
the few who were kindly inclined toward the stranger.

IV

*The diary of Mrs. Miriam Colt, Went to Kansas, starkly presents the
inflated hopes and grandiose dreams that brought families to
the West and kept them moving. The Colt family traveled from
western New York to Kansas under the auspices of the Vegetarian
Settlement Society, and while there was certainly something odd
about this sponsorship, there is nothing unusual in the society's
promises to prospective settlers. Railroad companies and real estate
promoters did very much the same thing. The site, according to
the prospectus, was to have an agricultural college and several
common schools among its first institutions. Settlers would on
arrival find mills in operation, houses built, and a city under way.
What they found when they arrived, and how they dealt with it,
emerges all too poignantly in Mrs. Colt's account.*

WENT TO KANSAS, 1862

MIRIAM COLT

May thirteenth

Can anyone imagine our disappointment [when arriving] this morning, on learning from this and that member that no mills have been
built; that the directors, after receiving our money to build mills,
have not fulfilled the trust reposed in them, and that in consequence,
some families have already left the settlement.

Now *we all have come!* Have brought our fathers, our mothers, and
our little ones, and find no shelter sufficient to shield them from the
furious prairie winds, and the terrific storms of the climate!

In *Went to Kansas: Being a Thrilling and Ill-Fated Expedition to That Fairy
Land—Its Sad Results*, by Miriam Colt (Boston, 1862), pp. 45–47, 52–55,
70–73, 98–99, 134–35, 140–41, 144–45, 278–85.

For a moment let me contrast the two pictures—the one we had made provision for and had reason to believe would be presented to us, with the one that meets our eyes:

Expected a sawmill would be in operation, a gristmill building, and a temporary boardinghouse erected to receive families as they should come into the settlement, until their own houses could be built.

Wherever there are mills in this southwestern world, there surely is to be a town. And how much of life, active life, would resound through a new settlement, from the noisy sawmill. How soon could comfortable houses be built. As it is, we find the families, some living in tents of cloth, some of cloth and green bark just peeled from the trees, and some wholly of green bark, stuck up on the damp ground, without floors or fires. These intelligent, but too confiding, families have come from the North, East, South, and West, to this *farther* West, to make pleasant homes; and now are determined to turn right about, start again on a journey—some know not where! Others have invested their all in the company. Now come lost means and blighted hopes.

We see that the city grounds, which have been surveyed (and a log cabin built in the center, where is to stand the large "central octagon building"), are one mile from here. It seems the company did not pitch their tents there on account of its being so wet, so chose this higher prairie until after the spring rains should be over. Two or three families of us, and a few single men, take to our wagons again, drive over the roadless prairie, and around the head of a creek, to become the first residents in the "Neosho, or Octagon City." Find the city, as we had seen, to contain only one log cabin, sixteen by sixteen, mudded between the logs on the inside, instead of on the outside; neither door nor window; the roof covered with "shakes" (western shingles), split out of

oak I should think, three and one-half feet in length, and about as wide as a sheet of foolscap paper.

The men have set themselves at work now to improve this dwelling. Some are laying a floor, or rather paving one, by drawing fresh dirt, spreading it all over the ground, then laying flat stones of irregular shape on to it, leaving them bound on all sides by the rich prairie soil. Others are laying a floor to the loft above of "shakes," which from their slivery sides and warping propensity, methinks, will present no very smooth surface to lie upon, when nothing, hardly, save one Indian blanket is to intervene between us and them.

May twenty-second

Members of the company who have concluded to remain in the Territory, think it time now to do what they can, under present disappointments, for the comfort of their families, and also for their future welfare. Some are building their cabins on their city lots, in their respective portions of the octagon; others, independent of the company, have become "squatter sovereigns," and will build their cabins on their claims.

Each claimant can claim and hold, by the preemption right, 240 acres of land—160 timber and 80 prairie. My husband, his father, and sister L. are each claimants; they have accordingly located their claims side by side, making 720 acres of land belonging to our family. It is two miles east from the "center octagon," and joining the Osage Indian lands. My husband says the timber on our claim is fine; there are different kinds of walnut and oak (some black walnuts four feet through), and that for several rods on the river is the prettiest bed of pebbles he ever saw, nice for walks. We intend, some time, to have walks made of them.

The Stewarts have located their claims two miles west from here; are building their cabin on a high prairie swell, where nature has planted the walnut and oak just sparsely enough for both beauty and shade.

Mr. Adams has made a cabin of "shakes" on his city lot, one-fourth of a mile north from the "center."

Mr. Herrimen, a little shed-like cabin of logs and bark, one-half mile a little west of north.

H. S. Clubb's dwelling is a cabin made of an old Indian wigwam and tenting, one mile southeast, on his city lot.

Father Cosgrove resides in a cabin one-half mile southeast, on his city lot, near the river.

The young men, and men without their families, board around in the cabins with the families. So we are all uncomfortably situated, for the want of proper building materials.

June fourth

Disappointment has darkened every brow, however hard they may have striven to rise above it. We are one hundred miles from a gristmill, and fifty from a post office. Mr. Clubb has petitioned to have the mail come here.

The Indians have gone away now on their hunt; it seems quiet and good to have our fear removed for a time. The people say we have had our hardest time here, but it does not seem so to me. I tell my husband, "We are a doomed ship; unless we go away, some great calamity will come upon us; and it is on me that the storm will burst with all its dark fury." Sometimes a voice speaks to me in thunder tones, saying, "Rise, rise! flee to the mountains—tarry not in all the plain. Haste away! Destruction's before thee, and sorrow behind." My husband says, "Miriam, don't feel so; I am afraid you will go crazy. I think it is your imaginings, caused by our disappointments and discomforts." I answer, "I hope it is, but I don't know why I should be so overpowered with such feelings; they come to me without being invited, and I cannot help giving them expression sometimes."

June seventh

My husband is up at his claim planting corn. Hopeful man! Whatever of calamity may be pent up in the black clouds for us, may Heaven grant that our lives may be spared! I can bear all pecuniary losses—go hungry, cold, barefoot, and sleep on the rough and uneven floor—but spare me my beloved husband and my darling children.

The *one plough* is broken. Father started off this morning to go twenty-five miles, down to the Catholic Mission, where is the nearest blacksmith, to get it mended.

June ninth

Father has returned with the mended plough—has had quite an interesting time going to and from the blacksmith's shop, a journey of fifty miles.

June tenth

Mr. Clubb has returned from Fort Scott, and the goods, groceries, seeds, and some provisions belonging to the company have arrived. They were bought with the company's money, still we are charged a very high price for them. Potatoes four dollars per bushel; can't afford to have even one meal of them—have cooked one for mother; they must, all that we have, be planted. Flour is dealt out to us in rations. Have just been to Mr. Clubb's with my small white bag; came home with a few pounds in one end strung over my shoulder. I must have resembled the Missourian woman, with her bag of cornmeal (for I felt as she looked), when I said, "shall I ever come to this?"

July thirteenth

Father's name is now added to the list of the sick. How can I stay this flood of tears, as I look about and see all but myself prostrated with sickness? So pale and weak, and amid so many discomforts. It is impossible for me to do for them as they require. I am weak myself; it seems when I go for water that I can never get back again. Have just been to the spring for my turn of water, one-half mile, which I bring in a six quart camp-pail and Indian coffee pot of the same dimensions.

It is all the way up hill from the spring. This is a long, long sabbath day. *"O, God, forsake us not utterly!"*

July sixteenth

Yesterday morning, father drove out to the settlement before his chill came on, and drove back last eve, after his fever was off. He went to see if he could get someone to stay with us for a few days. Our good neighbor, Mr. Stewart, sent his hired man, Mr. Buxton, this morning. He prepares wood, takes care of the oxen, cow and calf, and brings water. My husband is lying on our bed of prairie grass, on the floor; his fever is passing off. Mother lies on her bed in the other room; seems very sick.

August sixteenth

A letter has come over the long distance from our dear friend Mrs. V. She writes as follows:

Plainfield, Wis., July 22, 1856

My Dear Friends:

Arrived at home safely, and in much better health than when I left you. Arrived here at home just in two weeks from the time that we left the Neosho. Had a very pleasant journey. How happy I was, my dear friends, to find my father's family all well and happy, and O! how prosperous. They certainly have been signally blessed. The crops are most abundant; corn looks better than in Missouri. This is a beautiful country; it never looked so good to me before. I must tell you, Mr. Colt, that father says, and all the neighbors too, that there are thousands of acres of land to be taken in this vicinity, and any amount of wheat harvesting to be had on shares—no trouble. Father says there will be some place to stay in for the first few weeks. O, well, there is no *trouble*, no *difficulty* in the least; my parents and all the neighbors invite you to come; they will certainly insure you all profitable employment. Come, now! Schoolteachers are in great demand, both in the academies and district schools, around here. Oh! do come! The air is so pure and bracing—how can you be sick? It seems to infuse life and vigor immediately into me. Oh! if you would only come, you could live with us a while. Be sure to write immediately on the receipt of this. I must say again, oh! how I wish you would come! Our people here all want to see you; you certainly will not regret making a home here. How I hope you will come. That this may find you all well is the sincere wish and prayer of your friend,

E. V.

Dear, good friend. I could wish we were all transferred to your pleasant Wisconsin home; but my heart has so long vibrated between hope and fear that to get away from this place seems almost an impossibility. I ask my husband many times a day if he thinks we shall ever get away. He says, "I am determined to go now, let father do as he will."

August nineteenth

Have been saving a little water everyday now, for some days, to get enough to wash with, or make a pretension. Truly we are in a land where there is neither soap nor water; so how can we keep clean?

August thirtieth

Mr. Morris sent us word today that he will not be able to take us out of the Territory. He intends leaving with his family, in company with another, on account of the northern troubles.

Father has just returned from the cornfield, with a sledload of pumpkins that the Indians had not tugged away; he has piled them up in one corner of the cabin; says he is going to live on pumpkin pies after we go away. We know of no way now to get out of the Territory.

Sunday, August thirty-first

A bright, bright day! All nature is quiet; a silent adoration from prairie, wood, and dell.

My husband, though no dreamer, has just been relating to me the dream he dreamt last night. He said, "I dreamt that we left this place, and traveled a very long distance, until we came to a large river; then we stood on the bank considering how we were to get across it. Finally, we concluded to ford it; so you took one child and I the other, and soon came out on the other side. There we found a beautiful country—all kinds of fruit were growing spontaneously, and in abundance—every want was satisfied, and we were happy."

When we were expecting to leave, my husband gave the cow and calf to sister L.; told her that they were well worth forty dollars, and that the worth of them would take her out of the Territory anytime she wished to leave. His planes, augers, saws, and all such tools he has given to father; has divided the remainder of the money, keeping for ourselves just what, with the cheapest fare, would take us to some point on the other side of the Mississippi, either to Wisconsin or to New York.

September second

I was up this morning at early dawn, cooking for our journey, and bringing water to fill all empty vessels. Made myself and children ready again—got our good neighbor, Mr. Hobbs, to strap our trunks and take our bed of prairie grass from the loft, to be ready to place in the wagon, so that my husband and children can lie on it to ride through the days, and for us to sleep on nights. I then went for my last turn of water, and to pick my spike of flowers; bade farewell to all the windings of my path to the water, and to the trees, vines, grass, and flowers which had seemed to bow in silent sympathy at my sad lamentations. Soon the wagon was seen coming toward the creek, and the other two moving in a straight line on the prairie, with which we were soon to fall in rear. Our trunks were placed in the back end of the wagon, our bed in front, and our dinner pail so as to have it handy. Children were in a hurry to ride, and teamster to get up with the other wagons. I bade farewell to father, mother, and sister L. with a sad heart, and placed my children and self into the wagon; my husband still lingered; it was a time of heart-trial to him to leave his own father, mother, and sister in this wild land, when he had made such earnest appeals to them to leave. Father's tenacious will must bind his wife and daughter.

We start out upon the world again. Many a dark shade has passed over us since last spring. We move up along on to the high prairie.

Now I will take a look at the picture before me: here are my husband and children, very weak; we move along at a very slow pace; hundreds of miles are before us, and know not where we shall find a resting place. I must take the burden! How are we to reach the summit of the mountain that rises before us? May Heaven grant strength and courage!

V

One of the most famous outgrowths of frontier conditions was the vigilance committee, the posse that dispensed its own special brand of justice. These bands have been traditionally understood as more or less indistinguishable from the ruffians they pursued. But the story is actually far more complex. The vigilantes highlight the difficulty of establishing and maintaining order in a community where population growth has run far ahead of the transfer of institutions, where people settled in advance of courts, police, or other formal institutions of social control. In many ways, the bands stood outside the law because they had preceded the law.

A well-organized vigilance committee operated in the 1850s in San Francisco. In origin, the committee was a response to the sudden influx of thousands of migrants in search of gold in the hills. To a notable degree, it was composed of the most respectable classes of this new city, most typically the merchants, those who had most to lose in a reign of disorder. The documents below describe this venture, clarifying the motives and experiences of those who took the law into their own hands.

THE SAN FRANCISCO VIGILANCE COMMITTEE, 1851

Constitution of the San Francisco Vigilance Committee Instituted the Eighth of June 1851

Whereas it has become apparent to the citizens of San Francisco that there is no security for life and property, either under the regulations of society as it at present exists or under the laws as now administered, therefore the citizens whose names are hereunto attached do unite themselves into an association for the maintenance of the peace and good order of society and the preservation of the lives and prop-

Originally entitled "Papers of the San Francisco Vigilance Committee of 1851." In *Publications of Pacific Coast History* (Berkeley, 1919), vol. 4, pp. 1–3, 634–37, 825–27.

erty of the citizens of San Francisco and do bind themselves each unto the other to do and perform every lawful act for the maintenance of law and order and to sustain the laws when faithfully and properly administered but we are determined that no thief, burglar, incendiary assassin, professed gambler, and other disturbers of the peace shall escape punishment either by the quibbles of the law, the insecurity of prisons, the carelessness or corruption of the police, or a laxity of those who pretend to administer justice.

And to secure the objects of this association we do hereby agree:

First, that the name and style of the association shall be the "Committee of Vigilance for the protection of the lives and property of the citizens and residents of the City of San Francisco.

Secondly, that there shall be a room selected for the meeting and deliberations of the Committee at which there shall be some one or more members of the Committee appointed for that purpose in constant attendance at all hours of the day and night to receive the report of any member of the association or of any other person or persons whatsoever of any act of violence done to the person or property of any citizen of San Francisco and if in the judgement of the member or members of the Committee present it be such an act as justifies the interference of this Committee either in aiding in the execution of the laws or the prompt and summary punishment of the offender the Committee shall be at once assembled for the purpose of taking such action as a majority of the Committee when assembled shall determine upon.

Thirdly, that it shall be the duty of any member or members of the Committee on duty at the Committee room whenever a general assemblage of the Committee is deemed necessary to cause a call to be made by two strokes upon a bell.

Fourthly, that when the Committee have assembled for action the decision of a majority present shall be binding upon the whole Committee and that those members of the Committee pledge their honor and hereby bind themselves to defend and sustain each other in carrying out the determined action of this Committee at the hazard of their lives and their fortunes.

Fifthly, that there shall be chosen monthly a President, Secretary, and Treasurer and it shall be the duty of the Secretary to detail the members required to be in daily attendance at the Committee room. A Sergeant-at-Arms shall be appointed whose duty it shall be to notify such members of their detail for duty. The Sergeant-at-Arms shall reside at and be in constant attendance at the Committee room.

There shall be a standing Committee of Finance and qualification consisting of five each and no person shall be admitted a member of this association unless he be a respectable citizen and approved of by the Committee on qualification before admission.

[To this constitution were annexed the names of seven hundred and five citizens.]

Resignation of G. E. Schenck

Executive Chamber
San Francisco, September 14, 1851

To the Committee of Vigilance,
Gentlemen:

It is with great regret that we offer the annexed resignation of our Brother G. E. Schenck, who is about to leave the state. He has labored long and arduously with us throughout the trying scenes that have passed, has shown regard for their personal welfare, and for the lasting good and greatness, of this your adopted city and state.

With sentiments of great regard and esteem I beg to remain ever
Yours Truly etc.,
[Signed]   Geo. Everett Schenck

To,
Stephen Payran,
President Ex Committee

September 11, 1851
Executive Chamber

G. E. Schenck Esquire,
of the Committee of Vigilance of San Francisco
Dear Sir:

In the name and on behalf of my colleagues constituting the executive body of our association to express our sincere regret at a separation with one whom we so fondly esteem.

We can never forget when with us at the inception of our duties you joined us with a willing heart and firm hand to relieve our adopted city from the many impending evils that hung over it.

We had suffered much and suffered long. The torch of the

incendiary had destroyed us many times, ruin so frequently fell to our lot that we became dismayed, the lives of many of our valuable citizens had been destroyed by the hands of assassins, it was under such a state of things that we banded ourselves together, having no alternative, our judiciary and subordinates, had become corrupt, desperate offenders were allowed to go forth in our midst to riot on our lives and property for their pecuniary advantage.

Although the day was dark, and danger stared us in the face, we essayed to meet the storm and test the consequence, the spirits of our revolutionary sires prompted us, virtue guided our acts, corrupt representatives yielded, felons and incendiaries fled, light has taken the place of darkness, and a calm has succeeded the storm, peace and security are restored.

You are about to revisit the scenes of your youth, to see eye to eye those whom you love; and with you will attend the sincere wishes of your colaborers that your fondest expectations may be realized.

We humbly trust that if you ever feel disposed to revisit us, that you may find the good seed sown by us in honesty bringing forth all that we so ardently have desired, that California may be the abode of virtue and innocence, and that such confidence may be felt in its institutions that yourself and all our brethren may be induced to bring out their wives and children, and thereby to strengthen what we have done, as to bid defiance to the vicious and evil minded.

Assure your friends, sir, that we are worthy of all commendation, that hereafter they may treat with us commercially with confidence.

You are granted leave of absence and a remittance of all dues until your return.

[signed]　Stephen Payran
President Ex[ecutive] Committee

Prisoners Arrested by the Committee of Vigilance

George Adams; larceny; handed over to authorities.
Thomas Ainsworth; larceny; handed over to authorities.
Ahone; keeper of a suspicious house; discharged.
William Alderson; convict; deported.
Alo; keeper of a suspicious house; discharged.
J. J. Arentrue; larceny and murder; handed over to authorities.
George Arthur; larceny; handed over to authorities.
William Barclay; convict; deported.
James Burns, *alias* Jimmy from Town; larceny; handed over to authorities.
Thomas Burns; convict, keeper of a suspicious house; deported.
Capt. Canning; murder; handed over to authorities.
Samuel Church; horse thief and deserter; handed over to army.
William Clay; convict; deported.
William Cummings; larceny; discharged.
Theodore Dahlgrén; larceny; honorably discharged.
Peter Davis; "desperate character"; discharged.
John Donnelly; convict; discharged.
David Earl; larceny; ordered to leave California.

Aaron Gainesborough; convict; ordered to leave California.
Samuel Gallagher; murder; handed over to authorities.
Richard Garland; convict; deported.
John Goff; convict; ordered to leave California.
W. F. Hance; murder in Panama; sent back to Panama.
W. H. Hays; larceny; ordered to leave California.
James Hetherington; keeper of a suspicious house; deported.
Lawrence Higgins; convict immigrant; deported.
Mary Ann Hogan; keeper of a suspicious house; discharged.
Howard; deserter; handed over to army.
John Jenkins; larceny; convict (?); hanged.
Daniel Jenks; larceny, ordered to leave California.
Emma Jones; convict; ordered to leave California.
Dr. Kennedy; assault; handed over to authorities.
Francois Le Bras; murder; handed over to authorities.
William Leonard; larceny; handed over to authorities.
William Lovegrove; larceny; discharged.
John McDonald; drunk; discharged.
Robert McKenzie; larceny; hanged.
John Matson; arson; discharged.
Robert Ogden; convict; ordered to leave California.
John Olligin; murder; discharged.
Daniel Peterson; larceny; discharged.
Justo Reyes; larceny; whipped; ordered to leave California.
James Roach; convict; deported.
Ben Robinson; arson; discharged.
Michael Ryan; suspected immigrant; deported.
Martin Sanphy; "bad citizen"; ordered to leave California.
Mrs. Jane Sanphy; larceny; discharged.
Thomas Scott; "bad man"; deported.
Henry Smith; horse stealing; honorably discharged.
James Smith; larceny; discharged.

VI

*The frontier also bred its own peculiar brand of American religion—
revivalism. To many observers, evangelical preaching at camp
meetings represented the most primitive and crude form of religion.
They thought of revival meetings as excuses for drunkenness and
sexual license, and judged the revival ministers to be ignorant
rabble-rousers. But here, as in the case of vigilantees, Eastern
stereotypes miss the essential point. In fact, revivalism to an
extraordinary degree worked to uphold order on the frontier. It
also represented the triumph of a spirit of voluntarism. Here were
men and women organizing churches without state intervention,
and supporting them without state aid.*

The most important analysis of revivalism during these years

was made by Robert Baird, in his study Religion in the United
States (1844). *His effort to defend the revivalist spirit led him to
link this religious occurrence directly to the nature of frontier
community life.*

RELIGION IN THE UNITED STATES OF AMERICA, 1844

ROBERT BAIRD

Neither the general government nor that of the states does anything
directly for the maintenance of public worship. Religion is protected and
indirectly aided by both; but nowhere does the civil power defray the
expenses of the churches, or pay the salaries of ministers of the gospel,
excepting in the case of a few chaplains connected with the public
service.

Upon what then must religion rely? Only, under God, upon the
efforts of its friends, acting from their own freewill, influenced by that
variety of considerations which are ordinarily comprehended under the
title of a desire to do good. This, in America, is the grand and only
alternative. To this principle must the country look for all those efforts
which must be made for its religious instruction.

Let us look for a moment at the work which, under God's blessing,
has to be accomplished by this instrumentality.

The population of the United States at present (November 1842)
is not far short of 18,000,000. Upon the voluntary principle alone
depends the religious instruction of this entire population, embracing
the thousands of churches and ministers of the gospel, colleges, theological seminaries, sunday schools, missionary societies, and all the
other instrumentalities that are employed to promote the knowledge of
the gospel from one end of the country to the other. Upon the mere
unconstrained good will of the people, and especially of those among
them who love the Savior and profess His name, does this vast super-
structure rest.

At the first sight of this statistical view of the case, some of my
readers will be ready to exclaim that the prospect is hopeless. Others will
say, Woe to the cause of religion if the government does not put its
shoulders to the wheel! But I answer, not only in my own name, but
dare to do it in that of every well-informed American Christian: "No!
we want no more aid from the government than what we receive, and
what it so cheerfully gives. The prospect is not desperate so long as
Christians do their duty in humble and heartfelt reliance upon God."

Americans [have] been trained to exercise the same energy, self-
reliance, and enterprise in the cause of religion which they exhibit in
other affairs. Thus, when a new church is called for, the people first
inquire whether they cannot build it at their own cost, and ask help
from others only after having done all they think practicable among

In *Religion in the United States of America,* by Robert Baird (London, 1844),
pp. 288–89, 292, 298–99, 426–28, 433–44, 494–97.

themselves—a course which often leads them to find that they can accomplish by their own efforts what, at first, they hardly dared to hope for.

Besides, there has grown up among the truly American part of the population a feeling that religion is necessary even to the temporal well-being of society, so that many contribute to its promotion, though not themselves members of any of the churches.

These remarks point the reader to the true secret of the success of the voluntary plan in America. The people feel that they can help themselves, and that it is at once a duty and a privilege to do so. Should a church steeple come to the ground, or the roof be blown away, or any other such accident happen, instead of looking to some government official for the means of needful repair, a few of them put their hands into their pockets, and supply these themselves, without delay or the risk of vexatious refusals from public functionaries.

It is in the building of places of worship in the new settlements of the Western states, and in the villages that are springing up in the more recently peopled parts of those bordering on the Atlantic that we see the most remarkable development of the voluntary principle. Let me illustrate by a particular case what is daily occurring in both these divisions of the country.

Let us suppose a settlement commenced in the forest, in the northern part of Indiana, and that in the course of three or four years a considerable number of emigrants have established themselves within a mile or two of each other in the woods. Each clears away by degrees a part of the surrounding forest and fences in his new fields where the deadened trees still stand very thick. By little and little the country shows signs of occupation by civilized man.

In the center of the settlement a little village begins to form around a tavern and a blacksmith's shop. A carpenter places himself there as a convenient center. So do the tailor, the shoemaker, the wagon-maker, and the hatter. The merchant opens his magazine [store] there. And if there be any prospect of the rising city, though the deadened trees stand quite in the vicinity of the streets, becoming the seat of justice for a new county, there will soon be half a dozen young expounders of the law to increase the population and offer their services to those who have suffered or committed some injustice.

Things will hardly have reached this point before someone amid this heterogeneous population come from different points of the older states, intermixed with wanderers from Europe—Irish, Scotch, or German—proposes that they should think of having a church, or at least some place of worship. It is ten chances to one if there be not one or more pious women, or some pious man with his family, who sigh for the privileges of the sanctuary as once enjoyed by them in the distant east. What is to be done? Someone proposes that they should build a good large schoolhouse, which may serve also for holding religious meetings, and this is scarcely sooner proposed than accomplished. Though possibly made of mere logs and very plain, it will answer the purpose for a few years. Being intended for the meetings of all denominations of Christians, and open to all preachers who may be passing, word is sent to the nearest in the neighbourhood. Ere long some Baptist preacher in passing preaches in the evening, and is followed by a Presbyterian and a Methodist. Bye and bye the last of these arranges his circuit labors so as to preach there once in the fortnight, and then the minister of some Presbyterian congregation, ten or fifteen miles off, agrees to come and preach once a month.

Meanwhile, from the increase of the inhabitants, the congregations, on the sabbath particularly, become too large for the schoolhouse. A church is then built of framed beams and boards, forming no mean ornament to the village, and capable of accommodating some 200 or 300 people. Erected for the public good, it is used by all the sects in the place, and by others besides. But it will not be long before the Presbyterians, Methodists, or Baptists feel that they must have a minister on whose services they can count with more certainty, and hence a church also for themselves. And, at last, the house, which was a joint-stock affair at first, falls into the hands of some one of the denominations, and is abandoned by the others who have mostly provided each one for itself. Or, it may remain for the occasional service of some passing Roman Catholic priest, or Universalist preacher.

I have often been asked in Europe what measures are adopted by our churches in enforcing discipline—how unworthy persons, for instance, are prevented from coming to the Lord's table? The very question indicates familiarity with a state of things very different from what prevails in the United States—with a state of things in which the decisions of the ecclesiastical authority are enforced by the civil.

Church discipline with us, though wholly moral, is thought quite sufficient. The case must be rare, indeed, of anyone not the member of some recognized church coming forward to receive the sacrament in an evangelical church. But if he should, he does so on his own responsibility before God; the church is not to be blamed for his conduct. I know of one solitary occasion on which one of the office bearers whispered in the ear of a person who ought not to have been among the communicants that it would be better for his own soul, as well as due to the church, that he should retire, and he did so.

No difficulty whatever, I repeat, can arise on this subject. Our discipline is moral, and the people are too well instructed on the subject of their duties not to know what they should do, and what to abstain from doing. We have no *gens d'armes* or other police agents to enforce our discipline, and if such functionaries are ever seen about our churches in any character but that of worshippers, it is on extraordinary occasions, to keep order at the door; and their services are not often needed even for that purpose.

In regard to church members who subject themselves to censure for open sin, or gross neglect of duty, they are dealt with according to the established discipline of the body to which they belong; and that, in all our evangelical churches, is based upon the simple and clear directions given by our Lord and His apostles. Unworthy members after having been dealt with according to scriptural rule, are excluded until they give evidence of sincere contrition for their sin. Where the case is flagrant, and the sin persisted in, after all attempts to reclaim the offender have failed, he is openly excommunicated before the church and congregation. But whatever be the course pursued, unworthy men are excluded in all our evangelical churches as soon as their offense can be properly taken up by the church. I state this as a general fact. Once excluded, the world does not long remain ignorant of what has taken place, and the church thus avoids the charge of retaining persons of scandalous lives in her communion.

In order adequately to describe American preaching, one would require to be intimately acquainted with the churches of the country throughout its vast extent, but this knowledge it falls to the lot of few to possess. Some of the tourists from abroad that have visited the United States have affected to despise our "uneducated" and "ignorant" ministers, and have thought what they call the "ranting" of such men a fit subject of diversion for themselves. Such authors know little of the real worth of these humble, unlettered men. Their plain preaching, in fact, is often far more likely to benefit their usual hearers than would that of a learned doctor of divinity. Their language, though not refined, is intelligible to those to whom it is addressed. Their illustrations may not be classical, but they will probably be drawn either from the Bible or from the scenes amid which their hearers move, and the events with which they are familiar. To the labors of such men more than 10,000 neighborhoods in the United States are indebted for their general good order, tranquillity, and happiness, as well as for the humble but sincere piety that reigns in many a heart, and around many a fireside. To them the country owes much of its conservative character, for no men have inculcated more effectively those doctrines which promote obedience to law, respect for magistracy, and the maintenance of civil government, and never more than within the last year or two, during which they have had to resist the anarchical principles of self-styled reformers, both religious and political. No men are more hated and reviled by these demagogues, whose projects, I rejoice to say, find comparatively but a small and decreasing number of friends and advocates. To the influence of the pulpit, and that of the religious and sound part of the political press, we owe a return of better sentiments in several states. And in a late insurrectionary movement in Rhode Island, [Dorr's Rebellion] the leading journals of that state attest that the clergy of all denominations exerted a powerfully salutary influence.

A stranger upon visiting extensively our evangelical churches of all denominations would be struck, I am sure, with the order that prevails in them, and this applies equally to the smaller prayer meetings to be found in every parish and congregation that has any life in it, and to the greater assemblies that meet for public worship. Foreigners seem impressed with the idea that there is a great deal of disorder and lawlessness in the United States, and they infer that there must be no less insubordination in the religious commonwealth than they ascribe to the civil. But both opinions are totally unfounded. It does not follow because of a few disturbances arising from the disgraceful opposition made in some places to the slavery abolitionists, and the resentment of an exasperated populace against gangs of gamblers in others, that the whole country is a scene of continual commotion. In no part of the world have there been so few dreadful riots attended with loss of life as in the United States during those sixty years. There are bad men among us, and there are crimes, but after all, life is quite as safe among us as in any country I ever visited, and I have been in most of those that are considered civilized.

As for the church, a regard for law and order reigns to a degree not surpassed in any other country. There is no confusion of the respective rights of the ministry and people. The duties of both are well understood everywhere.

The little meetings of Christians held for prayer and the reading of the word—meetings so numerous, and almost always conducted by pious laymen! How seldom do private church members encroach by word or deed, at meetings of any kind, on the proper sphere of those who hold office in the churches! Indeed, on no one point are our churches more perfectly united in opinion than with respect to the necessity of maintaining due order and subordination. The ministry enjoys their full share of influence.

Experience has also taught us the necessity of maintaining order at meetings held during revivals—occasions on which, in consequence of the strong excitement of the most powerful feelings of the human heart, there is a special call for watchfulness in this respect. It is a sad mistake to multiply meetings unnecessarily during revivals, or to prolong them to unseasonable hours at night, to the exhaustion of strength, the loss of needed repose, and the unnatural and dangerous irritation of the nervous system. Yet these are the points in which the inexperienced are most liable to err. They begin a meeting, say, at seven o'clock in the evening. The preacher feels deeply, and the people are much interested. Instead of preaching for an hour, he is tempted, by the manifest attention of his hearers, to go on for an hour and a half or two hours, and instead of sending them home at half past eight o'clock, or at nine at the farthest, he dismisses them at ten or eleven o'clock, fatigued, yet excited, but here there is often a temptation of the adversary. Let the people be almost compelled to leave the house rather than unduly protract such meetings.

I consider hasty admissions to our churches to be the greatest of all the evils connected with revivals in some parts of the country, and among some denominations in particular. But this evil is not peculiar to revivals. It is quite as likely to occur when there is no revival as when there is. With all possible care it is difficult to keep a church pure, in a reasonable sense. The church must be kept as a living body of believers—a company of persons who have come out from the world and are determined to adorn the profession which they have made. In their organization and action, order, which is said to be "heaven's first law," must be maintained. In this opinion I am sure Christians of all denominations in the United States sincerely and entirely concur.

Chapter 8

The Common School

THE JACKSONIAN period witnessed the triumph of the common school, the establishment of free, tax-supported, public education. Before 1820, only a handful of communities took responsibility for primary education. By 1850, cities, towns, and villages all over the nation had founded schools. Education had become a primary responsibility of the state.

To later generations, schooling seemed so obviously a task for government to fulfill that it was difficult to imagine a time when citizens debated the propriety of using taxes to pay for such an enterprise. But in fact the establishment of the common schools was a controversial measure. It was the invention of one particular generation, not the inevitable culmination of colonial or Revolutionary developments. Why did the common school flourish in the Jacksonian period? What did proponents expect of it? Why was the controversy around the use of tax funds resolved so firmly and finally in favor of schooling?

The answers to these questions can be found first in the literature that supporters of public education produced during the antebellum decades. With great skill and sincerity, they tied the need for education to the fundamental welfare of the republic; so tight did they make this link that critics were hard pressed to challenge it. The founders of the common schools shared a very special view of childhood and human nature. This view assumed the power of the environment to effect change. It set forth a very particular definition of the needs of the republic (one which emphasized the prerequisites of virtue and intelligence for good citizenry) and had a very acute sensitivity to the problem of social order in the community (one which predicted the dissolution of the republic unless new means of social control were implemented). The foundation of the common schools rested on these premises.

Given the belief in the power of schooling to overcome the several dangers confronting the republic, education had to bear a heavy burden. It was not simply a matter of teaching students a basic knowledge of letters and numbers. Rather, the schools had to train students to political

participation, law-abiding behavior, and responsible community membership. In essence, the business of schools was not reading and writing but citizenship, not education but social control.

This orientation probably had an important effect on the day-to-day administration and conduct of the common schools. How did this special focus on social order affect the nature of the curriculum? How did it influence the routine of the classroom? What impact did it have on the way students were to learn and on the way they were to behave at school? The answers to these questions will enable us to measure the impact of educational rhetoric on classroom reality.

Moreover, it is not accidental that the popularity of the common school came at the same time that Americans began to rely upon institutions to care for the deviant and dependent. In the Jacksonian period, the states erected penitentiaries for the criminal, insane asylums for the mentally ill, and almshouses for the poor. In fact, many of the leaders of the common-school movement were in the forefront of the campaign to erect caretaker institutions, and the ways they defended these programs were not at all dissimilar to the ways that they argued for common schools. Yet why should schools have grown popular when prisons did? Why should proponents of one of these programs support the others? Did these similarities extend to the internal administration of the institutions as well? To what extent were schools similar to mental hospitals?

The materials that follow are addressed to these several considerations. The ideas of the common-school movement are captured effectively in the writings of such spokesmen as Noah Webster and Horace Mann. It is more difficult to re-create precisely the nature of the school day—variety was probably as great as record keeping was primitive. Still, the primers used in the classrooms do survive, as do some of the tests that students had to take; and there are also seating plans and curriculum outlines of the period. Finally, the prisons and hospitals published annual reports, informing legislators of what went on behind the walls. While clearly self-serving documents, they give us insights into the goals and the conduct of these institutions. Taken together, these documents trace the origins and implications of reform movements in the Jacksonian era.

I

Noah Webster was one of the first spokesmen in the new nation to link the welfare of the republic with common schooling. Webster exemplified the patriotic enthusiasm of many of the first republicans— in every endeavor, the United States was to exhibit its uniqueness and superiority to Europe. As one part of this effort, Webster helped to organize a common American spelling, and he also worked to codify a distinctly American language. His dictionaries were, in effect, nationalist endeavors. So, too, Webster sought to give a distinctly American character to education. His essay On the Education of Youth, *which appeared in 1790, announced many of the themes that would be popular a generation later during the movement for common schools.*

ON THE EDUCATION OF YOUTH, 1790

NOAH WEBSTER

The education of youth is, in all governments, an object of the first consequence. The impressions received in early life usually form the characters of individuals, a union of which forms the general character of a nation.

The mode of education and the arts taught to youth have in every nation been adapted to its particular stage of society or local circumstances.

In despotic states education, like religion, is made subservient to government. In some of the vast empires of Asia children are always instructed in the occupation of their parents; thus the same arts are always continued in the same families. Such an institution cramps genius and limits the progress of national improvement; at the same time it is an almost immovable barrier against the introduction of vice, luxury, faction, and changes in government. This is one of the principal causes which have operated in preserving national tranquility for incredible periods of time.

In the complicated systems of government which are established among the civilized nations of Europe education has less influence in forming a national character; but there is no state in which it has not an inseparable connection with morals and a consequential influence upon the peace and happiness of society.

In *On the Education of Youth in America,* by Noah Webster (Boston, 1790). Reprinted in *Essays on Education in the Early Republic,* ed. Frederick Rudolph (Cambridge, Mass., 1965), pp. 43–47, 52–67.

Education is a subject which has been exhausted by the ablest writers. I am not vain enough to suppose I can suggest any new ideas but perhaps the manner of conducting the youth in America may be capable of some improvement. Our constitutions of civil government are not yet firmly established; our national character is not yet formed; and it is an object of vast magnitude that systems of education should be adopted and pursued which may not only diffuse a knowledge of the sciences but may implant in the minds of the American youth the principles of virtue and of liberty and inspire them with just and liberal ideas of government and with an inviolable attachment to their own country. It now becomes every American to examine the modes of education in Europe, to see how far they are applicable in this country and whether it is not possible to make some valuable alterations, adapted to our local and political circumstances. Let us examine the subject in two views. First, as it respects arts and sciences. Secondly, as it is connected with morals and government. In each of these articles let us see what errors may be found and what improvements suggested in our present practice.

The first error that I would mention is a too general attention to the dead languages, with a neglect of our own.

Indeed it appears to me that what is now called a *liberal education* disqualifies a man for business. Habits are formed in youth and by practice, and as business is in some measure mechanical, every person should be exercised in his employment in an early period of life, that his habits may be formed by the time his apprenticeship expires. An education in a university interferes with the forming of these habits and perhaps forms opposite habits; the mind may contract a fondness for ease, for pleasure or for books, which no efforts can overcome.

But the principal defect in our plan of education in America is the want of good teachers in the academies and common schools. By good teachers I mean men of unblemished reputation and possessed of abilities competent to their stations. To those who employ ignorant men to instruct their children, permit me to suggest one important idea: that it is better for youth to have *no* education than to have a bad one, for it is more difficult to eradicate habits than to impress new ideas.

Yet abilities are not the sole requisites. The instructors of youth ought, of all men, to be the most prudent, accomplished, agreeable, and respectable. In order to give full effect to instructions, it is requisite that they should proceed from a man who is loved and respected. But a low-bred clown or morose tyrant can command neither love nor respect, and that pupil who has no motive for application to books but the fear of a rod will not make a scholar.

The rod is often necessary in school, especially after the children have been accustomed to disobedience and a licentious behavior at home. All government originates in families, and if neglected there, it will hardly exist in society, but the want of it must be supplied by the rod in school, the penal laws of the state, and the terrors of divine wrath from the pulpit. The government both of families and schools should be absolute. There should in families be no appeal from one parent to another, with the prospect of pardon for offenses.

In schools the master should be absolute in command, for it is utterly impossible for any man to support order and discipline among children who are indulged with an appeal to their parents. A proper subordination in families would generally supersede the necessity of severity in schools, and a strict discipline in both is the best foundation of good order in political society.

If parents should say, "We cannot give the instructors of our children unlimited authority over them, for it may be abused and our children injured," I would answer, "They must not place them under the direction of any man in whose temper, judgment, and abilities they do not repose perfect confidence." The teacher should be, if such can be found, as judicious and reasonable a man as the parent.

There can be little improvement in schools without strict subordination; there can be no subordination without principles of esteem and respect in the pupils; and the pupils cannot esteem and respect a man who is not in himself respectable and who is not treated with respect by their parents.

From a strange inversion of the order of nature, the most important business in civil society is in many parts of America committed to the most worthless characters. The education of youth, an employment of more consequence than making laws and preaching the gospel, because it lays the foundation on which both law and gospel rest for success, this education is sunk to a level with the most menial services. In most instances we find the higher seminaries of learning entrusted to men of good characters and possessed of the moral virtues of social affections. But many of our [lower] schools, which, so far as the heart is concerned, are as important as colleges, are kept by men of no breeding, and many of them, by men infamous for the most detestable vices.

It is idle to suppress such truths; nay more, it is wicked. The practice of employing low and vicious characters to direct the studies of youth is in a high degree criminal; it is destructive of the order and peace of society.

Our legislators frame laws for the suppression of vice and immorality; our divines thunder from the pulpit the terrors of infinite wrath against the vices that stain the characters of men. And do laws and preaching effect a reformation of manners? Laws can only check the public effects of vicious principles but can never reach the principles themselves, and preaching is not very intelligible to people till they arrive at an age when their principles are rooted or their habits firmly established.

The only practicable method to reform mankind is to begin with children, to banish, if possible, from their company every low-bred, drunken, immoral character.

For this reason society requires that the education of youth should be watched with the most scrupulous attention. Education, in a great measure, forms the moral characters of men, and morals are the basis of government.

A good system of education should be the first article in the code of political regulations, for it is much easier to introduce and establish an effectual system for preserving morals than to correct by penal statutes the ill effects of a bad system.

Another defect in our schools, which, since the Revolution, is become inexcusable, is the want of proper books. The collections which are now used consist of essays that respect foreign and ancient nations. The minds of youth are perpetually led to the history of Greece and Rome or to Great Britain. Every child in America should be acquainted with his own country. As soon as he opens his lips, he should rehearse the history of his own country; he should lisp the praise of liberty and of those illustrious heroes and statesmen who have wrought a revolution in her favor.

A selection of essays respecting the settlement and geography of America, the history of the late Revolution and of the most remarkable characters and events that distinguished it, and a compendium of the principles of the federal and provincial governments should be the principal schoolbook in the United States.

Two regulations are essential to the continuance of republican governments: 1. Such a distribution of lands and such principles of descent and alienation as shall give every citizen a power of acquiring what his industry merits. 2. Such a system of education as gives every citizen an opportunity of acquiring knowledge and fitting himself for places of trust.

In several states we find laws passed establishing provision for colleges and academies where people of property may educate their sons, but no provision is made for instructing the poorer rank of people even in reading and writing. Yet in these same states every citizen who is worth a few shillings annually is entitled to vote for legislators. This appears to me a most glaring solecism in government. The constitutions are *republican* and the laws of education are *monarchical.* The *former* extend civil rights to every honest industrious man, the *latter* deprive a large proportion of the citizens of a most valuable privilege.

In our American republics, where government is in the hands of the people, knowledge should be universally diffused by means of public schools. Of such consequence is it to society that the people who make laws should be well informed that I conceive no legislature can be justified in neglecting proper establishments for this purpose.

Every small district should be furnished with a school, at least four months in a year, when boys are not otherwise employed. This school should be kept by the most reputable and well-informed man in the district. Here children should be taught the usual branches of learning, submission to superiors and to laws, the moral or social duties, the history and transactions of their own country, the principles of liberty and government. Here the rough manners of the wilderness should be softened and the principles of virtue and good behavior inculcated.

A tour through the United States ought now to be considered as a necessary part of a liberal education. Instead of sending young gentlemen to Europe to view curiosities and learn vices and follies, let them spend twelve or eighteen months in examining the local situation of the different states with an attention to the spirit and manners of the inhabitants, their laws, local customs, and institutions. Such a tour should at least precede a tour to Europe, for nothing can be more ridiculous than a man traveling in a foreign country for information when he can give no account of his own.

Americans, unshackle your minds and act like independent beings. You have been children long enough, subject to the control and subservient to the interest of a haughty parent. You have now an interest of your own to augment and defend: you have an empire to raise and support by your exertions and a national character to establish and extend by your wisdom and virtues. To effect these great objects, it is necessary to frame a liberal plan of policy and build it on a broad system of education. Before this system can be formed and embraced, the Americans must *believe* and *act* from the belief that it is dishonorable to waste life in mimicking the follies of other nations and basking in the sunshine of foreign glory.

II

More than any other individual, Horace Mann led the movement to establish common schools. Born in 1796 into a family of limited means in a small Massachusetts town, Mann worked his way through school, graduated from Brown University, and began to practice law. He found himself quickly drawn to government service; and since no other cause held greater appeal to him than education, in 1837 he became the first Secretary to the Massachusetts Board of Education. In that capacity he exercised practical leadership over the schools, and his system became a model for other states to emulate. He also used his position to persuade others of the merits of the program. His Twelfth Annual Report *for the State Board of Education summarizes the ideas most central to his concern for education.*

REPORT FOR THE MASSACHUSETTS BOARD OF EDUCATION, 1848

HORACE MANN

According to the European theory, men are divided into classes—some to toil and earn, others to seize and enjoy. According to the Massachusetts theory, all are to have an equal chance for earning, and equal security in the enjoyment of what they earn. The latter tends to equality of condition; the former to the grossest inequalities.

Now two or three things will doubtless be admitted to be true, beyond all controversy, in regard to Massachusetts. By its industrial condition, and its business operations, it is exposed, far beyond any other state in the Union, to the fatal extremes of overgrown wealth and

Originally entitled *Twelfth Annual Report*, Massachusetts State Board of Education (Boston, 1848). Reprinted in *The Republic and the School*, ed. Lawrence Cremin (New York, 1957), pp. 80–92, 98–101.

desperate poverty. Its population is far more dense than that of any other state. It is four or five times more dense than the average of all the other states, taken together; and density of population has always been one of the proximate causes of social inequality. According to population and territorial extent, there is far more capital in Massachusetts—capital which is movable, and instantaneously available—than in any other state in the Union; and probably both these qualifications respecting population and territory could be omitted without endangering the truth of the assertion. If this be so, are we not in danger of naturalizing and domesticating among ourselves those hideous evils which are always engendered between capital and labor, when all the capital is in the hands of one class, and all the labor is thrown upon another?

Now, surely, nothing but universal education can counterwork this tendency to the domination of capital and the servility of labor. If one class possesses all the wealth and the education, while the residue of society is ignorant and poor, it matters not by what name the relation between them may be called; the latter, in fact and in truth, will be the servile dependants and subjects of the former. But if education be equally diffused, it will draw property after it, by the strongest of all attractions.

For the creation of wealth, then—for the existence of a wealthy people and a wealthy nation—intelligence is the grand condition. The number of improvers will increase as the intellectual constituency, if I may so call it, increases. In former times, and in most parts of the world even at the present day, not one man in a million has ever had such a development of mind as made it possible for him to become a contributor to art or science. Let this development precede, and contributions, numberless, and of inestimable value, will be sure to follow.

In the possession of this attribute of intelligence, elective legislators will never far surpass their electors. By a natural law, like that which regulates the equilibrium of fluids, elector and elected, appointer and appointee, tend to the same level. It is not more certain that a wise and enlightened constituency will refuse to invest a reckless and profligate man with office, or discard him if accidentally chosen, than it is that a foolish or immoral constituency will discard or eject a wise man. This law of assimilation, between the choosers and the chosen, results not only from the fact that the voter originally selects his representative according to the affinities of good or of ill, of wisdom or of folly, which exist between them, but if the legislator enacts or favors a law which is too wise for the constituent to understand, or too just for him to approve, the next election will set him aside as certainly as if he had made open merchandise of the dearest interests of the people, by perjury and for a bribe.

Moral education is a primal necessity of social existence. The unrestrained passions of men are not only homicidal, but suicidal; and a community without a conscience would soon extinguish itself. Even with a natural conscience, how often has Evil triumphed over Good! From the beginning of time, Wrong has followed Right, as the shadow the substance. As the relations of men became more complex, and the business of the world more extended, new opportunities and new temptations for wrong-doing have been created. With the endearing relations of parent and child came also the possibility of infanticide and parricide; and the first domestic altar that brothers ever reared was stained with fratricidal blood. Following close upon the obligations to truth, came falsehood and perjury, and closer still upon the duty of obedience to the divine law, came disobedience. With the existence of private relations between men came fraud; and with the existence of public relations between nations came aggression, war, and slavery. And so, just in proportion as the relations of life became more numerous, and the interests of society more various and manifold, the range of possible and of actual offences has been continually enlarging.

The race has existed long enough to try many experiments for the solution of this greatest problem ever submitted to its hands; and the race has experimented, without stint of time or circumscription of space, to mar or modify legitimate results. Mankind have tried despotisms, monarchies, and republican forms of government. They have tried the extremes of anarchy and of autocracy. They have tried Draconian codes of law; and, for the lightest offences, have extinguished the life of the offender. They have established theological standards, claiming for them the sanction of divine authority, and the attributes of a perfect and infallible law; and then they have imprisoned, burnt, massacred, not individuals only but whole communities at a time, for not bowing down to idols which ecclesiastical authority had set up. These and other great systems of measures have been adopted as barriers against error and guilt; they have been extended over empires, prolonged through centuries, and administered with terrible energy; and yet the great ocean of vice and crime overleaps every embankment, pours down upon our heads, saps the foundations under our feet, and sweeps away the securities of social order, of property, liberty, and life.

But to all doubters, disbelievers, or despairers in human progress it may still be said, there is one experiment which has never yet been tried. It is an experiment which, even before its inception, offers the highest authority for its ultimate success. Its formula is intelligible to all; and it is as legible as though written in starry letters on an azure sky. It is expressed in these few and simple words: *"Train up a child in the way he should go, and when he is old he will not depart from it."* This declaration is positive. If the conditions are complied with, it makes no provision for a failure. Though pertaining to morals, yet, if the terms of the direction are observed, there is no more reason to doubt the result than there would be in an optical or a chemical experiment.

But this experiment has never yet been tried. Education has never yet been brought to bear with one hundredth part of its potential force upon the natures of children and, through them, upon the character of men, and of the race. In all the attempts to reform mankind which have hitherto been made, whether by changing the frame of government, by aggravating or softening the severity of the penal code, or by substituting a government-created for a God-created religion—in all these attempts, the infantile and youthful mind, its amenability to influences, and the enduring and self-operating character of the influences it receives, have been almost wholly unrecognized. Here, then, is a new agency, whose powers are but just beginning to be understood, and whose mighty energies, hitherto, have been but feebly invoked; and yet, from our experience, limited and imperfect as it is, we do know that, far beyond any other earthly instrumentality, it is comprehensive and decisive.

III

The steps by which the common school established itself in the various states may be followed in the sequence of events in Philadelphia. The first legislation establishing the legal obligations and powers of the community, the problems subsequent administrators faced, and their hopes for the system are clarified in the annual reports of the school district officials. First intended to serve only the children of the poor, the Philadelphia schools soon expanded to give education without cost to all the children of the city. The reasons for this shift are at the heart of the common school movement.

REPORTS OF THE PHILADELPHIA PUBLIC SCHOOLS, 1819–1850

An Act To Provide for the Education of Children at Public Expense, within the City and County of Philadelphia

Passed March 3, 1818

Be it enacted by the Commonwealth of Pennsylvania that the city and county of Philadelphia shall be and hereby are erected into a district, for the purposes of this act, to be denominated the First School District of the state of Pennsylvania. And be it further enacted by the authority aforesaid that the common and select councils shall appoint the requisite number of qualified taxable inhabitants to be directors of the public schools, that is to say, the select and common councils of the city of Philadelphia shall, in joint meeting, elect by ballot twenty-four directors. And be it further enacted by the authority aforesaid that the said controllers of the public schools shall determine upon the number of schoolhouses which shall be erected and shall limit the expense of erecting and establishing every such schoolhouse. They shall have the power to establish a model school, in order to qualify teachers for the sectional schools, or for schools in other parts of the state. They shall also have power to provide such suitable books as they shall deem necessary. And be it further enacted by the authority aforesaid that it shall be the duty of the assessors of every ward and township within the said district to require and receive once in every year from parents

In *Annual Report[s] of the Controllers of the Public Schools of the First School District of the State of Pennsylvania* (Philadelphia, 1819), pp. 4–6; (1821), pp. 4–5; (1826), pp. 6–7; (1836), pp. 8–12; (1850), pp. 116–19.

and guardians the names of all the indigent orphan children—children of indigent parents residing within the said school sections respectively, that is to say, the names of boys between the ages of six and fourteen years, and girls between the ages of five and thirteen years—and to inform the said parents and guardians of such children that they may send the said children to the proper school within the section in which they reside respectively, free of expense.

Annual Report for 1819

The controllers were organized on the sixth day of April 1818, and proceeded to establish schools for both sexes.

The whole number of children belonging to the public schools, under the care of the board, at the last quarterly report, was two thousand eight hundred and forty-five.

The boys are instructed in reading, writing, and arithmetic; and the girls are taught the same branches, as well as needlework in its useful and economical departments. The pupils attend with much regularity to their business, and exhibit gratifying proofs of improvement in their learning, as well as encouraging evidence of advancement in their morals.

The controllers feel authorized to express their opinion that the system of education under their care appears to them to be worthy of public confidence and support, whether it be regarded as valuable for its economy—practical in its communication of useful learning—or an efficient means whereby the minds of youth may be impressed with those great principles of morality and virtue so conducive to their own happiness and the welfare of our country.

Annual Report for 1821

Each successive year confirms the utility of the mode of instruction which has been adopted, and it is only to be regretted that many parents whose children might be brought under its auspices *criminally* withhold their offspring. How far legislative enactments can remedy this evil it may be difficult to determine, but it will be worthy of consideration whether the guardians of the poor ought not to be forbidden to confer relief upon pensioners whose children of suitable ages are not in regular attendance at the school of the district in which they reside. If the population of this description now suffered to spend their juvenile years in idleness, and who are thereby liable to the temptation and commission of crimes peculiarly incident to large cities, were subjected to the wholesome discipline of these schools, the moral culture and literary information which they afford would essentially contribute to render those neglected beings useful members of society. Within the last six months, another cause has operated to lessen the number of our pupils. The increase of manufactories in Philadelphia and its vicinity has produced a great demand for the labor of young persons, and has consequently withdrawn many children from the public schools. This evidence of returning business, and general prosperity, always inseparable from the occupation of the laboring classes, must be gratifying to every reflecting individual;

but if the employment of youth in those establishments be not accompanied by due attention to their mental and physical health and improvement, they will grow up unfit to discharge the duties of social life, and from bodily infirmity, and vicious habits, become burdens upon the community.

Annual Report for 1826

Of those children who have entered the schools, many have been withdrawn by their parents owing to the inducement of wages, which vary from fifty to one hundred and twenty-five cents per week, according to the demand for labor by the manufacturers. The rising generation may thus sustain irretrievable loss, in the abandonment of means for acquiring useful learning, as well as in the moral and physical evils to which, it is to be feared, they are often subjected in their tender years, by these employments. It is also a fact that a short training in the public schools renders the subject of it more profitable in the occupation mentioned; and in proportion to this valuable preparation, the scholars are sought for and engaged.

Without desiring improperly to interfere with the operations of any department of industry, the controllers cannot forbear again suggesting the necessity of legislative enactments to protect our youth from the ignorance and vice, and bodily deterioration, which combined private interests may thus produce. It would seem to be indispensable to require, by law, of those persons who employ large numbers of young persons in manufactories, not only to furnish them with useful school learning, but also to adopt regulations for the preservation of their health and morals. It will be unwise to delay a measure so vitally important to the welfare of the community until the influence of circumstances may render interposition unavailing.

An Act To Establish a General System of Education by Common Schools

Passed April 1, 1834

Whereas, it is enjoined by the Constitution, as a solemn duty, which cannot be neglected without a disregard of the moral and political safety of the people: Be it enacted by the commonwealth of Pennsylvania that the city and county of Philadelphia, and every other county in this commonwealth, shall each form a school division. And each of said districts shall contain a competent number of common schools for the education of every child within the limits thereof, who shall apply, either in person or by his or her parents, guardian, or next friend, for admission and instruction.

Annual Report for 1836

But eighteen years have rolled away since the original board opened its first school, with a few pupils, in a hired room; now they point their fellow-citizens to eleven magnificent edifices for the accommodation of our children, of whom they can proudly point to twelve thousand actually enrolled in more than fifty schools. Of our colleagues in this noble undertaking—the directors of all the sections—we demand, shall this work be stayed in its onward course? We know no barrier, we will recognize no limits to the extension of our schools, until the blessings of moral and intellectual culture is tendered to every solitary pupils, of every age, within our district. An ignorant people always has been and always will be a degraded and oppressed people— they are always at the mercy of the corrupt and designing. In vain shall we trust to physical strength to guard us from foreign hostility or domestic violence—to a seacoast girt with a thousand fortresses—or a frontier bristling with countless bayonets—to armies, fleets, or military skill—if we fail to cultivate the *moral* strength of our people—which is only founded upon *knowledge* and *self-respect*—*if we fail by Education to awake—guide—confirm the moral energies of our people, we are lost!*

Annual Report for 1837

Upon the general review of the year, the controllers are gratified with all the departments of the system—with the general fidelity and efficiency of the teachers, the augmentation of the means of early instruction, the certain prospect of unquestionable improvements, and the undeniable certainty of a perfect adaptation of the present organization to the wants of the compact population of the city and districts.

May they not be permitted again most earnestly to invoke the attention and lively interest of their fellow-citizens to this all-important enterprise—to implore their aid and countenance, their energetic efforts for the prosecution of a work upon which is to depend mainly the happiness and the security of our social fabric. Will they not judge of what is practicable from what has been already done? The stigma of poverty—once the only title of admission to our public schools—has, at the solicitation of the controllers, been erased from our statute book, and the schools of this city and county are now open to every child that draws the breath of life within our borders. What may not be accomplished by this mighty lever of universal education?

Scarcely nineteen years have elapsed since a few public spirited and philanthropic individuals, disgusted with the miserable provisions and fraudulent execution of the then existing laws for the gratuitous education of the poor, determined to attain a melioration of the system. Through the midst of violent and selfish opposition, their disinterested zeal bore them onward to a perfect triumph. The act of March 3, 1818, was the prize of their conflict.

Annual Report for 1850

OCCUPATIONS

It is a matter of very general interest and inquiry to know to what classes in society the students of the high school belong. The only available means of information on this point are the occupations of their parents. This is not always a certain criterion. The term "merchant," for instance, is one not very well defined, and means sometimes a man with an income of a few hundred dollars, and again one with an income of as many thousands. Still, there are other cases where the name of an occupation defines pretty clearly the class and condition of those who pursue it. Everyone understands the classification meant by clergymen, judges, carpenters, blacksmiths, seamstresses, and others that might be named. When a candidate is admitted to the school, the occupation of his parent or guardian is always registered and published, together with his residence. In the absence of any temptation to deceive, and with the certain means of detecting any deception, the register of occupations may be relied on as evidence, and as indicating with sufficient accuracy the classes in the community most immediately benefited by the school.

Occupations of the Parents or Guardians of Pupils Admitted from the First Opening of the School, October 22, 1838 to July 26, 1850: Agents 6, Aldermen 2, Apothecary 1, Artists 3, Bakers 18, Barbers 2, Blacksmiths 26, Boardinghouse keepers 9, Bookbinders 10, Booksellers 4, Brassfounders 6, Brewers 9, Bricklayers 21, Brickmakers 12, Brokers 18, Brushmakers 9, Cabinetmakers 28, Carpenters 108, Chairmakers 5, Clergymen 32, Clerks and Accountants 123, Coachmakers 5, Coal-dealers 8, Coopers 12, Cordwainers 98, Curriers 14, Customhouse officers 3, Dealers 5, Dentists 10, Distillers 7, Druggists 19, Dry goods merchants 5, Dyers 9, Engineers 7, Engravers 17, Farmers 30, Fishermen 5, Furriers 3, Gardeners 4, Gentlemen 4, Gilders 4, Glassblowers 4, Grocers 78, Hardware merchants 4, Hatters 26, Innkeepers 41, Ironfounders 6, Jewellers 11, Judges 5, Laborers 48, Lawyers 24, Locksmiths 3, Lumber merchants 4, Machinists 29, Mantua makers 28, Manufacturers 62, Mariners 30, Merchants 125, Millers 10, Milliners 5, Painters 9, Pawnbrokers 4, Peddlers 2, Physicians 45, Plasterers 14, Plumbers 4, Portrait painters 2, Potters 2, Printers 21, Prison keeper 1, Saddlers 27, Sailmakers 4, Seamstresses 18, Sea captain 1, Shipwrights 28, Silversmiths 4, Stonecutters 13, Stonemasons 3, Storekeepers 113, Tailors 69, Tanners 5, Teachers 36, Tinsmiths 15, Tobacconists 14, Traders 4, Umbrella makers 6, Victuallers 16, Watchmakers 11, Watchmen 14, Weavers 28, Widows 117, Miscellaneous 217, Total 2,130.

Another point on which inquiry is frequently made relates to the occupations of the pupils after leaving the school. Each pupil on leaving is requested to make a record of the business which he is about to follow. It no doubt often happens that a boy after following one kind of business for a few months changes it for another. In some cases also we are not able to ascertain the occupation of pupils after leaving school. Still, as a general rule, the record is a safe guide to one inquiring into the tendencies of the course of instruction pursued. It was very early a matter of anxiety with the controllers to avoid the error, not of *over*educating the pupils, but of so educating them as to give them a distaste for business. It was feared that the gift of intellectual culture would be accompanied with a disrelish for anything but intellectual employment, if not with a dislike of employment altogether. Such, without doubt, is often the result of education misdirected. The tendency in this respect of the course of instruction prescribed by the controllers would seem to be of the most encouraging kind. The alumni of the high school are already found scattered through the city in almost every walk of useful industry.

Occupations of the 1,467 pupils who Graduated or Left during the Eight Years, ending July 26, 1850: Architects 2, Bakers 2, Blacksmiths 32, Blind makers 2, Bookbinders 16, Bricklayers 30, Brickmakers 5, Cabinetmakers 8, Cadets 3, Carpenters 120, Chairmakers 3, Chemists 6, Clergymen 6, Clerks 137, Conveyancers 44, Coopers 8, Cordwainers 50, Curriers 12, Cutlers 2, Dentists 5, Druggists 44, Dyers 2, Engineers 24, Engravers 37, Farmers 70, Gas fitters 2, Gilders 4, Glasscutters 2, Grocers 11, Hatters 11, Ironfounders 2, Jewellers 12, Lawyers 17, Locksmiths 2, Machinists 65, Manufacturers 13, Mariners 31, Masons 4, Merchants 3, Millwrights 3, Moulders 2, Painters 13, Paperhanger 1, Physicians 19, Plasterers 2, Printers 54, Saddlers 14, Sailmakers 2, Ship carpenters 6, Ship joiners 2, Shipwrights 22, Stereotypists 2, Stonecutters 4, Storekeepers 332, Tailors 12, Teachers 55, Tinsmiths 4, Tobacconists 3, Turners 4, Type founders 4, Watchmakers 4, Weavers 4, Wheelwrights 7, Not ascertained 29, Deceased 6, Miscellaneous 8, Total 1,467.

IV

The several documents that follow begin to construct an image of school life in the Jacksonian period. They include a school seating chart, an outline for instruction, and the general rules of behavior for the common schools of Cheshire, Connecticut, 1826–1827. Together they reveal how vital order and discipline were to these institutions.

SCHOOL CURRICULUM AND RULES, CHESHIRE, CONNECTICUT 1826–1827

Curriculum: Outline of Instruction, As Conducted in Cheshire Primary School No. 1, Winter Term, 1826–1827

EDUCATION		
MORAL: GENERAL PRINCIPLES	PHYSICAL: GENERAL PRINCIPLES	INTELLECTUAL: GENERAL PRINCIPLES
Affections	Senses	Observation
Obedience	Play games	Memory
Truth	Exercises	Judgment
Temper		Method
Approbation		Abstraction
Amusements		Association
Rewards and		Invention
Punishments		Taste
		Imagination

In *American Journal of Education*, 3 (1828): 86–91, 94.

Moral Education

GENERAL PRINCIPLES

Elicit the affections, and direct them to their appropriate objects; to

The Instructor,
Associates,
Mankind,
Brutes,
The Creator.

Mild and conciliating measures only are to be used in the education of the affections and passions.

Reason and conscience carefully trained, and made the only objects of appeal.

Confidence in the instructor, induced by the affections, and by example, made the foundation of obedience.

Obedience made the basis of truth.

Approbation, founded on truth, and obedience.

Amusements—rewards and punishments—internal police, and process, made to exert a strictly *moral* influence.

AFFECTIONS

Employ the language of nature—attitude, gesture, countenance expressing joy, gladness, cheerfulness, satisfaction, contentment, complacency, approbation, love, with correspondent tones of voice—caressing.

Amusements adapted to the development of the affections.

Social inclinations furnished with proper objects.

Dress, manners, habits.

Instructor acknowledge his faults frankly to scholars, as an example for their imitation.

Desired emotions excited, by oratory, address, action, countenance.

Characteristic affections frequently exercised.

Address pupils familiarly on all occasions.

Mutual sympathy.

No competition—never blaming one, while another is praised—the selfish sympathies of two or more being never brought to desire the same object, at the same time.

Character of rewards, and the manner of their distribution, considered.

Pupils made as happy as possible, by the address and arrangements of the instructor.

Selfish passions eradicated as much as possible.

No individual comparisons—equal, and exact, and public justice given to all.

Attainment, not *place*, made the standard of merit.

The Cheshire School Rules

LAWS

Members of the school are required to comply with the following rules:

1. That they appear at the schoolroom at the appointed hours for exercises to commence, or be denied entrance, unless a reasonable excuse from parents is preferred.
2. That they arrange their books, slates, etc., in good order on entrance.
3. That they keep their own, and so far as concerned, the books, and school apparatus of others, from defacement.
   That they do not soil, deface, or scatter any object in or near the schoolroom.
4. That they do not, without permission, address anyone during school exercises, save the instructor, and then, in all practicable cases, to prefer an address in writing, through the superintendent.
5. That they treat the superintendent with respect.
6. That they articulate their lessons in such voice as to be distinctly heard at any part of the schoolroom.
7. That they practice no deception in their lessons.
8. That they pursue their studies in silence.
9. That they follow the order of instruction faithfully.
10. That an excuse be given for imperfect lessons.
11. That they do not leave their seats without permission.
12. That they do not unnecessarily interrupt or retard the studies of their companions.
13. That they do not express inability to perform any given exercise previous to attempt.
14. That they suffer the consequences of forgetting and talebearing.
15. That they exercise mutual kindness and forbearance.
16. That they endeavor to promote the happiness of their companions.
17. That they *"Behave to their companions as they desire their companions to behave to them."*

OBEDIENCE

Induce the confidence of scholars, by affection and conduct, as the foundation for obedience.

Example—precept—practice, founded on reason.

Preventives, rather than punishments.

Few laws—those clearly defined, and rendered familiar by habitual practice.

Integrity, and honesty, without dissimulation, on the part of instructor.

Diminish temptations, by arrangement.

Self-government induced by appealing to reason and conscience.

Punishment, uniform, certain, immediate.

Ridicule, and raillery, used for the cure of little misdemeanors and habits.

Natural consequences of obedience and disobedience employed to encourage, or punish.

Punishments, private and solitary, to induce obedience.

TRUTH

Never require children to accuse themselves; ask them no questions where it is for their interest to deceive.

Clear ideas of right and wrong fixed in the minds of children.

Honesty and integrity respected, commended, rewarded.

Confidence deserved before it is given.

Avoid presenting temptations and dissimulation.

Fear banished; truth valued more than any pecuniary consideration.

TEMPER

Induce the affections which form and sweeten the temper.

Never irritate intentionally.

Appeal to hope and reason—not to fear.

Sympathy of surrounding persons.

APPROBATION

Train conscience, by frequent appeal to it.

Induce habitual obedience, as far as possible.

No personal emulation; general praise bestowed.

Beware of the counterfeits of approbation, pride, and vanity—cultivate the judgment carefully.

AMUSEMENTS

Controlled by the instructor.

Amusements *moralized* as much as possible, exercising a good influence on the affections and passions, improving and elevating the mind.

Adapted to the understandings, feelings, and habits of children.

REWARDS AND PUNISHMENTS

Moralized, of an intellectual nature, addressed to the understanding and the feelings.

REWARDS	PUNISHMENTS
Self-approbation	Self-condemnation
Affection of instructor	Loss of instructor's affection
Success	Defeat
Consequences of obedience	Consequences of disobedience
Caressing	Neglect
Encouragement	Ridicule; raillery
Self-government	Governed by the instructor
Proposed for imitation	Contempt
Hope; with attendants	Fear; and its attendants
Esteem; confidence; love	Aversion; jealousy
Perusal of library books	Wooden books
Knowledge; usefulness	Ignorance; beggary
Happiness	Misery; despair

Seating Chart

SCHOOL APPARATUS

Every scholar is furnished with a:

Slate, pencil, and sponge.
Desk.
Class books.

Writing books; pen, ink, but no
rule.
Cubes, beans, etc.

And for general use are furnished:

Books.
Cubes.
Tangible letters.

Prints.
Material substances, etc.

SCHOOLROOM

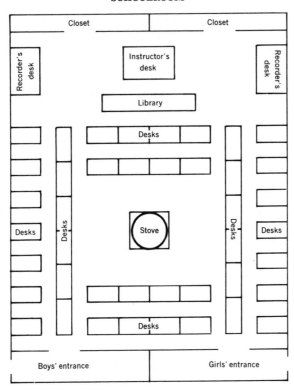

V

*Another indication of the character of the school experience in the
antebellum period comes from the textbooks most often read in the
classrooms. Lyman Cobb had the good fortune to compose one of
the most popular volumes; his* New North American Reader, *pub-*

lished in 1844, was used in many different regions of the country.
The passages below make quite clear that the teaching of reading
was part of a general exercise at teaching morality and good order.
And imagine what it was like for students to review these passages
day after day.

NEW NORTH AMERICAN READER, 1844

LYMAN COBB

READING LESSON

Danger of Bad Habits

A man's case may be pronounced to be desperate when his mind is brought into such a state as that the necessary means of reformation shall have lost their effect upon him; and, this is the natural consequence of confirmed habits of vice, and a long-continued neglect of the means of religion and virtue.

In order to be the more sensible of this, you are to consider that vice is a habit, and therefore of a subtle and insinuating nature. By easy, pleasing, and seemingly harmless actions men are often betrayed into a progress which grows everyday more alarming. Our virtuous resolutions may break with difficulty. It may be with pain and reluctance that we commit the first acts of sin, but the next are easier to us; and use, custom, and habit will at last reconcile us to anything, even things the very idea of which might at first be shocking to us.

Vice is a thing not to be trifled with. You may, by the force of vigorous resolution, break off in the early stages of it; but habits, when they have been confirmed, and long continued, are obstinate things to contend with, and are hardly ever entirely subdued. When bad habits seem to be overcome, and we think we have got rid of our chains, they may perhaps only have become, as it were, invisible; so that when we thought we had recovered our freedom and strength, so as to be able to repel any temptation, we may lose all power of resistance on the first approach of it.

A man who has contracted a habit of vice and been abandoned to sinful courses for some time *is never out of danger*. He is exactly in the case of a man who has long labored under a chronic disease and is perpetually subject to a relapse.

The reason is that a relapse does not find a person in the condition in which he was when the first fit of illness seized him. That gave his constitution a shock, and left him enfeebled, so as to be less able to sustain another shock.

In the very same dangerous situation is the man who has ever been addicted to vicious courses. He can never be said to be perfectly recovered, whatever appearances may promise, but is always in danger

In *New North American Reader, or Fifth Reading Book*, by Lyman Cobb (New York, 1844), pp. 25–28, 123–25.

of a fatal relapse. He ought, therefore, to take the greatest care of himself.

He ought, therefore, to have the greatest distrust of himself, and set a double watch over his thoughts, words, and actions, for fear of a surprise. For if once, through the force of any particular temptation, he should fall back into his former vicious courses, and his former disposition should return, his case will probably be desperate.

Questions—When may a man's condition or case be pronounced desperate? Of what is this the natural consequence? What is of a subtle and insinuating nature? How are men often betrayed into a progress which becomes alarming? To what will use, custom, and habit at last reconcile us? With what should we not trifle? Who is *never out of danger*? Why is a relapse very dangerous? Who is always in danger of *a fatal relapse*? Will all young persons remember that *habits*, whether *good* or *bad*, formed in youth, will generally remain with them through life, and never practice *any vice*, or contract *any bad habit*?

READING LESSON

The Schoolmaster

There are prouder themes for the eulogist than this. The praise of the statesman, the warrior, or the orator furnishes more splendid topics for ambitious eloquence; but no theme can be more rich in dessert or more fruitful in public advantage.

The enlightened liberality of many of our state governments, by extending the common school system over their whole population, has brought elementary education to the door of every family.

In this state, it appears, from the Annual Reports of the [New York] Secretary of the State, 1829, there are, besides the fifty incorporated academies and numerous private schools, about nine thousand school districts, in each of which instruction is regularly given. These contain at present half a million of children taught in the single state of New York.

Of what incalculable influence, then, for good or for evil, upon the dearest interests of society, must be the estimate entertained for the character of this great body of teachers, and the consequent respectability of the individuals who compose it!

What else is there in the whole of our social system of such extensive and powerful operation on the national character? There is one other influence more powerful, and but one. It is that of the *Mother*. The forms of a free government, the provisions of wise legislation, the schemes of the statesman, the sacrifices of the patriot are as nothing compared with these.

If the future citizens of our republic are to be worthy of their rich inheritance, they must be made so principally through the virtue and intelligence of their *mothers*.

But next in rank and in efficacy to that pure and holy source of moral influence is that of the *schoolmaster*. It is powerful already. What would it be if in every one of those school districts which we now count

by annually increasing thousands, there were to be found one teacher well informed without pedantry, religious without bigotry or fanaticism, proud and fond of his profession, and honored in the discharge of its duties? How wide would be the intellectual, the moral influence of such a body of men!

The schoolmaster's occupation is laborious and ungrateful; its rewards are scanty and precarious. He may indeed be, and he ought to be, animated by the conscientiousness of doing good, that best of all consolations, that noblest of all motives. But that too must be often clouded by doubt and uncertainty.

Obscure and inglorious as his daily occupation may appear to learned pride or worldly ambition, yet to be truly successful and happy, he must be animated by the spirit of the same great principles which inspired the most illustrious benefactors of mankind.

If he bring to his task high talent and rich acquirement, he must be content to look into distant years for the proof that his labors have not been wasted; that the good seed which he daily scatters abroad does not fall on stony ground and wither away, or among thorns, to be choked by the cares, the delusions, or the vices of the world. He must regard himself as sowing the seeds of truth for posterity and the care of heaven.

VI

The good order of the school was not very different from the good order of the new asylums for the mentally ill. Indeed, the psychiatrists of the nineteenth century diagnosed mental illness as a disease which resulted from disorder—the chaos that followed excessive ambition, or excessive concern with moneymaking, or excessive learning. Americans, they feared, were particularly liable to insanity—it was the price we paid for our free and open institutions. This diagnosis of the social causes of insanity led the psychiatrists to think that they had discovered a cure for the malady: in well-ordered and disciplined settings, the insane would learn the rigid rules for living that they had heretofore neglected. The description of the asylum routine comes from the Pennsylvania Hospital for the Insane, located in Philadelphia. It was a private hospital whose routine exemplified the best that was available for the treatment of the mentally ill in this period.

REPORT OF THE PENNSYLVANIA HOSPITAL FOR THE INSANE, 1843

The following is a sketch of the *regular duties of each day*.

The watchman rings the bell at a quarter before 5 A.M. when all persons engaged about the premises are expected to arise, and immediately commence the performance of their various duties. The attendants unlock the chamber doors, and give the patients a kind greeting, see that they are properly prepared for breakfast, and commence ventilating and arranging the halls and chambers, in which labor they receive voluntary assistance from many of the patients.

Half an hour before breakfast, which is at half past 6 A.M., they call at the physician's office for whatever medicine is to be given to the patients, and which they always find ready and in cups, labeled with each individual's name. No medicine is kept in the wards.

After breakfast, the beds are made, and every part of the wings placed in order, so as to be ready for inspection at the visit of the physician. At this visit, every patient is seen and spoken to, and all their rooms examined.

After the morning visit, the patients who are employed at outdoor labor commence their work—others engage in indoor employment—or walk, ride, or occupy themselves in reading, or various kinds of amusements. At half-past twelve, dinner is taken in different dining rooms. At all the meals, the attendants either wait upon the patients, or a portion of them preside at the different tables. In the afternoon, those who labor return to their work; and everyday in fine weather, some of the patients ride, and most of them take long walks in the open air, generally within but frequently outside of the enclosure. At 6 P.M., tea is ready, and no patients go out after sunset without special permission.

In the evening, the different parlors and halls are handsomely lighted, and the patients engage in reading, writing, or some of the various amusements, always at hand, among themselves or with some of the officers or attendants.

At half-past seven, medicine is given for the evening, and afterward such patients as wish it are allowed to retire. All are expected to do so by half-past nine. At 10 P.M., the house is closed, and all light in the wards extinguished.

In *Second Annual Report*, Pennsylvania Hospital for the Insane (Philadelphia, 1843), pp. 23–29, 34–35.

Remedial Means Employed in the Hospital

Of the strictly *medical* treatment, we can, of course, in a report of this kind speak only in a very general manner. In a large proportion of the recent cases that have been admitted, we have found derangement of the health of some kind, and the remedies have been varied according to circumstances.

In nearly all cases, our patients have a full and nutritious, but plain diet—they go to the dining rooms, where the tables are supplied with meats, and a great variety of vegetables, of which they are allowed to partake till satisfied.

In the *moral* treatment of the insane, so much may be effected by *attendants*, who are constantly in intercourse with the patients, who see them at all hours and under all circumstances, that although much has been done, we cannot help hoping the time is not far distant when greater inducements will be offered to persons of superior qualifications to engage in these stations, where active benevolence can be most profitably employed.

Printed rules are furnished to the attendants when entering upon the performance of their duties, and to which they are expected to conform in every particular. In these rules and on frequent occasions, we endeavor to impress the attendants with a true view of the importance and responsibility of their stations.

We insist on a mild and conciliatory manner under all circumstances, and roughness or violence we never tolerate. We are not satisfied with the simple performance of special duties, but wish to see an active interest felt in all the patients—a desire to add to their comfort, and to advance their cure—judicious efforts to interest or amuse them—a watchful care over their conduct and conversation, and a constant, sympathizing intercourse, calculated to win their attachment, and command their respect and confidence.

Employment and Amusements

The importance of furnishing the insane with suitable means of employment and amusement is now so well understood that we shall merely indicate those to which our patients have resorted during the past year.

At the head of the list, we place *outdoor labor*, on account of its importance in many of the curable cases, and its value in even those that are the most chronic and incurable. It is one of the means of treatment for which ample provision should be made in every well-conducted institution; and the importance of the farm can only be properly estimated by calculating the value of one of the best means for the restoration of the insane.

Although many of our patients previous to their admission had unfortunately never been accustomed to labor, nor to habits of industry, still a considerable number of the males have assisted in most of the operations connected with haymaking, and securing the harvest.

Farming and gardening are probably two of the very best means of giving exercise to insane patients; and the latter has this year produced the most pleasant effects in several instances. One of the regular gardeners before he commenced outdoor work was rarely more than a month without a period of excitement, requiring seclusion for several days, and during which he was guilty of nearly every description of mischief. During this summer he has had no recurrence of these attacks.

The incurable patients who labor show its good effects by their quietness in the halls—their orderly deportment and their sound rest at night.

The *workshop* is a valuable acquisition to our means of employment. It is a handsome frame building twenty by forty feet, two stories high, and situated near the gateway. The lower story is intended for carpenter work, turning, basket making, etc. The upper room is plastered, and may be used for mattress making, and other pursuits requiring space, or for some of the amusements of the patients.

Many of our cases, generally among the convalescent, have already been pleasantly and profitably employed in this building, and the interest they have felt in their work—the entire change in their thoughts, and the active use of their muscles—have rarely failed to contribute to the rapidity and certainty of their cure.

We have not as yet attempted any kind of work by which to ascertain the amount of income that might be derived from the workshop. Our great object thus far has been to induce our patients *to labor*; for the kind of work we have cared but little, and whatever object appeared most likely to excite a new train of thought has received our approbation.

Several of the patients, male and female, assist in keeping the house in order—preparing food for cooking and arranging the dining rooms; others take charge of particular departments of business—one attends the furnaces at the wash house, another superintends all the *mangling* in the ironing room; one who in the afternoon devotes himself to the classics, spends a part of each morning in cleaning the area around the whole building; and several are found always ready to assist where their services can be useful.

Simple seclusion in chambers properly secured has been resorted to during the past year, in by far the greater number of cases that have appeared to require restraint of any kind. In others, leather wristbands, secured by a belt around the body, or mittens of the same material, or of canvas, have been employed in rare cases, and two patients have occasionally been kept on their beds with much advantage, by an apparatus also of leather, but admitting of much freedom of motion.

The so-called tranquilizing chair has not been seen in our wards, nor is the muff or straitjacket among our regular means of restraint. The latter contrivance was used in two cases—only with the exceptions just indicated, no species of personal restraint has been resorted to, but those previously mentioned—and of these the use has been comparatively rare. For nearly three months after opening the house, not an article for restraint was used in the hospital. We have frequently, during the whole fortnight, had a family of more than one hundred

patients without any kind of restraint upon the person of a single individual—not more than two or three confined to their rooms, and not
more than half a dozen who were not able to take their meals in the
dining rooms, at tables regularly furnished with crockery, knives, forks,
and glasses.

From this freedom of action, and from these indulgences, we have
found nothing but advantage and encouragement to promote still less
dependence upon restraining apparatus as a means of controlling the
insane. To save the attendants trouble or labor is never admitted as a
reason for its application—the positive benefit of the patient is the
only one that is sound or justifiable, except under very peculiar
circumstances.

We allow restraint to be applied only by order of one of the
physicians—and even the seclusion of a patient is to be promptly
reported.

We have not dispensed with all restraining apparatus, because,
under some circumstances, mild means of the kind are much less annoying to the patient, and effect the object in view with less irritation and
more certainty, than the constant presence of even the best instructed
attendants.

The great objection to the employment of restraint, and the positive injury produced by it, does not come so much from its application,
as from its abuse, by being too long continued. Restraint or simple seclusion may be required for a week or a day, or it is possible that a single
hour will be more beneficial than either; and it ought never to be forgotten that when either ceases to be useful, from that moment it
becomes positively injurious.

VII

*Nowhere was the emphasis on obedience more pronounced than in the
child-rearing literature of the Jacksonian period. Practically every
tract instructed parents first and foremost to train their children
to respect authority, to obey commands immediately and without
argument. And in each instance, they held out the most dire
consequences should parents fail in this task, from children drown-
ing to children growing up to become criminals. Affection between
child and parent was important, not as an end in itself, but as a
way of securing more prompt and willing obedience. One of the
most widely read of the advice-to-parents books was John Abbott's
The Mother at Home. Abbott, like his fellow authors, insisted that
not only the good order of the family but also the good order of
society demanded this training to obedience. In no other way would
children learn to resist temptations at loose in the community, and
grow up to become law-abiding and hard-working citizens.*

THE MOTHER AT HOME, 1834

JOHN ABBOTT

It is a great trial to have children undutiful when young. But it is a tenfold greater affliction to have a child grow up to maturity in disobedience and become a dissolute and abandoned man. How many parents have passed days of sorrow, and nights of sleeplessness, in consequence of the misconduct of their offspring! How many have had their hearts broken, and their gray hairs brought down with sorrow to the grave, solely in consequence of their own neglect to train up their children in the nurture and admonition of the Lord! Your future happiness is in the hands of your children. They may throw gloom over all your prospects, embitter every enjoyment, and make you so miserable that your only prospect of relief will be in death.

That little girl whom you now fondle upon your knee, and who plays, so full of enjoyment, upon your floor, has entered a world where temptations are thick around. What is to enable her to resist these temptations but established principles of piety? And where is she to obtain these principles but from a mother's instructions and example? If, through your neglect now, she should hereafter yield herself to temptation and sin, what must become of your peace of mind? O mother! little are you aware of the wretchedness with which your beloved daughter may hereafter overwhelm you.

This is a dreadful subject. But it is one which the mother must feel and understand. There are facts which might here be introduced, sufficient to make every parent tremble. We might lead you to the dwelling of the clergyman, and tell you that a daughter's sin has murdered the mother; and sent paleness to the cheek, and trembling to the frame, and agony to the heart of the aged father.

No matter what your situation in life may be, that little child, now so innocent, whose playful endearments and happy laugh awaken such thrilling emotions in your heart, may cause you years of unalleviated misery.

And, mother! look at that drunken vagrant, staggering by your door. Listen to his horrid imprecations, as, bloated and ragged, he passes along. That wretch has a mother. Perhaps, widowed and in poverty, she needs the comfort and support of an affectionate son. You have a son. You may soon be a widow. If your son is dissolute, you are doubly widowed; you are worse, infinitely worse, than childless. You cannot now endure even the thought that your son will ever be thus abandoned. How dreadful then must be the experience of the reality!

I once knew a mother who had an only son. She loved him most ardently, and could not bear to deny him any indulgence. He, of course, soon learned to rule his mother. At the death of his father, the poor woman was left at the mercy of this vile boy. She had neglected her

In *The Mother at Home,* by John Abbott (New York, 1834), pp. 2–3, 10–15, 18–23.

duty when he was young, and now his ungovernable passions had become too strong for her control. Self-willed, turbulent, and revengeful, he was his mother's bitterest curse. His paroxysms of rage at times amounted almost to madness. One day, enraged with this mother, he set fire to her house, and it was burned to the ground with all its contents, and she was left in the extremest state of poverty.

You have watched over your child through all the months of its helpless infancy. You have denied yourself that you might give it comfort. When it has been sick, you have been unmindful of your own weariness and your own weakness, and the livelong night you have watched at his cradle, administering to all its wants. When it has smiled, you have felt a joy which none but a parent can feel, and have pressed your much-loved treasure to your bosom, praying that its future years of obedience and affection might be your ample reward. And now, how dreadful a requital for that child to grow up to hate and abuse you; to leave you friendless, in sickness and in poverty; to squander all his earnings in haunts of iniquity and degradation!

How entirely is your earthly happiness at the disposal of your child! His character is now in your hands, and you are to form it for good or for evil. If you are consistent in your government, and faithful in the discharge of your duties, your child will probably, through life, revere you. If, on the other hand, you cannot summon resolution to punish your child when disobedient; if you do not curb his passions; if you do not bring him to entire and willing subjection to your authority you must expect that he will be your curse. In all probability, he will despise you for your weakness. Unaccustomed to authority at home, he will break away from all restraints, make you wretched by his life, and disgraceful in his death.

"A good boy generally makes a good man," said the mother of Washington. "George was always a good boy." Here we see one secret of his greatness. George Washington had a mother who taught him to be a good boy and instilled into his heart those principles which raised him to be the benefactor of his country, and one of the brightest ornaments of the world. The mother of Washington is entitled to a nation's gratitude. She taught her boy the principles of obedience, and moral courage, and virtue. She, in a great measure, formed the character of the hero and the statesman. It was by her own fireside that she taught her playful boy to govern himself; and thus was he prepared for the brilliant career of usefulness which he afterward pursued. We are indebted to God for the gift of Washington; but we are no less indebted to Him for the gift of his inestimable mother. Had she been a weak, and indulgent, and unfaithful parent, the unchecked energies of Washington might have elevated him to the throne of a tyrant, or youthful disobedience might have prepared the way for a life of crime and a dishonoured grave.

The question has probably often presented itself to your mind "How shall I govern my children, so as to secure their virtue and happiness?" This question I shall now endeavor to answer.

Obedience is absolutely essential to proper family government. Without this, all other efforts will be in vain. You may pray with and for your children; you may strive to instruct them in religious truth; you may be unwearied in your efforts to make them happy, and to gain their affection. But if they are suffered to indulge in habits of disobedience, your instructions will be lost, and your toil in vain. And by obedience I do not mean languid and dilatory yielding to repeated threats, but prompt and cheerful acquiescence in parental commands. Neither is it enough that a child should yield to arguments and persuasions. It is essential that he should submit to your authority.

I will suppose a case in illustration of this last remark. Your little daughter is sick; you go to her with the medicine which has been prescribed for her, and the following dialogue ensues:

"Here, my daughter, is some medicine for you."
"I don't want to take it, mamma."
"Yes, my dear, do take it; for it will make you feel better."
"No it won't, mother. I don't want it."
"Yes it will, my child. The doctor says it will."
"Well, it don't taste good, and I don't want it."

The mother continues her persuasions, and the child persists in its refusal. After a long and wearisome conflict, the mother is compelled either to throw the medicine away, or to resort to compulsion, and force down the unpalatable drug. Thus, instead of appealing to her own supreme authority, she is appealing to the reason of the child; and, under these circumstances, the child of course refuses to submit.

A mother, not long since, under similar circumstances, not being able to persuade her child to take the medicine, and not having sufficient resolution to compel it, threw the medicine away. When the physician next called, she was ashamed to acknowledge her want of government, and therefore did not tell him that the medicine had not been given. The physician, finding the child worse, left another prescription, supposing the previous one had been properly administered. But the child had no idea of taking the nauseous dose, and the renewed efforts of the mother were unavailing. Again the fond and foolish, but cruel parent, threw the medicine away; and the fever was left to rage unchecked in its veins. Again the physician called, and was surprised to find the inefficacy of his prescriptions, and that the poor little sufferer was at the verge of death. The mother, when informed that her child must die, was in an agony, and confessed what she had done. But it was too late. The child died. And think you that mother gazed upon its pale corpse with any common emotions of anguish? Physicians will tell you that many children have thus been lost. Unaccustomed to obedience when well, they are still more adverse to it when sick. The efforts which are made to induce a stubborn child to take medicine often produce such an excitement as entirely to counteract the effect of the prescription; and thus is a mother often called to weep over the grave of her child, simply because she has not taught that child to obey.

The first thing therefore to be aimed at is to bring your child under perfect subjection. Teach him that he must obey you. Sometimes give him your reasons; again, withhold them. But let him perfectly understand that he is to do as he is bidden. Accustom him to immediate and cheerful acquiescence in your will. This is obedience. And this is absolutely essential to good family government. Without this, your family will present one continued scene of noise and confusion; the toil of rearing up your children will be almost insupportable; and, in all probability, your heart will be broken by their future licentiousness or ingratitude.

Chapter 9

The American Art Union

AN INTENSE ambivalence marked American attitudes toward culture and artistic production in the antebellum period. Americans were, on the one hand, acutely hostile to art and artists. They associated paintings with the overopulent walls of aristocratic and decadent Europeans; and they thought of artists as parasitic, as morally obnoxious as their upper-class patrons. Art, they believed, traditionally flourished amid gross disparities of wealth and power, disparities which they did not wish to re-create here. And yet other considerations blunted this hostility and suspicion. Americans, after all, wished to demonstrate the superiority of republican society in all its aspects. The best answer to European critics who labeled the new country rude and boorish would be to create splendid works of art, to make an esthetic contribution as notable and original as their constitutional one. Somehow, then, Americans had to turn out great art without corrupting themselves in the process.

Another stimulus to artistic production in the young republic was the eagerness of citizens to commemorate great moments in their history, to build appropriate monuments to the founding fathers and their victories. By 1820, most of those who had signed the Declaration of Independence or fought in the Revolutionary War had died, and those who had heard about these events firsthand, from parents or older siblings, were themselves advancing in age. The time had arrived, therefore, to celebrate the past; the nation's debt to these heroic figures had to be properly acknowledged. Furthermore, the monuments themselves would help to keep alive the spirit of the founding fathers. Veneration for George Washington was at once veneration for the republic. Appreciating the valor shown at Bunker Hill would perpetuate ideals of citizenship. In essence, monument building was one way to encourage and promote patriotic fervor.

This perspective on monument building carried over to other forms of artistic production as well. The solution to the paradox of producing great art without endangering republican values was to insist that art

193

self-consciously serve the nation. It was to be popularly supported and popularly oriented. The heroes on American canvases were to be Americans; the message of the painting was to promote the good order and solidarity of the society. Art, ultimately, was to serve social needs, not esthetic ones. The responsibility of the artist was not to some inner standard of taste, but to the moral character of the republic. Rather than endanger the society, the artist was to uplift it.

The character of American culture during the first half of the nineteenth century reflected this judgment. The artist was assured of support; his work was held in repute. But his position depended upon his willingness and ability to serve the public welfare. This solution clearly did not always enhance the quality of the artistic productions themselves.

These many themes were reflected in the formation of the American Art Union. The Union was an ingenious plan for supporting American artists and popularizing their works. A peculiarly American invention, the Union was the democratic answer to the problem of patronage and distribution. Under its influence, cultural needs were joined to social ones.

I

The organization and activities of the American Art Union reveal the connections between artistic productions and social goals. Under the Art Union plan, members were to purchase tickets for a lottery; the winner of the lottery would receive one large oil painting, and every subscriber would receive at least one print. The sums gathered through this scheme would be used to support worthy artists, and, at the same time, guarantee their works wide circulation. The selection below reveals how the Art Union viewed its own contribution to the state of American culture.

AMERICAN ART UNION BULLETIN, 1849

PLAN OF THE AMERICAN ART UNION

The American Art Union, in the City of New York, was incorporated by the Legislature of the State of New York for the promotion of the fine arts in the United States. It is managed by gentlemen who are chosen annually by the members, and receive no compensation. To accomplish a truly national object, uniting great public good with private gratification at small individual expense, in a manner best suited to the situation and institutions of our country, and the wants, habits, and tastes of our people, the Committee have adopted the following plan.

In *Bulletin for 1849*, American Art Union (New York, 1849), pp. 3–4, 8–11, 14–17.

Every subscriber of five dollars is a member of the Art Union for the year, and is entitled to all its privileges.

The money thus obtained (after paying necessary expenses) is applied:

First, to the production of a large and costly original engraving from an American painting, together with a set of outlines, or some other similar work of art.

Of this engraving every member receives a copy for every five dollars paid by him.

Members entitled to duplicates are at liberty to select from the engravings of previous years.

Second, to the purchase of paintings and sculpture, statuettes in bronze, and medals by native or resident artists.

These works of art are publicly exhibited at the Gallery of the Art Union till the annual meeting in December, when they are publicly distributed by lot among the members, each member having one share for every five dollars paid by him.

Each member is thus certain of receiving in return at least the value of the five dollars paid, and may also receive a painting or other work of art of great value.

Third, the institution keeps an office and free picture gallery always open, well attended, and hung with fine paintings where the members in New York receive their engravings, paintings, etc., and where the business of the institution is transacted.

What Has the American Art Union Accomplished?

The new gallery of the American Art Union has been opened to the public. The occasion is a proper one for "taking an observation," ascertaining where we are at present, whether we are sailing on our true course, and how much progress we have made in the voyage.

In material prosperity we have certainly abundant cause for self-congratulation. As a society, we have advanced with unexampled rapidity. So far as the number of members and the amount of subscriptions are concerned, the annual increase has been sufficiently large to gratify the expectations of the most sanguine. The change which a period of only eight years has brought about is believed to be unparalleled in the history of similar institutions. The six hundred and eighty-six members of the year 1840 have multiplied to sixteen thousand and upward in 1848, and the income of the former year, scarcely four thousand dollars, has grown in the same period to more than eighty-five thousand. Then the operations of the society beyond the city of New York were exceedingly limited; now many thousand letters are annually received and answered by the Corresponding Secretary, besides a great number of printed circulars and other communications which are constantly dispatched to our agents.

The contrast in the local habitations of the Art Union, at different periods, is not less striking. Only six years ago the Board held its meetings in a small dark apartment in the rear of a bookstore, which was thus used free of rent, through the courtesy of a friend of Art. We have at present in actual use for our own business, two galleries, also a committee chamber and office, besides large apartments in the basement for packing, storage, and other purposes; and all these properly lighted, warmed, ventilated, and furnished.

It is now apparent to all who examine the subject that a mode has been discovered by which Art may be encouraged to a proper extent as liberally in an economical republic as in a prodigal monarchy. That great moving principle of civilization which has effected such wonders in its application to traveling, to commerce, and to the useful arts; the principle of the combination of the limited means of many individuals to accomplish some great end has been found to serve equally well in the promotion of painting, sculpture, and engraving, and to be capable when carried out of supplying to these as generous a support as they have ever derived from crowned heads or wealthy aristocracies. The Art Union is now their steady and reliable patron. It expends a larger sum upon them than all other patrons upon the continent united; and under its auspices the most ambitious and laborious enterprises in their several departments may be undertaken and accomplished.

Has the Art Union Developed Talent among Artists?

Increasing subscription lists and growing revenues and large halls are not the only or the best tests of the benefits of any institution. A far more important matter to be settled is whether it advances the ends for which it was established. Does the American Art Union promote the development of artistic power? Does it elevate the taste and increase the knowledge of the people in matters of Art? We maintain the affirmative of both these questions. To the first of them we say that the association has already raised the compensation of artists for works of undoubted excellence to the rates paid in Europe for similar productions, and is always a ready and willing customer for such works at the advanced prices. It has stimulated many to attempt a higher range of subjects, and to bestow upon their paintings longer preparatory study, and more careful and laborious execution than heretofore. It has brought into notice a considerable number of men of decided ability who would have remained entirely unknown or, at any rate, advanced with much less rapidity excepting for this assistance. Great injustice is constantly done both to the Art Union and the artists by comparing the works of the latter, not with their own previous efforts, but either with the elaborate masterpieces of European schools or with some fanciful standard in the mind of the critic. This comparison is well enough when the abstract merit of our own men is to be estimated, but when the question relates to the progress they have made from year to year, and to the worth of any peculiar influence under which they have labored, a fairer mode is to compare each man with himself. It will be found that those who speak most contemptuously of Art Union pictures are persons who know nothing of the history of Art in America. They forget that genius has manifested itself here in many other departments, more conspicuously than in the fine arts—that at the time when our society commenced its efforts, the American School (if it may be so called) showed but little vitality, excepting in landscape and portraiture, that the most, after all, the Art Union could do was to offer generous prices and impartial judgments—it could not create genius, but only provide that genius, if it existed, should certainly be discovered and as certainly rewarded.

We must not forget to mention the immense benefit conferred by the Art Union in providing a sure and convenient avenue by which talent, no matter how obscure and humble its possessor, may make itself known to the public at large. This advantage is entirely independent of that conferred by the purchases of pictures by the committee, and must be conceded even by those who find the greatest fault with the character of these purchases. We allude to the great public galleries of this institution, which are well warmed, lighted, and ventilated, opened constantly to the public, and thronged daily by thousands of citizens. In these galleries any artist or amateur, whatever may be his station or his birthplace, the poor apprentice as well as the accomplished master, the unknown and friendless emigrant as well as the President of the Academy, may deposit his work (provided it be not utterly worthless) for public inspection. The only distinction recognized in these rooms is that of merit. As conspicuous a place is given to the nameless aspirant to fame, if his productions deserve it, as to the reigning favorite of the hour. No jealousies or secret enmities, no influential connections or low intrigues are allowed to control the arrangement of these apartments. We do not believe that in any part of the world, even among the most cultivated and refined nations of Europe, has there ever been afforded such an easy and accessible mode by which artists may bring their works before the people as this.

Has the Art Union Increased the Taste and Knowledge
of the People in Matters of Art?

So much for the question as to what the Art Union has done to develop artistic power; let us now attend to the equally important inquiry whether it has not also done much to elevate popular taste and increase the knowledge of the people in matters of Art. To answer this statistically, we may say that in the course of its ten year's existence, the society has distributed through the whole country nearly thirteen hundred paintings, seven hundred medals, more than fifty thousand engravings. It has constituted five hundred agencies in different parts of the country. It has kept open nearly ever since its institution a free gallery, in which not only have works been exhibited which were sent to the rooms to be purchased, but many others also, of the highest merit, belonging to individuals and deposited there for the gratification and improvement of the public. Finally, it has established a journal of the fine arts, which contains original and selected essays and much information respecting the progress of Art at home and abroad. This is given gratuitously to the members, and more than sixty-seven thousand copies of the different numbers have been printed and distributed.

It is well known to all who have studied the subject that a very general and strongly marked increase of interest in the fine arts has manifested itself within five or six years past in the United States. The growing subscription lists of the Art Union by themselves show this. Drawing is beginning to be taught in common schools. Exhibitions of paintings and statuary are more frequent and better attended. A greater number of houses are decorated with objects of taste. A decided improvement in the sale of prints is observed. Illustrated literature is eagerly welcomed and largely purchased. Societies upon the plan of the Art Union have sprung up in Philadelphia, Boston, Cincinnati, and elsewhere. Better taste is exhibited in architecture, both public and private, and in the furniture and adornment of houses. Books relating to Art have been sold in larger quantities than ever before in the same periods, and in parts of the country also where previously no interest had been felt in such matters.

Every unprejudiced mind must connect these novel manifestations with the progress of the American Art Union, and ascribe to its agency, in a very great degree, this newly awakened interest in the fine arts. After making due allowance for the great diffusion of illustrated books and newspapers, which have undoubtedly exercised an important influence, the greatest part of the credit for this movement must be awarded to our institution. Its secretaryships, its free gallery, its annual distribution of paintings, its various publications of prints and pamphlets have continually attracted public attention to the cause to which it is devoted. A periodic stimulus has been created which year after year has brought the subject freshly and pleasantly before the people.

II

The burdens of serving their society did not seem onerous to many American artists of the period. Indeed, to an astonishing degree, they found themselves comfortable with the charge. One such notable artist was the sculptor Horatio Greenough. Born in Boston in 1805, he was actually the first American to devote all his energies to sculpture. After graduating from Harvard in 1824, he studied in Rome, and then went to Florence, where he spent most of his later years. But his residence abroad did not in the least diminish his enthusiasm for an American art form. He executed an enormous statue of George Washington for the Capitol rotunda, and another piece for one of its entranceways. In 1851, a year before his death, he wrote a memoir of his life in art, giving clear expression to his national sentiments.

EXPERIENCES OF A YANKEE STONECUTTER, 1852

HORATIO GREENOUGH

The susceptibility, the tastes, and the genius which enable a people to enjoy the fine arts, and to excel in them, have been denied to the Anglo-Americans, not only by European talkers, but by European thinkers. The assertion of our obtuseness and inefficiency in this respect has been ignorantly and presumptuously set forth by some persons, merely to fill

In *Travels, Observations, and Experiences of a Yankee Stonecutter*, by Horatio Greenough (Boston, 1852), pp. 116–20, 122–26.

up the measure of our condemnation. Others have arrived at the same conclusions after examining our political and social character, after investigating our exploits and testing our capacities. They admit that we trade with enterprise and skill, that we build ships cunningly and sail them well, that we have a quick and far-sighted apprehension of the value of a territory, that we make wholesome homespun laws for its government, and that we fight hard when molested in any of these homely exercises of our ability; but they assert that there is a stubborn, antipoetical tendency in all that we do, or say, or think; they attribute our very excellence in the ordinary business of life to causes which must prevent our development as artists.

Enjoying the accumulated result of the thought and labor of centuries, Europe has witnessed our struggles with the hardships of an untamed continent, and the disadvantages of colonial relations, with but a partial appreciation of what we aim at, with but an imperfect knowledge of what we have done. Seeing us intently occupied during several generations in felling forests, in building towns, and constructing roads, she thence formed a theory that we are good for nothing except these pioneer efforts. She taunted us, because there were no statues or frescoes in our log cabins; she pronounced us unmusical, because we did not sit down in the swamp with an Indian on one side, and a rattlesnake on the other, to play the violin. That she should triumph over the deficiencies of a people who had set the example of revolt and republicanism was natural; but the reason which she assigned for those deficiencies was not the true reason. She argued with the depth and the sagacity of a philosopher who should conclude, from seeing an infant imbibe with eagerness its first aliment, that its whole life would be occupied in similar absorption.

It is true that before the Declaration of Independence Copley had in Boston formed a style of portrait which filled Sir Joshua Reynolds with astonishment; and that West, breaking through the bar of Quaker prohibition, and conquering the prejudice against a provincial aspirant, had taken a high rank in the highest walk of art in London. Stuart, Trumbull, Allston, Morse, Leslie, Newton followed in quick succession, while Vanderlyn won golden opinions at Rome, and bore away high honors at Paris. That England, with these facts before her, should have accused us of obtuseness in regard to art, and that we should have pleaded guilty to the charge, furnishes the strongest proof of her disposition to underrate our intellectual powers, and of our own ultra docility and want of self-reliance.

Artists have arisen in numbers; the public gives its attention to their productions; their labors are liberally rewarded. It seems now admitted that wealth and cultivation are destined to yield in America the same fruits that they have given in Italy, in Spain, in France, Germany, and England. It seems now admitted that there is no anomalous defect in our mental endowments; that the same powers displayed in clearing the forest and tilling the farm will trim the garden. It seems clear that we are destined to have a school of art. It becomes a matter of importance to decide how the youth who devote themselves to these studies are to acquire the rudiments of imitation, and what influences are to be made to act upon them. This question seemed at one time to have been decided. The friends of Art in America looked to Europe for an example, and with the natural assumption that experience had made the old world wise in what relates to the fine arts, determined upon forming academies as the more refined nations of the continent have ended by doing. We might as well have proposed a national church establishment. That the youth must be taught is clear—but in framing an institution for that object, if we look to countries grown old in European systems, it must be for warning rather than example.

The above reflections have been drawn from us by the oft-repeated expressions of regret which we have listened to, "that from the constitution of our society, and the nature of our institutions, no influences can be brought to bear upon art with the vivifying power of court patronage." We fully and firmly believe that these institutions are more favorable to a natural, healthful growth of art than any hotbed culture whatever. We cannot—as did Napoleon—make, by a few imperial edicts, an army of battle painters, a hierarchy of drum-and-fife glorifiers. Nor can we, in the lifetime of an individual, so stimulate this branch of culture, so unduly and disproportionately endow it, as to make a Walhalla start from a republican soil. The monuments, the pictures, the statues of the republic will represent what the people love and wish for—not what they can be made to accept, not how much taxation they will bear.

III

The social function of art was no less attractive a theme for the most talented painter in antebellum America, Thomas Cole. Cole (1801– 1848) was the founder and leading spirit of the Hudson River School, that group of artists who made the dramatic scenery of northern and western New York the focus of their painting. As Cole insisted, the choice of these rough and dramatic scenes was important for two reasons: first, it would focus Americans' attention on the sublime and beautiful, somehow making them more refined and less aggressive in their mutual dealings. Second, and no less important, this scenery was so appealing and attractive that it served to answer those European critics who argued that nothing of real value existed in this New World worthy of an artist's attention. Cole's statement clearly reflects both the social and patriotic concerns of the artists of the period.

ESSAY ON AMERICAN SCENERY, 1836

THOMAS COLE

The essay which is here offered is a mere sketch of an almost illimitable subject—American scenery. It is a subject that to every American ought to be of surpassing interest; for, whether he beholds the Hudson ming-

In *The American Monthly Magazine*, 1 (1836): 1–12.

ling waters with the Atlantic, explores the central wilds of this vast continent, or stands on the margin of the distant Oregon, he is still in the midst of American scenery—it is his own land; its beauty, its magnificence, its sublimity—all are his; and how undeserving of such a birthright, if he can turn toward it an unobserving eye, an unaffected heart!

The spirit of our society is to contrive but not to enjoy—toiling to produce more toil—accumulating in order to aggrandize. The pleasures of the imagination, among which the love of scenery holds a conspicuous place, will alone temper the harshness of such a state; and, like the atmosphere that softens the most rugged forms of the landscape, cast a veil of tender beauty over the asperities of life.

There are those who through ignorance or prejudice strive to maintain that American scenery possesses little that is interesting or truly beautiful—that it is rude without picturesqueness, and monotonous without sublimity—that being destitute of those vestiges of antiquity whose associations so strongly affect the mind, it may not be compared with European scenery. But from whom do these opinions come? From those who have read of European scenery, of Grecian mountains, and Italian skies, and never troubled themselves to look at their own; and from those traveled ones whose eyes were never opened to the beauties of nature until they beheld foreign lands, and when those lands faded from the sight were again closed and forever; disdaining to destroy their transatlantic impressions by the observation of the less fashionable and unfamed American scenery. Let such persons shut themselves up in their narrow shell of prejudice—I hope they are few—and the community increasing in intelligence will know better how to appreciate the treasures of their own country.

A very few generations have passed away since this vast tract of the American continent, now the United States, rested in the shadow of primeval forests, whose gloom was peopled by savage beasts and scarcely less savage men; or lay in those wide grassy plains called prairies. And, although an enlightened and increasing people have broken in upon the solitude, and with activity and power wrought changes that seem magical, yet the most distinctive, and perhaps the most impressive, characteristic of American scenery is its wildness.

It is the most distinctive because in civilized Europe the primitive features of scenery have long since been destroyed or modified—the extensive forests that once overshadowed a great part of it have been felled, rugged mountains have been smoothed, and the once tangled wood is now a grassy lawn; the turbulent brook a navigable stream, crags that could not be removed have been crowned with towers, and the rudest valleys tamed by the plough.

And to this cultivated state our western world is fast approaching; but nature is still predominant, and there are those who regret that with the improvements of cultivation the sublimity of the wilderness should pass away; for those scenes of solitude from which the hand of nature has never been lifted affect the mind with a more deep-toned emotion than aught which the hand of man has touched. Amid them the consequent associations are of God the Creator—they are His undefiled works, and the mind is cast into the contemplation of eternal things.

I will now venture a few remarks on what has been considered a grand defect in American scenery—the want of associations such as arise amid the scenes of the old world. He who stands on Mont Albano and looks down on ancient Rome has his mind peopled with the gigantic associations of the storied past; but he who stands on the mounds of the West, the most venerable remains of American antiquity, *may* experience the emotion of the sublime, but it is the sublimity of a shoreless ocean un-islanded by the recorded deeds of man.

Yet American scenes are not destitute of historical and legendary associations—the great struggle for freedom has sanctified many a spot, and many a mountain, stream, and rock has its legend, worthy of poet's pen or the painter's pencil. But American associations are not so much of the past as of the present and the future. Seated on a pleasant knoll, look down into the bosom of that secluded valley, begirt with wooded hills. You see no ruined tower to tell of outrage, no gorgeous temple to speak of ostentation; but freedom's offspring—peace, security, and happiness—dwell there, the spirits of the scene. On the margin of that gentle river the village girls may ramble unmolested, and the glad schoolboy, with hook and line, pass his bright holiday; those neat dwellings, unpretending to magnificence, are the abodes of plenty, virtue, and refinement. And in looking over the yet uncultivated scene, the mind's eye may see far into futurity. Where the wolf roams, the plough shall glisten; on the gray crag shall rise temple and tower— mighty deeds shall be done in the now pathless wilderness; and poets yet unborn shall sanctify the soil.

Yet I cannot but express my sorrow that the beauty of such landscapes are quickly passing away—the ravages of the ax are daily increasing—the most noble scenes are made desolate, and oftentimes with a wantonness and barbarism scarcely credible in a civilized nation. The wayside is becoming shadeless, and another generation will behold spots, now rife with beauty, desecrated by what is called improvement; which, as yet, generally destroys Nature's beauty without substituting that of Art. This is a regret rather than a complaint; such is the road society has to travel; it may lead to refinement in the end, but the traveler who sees the place of rest close at hand dislikes the road that has so many unnecessary windings.

I will now conclude, in the hope that the importance of cultivating a taste for scenery will not be forgotten. Nature has spread for us a rich and delightful banquet. Shall we turn from it? We are still in Eden; the wall that shuts us out of the garden is our own ignorance and folly.

IV

Probably the most perceptive and widely read art critic in mid-nine-teenth-century America was James Jackson Jarvis. A noted collector of art, Jarvis skillfully and persuasively helped to define the role of art and the artist in American society. For Jarvis, too, the link between esthetics and social order was at the heart of what he called the "art idea." As he put it, "We cannot make the world more beautiful without making it better, morally and socially."

THE ART IDEA, 1864

JAMES JACKSON JARVIS

The chief expressions in America of the art idea, under the forms of painting, sculpture, and architecture, traced to their present condition, we perceive a steady, and of late a rapid advance of each in quality and variety, showing that the unfolding of the art idea bears fruit in objects of taste and beauty, suited to all degrees of knowledge and feeling. Art, like nature, adds so much to enjoyment, and in such manifold ways, that we do not recognize the full extent of our obligations to her. But what she has done is as nothing compared with her power in reserve. Every good picture, statue, or bit of architecture is one more joy for the human race. We perceive that as a people or as individuals, it is a duty incumbent on all, in the interests of civilization, to make life as lovely as possible in manners, dress, and buildings; to adorn our homes, streets, and public places; in short, to infuse beauty by the aid of art into all objects, and to make unceasing war upon whatever deforms and debases, or tends to ugliness and coarseness.

We cannot make the world more beautiful without making it better, morally and socially. The art idea is the beautifier, an angel messenger of glad tidings to every receptive mind. Upward of four million visitors enjoyed Central Park, New York, the last year. We cite the park as an example of the carrying out of the art idea because, beside a barren site, it owes nothing to nature. Art here has done everything, even to

In *The Art Idea: Sculpture, Paintings, and Architecture in America,* by James Jackson Jarvis (New York, 1864). Reprint edition (Cambridge, Mass., 1960), pp. 247–53, 262–63, 266–67, 270–71.

nursing and training nature herself. An institution like this, combining art, science, and nature in harmonious unity, is a great free school for the people, of broader value than mere grammar schools; for, besides affording pleasing ideas and useful facts, it elevates and refines the popular mind by bringing it in intimate contact with the true and beautiful under circumstances conducive to happiness and physical well-being. What matter if it should cost a score of millions of money? Is it not so much saved from prisons, priests, police, and physicians? By it bodies are temporarily rescued from dirt and misery, and opportunities given the eye to look up to the clear vault of heaven, and take into the mind the healing significance of nature and art. In many it awakens the first consciousness of their spiritual birthright. To all it operates as a magnetic charm of decent behavior, giving salutary lessons in order, discipline, and comeliness, culminating in mutual goodwill and a better understanding of humanity at large, from its democratic intermingling of all classes, under quickening, many-sided, various refinements and delights. It is, too, a far cheaper amusement for the million than theaters, not to speak of the exchange of foul air for pure, noxious gaslight for health-giving sunlight, dubious morality and nerve-exhausting incitements for glorious music, invigorating games, boating, and exercise, the humanizing sight of merry childhood, the zoological and horticultural gardens.

In one direction we have already gone far enough. Anglo-Saxons, in their one-sided idea of home, are becoming selfish and unpatriotic. A home is a nursery and safeguard of domestic virtue, a protection of individuality, lest it be merged entirely into the mass. But man's selfhood being asserted and trained, he owes allegiance to the community. Home

is indeed the primary school of life and the sanctuary of its affections. As such it should be jealously guarded. We would make it as sacred in spirit as the holy of holies of the Temple itself. But any virtue pushed to excess becomes a vice. An American home has become something more than its original intent. It distracts the individual too much from mankind at large; tempts him to center therein wealth, luxury, and every conceivable stimulus of personal ease, pride, and display. The tendency is to narrow his humanity by putting it under bonds to vanity and selfishness. The family is made an excuse for neglecting the responsibilities of citizenship. As with trade, short-sighted, he forgets that the welfare of the neighbor in the code of Christian ethics is put upon the par with one's own, and that as he neglects it, the state drifts toward anarchy and turmoil. New Yorkers make too much money to care whether their city is given over or not to scoundrelism. They pay a blackmail to villainy, in order to shirk their duties as citizens and patriots, to make money as traders, or luxuriate as heads of fashionable families. Easy enough to see where this will end. Riots are the legitimate results. Home or business, viewed from the point of view of selfishness, becomes a curse instead of a blessing.

If we could expand the low-toned rivalry of individuals for wealth and power into a generous competition of cities and states in the growth of public institutions and the founding of parks, galleries of science and art, libraries, fine taste in architecture, schools of ideas, and whatever dignifies and advances human nature morally, intellectually, and esthetically, individuals competing with one another to be associated in noble enterprises with the same zeal and lavish expenditure they now devote to excel in costly houses, equipages, dress, and the gratification of appetites, we should shortly see the true golden age dawn. We are no illusionist. We do not look for this tomorrow, or the day after. But there are young minds to be formed on nobler ideas than have yet largely obtained. We are earnest in our advocacy of a larger measure of public spirit; of a collective local pride, and rivalry in good works; of the diminution of the selfishness of the home feeling by the substitution of a more generous sentiment, expanding love of the individual into a love of the people.

The inquiry now arises by what means, in America, may the knowledge and appreciation of art be best promoted?

The first duty of art, as we have already intimated, is to make our public buildings and places as instructive and enjoyable as possible. They should be pleasurable, full of attractive beauty and eloquent teachings. Picturesque groupings of natural objects, architectural surprises, sermons from the sculptor's chisel and painter's palette, the ravishment of the soul by its superior senses, the refinement of mind and body by the sympathetic power of beauty—these are a portion of the means which a due estimation of art as an element of civilization inspires the ruling will to provide freely for all. If art be kept a rare and tabooed thing, a specialty for the rich and powerful, it excites in the vulgar mind envy and hate. But proffer it freely to the public, and the public soon learns to delight in and protect it as its rightful inheritance. It also tends to develop a brotherhood of thought and feeling. During the civil strifes of Italy art flourished and was respected. Indeed, to some extent it operated as a sort of peace society, and was held sacred when nothing else was. Even rude soldiers, amid the perils and necessities of sieges, turned aside destruction from the walls that sheltered it. The history of art is full of records of its power to soften and elevate the human heart.

The desire for art being awakened, museums to illustrate its technical and historical progress, and galleries to exhibit its master-works, become indispensable. The most common means of popularizing art and cultivating a general taste is by galleries or museums. But even in Europe these have been only quite recently established.

To stimulate the art feeling, it is requisite that our public should have free access to museums, or galleries, in which shall be exhibited, in chronological series, specimens of the art of all nations and schools, including our own, arranged according to their motives and the special influences that attended their development. After this manner a mental and artistic history of the world may be spread out like a chart before the student, while the artist, with equal facility, can trace up to their origin the varied methods, styles, and excellences of each prominent epoch. A museum of art is a perpetual feast of the most intense and refined enjoyment to everyone capable of entering into its phases of thought and execution, and of analyzing its external and internal being and tracing the mysterious transformations of spirit into form.

Connected with it there might be schools of design for studying the nude figure, antique casts, and modern works. Also, for improvement in ornamental manufacture, the development of architecture, and whatever aids to refine and give beauty to social life.

Were we to wait long enough, fashion and interest here, as in England, would provide galleries and means of instruction in art for the people. But the spirit which animates such efforts is in the main ego-tistical. Better is it by far that the people act for themselves, supplying their own demands for esthetic enjoyment. Surely, the means already exist among us for beginning institutions which could in time grow to be the people's pride.

For immediate wants it would be sufficient to provide a suitable locality where such wealth of art as we possess could be got together in orderly shape. As the people grow into an appreciation of the value of art institutions, they will as freely provide for their permanent support and growth, either by private liberality or state aid, as they now do for more common education. That America possesses the population calculated to sustain and enjoy such institutions we have evidence in the progressively increasing interest awakened by every fresh appeal to its intellect and taste.

V

The federal buildings in Washington, D.C. provided some of the first opportunities for public sponsorship of artistic endeavors. Not surprisingly, Congress, in the role of patron, had very fixed ideas

*on the proper subject matter for decorating a government struc-
ture, and they did not invariably coincide with the particular
ambitions of the artist. One such conflict is described in the
correspondence of Washington Allston, one of the leading painters
of this period, and G. C. Verplanck, a New York congressman. Not
all artists, it is clear, flourished under a system in which art was
to serve the nation.*

THE LETTERS OF WASHINGTON ALLSTON, 1830–1832

From Allston to Verplanck

Cambridge, Mass., March 1, 1830

My Dear Sir:

I did not get your letter of the seventeenth until the night before
last and I shall endeavor to answer it in a businesslike manner.

I thank you for this additional instance of the friendship with
which you honor me. And yet I fear there are certain formidable,
and to my present apprehension, insurmountable obstacles to my
profiting by your kindness. The subjects from which I am to choose,
you say, are limited to American history. The most prominent of these,
indeed the only ones that occur to me, are in our military and naval
achievements. Herein lies my difficulty. I know that I have not any
talent for battlepieces; and, perhaps, because they have always appeared
to me, from their very nature, incapable of being justly represented,
for, to say nothing of the ominous prelude of silent emotion, when you
take away the excessive movement, the dash of arms, the deadly roll
of the drum, the blast of the trumpet, and the still more fearful din of
human thunder, giving a terrific life to the whole—and all this must
be taken from the painter—what is there left for his canvas?

Such being my opinion, you will easily believe that I could have
no hope of succeeding in subjects of this nature. Indeed I know from
past experience that I must fail when the subject is not of myself, that
is, in relation to the powers of my art, essentially exciting. In a pecuniary
view it has been, perhaps, my misfortune to have inherited a patrimony,
since it has lasted only just long enough to allow my mind to take its
own course till its habits of thought had become rigid and too fixed to
be changed when change was desirable. As an artist I cannot, in spite
of many troubles, regret this freedom of action, since I feel of such that
I owe to it whatever professional skill I may possess. But of late years,
since the source of this liberty has been dried up, and the cold current
of necessity has sprung up in its stead, I have sometimes, as a man,
almost felt the possession to have been a misfortune, for necessity,
I find, has no inspiration; she has not with me even the forcing power.

I trust you know me too well to doubt my patriotism because I
cannot be inspired to paint an American battle. I yield in love of country

In *The Life and Letters of Washington Allston,* ed. Jared B. Flagg (New York, 1922), pp. 230–39, 254–58.

to no man; no one has gloried more in the success of her arms, or more sincerely honored the gallant spirits whose victories have given her a name among nations. But they need not my pencil to make their deeds known to posterity.

But may there not be some eligible subject in our civil history? For myself I can think of none that would make a picture; of none, at least, that belongs to high art. But such a subject might possibly have occurred to you. If so, and I find it one from which I can make such a picture as you would have me paint, both for my own credit and that of the nation, be assured I will most gladly undertake it.

There is another class of subject, however, in which, were I permitted to choose from it, I should find exciting matter enough, and more than enough, for my imperfect skill, that is, from Scripture. But I fear this is a forlorn hope. Yet why should it be? This is a Christian land, and the Scriptures belong to no country, but to man. Should the government allow me to select a subject from them, I need not say with what delight I should accept the commission. With such a source of inspiration and the glory of painting for my country, if there be anything in me, it must come out. Would it might be so! But let us suppose it. Well, supposing such a commission given, there's a subject already composed *in petto*, which I have long intended to paint as soon as I am at liberty—the three Marys at the tomb of the Savior, the angel sitting on a stone before the mouth of the sepulcher. I consider this one of my happiest conceptions. I see now before me; I wish I could see them on the walls at Washington.

Now as to the price, should such a dream, I will not call it hope, be realized, it would be eight thousand dollars, which I believe was the price given to Colonel Trumbull for each of his pictures. I should not indeed refuse ten thousand, should Uncle Sam take the generous fit upon him to offer it; but eight is my price for that particular composition, which would consist of four figures, seven feet high; the picture itself (an upright) twelve or thirteen feet high and ten or twelve wide.

Pray do not let any part of this letter get into print. I beg you will not think from anything I have said that I intent any disrespect to the painters of battles. There are many of deserved reputation which show great skill in their authors; it would be unjust not to mention, as holding the very first rank, Mr. West's "Wolf," and the "Death of Warren and Montgomery," and the "Sortie," by Colonel Trumbull.

Ever most truly yours,

W. Allston

From Verplanck to Allston

Washington, March 9, 1830

My Dear Sir:

Your letter only convinces me the more that we must, if we can, have one specimen of "high art" on the wall of the Capitol. By American history mere revolutionary history is not meant. To Scripture I fear we cannot go in the present state of public opinion and taste. But does our anterevolutionary history present no subject? The "Landing of the

Pilgrims," a threadbare subject in some respects, has never been viewed with a poet's and painter's eye. What think you of that, or of any similar subject in our early history? Your townsman, Dr. Holmes, has recently published a very useful, though not important, book of "Annals." A hasty glance over the first volume of this would perhaps suggest some idea. If not, I still fall back upon the "Pilgrims."

Yours truly,
G. C. Verplanck

From Allston to Verplanck

Cambridgeport, March 29, 1830

My Dear Sir:

Your letter duly come to hand; as you full well know that I cannot be insensible to such persevering kindness I will not trouble you with a repetition of thanks, but proceed to answer them in as businesslike a way as I can.

To the first subject you propose, "The Landing of the Pilgrims" (not unpicturesque), I have a personal objection. It has already been painted by an old friend of mine, Colonel Sargent, a high-minded, honorable man, to whom I would on no account give pain; which I could not avoid doing were I to encroach on what, at the expense of several years' labor, he has a fair right to consider his ground.

I will not trouble you with my objections to the other subject, the "Leave-taking of Washington," lest I have no room for one of my own choosing, which I should be glad to have you approve, namely: "The First Interview of Columbus with Ferdinand and Isabella" at court after the discovery of America, accompanied by natives, and so forth, exhibited in evidence of his success. As you have read Irving's book it is unnecessary for me to describe the scene. Here is magnificence, emotion, and everything, the very truimph of "matter" to task a painter's powers. The announcement and the proof of the birth of a New World. This is not thought of now for the first time. I have long cherished it as one of the dreams which the future, if the future were spared to me, was one day to embody. But to business; the size of a picture from this would be not less than eighteen feet by twelve, perhaps twenty by fourteen; and the price fifteen thousand dollars. As to its class, I know not what subject could be said more emphatically to belong to America and her history than the triumph of her discoverer. We, who now enjoy the blessings of his discovery, cannot place him too high in that history which without him would never have been.

Faithfully yours,
W. Allston

From Verplanck to Allston

House of Representatives, May 29, 1830

My Dear Sir:

We (that is our Committee) had determined to try the taste and liberality of Congress by recommending an appropriation for a picture from you on your terms and choice, restricting you only to American history, in which Columbus would, of course, be included; but, unfortunately, for the present our bill for the improvement of the public buildings has been crowded out by the press of other business, and must lie over till next winter.

Though our proposed alterations in the buildings are important both to comfort and taste, there was nothing pressing in the bill now passing, and I only regret the delay on your account. Next winter we shall have the opportunity of taking up the bill early, and I hope with better success. But the extent to which Congress will go in these matters depends much on accidental circumstances.

Allston to Cogdell [Allston's Later Thoughts on the Incident]

Cambridgeport, February 27, 1832

Dear Cogdell:

It gives me great pleasure that I can bestow sincere praise on your group of Hagar and Ishmael. It is decidedly your best work, and much exceeds what I had expected; it really does you great honor. And though it has many faults, they are by no means of a kind to outweigh its merits. The attitudes of both mother and child are well conceived, and they group well together. But its chief merit lies in the general conception and the expression, which are certainly the principal points in a work of art. It has indeed great power of expression.

Now, after this praise, will you allow me, my friend, to say a few words of a prudential nature. Do not let it tempt you to give up a certainty for an uncertainty. I say this because my nephew informs me that when he left Carolina, you talked, as he had heard, of going to Italy, to make art your profession; if so, you must of course give up your office at the Customhouse, which, if I understand you aright, is now your principal means of support. What I am about to say, however, I do not give in the shape of advice; for I as much dislike giving advice as asking it. I shall merely express my opinion on the subject, leaving you to weigh it as you think fit, and to decide for yourself.

If by making the art your profession you are to depend on it as the means of support for yourself and family, I cannot but think that you look to a very precarious source. What may be the prospects of employment from private individuals you can judge as well as I, and I no better than you, for I can have no definite knowledge as to it unless I were myself a sculptor. It has often, however, been doubted by Greenough's friends here, notwithstanding the high and general estimation in which he stands as well for his private character as for his talents, whether he will be able to support himself in Boston from private employment alone. And if Boston cannot afford him sufficient, I know not in what other city of the Union he can expect it. His resource, they think, must be at Washington, in works for the government, or in Europe. Indeed, it seems to be the opinion of most persons that employment for the general government is the only hope for a sculptor who is to live by his profession in our country. And whether it is that people have been but little accustomed to it, or from some

other cause, so far as I have observed, the interest taken in sculpture
is by no means so general as that taken in pictures. Then the prices
which a sculptor must charge, even to defray his expenses, are such as
very few in our country are either able or willing to give for works of
art. So I do not see much prospect even of a bare support, unless he is
content to confine himself to busts that are portraits. But even supposing there were sufficient demand for sculpture, are you prepared to
coin your brain for bread—at all times and under all circumstances, of
depression, of illness, and the numberless harassments of unavoidable
debt? To produce an original work of the imagination, requiring of all
human efforts a pleasurable state of the mind, with a dunning letter
staring you in the face? With an honest heart yearning to give everyone
his due, and an empty purse, I know from bitter experience that the
fairest visions of the imagination vanish like dreams never to be
recalled, before the daylight reality of such a visitor. Poverty is no doubt
a stimulus to general industry, and to many kinds of mental effort, but
not to the imagination; for the imagination must be abortive—is a
nonentity—if it have not peace as its immediate condition. Pictures that
would have otherwise brought me hundreds, not to say thousands, have
crumbled into nothing under its pressure, and been thrown aside as
nothing worth. I say these things not querulously but that you might
know what it is to be an artist by profession, with no other income than
the product of the brain—which, to be at all available, must at least
be at peace. And I give them in their naked reality solely from a conscientious regard for your peace and happiness as a man. The love I
bear my art you well know; no one could love it more. And yet, with
all this love, which I still bear it, I thus speak of it as a profession.
Because I must speak the truth. But, understand me, when I speak of it
thus as a profession, it is when that profession is associated with
poverty.

Your office allows you, I suppose, the half of each day to yourself,
and secures to you the means of devoting one half of the year to the
pursuit of the art, in the way you like best, and independent of the
world. Ah, that word independent has a charm which I well know how
to value, from having known its reverse. But I still have hope, and I
look for repossession of it yet.

VI

Few military events were as famous in the United States as the Revolu-
tionary War battle at Bunker Hill, and it is not surprising that one
of the first proposed memorials was to commemorate this incident.
In 1824 a group of New Englanders, including Daniel Webster
and Edward Everett, tried to raise funds from the public for this
enterprise, and the following solicitation vividly captures the early
ideology of monument building.

THE BUNKER HILL MONUMENT ASSOCIATION, 1824

Fifty years have now nearly elapsed since the curtain rose on this momentous scene of our national drama, the battle of the seventeenth of June 1775. This long period has laid down in the soil which they combined to liberate most of the high-minded men who raised their hands or their voices in those trying times. A few only remain, the venerable witnesses of what we may do to show our gratitude toward those to whom we owe all "that makes it life to live," our liberty. The presence of these few Revolutionary patriots and heroes among us seems to give a peculiar character to this generation. It binds us by an affecting association to the momentous days, the searching trials, the sacrifices, and dangers, to which they were called. The feeble hands and gray hairs of those who, before we were living, faced death, that we, their children, might be born free, are a sight which this generation ought not to behold without emotion; a sight which calls upon us not to delay those public expressions of gratitude which soon will be too late for those we would most wish to honor.

Now, in the days of our independence, of our prosperity, of our growing internal wealth, of our participation in all the world's commerce, of our enjoyment of everything which can make a people happy, we ought to remember the sacrifices and losses of our fathers. No grateful mind can, from the fruits of this unexampled welfare, refuse to bestow a trifle upon a work proposed as a decent and becoming tribute to the memory of the great and good men to whose disinterestedness in putting to hazard their property and lives we owe our being, our rights, our property, our all.

The spot itself on which this memorable action took place is extremely favorable for becoming the site of a monumental structure. Competent judges have pronounced the heights of Charlestown to excel any spot on our coast, in their adaptation to the object in view. Their position, with the expanse of the harbor of Boston, and its beautiful islands in front, has long attracted the notice of the stranger. An elevated monument on this spot would be the first landmark of the mariner in his approach to our harbor; while the whole neighboring country, with their rich fields, villages, and spires, the buildings of the university, the bridges, the numerous ornamental country seats and improved plantations would be spread out as in a picture, to the eye of the spectator on the summit of the proposed structure.

Nor are these the only natural advantages of the spot. Though essentially rural in many of its features, it rises above one of our most flourishing towns, the seat of several important national establishments, where the noble ships of war of the American republic seem to guard the approach to the spot where her first martyrs fought and bled. Its immediate vicinity to Boston, and its convenient distance from Salem,

In *The History of the Bunker Hill Monument Association*, by George Washington Warren (Boston, 1877), pp. 112–13, 116–17.

makes the access to it direct from the centers of our most numerous, wealthy, and active populations, and will be the means of keeping continually in sight, or bringing frequently to view, to the great masses of the community, the imposing memorial of an event which ought never to be absent from their memory, as its effects are daily and hourly brought home to the business and bosoms of every American citizen.

In forming an estimate of the cost of the structure proposed, a single eye has been had to the principle which dictates its erection. Everything separated from the idea of substantial strength and severe taste has been discarded, as foreign from the grace and serious character both of the men and events to be commemorated. With this principle in view, it has been ascertained that a monumental column, of a classic model, with an elevation to make it the most lofty in the world, may be erected of our fine Chelmsford granite for about thirty-seven thousand dollars.

The general propriety and expediency of erecting public monuments of the kind proposed are acknowledged by all. They form not only the most conspicuous ornaments with which we can adorn our towns and high places, but they are the best proof we can exhibit to strangers that our sensibility is strong and animated toward those great achievements and greater characters to which we owe all our national blessings. There surely is not one among us who would not experience a strong satisfaction in conducting a stranger to the foot of a monumental structure rising in decent majesty on this memorable spot.

Works of this kind also have the happiest influence in exciting and nourishing the national and patriotic sentiment. Our government has been called, and truly is a government of opinion; but it is one of sentiment still more. It is not the judgment only of this people, which dictates a preference for our institutions, but it is a strong, deep-seated, inborn sentiment; a feeling, a passion for liberty. It is a becoming expression of this sentiment to honor, in every way, the memories and characters of our fathers; to adorn a spot where their noble blood was spilt, and not surrender it uncared for to the plough. Years, it is to be remembered, are rapidly passing away; and the glorious traditions of our national emancipation which we received from them will descend more faintly to our successors. The patriotic sentiment which binds us together more strongly than compacts or constitutions will, if permitted, grow cold from mere lapse of time. We owe these monuments, therefore, not less to the character of our posterity than to the memory of our fathers. These events must not lose their interest. Our children and our children's children have a right to these feelings, cherished and kept by a worthy transmission. It is the order of nature that the generation to achieve nobly should be succeeded by a generation worthily to record and gratefully to commemorate. We are not called to the fire and the sword; to meet the appalling array of armies, to taste the bitter cup of imperial wrath and vengeance proffered to an ill-provided land. We are chosen for the easier, more grateful, but not less bound duty of commemorating and honoring the labors, sacrifices, and sufferings of the great men of those dark times.

There is one point of view in which we seem to be strongly called upon to engage in the erection of works like that proposed. The beautiful and noble arts of design and architecture have hitherto been engaged in arbitrary and despotic service. The pyramids and obelisks of Egypt, the monumental columns of Trajan and Aurelius have paid no tribute to the rights and feelings of man. Majestic and graceful as they are, they have no record but that of sovereignty, sometimes cruel and tyrannical, and sometimes mild; but never that of a great, enlightened, and generous people. Providence, which has given us the senses to observe, the taste to admire, and the skill to execute these beautiful works of art, cannot have intended that, in a flourishing nation of freemen, there should be no scope for their erection. Our fellow-citizens of Baltimore have set us a noble example of redeeming the arts to the cause of free institutions, in the imposing monument they have erected to the memory of those who fell in defending their city. If we cannot be the first to set up a structure of this character, let us not be other than the first to improve upon the example; to arrest and fix the feelings of our generation on the important events of an earlier and more momentous struggle; and to redeem the pledge of gratitude to the high-souled heroes of that trying day.

For a work calculated to appeal, without distinction, to every member of the community, we trust we need no apology for respectfully soliciting your cooperation and interest. The monument must be erected by the union of all the classes and members of society, and the smallest assistance, by contribution or encouragement, will aid in the great design.

Daniel Webster,	Jesse Putnam,
H. A. S. Dearborn,	Isaac P. Davis,
Benjamin Gorham,	Seth Knowles,
George Blake,	Edward Everett,
John C. Warren,	George Ticknor,
Samuel D. Harris,	Theodore Lyman, Jr.,
William Sullivan,	*Directors*

Edward Everett, {*Secretary of the Standing Committee of the Directors*

Chapter 10

Abolitionist Societies

BEGINNING IN THE 1830s and continuing up to the outbreak of the Civil War, ardent opponents of slavery organized themselves into societies to further their cause. Under the organizational network of these societies, they urged the abolition of slavery in the United States in public meetings, newspapers, pamphlets, and petitions. Their impact far outweighed their numbers. Indeed, the content of their message and the ways in which they spread it were so novel that the movement created a furor among contemporaries, and to this day has remained the subject of heated debate among historians.

The rhetoric of the abolitionists is in and of itself worth close scrutiny. Abolitionism was part of a large reform effort; those eager to improve the condition of slaves also devoted their efforts to uplifting other disadvantaged groups, namely women, the criminal, the poor, and the insane. Hence, to understand the causes behind the concern for the slave is to explore the motives of other reform efforts as well. What view of society did the abolitionists share? How did they understand the possibility of social change within the United States? What constituted for them an optimal social organization, and how did they set out to achieve it?

Moreover, the activities of the abolitionists have sparked a heated debate on the issue of whether or not these leaders were "fanatics." Many contemporaries, and later historians, too, insisted that the abolitionists did far more harm than good. By exciting the passions of the people, by whipping up public emotions, they made reasoned compromise impossible. The tragedy of the Civil War is laid at their feet. If not for their frenzied activities, sensible statesmanship could have amicably settled the issues dividing North and South. The abolitionists themselves and their defenders offer a far different interpretation. For them, the very notion of a fanatic for freedom is absurd. Rather, abolitionists were the keepers of the American conscience. Their activities made it impossible for the country to tolerate the moral disgrace that was slavery. Hence, any effort to understand the coming of the Civil War must focus on the merits of the abolitionist movement.

The activities of the abolitionist societies command attention for they were, in many ways, notably modern. Abolitionists were among the first groups in American society to employ all available means to mold public opinion. In this way, their efforts clarify for us the mechanisms that could be used in the early republic for purposes of persuasion, and to break the barriers of regional insularity.

Finally, the public's response to the abolitionists was so violent as to prompt a whole series of questions about the forces of order and disorder operating in antebellum society. Abolitionists' meetings were often broken up by force, their presses smashed, their lives threatened, and several of them were actually murdered—all this in Northern not Southern, communities. Why did a movement so essentially verbal in its approach provoke such incredibly hostile physical reactions? Why did antislavery words lead men to take to the streets? By exploring this phenomenon, the underlying tensions in American society during the period before the Civil War are revealed.

I

An especially articulate statement of the abolitionists' ideology appeared in the writings and speeches of Wendell Phillips. Born in Boston in 1811, Phillips first became interested in the movement when a mob attacked abolitionist William Lloyd Garrison in Boston in 1835. Soon Phillips was writing for Garrison's paper, The Liberator, *and addressing innumerable public meetings as well. He was also concerned with other causes. Before the Civil War it was women's rights, and after the war, worker's welfare. His speech, reprinted below, delivered in Boston in 1853 before a meeting of the Massachusetts Anti-Slavery Society, presents the abolitionist's response to critics who labeled them uncompromising fanatics on the slavery issue.*

THE PHILOSOPHY OF THE ABOLITION MOVEMENT, 1853

WENDELL PHILLIPS

I wish, Mr. Chairman, to notice some objections that have been made to our course ever since Mr. Garrison began his career, and which have been lately urged again. I know these objections have been made a thousand times, that they have been often answered. But there are times when justice to the slave will not allow us to be silent. There are many

In *Speeches, Lectures, and Letters,* by Wendell Phillips (Boston, 1863), pp. 98–100, 105–111, 126–27, 151–53.

in this country who have had their attention turned, recently, to the antislavery cause. They are asking, "Which is the best and most efficient method of helping it?" Engaged ourselves in an effort for the slave, which time has tested and success hitherto approved, we are very properly desirous that they should join us in our labors, and pour into this channel the full tide of their new zeal and great resources. Long experience gives us a right to advise. They are our spiritual children.

The charges to which I refer are these: that, in dealing with slaveholders and their apologists, we indulge in fierce denunciations, instead of appealing to their reason and common sense by plain statements and fair argument; that we might have won the sympathies and support of the nation if we would have submitted to argue this question with a manly patience; but, instead of this, we have outraged the feelings of the community by attacks, unjust and unnecessarily severe, on its most valued institutions, and gratified our spleen by indiscriminate abuse of leading men who were often honest in their intentions, however mistaken in their views; that we have utterly neglected the ample means that lay around us to convert the nation, submitted to no discipline, formed no plan, been guided by no foresight, but hurried on in childish, reckless, blind, and hot-headed zeal, bigots in the narrowness of our views, and fanatics in our blind fury of invective and malignant judgment of other men's motives. I reject with scorn all these implications that *our* judgments are uncharitable, that *we* are lacking in patience, that *we* have any other dependence than on the simple truth, spoken with Christian frankness, yet with Christian love.

I claim, before you who know the true state of the case, I claim for the antislavery movement with which this society is identified, that, looking back over its whole course, and considering the men connected with it in the mass, it has been marked by sound judgment, unerring foresight, the most sagacious adaptation of means to ends, the strictest self-discipline, the most thorough research, and an amount of patient and manly argument addressed to the conscience and intellect of the nation, such as no other cause of the kind, in England or this country, has ever offered.

We must plead guilty, if there be guilt in not knowing how to separate the sin from the sinner. With all the fondness for abstractions attributed to us, we are not yet capable of that. We are fighting a momentous battle at desperate odds—one against a thousand. Every weapon that ability or ignorance, wit, wealth, prejudice, or fashion can command, is pointed against us. The guns are shotted to their lips. The arrows are poisoned. Fighting against such an array, we cannot afford to confine ourselves to any one weapon. The cause is not ours, so that we might, rightfully, postpone or put in peril the victory by moderating our demands, stifling our convictions, or filing down our rebukes, to gratify any sickly taste of our own, or to spare the delicate nerves of our neighbor. Our clients are three millions of Christian slaves, standing dumb suppliants at the threshold of the Christian world. They have no voice but ours to utter their complaints, or to demand justice. The press, the pulpit, the wealth, the literature, the prejudices, the political arrangements, the present self-interest of the country are all against us. God has given us no weapon but the truth, faithfully uttered, and addressed, with the old prophets' directness, to the conscience of the individual sinner. The elements which control public opinion and mold the masses are against us. We can but pick off here and there a man from the triumphant majority. We have facts for those who think, arguments for those who reason; but he who cannot be reasoned out of his prejudices must be laughed out of them; he who cannot be argued out of his selfishness must be shamed out of it by the mirror of his hateful self held up relentlessly before his eyes. We live in a land where every man makes broad his phylactery, inscribing thereon, "All men are created equal," "God hath made of one blood all nations of men." It seems to us that in such a land there must be, on this question of slavery, sluggards to be awakened, as well as doubters to be convinced.

What is the denunciation with which we are charged? It is endeavoring, in our faltering human speech, to declare the enormity of the sin of making merchandise of men, of separating husband and wife, taking the infant from its mother, and selling the daughter to prostitution, of a professedly Christian nation denying, by statute, the Bible to every sixth man and woman of its population, and making it illegal for "two or three" to meet together, except a white man be present! What is this harsh criticism of motives with which we are charged? It is simply holding the intelligent and deliberate actor responsible for the character and consequences of his acts. Is there anything inherently wrong in such denunciation or such criticism? All that we ask the world and thoughtful men to note are the principles and deeds on which the American pulpit and American public men plume themselves.

The South is one great brothel, where half a million of women are flogged to prostitution or, worse still, are degraded to believe it honorable. The public squares of half our great cities echo to the wail of families torn asunder at the auction block; no one of our fair rivers that has not closed over the Negro seeking in death a refuge from a life too wretched to bear; thousands of fugitives skulk along our highways, afraid to tell their names, and trembling at the sight of a human being; free men are kidnapped in our streets, to be plunged into that hell of slavery; and now and then one, as if by miracle, after long years, returns to make men aghast with his tale. The press says, "It is all right"; and the pulpit cries, "Amen." They print the Bible in every tongue in which man utters his prayers; and get the money to do so by agreeing never to give the book, in the language our mothers taught us, to any Negro, free or bond, south of Mason and Dixon's line. The press says, "It is all right"; and the pulpit cries, "Amen."

Prove to me now that harsh rebuke, indignant denunciation, scathing sarcasm, and pitiless ridicule are wholly and always unjustifiable.

Our aim is to alter public opinion. Did we live in a market, our talk should be of dollars and cents, and we would seek to prove only that slavery was an unprofitable investment. Were the nation one great, pure church, we would sit down and reason of "righteousness, temperance, and judgment to come." Had slavery fortified itself in a college, we would load our cannons with cold facts, and wing our arrows with arguments. But we happen to live in the world—the world made up of thought and impulse, of self-conceit and self-interest, of weak men and wicked. To conquer, we must reach all. Our object is not to make every man a Christian or a philosopher, but to induce everyone to aid in the abolition of slavery. To change public opinion, we use the very tools by which it was formed. That is, all such an honest man may touch.

But there are some persons about us who pretend that the anti-slavery movement has been hitherto mere fanaticism, its only weapon angry abuse. My claim is this: that neither the charity of the most timid of sects, the sagacity of our wisest converts, nor the culture of the ripest scholars, though all have been aided by our twenty years' experience, has yet struck out any new method of reaching the public mind, or originated any new argument or train of thought or discovered any new fact bearing on the question.

We are charged with lacking foresight, and said to exaggerate. This charge of exaggeration brings to my mind a fact I mentioned, last month. The theaters in many of our large cities bring out, night after night, all the radical doctrines and all the startling scenes of "Uncle Tom." They preach immediate emancipation, and slaves shoot their hunters to loud applause. Two years ago, sitting in this hall, I was myself somewhat startled by the assertion of my friend Mr. Pillsbury, that the theaters would receive the gospel of antislavery truth earlier than the churches. A hiss went up from the galleries, and many in the audience were shocked by the remark. I asked myself whether I could endorse such a statement, and felt that I could not. I could not believe it to be true. Only two years have passed, and what was then deemed rant and fanaticism, by seven out of ten who heard it, has proved true. The theater, bowing to its audience, has preached immediate emancipation, and given us the whole of "Uncle Tom"; while the pulpit is either silent or hostile, and in the columns of the theological papers the work is subjected to criticism, to reproach, and its author to severe rebuke.

Every thoughtful and unprejudiced mind must see that such an evil as slavery will yield only to the most radical treatment. If you consider the work we have to do, you will not think us needlessly aggressive, or that we dig down unnecessarily deep in laying the foundations of our enterprise. A money power of two thousand millions of dollars, as the prices of slaves now range, held by a small body of able and desperate men; that body raised into a political aristocracy by special constitutional provisions; cotton, the product of slave labor, forming the basis of our whole foreign commerce, and the commercial class thus subsidized; the press bought up; the pulpit reduced to vassalage; the heart of the common people chilled by a bitter prejudice against the black race; our leading men bribed, by ambition, either to silence or open hostility—in such a land, on what shall an abolitionist rely? On a few cold prayers, mere lip service, and never from the heart? On a church resolution, hidden often in its records, and meant only as a decent cover for servility in daily practice? On political parties, with their superficial influence at best, and seeking ordinarily only to use existing prejudices to the best advantage? Slavery has deeper root here than any aristocratic institution has in Europe. How shall the stream rise above its fountain? Where shall our church organizations or parties get strength to attack their great parent and molder, the Slave Power? Mechanics say nothing but an earthquake, strong enough to move all Egypt, can bring down the pyramids.

Experience has confirmed these views. The abolitionists who have acted on them have a "short method" with all unbelievers. They have but to point to their own success, in contrast with every other man's failure. To waken the nation to its real state, and chain it to the consideration of this one duty, is half the work. So much we have done. Slavery has been made the question of this generation. To startle the South to madness, so that every step she takes, in her blindness, is one step more toward ruin, is much. This we have done. Witness Texas and the Fugitive Slave Law. To have elaborated for the nation the only plan of redemption, pointed out the only exodus from this "sea of troubles," is much. This we claim to have done in our motto of *Immediate, Unconditional Emancipation on the Soil*. The closer any statesmanlike mind looks into the question, the more favor our plan finds with it. The Christian asks fairly of the infidel, "If this religion be not from God, how do you explain its triumph, and the history of the first three centuries?" Our question is similar. If our agitation has not been wisely planned and conducted, explain for us the history of the last twenty years! Experience is a safe light to walk by, and he is not a rash man who expects success in future from the same means which have secured it in times past.

II

The work of the Grimké sisters Angelina and Sarah, on behalf of abolitionism demonstrates many of the favorite tactics of these organizations. Trained by Theodore Weld (who later became Angelina's husband), the sisters went out in the 1830s to address and organize women's auxiliaries. They soon grew famous, stimulating controversy not only about slavery but also about women's rights. The pamphlet below, composed by Angelina Grimké upon her conversion to abolitionism, was addressed specifically to the women of the South. It presents the ideas and the techniques that the sisters used in their efforts to influence public opinion.

APPEAL TO THE CHRISTIAN WOMEN OF THE SOUTH, 1836

ANGELINA GRIMKÉ

Respected Friends,

It is because I feel a deep and tender interest in your present and eternal welfare that I am willing thus publicly to address you. Some

In *The Anti-Slavery Examiner*, 1 (1836): 1–3, 16–20, 23–24, 26, 28–30, 32–33, 35–36.

of you have loved me as a relative, and some have felt bound to me in Christian sympathy, and gospel fellowship; and even when compelled by a strong sense of duty, to break those outward bonds of union which bound us together as members of the same community, you were generous enough to give me credit, for sincerity as a Christian, though you believed I had been most strangely deceived. I thanked you then for your kindness, and I ask you *now*, for the sake of former confidence, and former friendship, to read the following pages in the spirit of calm investigation and fervent prayer. I have felt for you at this time, when unwelcome light is pouring in upon the world on the subject of slavery, light which even Christians would exclude, if they could, from our country, or at any rate from the southern portion of it, I know that even professors of His name would, if they could, build a wall of adamant around the Southern states whose top might reach unto heaven, in order to shut out the light. But believe me, when I tell you, their attempts will be as utterly fruitless as were the efforts of the builders of Babel; and why? Because moral, like natural light, is so extremely subtle in its nature as to overleap all human barriers. All the excuses and palliations of this system must inevitably be swept away, just as other "refuges of lies" have been, by the irresistible torrent of a rectified public opinion. All that sophistry of argument which has been employed to prove that although it is sinful to send to Africa to procure men and women as slaves, who have never been in slavery, that still is not sinful to keep those in bondage who have come down by inheritance, will be utterly overthrown. We must come back to the good old doctrine of our forefathers who declared to the world, "this self evident truth that *all* men are created equal, and that they have certain *inalienable* rights among which are life, *liberty*, and the pursuit of happiness."

But after all, it may be said, our fathers were certainly mistaken, for the Bible sanctions slavery, and that is the highest authority. Now the Bible is my ultimate appeal in all matters of faith and practice, and it is to *this test* I am anxious to bring the subject at issue between us. Let us then begin with Adam and examine the charter of privileges which was given to him. "Have dominion over the fish of the sea, and over the fowl of the air, and over every living thing that moveth upon the earth." In this charter, although the different kinds of *irrational* beings are so particularly enumerated, and supreme dominion over *all of them* is granted, yet *man* is *never* vested with this dominion *over his fellowman;* he was never told that any of the human species were put *under his feet. Man* then, I assert *never* was put *under the feet of man*, by that first charter of human rights which was given by God.

But perhaps you will be ready to query, why appeal to *women* on this subject? *We* do not make the laws which perpetuate slavery. *No* legislative power is vested in *us; we* can do nothing to overthrow the system, even if we wished to do so. To this I reply, I know you do not make the laws, but I also know that *you are the wives and mothers, the sisters and daughters of those who do;* and if you really suppose *you* can do nothing to overthrow slavery, you are greatly mistaken. You can do much in every way: four things I will name. 1. You can read on this subject. 2. You can pray over this subject. 3. You can speak on this subject. 4. You can *act* on this subject. I have not placed reading before praying because I regard it more important, but because, in order to pray aright, we must understand what we are praying for; it is only then we can "pray with the understanding and the spirit also."

1. Read then on the subject of slavery. Search the Scriptures daily, whether the things I have told you are true. Other books and papers might be a great help to you in this investigation, but they are not necessary, and it is hardly probable that your committees of vigilance will allow you to have any other.

In the great mob in Boston, last autumn, when the books and papers of the Anti-Slavery Society were thrown out of the windows of their office, one individual laid hold of the Bible and was about tossing it out to the ground, when another reminded him that it was the Bible he had in his hand. *"O! 'tis all one,"* he replied, and out went the sacred volume, along with the rest. We thank him for the acknowledgment.

Read the *Bible* then, it contains the words of Jesus, and they are spirit and life. Judge for yourselves whether *he sanctioned* such a system of oppression and crime.

2. Pray over this subject. Pray to your Father, who seeth in secret, that He would open your eyes to see whether slavery is *sinful,* and if it is, that He would enable you to bear a faithful, open, and unshrinking testimony against it, and to do whatsoever your hands find to do, leaving the consequences entirely to Him. Pray also for the poor slave, that he may be kept patient and submissive under his hard lot, until God is pleased to open the door of freedom to him without violence or bloodshed. Pray too for the master that his heart may be softened.

3. Speak on this subject. It is through the tongue, the pen, and the press that truth is principally propagated. Speak then to your relatives, your friends, your acquaintances on the subject of slavery; be not afraid if you are conscientiously convinced it is *sinful,* to say so openly, but calmly, and to let your sentiments be known. If you are served by the slaves of others, try to ameliorate their condition as much as possible; never aggravate their faults, and thus add fuel to the fire of anger already kindled, in a master and mistress's bosom; remember their extreme ignorance, and consider them as your heavenly Father does the *less* culpable on this account, even when they do wrong things. Discountenance *all* cruelty to them, all starvation, all corporal chastisement; these may brutalize and *break* their spirits, but will never bend them to willing, cheerful obedience. If possible, see that they are comfortably and *seasonably* fed, whether in the house or the field; it is unreasonable and cruel to expect slaves to wait for their breakfast until eleven o'clock, when they rise at five or six. Do all you can to induce their owners to clothe them well, and to allow them many little indulgences which would contribute to their comfort. Above all, try to persuade your husband, father, brothers, and sons that *slavery is a crime against God and man,* and that it is a great sin to keep *human beings* in such abject ignorance; to deny them the privilege of learning to read and write.

4. Act on this subject. Some of you *own* slaves yourselves. If you believe slavery is *sinful,* set them at liberty. If they wish to remain with

you, pay them wages, if not let them leave you. Should they remain teach them, and have them taught the common branches of an English education.

But some of you will say, we can neither free our slaves nor teach them to read, for the laws of our state forbid it. Be not surprised when I say such wicked laws *ought to be no barrier* in the way of your duty, and I appeal to the Bible to prove this position. What was the conduct of Shiphrah and Pauh, when the king of Egypt issued his cruel mandate, with regard to the Hebrew children? *"They* feared *God*, and did *not* as the King of Egypt commanded them, but saved the men children alive." Did these *women* do right in disobeying that monarch?

What was the conduct of Daniel, when Darius made a firm decree that no one should ask a petition of any man or God for thirty days? Did the prophet cease to pray? No!

Did Daniel do right thus to *break* the law of his king? Let his wonderful deliverance out of the mouths of the lions answer.

But some of you may say, if we do free our slaves, they will be taken up and sold, therefore there will be no use in doing it. Peter and John might just as well have said, we will not preach the gospel, for if we do, we shall be taken up and put in prison, therefore there will be no use in our preaching. *Consequences*, my friends, belong no more to *you*, than they did to these apostles. Duty is ours and events are God's. If you think slavery is sinful, all *you* have to do is to set your slaves at liberty, do all you can to protect them, and in humble faith and fervent prayer, commend them to your common Father.

I know that this doctrine of obeying *God*, rather than man, will be considered as dangerous, and heretical by many, but I am not afraid openly to avow it, because it is the doctrine of the Bible; but I would not be understood to advocate resistance to any law however oppressive, if, in obeying it, I was not obliged to commit *sin*. If for instance, there was a law which imposed imprisonment or a fine upon me if I manumitted a slave, I would on no account resist that law, I would set the slave free, and then go to prison or pay the fine. If a law commands me to *sin I will break it;* if it calls me to *suffer*, I will let it take its course *unresistingly*. The doctrine of blind obedience and unqualified submission to *any human* power, whether civil or ecclesiastical, is the doctrine of despotism, and ought to have no place among republicans and Christians.

But you will perhaps say, such a course of conduct would inevitably expose us to great suffering. Yes! my Christian friends, I believe it would, but this will *not* excuse you or anyone else for the neglect of *duty*. If prophets and apostles, martyrs and reformers had not been willing to suffer for the truth's sake, where would the world have been now? If they had said, we cannot speak the truth, we cannot do what we believe is right, because the *laws of our country or public opinion are against us*, where would our holy religion have been now?

The Ladies' Anti-Slavery Society of Boston was called last fall to a severe trial of their faith and constancy. They were mobbed by "the gentlemen of property and standing," in that city at their anniversary meeting, and their lives were jeopardized by an infuriated crowd; but their conduct on that occasion did credit to our sex, and affords a full assurance that they will *never* abandon the cause of the slave. The pamphlet, "Right and Wrong in Boston," issued by them in which a particular account is given of that "mob of broadcloth in broad day," does equal credit to the head and the heart of her who wrote it. I wish my Southern sisters could read it; they would then understand that the women of the North have engaged in this work from a sense of *religious duty*, and that nothing will ever induce them to take their hands from it until it is fully accomplished. Northern women may labor to produce a correct public opinion at the North, but if Southern women sit down in listless indifference and criminal idleness, public opinion cannot be rectified and purified at the South. It is manifest to every reflecting mind that slavery must be abolished; the era in which we live, and the light which is overspreading the whole world on this subject, clearly show that the time cannot be distant when it will be done. Now there are only two ways in which it can be effective, by moral power or physical force, and it is for *you* to choose which of these you prefer. Slavery always has and always will produce insurrections whenever it exists, because it is a violation of the natural order of things, and no human power can much longer perpetuate it. The opposers of abolitionists fully believe this; one of them remarked to me not long since, there is no doubt there will be a most terrible overturning at the South in a few years, such cruelty and wrong must be visited with divine vengeance soon. Abolitionists believe, too, that this must inevitably be the case if you do not repent, and they are not willing to leave you to perish without entreating you to save yourselves from destruction; well may they say with the apostle, "am I then your enemy because I tell you the truth," and warn you to flee from impending judgments.

The *women of the South can overthrow* this horrible system of oppression and cruelty, licentiousness and wrong. Such appeals to your legislatures would be irresistible, for there is something in the heart of man which *will bend under moral suasion*. There is a swift witness for truth in his bosom, which *will respond to truth* when it is uttered with calmness and dignity. If you could obtain but six signatures to such a petition in only one state, I would say, send up that petition, and be not in the least discouraged by the scoffs and jeers of the heartless, or the resolution of the house to lay it on the table. It will be a great thing if the subject can be introduced into your legislatures in any way, even by *women*, and *they* will be the most likely to introduce it there in the best possible manner, as a matter of *morals* and *religion*, not of expediency or politics.

Great fault has been found with the prints which have been employed to expose slavery at the North, but my friends, how could this be done so effectually in any other way? Until the pictures of the slave's sufferings were drawn and held up to public gaze, no Northerner had any idea of the cruelty of the system, it never entered their minds thas such abominations could exist in Christian, republican America; they never suspected that many of the *gentlemen* and *ladies* who came from the South to spend the summer months in traveling among them, were petty tyrants at home. To such hidden mourners the formation of Anti-Slavery Societies was as life from the dead, the first beams of hope which gleamed through the dark clouds of despondency and grief. Prints were made use of to effect the abolition of the Inquisition in Spain, and Clarkson employed them when he was laboring to break up the slave trade, and English abolitionists used them just as we are now doing. They are powerful appeals and have invariably done the work they were designed to do, and we cannot consent to abandon the use of these until the *realities* no longer exist.

Sisters in Christ, I have done. As a Southerner, I have felt it was my duty to address you. I have endeavored to set before you the exceeding sinfulness of slavery, and to point you to the example of those noble women who have been raised up in the church to effect great revolutions, and to suffer for the truth's sake. I have appealed to your sympathies as women, to your sense of duty as *Christian women*. I have attempted to vindicate the abolitionists, to prove the entire safety of immediate emancipation, and to plead the cause of the poor and oppressed. I have done—I have sowed the seeds of truth, but I well know "*God only* can give the increase."

Farewell—Count me not your "enemy because I have told you the truth," but believe me in unfeigned affection,

Your sympathizing Friend,
Angelina E. Grimké

Published by the American Anti-Slavery Society, corner of Spruce and Nassau Streets. Price 6¼ cents single. 62½ cents per dozen. $4 per hundred.—Please Read and Circulate—

III

The abolitionist societies produced capsule guides for would-be antislavery proponents. Anyone reading this fact sheet, they hoped, should be able to spread the message effectively, persuade his own audiences, and effectively rebut opponents. The manual reprinted here has a double significance for the reader today. It offers both insights into the content of the antislavery message and clarifies the ways by which proponents tried to extend its appeal.

ANTISLAVERY MANUAL, 1837

LAROY SUNDERLAND

Immediate Emancipation

We mean by this,

1. That the slave owner, so far as he is personally concerned, should *cease immediately* to hold or to use human beings as his *property*.

In *Anti-Slavery Manual Containing a Collection of Facts and Arguments on American Slavery,* by LaRoy Sunderland (New York, 1837), pp. 79, 100–101, 118–20, 129–33.

And is there one slave owner in the nation who cannot do this? If there be one, then he must be set down as *non compos mentis,* or an idiot.

2. That the master, so far as he is personally concerned, should immediately offer to employ those whom he has held as his property, as free hired laborers; he should not turn them loose upon society, uncared for and unprotected, but he should treat them as *men,* and give them the liberty of choice, whether to remain in his employ at fair wages, or not.

3. So far as the state is concerned, it should annihilate the right of man to hold man as property; and all who are now slaves should be *immediately brought under the protection and restraint of suitable and impartial laws.* But the want of action on the part of any state government should not, and need not, hinder anyone from doing his duty as above described.

Reasons for Discussing the Subject of Slavery at the North

1. Because it is *American* slavery.
2. Because the North contributes its share toward its support.

Its money in building prisons in the District of Columbia, where slaves are kept.

Its representatives and senators in Congress who virtually vote for its continuance.

Its portion of men, Christians and ministers of the gospel, who go to the South and become slaveholders.

3. We are obligated by the United States' laws to deliver up slaves who escape to us for refuge.

4. Because Northern blood is liable to be spilt in case of insurrection at the South.

5. Because the slaveholding principle exists at the North, as really as at the South. The continuance of the system is justified here by Christians and ministers, on the same ground on which it is justified there, by the slaveholders themselves.

6. We discuss this subject at the North, because as long as slavery exists in this nation our own liberties are insecure. See the case of Dr. Crandall, a citizen of New York, who was incarcerated in Washington jail, for eight months, merely on suspicion of his being an abolitionist. Other citizens from the North have, by simply venturing to the South, lost both their liberty and their lives.

7. Because it is our right and privilege to discuss this question. The United States and the state in which we live have guaranteed to us the freedom of speech, and of the press.

8. Because God has commanded his servants to open their mouths for such as cannot plead for themselves.

9. Because to neglect this subject would endanger the salvation of souls, for whom Christ died.

10. Because slavery is a reproach to the nation which every lover of his country should be anxious to do away.

11. Because we should do, as we would be done by.

12. Because, without discussion, slavery will never be abolished, and it must be discussed here or nowhere, in the nation.

Abolitionists

Their Principles

1. We hold that Congress has no right to abolish slavery in the Southern states.

2. We hold that slavery can only be lawfully abolished by the legislatures of the several states in which it prevails, and that the exercise of any other than moral influence to induce such abolition is unconstitutional.

3. We believe that Congress has the same right to abolish slavery in the District of Columbia, that the state governments have within their respective jurisdictions, and that it is their duty to efface so foul a blot from the national escutcheon.

4. We believe that American citizens have the right to express and publish their opinions of the constitutions, laws, and institutions of any and every state and nation under heaven; and we mean never to surrender the liberty of speech, of the press, or of conscience.

5. We have uniformly deprecated all forcible attempts on the part of the slaves to recover their liberty. And were it in our power to address them, we would exhort them to observe a quiet and peaceful demeanor, and would assure them that no insurrectionary movement on their part would receive from us the slightest aid or countenance.

6. We would deplore any servile insurrection, both on account of the calamities which would attend it, and on account of the occasion which it might furnish of increased severity and oppression.

7. We are charged with sending incendiary publications to the South. If by the term *incendiary* is meant publications containing arguments and facts to prove slavery to be a moral and political evil, and that duty and policy require its immediate abolition, the charge is true. But if this term is used to imply publications encouraging insurrection, and designed to excite the slaves to break their fetters, the charge is utterly and unequivocally false.

8. We are accused of sending our publications to the slaves, and it is asserted that their tendency is to excite insurrections. Both the charges are false. These publications are not intended for the slaves, and were they able to read them, they would find in them no encouragement to insurrection.

9. We are accused of employing agents in the slave states to distribute our publications. We have never had one such agent. We have sent no *packages* of our papers to any person in those states for distribution, except to five respectable resident citizens, at their own request. But we have sent, by mail, single papers addressed to public officers, editors of newspapers, clergymen and others.

10. We believe slavery to be sinful, injurious to this and every other country in which it prevails; we believe immediate emancipation to be the duty of every slaveholder, and that the immediate abolition of slavery, by those who have the right to abolish it, would be safe and wise.

11. We believe that the education of the poor is required by duty, and by a regard for the permanency of our republican institutions. There are thousands and tens of thousands of our fellow-citizens, even in the free states, sunk in abject poverty, and who on account of their complexion, are virtually *kept* in ignorance, and whose instruction in certain cases is actually prohibited by law! We are anxious to protect the rights and to promote the virtue and happiness of the colored portion of our population, and on this account we have been charged with a design to encourage intermarriage between the whites and blacks. This charge has been repeatedly, and is again, denied, while we repeat that the tendency of our sentiments is to put an end to the criminal amalgamation that prevails wherever slavery exists.

12. We are accused of acts that tend to a dissolution of the Union, and even of wishing to dissolve it. We have never "calculated the value of the Union," because we believe it to be inestimable; and that the abolition of slavery will remove the chief danger of its dissolution; and one of the many reasons why we cherish and will endeavor to preserve the Constitution is that it restrains Congress from making any law abridging the freedom of speech or of the press.

Such, fellow-citizens, are our principles. Are they unworthy of republicans and of Christians?

Objections Answered

1. "The Bible recognizes, and of course in some circumstances, justifies slavery."

One sentence is sufficient to dispose of this argument. *Slaveholders refuse the Bible to their slaves.* Strange that they should fear to add *moral chains* to the *physical!*

2. "Abolitionists are too sweeping in their denunciations. Slavery is not always, as they affirm, a *sin*, because slaves are often treated with kindness."

So are horses. Is it right to put a man to the place of a horse, provided that horse is a beloved and favorite one? And would you judge it kind treatment, if you were, under any circumstances, robbed of your liberty, and bought and sold like a beast?

3. "The slaves are unfit for freedom."

Are they all unfit? If not, then you must be an immediate abolitionist in regard to those who are fit. If they are, then how can any of them ever be made fit, for some, nay, many of them, have already enjoyed long enough all the possible influences which can be supposed to fit men for freedom while in a state of slavery.

4. "Slaves are paid wages, inasmuch as they receive from their masters food and clothing."

"It takes two to make a bargain." You might as well call the grease a man puts on his cart wheels the wages of the ox of the cart, as to call the food and clothing of the slave his wages.

5. "Many slaves have religious privileges. Their masters labor for the salvation of their souls."

So long as the slaves are kept in ignorance of the Bible, and of their own rights as *men*, and consequently of their duties to God and man; and so long as their persons and purity are not protected either by public opinion or by the laws, their piety must be of a doubtful character.

6. "Slaveholders know that slavery is a curse, and are opposed to it, but cannot get rid of it."

If they know it to be a curse, they seem not to believe that their slaves are curses, or, if they do, they are very loth to part with curses.

IV

In 1840, two brothers, Arthur and Lewis Tappan, having made fortunes as New York merchants, turned their energies to the antislavery campaign. Determined to bring as much organizational efficiency to the spreading of the antislavery message as to selling goods, they founded the American and Foreign Antislavery Society. Each year they issued an annual report to their members, describing the many activities that the society had carried out. It was, as the report of 1849 reprinted below demonstrates, an impressive list of activities, one indicator of the modernity of their techniques.

REPORT OF THE AMERICAN AND FOREIGN ANTISLAVERY SOCIETY, 1849

The past year has been distinguished for the increasing prevalence of antislavery sentiments, and especially for attention to the political aspects of the cause. Venal politicians have been rebuked, arrested in their career of iniquity, and taught a lesson that will never, it is believed, be forgotten. The people have been aroused, and have evinced a determination if not to put an end to slavery, to prevent its extension on this continent. At the same time, the moral and religious aspects of the cause have not been overlooked. Many friends of the Redeemer, heretofore repelled by the erroneous doctrines of persons advocating the antislavery cause, have been led to see that it is the cause of God and humanity, and that all who profess to be the friends of the slave are not disunionists, and do not speak the truth in unrighteousness.

It is now acknowledged, even by the opponents of abolitionists, that the abolition of American slavery is the great question of the age; and men who have hitherto remained passive upon the subject now feel that the encroachments of the slavocracy are becoming intolerable; that the point where inactive forbearance ceases to be a virtue is at hand; that the grasping spirit of slavery must be arrested, and the foul system overthrown and swept away forever.

The part taken by the Executive Committee of this Society the past year has been cautious, watchful, and prudent. With limited means, in the midst of political excitement, aware of the imprudence of those who call themselves, par excellence, the friends of the slave, they have not been eager to startle the community by new projects, or arouse them by spasmodic efforts; they have contented themselves by using the resources committed to them with economy, in diffusing truth with firmness and perseverance, and in aggressive movements both in the free and slave states, as opportunities and openings occurred. "Make haste slowly" has been their maxim, in the peculiar condition of the country and of the antislavery cause, in convincing of error and sin—in effecting reformation—leaving to others the odious task of vituperation, projects of disunion, efforts to rend the churches, destroy the constitution, and break down the government of their country. The Committee have been desirous of pursuing a course that would commend the cause to the approbation, and enlist the cooperation, of good men of all religious denominations and political parties. To accomplish this great object they have not deemed it necessary or wise to adulterate truth, to possess or exhibit a compromising spirit. Associates thus gained are not worth the pains taken to obtain their adhesion. The course pursued the past year will be continued, but the Committee hope with more abundant means at command, with more ability in their use, and with greater accessions to their members.

Some progress has been made in the plan, announced in the last

In *Annual Report for 1849*, American and Foreign Antislavery Society (New York, 1849), pp. 20–29.

Annual Report, of publishing the slave laws of the several states and territories. The laws of the District of Columbia relating to slaves and free people of color, under the title of the *Black Code of the District of Columbia,* have been published, prepared by William G. Snethen, Esq., counselor at law, Washington City, who has also in readiness for publication laws of similar character of the State of Maryland, to be followed by the slave laws of other states, and published whenever sufficient funds shall have been contributed for the object. A copy of the *Black Code* was sent to each member of Congress, and to each of the judges of the Supreme Court of the United States. Aid has been furnished Rev. John G. Fee, of Kentucky, in the publication of his work entitled "An Antislavery Manual," and in giving it an extensive circulation in that state and elsewhere.

The Committee published the past year, as usual, a large edition of the *Liberty Almanac.* In it they gave a succinct history of the formation of this Society, vindicated its founders in reference to the aspersions frequently heaped upon them by disappointed and selfish individuals and cabals from whom they had felt compelled to separate, and proved that the original object of the Society—the entire extinction of slavery and the slave trade, and the equal security, protection, and improvement of the people of color—had been pursued to the extent of the means furnished. This publication contained also valuable reminiscences respecting the restriction of slavery; discussions on the Wilmot Proviso and the Oregon Bill; the compromises of the Constitution; the slave power politically and morally considered—together with a mass of intelligence, antislavery, and miscellaneous. No better way can be devised, it is thought, for the dissemination of valuable matter relating to the great object of our association than by the cheap and popular method referred to.

A new and large edition of the Society's *Address to Non-Slaveholders of the United States* has been published, and a portion of it, with considerable additions, is in the press for distribution in New Mexico and California. Applications have been received and responded to, from different slave states, for books and pamphlets of an antislavery character; and the Committee are advised that native citizens of such states are circulating essays showing the safety and advantages of emancipation, with much effect; and they know of no way in which the friends of the cause can better aid the progress of antislavery principles than by liberal appropriations for such objects.

Applications have been received from several individuals for aid in sustaining newspapers in slave states and territories that will advocate, though not exclusively, the emancipation of slaves, or the prohibition of slavery; and the Committee are in possession of facts with regard to the prevalence of antislavery feeling and action in slave states, produced by Northern agitation, that are highly encouraging.

Under the advice of the Committee, and with funds furnished by its members and others, suits or other legal processes have been commenced for the liberation of persons claiming their liberty under the laws of the states in which they have been held in bondage. In one of these cases, where slaves, emancipated by the will of a slaveholder in Maryland, were kept in slavery nearly fourteen years by the unprincipled executor, a decree has been obtained, after an expensive and protracted litigation in the various courts, restoring fifteen persons to liberty. This result was achieved by the joint cooperation and at the mutual expense of members of this Committee and friends of justice in Maryland.

Correspondence has been maintained with other societies, and with individual friends of emancipation in this and other countries, and intelligence has been reciprocated. Publications have been received from various quarters.

Letters were recently addressed by the Corresponding Secretary to a considerable number of influential and intelligent abolitionists in different states, asking their opinion and advice with reference to the best course to be taken by the Society in the present position of the antislavery cause in this country. Great unanimity on the following sentiments was expressed in the replies: that the present is a favorable time to awaken the public conscience with regard to the moral and religious aspects of the cause; that an organization, based upon an earnest abhorrence of the sinfulness of slavery, and bringing its influence to bear upon the social, civil, and ecclesiastical defenses of the system, is greatly needed; a hope that judicious, prayerful, and persevering action may soon bring about an application of antislavery principles to Bible, tract, missionary, and Sunday-school operations, and induce all the organizations in these departments of benevolence to give the slave population an importance proportioned to their hard and bitter necessities.

V

For all their fervor, the abolitionists relied exclusively upon verbal persuasion to end slavery. Their critics, on the other hand, had frequent recourse to violence. In the 1830s, over one hundred incidents of violence were directed at the abolitionists, and all of these were in the North, not the South. Why did citizens, often led by business leaders in the community, react so violently to the abolitionist message? Why were the forces of law and order so ineffective in containing them? These questions emerge vividly in the incidents that surround the first murder of an abolitionist, the death of Elijah Lovejoy in Alton, Illinois, on November 3, 1837. Lovejoy was a Presbyterian minister, who at the age of thirty-one joined the abolitionist struggle. He published an antislavery newspaper in St. Louis, but in 1836, after public opposition to his writings there grew too great, he moved to Alton. Again he edited an abolitionist paper, but this time he was determined to ride out criticism. When in 1836 a mob destroyed his press, he ordered a second; when the second was smashed, he ordered a third; and when the third went the way of its predecessors, a fourth. The document below describes what happened when a fourth press arrived.

NARRATIVES OF RIOTS AT ALTON, 1838

EDWARD BEECHER

It often happens that events, in themselves of no great importance, are invested with unusual interest in consequence of their connection with principles of universal application or with momentous results. Of this kind are the events which preceded and led to the death of the Rev. Elijah P. Lovejoy: the first martyr in America to the great principles of the freedom of speech and of the press.

Of these events I propose in the following pages to give an account. The facts are of a nature sufficiently astounding in any age or at any time: the destruction of four printing presses in succession; the personal abuse of the editor, from time to time by repeated mobs; and his final and premeditated murder!

Still more astounding are they when we consider the country in which they occurred. Had it been in revolutionary France; or in England, agitated by the consequent convulsion of the nations; there had been less cause for surprise. But it was not. It was in America—the land of free discussion and equal rights.

Still more are we amazed when we consider the subjects, the discussion of which was thus forcibly arrested. Had it been an effort to debauch and pollute the public mind by obscenity and atheism; or by injurious and disorganizing schemes; the rise of public indignation had at least found a cause; though the friends of truth and righteousness are not the men who employ mobs as their chosen instruments of persuasion. But it was none of these. It was solely the advocacy of the principles of freedom and equal rights.

Were these principles of recent origin, and the opinions of a sect, it might have caused less surprise. But they are the sacred legacy of ages—the doctrines of our nation's birth; of natural justice; and of God.

All these things are astonishing: but there is one fact that may justly excite amazement still more deep and overwhelming; the opinions and feelings elicited by events like these. Had an earthquake of indignation convulsed the land; had the united voices of every individual of every party rebuked and remedied the wrong; all had been well. But during the progress of the scenes there have been found those in reputation as wise and good who have been unsparing in their censure on the sufferers, and stimulated the evildoers by sympathy or feeble rebuke. And after the final and dreadful catastrophe, only a faint tribute has been given *by them* to certain abstract principles of free inquiry as generally good; and a decent regret for their violation has been expressed. But the full tide of indignation has been reserved for the audacious man who dared to speak and act as a freeman; and though lawlessly inflicted, his penalty has been declared to be deserved.

What are we to say of facts like these? They at least open a deep chapter in human nature, and in the condition of our country. They are

In *Narratives of Riots at Alton* (New York, 1838). Reprint edition, (New York, 1965), pp. 3–4, 60–66.

the result of principles neither superficial nor accidental. They penetrate to the very vitals of society and indicate a crisis in our national life.

That as a nation we are radically unsound and lost, they do not to my mind indicate. But that there are in the body politic causes of tremendous power tending to that result, they do evince. And the question on which all turns is now before us as a nation; and on its decision our life or death depends. Have we coolness of thought left sufficient to discern them, and energy of moral feeling enough to react?

As these events are of a nature to rouse and demand public attention, I hope that an impartial narration of them will be candidly and thoughtfully read; and as I have been an actor in the leading events from the beginning—an eyewitness of most that I describe—I feel that no one who speaks only from hearsay can have so full a knowledge of all the causes of these events as I; and as perhaps no one has been more severely censured by enemies, or regarded in greater error by some sincere and valued friends, I feel that not only a regard to truth and the general good, but decent regard to the opinions of others, requires me to speak.

Mr. Lovejoy having decided on his course, the friends of law and order made their arrangements for the defense of his press. Personal violence or an attempt to murder him was not expected. It was supposed that the main effort, if any were made, would be to destroy the press as it was landed. We all felt that if once deposited in Godfrey and Gilman's store it would be safe. Great difficulty was encountered in obtaining a special constable to direct the friends of law in case of an attack, under the authority of the Mayor. The Mayor himself did not refuse to act; but as it might be inconvenient to find him when most needed, it was considered important to have one of the supporters of the press appointed as special constable on any sudden emergency. Though the Mayor acceded to the proposal, it was from time to time delayed, and finally it was not carried into effect. The Mayor, however, still consented to direct their movement when called upon.

On Monday, Mr. W. S. Gilman was informed that the press was at St. Louis on board a boat which would probably arrive at Alton about evening. He immediately sent an express to the captain of the boat requesting him to delay the hour of his arrival until three o'clock at night, in order to avoid an affray with the rioters. This movement was successful. The spies of the mob watched for the arrival of boats for some time; but late in the evening seemed to give up the expectation of any arrival that night, and retired.

Meantime the supporters of the press met at Mr. Gilman's store to the number of thirty or more; and, as before stated, organized themselves into a volunteer company according to law, and spent the night in the store. At the appointed hour the boat arrived, and the press was safely landed; the Mayor being present. All arrangements had been made with such judgment, and the men were stationed at such commanding points, that an attack would have been vain. But it was not made. A horn was indeed sounded, but no one came.

Shortly after the hour fixed on for the landing of the boat, Mr. Lovejoy arose and called me to go with him to see what was the result.

The moon had set and it was still dark, but day was near; and here and there a light was glimmering from the window of some sickroom or of some early riser. The streets were empty and silent, and the sounds of our feet echoed from the walls as we passed along. Little did he dream, at that hour, of the contest which the next night would witness: that these same streets would echo with the shouts of an infuriate mob, and be stained with his own heart's blood!

We found the boat there and the press in the warehouse; aided in raising it to the third story. We were all rejoiced that no conflict had ensued and that the press was safe; and all felt that the crisis was over. We were sure that the store could not be carried by storm by so few men as had ever yet acted in a mob; and though the majority of the citizens would not aid to defend the press we had no fear that they would aid in an attack. So deep was this feeling that it was thought that a small number was sufficient to guard the press afterward; and it was agreed that the company should be divided into sections of six, and take turns on successive nights. As they had been up all night, Mr. Lovejoy and myself offered to take charge of the press till morning, and they retired.

The morning soon began to dawn; and that morning I shall never forget. I passed through the scuttle to the roof and ascended to the highest point of the wall. The sky and the river were beginning to glow with approaching day, and the busy hum of business to be heard. I looked with exultation on the scenes below. I felt that a bloodless battle had been gained for God and for the truth; and that Alton was redeemed from eternal shame. And as all around grew brighter with approaching day, I thought of that still brighter sun, even now dawning on the world, and soon to bathe it with floods of glorious light.

Brother Lovejoy, too, was happy. He did not exult: he was tranquil and composed; but his countenance indicated the state of his mind. It was a calm and tranquil joy, for he trusted in God that the point was gained: that the banner of an unfettered press would soon wave over that mighty stream.

Vain hopes! How soon to be buried in a martyr's grave. Vain! did I say? No: they are not vain. Though dead he still speaketh; and a united world can never silence his voice. Ten thousand presses, had he employed them all, could never have done what the simple tale of his death will do. Up and down the mighty streams of the West his voice will go; it will penetrate the remotest corner of our land; it will be heard to the extremities of the civilized world. From henceforth no boat will pass the spot where he fell, heedless of his name, or of his sentiments, or of the cause for which he died. And if God in his mercy shall use this event to arouse a slumbering nation to maintain the right for which he died, he will look down from the throne of his glory on the scene of his martyrdom and say, "It is enough: truth is triumphant; the victory is gained."

We returned to his house, and before my departure we united in prayer. His wife, through weakness, had not risen. In her chamber we met in the last act of worship in which we were to unite on earth. I commended him and his family to the care of God. As I left her I cheered her with the hope that her days of trial were nearly over and that more tranquil hours were at hand. Cheered by these hopes I bade them and my other friends farewell, and began my journey homeward. On my way I heard passing rumors of a meditated attack on the store, but gave them no weight. The events of a few hours proved them but too well founded.

Of the tragic catastrophe I was not a spectator; but after careful inquiry of eyewitnesses I shall proceed to narrate the leading facts.

From the statement of the Mayor it seems that an attack was apprehended; and that the matter was laid before the common council, and that they did not deem it necessary to take any action on the subject.

On account of the fatigue and watching of the preceding night, most of the defenders of the press who were in the store the night before were absent; and others took their place. The number was larger than at first intended in consequence of an increased apprehension of an attack. Their apprehensions were realized. An attack was commenced at about ten o'clock at night.

In order to render the narrative more clear, it is necessary to say a few words concerning the structure and location of the store. It consisted of two long stone buildings, side by side, in one block, extending from the landing in Water Street back to Second Street; with doors and windows at each gable end, but with no windows at the sides. Hence it can be defended at the ends from within, but not at the sides. The roofs are of wood. The lots on each side being vacant, these stores form a detached block, accessible on every side.

About ten o'clock a mob, *already armed*, came and formed a line at the end of the store in Water Street, and hailed those within. Mr. Gilman opened the end door of the third story, and asked what they wanted. They demanded the press. He, of course, refused to give it up; and earnestly entreated them to use no violence. He told them that the property was committed to his care, and that they should defend it at the risk and sacrifice of their lives. At the same time they had no ill will against them, and should deprecate doing them an injury. One of them, a leading individual among the friends of free inquiry at the late convention, replied that they would have it at the sacrifice of their lives, and presented a pistol at him: upon which he retired.

They then went to the other end of the store and commenced an attack. They demolished two or three windows with stones and fired two or three guns. As those within threw back the stones, one without was distinctly recognized and seen taking aim at one within: for it was a moonlight evening, and persons could be distinctly seen and recognized.

A few guns were then fired by individuals from within, by which Lyman Bishop, one of the mob, was killed. The story that he was a mere stranger waiting for a boat, and that Mr. Lovejoy shot him, are alike incapable of proof. He was heard during the day, by a person in whose employ he was, to express his intention to join the mob.

After this the mob retired for a few moments, and then returned with ladders which they lashed together to make them the proper length, and prepared to set fire to the roof.

About this time the Mayor, having been informed of the riot, came on to the ground; but having few to sustain him, was unable to compel the rioters to desist by force. They requested him to go into the store, and state to its defenders that they were determined to have the press, and would not desist until they had accomplished their object; and agreed to suspend operations until his return. Attended by a Justice of the Peace, he entered and delivered the message of the mob.

Suppose now it had been delivered up by its defenders and destroyed. How remarkable the narrative must have been, of a press given up to the mob to be destroyed by the agency of the Mayor and a Justice of the Peace!

However, they did not give it up. Mr. Gilman requested the Mayor to call on certain citizens to see if they could not prevent the destruction of the building. He said he could not: he had used his official authority in vain. He then asked him whether he should continue to defend the property by arms. This the Mayor, as he had previously done, authorized him to do. The Mayor and the Justice were then informed that the press would not be given up, and the decision was by them communicated to the mob. They then proceeded to fire the roof, taking care to keep on the side of the store where they were secure from the fire of those within.

It now became evident to the defenders that their means of defense, so long as they remained with, was cut off; and nothing remained but to attack the assailants without. It was a hazardous step; but they determined to take it. A select number, of whom Mr. Lovejoy was one, undertook the work. They went out at the end, turned the corner, and saw one of the incendiaries on the ladder, and a number standing at the foot. They fired and it is supposed wounded, but did not kill him; and then, after continuing their fire some minutes and dispersing the mob, returned to load their guns. When they went out again no one was near the ladder, the assailants having so secreted themselves as to be able to fire, unseen, on the defenders of the press as they came out. No assailant being in sight Mr. Lovejoy stood, and was looking round. Yet, though he saw no assailant, the eye of his murderer was on him. The object of hatred, deep, malignant, and long continued, was fully before him—and the bloody tragedy was consummated. Five balls were lodged in his body, and he soon breathed his last. Yet after his mortal wound he had strength remaining to return to the building and ascend one flight of stairs before he fell and expired. They then attempted to capitulate, but were refused with curses by the mob, who threatened to burn the store and shoot them as they came out. Mr. Roff now determined at all hazards to go out and make some terms, but he was wounded as soon as he set his foot over the threshold.

The defenders then held a consultation. They were shut up within the building, unable to resist the ferocious mode of attack now adopted, and seemed devoted to destruction. At length Mr. West came to the door, informed them that the building was actually on fire, and urged them to escape by passing down the riverbank; saying that he would stand between them and the assailants so that if they fired they must fire on him. This was done. All but two or three marched out and ran down Water Street, being fired on by the mob as they went. Two, who were wounded, were left in the building, and one, who was not, remained to take care of the body of their murdered brother. The mob then entered, destroyed the press, and retired. Among them were seen some of those leading "friends of free inquiry" who had taken an active part in the convention.

Before these tragic scenes were ended, the streets were crowded with spectators. They came out to see the winding up of the plot, but not to aid in repressing violence or maintaining the law. The vote to aid the Mayor in suppressing violence they had refused to pass, because it was their duty to aid without it; and here we see how powerful their sense of duty was. The time of the conflict was from one hour and a half to two hours. During this time the bells were rung, and a general notice given; and yet none came to the rescue. It has been said, however, in extenuation of this inactivity that it was owing to a want of concert and arrangement among the citizens or by the police. No man knew on whom he might call to aid in suppressing the riot; and some who have professed that it was their desire to do so say that they were hindered by the apprehension that they might be only rallying the mob in the attempt to quell it.

The feelings exhibited by the mob were in keeping with the deed on which they were intent. Oaths, curses, blasphemy, and malignant yells broke upon the silence of the night as they prosecuted their work of death. But even passions so malignant were not enough to give them the hardihood and recklessness needed for their work. To drench conscience, blind reason, and arouse passion to its highest fury by the intoxicating cup was needed to fit them for the consummation of their work. The leaders in this business were adepts; they knew what means were adapted to their ends, and used them without stint or treason.

Thus closes a tragedy without parallel in the history of our land. In other popular excitements, there has been an equal amount of feeling: in some, blood has been shed. But never was there an avowed effort to overthrow the foundations of human society pushed to such bloody results: and that, on principles adapted so utterly to dissolve the social system, and plunge the nation into anarchy and blood.

SUGGESTIONS FOR
FURTHER READING

The special characteristics of the *Lowell Factory* are described in H.J. Habbakkuk, *American and British Technology in the 19th Century* (Cambridge, Eng. 1962). For a survey of the rise of industrialization in America informed by economic theory, see Douglas North, *Economic Growth in the United States, 1790–1860* (New York, 1966).

The most important works on the *Southern Plantations* include: Stanley Elkins, *Slavery* (Chicago, 1968, 2d. ed.) and Kenneth Stampp, *The Peculiar Institution* (New York, 1956). For a new view that is heavily based on quantitative techniques see, Robert Fogel and Stanley Engerman, *Time on the Cross* (Boston, 1974). A remarkably thorough account of slave life, more traditional in approach, is Eugene Genovese, *Roll, Jordan, Roll* (New York, 1974).

The nature of the *Frontier Community* is analyzed from a social science point of view in the collection of essays edited by Richard Hofstadter and Seymour Lipset, *Turner and the Sociology of the Frontier* (New York, 1968). A very detailed look at life in one American frontier community, based on quantitative materials, is Merle Curti, *The Making of an American Community* (Stanford, 1959).

The quality of the American *Common School* and the motives of its founders are analyzed in Michael Katz, *The Irony of Early School Reform* (Cambridge, Mass., 1968). Like Katz, Stanley Schultz, *The Culture Factory* (New York, 1973) is also suspicious of the benevolence of the program. For similarities between schools and custodial institutions see David J. Rothman, *The Discovery of the Asylum* (Boston, 1971).

The history of the *American Art Union* in particular and American artistic productions in general is imaginatively described in Neil Harris, *The Artist in American Society* (New York, 1966). A well-illustrated volume on the subject is Oliver Larkin's *Art and Life in America* (New York, 1949).

A revisionist collection of articles treating *Abolitionist Societies* is edited by Martin Duberman, *The Anti-Slavery Vanguard* (Princeton, 1965). Richard Hofstadter and Michael Wallace, *American Violence: A Documentary History* (New York, 1970) puts anti-abolitionist violence in a broader perspective. On anti-abolitionist mobs in particular see, Leonard Richards, *Gentlemen of Property and Standing* (New York, 1970).

The Making of Modern America, 1865–1920

THE DEPARTMENT STORE

THE COMPANY TOWN

THE NEW RICH

THE COUNTRY TOWN

THE IMMIGRANT GHETTO

THE SETTLEMENT HOUSE

INTRODUCTION

I N THE closing decades of the nineteenth century, American society became modern, that is, many of the nation's institutions took on the form and characteristics which they possess today. There is a familiar quality for us about the nature of American society as of 1900. It seems not at all distant from the world in which we live.

Perhaps the most crucial element promoting this familiarity is the growth of American industry. By 1900, the giant firms still powerful today such as Standard Oil and Anaconda Copper had already achieved dominance. Moreover, the organizations devoted to distributing the new industrial wealth were also flourishing. By 1900, department stores like Wanamakers, chain stores like the A&P, and mail-order companies like Sears Roebuck dominated the marketplace. So, too, the character of factory work became modern—and laborers took their first steps to organization. Finally, an unprecedented accumulation of personal wealth occurred during these years; this was the time that the new rich emerged, and the Carnegies and the Rockefellers took their positions of leadership in the economy and in society.

To explore the nature of these changes, it is appropriate to focus first on the distribution of industrial products, on the creation of that new and powerful institution of selling, the *department store*. In many ways, the department store occupied a unique place not only in the economy but also in American society, for it both encouraged and reflected a new ethos of consumerism. Material welfare became identical with social welfare—citizens who enjoyed a high standard of living would be loyal to the new system, or so contemporaries believed. How did this ethos spread? Did all classes in fact come to experience a real rise in their standard of living? What role did advertising play in this development? The revolution in ways of selling had a crucial impact on ways of buying—and the results are central to an understanding of social reality and social thought in this era.

The new power of the industrial producers had obvious consequences for industrial workers. With the increasing ability of factory owners to replace skilled workers with machines that required little skill to run, and with a growing pool of surplus laborers eager to work at any wage level, the position and power of workers against owners deteriorated. One response to this change was the effort on the part of labor to organize, to gain a strength in numbers that they did not have as individuals. But that effort, at least in this period, was not often successful. The experience of the workers at Pullman, Illinois, home of George Pullman's railroad car manufacturing plant, reveals in stark fashion the new relationship between capital and labor. Pullman was a *company town*, following to a degree in the Lowell tradition. But the differences between Lowell and Pullman point to the new character of industry in the modern nation.

The life style of the *new rich* also warrants attention. For the first time an elite lived in ways totally apart and different from their fellow Americans. So new and unusual were their circumstances that social philosophers, and the new rich themselves, evolved a whole ideology to justify their wealth, under the label of Social Darwinism. The relationship between the premises of Social Darwinism and the reality of American society must be tested and explored. Finally, the new rich also had a crucial impact on the other institutions in society, particularly cultural ones. They founded museums, opera houses, and libraries —and thereby fundamentally altered the nature of American culture. Once again, the culture of the country was intimately bound to its social development.

Two other factors make the period 1865–1920 a time of modernization for the United States. In these years, urbanization and immigration reached new heights. Countless numbers of rural Americans moved to the city, sparking a crisis in country life. Commissions proliferated, all attempting to analyze the nature of the *country town*, and their findings shed light both on the attraction of the new urban environments and on the essential characteristics of rural ones. The story is quite different from popular conceptions of it: for all the praise given to the simple and good country life, the reality was much more grim.

Moreover, urban life, as experienced by the first immigrants, was far less demoralizing and corrupting than we might think. The *immigrant ghetto* must be understood both for what it did, as well as for what it did not, provide. The ghettos were much more than slums and centers of crime and vice. In many ways, they shielded the immigrants from the harsher realities of life in a strange country. The ghetto was a complex form of social organization and, as such, demands close and full analysis.

An understanding of the nature of the ghetto community also shed new light on the nature of the Progressives' response to it. The period 1900–1920 is properly considered a reform era, when Americans attempted to come to grips with all the changes that we have been discussing here. The *settlement house* represents one major Progressive effort to deal with new urban and immigrant conditions. Again, reform turns out to be closely linked to the issue of social order. At times efforts at uplift seem to be more intent on keeping the lower classes in line than on improving their life chances. But such a view fails to give proper weight to genuinely benevolent motives. The work of the settlement house provides an important test case for helping to strike the right balance.

Chapter 11

The Department Store

BETWEEN 1870 and 1900, American industry underwent a radical transformation. In the 1870s the techniques of manufacturing and the quantity of industrial output were not very different from what they had been in the 1850s. By 1900, industry had become modern, closely resembling the system we know today. As late as 1870, American manufacturing firms were small in size: they employed few workers (typically less than twenty-five), operated with minimal amounts of capital, were run by an owner-boss, and produced goods almost exclusively for a local market. Three decades later, industries employed armies of laborers, functioned with enormous reserves of capital, were largely bureaucratic in organization, and produced for a national market. This crucial shift catapulted the United States to world economic leadership. By 1900, this country produced more steel and had laid more miles of railroad than any other nation.

How are we to understand the causes and implications of these changes? Although the growth of industry certainly did reflect the satisfaction of certain technical, economic factors (there had to be, for example, sufficient capital available in the country to fund these enterprises), the impact of social considerations was at least as important. Why were investors prepared to support these enterprises? Why were laborers ready to accept the discipline of the factory? Why were citizens both able and eager to consume the products of the machines? In essence, modernization did not take place in a vacuum. One must look beyond the narrow confines of the marketplace to the larger society in order to understand fully the nature of this change.

When one analyzes the first firms to become "modern," to expand in size and scale of operation, it becomes quickly apparent that they shared one crucial attribute: they had captured a national market for their products. They were not manufacturers just for New England, but for the nation. Firms became giants of industry not because of some technological breakthrough, not because they had invented a new pro-

cess to produce steel or a new refining technique for oil, but because of marketing innovations. The key to success rested not with invention but with distribution. Entrepreneurs who for one reason or another were able to exploit the availability of large markets were the ones who increased their scales of operation in dramatic ways. It was breakthroughs in selling, not in producing, that made the difference.

Several examples of this process are worth noting. It was Gustavus Swift who recognized the potential of an urban market for the consumption of beef products; he was the first to use refrigerated railroad cars to ship meat from the Midwest to urban Eastern depots—and it was this breakthrough that gave Swift and Company (and likewise Armour and Company) their advantage. James Duke also recognized the potential of the urban market. City people, he resolved, would be more prepared to buy a prerolled cigarette than to roll their own—and American tobacco went into the business of packaging cigarettes in new ways. The achievement of the National Biscuit Company lay not in inventing a better tasting cookie, but in mastering the techniques for distributing its baked products in cities all over the land.

One crucial implication of this change was that the fortune of the company was inexorably tied to its ability to capture a huge market, or, put another way, the willingness of Americans to buy their products. The company had to make selling more efficient and desirable, and citizens had to act to a new degree as consumers. The period 1880–1910, therefore, witnessed not just a revolution in the size of manufacturing enterprises but also in the importance of consumption.

One of the most dramatic manifestations of this change was the rise and growth of department stores—the creation of cathedrals to the rational distribution of goods. Its advertisements encouraged customers to enter the store, and its floors displayed in attractive fashion the goods to be purchased. The rise of department stores was coincidental with the growth of mail-order companies, like Sears Roebuck, and the appearance of chain stores, like the A&P. At the same time, brand names grew popular as manufacturers attempted to distinguish their products from others by means of a label. These shifts in the organization of selling reflected and reinforced the triumph of an ethic of consumerism in the nation. The implications of this new ethic to social ideas and realities is the focus of the materials that follow.

I

The Wanamaker Stores exemplified the new spirit of merchandising. Their founder, John Wanamaker, born in Philadelphia in 1838, began his career by selling clothing, and then expanded the network of his operations. By 1900, he was operating a very efficient department store, improvising a series of strategies to increase sales. The selections below not only illuminate the cause of Wanamaker's economic successes but also cast light on the social attitudes that at once stimulated and were stimulated by the growth of department stores. It is no exaggeration to say that proponents viewed the department store as a major guarantor of the future stability and well-being of the republic. In the first selection, Wanamaker himself explains the evolution and social role of the department store. In the second, President William Taft offers his words of praise at the fiftieth year celebration of the enterprise.

THE EVOLUTION OF MERCANTILE BUSINESS, 1900

JOHN WANAMAKER

As late as forty years ago, or before the [Civil] War, the transaction of business in producing and distributing merchandise required many agencies: the manufacturer, importer, commission men, bankers, jobbers, commercial travelers, and retailers.

The conditions governing the placing of goods in the retailer's hands were not only heavily weighted with expense, but, in the main, the retail merchant was badly handicapped as a rule by:

1. Small capital, commonly borrowed by long credit for merchandise.
2. Necessity of selling upon credit.
3. Necessity for larger percentage of profit.
4. Impossibility of utilizing to advantage store and people all seasons of the year.
5. Nonaccumulation of capital.

In *Corporations and Public Welfare*, American Academy of Political and Social Science (Philadelphia, 1900), pp. 124–28, 130.

The consequence was, that but four out of every hundred merchants succeeded in business. Naturally, an undercurrent of discontent with these conditions manifested itself, protesting against two or more prices for the same article, meager assortments of goods, high prices, and the custom that probably grew out of one rate to cash buyers and a different rate to buyers upon credit.

Up to 1877, so far as now known, no extensive, well-systemized mercantile retail establishment upon a large scale existed in the United States. The nearest approach was the A. T. Stewart store in New York, which limited itself to dry goods of the higher class.

The tendency of the age toward simplification of business systems and to remove unnecessary duplication of expenses, awakened throughout the United States a keen study of means to bring about a closer alliance with the producer and consumer. Almost simultaneously in a number of cities, long-established stores gradually enlarged and new stores sprang up to group at one point masses of merchandise in more or less variety.

Though there probably was never a time in any city that there were not bankruptcies of merchants and vacant stores, yet after the opening of the large stores, it everywhere became common with storekeepers and renters to charge all the causes of disaster to the large stores, then and now commonly called department stores, and an unsuccessful effort was made to decry them as monopolies. The inequality of talents and the unequal application of individuals must always carry some to the top and others to the lower places in all pursuits of life. The highest statesmanship thus far known has not been able anywhere in the world to maintain a permanent equilibrium for the slow, slovenly, and misplaced workers with the thrifty, well-trained, and properly fitted toilers.

Whoever conquers a higher place than his neighbor is supposed to face a commanding position, that at least makes his business way more difficult with his fellow tradesmen. Doubtless there must be some disadvantages arising from large single businesses of every kind. The trolley affected the business of the horse dealer. The large stores certainly affect a certain part of the small stores. The thing to be considered, and considered fairly from every point of view, is what the large single-ownership businesses contribute to the well-being of the public to counterbalance any disadvantages arising from them.

First of all it must be remembered that society is not constituted for the benefit of any one particular class of the population. Without sentiment or prejudice, the interests of all must be justly weighed and the greatest good of the greatest number must be gained.

I respectfully submit that the evolution in mercantile business during the last quarter of a century has been wrought not by combinations of capital, corporations, or trusts, but by the natural growth of individual mercantile enterprises born of new conditions out of the experience, mistakes, and losses of old-time trading; that the underlying basis of the new order of business and its principal claim for favor is that it distributes to the consumer in substance or cash compounded earnings hitherto wasted unnecessarily on middlemen; that the establishing of direct relations with mills and makers proves to be not only desirable for the saving of such costs as are dispensed with, but because less risks are incurred in preparing products and finding quick markets, thereby favoring lower prices; that the people must be taken into the equation when considering the right of certain businesses to a title of life, as they are responsible for the new conditions, highly value, and heartily support them.

I contend that the department store development would not be here but for its service to society; that it has done a public service in retiring middlemen; that its organization neither denies rights to others nor claims privileges of state franchises, or favoritism of national tariff laws; that if there is any suffering from it it is by the pressure of competition, and not from the pressure of monopoly.

Philadelphia is believed to be a buying center for three million people. If each of them in a year's purchase of personal needs and home necessities saves on an average ten cents a day, the saving is $10,095,000 in a year. Suppose it be but half that amount, there is still five millions to the good of the people to be put into their savings or their pleasures.

I believe the new American system of storekeeping is the most powerful factor yet discovered to compel minimum prices. It is a noticeable fact that lowered prices stimulate consumption and require additional labor in producing, transporting, and distributing. The care of such large stocks, amounting in one single store upon an average at all times to between four and five millions of dollars, and the preparation of and handling from reserves to forward stocks, require large corps of men. The new systems make shorter hours of duty and thus the number of employees is increased, while many entirely new avenues of employment for women are opened, as typewriters, stenographers, cashiers, check-clerks, inspectors, wrappers, mailing clerks, and the like. The division of labor creates many places for talented and high-priced men, whose salaries range alongside of presidents of banks and trust companies and similar important positions. It is universally admitted that the sanitary conditions that surround the employees of the large stores are better than in the old-time smaller stores and that employees are considerably better paid.

I hold that the evolution in trade was inevitable, because it was waterlogged by old customs that overtaxed purchasers; that there was at work for a long time a resistless force moving toward the highest good of humanity; that the profit therefrom to individuals who have risked their own capital, as any man may still do if he chooses, has been insignificant, compared to the people benefited both by the cheapening of the comforts of life and by the improved condition of persons employed.

[*Wanamaker's Principles*]

A GREAT STRIDE UP AND OVER BUSINESS CUSTOMS

Old methods found to be faulty or objectionable, discarded. A new and advantageous plan hereby adopted.

Already the largest clothing concern in America, and leading the trade,

NOW STARTS ON A NEW CAREER

Thoroughly reorganized on a greatly improved plan.

Silencing objectors! Assuring equal rights to all! Ruling out the possibility of unfairness! Securing a scale of still lower prices! Dropping every feature liable even to criticism! Guaranteeing purchasers against

MISFITS, MISTAKES, MISREPRESENTATIONS, MISUNDERSTANDINGS.

Dissatisfaction with price or purchase rendered impossible.

Thirteen years of interested and eager observation of different methods of doing business, while establishing and extending the largest clothing trade in the United States, have brought us to the following *conclusion*:

1. That a customer has a right to some guarantee that his purchase shall prove exactly as represented.
2. That cash throughout is the only basis consistent with the very lowest prices, as credit in every case necessitates higher prices to cover losses by bad debts, interest, lawsuits, hire of collectors, increased number of bookkeepers, etc.
3. That, though justice does not require it, comfort and actual security in dealing are greatly promoted by giving to the purchaser the privilege not only of exchange of goods, but of returning the same within a given time, and having promptly paid back the cash in full.
4. That all customers buying at the same time should pay precisely the same price for the same quality of goods.
5. That the interest of customers will be best served by abandoning the practice of paying salesmen a percentage on each sale, as it leads to "hurrying-up," and sometimes "over-persuading" buyers to take goods with which they are not fully suited.
6. That as customers naturally inquire into the character and quality of articles offered for sale, and may not always be correctly informed, or fully understand the clerks, a label, made under the authority and guarantee of the firm, bearing a printed description of the name and quality of the goods, should be attached to each article.

Businessmen thoroughly bent on upright dealing have been thinking over, working out, and experimenting on propositions similar to the above, and here and there is an establishment which has accepted one or another of these conclusions, and ordered their business accordingly. But

WE UNHESITATINGLY ADOPT THEM ALL.

And confidently relying on the approval and support of an intelligent and discriminating public, we inaugurate what we believe to be the best system in the world, and we now

Announce these as the
FOUR CARDINAL POINTS
by which we will hereafter
steer our craft:

FULL GUARANTEE   CASH PAYMENT
ONE PRICE   CASH RETURNED

THE DEDICATION OF WANAMAKER'S, 1911

WILLIAM HOWARD TAFT

Address of the President of the United States, William Howard Taft,
Dedicating the Wanamaker House of Business, December 30, 1911

Mr. Wanamaker, Mr. Mayor, and Governor Tener, ladies and gentlemen of Philadelphia, my fellow-citizens: It is now twenty years ago since I had the pleasure of becoming acquainted, with John Wanamaker of Philadelphia.

It has been a great pleasure to me to know and to feel that the friendship and mutual respect there begun have continued until the present day, and it has given me the greatest pleasure to take part in this ceremony at the moment of the greatest triumph of John Wanamaker's long and useful life.

We are here to celebrate the completion of one of the most important instrumentalities in modern life for the promotion of comfort among the people. The department store—which brings under one roof the opportunity to purchase, at the lowest reasonable, constant, and fixed price, everything that is usually needed upon the person or in the household for the sustaining of life, for recreation, and for intellectual enjoyment (except food alone)—means a reduction in the cost of living and necessary effort that we do not always appreciate.

It has been given to Mr. Wanamaker, the founder of this great institution, to begin the formation of this new instrumentality for the betterment of the condition of men, and to pursue the work of its improvement for fifty years, until now the end crowns his labor. The introduction into the conduct of his business of rigid rules as to the fixedness of the price; accuracy of representation as to the quality; the conveniences accorded to all in the return of unsatisfactory goods; and the delivery without cost, or at a reasonable cost according to the distance, of the goods to the home of the purchaser; together with such economical arrangement in sales as to reduce to a minimum the effort necessary to examine the goods to be purchased; the concentration and cooperation of the different branches of the business to reduce expense and increase efficiency all call for an executive genius that hardly finds its counterpart.

With no adventitious aid, with no combinations in restraint of competition, but simply by a natural growth and aggregation of means to an end, this great business was built up here in Philadelphia, and there in New York, to form a model for all other stores of the same kind throughout the country and throughout the world.

On this day, when we can look back half a century to the humble beginnings of this enormous business machine with its thirteen thousand employees and its millions of constant customers, it is right that there should be a ceremony dedicatory and congratulatory to show the

In *Golden Book of the Wanamaker Store, Jubilee Year, 1861–1911* (Philadelphia, 1911), vol. 2, pp. 3–5.

appreciation that the country at large has for the successful creation of an aid to the happiness of the people that is substantial and permanent.

II

The symbolic significance of the department store emerges with striking clarity in the architecture of the structures. The design of the buildings was anything but functional—Greek areas here, Egyptian style there. And yet the business organization within the walls was dedicated to maximizing sales. The document below presents both sides of the venture and helps to explain why such eclectic architecture should have accompanied so rational an enterprise as Wanamaker's.

GOLDEN BOOK OF THE WANAMAKER STORE, 1911

Section by section the great building arose and in 1911 it was completed, its construction having taken about nine years. Wonderful years they were, as the army of workers erecting the new building and the other army carrying forward the business in the old building could testify. Years they were of stress, of strain. But the great temple of business and all of which it is the embodiment in the business world came from that travail; and was well worth it.

When planning it, Mr. Wanamaker said to the architect,

> What you must do for me is to strive to say in stone what this business has said to the world in deed. You must make a building that is solid and true. It shall be of granite and steel throughout. It shall stand four square to the city—simple, unpretentious, noble, classic—a work of art, and, humanly speaking, a monument for all time.

One of the most notable features is the Grand Court. It soars one hundred and fifty feet in height without a break. Its proportions, its spaciousness, its towering marble columns with their capitals of dark Greek marble, the graceful balustrades of the various stories, the bronze torchierres for lighting, the famous great bronze eagle, and, above all, the magnificent organ set the Grand Court.

Throughout the building are various specially designed halls and rooms unusual in mercantile establishments. One of these, Egyptian Hall, has a magnificent auditorium seating almost two thousand, a gallery composed of private boxes, a stage on which a chorus of five hundred can sing at one time, and a pipe organ of nearly three thousand pipes.

In *Golden Book of the Wanamaker Store, Jubilee Year, 1861–1911* (Philadelphia, 1911), vol. 2, pp. 150–52, 277–79, 283–85.

Adjoining Egyptian Hall is Greek Hall, which seats six hundred people, has a large stage, and a two-manual pipe organ, and is exquisite in its architecture.

Another novel feature is the famous House that Budget Built planned to help those who wish to furnish either a house or a room to the best advantage on a specified amount of money. In addition to the practical demonstration given by the beautiful little home, a corps of experts is on hand to help in individual problems. To this corps of workers come high and low, rich and poor, old and young, with their problems. In the course of a year thousands seek them, asking for help to furnish artistically and practically on the amount of money each has to spend.

There is romance also in the very quantities of merchandise handled daily. It gives one a thrill to be part of a big thing. In store records, one comes across from time to time such statements as these:

> The most recent Wanamaker order for hairpins required fourteen tons of wire to fill.
>
> A single purchase of pins for the Wanamaker store required an entire freight car to transport.
>
> Every year in the Wanamaker Grand Crystal Tea Room six hundred thousand meals are served.
>
> The Wanamaker Jewelry Store owns enough clocks and watches to tick off, if they were all going at once, sixty thousand minutes in an hour.

The decoration of the stores both in New York and Philadelphia is a feature of the store life that is educational and enjoyable for both workers and customers. Though it has its value from the selling point, the commercial spirit by no means rules it. Art is its basis, and the thought of display for selling purposes only gives way always, if there is a conflict, to the artistic result. The decorations are always unusual and original. Stereotyped schemes or ornaments never are admitted.

As in other things, Mr. Wanamaker was a pioneer in house delivery. At a time when other stores asked customers to carry their packages, Mr. Wanamaker inaugurated the practice of delivering, thus carrying out his theory of service to the customer in every way possible. In the matter of delivery Mr. Wanamaker kept on pioneering. He inaugurated the suburban and seashore delivery.

Mr. Wanamaker was the first to use pneumatic tubes as cash carriers; the first to install continuous telephone service, night and day, for the use of customers; the first to open the store one evening a week, merely to let the people enjoy its sights, no selling being done; the first to set aside a day for the "little people," this being the forerunner of Children's Day.

Advertising, when Mr. Wanamaker started business, was almost a negligible factor in mercantile fields. The merchants thought it a waste of money. It was given as a sort of charity, and not with the exception of receiving a return commensurate with the expenditure.

Mr. Wanamaker changed all this, although the change was not instantaneous. His method unfolded naturally, but there was steady progress.

His first efforts seem crude in the light of today. But they fulfilled one law of advertising. They attracted attention and then drove home the point he wished to make. At different places in the city were erected immense billboards, each more than one hundred feet long and at that time the largest ever put up, and on them in large letters were announcements about men's clothing and Oak Hall. On fences, or wherever space could be found, were posters with simply "W. & B." on them in big wood type. Everybody at once inquired of everybody else, "What does W. & B. mean?" It soon became known that it stood for the firm at Sixth and Market Streets.

He gave away clocks bearing the legend "Wanamaker and Brown, Sixth and Market Streets." Picture cards were distributed. These were often perfumed, so as to be kept by those who received them, possibly laid away among clothing and thus seen whenever dressing.

In addition to these methods, he was advertising as largely as he could afford in the newspapers. Speaking of these first advertising efforts he said once: "When this little store [Oak Hall] closed its doors on its first day's business away back in 1861 the sum of $24.67 was found in the old-fashioned till under the counter. The sixty-seven cents were left there for making change the next morning and the twenty-four dollars were taken out by the founder and spent with the newspapers, which were asked simply to say that the new store was open and doing business and had a good stock of goods useful to the public."

Having decided that newspaper advertising was the most profitable, he suddenly took a daring leap and became the most talked-about advertiser in the country. This leap he did not take wildly. But when he saw he could take it and that the thing itself would be an advertisement because it was far ahead of anything that had yet been done, he leaped into the full-page advertisement. This first full-page advertisement appeared in the Philadelphia *Record* in December 1879. This, again, was an innovation that startled the business world, for at this time no store had taken so much space for advertising and eventually held to it continuously.

Not only did he attract attention by his methods and his mediums, but the matter published was in itself so interesting that the Wanamaker advertising page became a popular feature of the Philadelphia newspapers. It is no exaggeration to say that many women of the city and suburbs refused to take a daily paper that did not contain the Wanamaker advertisement.

III

The country store was a rather relaxed place to shop. Social conversations between clerks and customers went on regularly, interposed occasionally with a bit of bargaining over the price of goods. Compare this style with that which department store owners were eager to establish. The rules for the employees of Siegel and Cooper, one of New York City's new enterprises, includes impersonal shopping, fixed prices, rapid transactions, punctuality, and discipline. The store seemed to be modeled on the factory. The setting in which workers produced the goods was surprisingly similar to the setting in which customers purchased them.

RULES AND REGULATIONS FOR THE SIEGEL AND COOPER EMPLOYEES, *c.* 1900

General Instructions

DEPORTMENT

We want it said of our employees, that they are a credit to the house. Be civil and polite to your superiors. Should those in authority not be civil to you, *obey,* and if grievance warrants, see Superintendent. Under no circumstances are you to refuse to do what you are told to do by one superior in authority. Should you be reported for not obeying, you will lose your position, even if circumstances warranted your actions.

NOT PERMITTED

Buyers and floor managers will be held accountable and blamed if anyone under their control is found chewing gum, tobacco, or eating while back of counters. Anyone acting thus will be discharged.

THINGS NOT TO DO

Do not stand in groups.
Do not chew gum, read books, or sew.
Do not giggle, flirt, or idle away your time.
Do not walk together through the store.
Do not be out of your place.
Do not be late at any time.
Do not take over fifteen minutes on a pass.
Do not make a noise when going up in elevators.
Do not push when going into elevators, but always stand in line.
Do not talk across aisle, or in a loud voice.
Do not gossip; mind your own affairs, and you will have enough to do.
Do not sit in front of counter.

TRY TO BE

Polite, neat; dress in black.
Serious in your work.
Punctual, obliging, painstaking.
Keep your stock in good order, and follow the rules of the house, which, if obeyed, simply means that you are doing right, and if you do what you feel *is right* you will find that you are obeying the rules.

SYSTEM OF THE HOUSE

Learn all the details.
Know how to make out all checks.

In *Rules and Regulations for the Government of the Employees,* Siegel and Cooper Company of New York (New York, *c.* 1900), pp. 4–7, 36–37.

If you don't know, ask.

Always write legibly. If the week's sales show carelessness or incompetence, clerk will be dismissed, as we cannot permit illegible records.

LATE

If we opened at 10 A.M. some people would come late. We are rigid in our rule that you be on time. You should be here by 8 A.M.; after 8:05 you will be "late." Doors will be closed at 8:10, and employees coming after 8:10 will be told to come at noon, and therefore lose half a day's pay.

RULES REGARDING TIME CARD

Name, number, date, and lunch hour must be written in ink on time card before noon on each Monday. Cards must be carried on person.

When coming late, cards must be surrendered to time keeper at once.

To Our Employees in General, a Few Words of Advice

CHARACTER AND HABITS

You may be bright, energetic, and a valuable employee, yet your services may be undesirable if you haven't a good character, or if your habits are questionable. You stand or fall by your own actions. Remember that judgment is passed on truth, and right will always triumph.

As you rise step by step, it is because of ability and character, but no matter how high you do get, laxity in either may be your downfall and ruination for life.

You would be very much surprised if you knew the trouble and expense we go to to find out "character and habits." Detectives you don't know often are detailed to report all of your doings for a week.

Don't flirt. Remember the esteem which is due to all self-respecting persons; and ever remember the ill comments which follow idle gossip.

Don't lie. It takes more lies to back it up, which finally brings the house down on your head.

Don't live beyond your income, or go into debt. Cultivate saving. No matter what your wages are, you should save a part for a rainy day. It is not only the amount, but the habit formed, which will prove valuable to you.

DON'T BORROW OR LEND

Don't loan money even to your best friend. You are apt to lose both your money and your friend if you do.

FAMILY AND SOCIAL FRIENDS

A short stop for inquiry is not objectionable, but your family and friends do the house harm by extended visits, and they will not be tolerated. Entertaining, even while selling goods in a long drawn-out way, will not be allowed. Floor managers are particularly instructed to enforce this rule and are to remember that they are to guard the young ladies from annoying visitors.

IV

The market orientation of the new large-scale industries gave an unprecedented importance to the role of advertising. Its most obvious function was to persuade customers to buy in order to keep the rate of consumption in line with rates of production. But its significance to the manufacturer was even more basic and subtle. Traditionally, the manufacturer who wished to expand his operation, who wanted to carve out new markets, had to win out over competitors by one of several strategems: he could sell his goods cheaper than other firms, he could markedly improve the quality of his goods, or he could buy out his competitors. But each of these devices was costly: lower prices or higher quality could mean lower profits, and buying out other firms was always expensive. Advertising actually provided a new, and less costly, means of expanding control over a market. Prices could be kept constant and competitors need not be bought out; rather, a slogan that proclaimed the superiority of your product over others would attract new customers. In succinct but clear fashion, the directors of the National Biscuit Company announced their pursuit of just such a policy. The document below clarifies why Americans soon came under the unremitting influence of advertising.

NATIONAL BISCUIT COMPANY ANNUAL REPORT, 1901

To the Stockholders of National Biscuit Company

This company is four years old, and it may be of interest to shortly review its history. Its sales and profits year by year, have been as follows:

	SALES	PROFITS
1898	$34,051,279.84	$3,292,143.10
1899	35,651,898.84	3,302,155.00
1900	36,439,160.00	3,318,355.19
1901	38,625,134.78	3,670,445.05

In *Annual Report for 1901*, National Biscuit Company, pp. 1–4.

When the company started, it was an aggregation of plants. It is now an organized business. When we look back through the four years, we find that a radical change has been wrought in our methods of business. In the past, the managers of large industrial corporations have thought it necessary, for success, to control or to eliminate competition. So, when this company started, it was believed that we must control competition, and that to do this we must either fight competition or buy it. The first meant a ruinous war of prices and great loss of profits; the second, constantly increasing capitalization. Experience soon proved to us that, instead of bringing success, either of these courses, if persevered in, must bring disaster. This led us to reflect whether it was necessary to control competition. We asked ourselves whether this company, to succeed, must not be managed like any other large mercantile business. We soon satisfied ourselves that within the company itself we must look for success.

We turned our attention and bent our energies to improving the internal management of our own business, to getting the full benefit from purchasing our raw materials in large quantities, to economizing the expense of manufacture, to systematizing and rendering more effective our selling department, and, above all things and before all things, to improving the quality of our goods and the conditions in which they should reach the consumer.

It became the settled policy of this company to buy out no competition, and to that policy, since it was adopted, we have steadfastly adhered, and expect to adhere to the end.

We do not aim to sell all the biscuit consumed in this country. A monopoly in any product made from such raw materials as we use in the manufacture of our goods is an impossibility.

Upon our standard goods we fix prices which will render us a fair and sufficient profit, and in fixing such prices we pay no attention to the prices which other persons may make for their goods. But no one attempts to get the same prices which we get for our standard goods, because no one else offers for sale goods of the same quality. In fact, on such goods we have no real competition.

The consumer is not obliged to buy our goods; there are plenty of the biscuit of other manufacturers on the market, which he can buy at any time, if he so desires; but he does, in fact, buy our goods in increasing quantities, because the quality suits him and the price is satisfactory.

We do not aim to control all the biscuit business, but we are striving by every legitimate means to gather into this company all the *best* business possible in our line of manufacture. We do not pretend to sell our standard goods cheaper than other manufacturers of biscuit sell their goods. They always undersell us. Why do they not take away our business?

First, because they cannot make goods equal in quality to ours.

Second, because they cannot put them in the In-er-seal patent package.

Third, because they cannot give the trade the efficient service we furnish.

On the package business we have practically no competition—*not* because the field is not open to all, *not* because we have had any special privileges, except such as were granted by the United States. These privileges lie in the patents we control and in our trademarks. *The trademarks we adopted.* Their value we created.

When the company started, our goods were sold almost entirely in bulk, and the package business was in its infancy. We determined that the true way to sell certain of our goods was to sell them in small, airtight, moisture-proof packages. The first result of this determination was the Uneeda Biscuit, a five-cent package of soda biscuit put up in a package protected by United States patent. The idea was novel, and we soon found we had struck the taste of the people. The introduction of the Uneeda Biscuit was followed by many other packages put up in the same manner and sealed with the In-er-seal trademark design.

The next point was to reach the consumer. Knowing that we had something that the consumer wanted, we had to advise the consumer of its existence. We did this by extensive advertising.

The results have exceeded even our expectations. The consumers are not obliged to buy many millions of our packages every month, but they have done so because they wanted them, and the consumer is the final arbiter. The great body of the consumers have become our allies in this great enterprise. So far as we have any monopoly in this business, it is one that the people have voluntarily conferred upon us.

It is said that imitation is the sincerest form of flattery. If this be so, then, since the introduction of our In-er-seal patent package, we have not been wanting in a constant stream of flattery. More than thirty imitations of Uneeda Biscuit have been put upon the market. One after another in constant procession they have appeared, have lived a short, uneventful life, and disappeared. The Uneeda Biscuit still remains, with increasing sales and with increasing value to this company. So have our other advertised packages been imitated—but the consumer buys our packages in ever-increasing numbers. This business is *our* business, which no one can take away.

So rapidly has our package business increased that our facilities have become inadequate, and we are now planning to build, this year, two large biscuit works to take care of this increasing business.

The spirit throughout the company is of the best. We are like a great army, all animated with a like spirit, and with but one aim—100 percent efficiency in every department of the company. We may never reach that efficiency, but we prefer to aim for it rather than to be satisfied with less.

The past year has successfully demonstrated the soundness of the policy we have adopted for the management of this company. The margin between the prices of raw material and prices obtained for our goods has been generally less during the preceding year; but our sales have increased, and the economies we have introduced into our business have brought better and quicker results than we ourselves anticipated.

That the officers and managers of this company have confidence in its continued prosperity is shown by the fact that they are themselves the owners of many millions of both the common and preferred stock, and that, notwithstanding the advance in price, the amount held by them is larger than it was a year ago. That our employees share with the management in loyalty to the company and faith in its future is shown by the result of the plan adopted by our board of directors in February of last year enabling employees to buy our preferred stock in single shares, paying for it in installments.

The total number of stockholders of the company, immediately after its organization, was about 1,300. The total number now is 5,153, of which 1,860 are women.

Trustees as we are for this large and constantly increasing body of stockholders, many of them women, some of them the widows and children of former associates, all of them entitled to the best service we can give them, we must and do feel that the administration of this great property is a trust of the highest and most sacred character, and while it is in our charge we shall ever strive to administer it in this spirit.

V

Increasing expenditure on advertising soon led to efforts to understand the sudden prominence of this enterprise, and to justify it. To a society accustomed to an ethic of thriftiness, there was something suspect about messages to buy. One way to quiet these fears was to emphasize how vital advertising was to the well-being of the economy and that the well-being of the economy was crucial to the good order of the society. The analysis below, by Joseph Appel, a long-time associate of John Wanamaker, was one effort in this direction.

GROWING UP WITH ADVERTISING, 1940

JOSEPH H. APPEL

In 1924, from my growing practical experience in business, I formulated for educational use my conception and understanding of advertising as it then appeared and as here presented in unified and primer form:

Attracting attention is the primary meaning of the word advertising.

Anything that attracts attention, either unfavorable or favorable, is advertising.

When advertising attracts unfavorable attention, it is bad.

When advertising attracts favorable attention, it is good.

But all arresting of attention, good or bad, is advertising.

In *Growing Up with Advertising*, by Joseph H. Appel (New York, 1940), pp. 106–107, 112–17, 126–29.

It is well to remember this fact at the outset, because it links everyone in business with the whole organization itself, with its advertising, its selling, its making of profits, its good will, its success or failure as a going concern.

The newspaper is the natural medium for a store's advertising because it offers concentrated home circulation in the most fertile selling field, in centers where population is thickest, need of goods most urgent, and money most plentiful.

Merchants in cities and towns who advertise in the daily newspapers reach the largest percentage of money-spending people most directly and efficiently.

Yet it required a long time for merchants to learn how to use newspapers in the most efficient way.

At first newspaper advertising consisted only of announcements— the store name and location, the mere mention of goods on sale, perhaps of a new shipment.

This sort of advertising made very dry reading. It lacked human interest. It was not even news, because the same announcement was repeated day after day. Merchants even announced Christmas goods in January because they forgot to change their advertisement.

Little by little merchants began to wake up to the fact that advertising, properly done, in a human-interest way, could be made a great force in attracting business, and advertising came to be studied in a scientific way.

Today, advertising by the printed word is recognized as both a science and an art and the business of advertising is recognized as a profession like the profession of law, of medicine, of teaching, even of preaching. Great advertising agencies are established to study the science and practice the art of distribution of merchandise by means of advertising. Schools of advertising are established in colleges and universities.

There are those who say that too much money is being expended in advertising; that such expenditure is not warranted by the business that it attracts; that advertising is overdone; that much advertising is waste; that it forces people to buy too much, more than they need, and thus makes them extravagant.

Some of this criticism may be true but, on the other hand, it is also true that without advertising business would not have developed anywhere near the volume in which it operates today; merchandise would not be so well made and standardized; and prices would not be so low, quality considered.

Advertising makes possible the multiple merchant because advertising is the million-tongued salesman.

Advertising distributes the merchandise of the world, and then produces demand for still more.

Advertising both creates wants and supplies them.

Advertising is capital, not expense. It is an asset, not a liability.

Advertising is a real producer of wealth. It lights factory fires, keeps the wheels of industry amove, spans continents with railroads, sends the ships of commerce in never-ending circles around the globe.

Advertising is a great builder. It builds businesses. It builds fortunes. It builds homes and communities and cities and nations.

Advertising even upbuilds humanity, for advertising is a great educator, a great humanizer, a great civilizer.

Advertising teaches a better way of living, a better way of furnishing homes, a better way of managing our affairs.

Advertising, as known the world over today, is largely the product of America, of the last half-century of America's young life.

Advertising is the creative power of this, the most wonderful business age the world has ever seen.

Like merchandising itself, advertising finds a true foundation only as it becomes a public service.

Unless advertising renders a real service to the people in lowering and stabilizing prices, in raising qualities, and maintaining standards of products, in giving useful information which leads to intelligent buying, or in building great businesses which in themselves become a service to the people, it becomes an evil and should be kept out of the business system.

The mental stages in the operations of advertising are much the same as the mental stages in salesmanship. They are:

1. *Get seen.*
2. *Get read.*
3. *Get believed.*
4. *Get into the store people with a desire for the goods.*
5. *Get satisfaction into the minds and hearts of your customer.*
6. *Get the good will of the community.*

First, we must look squarely in the face this fact: *Advertising is not to sell goods but to help people buy goods.* This changes its entire aspect. It takes a new point of view.

The advertiser must actually stand in the shoes of the customer.

The advertiser must stand on the outside of the counter. He must put on the customer's spectacles, for the time being. He will serve the firm all the better by serving the customer first.

An advertiser must become, at times, a millionaire, a struggling laborer, a man of affairs, a clerk, a mother, a father, a bachelor, an art lover, a miser, as the case may be; running the gamut of life in all its stages; appealing to each reader, if possible; if not, then appealing to some trait common to them all.

Economy is the touchstone for thousands—but not for everybody.

Uniqueness of goods appeals to some.

Extravagance appeals to a few.

Exclusiveness appeals to many.

Newness of goods appeals to very many.

Quality and style are perhaps the strongest magnets of all.

The advertiser must use his own imagination to arouse the imagination of the reader. Analysis shows that of the total volume of merchandise bought at retail annually in the United States, nine-tenths is bought by women.

Woman is a creature of the imagination. We pay her a compliment when we say this, for imagination comes from the feelings, feelings come from what we call the heart, and the heart type of mankind is the highest of all.

And so the advertising appeal, to reach women, must not disregard the first great quality of the heart, which is love. Love is a product of the imagination; we love each other because we see things in the same light; we have the same ideals.

Most advertisers do not disregard the quality of love. There, unmistakably, in almost every advertisement is a reference, in word, or picture, to mother love, to the home, to children, to sentiment.

While it might be unwise to mix too much sentiment and imagination with reason in an advertisement to reach men, there can scarcely be too much sentiment or too much imagination in an advertisement to reach women. In fact, many advertisements for women should be pointed directly at the heart side of their nature.

Even vanity comes from the heart and vanity buys many articles of merchandise.

Chapter 12

The Company Town

THE CONSUMPTION ETHIC spread rapidly through industrial America, promoting, at least among the middle and upper classes, a new confidence in the future stability of the society. As the favored groups viewed it, consumerism would insure social harmony, first, because the rise in the standard of living that would result from the widespread distribution of goods would minimize the felt need for protest or discontent; and, second, because in this system, the diligent and ambitious worker could make his way up the social ladder, his success limited only by talent and energy. In brief, property accumulation and social mobility would eliminate the seeds of discontent and protest from below.

How valid were these assumptions? How wide was the actual distribution of goods through social classes in industrial America? To what degree did social mobility operate? In brief, was rags-to-riches really part of the American story?

For the middle and upper classes, the consumer orientation of the economic system clearly was advantageous. Their wants were satisfied, and the rhetoric of advertising made their buying seem almost patriotic. Occasional critics like Thorstein Veblen bemoaned "conspicuous consumption," but his was an isolated complaint. Spending, whether for frills or necessities, had become a virtue. The more difficult question, however, concerns the fate of the working classes. How did they fare in this economic system? Did grandiose promises have any meaning in their lives?

A useful way to approach this issue is to examine closely one economic enterprise in which workers reputedly fared very well. In supposedly favored circumstances, did workers have the ability to determine their wages, to improve employment conditions, to share in the products of the system? Or, in fact, were they ultimately helpless against the power of employers who were far more concerned with the profit and loss ledgers than with their workers' standards of living? The enterprise analyzed here is the Pullman company town, located on the out-skirts of Chicago and, by reputation at least, one of the most enlightened and benevolent of American industrial organizations.

In 1867, George Pullman went into the business of manufacturing railroad cars for passengers, and he quickly made a success of it. (Well after World War II, people still talked about going "Pullman.") The scope and profitability of his enterprise made it possible for him in 1880 to build his own town and move his factories and workers there. The effort, in many ways reminiscent of Lowell, received much favor-able publicity. Yet, when put under scrutiny, Pullman town reveals not only the idiosyncrasies of its particular design but also the severe limits on the power of the workers to determine their own fate. Pull-man's goals were certainly not just philanthropic. The company town banned taverns from its premises in an effort to preserve the health and moral of the workers and to maintain rigid discipline in the work force. The very idea of the isolation of workers in one town worked to stabilize Pullman's work force. Given the absence of any other industry in town, the worker who would leave Pullman's factory would have to leave the town, a decision often difficult to make. Indeed, the character of the Pullman system became far clearer after the recession of 1893. Pullman immediately moved to cut back his workers' wages, while at the same time keeping constant the rents for company houses. The workers went out on strike. The events that then transpired are re-ported in full detail in the report of the subsequent Congressional investigation. Here we can see where the balance of power actually rested between worker and owner.

I

The enthusiasm with which observers greeted the building of Pullman town emerges vividly in this 1884 survey of conditions by the Illinois Bureau of Labor Statistics. The Bureau was, on the whole, very impressed with what they found. Their only regret was that more workers did not enjoy such benefits.

INDUSTRIAL, SOCIAL, AND ECONOMIC CONDITIONS AT PULLMAN, ILLINOIS, 1884

Our object in making the investigation was to give to the manufacturers and capitalists of our respective states official information relative to one of the most attractive experiments of the age seeking to harmonize the interests of labor and capital. It is no part of our duty to eulogize individuals; we have endeavored to learn results.

In *Third Biennial Report: Industrial, Social, and Economic Conditions at Pullman, Illinois,* Illinois Bureau of Labor Statistics (Springfield, Ill., 1884), pp. 638–54.

Pullman's Palace Car Co. was founded in 1867, with a capital of one million dollars; its extended operations have been conducted on the strictest business principles, and have, from time to time, necessitated increases in its capital stock, until now its capital represents nearly sixteen million dollars; its palace cars are operated on upwards of seventy thousand miles of railway in America and Europe. Its capital stock has been paid in dollar for dollar and no watering processes have ever entered into the financial operations of the company. Its dividends have been regular and ample.

Four or five years ago Mr. Pullman determined to bring the greater portion of the works of the company into one locality. It was essential that a site should be selected where communication could be had with the whole country, and near some metropolitan place like Chicago. He wished above all things to remove his workmen from the close quarters of a great city, and give them the healthful benefits of good air, good drainage, and good water, and where they would be free, so far as it would lie in the power of management to keep them free, from the many seductive influences of a great town.

He was fortunate in securing about four thousand acres of land on the Illinois Central Road, a dozen miles to the south of Chicago. This land was located in the town of Hyde Park, and here he built his city.

On the twenty-fifth day of May 1880, ground was first broken for the building of the Palace Car Works, and the city of Pullman. The land was an open and not over-promising prairie.

The first efforts were directed toward the scientific drainage of the future town.

The city of Pullman is exception in respect to drainage and sewerage if in no other regard. For here the drainage preceded the population, and the soil is now as free from organic contamination as when it formed a portion of the open prairie. Every house has been constructed from approved plans, and under the supervision of competent builders and engineers.

The perfection of the site selected was accomplished through surface drainage, and the construction of deep sewers. With the scientific drainage and sewage system, in the construction of which nearly one million dollars ($1,000,000) were expended underneath the ground before anything appeared on its surface, came the erection of the works and the dwellings of the town. It is sufficient to say that the same care exercised in guarding the future health of the place has been bestowed in the erection of works and dwellings.

In the center stands the water tower which takes a supply of water from Lake Michigan and distributes it through the town. Around the tower are located the principal works; to the south and north of the works, chiefly to the south, are the dwellings.

The appearance from the railroad as one approaches from Chicago is effective. The neat station; the water tower and the works in front; the park and artificial lakes intervening; to the right a picturesque hotel backed by pretty dwellings; the arcade containing stores, library, theatre, offices, etc.; still further to the right, and beyond, a church which fits into the landscape with artistic effect.

The laying out of the whole town has been under the guidance of skilled architects aided by civil engineers and landscape gardeners.

The dwellings present a great variety of architecture, yet give harmonious effects. They are not built like the tenement houses of ordinary manufacturing towns, but a successful effort has been made to give diversity to architectural design.

The streets are wide, well built, and wherever possible parked. The lawns are kept in order by the company; the shade trees are cared for, and all the police work is done under competent supervision.

Every care has been taken to secure convenience inside as well as outside the dwellings. The cheapest tenement is supplied with gas and water and garbage outlets. The housekeeper throws the garbage into a specified receptacle and has no more care of it.

The testimony of every woman we met was that housekeeping was rendered far more easy in Pullman than in any other place. In fact the women were in love with the place: its purity of air, cleanliness of houses and streets, and lessened household burdens are advantages over their former residences which brought out the heartiest expressions of approval. Pullman has really wrought a greater change for the women than for any other class of its dwellers.

There are 1,520 brick tenements in houses and flats. The frontage of all the buildings extends along five miles of solid paved streets, and there are fourteen miles of railroad track laid for the use of those in the shops and the town. The buildings are of brick or stone.

The industries carried on and for which the city was built comprise the manufacture of Pullman Palace Cars, and all classes of passenger and freight cars.

Gradually the manufacture of all the parts necessary to the construction of cars in every condition is being added to the enterprise of the town. A laundry is being established for cleansing the vast quantities of linen used in the palace car service which will give employment to women; it is the policy of the company to encourage the employment of women and young persons.

The wages paid in the works at Pullman are somewhat higher than those paid for like work in other places. They have been adjusted on the hour basis, and from such basis piece wages have been arranged. The attempt to justly equalize and adjust wages has sometimes caused complaint amongst the workmen, and in one instance a strike of small moment. With this exception no strikes have occurred at Pullman city, and so far as we could learn there was no complaint regarding wages paid.

It costs quite as much to live in Pullman as in any other locality with which it can be reasonably compared. A two-room tenement in a second story flat, but having all the conveniences of water and gas, and for sewage and garbage, rents for $4 per month, and a three-room tenement, similarly situated, for $4.50 per month. Two-room flats in small houses, large enough to accommodate five families, rent all the way from $5 to $8.50 per month, while two-, three-, and four-room tenements in large blocks rent from $6.50 to $10 per month.

The rentals at Pullman are a little higher for the same number of rooms than in Chicago, but in Chicago the tenement would be in a narrow street or alley, while in Pullman it is on a broad avenue where no garbage is allowed to collect, and where beauty, order, and cleanliness prevail, and fresh air abounds.

The tenant is under no restrictions beyond those ordinarily contained in a lease, except that he must leave his tenement at ten day's notice, or he can give the same notice and quit. This short limitation has been established in order that no liquor saloons, objectionable houses, or anything likely to disturb the *morals* of the place can become fastened on the community.

All the houses in Pullman city are owned by the company. This policy has been considered the best in the early years of the city in order that a foundation may be securely laid for a community of good habits and good order.

The men are employed without restriction. There are no conditions laid upon their freedom; they are paid fortnightly, and they expend their wages when and where they see fit, their rent being charged against their wages. This, at first, caused some complaint, but the system is now generally liked, for when wages are paid there is no bother about rent bills, and the wife and the children know that the home is secure. Repairs, if due to the carelessness or negligence of the tenant, are made by the company at the lowest possible expense, and charged against the tenant. Of course, the company, like all landlords, expects to keep the houses in tenantable condition.

The company has erected a very fine school building having fourteen commodious rooms, which now contain about 900 pupils.

There are two or three religious societies and the beautiful church which has been built by the company, while occupied by any sect or by anybody that wishes to hold meetings there, is awaiting the occupancy of some society that chooses to lease it at a fair rental.

The company has also provided a gymnasium, an amphitheater for games, baseball grounds, and in the arcade is one of the most aesthetic theaters in the country.

There is but little crime or drunkenness in Pullman, and one policeman, an officer appointed by the authorities of Hyde Park, constitutes the police force for 8,500 people.

There is no pauperism; two or three families, where the head had been taken away, or where some accident or misfortune had rendered it necessary, have been aided; but pauperism, as such, does not exist at Pullman.

We found the *morale* of the place even better than we expected. Merely external appearances may not clearly indicate social conditions nor the motive and the policy of the management in such an establishment; yet, if the commissioners did not find that the whole plan was conceived and executed in a spirit of broad and unostentatious philanthropy, our observations and conclusions were at fault throughout.

If the workman at Pullman lives in a "gilded cage," we must congratulate him on its being so handsomely gilded; the average workman does not have his cage gilded. That there is any cage or imprisonment about it is not true, save in the sense that all men are circumscribed by the conditions with which they surround themselves and imprisoned by the daily duties of life.

II

*A more cautious yet still favorable estimate of the virtues of Pullman
town emerged in the analysis of the economist Richard Ely. Born
in 1854, Ely had been trained in Germany. He returned to the
United States to teach first at Johns Hopkins and then at the University of Wisconsin. A reform-minded scholar, one who was not
trapped in the rigidities of classical economic doctrines, Ely also
helped to organize the American Economic Association. That he
also found much to praise in Pullman suggests just how appealing
the venture was to contemporaries.*

PULLMAN: A SOCIAL STUDY, 1885

RICHARD ELY

Much could be said of Pullman as a manufacturing center, but the
purpose of this article is to treat it as an attempt to furnish laborers
with the best homes under the most healthful conditions and with the
most favorable surroundings in every respect, for Pullman aims to be
a forerunner of better things for the laboring classes.

The questions to be answered are these: Is Pullman a success from
a social standpoint? Is it worthy of imitation? Is it likely to inaugurate
a new era in society? If only a partial success, what are its bright
features and what its dark features?

One of the most striking peculiarities of this place is the all-pervading air of thrift and providence. The most pleasing impression of
general well-being is at once produced. Contrary to what is seen
ordinarily in laborers' quarters, not a dilapidated doorstep nor a broken
window, stuffed perhaps with old clothing, is to be found in the city.
The streets of Pullman, always kept in perfect condition, are wide and
finely macadamized.

Unity of design and an unexpected variety charm us as we saunter
through the town. The streets cross each other at right angles, yet here
again skill has avoided the frightful monotony of New York, which must
sometimes tempt a nervous person to scream for relief. A public square,
arcade, hotel, market, or some large building is often set across a street
so ingeniously as to break the regular line, yet without inconvenience
to traffic. Then at the termination of long streets a pleasing view
greets and relieves the eye—a bit of water, a stretch of meadow, a
clump of trees, or even one of the large but neat workshops. All this
grows upon the visitor day by day. No other feature of Pullman can
receive praise needing so little qualification as its architecture.

Pullman is only a part of the large village and town of Hyde Park,
but the latter appears to have relinquished the government of this por-

In *Harper's New Monthly Magazine*, 70 (1885): 452–66.

tion of its territory bearing the name of Pullman to private corporations, and the writer was not able to find that a single resident of Pullman, not an officer of the Pullman companies, was either in the board of trustees of Hyde Park or in the staff of officers. The town clerk and treasurer are both officers of the Pullman Palace Car Company, and the directory of Hyde Park reveals the fact that with one exception every member of the board of education of the Pullman school district is an officer of the Palace Car Company or some concern which bears the name of Pullman.

One of Mr. Pullman's fundamental ideas is the *commercial value of beauty*, and this he has endeavored to carry out as faithfully in the town which bears his name as in the Pullman drawing room and sleeping cars. He is one of the few men who have thought it a paying investment to expend millions for the purpose of surrounding laborers with objects of beauty and comfort. In a hundred ways one sees in Pullman today evidences of its founder's sagacious foresight. One of the most interesting is the fact that the company finds it pays them in dollars and cents to keep the streets sprinkled with water and the lawns well trimmed, the saving in paint and kalsomine more than repaying the outlay.

For the rest, the neat exterior is a constant example, which is sure sooner or later to exert its proper effect on housewives stimulating them to exertion in behalf of cleanliness and order.

It should be constantly borne in mind that all investments and outlays in Pullman are intended to yield financial returns satisfactory from a purely business point of view. The minimum return expected is six per centum on expenditure, and the town appears to have yielded a far higher percentage on cost up to the present time. The extreme reluctance of the officers of the company to make precise statements of any kind renders it impossible to obtain the accurate information desired. Yet there seems to be no reason to doubt the emphatic assertion that the whole establishment pays handsomely.

It pays also in another way. The wholesome, cheerful surroundings enable the men to work more constantly and more efficiently. The healthy condition of the residents is a matter of general comment.

If what is done for the residents of the town were simply a generous gift, another might argue, "If Mr. Pullman chooses to spend his money this way, very well! I have no objection, but I prefer to keep a stable of blooded horses. Each one according to his taste!" But certainly it is a great thing to have demonstrated the commercial value of beauty in a city of laborers.

But admirable as are the peculiarities of Pullman which have been described, certain unpleasant features of social life in that place are soon noticed by the careful observer, which moderate the enthusiasm one is at first inclined to feel.

One just cause of complaint is what in government affairs would be called a bad civil service, that is, a bad administration in respect to the employment, retention, and promotion of employees. Change is constant in men and officers, and each new superior appears to have his own friends, whom he appoints to desirable positions.

The resulting evil is very naturally dissatisfaction, a painful prevalence of petty jealousies, a discouragement of superior excellence, frequent change in the residents, and an all-pervading feeling of insecurity. Nobody regards Pullman as a real home, and, in fact, it can scarcely be said that there are more than temporary residents at Pullman. The nature of the leases aggravates this evil. Every tenant holds his house on a lease which may be terminated on ten days' notice. It is not necessary that any reason be assigned for the notice.

Furthermore, three-fourths of the laborers in Pullman are employed by the Palace Car Company, and many of those who do not work for it are employed in establishments in which the company as such or a prominent member of it is interested. The power of Bismarck in Germany is utterly insignificant when compared with the power of the ruling authority of the Pullman Palace Car Company in Pullman. Whether the power be exercised rightfully or wrongfully, it is there all the same.

It is impossible within the realm of Pullman to escape from the overshadowing influence of the company, and every resident feels this, and "monopoly" is a word which constantly falls on the ear of the visitor. Large as the place is, it supports no newspaper, through which complaints might find utterance, and one whose official position in the town qualified him to speak with knowledge declared positively that no publication would be allowed which was not under the direct influence of the Pullman Company.

It is indeed a sad spectacle. Here is a population of eight thousand souls where not one single resident dare speak out openly his opinion about the town in which he lives. One feels that one is mingling with a dependent, servile people. There is an abundance of grievances, but if there lives in Pullman one man who would give expression to them in print over his own name, diligent inquiry continued for ten days was not sufficient to find him.

The men believe they are watched by the "company's spotter," and to let one of them know that information was desired about Pullman for publication was to close his lips to the honest expression of opinion. The women were inclined to be more outspoken. The free discussion of local affairs, and the full responsibility for what is done and not done, have ever been held to be an education of the mind, a means to develop the qualities most useful in a citizen of a republic. Yet in Pullman all this disappears. The citizen is surrounded by constant restraint and restriction, and everything is done for him, nothing by him.

The desire of the American to acquire a home is justly considered most commendable and hopeful. It promotes thrift and economy, and the habits acquired in the effort to pay for it are often the foundation of a future prosperous career.

Again, a large number of house owners is a safeguard against violent movements of social discontent. Heretofore laborers at Pullman have not been allowed to acquire any real property in the place. There is a repression here as elsewhere of any marked individuality. Everything tends to stamp upon residents, as upon the town, the character expressed in "machinemade." Individual initiative, even in affairs which concern the residents alone, is repressed. Once several of the men wanted to form a kind of mutual insurance association to insure themselves against loss of time in case of accident, but it was frowned down by the authorities, and nothing further has been heard of the matter.

In looking over all the facts of the case the conclusion is unavoidable that the idea of Pullman is un-American. It is a nearer approach than anything the writer has seen to what appears to be the ideal of the great German Chancellor. It is not the American ideal.

III

In May 1894, one of the most famous strikes in the nation's history occurred at Pullman. The workers protested a series of wage cuts, especially angry that the rents in company-owned houses had not been reduced proportionately. After a delegation called on the Pullman management and received no satisfaction, the men went out on strike. They quickly won the sympathy and support of the American Railways Union, headed by Eugene Debs. The union decided not to move any trains that had Pullman cars on them. For their part, the owners refused to remove the Pullman cars, provoking an impasse, and railroad transportation ground to a halt. At this point, the managers applied for and received an injunction from the federal courts ordering the union to end its strike. Since the strike prevented the movement of the mail, argued the court, the federal government had the right to intervene on behalf of the owners. When Debs and his followers disobeyed the order, and violence broke out between some of the strikers and the company guards, Pullman appealed to President Grover Cleveland for assistance. Cleveland dispatched troops to break the strike. In short order, Debs was in jail and the company had its victory.

A congressional investigation of the strike examined in detail not only the events surrounding May 1894, but also the working conditions at Pullman. The result is an extraordinarily enlightening document, clarifying the realities with which labor lived. Clearly the balance of power rested with management. It did win its final victory in the courts, but the result was clear from the start.

REPORT ON THE CHICAGO STRIKE
OF JUNE–JULY 1894

TESTIMONY ON THE PART OF THE STRIKING EMPLOYEES AT THE TOWN OF PULLMAN

Testimony of Thomas W. Heathcoate

August 16, 1894, Thomas W. Heathcoate, being first duly sworn, testified as follows:

In *Report on the Chicago Strike of June–July 1894*, United States Strike Commission, 53rd Congress, 3rd session, U.S. Senate Document, no. 7 (1894), pp. 416–79, 508–16.

Commissioner Wright: State your name, age, residence, and occupation.

Mr. Heathcoate: My name is Thomas W. Heathcoate; am fifty-eight years of age; reside at Pullman, Ill. I was employed at the Pullman shops until the recent strike; have been at Pullman as a car builder five years; am a member of the American Railway Union and am president of local union, No. 208, at Pullman; the membership of that local union is 656.

Commissioner Wright: State what you know of the causes which led to that strike by the local unions at Pullman.

Mr. Heathcoate: In May 1893, we were getting good wages. Along about September 1893, our wages began to be reduced because work was slack, and they kept reducing our pay each month. They kept reducing the price of piecework until it was almost impossible for us to live; in January 1894, the men wanted to strike, but we were not organized at that time; and in order to succeed in securing a higher rate of pay it became necessary for us to organize in some way; we could not see any more feasible plan than to organize in the American Railway Union, for the reason, we believed, that union was stronger than any other organization in the country.

Along about the first of April 1894, we began to organize, and in order to do so we had to go to Grand Crossing, as the Pullman company would not tolerate any union in their shops. If a man belonged to a union, if the company knew it, he was discharged. Then we held meetings over in Kensington. At about the first meeting that was held I think about two hundred signed their names as members of the American Railway Union. The conditions became worse; in April there was another cut, which made it impossible for us to maintain our families and pay our rent; we had to do something; times were hard and men could not get money enough to move away from Pullman; we did not know really what to do. I used my utmost endeavors to keep the men from striking. I knew the condition of the times. We then held meetings until we had about 35 percent of the men organized; and on the tenth of May, after this committee had been down to see the Pullman officials, after they had used every effort with the Pullman company to make some concessions toward the raising of wages or reduction of them, the mediation board, which was a committee composed of three members from each local union, then organized, met in Turner Hall, and were in session all night discussing what to do, and that night a strike was ordered.

The strike occurred on May 11, 1894, and we then met and appointed what is called a central strike committee for the purpose of conducting the strike. We then appointed committees to watch the Pullman property, so as to protect it. We kept them there night and day, changing the men, until the United States Government sent troops there.

Commissioner Wright: Did any violence or destruction of property take place at Pullman?

Mr. Heathcoate: No, sir.

Commissioner Wright: What wages were you receiving at time of and prior to the strike?

Mr. Heathcoate: Now I was foreman of a gang. In June 1893, my pay for two weeks' work was $43.55 at piecework; in July 1893, my pay for two weeks' work was $34.65. In the first two weeks of September my pay was $32.70, and for the last two weeks of September, $12.25. We were laid off from the twenty-second to the last of September, that is, the foreman laid all the gang off, so I only earned $12.25 that two weeks. During the month of October we had no work at all. The first two weeks in November I received $8.05; the second two weeks $20.10. There was another cut. During the last two weeks of December 1893, I worked everyday except seven hours and earned $21.15; in January 1894, I worked full time with the exception of five hours and earned $20.85.

Commissioner Kernan: What would you have earned for the same time in June 1893?

Mr. Heathcoate: Forty-eight dollars. In March 1894, the first two weeks I made $24.75, and the next two weeks, $26.50.

Commissioner Kernan: What would you have earned for the same work in June 1893?

Mr. Heathcoate: About $43. We were making in June 1893, from 28½ to 32½ cents per hour on piecework, and now we are making 19 cents and hour, and 18, 15, and 14 cents.

Commissioner Kernan: What do you mean by now?

Mr. Heathcoate: In the months of March, April, and May 1894. I worked up to April 4, and we appointed a committee to go and see Mr. Wickes. On the fifth that committee returned to Pullman. We waited two days to have an answer from Mr. Wickes in regard to what should be done, and on the ninth we returned again to Mr. Wickes.

Commissioner Kernan: You have not given us what you said to Mr. Wickes?

Mr. Heathcoate: We went down and saw him, stated our case to him, and he said he could not do anything, that the company could not pay any more wages, that they were losing money. I asked Mr. Wickes why it was that railroad companies were paying $2.50 per day for the same work the Pullman company were only paying $1.90 for. He said he was not aware of anything of that kind. I had gotten that information from the master car builder of the Great Western road and the Northern Pacific. Only ours was piecework and theirs was day work.

A man has to do about four times as much work at piecework as he has to do at day work, because the prices are cut down so low it is almost impossible for a man, unless he is an expert, to make $1.90 per day at the work.

Commissioner Wright: Do you live at Pullman now, and occupy one of the Pullman houses?

Mr. Heathcoate: Yes, sir.

Commissioner Wright: What rent do you pay?

Mr. Heathcoate: $17.71 per month.

Commissioner Wright: What is the size of the house?

Mr. Heathcoate: Five rooms, a cellar, and a back yard.

Commissioner Wright: What would you have to pay in this city for the same accommodations, or say in Kensington or Hyde Park?

Mr. Heathcoate: There are seven and eight room cottages that are renting there today for $7, $8, and $9 per month.

Commissioner Wright: What was the price last year for such accommodations as you have at Pullman?

Mr. Heathcoate: The same as it is now.

Commissioner Wright: Has there been any change in the rental since you have been working there?

Mr. Heathcoate: No, sir. When we left the Pullman service we owed George M. Pullman $70,000 rent, and our pay was such we could not pay our rent and have sufficient to eat. I have known men to drop down by the side of a car when they were working for want of food; and there were hundreds of men in that condition at the Pullman shops when we quit.

Commissioner Worthington: Do I understand you to say that all the operatives who live in Pullman and are housekeepers live in houses owned by the Pullman company?

Mr. Heathcoate: Whenever a man is employed in the Pullman shops he is supposed to live in a Pullman house until the Pullman houses are filled. I have known men who owned property in Roseland who had to leave their property not rented and come down to Pullman and hire houses in order to fill up the Pullman houses.

Commissioner Kernan: How was that rule made and enforced?

Mr. Heathcoate: Suppose you made application to a foreman for a job; if the houses in Pullman were not filled he would give you a job, provided you moved into Pullman; that was made a condition of the job.

Commissioner Kernan: You spoke about owing $70,000 back rent; during how long a period has that accumulated?

Mr. Heathcoate: The accumulation of the back rent commenced about the first of November. I do not think there was a man in the Pullman shops that owed any rent up to November 1, 1893.

Commissioner Kernan: Do you know what, if any, attempts have been made to collect those rents during the last three or four months?

Mr. Heathcoate: They have been around twice after the rent within the last three months; there have not been any attempts at eviction as yet; when we used to get our pay our pay was in two checks, one check for the rent, the other for the amount we had left.

Commissioner Kernan: How would the check be made out for the rent?

Mr. Heathcoate: It would be made out in full for the current rent; that is, two weeks in advance.

Commissioner Kernan: Was the check payable to your order?

Mr. Heathcoate: Yes, and I would have to endorse the rent check.

Commissioner Kernan: And that check would be good anywhere?

Mr. Heathcoate: They have a paymaster and a rent collector that goes with him.

Commissioner Kernan: Could you get the rent check cashed anywhere in town?

Mr. Heathcoate: Not without I was to keep it and not sign it. If I was in such a condition that I could not pay my rent, or any part of it, of course the law of the State is that I must be paid in full; of course they could not compel me to pay the rent, but if I had only $9 coming to me, or any other amount, the rent would be taken out of my pay; that is, the rent check would be left at the bank and I would have to leave my work in the shop, go over to the bank and have an argument there for a few minutes to get the gentleman to let me have money to live on, and sometimes I would get it and sometimes not. I have seen men with families of eight or nine children to support crying there because they only got three or four cents after paying their rent; I have seen them stand by the window and cry for money enough to enable them to keep their families; I have been insulted at that window time and time again by the clerks when I tried to get money enough to support my family, even after working everyday and overtime.

Commissioner Wright: Do you know how many liquor saloons there are in Kensington and vicinity?

Mr. Heathcoate: There must be somewhere in the neighborhood of one hundred, and one in Pullman at the Hotel Florence.

Commissioner Wright: Is the prohibition or temperance question, in relation to whether saloons shall or shall not be licensed at Pullman, regulated by vote?

Mr. Heathcoate: I don't know that there has been any vote in regard to the liquor question there since I have been in Pullman. The management get their drinks at the hotel, but the men have to go to Kensington and Roseland.

Commissioner Wright: To what extent do they go to Kensington for that purpose?

Mr. Heathcoate: There are quite a number of Germans there who indulge in drinking beer, more or less.

Commissioner Wright: Has there been much of that since the strike began?

Mr. Heathcoate: No, sir; I have advocated in all my speeches to the strikers not to carry any pails of beer over to Pullman.

Commissioner Kernan: The number of saloons there seems to be regulated by public sentiment, does it not?

Mr. Heathcoate: I don't know as to that, but I don't think public sentiment would favor so many saloons as there are at Kensington and Roseland.

Commissioner Kernan: I am speaking of Pullman?

Mr. Heathcoate: Oh, no; George M. Pullman regulates that himself.

Testimony of Rev. William H. Carwardine

August 17, 1894, Rev. William H. Carwardine, being first duly sworn, testified as follows:

Commissioner Wright: State your name, profession, and residence.

Mr. Carwardine: William H. Carwardine; am a clergyman of the Methodist Episcopal Church, Pullman, Ill.

Commissioner Wright: How long have you been at Pullman?

Mr. Carwardine: It will be two years the first of October.

Commissioner Wright: State what you know of your own knowledge relative to the causes of the strike there.

Mr. Carwardine: Last year we had a very prosperous year at Pullman and the men were apparently doing very nicely; along toward September, we entered into a very dull season. During the winter I realized that there was a great deal of dissatisfaction among the employees. I also realized there was a great deal of distress by reason of the hard times, and here and there cases of destitution were shown. Toward the spring I realized that the dissatisfaction was about to break out—it is simply the old story—they took the matter to Mr. Pullman and Mr. Wickes, talked the matter over with them and did not get any redress there. I watched them go out and felt very sorry. I saw the employees were being condemned very much by the press, and a brother clergyman in the town told them he thought they had done a very unwise thing; that he thought they were better off in the shops, etc., and knowing the state of affairs as I had seen it, I felt I must preach upon the subject, as the other pastor had done, and state my views on the question. I judge from all I have found out in regard to the matter that in the first place the wages were cut very severely. I also realize that one cause of the strike was that while they were cutting wages, they did not at the same time make a reduction in the rents, and when the employees made their appeal for an investigation they were very suspicious; they were in a state of suspicion regarding the company. They had come to feel that they could get no justice. I have felt that the great trouble has been, that the difficulty lies, with the local administration. I have felt, however, that Mr. Pullman is to blame for this; he has not kept himself in touch with the laboring men. I feel free to make the statement that there never would have been a strike in Pullman if Mr. Pullman had been in closer relations to his men, and if the rents had been reduced at the same time the wages were cut.

Commissioner Wright: If the works cease entirely to operate, would you have the rents cease entirely, too?

Mr. Carwardine: Of course if the works ceased at Pullman that would end the whole matter.

Commissioner Wright: It would end the relation of employer and employee?

Mr. Carwardine: Yes, sir; it would to a great extent; but the reason I criticize the Pullman company is this: They started out upon the basis that their system is paternalistic, and they founded their system upon a desire to improve the workingmen and to solve the industrial situation, for instance, on a basis of a mutual recognition. Now, I contend that a company making as much money as the Pullman company does out of one part of its plant, that when they come to reduce in another part of their plant—having old employees who have been with them so long—it ought not at least to cut them so severely, but share up a little bit with them, from the standpoint that it is a paternalistic system.

Commissioner Wright: You have been charged with being both a socialist and an anarchist?

Mr. Carwardine: Yes, sir.

Commissioner Wright: You of course understand the difference in the terms?

Mr. Carwardine: Yes, sir.

Commissioner Wright: I thought it fair to allow you to define your position relative to these difficulties, and that is why I asked the question.

Mr. Carwardine: I confess I am surprised at the prejudice which exists on the part of a great many people toward this whole matter. I was a clergyman in the town of Pullman and had to do one of two things: I had to keep quiet and say nothing, and at the same time realize that these men were not being rightly treated, or else I had to speak out my convictions, and that is the reason I have been interested as a clergyman in this matter. I will also say there has been a good deal said on the part of the clergy about reaching the masses, getting hold of the workingmen and getting them into our churches, and I have thought if as clergymen, without endorsing all that the workingmen do, we would show our sympathy for them in their desire to better their condition we would probably be able to reach them on other lines if we would help them practically on these lines.

Commissioner Kernan: What are the conditions in Pullman as to the building of churches for the accommodation of the people?

Mr. Carwardine: When Mr. Pullman built the town of Pullman he decided that there should be one church building, and he built that church, a very handsome structure indeed, and they are renting it today at $100 per month, and the parsonage, which is part of the church, rents for $65 per month; but no minister, so far as I have ever been able to find out, has received salary enough to permit him to live in that parsonage.

Commissioner Kernan: What is the membership of that church?

Mr. Carwardine: I could not state; I should judge there were from two hundred to two hundred and fifty, but I do not think they have that membership now.

Commissioner Kernan: What I want to know more particularly is whether churches can acquire title to property there at all?

Mr. Carwardine: No, sir; they cannot, in the town of Pullman proper; but across the tracks on Pullman's property, but not really recognized as Pullman proper, the Roman Catholic people have got a lease for ninety-nine years and have a very handsome church there, and the Swedish Evangelical Lutherans have got a church, also. Nobody, however, can buy property to build a church. We have made several efforts to get Mr. Pullman to sell us property to build a church, but could not.

Testimony of Rev. Morris L. Wickman

August 21, 1894, Rev. Morris L. Wickman, being first duly sworn, testified as follows:

Commissioner Wright: State your name and profession?

Mr. Wickman: Morris L. Wickman; minister of the gospel.

Commissioner Wright: Where are you located?

Mr. Wickman: On the borders of Pullman. It is called the Pullman Swedish Methodist Church.

Commissioner Wright: How long have you been pastor of that church?

Mr. Wickman: Five years.

Commissioner Wright: Are you familiar with the condition of the people as to their tenements in Pullman and surrounding places?

Mr. Wickman: Yes, sir; during the time of my pastorage I have made about 1,500 visits, I should judge, to the families in Pullman, and have visited families in Kensington and Roseland also.

Commissioner Wright: State what you found comparatively as to conditions in those three places.

Mr. Wickman: I find that the people in Pullman are compelled to pay about one-third at least more rent than the people in Kensington and Roseland for like accommodations.

Commissioner Kernan: Do employees of the Pullman shops live in Kensington?

Mr. Wickman: Yes, sir; but when the work begins to be slack in Pullman the outside workmen receive orders to move into Pullman if they wish to retain their positions. I am acquainted with families that were compelled to do so last fall.

Commissioner Wright: Did you see the order from the Pullman company to that effect?

Mr. Wickman: No, sir; I did not. But they are not written; they are given verbally by the foremen of the different departments. I have a foreman belonging to my church that personally has given those orders by the orders of the company.

Commissioner Wright: You have observed, of course, the moral bearing of the people of Pullman, Kensington, and Roseland?

Mr. Wickman: Yes, sir.

Commissioner Wright: How does that of one place compare with that of the other?

Mr. Wickman: I think so far as the moral conditions go that the people in Roseland are better off than the people in Pullman. The families in Pullman, on account of the high rents, are compelled to keep roomers, and the rooms are so arranged that a roomer cannot go to his room without going through the private rooms of the family, which breaks in upon the sanctity of the family, and there have been cases where immorality resulted from that cause.

Commissioner Wright: How is it as to conditions of temperance as between Kensington and Pullman?

Mr. Wickman: Kensington has the reputation of being a "bum" town, and the saloons are concentrated there.

Commissioner Wright: Is that reputation well earned?

Mr. Wickman: Yes, sir; but there is a steady stream of people pouring from Pullman into Kensington every night and every Sunday. There are kegs of beer carried over into Pullman, and the beer wagons have free permission to go through the streets of Pullman, and leave beer and liquor with the families and in the boardinghouses.

Commissioner Worthington: What would you say generally as to the habits of the Pullman employees, so far as sobriety is concerned, compared with the habits of employees in similar establishments?

Mr. Wickman: I think, taken as a whole, it is a very good community, and I think the conduct of the men during the strike would bear me out, until the rioting began on the railroads. We had more quiet, less rioting during that time than at any other time during the history of the town since I have been there.

Commissioner Kernan: How is it as to their providence as a class; I mean as to saving out of their wages?

Mr. Wickman: Speaking for my own people, there is a saving tendency among them. Quite a number of them have tried to obtain their own homes in Roseland.

Commissioner Kernan: How does the Pullman company, if at all, encourage this desire on the part of the men to get their own homes?

Mr. Wickman: I don't think the Pullman company tries to hinder it, at least I have never found it so; but of course when work begins to get slack these men are the first laid off; that is the only way the Pullman company hinders them, I believe.

Commissioner Kernan: The men can buy land in the adjoining towns and build homes if they desire?

Mr. Wickman: Yes, if they have the means.

Commissioner Kernan: Is it your observation that that course places them at a disadvantage as workmen?

Mr. Wickman: It does place them at a slight disadvantage, because workmen living in Pullman have the first chance.

Commissioner Kernan: Does the company keep a physician?

Mr. Wickman: Yes, sir.

Commissioner Kernan: To what extent does that physician look after the health of the people?

Mr. Wickman: Just when an accident happens in the shop. We have need of an emergency hospital in Pullman, and at one time took steps to get one some years ago. A committee was appointed, consisting of a preacher and two doctors, who called to see the Pullman company, stating that they would see that the expenses of the hospital were met and the doctors would furnish their services free, if the company would donate a cottage on Watt Avenue, but they refused, simply stating that the cottages were not built for that purpose; that they were built for residences.

Commissioner Kernan: Then an employee that is injured so he needs care has to be removed to some hospital in Chicago for treatment?

Mr. Wickman: Yes, sir.

Commissioner Kernan: I understand no provision is made for paying the expenses.

Mr. Wickman: No provision unless it is so clear that the injury was caused by the fault of the company or its agents that the company cannot get out of it.

Testimony of L. H. Johnson

August 22, 1894, L. H. Johnson, being first duly sworn, testified as follows:

Commissioner Worthington: State your name, age, residence, and occupation.

Mr. Johnson: L. H. Johnson; 68; Pullman, Ill.; hardware and furniture.

Commissioner Worthington: Are you doing business for yourself there?

Mr. Johnson: Yes, sir.

Commissioner Worthington: Do you own your property or rent it?

Mr. Johnson: I rent it from the Pullman company.

Commissioner Kernan: What line are you in? Answer: Hardware and furniture.

Commissioner Kernan: How many are there in competition with you?

Mr. Johnson: There is no one in competition in that line in Pullman proper, but we have plenty of competitors close by in Roseland and in Kensington.

Commissioner Kernan: Do you know whether or not the Pullman company undertakes to restrict the stores in that way by renting to but one at a time?

Mr. Johnson: I don't think they do now, but there was a time a good many years ago when they did.

Commissioner Kernan: You say there is no understanding or agreement between you and the company by which they would refuse to rent to other hardware stores joining you?

Mr. Johnson: No, sir; there is not. Some years ago I paid the Pullman company a good deal more rent than I do now. I made a complaint; the company sent an agent to my store and wanted to know what I thought would be a fair rental for the stores in the Arcade. There are a good many of them, and he came to me, because I was about the oldest tenant, to see about it. I told him what I thought would be a fair rental for the stores, and he said that would be satisfactory.

Commissioner Kernan: You are familiar with the business of the town; has there been any similar reduction in your experience there?

Mr. Johnson: I think when they made this reduction to me they made a general reduction to all the tenants in what is called the Arcade, where all the stores are; that is, so far as I know they did.

Commissioner Kernan: What did you pay for your house after that?

Mr. Johnson: Just the same.

Commissioner Kernan: So in the house rent they made no change?

Mr. Johnson: No, sir. I have always been of the impression if the Pullman employees had gone to the company in the right way they would have got a reduction of rent like I did. The company might be a little slow in such matters, but if you have patience they will come around and look into the thing, and if you are right they will accede to you. That is the way I found it, and for that reason I have been of the impression the employees were a little too hasty and that these matters would have been remedied if they had been more patient.

Commissioner Kernan: That is, you think there would have been a readjustment of rents?

Mr. Johnson: I could not say about a readjustment, but probably there would have been some equalizing of wages. I think there has been in the shops sometimes some parts which paid a little more than other parts in proportion, and those things, if adjusted, would make it more just to all parties.

Testimony of Edward F. Bryant

August 27, 1894, Edward F. Bryant, being first duly sworn, testified as follows:

Commissioner Wright: State your name and place of residence.

Mr. Bryant: My name is Edward F. Bryant; I reside at Pullman, Ill.

Commissioner Wright: What is your occupation?

Mr. Bryant: I am manager of the Pullman Loan and Savings Bank —cashier and manager. I have been connected with that bank for nearly nine years.

Commissioner Wright: Is that bank an organization independent of the Pullman company?

Mr. Bryant: Yes, sir; it is. It was organized under the laws of the State of Illinois as a state bank; it has a capital of one hundred thousand dollars.

Commissioner Wright: Are the Pullman officials stockholders in the bank?

Mr. Bryant: Some of them are.

Commissioner Wright: To what extent—not exactly, but about to what extent?

Mr. Bryant: The capital stock is divided into one thousand shares of one hundred dollars each, and of those one thousand shares I think that probably two hundred or three hundred are held by officials of the Pullman company, if such term includes directors of the company, not the active officials.

Commissioner Wright: But including all active and advisory officials?

Mr. Bryant: Yes, sir.

Commissioner Wright: What is the character of the remaining stockholders?

Mr. Bryant: The remaining stock is held by the Pullman Southern Car Company.

Commissioner Wright: Just what is the office of that company and where are its headquarters?

Mr. Bryant: To the best of my knowledge that company is now owned by the Pullman Palace Car Company.

Commissioner Wright: Do you have any relation to the Pullman company in reference to the collection of its rents?

Mr. Bryant: Well, in the course of our business we collect for different individuals drafts, notes, and whatever bank items are sent to us for collection, and, included in such general business, are rent accounts from the Pullman Palace Car Company.

Commissioner Wright: You collect them in what manner?

Mr. Bryant: The bills of nonemployees of the Pullman company and the bills of tenants who are behind in their rent are sent to the Pullman Loan and Savings Bank for collection; I employ several men as collectors to present these bills for payment and secure such money as the tenants are able to pay.

Commissioner Wright: You have the supervision of the work of collecting rents generally for the whole company from its tenants, do you?

Mr. Bryant: Only in such capacity as a bank collects accounts; owing to the location of our business, we do such business as comes to us from that locality.

Commissioner Wright: But any matters connected with the collection of rents, such as evictions, do they come under your charge in any way?

Mr. Bryant: They do not; we simply present a bill to a tenant and if he does not pay it such bill is returned to the Pullman Palace Car Company.

Commissioner Wright: But are the rents payable to you through checks given to the employees for wages?

Mr. Bryant: No, sir.

Commissioner Wright: Are there not two kinds of checks given to an employee for his wages or earnings, one to cover rent and the other to cover any balance which may be due him after the rent is paid.

Mr. Bryant: There are two such checks given, but their character is exactly the same, as, for instance, if a man has earned fifteen dollars and he owes five dollars for rent there are two checks made, one for ten dollars and one for five dollars, both given to the man, and it is entirely at his discretion whether he uses the check for the amount of his rent in payment thereof or not; it is payable to his order and cannot be used until he voluntarily endorses it, which is the only way that it can be made good.

Commissioner Wright: That is, he could endorse both checks and use them in ordinary business transactions other than the payment of rent, could he?

Mr. Bryant: He could; yes, sir.

Commissioner Wright: Are these checks on your bank?

Mr. Bryant: Yes, sir.

Commissioner Wright: Are all wages paid in that way?

Mr. Bryant: All wages of employees at Pullman are.

Commissioner Kernan: What is the arrangement between the bank and the Pullman Palace Car Company by which the bank acts as agent for the collection of rents for the Pullman Palace Car Company?

Mr. Bryant: Prior to the passage of the "Truck act," or before June 1891, it was customary to give an employee who was a tenant, in payment for his earnings of every two weeks, a check for the difference between the amount of his earnings and one-half of the amount of his monthly rent. If a tenant employee got behind in his rent the amount of one-half of his monthly rent deducted was increased by a small amount when he again went to work until his back rent was paid.

Since the passage of the "Truck act" the full amount of earnings for every two weeks has been given to each tenant employee by the paymaster of the company in two checks. One for the amount of one-half the month's rent, and the other for the balance of wages earned. It has been customary for the men on receiving these two checks to endorse and deliver to the rent collector, who was near at hand during the pay days, the check representing the rent.

During the past year the decrease of work has been such that many of the tenant employees could not easily pay the amount of their current rent or their back rent. For the purpose of dealing considerately with such tenants, the collector requested the paymaster of the company to send both checks due such employee to him for delivery. Upon their calling their checks were handed them, with the request that they make some payment upon their rent. For months during the last year, several hundred men in this way paid but one dollar each every two weeks for rent, the remainder of the amount of both checks being paid to the employee. In some cases no rent at all was paid by the employees.

Commissioner Kernan: For the benefit of those in the dark, tell me what the "Truck act" is.

Mr. Bryant: The "Truck Act," which is part of the laws of Illinois—I believe it has since been declared unconstitutional—forbids the deducting from a man's earnings what he might owe his employer.

Testimony of George M. Pullman

August 27, 1894, George M. Pullman being duly sworn, testified as follows:

Commissioner Wright: You are the president of the Pullman Palace Car Company?

Mr. Pullman: Yes, sir.

Commissioner Wright: How long have you been president of that company?

Mr. Pullman: Twenty-seven years on the first day of August.

Commissioner Wright: State generally what the idea was of establishing the town in connection with your manufacturing plant.

Mr. Pullman: Anticipating that question, if the commission will allow me, I would like to state, from memoranda that I have, which are very brief, an answer to your question.

The object in building Pullman was the establishment of a great manufacturing business on the most substantial basis possible, recognizing, as we did, and do now, that the working people are the most important element which enters into the successful operation of any manufacturing enterprise. We decided to build, in close proximity to the shops, homes for workingmen of such character and surroundings as would prove so attractive as to cause the best class of mechanics to seek that place for employment in preference to others. We also desired to establish the place on such a basis as would exclude all baneful influences, believing that such a policy would result in the greatest measure of success, both from a commercial point of view, and also, a tendency toward continued elevation and improvement of the conditions not only of the working people themselves, but of their children growing up about them. Accordingly, the present location of Pullman was selected.

It was not the intention to sell to workingmen homes in Pullman, but to so limit the area of the town that they could buy homes at convenient distances from the works if they chose to do so.

If any lots had been sold in Pullman, it would have permitted the introduction of the baneful elements which it was the chief purpose to exclude from the immediate neighborhood of the shops, and from the home to be erected about them.

The relations of those employed in the shops are, as to the shops, the relations of employees to employer; and as to those of them and others living in the homes, the relations are simply and only those of tenant to landlord. The company has not now, and never has had, any interest whatever in the business of any of the stores or shops in the town. They are rented to and managed by outside parties, free from any control by the company. The people living in the town are entirely free to buy where they choose.

The basis on which rents were fixed was to make a return of 6 percent on the actual investment, which at that time, 1881, was a reasonable return to be expected from such an investment; and in calculating what, for such a purpose, was the actual investment in the dwellings on the one hand and the other buildings on the other, an allowance was made for the cost of the streets and other public improvements, just as it has to be considered in the valuation of any property for renting anywhere.

Commissioner Worthington: Let me ask you if any attempts were made by approaching you, either in writing or orally, by different parties to secure an arbitration of the differences between the Pullman company and the strikers there?

Mr. Pullman: I don't recollect of any formal attempt at arbitration with me. I think some committees waited upon Mr. Wickes.

Commissioner Worthington: Did you, as president of the company, ever express to any parties your willingness or unwillingness to submit these matters to arbitration?

Mr. Pullman: I expressed my unwillingness to submit these matters to arbitration.

Commissioner Worthington: I think you are quoted in this pamphlet. Yes, I see it here (reading):

> The demand made before quitting work was that the wages should be restored to the scale of last year, or, in effect, that the actual outgoing money losses then being daily incurred by the company in car building should be deliberately increased to an amount equal to about one-fourth of the wages of the employee. It must be clear to every businessman and to every thinking mechanic that no prudent employer could submit to arbitration the question whether he should commit such a piece of business folly.

Was that your language?

Mr. Pullman: Yes, sir.

Commissioner Worthington: Were those the only losses that the company was sustaining in the employment of its workmen during that year?

Mr. Pullman: Well, those were the losses pertaining to the work. What I wish to be understood is that the question with me was whether the shops at Pullman should be closed or whether we could, by putting the prices so low as to command whatever work was to be let anywhere in the country, secure it, thus keeping our people employed, and the amount which I was willing to contribute in that way—willing to sacrifice—was a varying amount according to my idea of how low it was necessary to make the bid in order to get the work.

Commissioner Worthington: I wanted to know what you had in

mind at the time you made this statement that "it was very clear that no prudent man could submit to arbitration in this manner" when you were referring to your daily losses as a reason why any prudent man could not submit to arbitration?

Mr. Pullman: The amount of the losses would not cut any figure; it was the principle involved, not the amount that would affect my views as to arbitration.

Commissioner Worthington: Then it was not the amount of losses that the company was then sustaining.

Mr. Pullman: It was the principle that that should not be submitted to a third party. That was a matter that the company should decide for itself.

Commissioner Worthington: Now, let me ask you if, taking all the revenues of the Pullman company for the last year, so far as you are advised, if the company has lost money or made money during the last year?

Mr. Pullman: The company has made money during the last year.

Commissioner Worthington: What amount of dividends was declared during the last year?

Mr. Pullman: The usual dividend of 8 percent.

Commissioner Worthington: What is the gross amount?

Mr. Pullman: I can't tell now.

Commissioner Worthington: It is upward of $600,000, is it not? It has paid out about $2,800,000 in dividends during the last year, has it not?

Mr. Pullman: It has, for the full year.

Commissioner Worthington: That is out of its earnings of the last year, is it not?

Mr. Pullman: Yes sir; out of the earnings.

Commissioner Worthington: And you have no idea of the losses you sustained on account of this car building?

Mr. Pullman: I have told you that on the contracts we took the losses were something over $50,000.

Commissioner Worthington: Don't you think it would have been right that a corporation that has been so successful financially as the Pullman corporation—and of which we have all been proud—declaring a dividend of $2,800,000, should not have borne some losses for employees who had been working for a long time—shared your profits to that extent with them?

Mr. Pullman: The manufacturing business at Pullman is a perfectly distinct and separate branch of business from the manufacturing business at Detroit. The profits and losses of that business are kept entirely separate and by itself. I can see no reason why I should take the profit belonging to the 4,200 shareholders and that comes as the result of their investment in this company years ago and pay one set of men a higher rate of wages than I was paying other men in different parts of the country, or than other people were paying men, because the manufacturing business happened to belong to the same company that the business of operating cars did, or that we happened to be able to pay the $2,800,000; because during all the years we have been prudent and put our surplus earnings into property that has helped earn this money, that we should be called upon now to pay them out to give exceptional wages to a certain class of men who happen to be living at Pullman.

We have many men at Pullman that have been there for a number of years. We have a great many men who had been there but a very few months at the time of the strike. The claims of those men would be the same upon us with the men who live at Wilmington, or at St. Louis, or at Ludlow, or at any of our shops. There was no complaint of wages there. The effort of the American Railway Union to cause a strike there was a failure, although they made repeated efforts to get the men out. They were satisfied with their wages. The wages were equal to those paid by other people. I could see no reason why because the Pullman company happened to be prosperous, as you say, that it should pay a higher rate of wages than other establishments in the same business.

Commissioner Worthington: Did the Pullman company during its years of prosperity ever voluntarily increase the wages of any class or of all classes of its employees?

Mr. Pullman: Not specially on account of prosperous business. It has always paid its employees liberal wages.

Commissioner Worthington: But it has never increased the wages of its employees voluntarily?

Mr. Pullman: Certainly it has not increased them any other way.

Commissioner Worthington: It has never divided any of its profits with them in any shape or form?

Mr. Pullman: The Pullman Company divides its profits with the people who own the property. It would not have a right to take the profits belonging to the people who own that property—

Commissioner Worthington: Well, we will not discuss that question. If you will answer my questions we will get along faster.

Commissioner Worthington: Suppose a board of arbitration had examined into the matter and had said: "Yes, we accept your statement that you are losing money on these jobs and that the times are hard, and you are not receiving as much money on car mileage as heretofore; but with a body of workmen who had been with you some time—and a person would imagine it would be a good thing to do that under all the circumstances—you ought to divide with them a little, give them at least enough to make a good living"—wouldn't that have been a fair matter to be considered?

Mr. Pullman: I think not. How long a time should a man be with a company before he would be entitled to a gift of money? For that is what this would mean. The wage question is settled by the law of supply and demand. We were obliged to reduce wages in order to get these cars—to compete with other people in the same business, that were doing the same thing. I suppose the wages are practically uniform. I assume that the people who are bidding for the same class of cars, bidding for the same lots of cars that this company was bidding for, and obtained them against our bid until we finally reduced them to a point away below cost—I suppose the wages that we were paying were practically the same wages they were paying. Of course, that I am not certain of.

Commissioner Worthington: In other words, you insisted upon a right which is conceded to you, of course, or your company, of getting the labor as cheap as you could, and of reducing the wages there to correspond with the reduction that you made in contracts that you took?

Mr. Pullman: I beg your pardon; my point at the time was to work in conjunction with the men at Pullman to secure the disbursement of the large amount of money involved in these contracts. I was willing to contribute, or the company lose money for the sake of getting them, if the men were willing to do their work at a less price; I believe it amounts to 20 or 25 percent. If they were willing to do that rather than to have the work go to Detroit or Dayton, Ohio, or Springfield, Mass., or Wilmington, Del., in order to bring it to Pullman, and give the people at Pullman the benefit of the disbursement of that money; to let it permeate the channels of trade—to do that, a mutual sacrifice must be made. The men must work a little harder and the Pullman company must use its profits that it has made in its business to secure that object.

Commissioner Worthington: Is not this American Railway Union the first labor organization that your employees as employees have belonged to that has come to your knowledge?

Mr. Pullman: That has come to my direct knowledge?

Commissioner Worthington: Yes.

Mr. Pullman: I have no recollection of any contact with labor organizations other than the railway union.

Commissioner Worthington: And the policy now, as I understand it, of the Pullman Palace Car Company is that it will retain no one in its employ that belongs to this branch of organized labor?

Mr. Pullman: The policy is that it will retain no one that belongs to the American Railway Union. It has not discriminated against any other labor organizations.

Commissioner Worthington: And you do not know that there is any other one out there to discriminate against?

Mr. Pullman: I don't know as a fact, but I presume there is.

Commissioner Worthington: But if there was one you would not have discriminated against it?

Mr. Pullman: I say we have never discriminated against other labor organizations.

Commissioner Wright: Who has the power to reduce rents at Pullman?

Mr. Pullman: Any question of that kind would come to me.

Commissioner Wright: It would come to you?

Mr. Pullman: Yes, sir; it would come to me—a question of that kind.

Commissioner Wright: Was the question of reducing rents when wages were reduced one that came under discussion at all?

Mr. Pullman: No. sir; the question of reducing rents did not come under discussion between the officers of the company. The income from the rent was so low that there was no room for reducing the rent and bringing any income from it; and, as I explained to the men, there was no necessary connection between the employment of men and the renting of homes; that they had the privilege of living where they chose. As a matter of fact, only one-third of the men who struck lived in Pullman tenements at the time. There were 560-odd of them that lived in their own houses at the time of the strike, so that the rent question did not seem to me to be an important one as bearing on the strike, because two-thirds of the people lived outside of Pullman.

Commissioner Worthington: They claimed to you, did they not, that at those wages they could not support themselves and pay their rent? Was not that the claim; or, in other words, that it was below what is known to workmen as the living wage?

Mr. Pullman: No, sir; they said only that they wanted the wages of 1893, and, in fact, the claim that they were not working at a living wage is not true, because they are working for it now, and so are the people all over the country. I would be very glad to pay the men very much higher wages if the conditions of business warranted it. I do not know where I am going to get cars enough to be built to keep the people at work at these present wages. That is a problem I have now.

Commissioner Kernan: When this reduction of wages was made was your salary reduced and that of the other officers?

Mr. Pullman: No, sir.

Commissioner Kernan: Were the salaries of the superintendents and foremen reduced?

Mr. Pullman: No, sir.

Commissioner Kernan: Now, let me ask you why, in this general reduction, that was not done?

Mr. Pullman: Because it is not easy for the manager of a corporation to find men to fill the positions. Men that have been with a corporation for twenty-five years, it don't lie with me to go to him and say to him, "I am going to reduce your salary one thousand dollars," because he will say, "Very well; you will find somebody else to take my place." And there are very few officers of a corporation, comparatively, to the number of employees, and they are able to command their salaries. It would be a matter of agreement whether they would take less, and it is a matter, then, whether a corporation could afford to dispense with their services.

Commissioner Kernan: In other words, a corporation could not afford to make a reduction of their salaries?

Mr. Pullman: It would be impossible for me, as the president of a corporation, to reduce the salaries of my officers arbitrarily, because I would find myself possibly without them.

Commissioner Kernan: You might reduce your own, perhaps, but not theirs.

Mr. Pullman: I might, if I chose, but the difference that it would make on the cost of a car would be so infinitesimal and fractional that it would not be worth considering.

Commissioner Kernan: Under the circumstances, don't you think that you ought to have, fairly and in justice to the other classes, attempted to reduce those salaries?

Mr. Pullman: That might come, we cannot do everything at once, and we cannot tell how long this depression is going to last.

IV

The events surrounding the Pullman strike demonstrate that workers in industry would not be able to coerce management into paying them higher wages. And managers were not likely to pay workers, out of their own sense of benevolence, anything more than the market would demand. Are we then to conclude that the promise of distribution of goods to the working classes went largely unfulfilled? The documents reprinted below were issued by the Illinois Labor Bureau following an investigation of workingman's budgets in 1884. They reveal some of the important variables determining worker's standards of living. Some families, with young children to feed and wives unable to enter the job market, lived on the margin of subsistence. But others, families accumulating the wages of father, children, and perhaps wife as well, managed to live at substantially higher levels. Their comforts, however, were purchased at a high price—often the education of their children had to be sacrificed in order to satisfy needs. And, without education, the prospect of the children's improving on their fathers' position, of enjoying upward mobility, a change from unskilled to skilled labor, was minimal. Still, these sacrifices may not have been perceived as sacrifices; immediate returns, the satisfaction of living better than they had before, may well have helped to wed American workers to the industrial system. Remember, too, that many of the workers were immigrants; as the comparison in the table below between British and American wages demonstrate, these people were in fact substantially better off in this country. The American dream, then, was not all myth.

CONDITION OF LABORERS, 1884

ITALIAN LABORER

EARNINGS: Of father $270

CONDITION: Family numbers 5—parents and three children, all boys, aged one, three, and five. Live in one room, for which they pay $4 per month rent. A very dirty and unhealthy place, everything perfectly filthy. There are about fifteen other families living in the same house. They buy the cheapest kind of meat from the neighboring slaughterhouses and the children pick up fuel on the streets and rotten eatables from the commission houses. Children do not attend school. They are all ignorant in the full sense of the word. Father could not write his name.

FOOD: *Breakfast*—Coffee and bread.

      Dinner—Soups.

      Supper—Coffee and bread.

In *Third Biennial Report*, Illinois Bureau of Statistics (Springfield, Ill., 1884), pp. 333, 342–43, 369–71, 383.

(ITALIAN LABORER)

COST OF LIVING:

Rent	$48	
Fuel	5	
Meat and groceries	100	
Clothing, boots and shoes, and dry goods	15	
Sickness	5	
Total		$173

SCANDINAVIAN LABORER

EARNINGS:

Of father	$240	
Of daughter, aged seventeen	340	
Of son, aged fifteen	200	
Total		$780

CONDITION: Family numbers 5—parents and three children, two boys, aged fifteen and seven, and a girl, aged seventeen. Live in a 4-room house, and pay $10 per month rent for the same. House is comfortable, but poorly furnished, and is in unhealthy location. Family attends church. Their expenditures exceed their income.

FOOD: *Breakfast*—Meat, potatoes, bread, and coffee.
  Dinner—Lunches.
  Supper—Soup, bread, and meat.

COST OF LIVING:

Rent	$120	
Fuel	15	
Meat and groceries	300	
Clothing, boots and shoes, dry goods	120	
Books, papers, etc.	5	
Sickness	40	
Sundries	250	
Total		$850

IRISH LABORER

EARNINGS: Of father $343

CONDITION: Family numbers 5—parents and three children, two girls, aged seven and five, and boy, eight. They occupy a rented house of 4 rooms, and pay a rental, monthly, of $7. Two of the children attend school. Father complains of the wages he receives, being but $1.10 per day, and says it is extremely difficult for him to support his family upon that amount. His work consists in cleaning yards, basements, outbuildings, etc., and is, in fact, a regular scavenger. He also complains of the work as being very unhealthy, but it seems he can procure no other work.

FOOD: *Breakfast*—Black coffee, bread, and potatoes.
  Dinner—Corned beef, cabbage, and potatoes.
  Supper—Bread, coffee, and potatoes.

COST OF LIVING:

Rent	$84	
Fuel	15	
Meat and groceries	180	
Clothing, boots and shoes, and dry goods	40	
Sundries	20	
Total		$339

AMERICAN COAL MINER

EARNINGS: Of father $250

CONDITION: Family numbers 7—husband, wife, and five children, three girls and two boys, aged from three to nineteen years. Three of them go to the public school. Family live in 2-room tenement, in healthy locality, for which they pay $6 per month rent. The house is scantily furnished, without carpets, but is kept neat and clean. They are compelled to live very economically, and every cent they earn is used to the best advantage. Father had only thirty weeks work during the past year. He belongs to trade union. The figures for cost of living are actual and there is no doubt the family lived on the amount specified.

FOOD: *Breakfast*—Bread, coffee, and salt meat.
   Dinner—Meat, bread, coffee, and butter.
   Supper—Sausage, bread, and coffee.

COST OF LIVING:

Rent	$72	
Fuel	20	
Meat	20	
Groceries	60	
Clothing	28	
Boots and shoes	15	
Dry goods	20	
Trade union	3	
Sickness	10	
Sundries	5	
Total		$253

IRISH COAL MINER

EARNINGS:	Of father	$420
	Of son, twenty-one years of age	420
	Of son, eighteen years of age	420
	Of son, sixteen years of age	150
	Total	$1,410

CONDITION: Family numbers 6—parents and four children, three boys and one girl. The girl attends school, and the three boys are working in the mine. Father owns a house of six rooms, which is clean and very comfortably furnished. Family temperate, and members of a church, which they attend with regularity. They have an acre of ground, which they work in summer, and raise vegetables for their consumption. They have their house about paid for, payments being made in installments of $240 per year. Father belongs to mutual assessment association and to trade union.

FOOD: *Breakfast*—Steak, bread, butter, potatoes, bacon, and coffee.
   Dinner—Bread, butter, meat, cheese, pie, and tea.
   Supper—Meat, potatoes, bread, butter, puddings, pie, and coffee.

(IRISH COAL MINER)

COST OF LIVING:

Rent	$240
Fuel	10
Meat	200
Groceries	700
Clothing	80
Boots, shoes, and dry goods	70
Books, papers, etc.	15
Life insurance	18
Trade union	3
Sickness	4
Sundries	75
Total	$1,415

ENGLISH IRON AND STEEL WORKER

EARNINGS: Of father $1,420
          Of son, aged fourteen   300
             Total $1,720

CONDITION: Family numbers 6—parents and four children; two boys and two girls, aged from seven to sixteen years. Three of them attend school, and the other works in the shop with his father. Family occupy their own house, containing 9 well-furnished rooms, in a pleasant and healthy locality. They have a good vegetable and flower garden. They live well, but not extravagantly, and are saving about a thousand dollars per year. Father receives an average of $7 per day of twelve hours, for his labor, and works about thirty-four weeks of the year. Belongs to trade union, but carries no life insurance. Had but little sickness during the year.

FOOD: *Breakfast*—Bread, butter, meat, eggs, and sometimes oysters.
       Dinner—Potatoes, bread, butter, meat, pie, cake, or pudding.
       Supper—Bread, butter, meat, rice or sauce, and tea or coffee.

COST OF LIVING:

Fuel	$55
Meat	100
Groceries	300
Clothing	75
Boots and shoes	50
Dry goods	50
Books, papers, etc.	10
Trade union	6
Sickness	12
Sundries	50
Total	$708

Showing the Proportion of the Family Income Derived from the Labor of Wives and Children

OCCUPATIONS	WHOLE NUMBER OF FAMILIES	NUMBER SUPPORTED BY FATHER ALONE	NUMBER ASSISTED BY WIVES AND CHILDREN	AVERAGE EARNINGS OF FATHER ALONE	AVERAGE EARNINGS OF OTHER MEMBERS OF FAMILY	PERCENT OF THE WHOLE	TOTAL EARNINGS OF FAMILY	TOTAL EXPENSES OF FAMILY
Blacksmiths	75	58	17	$622	$54	.08	$676	$540
Bricklayers	46	36	10	638	61	.09	699	601
Butchers	27	21	6	515	43	.08	558	470
Cabinet makers	15	9	6	466	70	.13	536	463
Carpenters	111	73	38	552	73	.12	625	532
Cigar makers	79	63	16	492	85	.15	577	528
Clerks	46	40	6	641	46	.07	687	587
Coal miners	232	159	73	385	86	.18	471	435
Coopers	22	16	6	432	52	.11	484	474
Harness makers	31	25	6	547	58	.08	605	548
Laborers	397	253	144	344	70	.17	414	388
Machinists	35	29	6	661	10	.015	671	563
Marble workers	17	14	3	570	48	.08	618	552
Millers	16	13	3	872	37	.04	909	656
Molders	49	41	8	712	32	.043	744	622
Painters	62	51	11	503	29	.054	532	486
Plasterers	23	18	5	626	27	.04	653	595
Printers	26	21	5	654	49	.07	703	647
Shoemakers	32	25	7	467	37	.07	504	458
Stone masons	19	16	3	467	21	.04	488	478
Stone cutters	28	27	1	627	1	—	628	560
Tailors	16	9	7	543	155	.22	698	620
Teamsters	66	57	9	460	25	.05	485	435
Tinners	21	16	5	595	35	.055	630	536
Wood machinists	20	18	2	739	14	.02	753	627
Wood workers	17	16	1	654	18	.026	672	557
Totals	1,528	1,124	404	$14,784	$1,236	—	$16,020	$13,958
Averages	—	—	—	$568.61	$47.54	.08	$616.15	$536.85

Showing Average Prices of Food Supplies and Fuel for the State

ARTICLES	AVERAGE PRICES	ARTICLES	AVERAGE PRICES
Family flour, per barrel	$6.26.	Mutton, per pound	$ 12.1
Cornmeal, per hundred-weight	1.54.	Poultry, per pound	12.6
		Salt pork, per pound	12.
Bread, white, per loaf	05.6	Hams, smoked, per pound	15.3
Bread, brown, per loaf	05.8	Codfish, dry, per pound	09.8
Crackers, per pound	09.	Mackerel, salt, per pound	10.3
Milk, per quart	05.8	Fresh fish, per pound	10.5
Coffee, roasted, per pound	20.5	Potatoes, per bushel	45.8
Tea, common, per pound	51.7	Beans, per quart	09.7
Sugar, brown, per pound	08.7	Onions, per bushel	81.9
Eggs, per dozen	17.4	Dried apples, per pound	10.3
Butter, per pound	25.8	Dried peaches, per pound	13.4
Cheese, per pound	17.	Canned fruit, per can	18.2
Molasses, per gallon	62.2	Raisins, per pound	13.4
Soap, common bar, per pound	06.	Lard, per pound	12.4
Salt, per sack	10.6	Vinegar, per gallon	26.
Baking powder, per pound	38.9	Kerosene, per gallon	19.6
Bacon, per pound	13.7	Soft coal, per ton	2.95.
Beef, corned, per pound	09.7	Hard wood, per cord	4.80.
Beef or pork, roast, per pound	12.3		

Showing the Earnings and Expenses of Sixteen Representative Families of Workingmen in Great Britain

NUMBER OF PERSONS		EARNINGS OF HEADS OF FAMILY	EARNINGS OF MEMBERS OF FAMILY	TOTAL EARNINGS	TOTAL EXPENSES	SURPLUS OR DEBT
IN FAMILY	AT WORK					
6	1	$282.24	—	$282.24	$282.24	—
5	3	126.52	$666.64	793.16	647.18	+$145.98
5	3	243.30	209.24	452.54	452.64	—
4	2	277.36	101.21	378.57	378.57	—
7	3	326.02	192.21	518.23	518.23	—
7	2	227.73	88.56	316.29	316.29	—
6	3	253.03	253.04	506.07	506.07	—
8	4	291.96	340.62	632.58	632.58	—
7	3	248.17	327.49	575.66	575.66	—
6	2	417.50	151.82	569.32	569.32	—
8	3	399.01	272.50	671.51	671.51	—
5	3	462.27	321.16	783.43	783.43	—
6	3	301.69	128.95	430.64	430.64	—
6	1	379.55	—	379.55	379.55	—
4	2	341.59	88.56	430.15	430.15	—
7	3	379.55	180.04	559.59	559.59	—
6.06	2.56	$309.84	$207.63	$517.47	$508.35	$9.12

The average size of family in this instance is 6.06 persons—a materially larger family than is found in either of the preceding tables. The earnings, however, are smaller than in either case, being $309.84 for the head of the family, $207.62 for the other members, and $517.47 for both. Of this amount, $508.35 is expended for the support of the family, leaving a surplus of $9.12. The head of the family earns 60 percent of the whole income; the other members 40 percent. They expend, in even figures, 98 percent for maintenance, and save 2 percent.

As compared with the English workingmen our advantages in both these respects are still more marked. The workingman in Great Britain derives 40 percent of his income from the labor of wife and children, while in this state only 8 percent of the average income is derived from that source. He can save from the combined earnings of his family less than 2 percent of his total receipts, while workingmen in Massachusetts show an average saving of 6.11 percent of their incomes, and those in Illinois 12.60 percent of their incomes.

To present these results more forcibly to the eye, we give the following arrangement of the respective percentages:

CLASSIFICATION	ILLINOIS		MASSACHUSETTS		GREAT BRITAIN	
	AVER-AGE	PER-CENT	AVER-AGE	PER-CENT	AVER-AGE	PER-CENT
Persons in family	4.49	—	5.21	—	6.06	—
Total earnings	$612.76	—	$803.47	—	$517.47	—
Earnings of head of family	566.15	92.39	558.68	69.53	309.84	59.88
Earnings of members of family	46.61	7.61	244.79	30.47	207.63	40.12
Total expenses	535.55	87.40	754.42	93.89	508.35	98.24
Surplus	77.21	12.60	49.05	6.11	9.12	1.76

We are led to the conclusion that, while the assistance demanded of wives and children by the average workingman in Great Britain is five times as great as that called for by the necessities of workingmen in Illinois, and the average savings of the latter is eight times as much as that of the former, the Illinois workingman enjoys a mode of life, in his home surroundings and general standard of living, 42.60 percent better than his neighbor in Great Britain.

Chapter 13

The New Rich

THE INDUSTRIAL REVOLUTION of the late nineteenth century created a new social class, businessmen with personal fortunes of unprecedented enormity. While at all times in our society some men have been wealthier than others, until this period the differentiations between the social classes were not very great. The better sort lived in more commodious homes, had more numerous comforts, dressed and ate more elaborately than others. But their life style did not isolate them from the rest of the community. As late as 1850 a businessman could proclaim himself wealthy if he had savings totaling fifty thousand dollars. By 1900, an annual income of that sum would not have qualified its holder for membership in the nation's financial elite.

The leaders of big business—the Rockefellers, Carnegies, Mellons, and Morgans—had such unlimited wealth at their disposal that they could not, in ordinary fashion, begin to expend a major portion of it. Such vast and unusual accumulations allowed, actually compelled, them to exercise not only economic and political power, but to exert a basic and crucial influence on the nature of social institutions and social thought of the period.

In attempting to understand, and perhaps to justify the emergence of the new rich, many theorists transferred into the social realm, a framework and system of thought initially developed by Charles Darwin in the biological realm. The Social Darwinists, as this group was called, insisted that society and the animal kingdom had much in common; the victors in the struggle for economic success were like those who won out in the struggle for biological survival. Clearly, in both instances, it was the fittest and strongest who dominated. Indeed, this doctrine seemed to fit so well with popular American attitudes toward success that Social Darwinism became more popular in this country than in any other.

The new rich sought to justify their amazing accumulations in still other ways. Some among them, notably Andrew Carnegie, turned

to philanthropy, endowing public libraries, hospitals, and universities. Members of this elite also began building art collections and founding museums, buying up European masterpieces, and, sooner or later, putting them on public display. J. P. Morgan was probably the most avaricious collector, and the Metropolitan Museum of Art in New York City profited from his activities. Opera houses and orchestras also received support, as did architects ready to build elaborate private residences.

In each instance, vanity and public service went hand in hand for the new rich. They refused to recognize the possibility that their self-interest and the public interest could conflict.

Finally, the gospel of success preached during this era insisted that any deserving man, honest and ambitious, could win the struggle for success. Not inherited privilege but talent and perseverance triumphed in America. This doctrine not only legitimated the position of the new rich, but also served to tie those in the lower class more firmly to the established order. The creed held out to them the possibility for success; and at the same time it implied that if they lived miserably, it was in all likelihood their own fault and not that of the system. But, in fact, as many historical investigations now demonstrate, the rags-to-riches experience was ever so rare. Indeed, even mobility from the ranks of the unskilled to those of the skilled did not occur in any great number. Only a small fraction of the laboring classes entered white-collar jobs; most of the business elite came from middle- and upper-class families. So one must return again to the ideology and social practices of the new rich to begin to understand why the claims of opportunity were believed. In all, their efforts at self-justification seemed to have worked surprisingly well.

I

The most important American exponent of the doctrine of Social Darwinism was William Graham Sumner, Professor of Political and Social Science at Yale. Sumner was a staunch advocate of laissez faire economics, insisting that government intervention would disturb the natural and proper order of the marketplace. Just as he was certain that the economy would work best when left to its own self-regulating devices, so was he confident that the men who profited most from the system fully deserved their rewards. His volume, What Social Classes Owe Each Other, *was the most famous defense of the new rich.*

WHAT SOCIAL CLASSES OWE TO EACH OTHER, 1883

WILLIAM GRAHAM SUMNER

That It Is Not Wicked To Be Rich; Nay Even, That It Is Not Wicked To Be Richer Than One's Neighbor

I have before me a newspaper slip on which a writer expresses the opinion that no one should be allowed to possess more than one million dollars' worth of property. Alongside of it is another slip, on which another writer expresses the opinion that the limit should be five millions.

These two writers only represent a great deal of crude thinking and declaiming which is in fashion. I never have known a man of ordinary common sense who did not urge upon his sons, from earliest childhood, doctrines of economy and the practice of accumulation. The object is to teach the boy to accumulate capital. If, however, the boy should read many of the diatribes against "the rich" which are afloat in our literature, and if he should take these productions at their literal sense, he would be forced to believe that he was on the path of infamy when he was earning and saving capital. It is worthwhile to consider which we mean or what we mean. Is it wicked to be rich? Is it mean to be a capitalist?

It is not uncommon to hear a clergyman utter from the pulpit all the old prejudice in favor of the poor and against the rich, while asking the rich to do something for the poor; and the rich comply, without apparently having their feelings hurt at all by the invidious comparison. We all agree that he is a good member of society who works his way up from poverty to wealth, but as soon as he has worked his way up we

In *What Social Classes Owe to Each Other*, by William Graham Sumner (New York, 1883), pp. 43–47, 52–57.

begin to regard him with suspicion, as a dangerous member of society. A newspaper starts the silly fallacy that "the rich are rich because the poor are industrious," and it is copied from one end of the country to the other as if it were a brilliant apothegm. Labor organizations are formed, not to employ combined effort for a common object, but to indulge in declamation and denunciation, and especially to furnish an easy living to some officers who do not want to work.

We have denunciations of banks, corporations, and monopolies, which denunciations encourage only helpless rage and animosity, because they are not controlled by any distinctions between what is indispensably necessary and what is abuse, between what is established in the order of nature and what is legislative error. Think, for instance, of a journal which makes it its special business to denounce monopolies, yet favors a protective tariff, and has not a word to say against trade unions or patents. Think of public teachers who say that the farmer is ruined by the cost of transportation, when they mean that he cannot make any profits because his farm is too far from the market, and who denounce the railroad because it does not correct for the farmer, at the expense of its stockholders, the disadvantage which lies in the physical situation of the farm! Think of that construction of this situation which attributes all the trouble to the greed of "moneyed corporations!" Think of the piles of rubbish that one has read about corners, and watering stocks, and selling futures!

The great gains of a great capitalist in a modern state must be put under the head of wages of superintendence. Anyone who believes that any great enterprise of an industrial character can be started without labor must have little experience of life. Let anyone try to get a railroad built, or to start a factory and win reputation for its products, or to start a school and win a reputation for it, or to found a newspaper and make it a success, or to start any other enterprise, and he will find what obstacles must be overcome, what risks must be taken, what perseverance and courage are required, what foresight and sagacity are necessary. Especially in a new country, where many tasks are waiting, where resources are strained to the utmost all the time, the judgment, courage, and perseverance required to organize new enterprises and carry them to success are sometimes heroic. Persons who possess the necessary qualifications obtain great rewards. They ought to do so. It is foolish to rail at them. Then, again, the ability to organize and conduct industrial, commercial, or financial enterprises is rare; the great captains of industry are as rare as great generals.

If Mr. A. T. Stewart made a great fortune by collecting and bringing dry goods to the people of the United States, he did so because he understood how to do that thing better than any other man of his generation. If, when he died, he left no competent successor, the business must break up, and pass into new organization in the hands of other men. Some have said that Mr. Stewart made his fortune out of those who worked for him or with him. But would those persons have been able to come together, organize themselves, and earn what they did earn without him? Not at all. They would have been comparatively helpless. He and they together formed a great system of factories, stores, transportation, under his guidance and judgment. It was for the benefit of all; but he contributed to it what no one else was able to contribute— the one guiding mind which made the whole thing possible. In no sense whatever does a man who accumulates a fortune by legitimate industry exploit his employees, or make his capital "out of" anybody else. The wealth which he wins would not be but for him.

The aggregation of large fortunes is not at all a thing to be regretted. On the contrary, it is a necessary condition of many forms of social advance. If we should set a limit to the accumulation of wealth, we should say to our most valuable producers, "We do not want you to do us the services which you best understand how to perform, beyond a certain point." It would be like killing off our generals in war.

There is every indication that we are to see new developments of the power of aggregated capital to serve civilization, and that the new developments will be made right here in America. We are to see the development of the country pushed forward at an unprecedented rate by an aggregation of capital, and a systematic application of it under the direction of competent men. This development will be for the benefit of all, and it will enable each one of us, in his measure and way, to increase his wealth. We may each of us go ahead to do so, and we have every reason to rejoice in each other's prosperity. There ought to be no laws to guarantee property against the folly of its possessors. In the absence of such laws, capital inherited by a spendthrift will be squandered and reaccumulated in the hands of men who are fit and competent to hold it. So it should be, and under such a state of things there is no reason to desire to limit the property which any man may acquire.

Many other avenues for the wise expenditure of surplus wealth might be indicated. I enumerate but a few—a very few—of the many fields which are open, and only those in which great or considerable sums can be judiciously used. It is not the privilege, however, of millionaires alone to work for or aid measures which are certain to benefit the community. Everyone who has but a small surplus above his moderate wants may share this privilege with his richer brothers, and those without surplus can give at least a part of their time, which is usually as important as funds, and often more so.

II

A very different image of the new rich also appeared in these years, influencing the rhetoric and programs of Populist and Progressive reformers. In this literature industrial leaders were robber barons prepared to adopt corrupt practices to accomplish their selfish ends. Their economic policies were threatening the very liberty of the nation. One of the most widely read of these attacks was Henry

Demarest Lloyd's Wealth Against Commonwealth *(1894). The title
itself sets the terms of the argument, and the text, focusing on the
actions of Rockefeller and Standard Oil, attempted to alert Americans to the dangers of the "corporate Caesars."*

WEALTH AGAINST COMMONWEALTH, 1894

HENRY DEMAREST LLOYD

Nature is rich; but everywhere man, the heir of nature, is poor. Never
in this happy country or elswhere—except in the Land of Miracle, where
"they did all eat and were filled"—has there been enough of anything
for the people. Never since time began have all the sons and daughters
of men been all warm, and all filled, and all shod and roofed. Never
yet have all the virgins, wise or foolish, been able to fill their lamps
with oil.

The world, enriched by thousands of generations of toilers and
thinkers, has reached a fertility which can give every human being a
plenty undreamed of even in the utopias. But between this plenty ripen-
ing on the boughs of our civilization and the people hungering for it step
the "cornerers," the syndicates, trusts, combinations, with the cry of
"overproduction"—too much of everything. Holding back the riches of
earth, sea, and sky from their fellows who famish and freeze in the
dark, they declare to them that there is too much light and warmth
and food. They assert the right, for their private profit, to regulate the
consumption by the people of the necessaries of life, and to control
production, not by the needs of humanity, but by the desires of a few
for dividends. The coal syndicate thinks there is too much coal. There
is too much iron, too much lumber, too much flour—for this or that
syndicate.

The majority have never been able to buy enough of anything; but
this minority have too much of everything to sell. Our bigness, cities,
factories, monopolies, fortunes, which are our empires, are the obesities
of an age gluttonous beyond its powers of digestion. Our size has got
beyond both our science and our conscience. The vision of the railroad
stockholder is not farsighted enough to see into the office of the
general manager; the people cannot reach across even a ward of a city
to rule their rulers; captains of industry "do not know" whether the men
in the ranks are dying from lack of food and shelter; we cannot clean
our cities nor our politics; the locomotive has more manpower than all
the ballot boxes, and mill wheels wear out the hearts of workers unable
to keep up beating time to their whirl. If mankind had gone on pursuing
the ideals of the fighter, the time would necessarily have come when
there would have been only a few, then only one, and then none left.
This is what we are witnessing in the world of livelihoods. Our ideals
of livelihood are ideals of mutual deglutition. We are rapidly reaching
the stage where in each province only a few are left; that is the key

In *Wealth Against Commonwealth*, by Henry Demarest Lloyd (New York,
1894), pp. 1-2, 4-7, 516-17, 519-21.

to our times. Beyond the deep is another deep. This era is but a passing phase in the evolution of industrial Caesars, and these Caesars will be of a new type—corporate Caesars.

Corners are "acute" attacks of that which combinations exhibit as chronic. First a corner, then a pool, then a trust, has often been the genesis. The last stage, when the trust throws off the forms of combination and returns to the simpler dress of corporations, is already well along. Some of the "sympathetical cooperations" on record have no doubt ceased to exist. But that they should have been attempted is one of the signs of the time, and these attempts are repeated again and again until success is reached.

The line of development is from local to national, and from national to international. The amount of capital changes continually with the recrystallizations in progress. Not less than five hundred million dollars is in the coal combination, which our evidence shows to have flourished twenty-two years; that in oil has nearly if not quite two hundred millions; and the other combinations in which its members are leaders foot up hundreds of millions more. Hundreds of millions of dollars are united in the railroads and elevators of the Northwest against the wheat growers. In cattle and meat there are not less than one hundred millions; in whiskey, thirty-five millions; and in beer a great deal more than that; in sugar, seventy-five millions; in leather, over a hundred millions; in gas, hundreds of millions. At this writing a union is being negotiated of all the piano makers in the United States, to have a capital of fifty millions.

What we call monopoly is business at the end of its journey. The concentration of wealth, the wiping out of the middle classes, are other names for it. To get it is, in the world of affairs, the chief end of man.

There are no solitary truths, Goethe says, and monopoly—as the greatest business fact of our civilization, which gives to business what other ages gave to war and religion—is our greatest social, political, and moral fact.

The men and women who do the work of the world have the right to the floor. Everywhere they are rising to "a point of information." They want to know how our labor and the gifts of nature are being ordered by those whom our ideals and consent have made captains of industry over us; how it is that we, who profess the religion of the golden rule and the political economy of service for service, come to divide our produce into incalculable power and pleasure for a few, and partial existence for the many who are the fountains of these powers and pleasures.

Thousands of years' experience has proved that government must begin where it ends—with the people; that the general welfare demands that they who exercise the powers and they upon whom these are exercised must be the same, and that higher political ideals can be realized only through higher political forms. Myriads of experiments to get the substance of liberty out of the forms of tyranny, to believe in princes, to trust good men to do good as kings, have taught the inexorable truth that, in the economy of nature, form and substance must move together, and are as inextricably interdependent as are, within our experience, what we call matter and spirit. Identical is the lesson we are learning with regard to industrial power and property. We are calling upon their owners, as mankind called upon kings in their day, to be good and kind, wise and sweet, and we are calling in vain. We are asking them not to be what we have made them to be. We put power into their hands and ask them not to use it as power. If this power is a trust for the people, the people betrayed it when they made private estates out of it for individuals. If the spirit of power is to change, institutions must change as much. Liberty recast the old forms of government into the republic, and it must remold our institutions of wealth into the commonwealth.

Liberty and monopoly cannot live together. What chance have we against the persistent coming and the easy coalescence of the confederated cliques, which aspire to say of all business, "This belongs to us," and whose members, though moving among us as brothers, are using against us, through the corporate forms we have given them, powers of invisibility, of entail and accumulation, unprecedented because impersonal and immortal, and, most peculiar of all, power to act as persons, as in the commission of crimes, with exemption from punishment as persons? Two classes study and practice politics and government: place hunters and privilege hunters. In a world of relativities like ours size of area has a great deal to do with the truth of principles. America has grown so big—and the tickets to be voted, and the powers of government, and the duties of citizens, and the profits of personal use of public functions have all grown so big—that the average citizen has broken down.

The secret of the history we are about to make is not that the world is poorer or worse. It is richer and better. Its new wealth is too great for the old forms. The success and beauties of our old mutualities have made us ready for new mutualities. The wonder of today is the modern multiplication of products by the union of forces; the marvel of tomorrow will be the greater product which will follow when that which is co-operatively produced is cooperatively enjoyed. It is the spectacle of its concentration in the private fortunes of our day which reveals this wealth to its real makers—the whole people—and summons them to extend the manners and institutions of civilization to this new tribal relation.

III

The philanthropic impulse among the new captains of industry was most clearly expressed in the actions and writings of Andrew Carnegie. The Scottish-born industrialist made his fortune in iron and steel; by 1900, his mills were producing one-third of the steel manufactured in America. In 1901, he sold his holdings (to U.S. Steel) for a staggering $250,000,000. Over the next years, he distributed large sums to philanthropic enterprises ranging from

*public libraries to societies working for the advancement of peace.
In 1899, he published an essay,* The Gospel of Wealth *which
spelled out his credo of the obligations facing the guardians of
wealth.*

THE GOSPEL OF WEALTH, 1900

ANDREW CARNEGIE

The Problem of the Administration of Wealth

The problem of our age is the proper administration of wealth, that
the ties of brotherhood may still bind together the rich and poor in harmonious relationship. The conditions of human life have not only been
changed, but revolutionized, within the past few hundred years. In
former days there was little difference between the dwelling, dress, food,
and environment of the chief and those of his retainers. The contrast
between the palace of the millionaire and the cottage of the laborer with
us today measures the change which has come with civilization. This
change, however, is not to be deplored, but welcomed as highly beneficial. It is well, nay, essential, for the progress of the race that the
houses of some should be homes for all that is highest and best in
literature and the arts, and for all the refinements of civilization, rather
than that none should be so. Much better this great irregularity than
universal squalor.

It is easy to see how the change has come. In the manufacture of
products we have the whole story. Formerly, articles were manufactured at the domestic hearth, or in small shops which formed part of
the household. The master and his apprentices worked side by side, the
latter living with the master, and therefore subject to the same
conditions.

The inevitable result of such a mode of manufacture was crude
articles at high prices. Today the world obtains commodities of excellent
quality at prices which even the preceding generation would have
deemed incredible. The poor enjoy what the rich could not before afford.

The price we pay for this salutary change is, no doubt, great. We
assemble thousands of operatives in the factory, and in the mine, of
whom the employer can know little or nothing, and to whom he is
little better than a myth. All intercourse between them is at an end.
Rigid castes are formed, and, as usual, mutual ignorance breeds mutual
distrust. Under the law of competition, the employer of thousands is
forced into the strictest economies, among which the rates paid to labor
figure prominently, and often there is friction between the employer
and the employed, between capital and labor, between rich and poor.
Human society loses homogeneity.

The price which society pays for the law of competition, like the
price it pays for cheap comforts and luxuries, is also great; but the

In *The Gospel of Wealth*, by Andrew Carnegie (New York, 1900), pp. 1–11,
24–27, 32–33, 36–41.

advantages of this law are also greater still than its cost—for it is to this law that we owe our wonderful material development, which brings improved conditions in its train. But, whether the law be benign or not, we must say of it: It is here; we cannot evade it; no substitutes for it have been found; and while the law may be sometimes hard for the individual, it is best for the race, because it insures the survival of the fittest in every department. We accept and welcome, therefore, as conditions to which we must accommodate ourselves, great inequality of environment; the concentration of business, industrial and commercial, in the hands of a few; and the law of competition between these, as being not only beneficial, but essential to the future progress of the race.

Objections to the foundations upon which society is based are not in order, because the condition of the race is better with these than it has been with any other which has been tired. Of the effect of any new substitutes proposed we cannot be sure. The socialist or anarchist who seeks to overturn present conditions is to be regarded as attacking the foundation upon which civilization itself rests, for civilization took its start from the day when the capable, industrious workman said to his incompetent and lazy fellow, "If thou dost not sow, thou shalt not reap," and thus ended primitive communism by separating the drones from the bees.

Upon the sacredness of property civilization itself depends—the right of the laborer to his hundred dollars in the savings bank, and equally the legal right of the millionaire to his millions.

We start, then, with a condition of affairs under which the best interests of the race are promoted, but which inevitably gives wealth to the few. Thus far, accepting conditions as they exist, the situation can be surveyed and pronounced good. The question then arises—and if the foregoing be correct, it is the only question with which we have to deal—what is the proper mode of administering wealth after the laws upon which civilization is founded have thrown it into the hands of the few? And it is of this great question that I believe I offer the true solution.

There are but three modes in which surplus wealth can be disposed of. It can be left to the families of the decedents; or it can be bequeathed for public purposes; or, finally, it can be administered by its possessors during their lives. Under the first and second modes most of the wealth of the world that has reached the few has hitherto been applied. Let us in turn consider each of these modes. The first is the most injudicious. In monarchical countries, the estates and the greatest portion of the wealth are left to the first son, that the vanity of the parent may be gratified by the thought that his name and title are to descend unimpaired to succeeding generations. The condition of this class in Europe today teaches the failure of such hopes or ambitions. The successors have become impoverished through their follies, or from the fall in the value of land.

As to the second mode, that of leaving wealth at death for public uses, it may be said that this is only a means for the disposal of wealth, provided a man is content to wait until he is dead before he becomes of much good in the world.

Bearing in mind these considerations, let us endeavor to present some of the best uses to which a millionaire can devote the surplus of which he should regard himself as only the trustee.

First. Standing apart by itself there is the founding of a university by men enormously rich, such men as must necessarily be few in any country. Perhaps the greatest sum ever given by an individual for any purpose is the gift of Senator Stanford, who undertakes to establish a complete university upon the Pacific coast, where he amassed his enormous fortune, which is said to involve the expenditure of ten millions of dollars, and upon which he may be expected to bestow twenty millions of his surplus. He is to be envied.

Here is a noble use of wealth. We have many such institutions— Johns Hopkins, Cornell, Packer, and others—but most of these have only been bequeathed, and it is impossible to extol any man greatly for simply leaving what he cannot take with him. Cooper and Pratt and Stanford, and others of this class, deserve credit and admiration as much for the time and attention given during their lives as for their expenditure upon their respective monuments.

Second. The result of my own study of the question, What is the best gift which can be given to a community? is that a free library occupies the first place, provided the community will accept and maintain it as a public institution, as much a part of the city property as its public schools, and, indeed, an adjunct to these. It is, no doubt, possible that my own personal experience may have led me to value a free library beyond all other forms of beneficence. When I was a working boy in Pittsburgh, Colonel Anderson of Allegheny—a name I can never speak without feelings of devotional gratitude—opened his little library of four hundred books to boys. Every Saturday afternoon he was in attendance at his house to exchange books. No one but he who has felt it can ever know the intense longing with which the arrival of Saturday was awaited, that a new book might be had.

Third. We have another most important department in which great sums can be worthily used—the founding or extension of hospitals, medical colleges, laboratories, and other institutions connected with the alleviation of human suffering, and especially with the prevention rather than with the cure of human ills. There is no danger in pauperizing a community in giving for such purposes, because such institutions relieve temporary ailments or shelter only those who are hopeless invalids. What better gift than a hospital can be given to a community that is without one—the gift being conditioned upon its proper maintenance by the community in its corporate capacity. If hospital accommodation already exists, no better method for using surplus wealth can be found than in making additions to it.

Fourth. In the very front rank of benefactions public parks should be placed, always provided that the community undertakes to maintain, beautify, and preserve them inviolate. No more useful or more beautiful monument can be left by any man than a park for the city in which he was born or in which he has long lived, nor can the community pay a more graceful tribute to the citizen who presents it than to give his name to the gift.

Fifth. We have another good use for surplus wealth in providing our cities with halls suitable for meetings of all kinds, and for concerts of elevating music. Our cities are rarely possessed of halls for these purposes, being in this respect also very far behind European cities.

Let no one underrate the influence of entertainments of an elevating or even of an amusing character, for these do much to make the lives of the people happier and their natures better. If any millionaire born in a small village which has now become a great city is prompted in the day of his success to do something for his birthplace with part of his surplus, his grateful remembrance cannot take a form more useful than that of a public hall with an organ, provided the city agrees to maintain and use it.

Sixth. In another respect we are still much behind Europe. A form of beneficence which is not uncommon there is providing swimming baths for the people. The donors of these have been wise enough to require the city benefited to maintain them at its own expense, and as proof of the contention that everything should never be done for anyone or for any community, but that the recipients should invariably be called upon to do a part, it is significant that it is found essential for the popular success of these healthful establishments to exact a nominal charge for their use.

Seventh. Churches as fields for the use of surplus wealth have purposely been reserved until the last, because, these being sectarian, every man will be governed in his action in regard to them by his own attachments; therefore gifts to churches, it may be said, are not, in one sense, gifts to the community at large, but to special classes. Nevertheless, every millionaire may know of a district where the little, cheap, uncomfortable, and altogether unworthy wooden structure stands at the crossroads in which the whole neighborhood gathers on Sunday, and which, independently of the form of the doctrines taught, is the center of social life and source of neighborly feeling. The administrator of wealth makes a good use of a part of his surplus if he replaces that building with a permanent structure of brick, stone, or granite from whose tower the sweet-tolling bell may sound.

IV

No observation is more commonplace about American life than that self-made men are common in businessmen's success stories, that the economic elite is made up to a large degree of men who began at the bottom of the ladder and worked their way up. Detailed studies of the business elite, however, fail to confirm this hypothesis. As the findings of William Miller make amply clear, the rags-to-riches story, for all the Horatio Alger novels, was exceptional. Most businessmen came from economically comfortable backgrounds, not from the lower classes.

THE BUSINESS ELITE, 1900–1910

WILLIAM MILLER

Had the "typical" American business leader of the first decade of the twentieth century been an immigrant? Was he best represented in manufacturing, for example, by Franz A. Assmann, the German-born President of the American Can Company; or in railroading by Edward T. Jeffery, the English-born President of the Denver and Rio Grande; or in insurance by Alexander E. Orr, the Irish-born President of the New York Life; or in banking by Jacob H. Schiff, the German-born Jew who became senior partner of Kuhn, Loeb, and Co.?

Simply to ask the question is to answer it. Of the 187 businessmen studied here whose birthplaces are known, only eighteen, or less than 10 percent, were born abroad. Surely these men were less "typical" of the topmost business leaders of their time than the 55 percent who were born in the eastern part of the United States, in New England and the middle Atlantic states.

*American Business and Political Leaders by Region of Birthplace**

BIRTHPLACE	BUSINESS LEADERS (PERCENT OF)	POLITICAL LEADERS (PERCENT OF)
New England	18 ⎫ 55	22
Middle Atlantic	37 ⎭	27
East north central	22	27
South	9	11
West	4	7
United States	90	94
Foreign	10	6
Total cases (= 100 percent)	187	188

* These are census regions. Combined in "South" are south Atlantic, south central, west south central; in "West" west north central, mountain, Pacific.

Of the eighteen business leaders who were foreign-born, moreover, scarcely two or three fit the historians' concept of the *poor* immigrant who made good, and even these men had been brought to the United States at such an early age that they may be said to have been bred if not born here. Two of the eighteen men were of rich, colonial American business families who happened to be residing temporarily in Canada when they were born. Four more, rich and highly placed abroad, either settled here as representatives of big foreign business firms or were brought over by fathers who represented such firms. At least two others had letters of introduction from their fathers or other relatives abroad to American bankers and merchants who helped to establish them here. Thus it appears to be unsafe in writing of elites to associate immigrant status, even where that fits, with the idea of poverty.

Originally entitled "American Historians and the Business Elite," by William Miller. In *Journal of Economic History*, 9 (1949): 200–208. Reprinted with permission.

If not typically poor immigrants, were these business and political leaders the sons of foreigners? More of them were, surely, but the next table shows that the typical leader in each field was born into an American family.

American Business and Political Leaders by Region of Father's Birthplace

FATHER'S BIRTHPLACE	BUSINESS LEADERS (PERCENT OF)	POLITICAL LEADERS (PERCENT OF)
New England	27	33
Middle Atlantic	31	28
East north central	4	5
South	12	17
United States, unspecified*	7	4
United States	81	87
Foreign	19	13
Total cases (= 100 percent)	176	176

* Fathers of none of these men were known to have been born in the "West" as defined in the preceding table. All those known to have been born in the United States, the exact region being unknown, are counted here.

Moreover, these families themselves had, in most instances, been in America for many generations. Almost three-fourths of the business and political leaders were at least of the fourth generation of their paternal lines to reside in America; many were of the seventh and even the eighth generations. Colonial families were represented by 73 percent of the business leaders and 79 percent of those in politics. Fifty-six percent of the former and 47 percent of the latter were of families that had settled in America in the seventeenth century.

Even were they not of colonial ancestry, most of these leaders could point to British, and many to English, forebears.

*American Business and Political Leaders by Paternal Family's Origin**

FAMILY ORIGIN	BUSINESS LEADERS (PERCENT OF)	POLITICAL LEADERS (PERCENT OF)
England and Wales	53	56
Ireland	14	13
Scotland	7	8
Canada	3	1
British Empire, other, or unspecified	5	5
British Empire	82	83
Germany	12	8
Other countries	6	9
Total cases (= 100 percent)	162	162

* Or country of leader's own origin if he was the first in the family to settle in America. In either case, *last country* before settlement in America.

They could claim Protestant, and often Episcopal or Presbyterian, backgrounds.

American Business and Political Leaders by Religious Background*

DENOMINATION	BUSINESS LEADERS (PERCENT OF)	POLITICAL LEADERS (PERCENT OF)
Episcopal	25	12
Presbyterian	21	17
Methodist	9	13
Baptist	5	7
Other Protestant	14	20
Protestant, unspecified	16	25
Protestant	90	94
Catholic	7	4
Jewish	3	2
Total cases (= 100 percent)	174	165

* In almost all instances this is the religion of the leader himself and most likely of his family as well. In a few instances where a shift in religion is known to have occurred, only the old religion is counted.

If not of recent foreign origin, was the typical American business leader of the early twentieth century a migrant from a farm?

[The following] table shows that the political leaders far more frequently than those in business came from rural areas, that almost 60 percent of the latter were recruited from the larger towns and cities. Indeed, more than 20 percent of them were born in cities that around the middle of the nineteenth century had populations of one-hundred thousand or more. Upon these men rural influences even in a predominantly rural society must have been at a minimum.

American Business and Political Leaders by Size of Birthplace

SIZE OF BIRTHPLACE	BUSINESS LEADERS (PERCENT OF)	POLITICAL LEADERS (PERCENT OF)
Rural (under 2,500)	41	75
Town (2,500–8,000)	19 ⎫ 59	9
City (over 8,000)	40 ⎭	16
Total cases (= 100 percent)	164	130

Yet more significant in answering the question are the occupations of the fathers of these business leaders. Here we find that even of those born in rural areas fewer than one-third (and only 12 percent of the whole group) had fathers who were mainly farmers. Fifty-six percent of all business leaders, on the other hand, had fathers who had been in business—often big business—before them; eight of ten, indeed, came from business or professional families.

American Business and Political Leaders by Father's Occupation*

OCCUPATION	BUSINESS LEADERS (PERCENT OF)	POLITICAL LEADERS (PERCENT OF)
Businessman	56 ⎱ 79	33
Professional	23 ⎰	18
Farmer	12	38
Public official	7	9
Worker	2	2
Total cases (= 100 percent)	167	167

° Some fathers engaged in more than one occupation. The one used here was dominant in the period in which each man was raised. In a few instances this was not clear so a choice was made more or less arbitrarily (considering our lack of knowledge of income and status factors in the early nineteenth century) by which business (including higher company positions as well as company ownership) took precedence over farming and professional or public-official positions over both. This conforms roughly to the ascending order of status used in classifying occupations today. In no instance was there a problem of a father who was a worker (including wage as well as salaried occupations). About one-third of the professionals were lawyers or engineers who might have been called businessmen, given the nature of their professional work; the others were clergymen, doctors, writers, etc. "Public official" includes professional politicians (even if not office-holders) and lawyers who were chiefly public men.

Darwin P. Kingsley, who was President of the New York Life Insurance Company from 1907 to 1931 and Chairman of the Board from 1931 to his death two years later, once said of his impoverished early years:

> On the forty-acre farm, in Vermont, where I was born, everything we wore and everything we ate was grown on the farm, except a little sugar once in a while in place of maple sugar, which was indigenous, and a little tea. From a dozen sheep came wool which was first spun and then woven by hand into winter clothing. Our garden supplied flax which was made into summer garments. . . . I well remember the first time my father took his wool and swapped it for fulled cloth. We all regarded that as an epochal advance into a higher state of civilization.
>
> At Alburg, where I was born, there were not then (1857) enough houses to form even a hamlet. In the summer I attended the old "deestrict" school, a primitive affair innocent of any suggestion of higher education. In our home were very few books. Life there was clean through and through, self-respecting, and full of moral and religious discipline. But it was extremely narrow, uninspiring, and unimaginative. There was little or nothing to fire a boy with ambition or enthusiasm or to acquaint him with the world that lay beyond his "cabined, cribbed, and confined" sphere.

Yet it was not this kind of poverty that Carnegie had in mind when he recommended his "sternest of all schools"; this kind of spiritual and intellectual poverty was probably most prevalent among the poor, but this much at least they shared with large segments of the population at all levels, including those born and raised among the very rich. Call Kingsley's family poor in material things as well; but compared with the sons of many urban and rural wage workers even in the 1850s he and other farmers' sons like him were not worse off.

Nevertheless, in the next table, showing the social status of the families of these business and political leaders, Kingsley and a few others with apparently similar or poorer backgrounds were classified as lower

class. Men were classified as of the upper class when it was clear that
their fathers, like those of August Belmont, Cornelius K. G. Billings, or
Charles Deering, were themselves big businessmen, or where their
families, like those of Robert Todd Lincoln or Winslow Shelby Pierce,
were politically eminent. Generally speaking, those in between—including some businessmen with no special claims to wealth or power or
professionals like the average clergyman, doctor, or lawyer—were
ranked as of middle-class origins. This does not mean that their fathers
were not of help to them. James B. Duke, for example, rose to wealth and
power with a company founded by his father; George W. Perkins
moved to a partnership in the House of Morgan—probably the acting
head of the house at one stage—from a Vice Presidency in the New York
Life Insurance Company in which his father, a minor executive there,
had given him his business start.

Not all the men ranked in the upper class, of course, had fathers as
rich and powerful as those of Belmont or Billings, or families as well
connected as those of Lincoln or Pierce. Many in the middle bracket,
likewise, probably were not as fortunate in their upbringing as Elbert
H. Gary, whose family is classified there; probably few so classified
were as poor in material things as the Harrimans.

American Business and Political Leaders by Family Status

STATUS	BUSINESS LEADERS (PERCENT OF)	POLITICAL LEADERS (PERCENT OF)
Upper	50	36
Middle	45	50
Lower	5	14
Total cases (= 100 percent)	179	180

Poor boys, as Carnegie rightly said, usually go to work early in life.
Clearly few of these business and political leaders were poor boys. And,
as the following table shows, few of them went to work at an early age.

American Business and Political Leaders by Age on Going to Work*

AGE	BUSINESS LEADERS (PERCENT OF)	POLITICAL LEADERS (PERCENT OF)
15 or under	20	13
16–18	35	10
19 and over	45	77
Total cases (= 100 percent)	179	182

* This is age on taking first business, professional, or other job (except work on father's or other
relative's farm) after leaving school or, in a very few instances, after leaving the Union or Con-
federate armies.

Only one in five of these business leaders had a job before he was
sixteen; slightly more than half of them had jobs before they were
nineteen. Delaying the business debuts of most of the others—their late
start, according to the tradition, being itself a handicap—was the pursuit

of higher education, an undertaking that should so have altered their characters as to make them even poorer prospects for business success. The educational levels attained by all the leaders studied here are shown in the following table.

American Business and Political Leaders by Highest Educational Level Attained*

EDUCATION	BUSINESS LEADERS (PERCENT OF)		POLITICAL LEADERS (PERCENT OF)	
Grammar school	22		18	
High school	37		27	
Some college	12	} 41	11	} 55
College graduate	29		44	
Total cases (= 100 percent)	183		188	

* I have reduced the many types of older schools to this modern terminology, including in "grammar school" institutions called by that name, as well as district, public, common, and similar schools; in "high school," academies and others of similar rank. Counted among grammar-school boys are those who had little or no formal education as well as graduates; among high-school boys, all those who attended whether graduates or not. A few who had private tutors well into their teens but did not attend college are counted with the high-school group.

Of the business leaders who did not go to work until they were nineteen or older, 76 percent had gone to college. Four out of five of these, in turn, were of the upper class. No group, if the traditional account of the origins and ascent pattern of the American business elite truly represented the facts, could have been worse off than this one in the competition for business eminence. Yet about 28 percent of the business leaders are found in it. These men shared *all* the alleged handicaps: upper-class upbringing, college education, a late business start; yet, if speed of ascent be taken as the measure of the *greatest* attainment, these men were actually the most successful of all. Not only did they spend less time after starting to work in getting to the top, but, as the following table shows, they got there on the whole earlier in life than those allegedly most favored. This table shows the ages at which the two polar groups attained the high positions that made them eligible for this study.

American Business Leaders by Age on Becoming President or Partner of Major Company*

AGE	LATE-STARTING, UPPER-CLASS, COLLEGE MEN (PERCENT OF)		EARLY-STARTING, MIDDLE- AND LOWER-CLASS NONCOLLEGE MEN (PERCENT OF)	
Under 45	43	} 66	26	} 48
45–49	23		22	
50 and over	34		52	
Total cases (= 100 percent)	40		53	

* Board chairmen are a special case in regard to age on attaining the position and were omitted from this table.

Still, one has to stretch a point to attribute to more than two or three general American historians *any* discussion of the speed of ascent of the business elite. More of them stress this elite's typically lower-class, foreign, or farm *origins* and speculate on the forces that impelled men upward from such insalubrious environs. Yet poor immigrant boys and poor farm boys together actually make up no more than 3 percent of the business leaders who are the subject of this essay. If men with such backgrounds had been in fact representative of the great entrepreneurs of the later nineteenth century, they must have been supplanted with extraordinary rapidity by the higher status, more highly educated bureaucrats of the following generation. More likely, poor immigrant and poor farm boys who become business leaders have always been more conspicuous in American history books than in the American business elite.

V

The origins of New York's Metropolitan Opera House illustrate well the close links between the social prestige sought by the new rich and cultural endowments. For many years, the Academy of Music, a small and not very sumptuous theater, served the city. Then, in the early 1880s the city's new rich, with great speed and facility, joined together to erect the Metropolitan Opera House. Their motives were not difficult to understand. As the design of the structure makes clear, social position may have been more fundamental to most of the patrons then musical appreciation.

OPENING THE METROPOLITAN OPERA-HOUSE, 1883

To many persons the Italian opera in its present estate makes no more appeal as a serious form of art than it did to Carlyle or to Wagner. The high-dizened, select populace is very apt to wear a bored aspect. The interest in opera is at least three parts social to one part musical. In what other cause of charity or of culture would it be possible so to enlist the men of business who have for years carried the New York Academy of Music, and cheerfully threw what, from a commercial point of view, was the good money of assessment after the bad of hopeless investment? In what other cause would it have been found so brief and easy a matter to induce seventy men of business to subscribe $20,000 each, in order to raise the $1,400,000 which the Metropolitan Opera House was estimated to cost? Here there was not only the certainty of no pecuniary return, but the additional prospect to the stockholders of paying their admission into their own building like the undistinguished throng. When we compare this alacrity with the struggles of the Metropolitan Museum of Art, or with the languishing condition of the project

Originally entitled "The Metropolitan Opera-House." In *Harper's Monthly Magazine*, 72 (1883): 877–80, 883–84.

for the erection of a cathedral by the richest Protestant denomination, it shows that whatever may be the nature of the hold of Italian opera upon the "high-dizened, select populace," it is at least very powerful.

The causing cause of the building of the Metropolitan Opera House was the demonstration that the volume of boxes in the old Academy of Music was unequal to the wants of society. Beggarly as was the account of these boxes in a commercial sense, and freely as their owners grumbled about their possessions to the reporters with the advent of each successive season, they showed no willingness to part with them to any of the increasing number of New Yorkers who were entitled to aspire to the financial and social distinction of an opera box, yearly reenforced as these were by persons who had made fortunes in other parts of the country. That this aspiration, which was probably more fervent in the breasts of the female members of the families whose heads competed for boxes than in the breasts of the actual competitors, was not a mere desire for the enjoyment of opera, seems plain enough. No actual hardship is attached to a seat in the parquet. In fact the music and the spectacle are at least as available from that humble station as from the coigne of vantage in the box tier.

The parquet, however, was rarely crowded, whereas the boxes were always taken, and the competition became so keen that the boxes of the Academy of Music quite lost their character of unprofitable investments. Just before the project of the new opera house was undertaken, $30,000 was offered for one of them. This condition of affairs culminated during the operatic season of 1880, and in the course of the following summer sundry gentlemen who had been unable to obtain suitable accommodations in the old building determined to build an opera house for themselves. The stately structure we are describing was the result of that determination. It was a very short and easy matter, as has been intimated, to raise the sum necessary to secure the building of a new opera house. Indeed, while the building has been under construction, a premium of $5000 has been offered for the title of a box. Seventy subscribers, whose investment at present is between $15,000 and $20,000 each, united themselves in the Metropolitan Opera House Company.

The interior form of an opera house is distinctly established by experience as the amphitheatrical, and very few innovations upon this typical form are possible. The amphitheater in this case seems elongated beyond what is usual, and then widens at the stage end so as to give it more nearly the form of a lyre than of "the glittering horseshoe's ample round," which belongs to the conventional temple of the lyric drama. The modification of the curve which produces this result is, however, slight. There is a more important departure from the conventional opera house, for the proscenium is altogether omitted. In the Fourteenth Street Academy the proscenium boxes have been objects of desire to achieve which there have been given whole seasons of intrigue and social politics. Inasmuch as the proscenium could not be extended so as to include the amphitheater, it was resolved to cut the Gordian knot of preference by abolishing the occasion of rivalry, and converting the stockholders into an oligarchy, indeed, but not into a graded hierarchy—into a republic of oligarchs with no precedence among themselves, nodding on equal terms all round Olympus. A widely splayed opening of a very few feet in depth, decorated with large pilasters at the reentrant angle, and still for convenience called the proscenium, is the only representative of the abolished feature.

The purpose of making any box as desirable as any other box has by no means been attained, however, when the proscenium has been abolished; and the study of "sight lines" and acoustics, so as in some measure to bring this about, is one of the chief of the many problems which beset the architect of an opera house. In the present case sight lines were drawn from every part of the house in each tier to the sides and the rear of the stage, to ascertain how much of the view of the stage would be lost from that point, and the contour of the auditorium and the pitch of each tier were modified in conformity with the results of these studies to the arrangement actually adopted. The result has been so satisfactory that it is safe to say that there is no theater in which there are fewer bad seats in proportion to its size, nor any opera house in which the difference between the best and the worst boxes is so small.

There are three tiers and a half of boxes—122 altogether. The boxes themselves are all of the same dimensions, seven feet front by thirteen deep, divided nearly midway of their depth by an upholstered partition into a salon so-called and a box proper, and they are intended for six persons each. They are screened from each other by panels set in iron frames against the partitions. It is plain that the intention has prevailed to make them as nearly of equal value as may be, and the same accommodations of smoking rooms, dressing rooms, and the like dependencies are given to each tier.

VI

Perhaps the most compelling evidence of the life style of the new rich survives in the architecture of their private residences. The sums invested in these structures were as great as their designs were unoriginal. But they did stand as monuments to the success of

their owners, their desire to establish themselves as unique in their
countrymen's eyes. The architectural details of their efforts are
described below in an astute contemporary reaction to the new
houses. The authors are rightly persuaded that the homes of the
rich tell us a good deal about the rich themselves and about the
nature of the society in which they flourished.

STATELY HOMES IN AMERICA, 1903

HENRY W. DESMOND
AND HERBERT CROLY

The Modern American Residence

The primary fact about the greater contemporary residence is that it is the house of a very rich man. All the greater residences of the past have been conditioned upon the possession of wealth; but they have primarily expressed something different—an established and impressive social position or some sort of propriety or luxury of life.

Our American residences, on the other hand, will not be understood unless it is frankly admitted that they are built for men whose chief title to distinction is that they are rich, and that they are designed by men whose architectural ideas are profoundly modified by the riches of their clients. This is an aspect of the matter upon which it is not pleasant to dwell; but it is also an aspect, both of American residential architecture and of American life generally, which it is impossible and even dangerous to ignore. If wealth, whether widely distributed or concentrated in a few hands, or both, is as bad a thing as some passages in the prophets and the gospels make it out to be, there is little hope for American civilization, for our civilization is assuredly conditioned on the belief that a high standard of comfort is not of necessity morally stupefying, or the possession of large fortunes inevitably a source of evil and corruption.

There is something very palpable, and not in the least subtle, about the impression of wealth afforded by the greater contemporary residence. It has as little modesty about it, and makes as loud a proclamation of its own merit as any other characteristic American achievement. Nevertheless it does so much to deserve its frank splendor that it generally escapes the danger of showy and costly things—the inexcusable fault, that is, of being both wasteful and worthless.

Since, however, these houses are built primarily to be inhabited by rich men and to please them, some short account of the American millionaire is a natural accompaniment of a description of his habitation.

The architecture of these buildings, meritorious as in some respects it is, has not become well enough formed and technically disinterested to justify an exclusively technical consideration. It remains architecturally in an experimental stage—the nature of the experiment being explained chiefly by the disposition and wealth of the owner.

In *Stately Homes in America,* by Henry W. Desmond and Herbert Croly (New York, 1903), pp. 247–48, 251–52, 255–56, 267–68, 271.

If the wealth were any less than it is, and if it were not such an inexorable fact in the interpretation both of the owner's personality and his dwelling, this aspect of the matter could be passed over with less emphasis; but it is the essence of the whole situation that these fortunes are fairly overpowering. Their influence is not to be denied.

The American millionaire is born into a plastic society. The fluid nature of its economic forms gives him his extraordinary opportunity of making money; the fluid nature of its social forms allows and even encourages him to take full advantage of these opportunities. He is in no danger of being overshadowed by an aristocracy; he has as yet no strong social motives for abandoning his work after he has accumulated a certain income. On the contrary, whatever social prestige exists in American society attaches to the possession of a large fortune; but this motive has been rather a condition than an effective cause of the accumulation of such fortunes.

The man who erects the greater contemporary residence is necessarily a man of great concentration of purpose, of intense and continuous activity, and of somewhat exclusive interests. He has had neither time nor need to be an all-around man, who has leisure for many things or who has many different ways of living. All his associations and habits tend to make him a man who is specially and continually occupied with the prosecution of large business affairs, and who finds his occupation excitement and perhaps no little amusement in planning and consummating such schemes.

The house the millionaire has built is assuredly the product of a civilizing and constructive rather than a decadent and corrupting impulse. More than ever before he wants something really admirable. His ideas as to what are admirable are somewhat barbaric and are wholly lacking in that sense of economy which is such a necessary corrective of artistic extravagances and which lies so near to a native love of beautiful things; but what else can be expected? The strong, successful man wants to have his personal success strikingly but adequately commemorated. This "adequate" commemoration must be striking, because his success has been dazzling; and it must be admirable, because he wants this commemoration to be approved.

But he is a busy man, and generally has neither time nor inclination to take much interest in the details of the movement. Well aware that he knows nothing about architecture, he employs the services of the men who are recommended to him as the best architects; and, habituated as he is to trusting his interests to competent subordinates, he allows his architects within certain limits to have much their own way. His ideas about the house he wants will generally be very vague, and, in case they are definite, will be formed partly by those European reminiscences and partly by the kind of houses which his associates have been building. As these houses being themselves suggested by European reminiscences, there is no contradiction between the two sources of effect.

The architect, in designing dwellings of this kind, is not doing any violence to his taste. He is even more overflowing with architectural memories than is the millionaire; and he preserves them systematically in great big books. Like his client, also, he does not want to dispense with architectural traditions. Indeed, he clings to them; his work is devoted to domesticating them in his native country. The use of these memories is still somewhat indiscriminate. If he does not attempt to blend an Oriental pagoda with a medieval castle, he also does not bother himself much about archaeological consistency—provided he can obtain a consistent and striking effect. It is these striking effects for which he is always seeking, and that is the reason why he and his client generally get along very well together. In the pursuit of the striking effect money is spent with unparalleled generosity. The rich man does not stint his architect, but he insists on getting a million dollars' worth of good looks for a million dollars. The inconspicuous refinement, the modest understatement, the scrupulous economy of colonial architecture rarely appeals to him; and it happens to appeal just as little to his favorite designers. Economy, indeed, of any kind is not characteristic of the American disposition. Our countrymen want a big result in a short time; and even things artistic, unless they conform to this demand, are neglected. The architect instinctively feels that for the good of American art people must be startled into noticing and admiring these "palatial" mansions. At the present stage of American architectural esthetics they have the effect of monumental "posters," advertising to the world both American opulence and American artistic emancipation.

An account of the transformation which is now beginning to take place will be more accurate and instructive, in case we deal with specific names and instances. Neither the first of the Vanderbilts, the first of the Goulds, the first of the Astors, or the first of the Rockefellers evinced any interest in domestic or any other kind of architecture. They were or are content with respectable, comfortable, and ugly houses, which might or might not be on Fifth Avenue. The same statement is not true of Mr. Carnegie, who late in life built himself a handsome city house, something in the modern style; but he showed a survival of the thriftiness of his early habits, as well as his personal opinion of the big modern dwellings, by carefully instructing his architects to avoid designing a "palatial" building. On the other hand, in many cases, particularly among men who have made their money more recently, the very first generation of rich men, who are still entirely devoted to business, started in to erect really magnificent dwellings, and among them may be mentioned the late C. P. Huntington, Charles M. Schwab, a number of the steel and Standard Oil millionaires, Mr. Charles T. Yerkes, Mr. Marshall Field, and many others.

If the craving for a "palatial" residence, however, sometimes escaped the first generation of millionaires, it rarely escaped the second generation. These gentlemen, of which George Gould, the late William H. Vanderbilt, and Mr. J. P. Morgan may be considered as types, remained as faithful to the vast business interests they inherited as did their fathers before them. They have succeeded frequently in making even bigger reputations for themselves as industrial organizers than their fathers possessed. At the same time, however, they have also taken a much more positive interest in the spending of their money, and have almost without exception allowed themselves the characteristic American esthetic luxuries and extravagances.

Chapter 14

The Country Town

THE DECADES 1870 to 1910 were difficult for many rural Americans. Their economic position declined as they increasingly lost control over the shipping and marketing of their farm crops. They also suffered social deprivations. The country town, in the view of many of its residents, had become a narrow and stultifying place. In part, this perception pointed to a real change in rural conditions, but in part it reflected also the dominance of a new standard of judgment—the diversity and freedom of the city.

In the post-Civil War period, both the number of farms and the amount of agricultural goods increased substantially. Nevertheless, the level of farmers' protest mounted steadily, reaching fever pitch in the Populist movement of the 1890s. The problems lay in several areas. Individual farmers were unable to influence the prices they received for their goods; market conditions, reflecting demand not only in this country but abroad, were immune to any strategy they could mount. Should an individual farmer cut back production in bad times (which was the standard practice of industrial concerns), there was no certainty that his prices would rise; too many other farmers produced for the same market.

Moreover, American farmers were ambitious and commercial minded. Rather than rest contentedly with subsistence production, they eagerly bought new lands and new machinery, hoping to achieve economic success. But the interest they paid on the loans incurred for these purchases was high; and when several bad years followed a good one, they sank deeper into the red. Remember, too, that the farmer could not, like the businessman, declare bankruptcy and start all over again. Farming was not simply an expendable economic operation. The farm was also the home, and no one wanted to surrender it.

As severe as the financial problems were, the social ones were equally acute. Farming was a hard life, and the small population of rural villages did little to enhance its satisfactions. One result was a large migration from country to city. In the course of these years, the United States became increasingly an urban nation. In 1860, only one citizen in four lived in a city; by 1890, the number had risen to one in three. By 1910, it stood at nearly one in two. Part of this growth reflected the large number of immigrants who flocked to urban centers. But it also reflected a steady march of the young from the farm to the city, a march that may further have demoralized those who remained behind.

The problem of migration out of rural centers sparked a good deal of governmental and sociological investigation. Presidential task forces, as well as a growing number of rural sociologists, tried to fathom its causes and to suggest antidotes. Their research gives a very detailed picture of the conditions of rural life. It also provides very interesting and useful comparisons to urban conditions. For many years, the popular as well as sociological assumption was that village life was well knit, cohesive, consistent, personal, meaningful, and satisfying. By comparison, urban life seemed disjointed, alienating, and generally destructive of inherited traditions. A close reading of the materials below raises many questions about the rural part of this proposition. Despite a long tradition in America of glorifying the virtues of rural living and denigrating urban conditions, the historical reality is not quite so simple.

I

One of the first sociological studies of a rural township was conducted by Carl W. Thompson and G. P. Warber in 1913. They focused on a settlement in southern Minnesota, one with a population of slightly over three thousand people. The village was a conglomerate of nationalities—11 percent of the population was American born, 21 percent of mixed American and foreign-born parentage, 24 percent Norwegian, and 31 percent German. While some traits may have been idiosyncratic to this township, the Thompson and Warber study presents a detailed picture of an ordinary farm settlement. Note especially here the daily style of life—the work hours, the leisure hours—and imagine the impact of this routine day after day, and year after year, on the men, women, and children.

A RURAL TOWNSHIP IN MINNESOTA, 1913

CARL W. THOMPSON

AND G. P. WARBER

Work

The "old-timers" are right in saying that farming is "not what it used to be," so it is with the work on the farm. The early wheat farmer of the sixties or the seventies had different tasks from the present-day diversified crop or dairy farmer. The census records for the county show that in 1870 the average value of machinery per farm was but one hundred and seventy-four dollars, whereas in 1910 it had increased to three hundred and five dollars.

Late hours are no longer the rule, the average working day is about ten hours in the field. But there are several hours required for chores. The thrifty well-to-do farmer rises at four-thirty in the morning during the season of field work. The chores are done by six or six-thirty, depending upon the number of cows, and the number of hands to milk them. Breakfast is a matter of only fifteen minutes and by seven o'clock every good farmer has to be starting his field work. Most farmers want their dinner regularly at twelve o'clock. The housewife must have the meal ready at that time, though occasionally she will be kept waiting until one o'clock or after before the men feel that they can drop the job on hand and take time to eat. One hour's time is ordinarily allowed for dinner. This noon hour may include ten or fifteen minutes for scanning the daily paper, but there is no time for recreation. First, the horses must be fed and, then, the men wash up and sit down for their own meal. At one o'clock, or as soon after as possible, "it's get out the horses and back into the field again." The afternoon's work drags on until six o'clock, which is the approved quitting time. However, the chores remain to be done after supper is over. By eight, or eight-thirty ordinarily, most farmers are through with the day's work.

Woman's work, too, has changed from what it used to be. At first thought many of the country women are inclined to deny this, but at a second consideration they see that it is so. Though the routine of household duties is much the same as it used to be, there have been modifications. Soft water, running water, furnaces, modern range stoves, oil stoves, and gasoline engines are some of the innovations that have tended to make housework more congenial. The following figures show the percentage of homes into which certain conveniences have been introduced: oil stoves, fifty-seven; furnaces, fifteen; hard-coal stoves, forty-four; soft-coal heaters, thirty-one; washing machines, thirty-three; washing machines run by engine, ten; drinking water in house, eleven; soft water in the house, sixty-three; soft water beside house, ten. Food

In *Social and Economic Survey of a Rural Township in Southern Minnesota*, by Carl W. Thompson and G. P. Warber, University of Minnesota Studies in Economics, no. 1 (Minneapolis, 1913), pp. 2–3, 6–7, 16–17, 36–39, 45–51, 58–65.

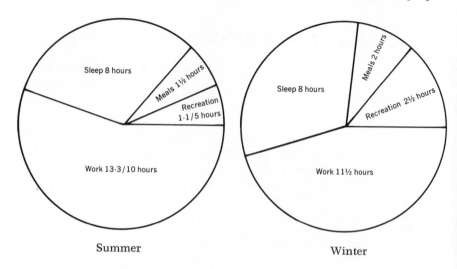

Summer   Winter

Diagram Showing the Average Farmer's Day

purchased: canned vegetables, sixteen; fruit, fifty-four; fresh meat, fifty-nine; prepared breakfast food, thirty-three.

With heavy outside tasks as a part of the regular household duties it is clear that the women are not run-down from lack of exercise. Even the indoor work is of the heaviest nature. There are big milk cans, separator, and all the milking utensils to cleanse by washing and rinsing with boiling hot water. This morning task itself together with doing the dishes lasts for an hour in many places. There is always much sweeping to be done, for feet cannot be kept clean in fields and barnyards. Preparing dinner is no longer the simple work it used to be. A woman has to be able to put up a little variety nowadays, although pork, potatoes, and gravy together with butter, bread, and coffee, are still the main diet of the toiling farmer. A good housewife has to be able to attend to all and yet get dinner ready on time. Nothing could be much more of an offense to her good husband than that she should accidentally keep a hungry score of threshing men waiting for their noonday meal. In only ten percent of the places was a hired girl kept. Sixty-nine percent of the families were without any girl help of sixteen years of age or over, and in forty-six percent of the families there were from one to four children under seven years of age who required care to keep them safe from mischief and out of harm's way. Thus the good women are kept "on the go" from five o'clock in the morning until nine at night.

Education

The aids to education among farmers may be shown by such factors as communication with the outside world, lectures and institutes attended, and the periodicals or magazines read, quite as much as by the interest manifest in the support of schools.

The rural mail service has greatly increased the amount of reading matter kept by farmers. In this township fifty-eight percent of the farmers kept a daily paper. The influence of these city publications has not only widened the mental horizon of the rural people, but also given the farmer a world outlook on markets and changed his attitude toward politics. The number of homes reached by popular magazines, such as *McClure's, Cosmopolitan, Ladies' Home Journal, Youth's Companion*, etc., is far less. In only twenty-seven percent of the homes of this township were any of the above class of periodicals read. Of the cheaper class of magazines, such as the *Woman's World* and *Good Stories*, thirty-two percent of the homes were readers. Eight homes contained a collection of books sufficient to be designated "a library." Five families had drawn books from the library. It is mainly the women who read anything outside of the daily papers or the farmers' publications.

The condition of country schools compared with town or city schools is admittedly poor, although there has been a general increase of interest and financial support.

The equipment of these schools is usually limited to a soft-coal stove in one corner of the room, a bit of blackboard, and a chart. Some have a set of maps and a globe. Most of them still have double seats. Only two of the country schools were well-enough equipped to get first-class state aid. Only three districts employed a first-grade teacher. Whatever others may think of the school situation as it presents itself, the farmers themselves are generally dissatisfied with the results.

A general criticism that is met with is that the school curriculum is loaded down with "too many subjects, which may be interesting and good enough for those who can go to school until they are through high school and college, but which are of little use to the boy who has to quit school as soon as he is sixteen to get to work. Why not teach something that a farmer can make use of?"

Furthermore it is charged that the schools are responsible for the outflow of youths from the country to the city. An old farmer who evidently had thought much on the subject said, "The things they take up in school all tend to direct the thought toward what man has done and is doing in cities. The boy who reads much at all begins to think that the only place where brains can be applied is in the city. Instead of leading the youth to think about the natural sciences as they connect up with the hills, the woods, and all the well-known life about them, the schools direct the newborn power of thought and reason into the realms of man-made conditions, which always gravitate toward the city. It is only natural that the boys and girls who are studious and thoughtful should begin to busy their minds with schemes of how they may get into that life where all big things seem to be accomplished. Small wonder that the brightest of our boys want to be lawyers, doctors, or engineers; and if they can't go to college, they leave the farm anyway to try to work their way up in business, like Marshall Field or Jim Hill."

Social Activities

That most evenings are spent at home is indicated by the popularity of reading and music as recreation during the winter months. Only forty-seven percent of the families in this township exchange evening visits, "which used to be so popular in the early days." Most of the families who still make those evening visits are "those with whom card playing is the chief social pastime." It is true that every farmer does some visiting during the year. However, most of them usually do it on Sundays. Among fifty-three percent of the families, Sunday visits were the only ones made. These visits were usually exchanged between two or three neighbors, or relatives living nearby, and once or twice a month was considered a fair average of the visits thus made.

As we have seen in our consideration of the routine of work of the present-day progressive farmer, he is forced to keep regular hours the year round on account of the importance of giving the right kind of care to his high-grade livestock. Hence, when chores are done in the evening, he takes up a farm journal or magazine and spends the evening reading, not because he is by nature antisocial and does not care to mingle in company with his neighbors, but he feels that "you can't afford to go away and tear around all night when you've got to get up at the usual time the next morning and keep on the go all day, just as if you had gotten your regular amount of sleep."

Another thing conducive to a decrease of social gatherings in the evenings is that "there has grown up a difference among country people." One old settler stated that "in the early days people were more social, because they were more alike." He explained that "nowadays, even if people do speak the same language, they don't associate with each other, except in a business way, unless they belong to the same church, have had the same education, and are about equally rich. There were no rich and poor people in the country then. All those of the same nationality, at least, had the same education, and the same social standards and tastes. There were no social classes in the country, as now; and that is why people got together more."

That these differences between the various families in a community do make for more or less of a social cleavage is evident from the fact that the social standards of formal etiquette, as well as questions of moral propriety, differ, not only with nationality and church affiliations, but also with wealth and education. To illustrate, while some families consider it "not in accordance with the spirit of the sabbath to allow boys to play baseball or even to go visiting on Sundays," many of their neighbors "see no harm in that kind of play," and "find no time to visit any other time than Sundays." So also some families "will not associate with a class of people who drink beer at their parties, and whose pleasure consists in listening to Uncle Josh's funny sayings run off on a phonograph, alternated with ghastly narrations of somebody's sickness or death."

The tendency seems to be toward more and more exclusiveness. In some places these differences have developed a sort of a clan spirit. The extent of this is indicated somewhat by the fact that twenty-six percent of the families visited "only with relatives." In some cases this clannishness had gone so far that children ten years of age did not know "the given names" of their nearest neighbors, although they had "been born and brought up" on adjoining farms. "While the members of these clans are very sociable among themselves, an outsider has no show of getting in with them except on business." One instance may be cited in which a new family had come into one of these neighborhoods, and they "lived there three years and not a single neighbor woman had called on the newcomer."

That this is a different spirit from that which prevailed "in the early days" is shown by the testimony of another old settler: "People used to get together much more than now; in those days they didn't wait to be invited, they just went and got acquainted. Nowadays nobody gets a chance to help out a neighbor any more. Even though everybody has the telephone, there may be someone taken sick at the neighbors, and instead of letting the women come and help them, they quietly hire doctors and nurses, and the first time that you hear of anybody having been sick is after the person is dead and they are getting ready for the funeral."

Most of the older people feel that "the country is all right if you aren't afraid to work; you at least get enough to eat." The growing generations, however, soon come to the conclusion that "the country means work and little else." Small wonder it is that many boys try to see if they can't "get a little of real life." "Plenty to eat," doesn't satisfy them, if they have read of the life of the great "White Way," as it is pictured in magazine stories. They feel that "there is nothing in the country for a fellow to enjoy." "People say: 'Hard work is the key to success.' The farmer gets the hard work all right, but what is the farmer's success? To have plenty to eat! To lay by a little money so that he may start out his boy in the same kind of a life that he has lived! And then to retire to town to die! That's a successful farmer's life! But is that really life?" Many farmers' boys who have read and "seen something of a different kind of existence" do not feel that they "care to repeat the old man's experiences." "Oh yes," say some, "you may tell us that we ought to be glad to hear the birds singing in the treetops; see the beautiful springtime blossoms and enjoy the fragrance of blooming orchards and budding roses! But you just put one of those poet fellows to work on a farm. Let him buckle in and get down to work, shocking barley for a while, and see what he feels most, the prickling itch or the beauties of a July sunset; and just notice how many birds he hears singing as he gets up at four-thirty or five o'clock the next morning. See how your budding poet enjoys the fragrance of springtime blossoms while he is swilling the hogs in the morning dew! Oh yes, we've got the fellows in the country who say that they can see all those beauties there, but it's funny that they never stay in the country to make their living."

II

In the first decades of the twentieth century, Cornell University organized the most innovative and active department of rural sociology. One of the leading members of the department was E. L. Kirkpatrick. In 1918–1919, he investigated the quality of life in an upper New York rural township; he compiled statistics on the conveniences that farmers in this comparatively prosperous region enjoyed. As a careful researcher, Kirkpatrick distinguished between the conditions prevalent among the owners of the farms, and those of the tenants and day laborers. The result is a sophisticated picture of prevailing standards of life in a rural township, one that ultimately helps explain why growing numbers of rural Americans moved to the city.

FARM LIFE IN NEW YORK, 1923

E . L . K I R K P A T R I C K

Methods of Study

Data for the study were obtained by the survey method. The field-work for the study of the farm business for the year April 1, 1918, to March 31, 1919, was conducted by the Department of Agricultural Economics and Farm Management at Cornell University, during the summer of 1919. Records of the farm business were taken on farms of Geneseo, York, Caledonia, Avon, and Lima towns, Livingston County, New York.

Location and Description of the Area Studied

LOCATION

The towns represented in the study constitute the northern part of Livingston County, situated in the west-central part of New York approximately halfway between the Pennsylvania border and the southern shore of Lake Ontario. The area lies, on an average, about twenty-five miles south of Rochester, the nearest market for milk and other perishable produce.

For practically all purposes of the study, the four hundred and two records were sorted into owner and tenant groups, the basis of classification being ownership or nonownership of the home in which the family lived. Farmers owning their homes and renting additional land were classed as owners. Of the four hundred and two homes studied in the analysis, two hundred and ninety-five were classed as owner and one hundred and seven as tenant.

MODERN IMPROVEMENTS

Only twelve (4.1 percent) of the owner homes and three (2.8 percent) of the tenant homes were fully modern, that is, were equipped with finished floors, heating and lighting systems, running hot and cold water, bathroom and flush toilet, sewage disposal, and power equipment for laundry. Modern conveniences of the various kinds, with the number and the percentage of homes having or lacking them, are listed in the following table.

In *Standard of Life in a Typical Section of Diversified Farming*, by E. L. Kirkpatrick (Ithaca, New York, 1923), pp. 8–11, 22–30.

Modern Conveniences in Farm Homes

	OWNER (295)		TENANT (107)		OWNER AND TENANT (402)	
	NUM-BER	PER-CENT	NUM-BER	PER-CENT	NUM-BER	PER-CENT
Floors:						
Floors finished throughout	34	11.5	11	10.3	45	11.2
Part of floors finished; carpets, congoleum, or linoleum	186	63.1	73	68.2	259	64.4
No finished floors; carpets, congoleum, or linoleum	75	25.4	23	21.5	98	24.4
Heating system:						
Steam or hot water	25	8.5	4	3.7	29	7.2
Hot air:						
Pipe	40	13.6	13	12.1	53	13.2
Pipeless	58	19.7	13	12.1	71	17.7
Gas	3	1.0	2	1.9	5	1.2
Stove heat only	169	57.3	75	70.1	244	60.7
Water system:						
Running cold and hot water	42	14.2	10	9.3	52	12.9
Running cold water	21	7.1	7	6.5	28	7.0
Well pump and cistern pump inside	16	5.4	10	9.3	26	6.5
Well pump only, inside	2	0.7	2	1.9	4	1.0
Cistern pump only, inside	173	58.6	58	54.2	231	57.5
No water inside	41	13.9	20	18.7	61	15.2
Bathroom:						
Bathroom fully equipped	48	16.3	13	12.1	61	15.2
Room, portable tub	2	0.7	2	1.9	4	1.0
Bathroom, no tub	2	0.7	0	0	2	0.5
No bathroom, no bathtub	243	82.4	92	86.0	335	83.3
Indoor toilet:						
Water flush, inside	33	11.2	13	12.1	46	11.4
Chemical, inside	14	4.7	5	4.7	19	4.7
Toilet outside	248	84.1	89	83.2	337	83.8
Kitchen sink:						
Kitchen sink with drain	222	75.3	79	73.8	301	74.9
Kitchen sink, no drain	19	6.4	6	5.6	25	6.2
No sink	54	18.3	22	20.6	76	18.9
Sewer system:						
Septic tank	16	5.4	3	2.8	19	4.7
Cesspool	23	7.8	6	5.6	29	7.2
Pipe to creek	1	0.3	0	0	1	0.2
Drain into ground from kitchen sink only	6	2.0	3	2.8	9	2.2
No sewage disposal	249	84.4	95	88.8	344	85.6
Lighting system:						
Electric lights:						
Commercial circuit	13	4.4	7	6.5	20	5.0
Farm plants	12	4.1	4	3.7	16	4.0
Gas lights	27	9.2	4	3.7	31	7.7
Acetylene lights	28	9.5	4	3.7	32	8.0
Gasoline lamps	12	4.1	5	4.7	17	4.2
Aladdin lamps	16	5.4	6	5.6	22	5.5

	OWNER (295)		TENANT (107)		OWNER AND TENANT (402)	
	NUM-BER	PER-CENT	NUM-BER	PER-CENT	NUM-BER	PER-CENT
Ordinary kerosene lamps	187	63.4	77	72.0	264	65.7
Laundry equipment:						
Laundry sent out	12	4.1	10	9.3	22	5.5
Power washer and electric or gas iron	15	5.1	7	6.5	22	5.5
Power washer only	35	11.9	12	11.2	47	11.7
Electric iron only	11	3.7	2	1.9	13	3.2
Gas iron only	13	4.4	5	4.7	18	4.5
No laundry equipment except hand-power washing machine and sadiron	209	70.8	71	66.4	280	69.7
Separate room for laundry	51	—	12	—	63	—
Equipment for cleaning:						
Power vacuum cleaner	10	3.4	3	2.8	13	3.2
Hand-pump vacuum cleaner	64	21.7	24	22.4	88	21.9
Sweeper vacuum	82	27.8	28	26.2	110	27.4
None other than carpet sweeper or brooms	139	47.1	52	48.6	191	47.5
Other equipment:						
Fireless cooker	5	1.7	1	0.9	6	1.5
Pressure or steam cooker	2	0.7	3	2.8	5	1.2
Bread mixer	46	15.6	11	10.3	57	14.2
Homes with none of the above	242	82.0	92	86.0	334	83.1

ITEMS OF COMFORT

The telephone, the automobile, musical instruments, and reading matter, some of which are regarded in general as luxuries, contribute as much to the standard of life as do modern improvements or conveniences. They may be regarded as constituting a part of living conditions (home equipment), and are here designated as items of comfort. A summary of these items as found in the homes included in the survey is given in the table below.

Items of Comfort

HOMES HAVING	OWNER (295)		TENANT (107)		OWNER AND TENANT (402)	
	NUM-BER	PER-CENT	NUM-BER	PER-CENT	NUM-BER	PER-CENT
Telephone	199	67.5	73	68.2	272	67.7
Automobile	228	77.3	76	71.0	304	75.6
Camera	105	35.6	48	44.9	153	38.1
Musical instruments:						
Piano, victrola, or phonograph, and other musical instruments	10	3.4	4	3.7	14	3.5
Piano and victrola only	43	14.6	18	16.8	61	15.2
Piano and other musical instrument than victrola	30	10.2	7	6.5	37	9.2

	OWNER (295)		TENANT (107)		OWNER AND TENANT (402)	
	NUM-BER	PER-CENT	NUM-BER	PER-CENT	NUM-BER	PER-CENT
Victrola and other musical instrument than piano	13	4.4	5	4.7	18	4.5
Piano only	83	28.1	21	19.6	104	25.9
Victrola only	37	12.5	19	17.8	56	13.9
Other musical instruments only	23	7.8	9	8.4	32	8.0
No musical instrument	56	19.0	24	22.4	80	19.9
Books in library:						
0– 49	133	45.1	58	54.2	191	47.5
50– 99	80	27.1	21	19.6	101	25.1
100–149	37	12.5	14	13.1	51	12.7
150–199	11	3.7	2	1.9	13	3.2
200 and over	34	11.5	12	11.2	46	11.4
Average number of books	72.8	—	64.4	—	70.5	—
Newspapers and magazines:						
No local paper	104	35.3	40	37.4	144	35.8
1 local paper	156	52.9	50	46.7	206	51.2
2 or more local papers	35	11.9	17	15.9	52	12.9
No daily	18	6.1	8	7.5	26	6.5
1 daily	262	88.8	93	86.9	355	88.3
2 or more dailies	15	5.1	6	5.6	21	5.2
No farm journal	38	12.9	13	12.1	51	12.7
1 farm journal	55	18.6	21	19.6	76	18.9
2 farm journals	76	25.8	34	31.8	110	27.4
3 farm journals	57	19.3	23	21.5	80	19.9
4 farm journals	36	12.2	8	7.5	44	10.9
5 or more farm journals	33	11.2	8	7.5	41	10.2
No general magazine	65	22.0	24	22.4	89	22.1
1–2 general magazines	130	44.1	46	43.0	176	43.8
3–4 general magazines	70	23.7	26	24.3	96	23.9
5 or more general magazines	30	10.2	11	10.3	41	10.2
No papers or magazines	3	1.0	1	0.9	4	1.0
At least 1 local, 1 daily, 1 farm journal, 1 general magazine	130	44.1	53	49.5	183	45.5
Average number of local papers taken	0.8	—	0.8	—	0.8	—
Average number of dailies taken	1	—	1	—	1	—
Average number of farm journals taken	2.4	—	2.2	—	2.4	—
Average number of general magazines taken	2.1	—	2.1	—	2.1	—

COMPARISON OF LIVING CONDITIONS WITH THOSE IN OTHER SECTIONS

Few data are available for comparison of living conditions on farms. Two studies made in Blackhawk and Clay Counties, Iowa, respectively, in 1918 and 1920, give summaries of housing conditions and home environment (Von Tungeln, 1918 and 1920). Comparison of certain factors contributing to home environment in these two Iowa areas with the same factors in the Livingston County area is possible from data presented in the following table.

Comparison of Home Environment, Iowa and New York Areas

HOMES HAVING	LIVINGSTON COUNTY, NEW YORK (402 FARM HOMES)				BLACKHAWK COUNTY, IOWA (142 FARM HOMES)				CLAY COUNTY, IOWA (85 FARM HOMES)			
	OWNER (295)		TENANT (107)		OWNER (86)		TENANT (56)		OWNER (30)		TENANT (55)	
	NUMBER	PER-CENT	NUMBER	PER-CENT	NUMBER	PER-CENT	NUMBER	PER-CENT	NUMBER	PER-CENT	NUMBER	PER-CENT
Running water	42	14.2	10	9.3	46	53.5	11	19.6	14	46.7	1	1.8
Bathroom	48	16.3	13	12.1	39	45.3	8	14.3	14	46.7	1	1.8
Indoor toilet	47	15.9	18	16.8	30	34.9	4	7.1	14	46.7	1	1.8
Electric lights	27	9.2	11	10.3	12	14.0	4	7.1	4	13.3	1	1.8
Gas lights	55	18.6	8	7.5	35	40.7	12	21.4	8	26.7	5	9.1
Power washer	50	16.9	19	17.8	52	60.5	16	28.6	15	50.0	19	34.5
Electric or gas iron	39	13.2	14	13.1	28	32.6	8	14.3	9	30.0	5	9.1
Vacuum cleaner	74	25.1	27	25.2	55	64.0	21	37.5	15	50.0	9	16.4
Heating system	123	41.7	30	28.0	51	59.3	21	37.5	15	50.0	3	5.5
Telephone	199	67.5	73	68.2	77	89.5	55	98.2	28	93.3	46	83.6
Piano	166	56.3	50	46.7	60	69.8	20	35.7	11	36.7	7	12.7
Automobile	228	77.3	76	71.0	50	58.1	25	44.6	24	80.0	25	45.5
Average of:												
Rooms per house	8.9		8.5		8.6		8.5		7.6		7	
Books in library	72.8		64.4		106.6		95.4		73.6		44.6	
Daily papers	1.0		1.0		1.3		1.3		1.6		1.0	
Farm journals	2.4		2.2		2.8		2.7		2.4		1.3	

III

Alarmed by the extent to which farmers were leaving the countryside, President Theodore Roosevelt appointed a special committee to investigate the causes of this out-migration. The ensuing report was both a diagnosis of the quality of community rural life and a series of recommendations for improvement. The implications of their findings question the accuracy of the traditional image of rural stability and cohesion.

REPORT OF THE COMMISSION ON COUNTRY LIFE, 1911

The ultimate need of the open country is the development of community effort and of social resources. Here and there the Commission has found a rural neighborhood in which the farmers and their wives come together frequently and effectively for social intercourse, but these instances seem to be infrequent exceptions. There is a general lack of wholesome societies that are organized on a social basis.

There is need of the greatest diversity in country life affairs, but there is equal need of a social cohesion operating among all these affairs and tying them all together. This life must be developed, directly from native or resident forces. The problem before the Commission is to suggest means whereby this development may be directed and hastened directly from the land.

The social disorder is usually unrecognized. If only the farms are financially profitable, the rural condition is commonly pronounced good. Country life must be made thoroughly attractive and satisfying as well as remunerative, and able to hold the center of interest throughout one's lifetime. With most persons this can come only with the development of a strong community sense or feeling. The first condition of a good country life, of course, is good and profitable farming. The farmer must be enabled to live comfortably.

The economic and industrial questions are, of course, of prime importance, but they must all be studied in their relations to the kind of life that should ultimately be established in rural communities.

We must begin a campaign for rural progress. It is specially necessary to develop the cooperative spirit, whereby all people participate and all become partakers.

The cohesion that is so marked among the different classes of farm folk in older countries cannot be reasonably expected at this period in American development. We are as yet a new country with undeveloped resources. Our farmers have been moving and numbers of them have

In *Report of the Commission on Country Life*, 60th Congress, 2nd session, U.S. Senate Document, no. 705 (1909). Reprint edition, (Chapel Hill, N.C., 1911), pp. 78–80, 90–102, 114–17, 121–23, 128–29, 137–43.

not yet become so well settled as to speak habitually of their farm as "home."

Even when permanently settled, the farmer does not easily combine with others for financial or social betterment. The training of generations has made him a strong individualist, and he has been obliged to rely mainly on himself. Self-reliance being the essence of his nature, he does not at once feel the need of cooperation for business purposes or of close association for social objects. In the main, he has been prosperous, and has not felt the need of cooperation.

If he is ambitious for social recognition, he usually prefers the society of the town to that of the country. He does not as a rule dream of a rural organization that can supply as completely as the city the four great requirements of man—health, education, occupation, society.

The correctives for the social sterility of the open country are already in existence or underway, but these agencies all need to be strengthened and especially to be coordinated and federated; and the problem needs to be recognized by all the people. The good institutions of cities may often be applied or extended to the open country. It appears that the social evils are in many cases no greater in cities in proportion to the number of people than in country districts; and the very concentration of numbers draws attention to the evils in cities and leads to earlier application of remedies.

It is of the greatest consequence that the people of the open country should learn to work together, not only for the purpose of forwarding their economic interests and of competing with other men who are organized, but also to develop themselves and to establish an effective community spirit.

At present the cooperative spirit works itself out chiefly in business organizations, devoted to selling and buying. So far as possible, these business organizations should have more or less social uses. There is a great need of associations in which persons cooperate directly for social results. The primary cooperation is social and should arise in the home, between all members of the family.

In every part of the United States there seems to be one mind, on the necessity of redirecting the rural schools. Everywhere there is a demand that education have relation to living, that the schools should express the daily life.

The schools are held to be largely responsible for ineffective farming, lack of ideals, and the drift to town. This is not because the rural schools, as a whole, are declining, but because they are in a state of arrested development and have not yet put themselves in consonance with all the recently changed conditions of life. The country communities are in need of social centers—places where persons may naturally meet, and where a real neighborhood interest exists. Inasmuch as the school is supported by public funds and is therefore an institution connected with the government of the community, it should form a natural organic center. If the school develops such a center, it must concern itself directly with the interests of the people. The school must express the best cooperation of all social and economic forces that make for the welfare of the community. Merely to add new studies will not meet the need. The school must be fundamentally redirected, until it becomes a new kind of institution.

Any consideration of the problem of rural life that leaves out of account the function and the possibilities of the church, and of related institutions, would be grossly inadequate.

The country church doubtless faces special difficulties. As a rule it is a small field. The country people are conservative. Ordinarily the financial support is inadequate. Sectarian ideas divide unduly and unfortunately. While there are many rural churches that are effective agents in the social evolution of their communities, it is true that as a whole the country church needs new direction and to assume new responsibilities. Few of the churches in the open country are provided with resident pastors. Without a resident minister the church work is likely to be confined chiefly to services once a week. The Sunday school is sometimes continued only during the months of settled weather. There are young people's organizations to some extent, but they are often inactive or irregular. The social activity of the real country church is likely to be limited to the short informal meetings before and after services and to suppers that are held for the purpose of raising funds. Most of the gatherings are designed for the church people themselves rather than for the community. The range of social influence is therefore generally restricted to the families particularly related to the special church organization, and there is likely to be no sense of social responsibility for the entire community.

The rural church must be more completely than now a social center. This means not so much a place for holding social gatherings, although this is legitimate and desirable, but a place whence constantly emanates influences that go to build up the moral and spiritual tone of the whole community. The country church of the future is to be held responsible for the great ideals of community life as well as of personal character.

Theoretically the farm should be the most healthful place in which to live, and there are numberless farmhouses, especially of the farmowner class, that possess most excellent modern sanitary conveniences. Still it is a fact that there are also numberless other farmhouses, especially of the tenant class, and even numerous rural schoolhouses, that do not have the rudiments of sanitary arrangement. Health conditions in many parts of the open country, therefore, are in urgent need of betterment. There are many questions of nationwide importance, such as soil, milk, and water pollution; patent medicines, advertising quacks, and intemperance; and general unsanitary conditions of those houses not under federal or other rigid sanitary control; in some regions unwholesome and poorly prepared and monotonous diet; lack of recreation; too long hours of work.

In general, the rural population is less safeguarded by boards of health than is the urban population. The physicians are farther apart and are called in later in case of sickness, and in some districts medical attendance is relatively more expensive. The necessity for disease prevention is therefore self-evident.

Realizing that the success of country life depends in very large

degree on the woman's part, the Commission has made special effort
to ascertain the condition of women on the farm.

The routine work of women on the farm is to prepare three meals
a day. This regularity of duty recurs regardless of season, weather,
planting, harvesting, social demands, or any other factor. It follows,
therefore, that whatever general hardships, such as poverty, isolation,
lack of labor-saving devices, may exist on any given farm, the burden
of these hardships falls more heavily on the farmer's wife than on the
farmer himself. In general her life is more monotonous and the more
isolated, no matter what the wealth or the poverty of the family may be.

The relief to farm women must come through a general elevation
of country living. The women must have more help. In particular, these
matters may be mentioned: development of a cooperative spirit in the
home; the building of convenient and sanitary houses; providing
running water in the house, and also more mechanical helps; a less
exclusive ideal of money getting on the part of the farmer; providing
better means of communication, as telephones, roads, and reading
circles; and developing of women's organizations. The farm woman
should have sufficient free time and strength so that she may serve the
community by participating in its vital affairs.

The farm labor problem is complicated by several special conditions, such as the fact that the need for labor is not continuous, the
lack of conveniences of living for the laborer, long hours, the want
of companionship, and in some places the apparently low wages. Because of these conditions, the necessary drift of workmen is from the
open country to the town.

The most marked reaction to the labor difficulty is the change in
modes of farm management, whereby farming is slowly adapting itself
to the situation. In some cases this change is in the nature of more
intensive and businesslike methods whereby the farmer becomes able
to secure a better class of labor and to employ it more continuously.
More frequently, however, the change is in the nature of a simplification of the business and a less full and active farm life.

The only real solution of the present labor problem must lie in
improved methods of farming. The excessive hours of labor on farms
must be shortened. This will come through the working out of the
better farm scheme and substituting planning for some of the muscular
work. Already in certain regions of well-systematized diversified farming the average hours of labor are less than ten.

The most difficult rural labor problem is that of securing household
help on the average farm. The larger the farm, the more serious the
problem becomes. The necessity of giving a suitable education to her
children deprives the farm woman largely of home help; while the lure
of the city with its social diversions, more regular hours of labor, and
its supposed higher respectability deprives her of help bred and born
in the country. Under these circumstances, she is compelled to provide
the food that requires the least labor. This simple fact explains much
of the lack of variety, in the midst of the greatest possible abundance.

There is widespread conviction that the farmer must give greater
attention to providing good quarters to laborers and to protect them from

discouragement and from the saloon. The shortage of labor seems to be the least marked where the laborer is best cared for. It is certain that farming itself must be so modified and organized as to meet the labor problems at least halfway. While all farmers feel the shortage of help, the Commission has found that the best farmers usually complain least about the labor difficulty.

The liquor question has been emphasized to the Commission in all parts of the country as complicating the labor question. It seems to be regarded as a burning country life problem. Intemperance is largely the result of the barrenness of farm life, particularly of the lot of the hired man. The Commission is impressed, from the testimony that has accumulated, that drunkenness is often a very serious menace to country life, and that the saloon is an institution that must be banished from at least all country districts and rural towns if our agricultural interests are to develop to the extent to which they are capable.

There is most urgent need for a quickened public sentiment on this whole question of intoxication in rural communities in order to relieve country life of one of its most threatening handicaps. At the same time it is incumbent on every person to exert his best effort to provide the open country with such intellectual and social interests as will lessen the appeal and attractiveness of the saloon.

IV

Some observers of rural life wondered whether the unhappy picture that emerged from presidential commissioners and rural sociologists was not overdrawn. One such figure, E. R. Eastman, editor of the popular farm journal the American Agriculturist, *disputed these findings. His article, "The Fundamental Satisfactions of Rural Life," was a self-conscious effort to present the other side of the story.*

THE FUNDAMENTAL SATISFACTIONS OF RURAL LIFE, 1927

E. R. EASTMAN

One of the fascinating things to me as a small farm boy was to kick the top of an anthill on my way to the back pasture after the cows and to watch the little creatures hurry hither and thither, apparently without any aim or goal. Time and again I have stood on a city street or in one of the great railroad terminals in New York City, watching the

Reprinted from "The Fundamental Satisfactions of Rural Life," by E. R. Eastman. In *Farm Income and Farm Life: A Symposium*, ed. Dwight Sanderson (Chicago, 1927), pp. 24–29, by permission of The University of Chicago Press. Copyright 1927 by the University of Chicago.

people rushing around, all going in different directions, with their strained and serious faces, and remembered the ants and the anthill. The thought always comes that so far as any real fundamental object in life is concerned, the rushing back and forth of people in this hurrying age is often as hopeless and futile as was the aimless hurrying of the ants.

Of these finer possessions, the farmer has a bountiful share. In mentioning a few of them, I in no way fail to recognize the farmers' problems and troubles, of which he has many, but I sometimes think that farm people themselves and their friends have emphasized the problems and the troubles of country life without giving due credit to the compensations and the satisfactions which serve in some measure to balance the darker side.

First of all, there is the privilege of association with the soil and with the plant and animal life, an association that strengthens character and cleanses the spirit.

Ole Hansen, manager of a cooperative creamery company in Nebraska, compares the hanging gardens of Babylon to a modern alfalfa field. "As I travelled," he says,

> through this fertile valley with its thousands of acres of alfalfa in bloom, and as I inhaled the sweet scent coming off those floating fields, I could not help but think about what a wonderful garden spot this Nebraska alfalfa field really was. I thought about the ancient gardens of Babylon, and I realized that right here we can discount it a million times with our valleys full to the brim with the sweet smelling alfalfa.

That fine old Southern farm paper called *The Progressive Farmer* has been running a little series of letters from country folks on the subject "Country Things I Love Most." These letters state so well from actual experience some of the fundamental country things which make for happiness that I quote portions of them here.

One country woman writes:

> These things I love:
> The sound and sight of wild geese in a snakelike line against a dull November sky.
> Roaring fires in stoves and fireplaces.
> The distant sound of a woodman's axe.
> The nicker of a horse for his corn.

Another farm woman says:

> I love the awakening of spring, heralded by the bluebirds, robin redbreasts, and whippoorwills.
> I love the green tips of buds and leaves, the pure white fragrant blossoms of the syringa, and I love to watch my winter window revealing new growth and beauty.
> Last but not least, if I cannot have what I like, I love to like what I have.

No business in the world is a closely associated with the home as is farming. No business gives the father such an opportunity to personal contact with his children. In the city, the father leaves in the morning before the younger children are up, and often he gets home so late that the children are in bed. If he sees them at all, it is when he is tired and worn from the labors of the day.

No place in the world equals the farm home for the rearing of children and for the opportunity of giving them the association with natural, growing things of both plant and animal life, a place to play in the open air under natural conditions, and the fresh air and food of the farm to build their young bodies. No place in the world is so good as the farm in the training of both the boy and the girl in habits of work and responsibility that will mean their success later on in life.

So, too, the farm home, perhaps in larger proportion than other homes, is the place where love abides. Problems of the business are mutual problems to be worked out by both father and mother together. Perhaps it is the soil and the natural things of life which surround the men and women of the farm which give them a deeper sense of responsibility and steadfastness toward each other, toward their community, their country, and their God.

These are some of the things that the farm boy who has gone to the city never forgets. No matter what his so-called success may be, deep in his heart these things are ever calling him back, for no matter how high he has climbed in worldly power and material attainment, he never again is able to touch the high spots of happiness that come to those who work and live upon the land and who are able to appreciate and enjoy the happiness that comes from simple, fundamental things.

V

The most famous and important voluntary association in rural America was the Grange. Organized in 1868, it attempted to improve both the economic and social welfare of the rural population. Its financial endeavors are well known—especially its effort to organize marketing cooperatives. But less attention has been paid to its efforts to bring fellowship and excitement to farmers' lives. Reprinted below are the first circular issued by the National Grange and the standard format for initiating new members. The exotic Grange ritual suggests, albeit indirectly, how exceptionally drab and dull ordinary days were.

THE GRANGE JOURNAL, 1868

The first circular which was issued by the National Grange immediately after its organization, and printed in January 1868.

We solicit attention to an organization now being established for

Reprinted in *Journal of Proceedings, Fourteenth Session*, National Grange of the Patrons of Husbandry (Philadelphia, 1880), pp. 10–11.

the purpose of increasing the general happiness, wealth, and prosperity of the country. It is based upon the axioms that the products of the soil comprise the basis of all wealth; and that the wealth of a country will depend altogether upon the general intelligence and mental culture of the producing classes.

All existing popular modes of creating an interest in agriculture have been carefully studied. Agricultural fairs enlist attention, and to a certain extent excite competition, but these associations are gradually losing their influence, and the novelty and excitement of horse racing, and other scenes still less commendable, are looked upon as essential to their success, if not to their very existence. Clubs for mutual instruction seem to lose their interest as soon as the first excitement of organization is passed.

The incentive to the formation of these societies results from a recognition of the well-known principles that *unity of action* is necessary to secure success. This unity must be made solid and permanent, not trivial and spasmodic, and from a preponderance of the latter we may trace the main cause of failure in these organizations. On the other hand, when we reflect upon the fact that certain associations have stood the test of ages and even of centuries, as for example, the Masonic order, we may well ask: "In what does their permanency consist?" We can only find one satisfactory answer to this question, and that is, their secrecy. If then, this is the great element of eminent success, why not embrace it? If this simple principle is the keystone of a permanent foundation, why not secure it? If such a slender thread as a secret or exclusive ceremony of initiation before membership can be secured will bind a society, then let us adopt *that* mode of forming the farming community into bodies where unity of action can be enforced by discipline, and where discipline can be secured by significant organization.

Reflections similar to the above have resulted in the formation of an Order known as the "Patrons of Husbandry." A constitution for the guidance of the Order has been prepared; four initiatory degrees, representing the four seasons, have also been completed, and they contain the novel beauty and secrecy that will make the Society "ever budding, ever new." Women are admitted, as well as young persons; it is hoped by this means a love of rural life will be encouraged, the desire for excitement and amusement so prevalent in youth will be gratified instead of being repressed; not, however, in frivolities, but by directing attention to the wonder workings of nature, and leading the mind to enjoy and appreciate these studies. Young men are constantly being attracted to the cities from the country. There are, undoubtedly, good reasons for this migratory tendency, and a want of attractions for the mind is one of the chief.

With regard to the modes of education, mention may be made of mutual instruction through the reading of essay and discussions, lectures, formation of select libraries, circulation of magazines treating directly upon subjects inculcating the principles governing our operations in the field. It may be remarked that all of these measures are now in existence. To this we answer that their direct application under a comprehensive and controlling principle is both new and novel, and one that has not been employed previously for the same objects.

THE GRANGE MANUAL, 1895

First Degree—Laborer

Alarm from the A. S. [Assistant Steward].

S. [Steward] Worthy Overseer, an alarm at the gate.

O. [Overseer] See who approaches.

A. S. Men seeking employment.

S. Are they unconstrained and willing?

A. S. They are.

S. Have they been tried and found worthy?

A. S. They have.

O. Admit them for examination.

S. [*Opens the door.*] It is the pleasure of our Worthy Overseer that you enter the field with this caution: use discretion, respectfully obey all orders and, should work be assigned you, labor with diligence.

A. S. Let our future conduct prove us.

O. Who comes here?

A. S. Worthy and honest men seeking wisdom, who desire to become laborers in the field.

O. What wages do they expect?

A. S. Wisdom, and not silver; knowledge, rather than fine gold.

O. Are you satisfied of their integrity?

A. S. I am.

O. Friends, is it of your own freewill that you ask the position?

Cand. [Candidate] It is.

O. It is well. Conduct them to our Worthy Master; from him you will receive further instruction.

M. [Master] In the presence of our heavenly Father and these witnesses, I do hereby pledge my sacred honor that, whether in or out of the Order, I will never reveal any of the secrets of this Order, unless I am satisfied by strict test, that they are lawfully entitled to receive them, that I will conform to and abide by the Constitution, rules, and regulations of the National Grange, and of the State Grange under whose jurisdiction I may be, that I will never propose for membership in the Order, anyone whom I have any reason to believe is an improper person; nor will I oppose the admission of anyone *solely* on the grounds of a personal prejudice or difficulty. I will recognize and answer all lawful signs given me by a brother or sister of the Order, and will render them such assistance as may be needed, so far as I may be able and the interest of my family will permit. I will not knowingly wrong or defraud a brother or sister of the Order, nor will I permit it to be done by another, if in my power to prevent it. Should I knowingly or willfully violate this pledge, I invoke upon myself suspension or expulsion from the Order, and thus be disgraced among those who were my brothers and sisters.

M. Brothers and Sisters, is this your Obligation?

Originally entitled *Manual of Subordinate Granges of the Patrons of Husbandry*, 7th ed. (Philadelphia, 1895), pp. 7–9, 11, 46–49.

Candidates. (All answer in a clear voice,) It is.

[*Song.*]

A. S. I will now introduce you to our Worthy Chaplain.

Chap. Worthy Brothers, agriculture is the first and noblest of all occupations. It is the only one directly instituted by our Creator. God planted the Garden of Eden, and placed man therein to tend and keep it. He caused to spring forth out of the ground every tree and plant that is pleasant to the sight and bearing fruit good for food. It was a command of the Almighty that man should till the ground. History proves that where agriculture has been fostered, that nation has prospered and reached a high degree of perfection; but where it has been neglected, degeneracy began. Let us heed the warning and escape the doom.

Fourth Degree—Husbandman

S. Worthy Overseer, an alarm at the Gate.

O. See who approaches.

A. S. Brothers, who, having finished their labor in the harvest field, seek advancement.

S. Do you vouch for them?

A. S. I do.

A. S. Worthy Overseer, brothers, who have served faithfully, desire to become Husbandmen.

O. Brothers, your industry, zeal, and efficiency have gained you the approbation of your companions in our Order; and the uprightness of your conduct, and your fidelity to your pledges, are evidences of your moral worth and fitness to be received among honorable Patrons. The position of Husbandmen further confers upon you great privileges, and binds you in a closer tie of brotherhood. It is your desire to proceed?

Cand. It is.

A. S. Worthy Master, brothers, true, worthy, and well qualified, are prepared to give the pledge of the Fourth Degree.

[*M. administers the pledge*] I hereby renew and confirm the obligations I have heretofore taken in this Order; and solemnly declare that I will never communicate the secrets of this Order to anyone unless legally authorized to do so; and that I will endeavor to be a true and faithful Patron of Husbandry, perform the duties enjoyed in this Order, and aid others in the performance of the same.

O. Brothers, you are now about to receive your reward as faithful Harvesters. It is to be made Husbandmen in our Order—a position reached by merit alone. There are duties devolving upon you and, in their proper observance, your example will reflect credit upon you and our Order.

As a Husbandman, look with earnest solicitude upon children and their welfare; and remember that they are to follow in our footsteps. If we desire to encourage them to love rural life, we must make its labors cheerful. We may tell them of the pleasures and independence of the farmer's life; but if their daily intercourse with us shows it to be tedious, irksome, laborious, without any recreation of body or mind, they will soon lose all interest in it, and seek enjoyment elsewhere. Therefore, strive to make your homes pleasing.

Adorn your grounds with those natural attractions which God has so profusely spread around us; and especially adorn the family circle with the noble traits of a kind disposition—fill its atmosphere with affection, and thus induce all to love and not to fear you; for love is the only enduring power.

[*Song*.]

Suggesions to Officers and Members of Subordinate Granges in Relation to Degree Work and Paraphernalia

1. All Officers of Subordinate Granges, before attempting to confer degrees, should make themselves thoroughly familiar with the *ritual* —not only the *lectures*, but the preparations and directions.

     In order to attain the highest degree of proficiency and discipline, *special drill* meetings should be held by the officers.
2. They should see that the room is in order, with the officers' desks as located in the diagram in late editions of the Manual.

     The regalia should be kept in wardrobe in anteroom, and no one be allowed to pass the inner gate unless attired in regalia.
3. The altar should be in position and have the open Bible upon it. There should be a neat oilcloth or an appropriate rung in front of O.
4. All officers should be supplied with their proper emblems and use them in the discharge of official duties.
5. The S. has the general charge of the arrangement and preparation of the room for conferring degrees, also of the decorations.
6. While the candidates are being prepared in preparation room, the M. should caution officers and members to strive to make the degree as impressive as possible. The choir should be ready to sing when needed, and instrumental and vocal music should accompany the movement of candidates upon the floor, unless *silence* is required in the instructions.
7. *The italic instructions in the Manual must be carefully observed.*

Instructions in General Decorations

Directions for Stage and Court. To give an impressive effect to the court in the several degrees, the stage should not be less than ten feet deep and fifteen feet wide for an ordinary good sized Grange Hall.

If stage scenery is used, which adds much to the effect of the court, the deeper the stage the better the effect.

In almost any good-sized town a professional stage-fitter can be found who would be glad to take the contract to put in the slides and scenery similar to those used in opera houses.

Curtains. The curtains for the stage should not be less than seven feet high. They can be made of two-faced, maroon-colored, cotton flannel, which will cost through our Grange Houses, about fifteen cents per yard.

The Robe. Material, navy blue cheesecloth, or calico, made sailor fashion, trimmed with white braid. A white cord and tassel confines it at the waist. A shepherdess' hat completes the costume. Requires about ten yards of material. The same suit is worn throughout all the degrees.

Directions for Making Court Robes. The robes can be made so that they may be worn as over-dresses; fitting anyone.

First, make a sack, with flowing sleeves; with draws of cord at the neck and waist; next make the overdress. Next cut two widths, from the waist down, allowing for a train, and complete the skirt, by sewing to front piece at waist. Such a stage robe will fit anyone.

These robes can, of course, be made by any other method preferred, so that the ideal of the colors is preserved.

The cheesecloth is wide and soft, consequently makes up and drapes very nicely, and will take about eight yards for a suit.

The whole outfit will probably cost from twenty-five to thirty-five dollars; costlier material can, of course, be used.

VI

Although most observers assumed that styles of rural life and urban life were not only different but also opposed one to the other, an occasional student recognized a bond of deep affinity between the two. One such figure was A. C. True, the director of the Department of Agriculture Experiment Stations. He insisted that there was a congruence of interest between farm and town, and the arguments he raises in his imaginative article are well worth considering. They offer a fresh way of understanding the character of the urban-rural nexus.

THE SOLIDARITY OF TOWN AND FARM, 1897

A . C . T R U E

Between 1870 and 1890, speaking relatively and in round numbers, two million men gave up farming and went to join the great army of toilers in our cities. In 1870, 46.72 percent of all the persons engaged in gainful occupations were employed in farming. In 1890 only 36.44 percent were so employed. The farms lost 10 percent in these twenty years.

Many good people have thought that if we could in some way surround the country youth with more comforts and pleasures, if we could relieve the solitude and monotony of the farm, he would stay at home and become a wiser and a better man. Various schemes to this end have been devised, and have come to naught. They have even hoped to make country life so attractive that great numbers of city people would move out of town, and thus relieve the congestion in certain districts and industries of the city. Nothing is more common than to revile poor people in the slums of our great cities because they will be so foolish as to herd together in tenement-houses when they might be out

In *The Arena*, 17 (1897): 538–48.

on quarter-sections breathing the pure air of heaven. Still, the talk about preventing the rush to the cities goes on. Lately, however, a few students of modern life have come to see and to say that, while present industrial conditions continue, the movement of populations to cities will continue. The fact is that, broadly speaking, men leave the farms because they are not needed there.

The introduction of labor-saving machinery and rapid transportation has produced the same result in agriculture as in other kinds of manufacturing. A smaller number of men working in our fields turn out a much greater product than the greater number of laborers could possibly secure in olden times, and the products of all lands are easily carried to where they are needed. Gradually, and more rapidly within the past twenty-five years, invention has gained the mastery in agriculture as in other arts. The brain of man has triumphed over his hand here as elsewhere. Enough is produced to feed and clothe the world. Fewer workers per acre are required. The horse or the machine, steam or electricity, has taken the place of the boy or the man.

It is not love of the town so much as necessity to earn a livelihood off the farm which drives boys to the town and makes them competitors in the great industrial struggles at the centers of population.

The clear apprehension of the great fundamental fact that the conditions of agriculture are steadily approximating to those of our other great industries is very important at this crisis in the industrial life of the world. The individual farmer needs to see this in order that he may conform in his business to those sound rules of procedure which experience has shown to be necessary to success in other branches of industry. To be successful today the farmer must think and work as other businessmen think and work. In order that he may come into sympathy with the workers in other lines who are studying and struggling to improve their industrial environment, he needs to see that the industrial problem of agriculture is the same as that of other industries. Hitherto it has been common among a certain class of conservative thinkers on industrial problems to set the farmers off by themselves as

a class firmly fixed in old ways and traditions, who could be safely counted on to oppose change, and who could be used politically and otherwise to counterbalance the radicalism of workers in other industries. The farmer is beginning to arouse himself to the real merits of the great labor controversy, to feel that he cannot afford to be a mere buffer against which agitation may recoil, to see that at bottom his interests are one with those of the toilers in the factory and the mart.

As long as the farmer says to himself, "I am not needed on the farm, there must be place for me in the town. I will go and mingle in the busy life there, trusting to my superior vigor to gain me the mastery over my sharp-witted city competitor"—regardless of the fact that there are too many workers in the town already—there will be disappointment for the newcomer, or suffering for the man whom he displaces. As long as the city man says to his unsuccessful brother, "Go out into the country and raise cabbages. There is plenty of air and work out there. Why will you starve in your miserable garret in the town?"—regardless of the fact that farm products are already a drug in the market, and farm machines are daily crowding more workers off the farm—there will be little hope of bettering the condition of industrial life in either city or county. But when both city and country workers say, "We are in the same fix. There are too many of us working at one thing. We must devise methods to diversify our industries, to raise the level of wages and expenditures, to more fully organize and perfect the system of distribution of products so that the wants of all men will be more fully met and the general conditions of life be more comfortable," then there will at least be greater reason to hope that in some way men will find a solution for problems which our age seems to find insoluble.

It is, I think, very desirable to lay stress upon the great common interests of town and farm at this time, because in some important ways the superficial tendencies of modern industrial development have seemed to widen the breach between city and country life.

The increase and concentration of wealth in large towns have produced complex social habits and distinctions which make the country man feel less and less at home there. The country man, coming infrequently to town, hardly knows how to act in the city, and is mystified and distressed by the unexpected situations of city life which confront him at every turn. This has been intensified by the efforts of our "smart set" in recent years to ape the manners of transatlantic society. In fact, we may say that in certain quarters there has been a studied effort to build the artificial barriers of caste, to create here, as in the Old World, a class of peasants, and put into it all tillers of the soil.

And so in various ways the disparities between city and country life have been magnified, until many have really thought that farm and town had no interests in common, but that one should be set over against the other in an eternal industrial enmity, and that the farmer was being relegated to a position of obscurity and menial service. But I believe that these separating tendencies which occupy so much of the attention of the popular mind today are only superficial, and that down underneath them is an irresistible current of common interest and sympathy which is drawing men closer together to work for human elevation and welfare. However much the relative importance of agriculture may decline as our industrial system grows more complex, it must always remain one of our greatest industries. The farm will always be a large factor in the commercial prosperity of the town. What folly then to propose or attempt any scheme of trade, transportation, or finance based on the selfish interests of either town or farm alone!

The business interests of both farm and town can only rest on a solid basis of enduring prosperity when all join together to devise and carry out an honest and just policy. The great problem of the equitable distribution of the products of labor on farm and in factory will not be settled until the common concern of both town and farm, in a just settlement, is acknowledged and acted upon.

From the farm come in large measure the strength and vigor of great cities. Call the roll of great manufacturers, merchants, bankers, teachers, preachers, and officials in any large city, and you will be surprised to find how many of these leaders in metropolitan enterprise are graduates of the farm. It is not a matter of some concern to the town in what atmosphere that strong body of its citizens sure to come to it from the country is reared? Can the city afford to do anything to destroy the purity or independence of farm life, or to reduce the farmer's family to the condition of a stolid and unprogressive peasantry?

To a greater extent than most men are aware of, the health of a great city depends on the quality of the products which it receives from the farm. Boards of health insist on inspecting dairy farms. The United States Government inspects the meat as it is received at our great cities. Is not the town interested to know whether hog cholera, or trichinosis, or tuberculosis is raging among the livestock on the farm? What kind of bacteria makes the flavor of your butter, or whether milk or oleomargarine fills your cheese, is a matter of some concern to the city dwellers. I happen to be the representative of the United States Government in its efforts to make more intelligent farmers by means of agricultural colleges and experiment stations. Are not the interests of town and farm in such questions mutual? When we seek to train better farmers, and to produce better food, do we not at the same time subserve the welfare of the city dwellers? I am glad to note that people are beginning to appreciate the interrelation of farm and town in these fundamental matters.

Efforts to better the conditions of farm life need the help of the cities. The cities should interest themselves in giving the country places good schools, libraries, and postal facilities. The wealth of the cities should contribute toward the bettering of farm life. They have a duty toward the rural communities, not simply to yield to the demand of the farmers whether what they ask for is wise or not, but to take an active interest in their affairs and counsel with them, so that the best plans for mutual benefit may be devised.

The attempt to purify city politics and revive civic pride and self-respect is very encouraging. But this must not be done to the neglect of the interests of the state, which, after all, is the great unit of our national life. The state government deals with the great problems of marriage, education, health, transportation, industrial organization, etc., which profoundly affect the daily life of all the people.

In general, to sum up, the problem of our times is not how to send men back to the farms where they are not needed, not how to scatter population into myriads of little communities, but how to raise the level of farm life and farm product, to more thoroughly organize the great towns, to improve the means of communication between farm and town, and to harmonize the manifold elements which compose the modern state, so that each will do its appointed work in the best manner, and the interests of all the people will be conserved.

There is a grand old word used in Thanksgiving proclamations in Massachusetts which, taken to heart, should bring town and farm into closest sympathy. Let us never forget that, wherever we may dwell, strong bonds unite us as members of the "Commonwealth."

Chapter 15

The Immigrant Ghetto

AT THE CLOSE of the nineteenth century and at the opening of the twentieth, the United States became the home for millions of immigrants. While foreigners in some numbers had always come to these shores (between 1815 and 1865, some six million had arrived), this influx was unprecedented in its magnitude. Between 1890 and 1910, thirteen million immigrants landed here; over one million aliens arrived in each of the years 1905, 1906, and 1907. No less unusual were the countries from which these immigrants came. In the nineteenth century, England, Ireland, Germany, and other Western European countries had supplied the bulk of the immigrants. After 1890, the great majority of newcomers came from Southern and Eastern Europe. Italians, Slavs, and Russians were numerous, as were Greeks and Armenians. Some one million Jews migrated here from Russia and Poland.

While some immigrants, particularly those from Scandinavia, settled on farmland in the Midwest and on the Great Plains, the bulk of the immigrants remained in the cities. In fact, the foreign-born populations in places such as New York and Chicago, quickly came to outnumber the native-born Americans. Within these cities, the immigrants tended to cluster together residentially. The North End in Boston became a center for Italians; the Lower East Side in New York, for Jews; and the North End of Chicago, for the Slavs. Immigrant ghettos became familiar pockets in the urban landscape.

Native-born Americans were, to varying degrees, uncomfortable with this development. Some groups, for example, unskilled workers, who feared immigrants' competition for their jobs, were eager to restrict or eliminate the flow of aliens here altogether. Others, less prepared to take such a rigid stand, nevertheless insisted or anticipated that the newcomers could be rapidly assimilated to American ways. The immigrants, they believed, should be encouraged to surrender foreign customs for American habits; the strange components of Old World dress and diet and custom had to be abandoned as quickly as possible.

No barrier to that accomplishment seemed more serious than the ghetto, and hence they deplored and criticized the very idea of such insular and idiosyncratic communities. From their perspective, the ghetto was a breeding ground for social problems, a dangerous, subversive form of social organization. It was the ghetto that encouraged immigrants to retain traditional habits and customs; that encouraged immorality, vice, and crime; and that kept the children of immigrants from becoming Americans. The quicker one managed to eliminate it, the better for both the immigrant and the nation.

This popular distrust of the influence of the ghetto reappeared in more sophisticated form in the writings of sociologists and historians. They, too, defined the ghetto as a deviant form of social organization. They painstakingly described the poor housing, wretched working conditions, crime, and unsanitary health conditions, and concluded that the ghetto was nothing more or less than a slum. And, in a curious way, many of the second generation immigrants, looking back on the hardships of their youth, agreed with this assessment. By comparison with their new neighborhoods, the ghetto seemed miserable. They had been right to escape from it.

But these accounts were one-sided, and failed to raise some very crucial questions about other characteristics of the ghetto experience. The ghetto, for one, did cushion the immigrant from the impact of massive change; it did protect him from the crisis of adapting immediately to an alien culture. The ghetto also gave economic and political benefits to its residents, providing livelihoods and some modicum of influence to immigrants. It also helped to keep alive inherited traditions, in a sense giving the immigrants a self-identification apart from the native-born view of them as "the wretched refuse of a teeming shore." In many ways, the ghetto was a composite of institutions some of which insulated the immigrant from the new culture, while others promoted his assimilation. Certainly it was more than a slum, and its residents something other than aliens on their way to becoming homogeneous Americans.

I

The voyage from the Old World to the New was difficult and exhausting for the immigrants. The ship fares were not very high, and the trip usually did not last over two weeks, but conditions in steerage were miserable. Under the best of circumstances, arriving in a strange land far from home and relatives, with no knowledge of the language, was a traumatic experience. Imagine, then, how the newcomer must have felt after a journey such as the one described below. The narrator, Anne Herkner, was a researcher for the United States Immigration Commission, which investigated the various problems raised by the influx of so many immigrants. To get a first-hand sense of the experience, she traveled incognito across the Atlantic with a group of newcomers.

THE IMMIGRATION COMMISSION—
STEERAGE, 1911

TESTIMONY OF ANNA HERKNER

All the steerage berths were of iron, the framework forming two tiers and having but a low partition between the individual berths. Each bunk contained a mattress filled with straw and covered with a slip made of coarse white canvas, apparently cleaned for the voyage. There were no pillows. Instead, a life preserver was placed under the mattress at the head in each berth. A short and light-weight white blanket was the only covering provided. This each passenger might take with him on leaving. It was practically impossible to undress properly for retiring because of insufficient covering and lack of privacy. Many women had pillows from home and used shawls and other clothing for coverings.

Our compartment was subdivided into three sections—one for the German women, which was completely boarded off from the rest; one for Hebrews; and one for all other creeds and nationalities together. The partition between these last two was merely a fence, consisting of four horizontal six-inch boards. This neither kept out odors nor cut off the view.

The single men had their sleeping quarters directly below ours, and adjoining was the compartment for families and partial families—that is, women and children. In this last section every one of the sixty beds was occupied and each passenger had only the one hundred cubic feet of space required by law. The Hebrews were here likewise separated from the others by the same ineffectual fence, consisting of four horizontal boards and the intervening spaces. During the first six days the entire sixty berths were separated from the rest of the room by a similar fence. Outside the fence was the so-called dining room, getting all the bedroom smells from these sixty crowded berths. Later the spaces in, above, and below the fence were entirely boarded up.

The floors in all these compartments were of wood. They were swept every morning and the aisles sprinkled lightly with sand. None of them was washed during the twelve days' voyage nor was there any indication that a disinfectant was being used on them. The beds received only such attention as each occupant gave to his own. When the steerage is full, each passenger's space is limited to his berth, which then serves as bed, clothes and towel rack, cupboard, and baggage space. There are no accommodations to encourage the steerage passenger to be clean and orderly. There was no hook on which to hang a garment, no receptacle for refuse, no cuspidor, no cans for use in case of seasickness.

Two washrooms were provided for the use of the steerage. The first morning out I took special care to inquire for the women's washroom. One of the crew directed me to a door bearing the sign "Washroom for men." Within were both men and women. Thinking I had been mis-

In *Reports of the Immigration Commission*, 61st Congress, 3rd session, U.S. *Senate Document*, no. 753 (1911), vol. 37, pp. 14, 16, 19–20, 23.

directed, I proceeded to the other washroom. This bore no label and was likewise being used by both sexes. Repeating my inquiry another of the crew directed me just as the first had done. Evidently there was no distinction between the men's and the women's washrooms. These were on the main deck and not convenient to any of the sleeping quarters. To use them one had to cross the open deck, subject to the public gaze. In the case of the families and men, it was necessary to come upstairs and cross the deck to get to both washrooms and toilets.

Steerage passengers may be filthy, as is often alleged, but considering the total absence of conveniences for keeping clean, this uncleanliness seems but a natural consequence. Some may really be filthy in their habits, but many make heroic efforts to keep clean. No woman with the smallest degree of modesty, and with no other conveniences than a washroom, used jointly with men, and a faucet of cold salt water can keep clean amidst such surroundings for a period of twelve days and more. It was forbidden to bring water for washing purposes into the sleeping compartments, nor was there anything in which to bring it. On different occasions some of the women rose early, brought drinking water in their soup pails, and thus tried to wash themselves effectively, but were driven out when detected by the steward. Others, resorting to extreme measures, used night chambers, which they carry with them for the children, as wash basins. This was done a great deal when preparation was being made for landing. Even hair was washed with these vessels. No soap and no towels were supplied.

During the twelve days only about six meals were fair and gave satisfaction. More than half of the food was always thrown into the sea. Hot water could be had in the galley, and many of the passengers made tea and lived on this and bread. The last day out we were told on every hand to look pleasant, else we would not be admitted in Baltimore. To help bring about this happy appearance the last meal on board consisted of boiled eggs, bread, and fried potatoes. Those who commented on this meal said it was "the best yet." None of this food was thrown into the sea, but all was eagerly eaten. If this simple meal of ordinary food, well prepared, gave such general satisfaction, then it is really not so difficult after all to satisfy the tastes of the various nationalities. A few simple standard dishes of fair quality and properly prepared, even though less generously served, would, I am positive, give satisfaction. The expense certainly would not be greater than that now caused by the waste of so much inferior food. The interpreter, the chief steerage steward, and one other officer were always in attendance during the meals to prevent any crowding. When all had been served, these three walked about among the passengers asking: "Does the food taste good?" The almost invariable answer was: "It has to; we must eat something."

The daily medical inspection of the steerage was carried on as follows: The second day out we all passed in single file before the doctor as he leisurely conversed with another officer, casting an occasional glance at the passing line. The chief steerage steward punched six holes in each passenger's inspection card, indicating that the inspection for six days was complete. One steward told me this was done to save the passengers from going through this formality every day. The fourth day out we were again reviewed. The doctor stood by. Another officer holding a cablegram blank in his hand compared each passenger card to some writing on it. There was another inspection on the seventh day, when we were required to bare our arms and show the vaccinations. Again our cards were punched six times and this completed the medical examination. Just before landing we were reviewed by some officer who came on board and checked us off on a counting machine operated by a ship's officer.

To sum up, let me make some general statements that will give an idea of the awfulness of steerage conditions on the steamer in question. During these twelve days in the steerage I lived in a disorder and in surroundings that offended every sense. Only the fresh breeze from the sea overcame the sickening odors. The vile language of the men, the screams of the women defending themselves, the crying of children, wretched because of their surroundings, and practically every sound that reached the ear, irritated beyond endurance. There was no sight before which the eye did not prefer to close. Everything was dirty, sticky, and disagreeable to the touch. Every impression was offensive. Worse than this was the general air of immorality. For fifteen hours each day I witnessed all around me this improper, indecent, and forced mingling of men and women who were total strangers and often did not understand one word of the same language. People cannot live in such surroundings and not be influenced.

II

Given the hardships, both economic and psychological, that immigrants confronted in their new country, it is not surprising that they often banded together for mutual aid and protection. Some of their organizations were ad hoc, others had a more formal structure. But, almost always, they rested on the immigrant's sense of identification with those who shared his religion, language, and customs. The U. S. Immigration Commission, when investigating social conditions in the ghetto, discovered the operation of immigrant "banks." This type of organization, typical of many voluntary associations, clarifies one way by which the ghetto alleviated the problem of adjustment for the immigrants.

THE IMMIGRATION COMMISSION— IMMIGRANT BANKS, 1911

The "Immigrant Bank" is an institution which flourishes in every part of the United States where immigrants are gathered in any considerable numbers. These banks bear little resemblance to regular banking institutions. They are without real capital, have little or no legal responsibility, and for the most part are entirely without legal control. Immigrant bankers, as a rule, are also steamship-ticket agents, and usually conduct some other business as well. Consequently the "banks" are, for the most part, located in groceries, saloons, or other establishments which are natural gathering places for immigrants.

Besides handling the savings of his patrons, the immigrant banker performs for them many necessary services. He writes their letters, receives their mail, and is their general adviser in what to them are important affairs. The ability and willingness of the banker to render such services naturally give him an advantage over regular banking institutions, which would not, and, in fact, could not, attend to such matters. In this way immigrant banks and immigrant bankers are important factors in the life of the newer immigrants.

The financial transactions of these bankers are confined mainly to the receiving of deposits and the transmission of money abroad. Deposits are not held as ordinary savings but represent, instead, sums of money left with immigrant bankers merely for temporary safekeeping. They are not subject to check, and as a rule no interest is paid upon them.

The question arises, "How have financial functions become confused with other lines of business?" The answer is found in the manner in which these banks originate. Out of the total of one hundred and sixteen establishments examined, one hundred and seven were steamship agencies, and of this number all but six did an immigrant banking business. In other words, 94 percent of the concerns engaged in the business of selling steamship tickets were at the same time engaged in the business of immigrant banking. This shows that the relation between the two is so close as to warrant the characterization of them as interdependent. In the mind of the immigrant the two are almost inseparable. To him the steamship agent is the sole connecting link with the fatherland. Nothing is more natural than that the immigrant

In *Reports of The Immigration Commission,* 61st Congress, 3rd session, Senate Document, no. 753 (1911), vol. 37, pp. 203, 212–19, 314.

should take his savings to the agent and ask that the agent send them home for him. Having made the start, it is natural that he should continue to leave with the agent for safekeeping his weekly or monthly surplus, so that he may accumulate a sufficient amount for another remittance or for the purpose of buying a steamship ticket to bring his family to this country or for his own return to Europe. It is not long before the agent has a nucleus for a banking business, and his assumption of banking functions quickly as follows. The transition is then complete—the steamship agent has become an immigrant banker.

Those proprietors who confine their operations to bank and steamship agency, as distinguished from those who conduct such in connection with some other business, are usually the most intelligent men of the immigrant population of any colony or locality. They are always possessed of considerable influence, and may be political leaders in the older and more established immigrant communities. Almost without exception, they are able to speak English and have some degree of education. In most cases the basis of their success lies in a native ability which is by no means necessarily the product of business experience or financial training.

On the other hand, quite the contrary is true of the great number of those who, in a purely personal way, are acting as custodians of their countrymen's funds. Numerous instances are at hand where strangers have gone into communities and established themselves as steamship agents and foreign-exchange dealers. Their only qualification was that they were Italians among Italians, or Magyars among Magyars. Hundreds of saloon keepers and grocers act as bankers without the least fitness or equipment. Although banking functions are more or less forced upon men of this character, and although they may be exercised in a thoroughly honorable way by many, hundreds of thousands of dollars belonging to immigrant laborers are handled by ignorant, incompetent, or untrustworthy men.

Why has not the immigrant laborer turned to American institutions to satisfy his banking needs, rather than to the less responsible men of his own race? The causes for his failure to do this are threefold: (1) the ignorance and suspicion of the immigrant; (2) the fact that American institutions have not developed the peculiar facilities necessary in the handling of immigrant business; (3) the ability and willingness of the immigrant proprietor to perform for his countrymen necessary services that it would be impossible for them to obtain otherwise.

The great hindrance in securing immigrant patronage for American banks lies in the alien's ignorance of the English language. Inability to read and write, combined with a poor comprehension of the checking system and other banking devices, is apt to cause him to prefer the money belt to the bank, the saloon keeper to the trust company. A natural hesitancy to place confidence in strangers of other races is augmented in many cases by a positive suspicion of American institutions. It was said of the Greeks in a certain locality that they stood somewhat in awe of the magnificent proportions and equipment of the modern city bank. They are usually suspicious of any attempt on the part of

Americans to influence the place or manner of their savings. Their very suspicion is the opportunity of designing persons among their countrymen, who, under the guise of friendly intervention, secure their little savings and use them for their own benefit. The average immigrant is easily excited in money matters. He is quicker to accept the assurances of irresponsible persons that his money will at all times and under any conditions be available. This assurance he obtains from the immigrant banker.

It is true that of recent years there has been a tendency among the banks in the financial districts of St. Louis, Pittsburgh, Chicago, Cleveland, and other large cities to establish foreign departments with competent managers and clerks of the various races of recent immigration. On the whole, however, there has been a decided disposition among American institutions not to solicit the patronage of the alien directly, especially in view of the fact that his deposits are often for temporary safekeeping only, to handle which would require an unwarranted amount of bookkeeping. Ignorance of foreign languages on the part of clerks of the average savings bank and unwillingness and inability to extend to the immigrant depositor the very necessary accommodation of patient assistance do not tend to attract immigrant patronage.

Strange as it may seem, its very equipment prevents the American bank from entering into a fair competition with the immigrant banker. A Slovak immigrant banker, in apologizing somewhat for the appearance of his banking room, stated that it was necessarily ill kept because the men would come in in their working clothes, often covered with mud, frequently intoxicated, which, together with smoking and spitting, kept the room in a constant state of disorder. Such a condition would not be tolerated by an American bank. Moreover, the average immigrant feels a certain hesitancy in entering in his working clothes a building of the character of some city banks.

By reason of his position of power and influence, the immigrant banker is often called upon to perform many other services. Not infrequently as saloon keeper or licensed labor agent he secures work for his patrons, and as grocer keeps them supplied with provisions. The banker's place of business is in a number of instances practically a labor headquarters, where the idle men congregate and where agents or contractors in need of laborers come to secure them. A notable feature is the extent to which customers are carried on credit through the winter and dull seasons. Book credits aggregating five or six thousand dollars are not unusual, while even larger sums were found to be due some grocer-bankers.

In forwarding mail, in writing letters for the illiterate, and in many other ways, the banker performs necessary and efficient service. He cashes pay checks, and acts as interpreter, intermediary, and, in some cases, legal adviser. He often furnishes lodging and board at a moderate cost. As notary public he prepares legal documents for his patrons and assists them in the disposition or management of their property.

The immigrant banker does not, of course, extend such accommodations without compensation. Even if there is not immediate remuneration, such services lead to ultimate gain. By the methods described the banker obtains a distinct hold over his "clients," as they are usually termed, and is in a position to turn their needs to his own advantage. The simple-minded laborers with whom he deals look to him for advice and guidance. Such is their ignorance of monetary affairs and such is the power and influence which the banker may acquire over them that it is a comparatively easy matter for him to use their confidence as a source of profit.

With a system so utterly at variance with all recognized principles of banking it is inevitable that losses should occur, and there are, without doubt, frequent cases of fraud. Banks conducted by immigrants are usually unincorporated and privately operated, and that, except in two states, they have not been subjected to any definite state control and have not effectively been brought within the province of existing laws regulating private banks.

[Copy of an Advertising Circular for an Immigrant Banker]

Very Esteemed Countrymen:

The chief purpose of my business is to endeavor with all my power to protect my countrymen here from the Old Country against suffering losses and to offer them means of transmitting their money—earned here by the sweat of the brow—safely and most quickly to their families or relatives left at home; that when traveling hither to America or hence to the Old Country they shall not be exploited by imposters and extorters, but be watched over until such time as they reach the end of their journey.

I have reached the point, through my great experience and connections, where I am able promptly and continually to serve, at the smallest expense, my countrymen who turn to me.

If, therefore, you wish to travel in the Old Country notify me with the enclosed envelope on what day and what train you depart, and I will meet you at the New York depot, conduct you to my office, and take care of you; then I will accompany you to the boat and through my agents will guard you until you reach home.

If you would send passage tickets to the Old Country, then I will, in detail, notify the passenger how to travel; I will recommend him to the attentions of my trusted representatives at the European ports, and when he arrives in America I will direct him to the place to which he is bound.

If you transmit money through me to the Old Country, I will forward the same to its place of destination on the day of its arrival, and at the cheapest daily price, so that it will be in the hands of the addressee in eleven days at the latest, upon which I will send you, without request, the original delivery receipt.

To deserve further the approval of my countrymen, and to reach the highest point of efficiency, I request you to patronize me with united and allied zeal, and to impart to me the addresses of your friends, for which I will surprise you with a nice present for over twenty-five addresses sent to me.

III

*Many immigrants were able to perceive the protective function of the
ghetto in ways that eluded outsiders. The account of Abraham
Rihbany, an immigrant from Syria in 1891, of his first days in
New York offers just such a view. Immediately on landing, Rihbany
sought out the Syrian ghetto, and his account below describes the
subsequent events. Here is a personal account of how the ghetto
served to bridge the gap between Old World and New World
experiences.*

A FAR JOURNEY, 1913

ABRAHAM M. RIHBANY

My friend, Moses, did not forget his promise to be on the lookout for
a position for me in some Syrian store, for on my tenth day in New
York he told me of a merchant who needed a *katib*—bookkeeper.
Realizing that I had never had any experience in bookkeeping, he
instructed me not to be overconscientious in confessing my ignorance.
The customers of the store were peddlers of "jewelry and notions," and
almost all the transactions were carried on in the Arabic language.

In company with my beneficent friend I proceeded to the store of
Khawaja Maron. Moses introduced me to the proprietor and departed.
Maron told me that the salary of the position I was seeking was twenty
dollars per month. Recalling the time when as a schoolteacher in Syria
my salary was three dollars a month and my board, twenty dollars
seemed to me a species of "frenzied financiering." I had every reason to
imagine that my new position was the gateway to riches and honor.

Our store was put to other uses not strictly commercial, which the
social habits of our Syrian customers demanded. On rainy days it fell
to me to entertain groups of peddlers who sat around the stove and
indulged themselves in their simple but boisterous pleasures. At times
they would buy a wash-pitcherful of beer and drink to one another's
health out of one common glass. Some of those simple-minded peddlers
had succeeded in observing that domestic and social life in America
was not so homogeneous as in Syria, that in this country the individual
was much freer and much more sharply defined.

"Hear, and I will tell you," said Abdu, especially to new arrivals
from Syria; "in this country the husband and wife live each one alone.
He has his room and she has hers. They say that he has to knock at
her door like a stranger, and she doesn't have to let him inside. He
has to say 'Shkooz me,' which means, 'Forgive me'!"

"But how can they live that way?" Anton would inquire. "Give me

In *A Far Journey,* by Abraham M. Rihbany (Boston, 1913), pp. 208–223,
242–45.

Syria and its submissive women. Let me tell you, our country knows something."

Then some genius would do human nature no little credit by remarking, "Your words are empty. No matter how they live, the Americans look clean and well-fed, and we are dirty and hungry; shorten your speech until you know what you are talking about."

On one occasion Maron offered the store to one of his customers for the celebration of a genuine Syrian wedding. The offer was accepted and our commercial establishment resounded with joy. We seated the bridegroom (the bride was in another building) in the place of honor— behind the counter. Beer and *arak* flowed like water. The men sang *aataba* and the women *zelaghet,* and we all partook of a bounteous feast.

I soon also made the acquaintance of the few college men in the Syrian colony. I proposed the organizing of a society whose purpose should be the mutual benefit of its own members and the advancement of the various interests of the Syrians in general. The suggestion met with favor among the leaders of thought in the colony, and the "Syrian Scientific and Ethical Society" was organized. The subjects of our debates and discussions were large and various. History, philosophy, the good and evil of immigration, the greatness of the United States of America, the superiority of the Syrian to the Irish population of Washington Street.

I was expected to make an "oration" at any time and on any subject. My most impassioned appeals in those "orations" were for the stronger cohesion of the Syrian population in the great city in which we lived, and the endeavor on the part of our people to adopt the noble principles of American civilization, of which, however, I knew nothing at the time.

The Syrian colony in New York seemed to me to be simply Syria on a smaller scale. During my stay of nearly eighteen months in it I did not have occasion to speak ten sentences in English. We ate the same dishes, spoke the same language, told the same stories, indulged in the same pleasures, and were torn by the same feuds, as those that had filled our lives on the eastern shores of the Mediterranean. I seemed to be almost as far from the real life of America as if I had been living in Beirut or Tripoli.

The sum total of my experience in New York convinced me that it was most difficult, if not impossible, for a foreigner to become really Americanized while living in a colony of his own kinsmen.

The Syrian colony in New York rendered me all the service it could by providing me with a home for about eighteen months among those whose language was my language and whose habits were my habits. Its Oriental atmosphere with its slight Occidental tinge protected me from the dangers of an abrupt transition. Had I been thrust into American society upon my arrival in this country, penniless and without serviceable knowledge of the English language, the change in environment might have proved too violent for me to endure with any comfort. To me the colony was a habitat so much like the one I had left behind me in Syria that its home atmosphere enabled me to maintain a firm hold on life in the face of the many difficulties which confronted me in those days, and just different enough to awaken my curiosity to know more about the surrounding American influences.

IV

The ghetto was also a place of work for most immigrants. Manufacturing enterprises frequently located themselves as near as possible to this ready pool of cheap labor; and, as was the case in clothing manufacturing on New York's Lower East Side, some of the enterprises were located right in the tenements themselves. Immigrants quickly discovered that the images of the good life in America that had circulated in the European villages were exaggerated. Tales about streets lined with gold spread by railroad and steamship promoters hardly prepared them for the reality of the sweatshop. The first day on the job was a rude awakening.

There can be no doubt that working conditions were frequently exploitative. Jacob Riis, himself an immigrant from Denmark in 1870, learned this when covering the city as a police reporter. How the Other Half Lives was his attempt to bring the story to the public, and the book's fame points to his success. The degree to which the "sweaters" took advantage of the immigrant emerges here in vivid detail. Whether the immigrant found these conditions any less intolerable because he was working among fellow countrymen is an open question.

HOW THE OTHER HALF LIVES, 1890

JACOB A. RIIS

Many harsh things have been said of the "sweater" that really apply to the system in which he is a necessary, logical link. It can at least be said of him that he is no worse than the conditions that created him. The sweater is simply the middleman, the subcontractor, a workman like his fellows, perhaps with the single distinction from the rest that he knows a little English; perhaps not even that, but with the accidental possession of two or three sewing-machines, or of credit enough to hire them. Of workmen he can always get enough. Every shipload from German ports brings them to his door in droves, clamoring for work. Often there are two, sometimes three, sets of sweaters on one job. They work with the rest when they are not drumming up trade, driving their "hands" as they drive their machine, for all they are worth, and making a profit on their work, of course, though in most cases not nearly as

In *How the Other Half Lives: Studies Among the Tenements of New York,* by Jacob A. Riis (New York, 1890), pp. 88-99.

extravagant a percentage, probably, as is often supposed. If it resolves itself into a margin of five or six cents, or even less, on a dozen pairs of boys' trousers for instance, it is nevertheless enough to make the contractor with his thrifty instincts independent. The workman growls, not at the hard labor, or poor pay, but over the pennies another is coining out of his sweat, and on the first opportunity turns sweater himself, and takes his revenge by driving an even closer bargain than his rival tyrant, thus reducing his profits.

The sweater knows well that the isolation of the workman in his helpless ignorance is his sure foundation. In this effort to perpetuate his depotism he has had the effectual assistance of his own system and the sharp competition that keep the men on starvation wages; of their constitutional greed, that will not permit the sacrifice of temporary advantage, however slight, for permanent good, and above all, of the hungry hordes of immigrants to whom no argument appeals save the cry for bread. As long as the ignorant crowds continue to come and to herd in these tenements, his grip can never be shaken off.

The bulk of the sweater's work is done in the tenements, which the law that regulates factory labor does not reach. To the factories themselves that are taking the place of the rear tenements in rapidly growing numbers, letting in bigger day crowds than those the health officers banished, the tenement shops serve as a supplement through which the law is successfully evaded. Ten hours is the legal workday in the factories, and nine o'clock the closing hour at the latest. Children under sixteen must not be employed unless they can read and write English; none at all under fourteen. The very fact that such a law should stand on the statute book shows how desperate the plight of these people. But the tenement has defeated its benevolent purpose. In it the child works unchallenged from the day he is old enough to pull a thread. There is no such thing as a dinner hour; man and women eat while they work, and the "day" is lengthened at both ends far into the night. Factory hands take their work with them at the close of the lawful day to eke out their scanty earnings by working overtime at home. Little chance on this ground for the campaign of education that alone can bring the needed relief.

Take the Second Avenue Elevated Railroad at Chatham Square and ride up half a mile through the sweaters' district. Every open window of the big tenements gives you a glimpse of one of these shops. Men and women bending over their machines, or ironing clothes at the window, half naked. Proprieties do not count on the East Side; nothing counts that cannot be converted into hard cash.

Morning, noon, or night, it makes no difference; the scene is always the same. Men stagger along the sidewalk groaning under heavy burdens of unsewn garments. Let us follow one to his home and see how Sunday passes in a Ludlow Street tenement.

Up two flights of dark stairs, three, four, with new smells of cabbage, of onions, of frying fish, on every landing, whirring sewing machines behind closed doors betraying what goes on within, to the door that opens to admit the bundle and the man. A sweater, this, in a small way. Five men and a woman, two young girls, not fifteen, and a boy who says unasked that he is fifteen, and lies in saying it, are at the machines sewing knickerbockers, "knee-pants" in the Ludlow Street dialect. The floor is littered ankle-deep with half-sewn garments. The faces, hands, and arms to the elbows of everyone in the room are black with the color of the cloth on which they are working.

They are "learners," all of them, says the woman, who proves to be the wife of the boss, and have "come over" only a few weeks ago. How much do they earn? She shrugs her shoulders with an expressive gesture. The workers themselves, asked in their own tongue, say indifferently, as though the question were of no interest: from two to five dollars. They turn out one hundred and twenty dozen "knee-pants" a week, for which the manufacturer pays seventy cents a dozen. Five cents a dozen is the clear profit, but her own and her husband's work brings the family earnings up to twenty-five dollars a week, when they have work all the time. But often half the time is put in looking for it. They work no longer than to nine o'clock at night, from daybreak. There are ten machines in the room; six are hired at two dollars a month. For the two shabby, smoke-begrimed rooms, one somewhat larger than ordinary, they pay twenty dollars a month. She does not complain, though "times are not what they were, and it costs a good deal to live." Eight dollars a week for the family of six and two boarders. How do they do it? She laughs, as she goes over the bill of fare, at the silly question: Bread fifteen cents a day, of milk two quarts a day at four cents a quart, one pound of meat for dinner at twelve cents, butter, one pound a week at "eight cents a quarter of a pound." Coffee, potatoes, and pickles complete the list. At the least calculation, probably, this sweater's family hoards up thirty dollars a month, and in a few years will own a tenement somewhere and profit by the example set by their landlord in rent collecting. It is the way the savings of Jewtown are universally invested, and with the natural talent of its people for commercial speculation the investment is enormously profitable.

We have reached Broome Street. The hum of industry in this six-story tenement on the corner leaves no doubt of the aspect Sunday wears within it. One flight up, we knock at the nearest door. The grocer, who keeps the store, lives on the "stoop," the first floor in East Side parlance. In this room a suspender maker sleeps and works with his family of wife and four children. For a wonder there are no boarders. His wife and eighteen year old daughter share in the work, but the girl's eyes are giving out from the strain. Three months in the year, when work is very brisk, the family makes by united efforts as high as fourteen and fifteen dollars a week. The other nine months it averages from three to four dollars. The rent is ten dollars a month for the room and a miserable little coop of a bedroom where the old folks sleep. The girl makes her bed on the lounge in the front room; the big boys and the children sleep on the floor.

Up under the roof three men are making boys' jackets at twenty cents apiece. They bunk together in a room for which they pay eight dollars a month. All three are single here, that is: their wives are on the other side yet, waiting for them to earn enough to send for them. Their breakfast, eaten at the workbench, consists of a couple of rolls at a cent apiece, and a draught of water, milk when business has been very good, a square meal at noon in a restaurant, and the morning meal over again at night. At this rate the lodger of Jewtown can "live like a lord," as he says himself, for twenty-five cents a day, including the price of his bed, that ranges all the way from thirty to forty to fifty cents a week, and save money, no matter what his earnings. He does it, too, so long as work is to be had at any price, and by the standard he sets up Jewtown must abide.

It has thousands upon thousands of lodgers who help to pay its extortionate rents. At night there is scarce a room in all the district that has not one or more of them, some above half a score, sleeping on cots, or on the floor. It is idle to speak of privacy in these "homes." The term carries no more meaning with it than would a lecture on social ethics to an audience of Hottentots. The picture is not overdrawn. In fact, in presenting the home life of these people I have been at some pains to avoid the extreme of privation, taking the cases just as they came to hand on the safer middle-ground of average earnings.

These are the economical conditions that enable my manufacturing friend to boast that New York can "beat the world" on cheap clothing.

V

To the consternation of many native-born Americans, the ghetto was also a place of amusements where immigrants pursued some pleasures that were legal, and some which were not. Indeed, the immigrants could often find some pastimes harmless which to the native-white population seemed all too deviant. The description below, by Robert Woods, of the quality of life in the Italian section of Boston's North End exemplifies the differences in cultural perceptions. Woods was one of the leaders and founding spirits of the settlement house movement, a movement which we shall see was caught between an eagerness to do good on behalf of the immigrants and a basic distrust of the immigrant style of life. Woods' reporting of ghetto activities informs us not only about the reality of life in the ghetto but also about American attitudes as well.

AMERICANS IN PROCESS, 1902

ROBERT A. WOODS

The [Boston] North End makes up Police Division 1. From the first of December 1900, to the first of December 1901, the total number of arrests in this division for all offenses was 4,300 males and 575 females, or 4,875 altogether. Of these, 3,124 were for drunkenness, 306 for assault of one kind or another, 232 for simple larceny, 37 for breaking and entering dwellings and buildings, 77 for offenses against chastity,

In *Americans in Process*, by Robert Woods (Boston, 1902), pp. 191–211.

including night-walking and the keeping of a noisy and disorderly house, 75 for gaming on the Lord's Day. There were taken into custody, also, 203 suspicious persons, and 37 vagrants and tramps of both sexes; 87 disturbances were suppressed; 368 sick and injured persons were assisted.

But the North End is bordered and crossed by great highways of travel and traffic from one part of the city to another. As a matter of fact, of the entire number of persons arrested in this division, fully two-thirds live outside the limits of Boston. Naturally, the majority of these nonresidents are arrested for drunkenness or immorality since a great number from neighboring cities and towns resort to the North End for purposes of wrong doing. Thus it appears that out of the 4,875 persons arrested in the division, fully 3,250 did not belong in Boston at all, and only about 825 resided at the North End. In view of the fact that this last-mentioned number comprises all who were arrested for any offense whatever, in a population of nearly 30,000, it seems astonishingly small. According to the police showing, therefore, the North End, so far from being exceptionally lawless, is, on the contrary, law-abiding to a degree that is not generally supposed.

Certain measures recently taken by the police in the North End have had an important bearing on the moral welfare of this section of the city. One of these was the closing of the last of the dance halls in the spring of 1900. Haunts of vice and crime were broken up, law-breakers of every sort were driven away or taken into custody, and life and property were safeguarded. Nevertheless, the police force in this part of the city was far too small for the situation that it tried to meet.

The closing of the dance halls really registered the moral change that had taken place at the North End within the last quarter of a century. The conditions out of which such resorts had sprung, and upon which their continuance really depended, had ceased to exist. A rapidly decreasing number of their women *habituées*, and a smaller and smaller percentage of their patronage, came from the neighborhood. The changed moral situation has been due, for the most part, to the change of the population. The moral decadence began with the incoming of the vicious and criminal of all races to take the places left vacant by the departure of the people of the better grades; with the coming of the self-respecting and industrious foreign immigrant began the moral revival.

This should not be construed as meaning that coercive agencies have not been at work all along. On the contrary, they have done much to keep the North End from sinking to any lower point of moral degradation, and to aid it in its moral recuperation.

The immigrants, who form the resident population of the North End, have brought certain evil ways of their own; they are also inevitably affected by the moral contagion in their surroundings. The Italian men, especially those of the so-called lower classes, are as a rule very lax morally, and the younger Jewish men are becoming so more and more.

The women of both races, on the other hand, are chaste with comparatively few exceptions. In the café of the hotel described, a Jewish girl rarely appeared, and an Italian girl almost never. No girl of either race frequented the dance halls. In the case of the Jewish women, chastity is due to religious and home influences; in that of the Italian, there is, in addition, the special protecting and avenging arm of the male members of the family. Any man attempting to lead an Italian woman astray is liable to be visited with a severe penalty from her father, brother, or other male relative. The custom still obtains among the Italians that a girl, especially if she is of marriageable age, shall never appear upon the street without a chaperon.

The number of liquor licenses held in Police Division 1 is 128. But with the exception of the Italian saloons, a few of them derive any considerable part of their trade from people living in the North End. The Jews, who with the Italians constitute the great mass of the population, are not frequenters of the saloon.

The great bulk of saloon patronage at the North End is by non-residents. All but about 450 of the 3,124 persons taken into custody for drunkenness during the twelve months ending December 1, 1901 had their places of abode outside this section of the city.

There are no gaming-places, strictly speaking, in the North End. Men play for drinks or even for small sums of money in the poolrooms and in some of the saloons; but whatever gaming is carried on here is of a comparatively harmless character, and is confined for the most part to the resident population.

Groups of boys may be seen at almost any time in side streets, doorways, and elsewhere, shooting craps. Here they congregate in considerable numbers, stationing sentinels on the street at either side to guard against surprise by the police. Occasionally the police make a descent upon the boys and take one or more into custody as a warning to the rest. Of the seventy-five persons arrested in this section of the city for gaming during the year 1901, the majority were juveniles.

Strangely enough, crime at the North End, while comparatively small in amount, is to a considerable extent of the most serious character. During the last eight years twenty murders, whose perpetrators were found out and convicted, have been committed in this section of the city. Of these murderers fourteen had their homes here. During the twelve months, three men were arrested for murder and four for assault with intent to murder—all residents of the North End. Thus a population that on the whole is orderly and law-abiding almost to an exceptional degree includes an element of a strikingly different character.

But these murderers and would-be murderers are of a single race—the Italian, and of the Sicilian branch of that race, and they by no means are representative of the population, or even of the Italian people. Moreover, while some of them premeditated their crimes, the majority acted on the impulse of the moment; hence are homicides rather than murders. Only one was convicted of murder in the first degree. Some of the murders were to satisfy a blood feud perhaps of long standing, or to avenge an insult or injury to a kinswoman of the murderer.

Other than murder, and assault with intent to murder, there is but little serious crime at the North End. Burglary is of infrequent occurrence. Italian boys, and to a less extent Jewish boys, steal junk whenever an opportunity presents itself, and commit other minor offenses. In the Italian rising generation especially, an increasing spirit of lawlessness is very noticeable. Gangs of these boys are beginning to present a serious problem, the so-called American spirit appearing to have peculiar possession of them.

The Jews seldom fall into the hands of the police, but they cannot be called a race "void of offense against the public order and welfare." They are especially prone to contentions with one another, as well as with their Gentile neighbors. No other people come to the police station so often to make complaints and demand redress. In nearly all cases their feelings have been hurt more than their bodies. In general, the law of the land is feared rather than respected by Jewish immigrants. On the whole, however, the Jewish community is law-abiding to a marked degree.

VI

Of all the settlement houses of the Progressive period, Hull House was probably the most famous. The writings of its founder, Jane Addams, attracted a wide readership, as did the various reports and studies issued by the House itself. Their descriptions of ghetto life were especially well-balanced. Somehow, Addams and her coworkers were able to see immigrant conditions more sympathetically than many other observers. The account below of Chicago's Slavic-Bohemian section is a sensitive analysis of the institutions, both protective and the assimilative, that were at work in the ghetto.

HULL HOUSE MAPS AND PAPERS, 1895

The first Bohemian emigrants came to Chicago in 1851 and 1852. Soon after the revolution in 1848, many of the enthusiastic patriots, forced to flee from their fatherland, sought homes in this country. The emigration from Bohemia increased after every continental war. This time not only the political refugees sought new homes, but artisans and peasants also began emigrating.

The social and political upheavals, the exaggerated stories of American wealth, were, and still are, the causes of Bohemian emigration. One of the chief causes now is the military law, which drives into this country a steady stream of strong, healthy, and able-bodied men. Bohemia has never sent her "slums" because her slums, like the slums of other nations, never like to "move on"; they are too contented in their indolence and filth to take the trouble of a sea voyage.

Often good artisans were compelled to work for low wages, even $1.25 a day; still, out of this meager remuneration they managed to lay a little aside for that longed-for possession—a house and lot that they

In *Maps and Papers*, Hull-House (New York, 1895), pp. 116–28.

could call their own. When that was paid for, then the house received an additional story, and that was rented, so that it began earning money. The landlord, who had till then lived in some unpleasant rear rooms, moved into the best part of the house; the wooden chairs replaced by upholstered ones, and the best room received the added luxury of a piano or violin.

To form at least a small estimate of the value of property owned by the Chicago Bohemians, it may be interesting to note how much the workingpeople have invested in property within the last eight years. They have saved it in the Bohemian building and loan associations. We can safely estimate that within the last eight years these societies have disbursed over four millions of dollars, which is all invested in property by the workingpeople.

Before 1878 the majority of the Bohemians were engaged in the various building trades; others, again, were tailors, and many ordinary laborers working in the lumberyards; but after 1878 they began entering as clerks into stores, law offices, and various other business enterprises. The majority of the Bohemians are artisans, and only some of the peasants are contented to be ordinary laborers. Businessmen dealing with them readily acknowledge the "bad debt" among the Bohemians to be very rare.

Social Life

Although the Bohemians have better food and more of it than they had at home, they lack the social life. They miss the free garden concerts that are given in almost every large city in Bohemia; the Sunday walks, and various holiday feasts.

This yearning after more social life has led them into various schemes for entertainment which are not always wholesome. The picnics, with uniformed processions, led by brass bands, that are so common and perfectly proper in Bohemia, appear strange and almost ridiculous. The Sunday dances, theaters, and concerts that stand substitute for the walks in the fields; the home entertainments, when families make calls, and amuse themselves by singing, eating, drinking, and telling stories—are to the conservative American desecrations of the sabbath.

Similar amusements are popular with the newcomers; but as they live here longer, and become more Americanized, this social life changes and becomes more formal, more affected, and gradually becomes a mixture of American and European, something unlike the real Bohemian, and foreign to the American; entirely original, the "Bohemian-American."

The love of social life is the predominating feature in the Bohemian settlement. Almost every Bohemian, man and woman, belongs to some society, and many are members of several orders. Unlike any other Slavonic nation, the Bohemian women have a great many organizations, both educational and benevolent. The secret societies of "Jednota Ceskych Dam" are among the most popular and influential. Their object is at once educational, social, and benevolent; and they pay yearly thousands of dollars to aid the orphan children of their former members.

Family Life

The family life is very affectionate. It is a prevailing custom among the working-class that the father and children should give all their wages to the wife or mother. Seldom do the children keep their earnings and pay board; they usually all work and live together, and then at marriage each child receives a portion, or after the death of the parents all is equally divided among the children. The Bohemian women are clean and thrifty, economical housekeepers, and very good cooks. They know the art of making a little go far; and this enables them to feed large families with comparatively meager sums.

The Illinois State factory inspector has said that of all the children who come to her for medical examination, the Bohemian and Jewish children are the best fed.

It is not the general custom for the mothers and wives of Bohemians to go out working; but more and younger children go out to work here than in any other Bohemian community. There is a greater demand for child labor in Chicago, the supply for which is recruited from the ranks of the needy families of all nationalities. It is a great temptation to all foreigners to sacrifice their children; for the little ones can often get work when grown people, slow to learn a new language, are forced to be idle.

Religion

It is estimated that the larger half of the Bohemian population in Chicago is Catholic, while the rest are non-churchgoers. In every parish there is a Bohemian school, where a half-day is devoted to teaching the English branches, and the afternoon to teaching the Bohemian language, grammar, and catechism. The pupils in these number not less than two thousand seven hundred.

The remainder of the Bohemian people are simply non-churchgoers, and call themselves "freethinkers," most of them having no definite philosophy, only cherishing antagonism against church institutions. The freethinkers have four Bohemian-English schools, where both Bohemian and English are taught. The children usually go for a year or two to the Bohemian school, where they learn to read and write in Bohemian, and then enter the public schools. They have separate halls, theaters, and societies.

Citizenship

In political life almost all the old settlers were Republicans. After the year 1880 some began to vote the Democratic ticket; and when in 1883 this party nominated a Bohemian for the office of alderman, it got the first real hold on the people in Chicago. The first political recognition given them was a stroke on the part of the Democratic wire-pullers to win the Bohemian vote. The politicians work on the people's feelings, incite them against the men of the other party as their most bitter enemies; and if this doesn't succeed, they go to work deliberately to buy some.

Thus adding insult to injury, they go off and set up a pharisaic cry about the ignorance and corruption of the foreign voters.

The Bohemian people in Chicago are called "clannish." They may deserve that epithet; but who is to be blamed for that? In the early days it was natural that they should settle near their kinsmen or relations. Their language, being Slavonic, was unlike any other about them; and they were at a disadvantage as compared with the Germans, whose native tongue is so closely allied to the English. Then, too, the Germans, being their traditional enemies, tried to disparage them in every way, until the poor inoffensive Bohemian was insulted by all around him; so that in time he began to regard everyone non-Bohemian as his enemy. '. goodly portion of the blame for this rests upon the American press; for in times of political campaigns it heaps insult or flattery without discrimination. Left alone, the foreigners are harmless, for they are too divided by their petty traditional national hatreds; but this constant aimless baiting of the American press gives these great masses one theme, one bond of sympathy, on which they can all unite; and that is— hatred of Americans.

So far, the Bohemians are free from any such feeling, and, to the sorrow of their European brothers, Americanize almost too rapidly; so that frequently the second and third generations do not even speak their own native language. They constitute only a drop in the mighty artery of foreign blood in America; but their leaders are anxious that this shall in its way contribute the very best to the life of this new and mighty nation.

VII

Each immigrant group had its own newspapers, written in the Old Country language. Some of the papers (particularly the Chinese), were almost exclusively concerned with news from back home; but most tried to balance their coverage between developments here and abroad. The immigrants' press certainly did help to keep alive the Old World language and traditions. At the same time, they introduced newcomers to the United States in ways that they could understand.

The press fulfilled another function as well. It allowed immigrants to share their experiences. Letters to the editor asking for advice not only gave the newspaper a chance to offer counsel, but allowed others, in more or less similar circumstances, to measure their own problems by a wider standard. The following letter from a distraught mother to The Jewish Daily Forward *is a classic statement of the conflict of generations in an immigrant group. Yet imagine how other parents felt as they read this letter. They may have begun to see that what they had thought of as their own special dilemma was really reflective of a mere general social process.*

THE JEWISH DAILY FORWARD, 1919

We sent our sixteen-year-old daughter to America and we remained at home. I cannot describe to you the way I felt when my daughter left us. Many nights I did not sleep and shed many tears before I received a letter from her that she had arrived safely. We thought that we should be able to follow her within a short time, but it was not so. My daughter came to America, but she did not meet with luck and it happened that our condition improved, so we wrote to our child to come home.

We wrote and we begged her to return, but she did not want to. She wrote that she liked America and did not even think of returning home. I am a mother, and when I saw that she did not want to return, we emigrated to America. It was not so soon; a few years had passed, and when we arrived we did not recognize our daughter. She was grown-up, tall, pretty—a pleasure to look at her.

My husband began to earn little by little. We fixed up a nice home and I was happy because I could see my daughter. But soon I realized that my big pretty daughter is not the girl I knew; she has changed entirely. During the few years that she was here without us she became a regular Yankee and forgot how to talk Yiddish. I talk to her in Yiddish and she replies in English.

So I ask her: "Daughter of mine, talk Yiddish to me and I will understand you." She says that it is not nice to talk Yiddish and that I am a greenhorn. And that is not all. She does worse things. She wants to make a Christian woman out of me. She does not like to have me light the Sabbath candles. When I light the candles she blows them out. And she argues with me. She says that because I and my husband are pious and have a Jewish home, she can never invite a boy acquaintance to her house; she is ashamed. She makes fun of me and her father. She calls us greenhorns and is ashamed of us. Once I saw her standing on the stoop with a boy, so I went up to her and asked her when she would come up. She did not even reply, and later when she came up she screamed at me because I had called her by her Jewish name. But I cannot call her differently. I cannot call her by her new name.

Dear Editor, it is impossible to describe the troubles that she causes us, and as much as I ask her to be a good daughter, it does not help. Please write a few words for my daughter.

In *The Jewish Daily Forward*, July 9, 1919.

Chapter 16

The Settlement House

THE SETTLEMENT HOUSE movement exemplified the spirit of Progressive reform. Although the model for this type of institution originated in England, at London's Toynbee Hall, Americans quickly became its foremost proponents. By 1900, nearly one hundred settlement houses operated in the nation's cities, including Hull House in Chicago, South End House in Boston, and the University Settlement in New York. The central idea of the movement was to have its members live among the poor immigrants so that they might learn about the causes and conditions of poverty; this knowledge, in turn, would equip them to design and enact corrective programs to alert the society to the problems of ghetto life and to enhance the ability of the poor to help themselves. A curious mixture of innovative social analysis, which blamed the economic system for the problem of poverty, combined with an older moralism, which looked to the personal virtues and vices of the needy to understand their condition, gave the settlement house program its peculiar character.

One of the compelling motives bringing comfortable and well-off Americans into the settlement house movement was a keen desire on their part to escape middle-class life, to encounter what they thought of as the real and authentic experience of the ghetto. Thus, many of the first members of the settlement houses were college-educated women, graduates, for example, of Vassar, Mt. Holyoke, and Smith. Having left the restrictive parlors of their middle-class families for the more spacious college dormitories, they had no desire, once their education was completed, to return home. With other opportunities limited (it was yet unheard of for respectable girls to live on their own), settlement house life presented an excellent solution. Here women could live and work in the real world, do service, and yet remain in a setting protective enough to satisfy fastidious parents.

But the public role of the settlement house was probably more important than the personal motives of its members. The residents came to understand that the plight of many of the ghetto poor had its origin in circumstances beyond their control. They soon recognized that the health conditions in overcrowded and poorly ventilated tenements, and the lack of safety measures in badly designed factories, disabled many a willing worker and cast his family into poverty. Testifying before state investigatory committees, they argued constantly and convincingly for protective legislation for women, for pensions for widowed mothers and dependent children, and for compensation for injured workers. Settlement house residents thus contributed substantially to the Americans' discovery of poverty in the Progressive era, laying the foundation for many programs that would be expanded during the New Deal.

Settlement workers also shared another ambition: to elevate the condition of the immigrant by teaching him American ways. Some of the roots of poverty, they believed, were to be found in the vices and superstitions of the immigrants. The sooner they became Americans, the quicker they would prosper. An occasional observer, like Jane Addams, had a genuine respect for the immigrants' traditions. But most of her colleagues assumed that the nation and the individual immigrant would benefit when American customs replaced Old World ones. As a result, settlement houses designed club programs to teach immigrant children and parents American ways. They emphasized also the potential of the public school to help assimilate foreign-born pupils. So, too, the movement tried to ferret out the corruptors of the municipal government, the ward boss, or the local policeman. The immigrant, they insisted, was learning the wrong lessons in political life.

The settlement house movement, in brief, represented both the spirit of benevolence and the ethnocentrism of Americans in the Progressive era. It aimed to do good—on its own terms.

I

One of the most prominent settlement house workers was Robert Woods. Born in 1865, Woods graduated from Amherst, and then went off to live for six months in London's Toynbee Hall. Upon his return to the United States in 1891, he organized its equivalent in Boston's South End House, remaining at the head of the institution for many years. Toward the end of his life, he looked back over the movement and set down its guiding principles. Here is an effective summary of the philosophy of the settlement house.

THE NEIGHBORHOOD
IN NATION BUILDING, 1923

ROBERT A. WOODS

Civilization is overreaching itself. Certain of its tendencies develop rankly, before corrective tendencies have begun to operate. The result is congestion in some places, and atrophy in others. We must find ways of uniting the parts of the social body, under the bonds of civilization, so that its vital influence shall run strongly out into every distant extremity.

We find ourselves compelled to see that the influences of civilization penetrate into all the ramifications of society. The great city—the typical product of civilization—shows by multiple effects the danger of having people cut off from the better life of society, and breeding with phenomenal rapidity all the evils with which society is cursed. The poverty of the means of life is felt in other sections of cities besides those called the slums, among grades of people above those called the workingpeople. Factory towns grow quickly, and mass together a large population with very little care that they shall live in a human way. And country villages, cut off by distance from elevating influences as crowded city quarters are by their numbers, offer a problem almost as serious as that of the cities themselves.

Only modern civilization could have brought about the difficulty; only modern civilization could have understood it; only modern civilization can overcome it. The task is to make provision so that every part of society shall not only have a full supply for its fundamental human wants, but shall also be constantly refreshed from the higher sources of happier and nobler life. The great social evil is that the resources of society are so illy applied to the supplying of its needs. There must be a shifting of resources to meet needs. The forces of civilization must be mobilized until every tenement block, every country hamlet, may be able to summon for its use all that can make life what it is designed to be. From the point of view of the individual, and at close range, this is philanthropy; from the point of view of society, this is only far-sighted social statesmanship.

If we are bold enough to hold that civilization must do its work for the whole of society, and for every class and every section of society, we must, I think, see that it is essential that such effort as has been indicated should be undertaken. It is for this reason one dares to believe that the university settlements, small in number and slight in results as yet, are destined to fill an important part among the many forces which are making for social progress. They come near to fulfilling the conditions that have been laid down. Their workers, like the people of the neighborhood, not only work there. As college men and women,

In *The Neighborhood in Nation Building*, by Robert A. Woods (Cambridge, Mass., 1923), pp. 2–3, 9–27. Reprinted by permission of the National Federation of Settlements and Neighborhood Centers.

they have learned to a degree how to live the good and beautiful life. As cultured persons, they believe in the saving quality of every sort of influence which tends to make men and women true to the human pattern.

For the present, the work must be done by amateurs, for there are no professionals. It must not now and it may never be too closely organized, because it consists so largely of turning to social account delicate kinds of influence which cannot be borne through the channels of organization.

The prime requisite in the minds of educated men in undertaking any task is to know to a greater or less degree the situation in which they are to work and the material which they are to work upon. The close, scientific study of the social conditions in the neighborhood about a settlement is indispensable to its success. Of course, careful social analysis of a neighborhood demands the observation of months and years; but the task should be undertaken from the very beginning. Science and sympathy must unite if we are to have any living knowledge of the poor.

After the study of the social statics of the neighborhood comes the study of its social dynamics. What the people are accomplishing for themselves both in their individual and home life, and in local organizations for whatever purpose, is a matter of absolute importance to a settlement before launching into its more constructive activity. The presumption is always against having a settlement introduce any newly devised scheme. It is always in favor of falling in with the current of what is already advancing in the neighborhood. In an enterprise of the people's own, you find them under a kind of momentum which can never be so well artificially aroused. And so gradually by the united efforts of the residents, the settlement, as a whole, comes to be in sympathetic touch with the homes of its neighbors, and with all combined movements among them toward trade organization, cooperation, or thrift, or toward education and recreation. And a settlement is false to its purpose if it does not take knowledge also of the organized forces of sin that are at work in its vicinity.

The curse of the poor is their poverty; often the sacred hearthstone of honest poverty must be within sound of the revelry and debauchery of those to whom society is pleased to give its greater rewards. University settlements must be courageous enough and scientific enough to face the grim, inhuman evils that flaunt themselves in what are called the less respectable sections of cities, the horror of prostitution, the horror of drunkenness, and all their accompaniments and consequences. The time has come when the educated man and the educated woman must no longer merely shudder and turn away from the dark depths of life.

It is very important, for the first at least, that the settlements should be located with a view to the most favorable opportunity for studying what is distinctive of the great metropolitan poor quarters. The first settlements ought to be located where they can be within range of the variety of social problems which a city offers. The settlement is best located where it can easily look every way—toward the very poor, toward the regularly employed working people, and toward the criminal and vicious elements which are found in spots and streaks in all degrees of outward respectability. This is very important if the active work of the settlement for the improvement of the people is to have the value of a comprehensive experiment.

Of course, the question begins at once to rise, "What shall we do?" And though there is danger in settlement work of rushing too quickly into schemes, yet it is for the improvement of the neighborhood that the settlement has come. And the first thing to do is to strengthen the things which remain. Every kind of center of social life in the neighborhood should become the object of the wisest care that the settlement can give. First of all, the settlement should begin by being as nearly as possible a home. It is a disadvantage, I think, to have, from the first, easy public access to the house. The residents should be neighbors, and should become acquainted in the same natural way by which neighbors come to know one another in the simpler circles of society. The first and constant effort of the settlement should be to have its men or its women come into relations of friendliness and intimacy with the people in their homes. The bringing out of the possibilities of home life among the workingpeople is one of the most valuable results that a group of educated men or women could aim at; and, of course, the women residents can accomplish far more in this direction than the men. It is a good plan to have one resident especially to visit in each of certain groups of houses and then, without hurry, let him become thoroughly acquainted with the people living there, with the purpose of bringing the resources of the settlement to bear upon that quarter. As time goes on, the homes of the neighborhood will be better in their sanitary condition, in their food, in their reading, in their enjoyments, in their morals, and in their religious life.

Whatever trade unions, workingmen's clubs, temperance societies, and even political clubs there are, ought to receive the sympathy, and so far as is possible without compromise, the active support of the settlement. It is particularly important that the leaders of these organizations, and other influential persons of the neighborhood, should be made friends of, unless they are unworthy of friendship. It is perhaps needless to say that in all these relations the residents must be frank to recognize the ability and worth of the people whom they meet, acting naturally, whether as learners or teachers.

A work only second in importance is that of cooperating with all the good forces already active in the neighborhood which are not original developments of its own immediate life. In these would be included all the officers of the law, the teachers in the schools, the agents of charitable societies, and the clergymen in charge of the churches. The policy of the settlement ought to be, first, to make every possible effort to establish friendly relations with these men, and through such relations to secure a knowledge of the situation and increased effort for its improvement.

There are few persons in the community more deserving of the sympathy and support of good people than an honest policeman located in a bad city quarter. He has to stem the tide of the city's moral defilement as no other person is called upon to do; and he is almost wholly deprived of the uplift, which nearly every social worker now feels, that comes from knowing of a great body of true men and women who are glad of the work he is doing. Another class of persons who make a valuable moral contribution to society and receive very little moral return at the hands of society is the schoolteachers. The residents of a settlement can be of great use both in confirming them in what they already do well, and in assisting them to have better purposes and methods.

The study and practice of scientific charity is a most important line of effort for a settlement to undertake. Residents should join the local committees of such charities as are already organized; and while it is doubtful whether a settlement should become identified with any charity to the extent of having its local headquarters in the settlement house, yet certain members of the group ought to give themselves especially to becoming thoroughly acquainted with the state of the dependent and casual classes and to the skillful administration of relief.

One of the first and most obvious needs of the life of every poor neighborhood is healthful recreation. The dullness and dreariness of its life is only the reverse side of the brutality in it. Whatever is done among the children and youth will center in boys' and girls' clubs, the success of which will depend almost wholly upon the capacity of the persons who have charge of them. There are no proved and tried methods for carrying on a boys' club. But the person to lead a boys' club is born, not made. In dealing with boys it is almost necessary to have a gymnasium and drill hall where they can run off their surplus spirits and be taught physical and moral manhood at the same time. After that, the hope of boys' clubs lies in manual training. It is also practically settled that the big club of boys, managed by one or two men as with long poles, can never accomplish what needs being done.

The settlement should be a center for social gatherings which shall from time to time include the different members of each family, bringing men and women, boys and girls, together, that they may learn of the grace and sweetness of life.

On the educational side, a settlement may begin with some of the simplest and most popular forms of study, and from that even aspire to establish a workingmen's university; and as for lectures and concerts and art exhibitions, it may gradually build up a people's palace. On the industrial side, it can introduce experiments in the way of cooperative stores, cooperative industries, building and loan associations, benefit and insurance organizations; it will bring workingmen and university men together, in order that they may learn from each other about social questions.

On the ethical side it will try to bring to the people the influence of the lives and teachings of the world's great moral heroes. On the religious side—if it have an acknowledged religious side to its work—it will, in all wisdom, provide opportunities for those who will, to advance in the better life by refreshing the spirit of love from the springs of faith and hope.

Thus far I have referred only to the duty of a university settlement to its own neighborhood. But it has other duties—to the general section of the city in which it is placed, and to the city as a whole; to the men or women who are its residents and associated workers; to the body of its supporters. And it owes it to society at large to secure the spread of the principles for which it stands. For the general district, the settlement can mass its forces of residents and sympathetic neighbors, and enter into the movement for good citizenship, by urging the support of worthy candidates for municipal offices, by promoting measures for reform and improvement, and in general by organizing for action as to public matters that closely affect the life of the people.

A university settlement ought to be a stronghold of that rising municipal loyalty which is in some respects as noble as patriotism among the civic virtues. The method and trend of city government ought to be watched until it is thoroughly known, and then patient and constant efforts made to improve the type of officials, and the methods of legislation and administration.

The residents of a settlement ought to be men or women of some kind of liberal training. The association of the settlements with academical loyalties is meant to be inclusive, but not exclusive—I have used the term "university settlement" as being the original and generic one, hoping that it might embrace all the similar forms of effort. The colleges owe it to themselves to remove the popular impression that they are places where well-dressed and haughty young persons live and enjoy themselves for four years. The residents should live without any mark of asceticism about them—especially not if such things have to be artificially taken on. The life of simplicity and frugality which includes the usual necessities of civilized existence will be most easily understood by the people who come to the house. Parts of the house which are intended for hospitable use may well have kinds of adornment which the residents might consider too costly for their own private satisfaction, wherever they might be living.

So much for the diagnosis; what of the prognosis? What can the settlements accomplish, what future development is the idea likely to have, and what is it worth to society as a whole? University settlements are capable of bringing to the depressed sections of society its healing and saving influences, for the lack of which those sections are to so large an extent as good as dead. The settlements are able to take neighborhoods in cities and by patience bring back to them much of the healthy village life, so that the people shall again know and care for each other. The settlements stand for the fact that there is no short and easy road to a better society, and that for every social gain there must be some corresponding expenditure of personal effort. They also show not only that social work demands a far greater number and variety of workers than has before been understood to be necessary, but that it demands the best type of men and women acting under the highest motives they can feel. Thus the settlement movement strikes at the root of the tree. Not contrivances, but persons, must save society. And wheresoever society at all needs saving, there persons must go in ample number and of the best trained ability. The resources of society are largely in persons. The needs of society are in persons. There must be overturnings and overturnings, till everywhere the resourceful shall be filling the wants of the needy.

II

The annual reports of the University Settlement Society demonstrate both the range and the moral thrust of its programs. Play, to these reformers, was much more than just release of stored energy. The activities, both in form and content, were to introduce the immigrants to American customs. Note carefully how the clubs were designed, for the settlement workers hoped that the habits the immigrants learned in the settlement house would carry over into the larger society.

REPORT OF NEW YORK'S UNIVERSITY SETTLEMENT SOCIETY, 1894

Historical Sketch of the University Settlement

The University Settlement was organized in 1887 under the name of the Neighborhood Guild. Dr. Stanton Coit, who had rooms at 146 Forsyth Street, had already formed a club of six boys, known as the Lily Pleasure Club. The boys met in Dr. Coit's room in '86, before the Guild was started. A room for the club was secured, and debates were held. The club soon asserted its moral character by voting that no cards should be allowed in its rooms, though the managers had been prepared to grant it, with the limitation of no gambling. The following year a girls' club was introduced, and then a kindergarten and penny provident bank. The work was also more thoroughly organized, and the power of personal sympathy and personal influence became strongly felt through several of the workers, who devoted careful attention to many individual members of the club. The total membership in October 1889 was one hundred and forty-seven. In 1891 the work was seriously embarrassed by lack of funds. At that time, the organization since known as the University Settlement Society was called into existence, and the name of University Settlement was given it. Through the support of the University Settlement Society a house was taken at 26 Delancey Street, and the work was established on its present basis. Since then the growth has been constant and steady. The attachment of a regularly paid librarian has been the means of developing one of the most important educational features of the work, and the permanent establishment of the kindergarten has also emphasized the educational feature. The clubs which have been in existence since the foundation of the work have revealed in many ways the influence of the workers associated with them. The scheme of clubs has been based according to ages, though the lines are not strictly observed. It will be seen that the club

In *Annual Report for 1894*, University Settlement Society (New York, 1895), pp. 7–9, 12–17, 24–25.

has always been the central feature of the Settlement, and that most of the work within the house has gathered around this organization.

Annual Report for 1894

The work of the University Settlement has enlarged in many directions since last year. There are six residents now against two then. The work embraces two lines, that of the clubs, classes, library, penny provident bank, lectures and entertainments, in the house, and outside of the house the broad interests of the Settlement in the general welfare of the district.

The central object with the younger clubs has been to develop wholesome vitality. Next to physical development, which we regard as essential to all other work, we aim to develop orderliness and to furnish food for the growth of mind and character. We also provide a limited technical education, desiring to train our youth in securing special fitness for useful, independent lives.

With the older people we aim to enlarge their view of life, to increase the number of their interests and enjoyments, that life may be less dull and sodden, and to enable them to realize some of the pleasures which the mind can extract from itself.

But we hold besides that we have a large civic responsibility and opportunity. The greatest difficulties are not moral, but those which result from lack of wholesome physical conditions and uplifting social environment. Overcrowded tenement houses, deficient sanitary conveniences, inadequate street cleaning and house inspection are the mere external aspects of life in the Tenth Ward. We must also remember that there are no museums and art galleries, except our own modest attempts, no libraries, except those of the college and university settlements, no fine stores encouraging discriminating tastes, scarcely one in fact of all those elements which encourage a wholesome and intelligent living. Such is the life and work into which we have oriented ourselves.

The Tenth Ward Social Reform Club

A club of men and women of the neighborhood, meeting together for social enjoyment. Occasionally discussions have been conducted, but it has been found very practicable to direct the main attention to the development of wholesome social feeling and easy and simple social enjoyment. Much of the entertainment, singing, declamations, readings, amateur theatricals, etc. is given by various members of the club. It is perhaps the most satisfactory embodiment of the Neighborhood Guild idea with which this institution was founded.

The Improvement Club
Miss Mosenthal, Director

The club is composed of members of girls between the ages of eighteen and twenty-four. It has the usual executive officers, and conducts a business meeting every Thursday evening. There is at present membership of about forty-five.

The club has now settled to its work for the winter, having organized classes in physical culture, dress making, and hygienic home nursing. These classes are joined by a majority of the members, are well conducted, and regularly attended.

At the close of the spring last year, the class in physical culture gave an exhibition, showing remarkably good drilling and training. Last year a class in cooking was continued till the summer.

The Neighborhood Guild Cadets

Membership from fourteen to sixteen. The exercises consist of business meetings, in which there is practice in parliamentary law, with occasional debates on literary and social questions, gymnastic exercises, and military drill. During last spring and summer the club took a number of outings, visiting Governor's Island, the Brooklyn Navy Yard, and a number of public buildings and institutions. Frequently after these visits a discussion was held, and members gave their impressions and criticisms of the administration.

Potomac Cadets
Miss W. Buck, Director

"The Young Potomac Cadets" started as a club two years ago. It meets twice a week at the Guild (on Mondays and Wednesdays), from 3:30 to 5:30. The members are boys, between the ages of eleven and fifteen. There are twenty-three boys in the club and there is an average attendance of sixteen. The club has no object but the amusement and general improvement of its members. They spend the time in drill, games, and gymnasium and physical culture, for which they have a teacher. They always have a business meeting in which they decide all questions. They pay three cents apiece for two meetings. They expect to give an entertainment in February, for which they will charge ten cents a ticket. The money earned in this way is usually spent in trips to Central Park, or games for the club.

Mayflower Club
Miss L. Waterman, Director

The Mayflower Club has now its full number of twenty-five members. To our regret we have to turn little girls away at almost every meeting who beg to be allowed to join. But we realize that twenty-five must be the limit if the individuals are to receive attention. Sewing is taught for its own value, but also as a means to influence the girls to be neat, clean, and exact. Up to the present time the work has consisted of making underwear for small children. Each girl took the article of clothing she had made and gave it in person to the mother of some of these destitute little ones. It was a new experience in their lives, and while they at first rebelled and were reluctant to work for others, they are now eager to finish and have garments ready for any emergency.

The reading aloud of some tale with a telling moral has been introduced during the sewing, to prevent noisy conversation and occupy the minds of the children. After the story has been read, it is talked over and by means of questions and answers the lesson is brought out which is intended they should find. This also develops the faculty of close and intelligent attention. All things are decided by vote of the members, who manage their club according to parliamentary rules in a simple way, while they look for advice to the one who has them in charge.

Order Club
Miss C. Nichol and B. S. Johnson, Directors

The sixth year of the Order Club opened the first week in October 1893. The membership having increased to eighty, no more were admitted, except to fill the places of those resigning. At each meeting, the first half-hour was spent either in singing or a talk on any subject or in discussing club business. After that, the boys [from eight to twelve years old] drilled for half an hour, and the last hour was spent in the gymnasium and in playing games. For the first Thursday in each month, the boys themselves arranged a simple entertainment of song and recitation.

A little before the beginning of the latter part of the year, last May, the system of business meetings, conducted entirely by the members of the club, was initiated. Though started with some degree of apprehension, experience has demonstrated its utility and value. Hints have been given as to parliamentary usages and it is our aim to gradually eliminate all unparliamentary methods.

The club has been divided into two battalions, the first, composed of those who have had some experience in drilling; the others, of those who have not. These battalions are drilled by a member of the club, who have given his time and labor to qualify himself for this duty. He drills his companies after the most approved military tactics. The boys like the idea of being drilled as soldiers and not as boys.

Great stress is laid upon physical exercise. Since September we have had the services of a competent instructor. The whole club is drilled at the same time and carried through the same movements for half an hour, once a week. As dumbbells are used in this physical drill, we are handicapped by an inadequate number of them.

The Literary Society
Mr. Philip Mosenthal, Critic

The society is composed of young men and women who meet weekly for debates, declamations, essays, and other literary exercises. All subjects are discussed, but mainly political topics, purely literary subjects not arousing as much interest as it was hoped would be the case when the club was founded. The average work has been good, and most of the members have taken the work seriously, and given much thought and preparation for the parts assigned to them.

The Tenth Ward Sanitary Union
Mr. W. S. Ufford, Chairman

The Tenth Ward Sanitary Union is about to complete the second year of its history. Its object is street and tenement house inspection. Its method is to visit the houses of the people of the district, and to enlist their cooperation in working for better sanitary conditions of life for themselves and their neighbors. In some cases, where tenants have vainly asked for repairs necessary to wholesome living, we have been able to receive the complaints and to secure the correction of the abuses. Where the agents or housekeepers have been either unwilling or unable to act, appeal has been taken to the landlord. When he is obdurate, resort is had to the Board of Health or other city departments, within whose province the case falls. Rarely are such complaints ineffectual. Well-lighted and clean halls and stairways, walls and ceilings kalsomined and whitewashed according to law, clear fire escapes, clean sinks, proper disposal of ashes and garbage, and decent closets are the homely virtues striven for.

For purposes of record, it may be well to incorporate here the figures. From February 15, 1893, to March 1, 1894, one hundred and eighty-three tenements were visited. Ninety-three complaints were filed with the Board of Health and other departments. From March 1, 1894, to July 1, 1894, eighty-one tenements were inspected. One hundred and twelve fire escapes were cleared, fifty sinks cleaned, one sweating place closed, and six complaints made to the Board of Health and Factory Inspectors.

That which we are trying to do requires patience, tact, and courageous persistence. The membership of the Union has always been small, yet there must be many who would be glad to meet and know their fellows. At present, the Board of Health, through its inspectors, average scarcely more than one visit a year to each tenement house. The force of officials should be largely increased. Till then the work must be done, however imperfectly, by volunteers, or go undone. We call for reenforcements from those who read this report and their friends.

The Unemployed

Last winter a large portion of our attention was given to the relieving of the unemployed. Early in December, when rumors of the need were afloat, and accurate information was lacking, a meeting was called at the Settlement, and an investigation was planned with a view to obtain accurate information as to the amount and character of the need. A careful canvass of five hundred families was made, in which it was found that about 40 percent were unemployed, 40 percent more were partially employed, and only 20 percent of the wage earners were in regular employment. The average time out of employment was four months from the time of the canvass, taking it back therefore to the twentieth of August. The Bowery Savings Bank reported the withdrawal of two million dollars between July 1893 and January 1894. A visitation of the pawnshops showed that unusual drains had been made upon them, but that the drains had not been made in November and December, but only in September and October, showing that many of the people had pawned all they had even at that early season. These statistics were presented to a public meeting, and used extensively. Their accuracy was substantially confirmed by later examinations.

When the East Side Street Sweeping work was organized, mainly under the auspices of the College Settlement, 2,231 applications for this relief were received at our Settlement. Of this number 23 were male, unmarried; 1,091 married, 130 females. The majority were tailors. Permanent work was given to 23, street sweeping to 140, tailoring to 70, whitewashing to 6, sewing to 38, and wood yard tickets to 65. The total number of street sweeping tickets issued was 507, representing $3,042 in wages to recipients. Twenty-five hundred visits were made to investigate cases. Two hundred and sixty bags of flour were distributed to the most needy cases, several tons of coal, twenty dollars worth of meal tickets, and twenty dollars worth of five-cent food and fuel tickets. Clothing was supplied in 434 cases to the extent of 1,611 garments.

The need this winter is not so severe as last, as work has continued a much longer time, but certainly there will be more than the ordinary demand for relief from the public. It is felt that we should preserve our position as a noncharitable organization. At the same time we are prepared to recognize our responsibility in a particular emergency of any sort however remote from the regular line of our work, and we shall endeavor in this as in other such work to cooperate with every movement in our district.

III

A major contribution of settlement house workers was to alert public officials to the desperate need and clear right of the poor to public assistance. Although relief to the needy at home had been long in practice in American municipalities, officials thought of it as a dole; they were suspicious of the recipients and tried to keep the sums as small as possible. Settlement house workers, however, argued for a new perspective. They insisted that groups such as widowed mothers be relieved under special programs, with the aid more of a right than an act of charity. At the same time, they wished to force the state governments to take responsibility for the problems, not just to rely upon private associations. Their efforts bore fruit in public provisions for widows, and the principles that they established grew increasingly significant during subsequent decades. The findings below, of the 1914 New York State Commission on Relief for Widowed Mothers, reveal the triumph of their arguments.

REPORT OF THE NEW YORK STATE
COMMISSION FOR WIDOWED MOTHERS, 1914

Basic Principles

The Commission believes it to be fundamentally true that:

1. The mother is the best guardian of her children.
2. Poverty is too big a problem for private philanthropy.
3. No woman, save in exceptional circumstances, can be both the home-maker and the breadwinner of her family.
4. Preventive work to be successful must concern itself with the child and the home.
5. Normal family life is the foundation of the state, and its conservation an inherent duty of government.

The General Situation

The Commission finds that:

1. Widowhood is the second greatest cause of dependency, the first being the incapacity of the breadwinner.
2. The widowed mother is in peculiar need of adequate assistance, and is uniquely open to constructive educational endeavors.
3. Public aid to dependent fatherless children is quite different in theory and effect from "charity" or "outdoor relief."
4. The experience of twenty-one other states in the Union, and of the larger countries of Europe, proves that it is feasible to administer such aid wisely and efficiently by public officials.
5. The experience elsewhere has shown that such aid is the most economical as well as the most socially advanced method of caring for dependent children.

The Situation in New York State

This Commission finds that:

Two thousand seven hundred and sixteen children of 1,483 widowed mothers are at present in institutions at public expense, who were committed for destitution only; 933 children of 489 widows are at present in institutions because of illness of the mother, resulting often from overwork and overworry that might easily have been prevented.

Self-Support Impossible

The unskilled widowed mother is unable to support herself and her family at a reasonable standard of living by taking work into the home or going out into the broader fields of industry.

The work available to such women outside of the home inevitably breaks down the physical, mental, and moral strength of the family and disrupts the home life through an inadequate standard of living and parental neglect, due to the enforced absence of the mother at the time the children most need her care.

In *Report of the New York State Commission for Widowed Mothers* (Albany, 1914), pp. 6–9, 15, 26–27, 50–53, 106, 113, 116–17, 158.

The work available in the home results, equally inevitably, in the prevention of normal family life, by causing overwork, congestion, child labor, contagion, and a dangerously low standard of living.

Normal Childlife Impossible

This disruption of the home contributes largely and directly to the backwardness and delinquency of children.

Present Sources of Assistance Inadequate

Neither the public outdoor relief system extant in the state, nor the private charities in our larger cities, have sufficient funds to relieve adequately all widows of the grim burden of support so that they might remain at home to take personal care of their dependent children.

Present Assistance Wrong in Principle

That neither public outdoor relief nor private charity constitutes the proper method of carrying on the conservation of the good home.

First Recommendation

With these principles as a basis, and these facts as a reason, the Commission respectfully recommends the immediate enactment into law of the principle of state aid to the dependent children of widowed mothers.

Government Aid the Only Solution

Other solutions that have been suggested to and rejected by the Commission are:

1. That all such relief be left in the hands of private charity. By a review of the work done in individual families, and through the testimony presented by many charity experts, the Commission finds that private charity has not the funds, and cannot, in the future, raise the funds to give adequate relief in the home, nor to administer such funds in the efficient, wise, and sympathetic manner which it has itself set up as the ideal.
2. That the state grant aid through the volunteer relief societies or the private child-caring institutions.

The Commission finds that experience in other states demonstrates clearly that public officials can be found who can administer such assistance as wisely and as sympathetically as can private social workers.

Public Prevention of Poverty

The problem of the prevention of poverty is perhaps the most serious that confronts any civilized community today. That it is ultimately preventable is a fundamental doctrine of democracy, an axiom of civilization. The principle of public effort in this field is an inherent part of the tradition of our state and nation and is clearly recognized in our constitutions. The many laws which carry this great principle into effect must, from time to time, be modified and extended to keep pace with our increasing knowledge of the social needs of the community and our understanding of the methods of meeting such needs.

Alternatives Open to Widowed Mothers

There are today four alternatives open to such women; all of which tend to break down physical, mental, and moral welfare of the family, rather than to conserve it as the most precious asset of the community.

The Special Committee on Widows' Pensions of the New York Neighborhood Workers' Association stated that:

> The death of the wage earner brings many a family to the line of dependency. Heretofore we have either forced the mother of such a family to seek work outside or bring it into the home, or we have relieved her of the burden of the support of her children by placing them in public institutions or in other private families. All four methods are ineffectual and costly, and in most instances serve but to add to the misery and degeneracy of those from whom death took their natural protector. For years, the private relief societies have striven to relieve the distress of worthy widows but despite their most valiant efforts such relief had admittedly been inadequate. Thus even in those exceptional cases in which a plan of family rehabilitation can be worked out and put into practice there is not sufficient money to make unnecessary the use of these other makeshifts. As a consequence, society has almost forced the widow to earn sufficient for her children's training at the cost of the home, or to drive from that home the children whom she should train.

All common sense and human sympathy cry out in protest against such a conception. The care given in the asylum may be more hygienic and scientific, but it is not, nor can it ever be, better than the care of the average mother. Although always part of our previous conception of American life this axiom was formulated as recently as 1910 at the National Conference on Dependent Children summoned at Washington by President Theodore Roosevelt.

Home Care

> Home life is the highest and finest product of civilization. It is the great molding force of mind and of character. Children should not be deprived of it except for urgent and compelling reasons. Children of parents of worthy character, suffering from temporary misfortune and children of reasonably efficient and deserving mothers who are without the support of the normal breadwinner, should, as a rule, be kept with their parents, such aid being given as may be necessary to maintain suitable homes for the rearing of the children.

The Home the Best Institution

Without in any way discrediting the splendid work of our present child-caring institutions, we believe that every mother who is a proper moral guardian must, as a right and as a duty, be given the care of her own children, and that only under her care can they receive that training which will best develop their character.

Serious charges have been made against the asylums in that the graduates become criminals and dependents in later life. No proof is available to substantiate any such claim and the Commission does not believe it true. But that there is a serious impairment to the normal development of the child brought up in an institution cannot be doubted.

The Ohio Commission reported: "The institution usually does not develop the child's individuality nor give him the sort of training needed to fit him for the province of life outside the institution. There is a tendency to institutionalize the child."

Pensions a Forward Step

Despite the ever-weakening protests of the private charities, the administration of Mothers' Pension is entirely different than that of public relief. The difference lies in the new note of adequate treatment and the emphasis placed on the development of the child. Because of this these pensions have developed a new standard of constructive rehabilitation that included all the more modern ideals of social work and far surpasses the ordinary type of charity both public and private.

The fear of pauperizing the needy by giving them money has proven in most instances without foundation; the dangers of giving inadequate relief have come to be recognized as a far greater evil. But organized charity has been unable to raise funds sufficiently large to permit their meeting this higher standard of adequacy in any appreciable number of families. The rest must be content with aid that is insufficient for their needs, and the widowed mother must supplement it by her own earnings. Thus again she must work either in or out of her house to the detriment of the family's health and well-being.

IV

Few observers had a keener sense of the plight of the immigrant than Jane Addams. She stood well above her fellow-reformers in her ability to empathize with the newcomers. Not surprisingly, she perceived and articulated more clearly than anyone else the protective quality of the ghetto. Addams was first awakened to social action when visiting England and, like Robert Woods, put the principles she had discovered into practice here. In 1899 she moved into Hull House. From this vantage point she learned in intimate detail about ghetto conditions. Especially insightful was her analysis of the role of the ward boss. Addams made it quite clear that unless the state took greater responsibility for the welfare of the immigrant, no one would shake the hold of the local boss, the alderman.

WHY THE WARD BOSS RULES, 1892

JANE ADDAMS

Primitive people, such as the south Italian peasants who live in the Nineteenth Ward, deep down in their heart admire nothing so much as the good man. The successful candidate must be a good man according to the standards of his constituents.

He must not attempt to hold up a morality beyond them, nor must he attempt to reform or change the standard. Anyone who has lived among poorer people cannot fail to be impressed with their constant kindness to each other; that unfailing response to the needs and distresses of their neighbors. This is their reward for living in the midst of poverty. It seems to such a man entirely fitting that his Alderman should do the same thing on a larger scale—that he should help a constituent out of trouble just because he is in trouble, irrespective of the justice involved.

The Alderman, therefore, bails out his constituents when they are arrested, or says a good word to the police justice when they appear before him for trial; uses his "pull" with the magistrate when they are likely to be fined for a civil misdemeanor, or sees what he can do to "fix up matters" with the state's attorney when the charge is really a serious one.

Because of simple friendliness, the Alderman is expected to pay rent for the hard-pressed tenant when no rent is forthcoming, to find jobs when work is hard to get, to procure and divide among his constituents all the places which he can seize from the City Hall. The Alderman of the Nineteenth Ward at one time made the proud boast that he had two thousand six hundred people in his ward upon the public payroll.

The Alderman may himself be quite sincere in his acts of kindness. In certain stages of moral evolution, a man is incapable of unselfish action the results of which will not benefit some one of his acquaintances. The Alderman gives presents at weddings and christenings. He seizes these days of family festivities for making friends. The Alderman procures passes from the railroads when his constituents wish to visit friends or to attend the funerals of distant relatives; he buys tickets galore for benefit entertainments given for a widow or a consumptive in peculiar distress; he contributes to prizes which are awarded to the handsomest lady or the most popular man. Where anxious relatives are canvassing to secure votes for the two most beautiful children who are being voted upon, he recklessly buys votes from both sides. The moral atmosphere of a bazaar suits him exactly. He murmurs many times, "Never mind; the money all goes to the poor," or, "It is all straight enough if the church gets it."

If the Alderman seizes upon festivities for expressions of his good will, much more does he seize upon periods of sorrow. There is among the poor, who have few social occasions, a great desire for a well-

In *Outlook*, 57 (April 18, 1892): 879–82.

arranged funeral the grade of which almost determines their social standing in the neighborhood. The Alderman saves the very poorest of his constituents from that awful horror of burial by the county; he provides carriages for the poor, who otherwise could not have them; for the more prosperous he sends extra carriages, so that they may invite more friends and have a longer procession; for the most prosperous of all there will be probably only a large "flowerpiece." It may be too much to say that all the relatives and friends who ride in the carriages provided by the Alderman's bounty vote for him, but they are certainly influenced by his kindness, and talk of his virtues during the long hours of the ride back and forth from the suburban cemetery.

Indeed, what headway can the notion of civic purity, of honesty of administration, make against this big manifestation of human friendliness, this stalking survival of village kindness? The notions of the civic reformer are negative and impotent before it. The reformers give themselves over largely to criticisms of the present state of affairs, to writing and talking of what the future must be; but their goodness is not dramatic; it is not even concrete and human.

Last Christmas our Alderman distributed six tons of turkeys, and four or more tons of ducks and geese; but each luckless biped was handed out either by himself or one of his friends with a "Merry Christmas." Inevitably, some families got three or four apiece, but what of that? He had none of the nagging rules of the charitable societies, nor was he ready to declare that, because a man wanted two turkeys for Christmas, he was a scoundrel, who should never be allowed to eat turkey again.

The question does, of course, occur to many minds, "Where does the money come from with which to dramatize so successfully?" The more primitive people accept the truthful statement of its sources without any shock to their moral sense. To their simple minds he gets it "from the rich," and so long as he again gives it out to the poor, as a true Robin Hood, with open hand, they have no objections to offer. The next less primitive people are quite willing to admit that he leads "the gang" in the City Council, and sells out the city franchises; that he makes deals with the franchise-seeking companies; that he guarantees to steer dubious measures through the Council, for which he demands liberal pay; that he is, in short, a successful boodler. Even when they are intelligent enough to complete the circle, and to see that the money comes, not from the pockets of the companies' agents, but from the streetcar fares of people like themselves, it almost seems as if they would rather pay two cents more each time they ride than give up the consciousness that they have a big, warm-hearted friend at court who will stand by them in an emergency. The Alderman is really elected because he is a good friend and neighbor.

If we would hold to our political democracy, some pains must be taken to keep on common ground in our human experiences, and to some solidarity in our ethical conceptions. And if we discover that men of low ideals and corrupt practice are forming popular political standards simply because such men stand by and for and with the people, then nothing remains but to obtain a like sense of identification before we can hope to modify ethical standards.

V

Fully aware of the limits of their influence over immigrants, settlement house workers hoped to make an ally of the public school system. Rather than simply teach basic skills, the school was to inculcate broad American values. This meant an enlarged function for it, and Mary Simkhovitch, of Greenwich House, New York, carefully spelled out the new dimensions.

THE PUBLIC SCHOOL, 1904

MARY SIMKHOVITCH

The picture of education in our national past from which we are only now beginning to emerge, is too vivid to us all to need portrayal. The physical life of the child was developed through work and free play in ample spaces. The varied life of the seasons on the farm, the long walks to school and church, snowballing, swimming in the pond, all these diversions created physical vigor. The intimate knowledge of birds and trees, the solemn moonrise, the hush of the early dawn, these were the calls of nature to the youthful soul deepening its insight. As the boy grew older and work more serious, the variety of training that every day brought to him was indeed manifold. How to plant the garden, get in the hay, build the barn, in fact to know how to meet every difficulty that arose, with efficiency, this is what the discipline of work meant. This method turned out handy men with the adaptability which has made us famous as a nation and which is one of the springs of our economic prosperity. The pleasant hours at singing school, the exciting debate at the academy or lyceum, the church social, the warm winter evening around the fire at home, this was the social life where the ideals of American manhood and womanhood were formed.

If we turn from this picture to New York city life and ask ourselves how far the old methods of education are adequate to deal with new conditions, we find changes so vast that no theory is going to meet those changes adequately. Elements of weakness exist in the methods of dealing with the great immigrant population of New York both by the church and by the home. What the churches do to create high ethical standards is something, but I suppose no one will deny that in the complexity of life in New York, where people move from one place to another so frequently, where it is as easy to go to one church as to another, there is little of that feeling of stability which comes about in a village where everyone knows what everybody else is doing, and where practically everybody has some church connection.

With the home the situation is far more important and difficult.

Originally entitled "The Enlarged Function of the Public School," by Mary Simkhovitch. In *Thirty-First National Conference of Charities and Correction* (Portland, 1904), pp. 471–81, 487.

The home of the great body of New York's residents is the tenement. To be able to make a home in such surroundings is a wonderful work which many thousands have accomplished by dint of perseverence and courage and ability. But by no means all have been able to withstand the disintegrating influences that infest the congested life of New York. The rooms are so small that most of the members of the family prefer to go out rather than stay in. Where then are those pleasant evenings in the home where the man reads, the woman sews, the children play? They have gone, those pleasant evenings, and they are not likely to return. From all over the world New York has gathered in her big household. The habits of the old world soon disappear, the traditions of the past suffer a rude shock, and in the transition from the old to the new, as is inevitable everywhere, great dramatic and disintegrating changes necessarily take place. The old self-reliance is broken down, and a new kind takes its place. The ordinary order of events is often turned upside-down. Where the industrial life of the man is drawing to its close at forty, the child must be impressed into industrial service. The result of these changes is that the old home has disappeared and the new home has not yet come into being.

Where does the child get its physical education? Not on the farm but in the street. Instead of the moonrise and the fragrant walks, the boy goes to the theater for fifteen cents. The older sister cannot comfortably see her young man in the crowded tenement, so she meets him at the corner, and very often he is quite unknown to her mother. The friends of the children are not the friends of the parents. Grandparents and grandchildren cannot speak the same language. It may be that taking it for all in all, it is better that the break between the old and the new is as violent as it is. To bridge it over is perhaps a fanciful dream, but at least this is clear, that there must be some central and unified plan by which the strangers who come to our shores can learn what is good in American ways and ideals and can become as rapidly as possible part of our great national life. That means an ethical plan by which a varied population living under highly specialized economic conditions can gain not only the ground lost in the changes that have taken place from village to city life, but can make use of those changes to create positive values which the village could never have understood. For with all the darker aspects of city life, still there is an opportunity to develop manhood which perhaps country regions can never know. But to accomplish this means the development of a conscious purpose for that end, and not until it is the firm conviction of the majority of the citizens of New York that that is precisely what is the purpose of our educational system can we expect the best results. If the church and the home prove inadequate to supply that physical, social, and ethical training which the village church and home afford, to what then shall we look? The great and increasing interest in settlements, that is in the idea of attacking problems firsthand, of living the life of the neighborhood in order to meet its needs is worthy of notice. The settlement psychology has permeated institutional efforts of all sorts, and an inductive method of dealing with city problems as a whole is very promising. But however important centers for neighborhood improvement, conducted under private enterprise, may be, the settlements themselves are the very first to recognize their own limitations in adequately meeting the social and ethical needs of the communities in which they are situated. One instrument we have at hand is adapted to this purpose admirably. It is our educational system.

The social features of the public school system with which we are more immediately concerned are vacation schools and playgrounds. But let us glance at other ways apart from the round of daily instruction. In 1849 evening schools were first opened. From a small beginning the work of the evening schools was developed till this last year there was an average attendance (only 40 percent of the registered attendance), of 24,912. Special attention has been given to the teaching of English.

It was in 1889 that the free lectures were established. The average attendance at each lecture was about two hundred and fifty. One hundred and seventeen lecture centers are maintained with a lecture staff of five hundred. The subjects covered by the lectures are varied in range. "Physiology and Hygiene," "First Aid to the Injured," "Home Nursing and Care of Children," "The Prevention of Consumption," "Trade Unions, Why They Came, What They Do," "The Street Cleaning Department," Lectures on Shakespeare and Great Writers of the Nineteenth Century, Seven Courses of Lectures on American History, Lectures on Music and Art—these are samples of what this lecture course has undertaken to do. This last year also saw the inauguration of lectures given in Yiddish and in Italian as well as in French. These lectures were, naturally, especially for recently arrived immigrants, and stress was laid upon the rights of a citizen, and the duties of foreigners in their new country.

Other new features carried on are the introduction of baths in the public schools (in 1901). There are however at present only two public school buildings in Greater New York where baths have been installed. The very active use of these baths would certainly indicate the usefulness of their introduction into practically all the schools.

In 1892, libraries were established in the schools in connection with the state. The Department of Health has cooperated with the Department of Education by establishing nurses in the public schools who have greatly brought up the daily attendance by caring for children who have hitherto been excluded principally for eye infection. The nurses have treated pupils both at school and in the homes. The health and morale of the children have been further looked after by the formation of the Public School Athletic League during the past year.

Vacation schools were established by the Board of Education in 1899. These schools lay emphasis upon other features than those of the day school. We find kindergartens, nature study, clay modeling, charcoal drawing, water-coloring, sewing, wood work, iron work, and story telling, the principal features. They serve a double purpose, both caring for the children in the summer and giving them a fresh mental interest, and also indicating where these features can be most satisfactorily introduced into the day school system. The opening of the recreation centers was, perhaps, a more radical departure than the vacation features.

To recover some sort of a center and bond of fellowship and cooperation, under the changed conditions of life in all our cities and many of our smaller towns, and even country places, has been more and more of a social, political, and moral, not to say, human necessity. For it is those populations which have lost, or never have had, their centers of neighborhood and patriotic cooperation, that have been worst prey of the demagogue, the boss, and the machine gang.

Nothing less than the rediscovery of the America that is to be, is demanded by the bewildering cosmopolitanism of large masses of our population. The new birth into the composite citizenship, now so rapidly developing, is costing a travail as perilous to both native and foreign citizens, as it is to the distinctive institutions and polity of American society. To initiate a renaissance of neighborship, that is, the consciousness of, respect for, and the working with each other for the interests common to our homes and the local communities in which we live, has become as insistent as the instinct of self-preservation.

VI

One of the most important programs urged by Progressives was the improvement of the tenement house conditions. Convinced that the physical environment debilitated the poor, ruining their health and corrupting their morality, reformers tried to establish new standards for housing. They urged the construction of "model tenements," and attempted to enact building codes to eliminate the worst abuses. Two leading proponents of this effort were Robert W. Deforest and Lawrence Vieller, and their reports to the New York legislature influenced legislation in both their own state and others. Below is their description of the dangerous conditions in New York.

THE TENEMENT HOUSE PROBLEM, 1903

ROBERT W. DEFOREST
AND LAWRENCE VIELLER

Of all the great social problems of modern times incident to the growth of cities, none is claiming public attention in a greater degree than that of the housing of the working people. Mere housing, however, that is, merely providing shelter, does not solve this problem. It only aggravates it by herding men and women together under conditions which inevitably tend to produce disease and crime. It is only by providing homes for the working people, that is, by providing for them not only shelter, but shelter of such a kind as to protect life and health and to

In *The Tenement House Program*, by Robert W. Deforest and Lawrence Vieller (New York, 1903), vol. i, pp. 3, 6–10.

make family life possible, free from surroundings which tend to immorality, that the evils of crowded city life can be mitigated and overcome. Homes are quite as much needed to make good citizens as to make good men. According as the workingpeople are provided with better or poorer homes will the government, morals, and health of a city be better or worse.

In most cities the housing problem is the problem of the small house rather than of the large tenement. In New York, however, it is the problem of the tenement house—the problem of the five-, six-, or even seven-story building usually on a lot twenty-five feet in width and with as many as three or four families on each floor.

Nothing short of a personal inspection of the great tenement districts of New York can give any adequate realization of the importance of the questions involved—questions affecting not only the health, morality, and welfare of the people living in those districts, but also having a most potent influence upon the political conditions of the whole city and of the entire state. Of the 3,437,202 inhabitants of New York City, 2,372,079, or more than two-thirds, live in tenement houses.

Some knowledge of the prevailing kind of New York tenement house must necessarily precede any consideration of its evils and their remedies. It is known as the "double-decker," "dumbbell" tenement, a type which New York has the unenviable distinction of having invented. It is a type unknown to any other city in America or Europe.

The most serious evils may be grouped as follows:

1. Insufficiency of light and air due to narrow courts or air shafts, undue height, and to the occupation by the building or by adjacent buildings of too great a proportion of lot area.
2. Danger from fire.
3. Lack of separate water closet and washing facilities.
4. Overcrowding.
5. Foul cellars and courts, and other like evils, which may be classed as bad housekeeping.

The tall tenement house, accommodating as many as one hundred to one hundred and fifty persons in one building, extending up six or seven stories into the air, with dark, unventilated rooms, is unknown in London or in any other city of Great Britain. It was first constructed in New York about the year 1879, and with slight modifications has been practically the sole type of building erected since, and is the type of the present day. It is a building usually five or six or even seven stories high, about twenty-five feet wide, and built upon a lot of land of the same width and about one hundred feet deep.

The front apartments generally consist of four rooms each and the rear apartments of three rooms, making altogether fourteen upon each floor, or in a seven-story house eighty-four rooms exclusive of the stores and rooms back of them. Of these fourteen rooms on each floor, only four receive direct light and air from the street or from the small yard at the back of the building. Generally, along each side of the building is what is termed an "air shaft." This shaft is entirely enclosed on four sides, and is, of course, the full height of the building. The ostensible purpose of the shaft is to provide light and air to rooms which get no direct light and air from the street or yard; but as the shafts are narrow and high, being enclosed on all four sides, and without any intake of air at the bottom, these rooms obtain, instead of fresh air and sunshine, foul air and semi-darkness. Nor is this all, these shafts act as conveyors of noise, odors, and disease, and when fire breaks out serve as inflammable flues, often rendering it impossible to save the buildings from destruction.

A family living in such a building pays for four rooms of this kind a rent of from twelve dollars to eighteen dollars a month. Of these four rooms only two are large enough to be deserving of the name of rooms. The front one is generally about 10 feet 6 inches wide by 11 feet 3 inches long; this the family uses as a parlor, and often at night, when the small bedrooms opening upon the air shaft are so close and ill-ventilated that sleep is impossible, mattresses are dragged upon the floor of the parlor, and there the family sleep, all together in one room. In summer the small bedrooms are so hot and stifling that a large part of the tenement house population sleep on the roofs, the sidewalks, and the fire escapes. The other room, the kitchen, is generally the same size as the parlor upon which it opens, and receives all its light and air from the "air shaft." Behind these two rooms are the bedrooms, so called, which are hardly more than closets, being each about 7 feet wide and 8 feet 6 inches long, hardly large enough to contain a bed. These rooms get no light and air whatsoever, except that which comes from the "air shaft."

The tenement house system has become fraught with so much danger to the welfare of the community. The effect upon the city population of the form of congregated living found in our tenement houses is to be seen, not only in its results upon the health of the people, but upon their moral and social condition as well. The public mind is just now especially aroused over the manifestation of one special

form of vice in tenement districts. It is not to be wondered at that vice in various forms should manifest itself in the tenements; the wonder is that there is not more vice in such districts. The tenement districts of New York are places in which thousands of people are living in the smallest space in which it is possible for human beings to exist— crowded together in dark, ill-ventilated rooms, in many of which the sunlight never enters and in most of which fresh air is unknown. They are centers of disease, poverty, vice, and crime, where it is a marvel, not that some children grow up to be thieves, drunkards, and prostitutes, but that so many should ever grow up to be decent and self-respecting. All the conditions which surround childhood, youth, and womanhood in New York's crowded tenement quarters make for unrighteousness. They also make for disease. There is hardly a tenement house in which there has not been at least one case of pulmonary tuberculosis within the last five years, and in some houses there have been as great a number as twenty-two different cases of this terrible disease. From the tenements there comes a stream of sick, helpless people to our hospitals and dispensaries, few of whom are able to afford the luxury of a private physician, and some houses are in such bad sanitary condition that few people can be seriously ill in them and get well; from them also comes a host of paupers and charity seekers. The most terrible of all the features of tenement house life in New York, however, is the indiscriminate herding of all kinds of people in close contact, the fact, that, mingled with the drunken, the dissolute, the improvident, the diseased, dwell the great mass of the respectable workingmen of the city with their families.

SUGGESTIONS FOR
FURTHER READING

The changes that accompanied the rise of the *Department Store* are imaginatively discussed by David Potter, *People of Plenty* (Chicago, 1954). A solid history of one department store is Ralph Hower, *A History of Macy's of New York, 1858–1919* (Cambridge, Mass., 1943). Robert Wiebe's *Search for Order, 1877–1920* (New York, 1967) is a major interpretive essay on the late nineteenth century. A quantitative analysis of social mobility among lower class Americans is Stephan Thernstrom, *Poverty and Progress: Social Mobility in a 19th Century Community* (Cambridge, Mass., 1964).

For a description of the *Company Town* that was Pullman, see Stanley Buder, *Pullman* (New York, 1967). An insightful analysis of the balance of power between management and labor is found in David Brody, *Steelworkers in America* (Cambridge, Mass., 1950).

The ideology of the *New Rich* in later nineteenth-century America is portrayed skillfully in Richard Hofstadter, *Social Darwinism in American Thought* (rev. ed., New York, 1959). The popular mythology of rags to riches is analyzed in Irvin Wyllie, *The Self-Made Man in America* (New Brunswick, N.J., 1954).

A grim but enlightening work of fiction that portrays life in the *Country Town* well is E. W. Howe, *The Story of A Country Town* (Boston, 1884; paperback ed., New York, 1964). For a revisionist interpretation of the business of agriculture see, Alan Bogue, *Money at Interest* (Ithaca, New York, 1955).

On the *Immigrant Ghetto*, begin with Oscar Handlin's powerful *The Uprooted* (Boston, 1951). For understanding more about the experience of poverty in the United States, see David J. Rothman and Sheila M. Rothman, *On Their Own* (Reading, Mass., 1972). A sociological account of the ghetto is offered by Gerald T. Suttles, *The Social Order of the Slum* (Chicago, 1958). The New York experience is recounted in detail by Moses Rischin, *The Promised City: New York Jews, 1870–1914* (Cambridge, Mass., 1962).

The most thorough account of the *Settlement House Movement* is Allen F. Davis, *Spearhead for Reform* (New York, 1967). For the discovery of poverty in the Progressive Era, see Robert Bremner, *From the Depths* (New York, 1966). Roy Lubove, *The Progressives and The Slums* (Pittsburgh, 1962), explores the work of Progressive reformers in one particular area.

One might have expected the architecture of the department stores to be functional, as efficient in design as were the new rules for selling (see the Siegel and Cooper Company regulations, p. 255). Instead, as this illustration of the fountain inside the Siegel and Cooper department stores makes dramatically clear, the forms were monumental and cathedral-like in character. For the department store had a more grandiose purpose than merely to sell goods: It was to bring the blessings of American industry to all people, and thereby guarantee that everyone would unite in celebration of the American system. *The Fountain, Siegel and Cooper Company, New York City, reproduced from the collection of the Library of Congress.*

The concern of the new large-scale manufacturing enterprises to capture a national market led them directly into the business of advertising. The purposes of advertising, as Joseph Appel's memoir makes clear, (see p. 260) were two-fold: to stimulate demand for the product in general, and to encourage sales of the manufacturer's product in particular. Companies therefore gave their products brand names, hoping that consumers would enter the stores and ask for them expressly. This 1898 example of advertising by Proctor and Gamble for Lenox Soap is a good example of the styles of presentation. The tub of water is overflowing with suds; the housewife looks contented with the product. And the next time a woman entered her market to purchase soap, she might remember to ask for the product that "just fits the hand." *Reproduced from the collection of the Library of Congress.*

The concepts of Social Darwinism were spread through the society not only by the writings of social philosophers and the new rich themselves (see the statements of Sumner and Carnegie, pp. 299, 305), but through illustrations of such as this by Currier and Ives. The way to grow rich was to work hard and tend to your business; start from the bottom as a shoeshine boy or newspaper hawker, and someday you will reap the rewards for diligence. The poor, on the other hand, had only themselves to blame for their condition; they had gambled or speculated, looking to make easy money without hard work. The devil, blowing his pipeful of goldmine bubbles, had captured them. Here was a powerful ideology that not only justified the new wealth but taught the poor that failure was their own fault, not that of the system. *Currier and Ives, The Way to Grow Poor; the Way to Grow Rich, 1875, reproduced from the collection of the Library of Congress.*

THE WAY TO GROW POOR. ✳ THE WAY TO GROW RICH.

The degree of dissatisfaction of farmers with their lot in post–Civil War America is apparent in this poster printed by the Grange organizations. "I Pay for All," it declared, with the clear implication that somehow or other, through forces he could only dimly understand, the farmer was not rewarded adequately in turn. His work was central to the society: he fed the cities. Yet others reaped the financial rewards. The Grange, responding to these sentiments, attempted to bring farmers together in economic enterprises and social enterprises as well (see the selections on the Grange Journal and Manual, pp. 339, 341). But it may not have succeeded in either task. *Gift of the Grangers, 1873, reproduced from the collection of the Library of Congress.*

The early history of photography was intimately bound up with the history of poverty. The first outstanding photographers in this country frequently used their skills to awaken public awareness of the plight of the poor. Lewis Hine and Jacob Riis were two notable examples; very self-consciously they entered the slums and the factories to record conditions and to publicize them. Riis, for example, not only wrote about ghetto life (see How the Other Half Lives, p. 360), but also photographed it. And soon newspapers around the country were hiring photo-journalists to emulate this style. This photograph, taken around 1900 for a Detroit newspaper, is one typical result. This scene of a New York street, sarcastically entitled, "End of a Career," could not help but shock and dismay middle-class citizens and provoke them to ameliorative action. *Detroit Photo Company, reproduced from the collection of the Library of Congress.*

No photographer put the skills of his profession to work for reform more diligently or effectively than Lewis Hine. Accepting commissions from various Progressive groups, Hine was particularly interested in the evils of child labor and conditions (just as were Deforest and Veiller, see p. 393). This photograph of the tenement family at work had the express purpose of securing legislation to ban child labor; these children should be doing something else than making garters afternoons and evenings. *Jewish Tenement Workers, New York City, 1912, Lewis Hine, reproduced from the collection of the Library of Congress.*

HOMEWORK DESTROYS
FAMILY LIFE

Keeps the child
from school

Encourages father
to shirk responsibilities

Prevents proper
care of home

Allows unsupervised, greedy
manufacturers and parents
to make a mockery of childhood

WOULD YOU LIKE YOUR CHILD TO GROW UP
HERE OR HERE

With the Hine photographs in hand, Progessives designed posters which were quite reminiscent of those produced by the antislavery societies. But now, instead of using engravings to illustrate their point, reformers relied upon dramatic photographs to convey the same message. *Anti-Tenement Labor poster, Lewis Hine photographer, c. 1910, reproduced from the collection of the Library of Congress.*

"With the mask," announced one prominent Klan leader, "we hide our individuality and sink ourselves into the great sea of Klankraft" (see p.
414). And this photograph of a Klan gathering in West Virginia well documents the point. The members are grouped in formation—an inner ring, and
outer ring, all focused around the cross, with American flags on display. The
Klan members took what comfort they could in their own numbers, and in
their homogeneity. But they could not make the outside world over in their
own image. *Klan Demonstration, Beckley, West Virginia, 1924, reproduced
from the collection of the Library of Congress.*

Life

FEBRUARY 18, 1926 Teaching old Dogs new tricks PRICE 15 CENTS

This 1926 magazine cover, celebrating the new woman, exemplifies her changing public image in the 1920s. This drawing of the new-styled feminist portrays a woman who is anything but a mother in appearance or in action. She is thin, not robust; her legs are showing; she wears makeup and lots of jewelry; and she is dancing gaily and freely, not holding her infant in the nursery. Yes, she is sex-typed, and she appears frivolous. But somehow one also senses that she is more liberated than her predecessors. *Life Magazine cover, February 18, 1926, reproduced from the collection of the Library of Congress.*

The paradox of poverty amid plenty
—this was a recurrent theme among
many of the commentators on the
Great Depression. How was it possible that in a country of such wealth
and resources, people could go hungry? It is this paradox that the
most outstanding photographer of the
1930s, Dorothea Lange, captured. The
fancy billboard proclaims the glories
of comfort and convenience, while the
migrant family camped behind it is
trapped in misery and poverty. *U.S.99,
Kern County California, photograph
by Dorothea Lange, November 1938,
reproduced from the collection of the
Library of Congress.*

The stigma of poverty hardly decreased through the Great Depression.
As the interviews of E.W. Bakke made
clear (see p. 453) the unemployed
remained reluctant to go on relief, to
visit that dreaded office and announce
themselves in need of public support.
Ben Shahn's photograph of the door
of a relief office captures just how
hard it was to cross that threshold.
Indeed, from the stenciled message
on that door (reliefers: you come during these hours only, and not on
Saturday), it seems that once inside
the relief office, the claimants would
not receive very much sympathy, or
very much support. *Relief Office in
London, Ohio, Summer 1938, photograph by Ben Shahn, reproduced
from the collection of the Library of
Congress.*

Our Times, 1920 to the Present

THE KU KLUX KLAN

THE URBAN FAMILY

THE RELIEF OFFICE

THE BLACK GHETTO

THE WOMEN'S LIBERATIONIST
SOCIETIES

THE COUNTERCULTURE

INTRODUCTION

AT THE CLOSE of World War One, the United States stood first among the nations of the world in industrial and military power. Just as our entrance in the War had tipped the balance in favor of the Allies, so, over the next decades, American economic, diplomatic, and military decisions exerted a crucial influence on the course of world affairs. Yet, in many ways, the nation in 1920 was unprepared and unwilling to exercise its new authority. The reluctance to join the League of Nations, to recognize that we had an overwhelming stake in developments in Europe and Asia, was the most dramatic manifestation of this timidity and aloofness. But time quickly proved how impossible it was to maintain this posture. Our insularity, after all, did not protect us from the devastating effects of a worldwide depression in the 1930s; nor did it shield us from the consequences of Hitler's rise to power in Germany and the outbreak of World War Two. Not surprisingly, by 1945 the United States was spearheading the drive to found the United Nations. And over the subsequent decades, for better or for worse, this nation has exercised the leading role in shaping world conditions. In essence, then, our times are marked by the clear emergence of the United States as a superpower.

What has this new status meant to the lives of ordinary citizens? How has the nature of American society changed as a result of this superpower position? The details of war, diplomacy, economic growth, and political development have been well studied and analyzed. But our focus here is different: to trace out some of the implications of this massive change on the home front, to analyze its effects on the institutions that shape the attitudes and realities with which people live.

By 1920, it was abundantly clear that America was a very heterogeneous country, probably more diverse in terms of race, religion, and ethnic composition than any other nation in the world. As political revolution and economic turmoil affected many countries, particularly in Eastern Europe, during 1890–1920, more and more immigrants sought refuge and opportunity here. At first, as we have seen, native-born Americans were confident of their ability to mold this diversity into a common pattern—think back to the optimism of the settlement house movement, for example. But by the 1920s, much of this confidence was shaken. In a sense, the same outlook that kept the nation from joining the League of Nations spilled over into domestic affairs. For the first time, in the 1920s, Americans drastically restricted the number of immigrants allowed into the country. As uncomfortable as Americans were with world leadership, they were equally uncomfortable with the heterogeneous population at home. No organization better illustrates the nature of these fears and uncertainties than the *Ku Klux Klan*. Although many observers insisted that this was a lunatic fringe movement, the KKK cannot be so easily dismissed. Rather, it represented one very important response of the nation to the novelty of racial and ethnic diversity.

By the 1920s, the bureaucratic, impersonal, highly organized, and efficient character of American industrial life was firmly established. Work was in every sense modern. In factories, efficiency experts like Frederick Taylor taught management how to shave seconds off an assembly line sequence in order to maximize production. In offices, rows and rows of typists completed the paper work so necessary to a complicated distribution network of goods and services. Both blue-collar and white-collar workers were cogs in a machine. As work became more routinized, many Americans had to look elsewhere for rewards and satisfactions. It is no coincidence that the 1920s, therefore, witnessed a new intensity in the *urban family*. As the office became more impersonal, family life became more engrossing and vital. New definitions of the role of women, of the place of children, and of the nature of husband-wife relations all emerged. The story of the family in industrial society is not one of decline. To the contrary, it assumed an unprecedented importance. This change must be understood if we are to appreciate the implications of economic change to ordinary Americans.

No single event more dramatically and disturbingly revealed the crucial link between American and world economic conditions than the *Great Depression*. The United States was not some specially blessed and protected nation; it too was prone to all the traumas and turmoil of industrial disturbances. The 1930s were cataclysmic years, and we suffered as much as, maybe even more than, other highly developed nations. For a time, one out of every four workers was unemployed; we had bread lines, Hoovervilles (men sleeping in shacks or river banks and in city parks), and scenes of people rummaging through city dumps for scraps of food. It was unthinkable but nevertheless, terribly real. How did Americans, with their long-entrenched belief in the abundance and special destiny of this country, respond to such grim conditions? In many ways, this was a decade of depression in both senses of the word, economic and psychological. Men and women were down, in body and in spirit. Why was this not a more radical decade? Why did the public on the whole respond to the dislocations so sluggishly? Part of the answer may well rest with the personality of Franklin Roosevelt. He did promise deliverance, and he was believed and trusted. But part of the answer rests also with the personal responses of ordinary Americans to their own troubles. Typically, they blamed themselves, not the system, for their misfortunes. Rather than join together in anger, they remained isolated and apart in shame. So it was a cataclysmic decade in one sense, and a nonradical one in another, and the character of this era is rooted in this paradox.

In many ways, the pressing issues of the 1920s and 1930s re-emerged in new forms in the post-World-War-Two period. In the 1950s and 1960s the black ghetto, rather than the immigrant ghetto, posed the challenge of heterogeneity to the society. Beginning in the 1920s, and in steadily increasing numbers thereafter, blacks left the rural South to migrate to the urban North and West. New York, Chicago, Detroit, Cleveland, and Los Angeles all became centers of black migration; and once again, in ways reminiscent of the immigrant, the *black ghetto* developed within these cities. Could the nation integrate the blacks into the mainstream of American life? Could blacks share, without prejudice, the economic and social advantages that so many other citizens enjoyed? No series of events put this question into a more pressing framework than the riots that swept the black ghettos in the 1960s. The causes and consequences of these riots, the conditions that led the blacks to riot, and the responses of the wider society take us to the root of this issue.

Once again, changes in the family both mirrored and sparked changes in the society. The *women's liberationist societies* made the role of women the focus of concern. Were they carrying responsibilities that denied them the status of persons? Were they another minority group in the nation, as disadvantaged as the blacks or the poor, as much the victims of prejudice? Indeed, there were those who now asked, with unprecedented intensity, whether the family itself was a viable institution in this society. In a novel way, the family became the subject of attack. Was its mode of conduct actually working to the detriment of women, of children, in fact, to the detriment of the public welfare?

The critique of the family was actually part of a larger critique of many institutions in society. The 1960s and 1970s witnessed the emergence of what we might call an intense anti-institutionalism in the *counterculture*. Alienation from institutions became a rallying cry. The worker was alienated from his job, the student from his university, the woman from her family. Fundamental attacks on prisons, hospitals, schools, and corporations all grew stronger. A new drug culture was one symptom of this attack; the commune, another. Having surveyed both the ideology and reality of social institutions in the past, we are in good position to evaluate the nature of this new protest. From what roots does it draw its strength? Does it presage fundamental changes in our society? How novel is it actually? Here the past may well be a useful guide to the future.

Chapter 17

The Ku Klux Klan

THE FIRST Ku Klux Klan organization came into being during Reconstruction. Nervous that the newly freed slaves might become first-class citizens, bands of whites roamed the countryside with the aim of keeping blacks in economic, social, and political subjugation. On the whole, their efforts succeeded all too well. Poll laws and threats of violence kept the blacks away from the ballot box; farm tenancy arrangements kept them in a form of economic serfdom; and they did not dare violate the unwritten codes of segregation. Once the black was safely consigned to second-class citizenship, the KKK organization slowly disappeared.

Not until 1915 did the Klan reappear. In that year, William Simon and some fifteen supporters joined together in Atlanta to try to revive the Klan. Their efforts at first seemed highly idiosyncratic, and they enjoyed little success in recruiting members. By 1918, the ranks had grown slightly, but the Klan was still an obscure group.

Its importance changed dramatically as soon as Edward Clarke and Elizabeth Tyler took over the movement. In quick order, they brought organizational know-how to the Klan. They set up local chapters, linked them to a national office, and, with great skill, made the entire operation a highly profitable one. Members paid ten dollars to join the Klan— four dollars went to the local solicitor, one dollar went to the state Klan organization, fifty cents went to the regional office, and four dollars and fifty cents went to the Atlantic headquarters. Clarke and Tyler themselves may have pocketed as much as three dollars for each new recruit to the Klan. Clarke and Tyler also established the national Klan magazine. They sold subscriptions to the members. They even went into the robe and mask business, again to their profit. Under their supervision, the Klan rolls swelled. At the peak of its strength in the mid-1920s, Klan membership stood at close to two million.

But it was more than organizational skill that accounted for the Klan's growth. Its doctrines and rituals struck a responsive chord in many Americans. To understand the Klan's appeal, one must scrutinize the writings and activities of the organization. Marketing tells part of the story, but not its most important part.

It has long been popular to dismiss the Klan as the last and dying gasp of a group of Southern fanatics who were determined to beat blacks into submission all over again. And this, on the whole, is a comforting interpretation. It makes it seem that racism and violence are not in the mainstream of American life. But it is false comfort. The Klan, like it or not, was not so alien to American traditions. It had much more respectability and power than we might like to think, not only in the South but in the North as well.

The Klan flourished in Texas, and in Illinois and Indiana as well. It had rural appeal, and urban, too. Blue-collar workers joined its ranks, and so did white-collar workers. In Chicago, 39 percent of the Klan members worked in blue-collar occupations; 61 percent were white-collar. In Knoxville, 71 percent were blue-collar, 29 percent white-collar. Moreover, the Klan's message was more complicated than just a preachment of hate. In a society growing increasingly heterogeneous and complex, it elevated the virtues of uniformity and simplicity. The black was only one of its enemies—even more important to the Klan were the Catholics and the Jews. In essence, to comprehend the Klan appeal it is necessary to look beyond antiblack prejudices to the broader issues of immigration and urbanization in twentieth-century America.

The materials that follow explore the character of the Klan appeal. From the writings of one of its presidents, Hiram Evans, to the symbols that the Klan wrapped itself in, to the elaborate initiation rituals that members followed, the selections reveal the Klan's desperate effort to tie itself to American values. Ultimately, it did not succeed. Its rhetorical devotion to God, motherhood, patriotism, loyalty, and white Anglo-saxon superiority in the end could not carry the nation. Most contemporaries finally defined it as a stain on the fabric of the republic, a repudiation of democratic principles. But the battle was not so easily won, and we ought not to minimize the difficulty of the contest.

I

Like all secret societies, the Klan had an elaborate hierarchy of officers, degrees of membership, and initiation rituals. The Klansman's Manual, *reprinted below, spelled out these codes; new members were to learn the mysteries and swear never to reveal them. Clearly the ideals that the Klan set for itself did not match with much of what its members actually did. Nevertheless, if we are to understand the Klan's appeal, the* Manual *is the right starting point. Note how diligently the Klan codes tried to ally themselves with patriotic and Christian symbols and sentiments; note also the great effort to bring drama and excitement into the lives of its members. The organization of Klan leadership into wizards, dragons, and cyclops is part of that story. Finally, note the barely dis-*

*guised appeal to racism and prejudice, all wrapped up in respectable
language and rhetoric.*

KLANSMAN'S MANUAL, 1925

THE ORDER

I. *The Name*

"Knights of the Ku Klux Klan."
"Forever hereafter it shall be known as KNIGHTS OF THE KU
KLUX KLAN."

II. *Its Divisions*

"There shall be four Kloranic Orders of this Order, namely:

1. "The order of citizenship or K-UNO (Probationary)."
2. "Knights Kamellia or K-DUO (Primary Order of Knighthood)."
3. "Knights of the great Forrest or K-TRIO (The Order of American
   Chivalry)."
4. "Knights of the Midnight Mystery or K-QUAD (Superior Order of
   Knighthood and Spiritual Philosophies)."

III. *Its Nature*

1. *Patriotic.* One of the paramount purposes of this order is to
"exemplify a pure patriotism toward our country." Every Klansman
is taught from the beginning of his connection with the movement that
it is his duty "to be patriotic toward our country."

2. *Military.* This characteristic feature applies to its form of organization and its method of operations. It is so organized on a military
plan that the whole power of the whole order, or of any part of it, may
be used in quick, united action for the execution of the purposes of the
order.

3. *Benevolent.* This means that the movement is also committed to
a program of sacrificial service for the benefit of others. As a benevolent
institution, the Knights of the Ku Klux Klan must give itself to the task
of relieving and helping the suffering and distressed, the unfortunate
and oppressed.

4. *Ritualistic.* In common with other orders, the Knights of the Ku
Klux Klan confers ritualistic degrees and obligations, and commits its
grips, signs, words, and other secret work to those persons who so
meet its requirements as to find membership in the order. The ritualistic devices become the ceremonial ties that bind Klansmen to one
another.

5. *Social.* The Knights of the Ku Klux Klan endeavors to unite in
companionable relationship and congenial association those men who
possess the essential qualifications for membership. It is so designed that

In *Klansman's Manual* (n.p., 1925), pp. 9–17, 66–69, 74–81.

kinship of race, belief, spirit, character, and purpose will engender a real, vital, and enduring fellowship among Klansmen.

6. *Fraternal.* The order is designed to be a real brotherhood.

Klansmen have committed themselves to the practice of "Klannishness toward fellow-Klansmen." By this commitment they have agreed to treat one another as brothers. Fraternal love has become the bond of union. And this requires the development of such a spirit of active good will as will impel every Klansman to seek to promote the well-being of his fellow-Klansmen "socially, physically, morally, and vocationally."

IV. *Its Government*

The Constitution provides for and establishes that form of government that will best further the interests of the movement and develop to the highest possible efficiency all of its component elements.

1. *This form of government is military in character.* It will suffice to compare the Klan's form of government to the government of an army. As the United States Army is duly organized with its various officers and troops, so is the Knights of the Ku Klux Klan welded together as an organized force for the fulfillment of its patriotic mission. The Commander-in-Chief is the Imperial Wizard. The Divisional Commanders are the Grand Dragons. The Brigade Commanders are the Great Titans. The Regimental Commanders are the Exalted Cyclops. All of these Commanders have their respective staffs and other subordinate officers and aides.

2. *This form of government is necessary.* (a) For efficient administration: (b) For effectiveness in method and operation: (c) For the preservation of the order.

Fraternal order history records the failure of many patriotic societies that were organized on a so-called democratic basis. Without this feature of the military form of government which is designed to provide efficient leadership, effective discipline, intelligent cooperation, active functioning, uniform methods, and unified operation, quickly responsive to the call to put over the immediate task at hand, even the Knights of the Ku Klux Klan would degenerate into a mere passive, inefficient, social order. The military form of government must and will be preserved for the sake of true, patriotic Americanism, because it is the only form of government that gives any guarantee of success. We must avoid the fate of the other organizations that have split on the rock of democracy.

V. *Its Authority*

Is "Vested primarily in the Imperial Wizard." The organization of the Knights of the Ku Klux Klan provides, and its principle of government demands, that there shall always be *one* individual, senior in rank to all other Klansmen of whatever rank, on whom shall rest the responsibility of command, and whose leadership will be recognized and accepted by all other loyal Klansmen.

To be recognized by all Klansmen. The Constitution is very explicit: "And whose decisions, decrees, edicts, mandates, rulings, and instructions shall be of full authority and unquestionably recognized and respected by each and every citizen of the Invisible Empire."

The whole movement, fraught with its tremendous responsibilities and rich in its magnificent possibilities, makes stirring appeal to red-blooded American manhood. Every Klansman is an important, necessary, and vital factor in the movement. In this crusade there are few occasions for "individual plays." Success is possible only through the most unselfish "playing for the team."

OBJECTS AND PURPOSES (ARTICLE II, THE CONSTITUTION)

I. Mobilization

This is its primary purpose: "To unite white male persons, native-born, Gentile citizens of the United States of America, who owe no allegiance of any nature or degree to any foreign government, nation, institution, sect, ruler, person, or people; whose morals are good; whose reputations and vocations are respectable; whose habits are exemplary; who are of sound minds and eighteen years or more of age, under a common oath into a brotherhood of strict regulations."

II. Cultural

The Knights of the Ku Klux Klan is a movement devoting itself to the needed task of developing a genuine spirit of American patriotism. Klansmen are to be examples of pure patriotism. They are to organize the patriotic sentiment of native-born white, Protestant Americans for the defense of distinctively American institutions. Klansmen are dedicated to the principle that America shall be made American through the promulgation of American doctrines, the dissemination of American ideals, the creation of wholesome American sentiment, the preservation of American institutions.

III. Fraternal

The movement is designed to create a real brotherhood among men who are akin in race, belief, spirit, character, interest, and purpose. The teachings of the order indicate very clearly the attitude and conduct that make for real expression of brotherhood, or, "the practice of Klannishness."

IV. Beneficent

"To relieve the injured and the oppressed; to succor the suffering and unfortunate, especially widows and orphans."

The supreme pattern for all true Klansmen is their Criterion of Character, Jesus Christ, "who went about doing good." The movement accepts the full Christian program of unselfish helpfulness, and will seek to carry it on in the manner commanded by the one Master of Men, Christ Jesus.

V. *Protective*

1. *The Home.* "*To shield the sanctity of the home.*" The American home is fundamental to all that is best in life, in society, in church, and in the nation. It is the most sacred of human institutions. Its sanctity is to be preserved, its interests are to be safeguarded, and its well-being is to be promoted. Every influence that seeks to disrupt the home must itself be destroyed. The Knights of the Ku Klux Klan would protect the home by promoting whatever would make for its stability, its betterment, its safety, and its inviolability.

2. *Womanhood.* The Knights of the Ku Klux Klan declares that it is committed to "the sacred duty of protecting womanhood"; and announces that one of its purposes is "to shield . . . the chastity of womanhood."

The degradation of women is a violation of the sacredness of human personality, a sin against the race, a crime against society, a menace to our country, and a prostitution of all that is best, and noblest, and highest in life. No race, or society, or country, can rise higher than its womanhood.

3. *The Helpless.* "To protect the weak, the innocent, and the defenseless from the indignities, wrongs, and outrages of the lawless, the violent, and the brutal."

Children, the disabled, and other helpless ones are to know the protective, sheltering arms of the Klan.

4. *American Interests.* "To protect and defend the Constitution of the United States of America, and all laws passed in conformity thereto, and to protect the states and the people thereof from all invasion of their right from any source whatsoever."

VI. *Racial*

"To maintain forever white supremacy." "To maintain forever the God-given supremacy of the white race."

Every Klansman has unqualifiedly affirmed that he will "faithfully strive for the eternal maintenance of white supremacy."

OFFENSES AND PENALTIES

I. *Two Classes of Offenses*

"Offenses against this order shall be divided into two classes— major and minor offenses."

II. *Major Offenses*

"Major offenses shall consist of:
1. "*Treason against the United States of America.*"
2. "*Violating the oath of allegiance to this order or any supplementary oath of obligation thereof.*"
3. "*Disrespect of virtuous womanhood.*"

4. *"Violation of the Constitution or laws of this order."*
    (a) By conspiracy:
    (b) Relinquishment or forfeiture of citizenship:
    (c) Support of any foreign power against the United States of America:
    (d) Violating the bylaws of a Klan of this Order.
    (e) Habitual drunkenness:
    (f) Habitual profanity or vulgarity:

5. *Unworthy racial or Klan conduct:* "Being responsible for the polluting of Caucasian blood through miscegenation, or the commission of any act unworthy of a Klansman."

White men must not mix their blood with that of colored or other inferior races.

6. *The repeated commission of a minor offense:* "The repeated commission of a minor offense shall in itself constitute a major offense."

Minor Offenses

1. *Drunkenness.*
2. *Profanity or vulgarity.*
3. *Actions inimical to interests of the order.*
4. *Refusal or failure to obey.*
5. *Refusal or failure to respond.*
6. *Refusal or failure to surrender credentials.*

THE OATH OF ALLEGIANCE

This oath of allegiance is divided into four sections, and will be analyzed section by section.

I. Obedience

Every Klansman, by his own oath, is solemnly and unconditionally pledged:

1. *To obey faithfully the Constitution and laws of the order.*
2. *To conform to all regulations, usages, and requirements of the order.*
3. *To respect and support the Imperial Authority of the order.*
4. *To heed heartily.*
5. *The only qualification:* "I having knowledge of same, Providence alone preventing." This is the only qualification that mitigates in any way the failure of any Klansman to keep any part of this section of the oath of allegiance.

II. Secrecy

1. *The Klansman's pledge of secrecy pertains to all matters connected with the Knights of the Ku Klux Klan.*
    (a) He is sworn to keep solemnly secret the symbols of the order. This means that he will not disclose the signs, words, or grip.

(b) He is solemnly sworn to keep sacredly secret all information that he may receive concerning the order. The alien world is eager to learn all it can of the inner secrets and workings and plans of the organization. The Klansman who is enlightened as to these matters is obligated to keep his information both sacred and secret.

2. *These matters must never be divulged to the alien.* Klansmen must not publish or cause to be published such secret matters to any person in the whole world, except such person be a member of the order in good and regular standing, and not even then unless it be for the best interests of the order.

3. *A true Klansman will resist all enticements to betray.*

(a) He will not sell out. No price is great enough to buy a Klansman's honor.

(b) A true Klansman cannot be flattered into betraying the secrets of the order. He does not yield to wiles and coaxings of any kind.

(c) His resistance is to be unyielding. The true Klansman is a *man* and will not be moved by threats of enemies, or threats of punishment by any person or power whatsoever, or by persecution of any kind. He can be loyal and true in the face of every sort of impending danger. He will not yield his honor even for the price of his safety.

(d) His resistance will be unswerving. He has sworn, "I will die rather than divulge same, so help me God."

III. Fidelity

1. *Every Klansman is solemnly pledged to guard and foster every interest of the order.*

(a) He will protect the order in every respect. He will defend its honor. He will defend its principles.

Every Klansman should be a propagator of the Knights of the Ku Klux Klan, disseminating its principles and promoting its growth.

(b) He will maintain its social cast and dignity. Every Klan should be a body consisting of the best, most honorable, and outstanding men in every community. It is every Klansman's duty to live up to the highest and noblest standards prevailing among men of this character.

2. *Every Klansman must be faithful in fulfilling all obligations to the order.* He has pledged himself to pay promptly all just and legal demands made upon him to defray the expenses of his Klan and of the order, when same are due and called for. He will pay his dues, and will meet such other just demands as may be laid upon him, withholding nothing that rightfully belongs to the order.

3. *Every Klansman will be faithful in preserving peace and harmony in the assemblies of the order.* He will not introduce any disturbing element of any kind. Neither will he be a party to the introduction of any disturbing or insurrectionary matters, either in the assemblies of his Klan or in other gatherings of the order, or among Klansmen in any way whatsoever.

IV. Klannishness

1. *Social:*

(a) A true Klansman will not injure a fellow Klansman. He will not slander him. He will not defraud a Klansman.

2. *Physical:* Every Klansman is pledged to go at any time without hesitation to the assistance or rescue of a Klansman in any way. With uplifted hand, every Klansman has committed himself; "at his call I will answer." The Klansman is sworn to be Klannish toward Klansmen in all things honorable.

3. *Fraternal:*

The True Klansman will not permit his Klan or his order to be injured, either by himself or by others.

4. *Civic and Patriotic:*

(a) Every true Klansman is loyally patriotic. This means he is devoted to:

   (1) The government of the United States of America.
   (2) His state.
   (3) His flag.
   (4) The Constitution of the United States.
   (5) Constitutional laws.
   (6) Law enforcement.

(b) The true Klansman is pledged to absolute devotion to American principles. Before the sacred altar of the Klan, face to face with the Stars and Stripes, and beneath the holy light of the Fiery Cross, he pledged himself in these words; "I swear that I will most zealously and valiantly shield and preserve, by any and all justifiable means and methods, the sacred Constitutional rights and privileges of . . ."

   (1) Free public schools.
   (2) Free speech and free press.
   (3) Separation of church and state.

II

To heighten the mystery and drama of Klan life, the society devoted special attention to symbols: the cross and the flag as well as the robe and the mask. The interpretation of these symbols reveals the very special definition of virtue that the Klan preached. By its own light, the Klan was the defender of law and order, womanhood and brotherhood, selflessness and responsibility. But all this appeal to group solidarity rested on exclusion: whites would band together against blacks, Catholics, Jews, and immigrants. No sentence better illustrates the Klan's retreat from the heterogeneity of American life than its defense of the mask. By hiding our faces, the Klan wrote, "we hide our individuality and sink ourselves into the great sea of Klankraft."

THE SEVEN SYMBOLS OF THE KLAN, 1923

THE CYCLOPS OF TEXAS

In the sublime ceremonies of Klankraft, I take it that we use seven significant symbols, each of which conveys and inculcates a very beautiful lesson, and emphasizes a great Klan principle. They are, in the order of their importance: The Bible, the Cross, the Flag, the Sword, the Water, the Robe, and the Mask.

The Bible

This Book Divine signifies that there is a God. It is a constant reminder that God is our Father, life is our opportunity, and Heaven is our Home. It is a lamp unto our feet, a light unto our pathway, and the *only* sure guide to right living.

In a Klavern you will always find this wonderful Book opened at the twelfth chapter of Romans. This is the most practical and the most complete chapter in the whole Bible on Christian living.

The Cross

This old cross is a symbol of sacrifice and service, and a sign of the Christian religion.

It was once a sign of ignominy, disgrace, and shame; but being bathed in the blood of the lowly Nazarene, it has been transformed into a symbol of Faith, Hope, and Love. It inspired the Crusaders of the Middle Ages in their perilous efforts to rescue the Holy Land from the heathen Turks; and is today being used to rally the forces of Christianity against the ever increasing hoards of anti-Christ, and the enemies of the principles of a pure Americanism.

The Flag

This old flag, purchased by the blood and suffering of American heroes, represents the price paid for American liberties.

Its red is the blood of American heroes that stained a hundred battlefields. Its white symbolizes the purity of American womanhood and the sanctity of American homes. Its blue is but a patch of America's unclouded sky, snatched from the diamond-studded canopy that bends over our native land. Its stars represent an aggregation of undefeated states bound together in an inseparable union.

It has never been trailed in the dust, trampled in the mud, or defeated in battle. It has never led a retreat or been hauled down at the command of an enemy. It is the greatest and most glorious flag that ever floated in a breeze or waved over land or sea.

The Sword

This unsheathed sword of steel is a symbol of law enforcement. It represents the military, or enforcement powers of our government. Its

In *The Imperial Nighthawk*, December 26, 1923, pp. 6–7.

presence on our sacred altar signifies that we, as an organization, are solidly behind every enforcement officer in the land, to "help, aid, and assist in the proper performance of their legal duties."

This sword also signifies that we are set for the defense of our flag and all that it symbolizes, against the attack and invasion of every foreign power, or people in the whole world. We believe in America for Americans, and are sworn to defend it by all justifiable means and methods, from any encroachment whatever.

The Water

This is a symbol of the purity of life and the unity of purpose. With this divinely distilled fluid we have been dedicated and set apart, to the sacred, sublime, and holy principles of Klankraft.

The Robe

We use the robe to signify that we do not judge men by the clothes they wear, and to conceal the difference in our clothing as well as our personality. There are no rich or poor, high or low, in Klankraft. As we look upon a body of Klansmen robed in white we are forcibly reminded that they are on a common level.

This white robe is also a symbol of that robe of righteousness to be worn by the saints in the land of Yet-to-Come. Taking Christ as our criterion of character, and endeavoring to follow His teachings, Klansmen wear this white robe to signify that they desire to put on *that white robe which is the righteousness of Christ.*

The Mask

In the first place it helps to conceal our membership. The secret of our power lies in the secrecy of our membership. We are a great secret service organization to aid the officers of the law and we can do our best work when we are not known to the public.

It is also a symbol of unselfishness. With the mask we hide our individuality and sink ourselves into the great sea of Klankraft.

Who can look upon a multitude of white-robed Klansmen without thinking of the equality and unselfishness of that throng of white robed saints in the Glory Land?

III

The respectability of the Klan as well as its social club character are apparent in this excerpt from a weekly Klan bulletin. The Klan donated flags to schools, and appeared at funerals of its members. Its meetings were addressed by noted politicians and clergymen. It even tried to advertise the products and services of its members. Clearly, in many sections of the country, it was no disgrace to be a Klan member.

KLAN KOMMENT, 1923

At a recent meeting addressed by two members of the Imperial Kloncilium at Kansas City, Mo., and which was attended by ten thousand Klansmen a novel feature was introduced. Powerful searchlights suddenly illuminated a white-robed horseman, on a white steed standing on a hill near the meeting while an airplane bearing a huge fiery cross swooped low above the celebration.

*

A great Klan meeting was held at Clinton, Mo., a few days ago when Senator Zach Harris addressed seventy-five hundred people on the principles of the order. The meeting was under the direction of Clinton Klan, a very progressive organization.

*

Jacksonville Klan, Realm of Florida, is now one of the most active Klans in that section of the country. A few days ago representatives of the Klan called at the Calvary Baptist Church revival tent and expressed appreciation on the part of the order of the work of Evangelist Allen C. Shuler.

Bloxom Klan, Realm of Virginia, a few days ago presented an American flag and a forty-foot flagpole to Bloxom High School. The presentation speech was made by a local minister and the flag was accepted by the principal of the school.

*

Members of the Quincy, Ill., Klan visited Woodlawn Cemetery on the night of May 30 with the fiery cross and American flag. They laid a cross of red carnations on the grave of Virgil Jonhson as hundreds of people watched them.

York Klan Number 1, Realm of Pennsylvania, recently conducted the funeral services of Horace H. Heiney, a prominent and respected citizen and the first member of their Klan to pass on into the empire invisible. At the graveside a committee of Klansmen bore fiery crosses of roses, and one of the members in full regalia, who is a well-known York minister, offered prayer. The services in the cemetery were witnessed by a large number of people.

KLANSMEN SHOULD STOP
AT THE SISSON HOTEL

Klansmen who visit Chicago will make no mistake if they register at the Hotel Sisson, Lake Michigan at Fifty-third Street.

When the Unity League recently published a list of alleged Chicago Klansmen the name of Harry W. Sisson, proprietor of the hotel, appeared upon it.

As a consequence his hotel is boycotted by Jews and Catholics.

In *The Imperial Nighthawk*, June 13, 1923, p. 7.

IV

*The nostalgic, backward-looking character of Klan thought is apparent
in almost every public defense of its activities. There is a yearning
for an older America, for that simpler time when, ostensibly,
Americans were all sturdy, Anglo-Saxon pioneer types. That the
Klan was romanticizing the past, constructing an image that never
coincided with reality, did not weaken the power of this appeal to
many Americans. Indeed, the more unreal and idyllic the picture,
the greater its attractiveness. When Hiram Evans, head of the Klan,
justified its activities for a literate, middle-class audience, he developed this theme in all its splendor.*

THE KLAN: DEFENDER
OF AMERICANISM, 1925

HIRAM EVANS

It is hard to answer criticisms of the Ku Klux Klan directly and categorically, because what the Klan needs is not so much defense as explanation. Most attacks have been deliberately unfair and so misleading
that reply is impossible.

In the case of the Klan that main issue is usually missed because
the men who make the criticisms have lost contact with the deeper
emotions and instincts which, far more than their brains, control the
majority of men. Our "intellectuals," particularly, in the process of
becoming intellectualized, have cramped their emotional perception to
such an extent that they are crippled, like a bird dog that has lost the
sense of smell.

The Klan can be evaluated only by starting from the point of view
of what it means to the average Klansman. The real value of the Klan,
or the real evil, is to be found in the needs, the purposes, and the convictions of the great mass of Americans of the old stock. It is only because the Klan has met these needs and voiced these convictions that
it has won strength.

There is no possibility of trying to prove the soundness of the
Klan position, or of the controlling instincts and beliefs of the common
people of American descent, to any of those who insist on measuring
either by the purely theoretic philosophy of cosmopolitanism: of universal equality in character, social value, and current rights. I will not
attempt to argue about that doctrine. Science does not support it, and
certainly the average American does not believe it. Our attitude toward
the Orientals proves this, no matter what our oral professions may be,
as well as does our treatment of the Negro.

In fact, actual social equality between whites and any other race
is not practised to any important extent anywhere on earth. Facts prove

In *The Forum*, 84 (1925): 802–805, 810, 812, 814.

the idea unworkable. This beautiful philosophy, therefore, the Klan will not argue about. It merely rejects it, as almost all Americans do.

Neither will we argue at all about the questions of white supremacy. We may be intolerant in this, but we will not delude other races into looking forward to privileges that will, in truth, be forever denied. The Klan looks forward to the day when the union of a white person with one of any other race will be illegal in every state of the Union, and when the question of social supremacy will have been settled on a much safer basis than that of racial mongrelization.

We believe that the pioneers who built America bequeathed to their own children a priority right to it, the control of it and of its future, and that no one on earth can claim any part of this inheritance except through our generosity. We believe, too, that the mission of America under Almighty God is to perpetuate and develop just the kind of nation and just the kind of civilization which our forefathers created. Also, we believe that races of men are as distinct as breeds of animals; that any mixture between races of any great divergence is evil; that the American stock, which was bred under highly selective surroundings, has proved its value and should not be mongrelized; that it has automatically and instinctively developed the kind of civilization which is best suited to its own healthy life and growth; and that this cannot safely be changed except by ourselves and along the lines of our own character. Finally, we believe that all foreigners were admitted with the idea, and on the basis of at least an implied understanding, that they would become a part of us, adopt our ideas and ideals, and help in fulfilling our destiny along those lines, but never that they should be permitted to force us to change into anything else. That is the basic idea of the Klan. We hold firmly that America belongs to Americans, and should be kept American.

Plain recognition of facts supports our opposition to the Roman Catholic Church. I have watched with interest the discussion whether the Roman Church is fighting Americanism, but this is another case where facts are more eloquent than any argument. The facts are that the Roman Church has always opposed the fundamental principle of liberty for which America stands. It has made certain compromises, taking advantage of the tolerance we give but which the Roman Church itself denies, and is trying through these compromises to win control of the nation. But it has made no admission that it has abandoned its old position.

Another ground for our opposition to the Roman Catholic Church is that most of its members in this country are aliens, and that the Church not only makes no effort to help them become assimilated to Americanism, but actually works to prevent this and to keep the Catholics as a group apart. It is notable that few of the evils which so often stamp the Catholic in politics are to be found in Catholics of the English and French stocks who have been in this country for generations. It is notable, too, that these evils seldom appear in Catholics who have attended the public schools. But with most of its communicants the Roman Church strongly and only too successfully opposes that united, understanding, homogeneous "group-mind" which is essential to nationhood, *unless it can control that group-mind.*

The Jew the Klan considers a far smaller problem. For one thing, he is confined to a few cities, and is no problem at all to most of the country. For another thing, his exclusiveness, political activities, and refusal to become assimilated are racial rather than religious, based on centuries of persecution. They cannot last long in the atmosphere of free America, and we may expect that with the passage of time the serious aspects of this problem will fade away.

To sum up: The Klan speaks for the plain people of America, who believe in an American nation, built on that unity of mind and spirit which is possible only to an homogeneous people, and growing out of the purposes, spirit, and instincts of our pioneer ancestors. We know that the melting pot has failed; the reasons are unimportant now. We believe that definite steps must now be taken to prevent ours from becoming a mongrel nation, or a milling and distraught mass of opposed groups, in which the mental and spiritual qualities that made America great will be lost forever. Therefore, we oppose all alienism in any form and the excessive liberalism that supports it. We grant to all the right to their own ideas, but we claim the same right for ourselves, and a prior right to control America.

V

The Klan was a highly profitable enterprise for its leaders, and no account of its history should ignore this element. An early (1923) exposé of the Klan traced in painstaking detail just how Edward Clarke and Elizabeth Tyler reaped a whirlwind return from the Klan venture—there was good money to be made even from the sale of blankets with which to cover the Klansman's horse! For all the nostalgia inherent in the Klan's rhetoric, its leaders certainly brought some of the best twentieth-century selling and management techniques to the organization. C. Anderson Wright was in a good position to write the exposé: at one time, he had been a highly placed official of the KKK. But soon, growing disillusioned with the organization, he published this account of it.

THE KU KLUX KLAN EXPOSED, 1923

C. ANDERSON WRIGHT

Hardly had the contract been entered into by the terms of which the association owned jointly by Mrs. Elizabeth Tyler and Edward Young Clarke took over the management of the Invisible Empire, Knights of the Ku Klux Klan, Incorporated, when plans were laid for bringing in profits from every department of the organization.

In *The Ku Klux Klan Exposed,* comp. George Whitehead (n.p., 1923), pp. 14–15.

By the terms of the contract, Mrs. Tyler and Clarke cut up the "donation" or initiation fee in the following manner: the Kleagle (salesman) was alloted four dollars for each new member he brought in; the King Kleagle (sales manager) was to receive one dollar for each new member; the Grand Goblin (district sales manager) was to receive fifty cents. The Southern Publicity Association, known officially in the Klan as the Propagation Department, took a rake-off of three dollars from each initiation fee, and the balance, one dollar and fifty cents, went into the treasury of the Imperial Palace.

The four principal sources of income to Mrs. Tyler and Clarke were as follows:

From memberships, 700,000 in one year at $3 each	$2,100,000
From the manufacture of robes and helmets, total profits	8,400,000
From "Clarke's Canned Spirits"	3,500,000
From the *Searchlight* official organ of the Ku Klux Klan	1,400,000
Add to the above profits from the official printing plant of the Ku Klux Klan operated by Mrs. Tyler and Clarke, which could be counted upon for a yearly revenue of	250,000
Profits from furniture and other equipment for Klaverns or lodge rooms	1,000,000
Dues from 700,000 members at $2	1,400,000
Donations from 150,000 Daughters of the KKK at $3	450,000
Dues from 150,000 Daughters at $2	300,000
Total	$18,800,000

In round figures, then, Mrs. Tyler and Clarke have made about $19,000,000 or $9,500,000 each in a period of one year. I say, $19,000,000 because I have omitted some of the smaller pickings. When one is dealing in millions a mere quarter of a million is very easily overlooked.

I have not taken into account the dues, which amount to $5 minimum a year. The dues may run as high as the local Klan desires, but out of the dues of each member each year must be paid to the powers that be in Atlanta $3. This adds another $2,100,000 to the total given above.

Like the Klectokens or initiation fees, the dues are collected without payment of federal tax.

Coincidental with entering the Ku Klux Klan, every applicant in addition to ten dollars for his initiation fee and five dollars dues must pay fourteen dollars and fifty cents as follows:

1 mask and robe for himself	$6.50
1 robe for his horse	8.00
Total	$14.50

Nobody can become a klansman without purchasing this equipment. The total income from costumes in the last year has been $10,150,000 from the sale of robes, for every member in addition to the robe and helmet for himself must buy a robe for his horse, whether or not he owns a horse. I doubt if more than 50,000 out of the total membership of 700,000 own horses.

The robes and masks are manufactured by the Gate City Manufacturing Company of Atlanta. Clarke publicly has denied any interest in this company, but since his denial it has been shown that it is not a company at all, but an adjunct or branch subsidiary of the Southern Publicity Association owned by Mrs. Elizabeth Tyler and Edward Young Clarke. They make the robes and collect the profit.

The helmet and robe for a klansman cost $1.25 to manufacture and the horse robe cost another $1.25, a total of $2.50 for the outfit. The material is shipped f.o.b. Atlanta, the freight being paid by the local Klans on receipt of shipment. The price above $2.50, therefore, is net profit. It has cost Mrs. Tyler and Clarke $1,750,000 to manufacture the robes for the 700,000 members and horses in the last year. Subtract this amount from the $10,150,000 sales price; a net profit of $8,400,000 is apparent.

Out of the profits that the heads of the Ku Klux Klan have taken from the members in the last year, two residences have been purchased, one has been elaborately improved and enlarged, an Imperial Palace has been bought, and Lanier University has been purchased.

The two residences were bought, one for William Joseph Simmons, the Imperial Emperor, and the other for his chief of staff, Edward Young Clarke.

The residence improved is that of Mrs. Elizabeth Tyler, in the suburbs of Altanta, some twenty miles out on Milltree Road. The improvements have cost many thousands of dollars.

The Imperial Palace, headquarters of the Imperial Wizard and his executive staff, has cost $1,500,000 according to numerous estimates of unprejudiced experts.

VI

One of the earliest and most successful attempts to analyze the power of the Klan's message and ritual was that of John Mecklin, a sociologist, writing in 1927. Mecklin appreciated how the Klan's messages fit so well with the fears and anxieties of many Americans in the 1920s, particularly its appeal to what he called "the petty impotence of the small-town mind." Mecklin may, to a degree, have overemphasized the small-town, Southwestern character of the Klan's membership. But much of what he said is easily generalized to include city dwellers alarmed at the presence of blacks and immigrants on the very edges of their neighborhoods. In all, Mecklin placed the phenomenon of the Klan in the social history of the 1920s. His was an angry and passionate critique, but still very much on the mark.

THE KU KLUX KLAN, 1927

JOHN M. MECKLIN

The student of the Klan finds some curious paradoxes in the solution of which he is apt to go amiss unless he takes into consideration the mental processes of the Americans of the old native stock who compose the rank and file of the Klan membership. To read the newspaper accounts of alleged Klan outrages, such as the whippings of Texas, the un-Christian arraignment of Catholics and Jews by Klan preachers, the childish mummeries of hood and gown, the spectacular initiations in the light of blazing torches, and the solemn nightly parades in the presence of gaping thousands of mystery-loving Americans—to read of these and to listen to the arraignments of the Klan by its enemies inclines one to feel that the members of this order are a curious combination of ferocious cruelty, cowardly vindictiveness, superstitious ignorance, and religious bigotry. On the other hand, when one converses with the members of the Klan he finds them to be conventional Americans, thoroughly human, kind fathers and husbands, hospitable to the stranger, devout in their worship of God, loyal to state and nation, and including in many instances the best citizens of the community. What is the explanation of the apparent contradiction?

By a process of elimination it is possible to demarcate with a fair degree of accuracy the general class from which the Klan draws its members. The twenty millions of Catholics, the twelve millions of Negroes, the two millions and more of Jews, and the twenty millions of foreign-born are automatically excluded from membership by the Klan constitution. Organized labor is not in sympathy with the Klan. The Klan, as might be expected from its policy of opportunism, has on occasion, as in Kansas when it seemed to further Klan interests, championed the cause of labor. But there is little in common between Klan doctrines and those of organized labor. The average Klansman is far more in sympathy with capital than with labor. There are sporadic instances of workers, generally skilled workers, identifying themselves with the Klan, but the Klan has made no great inroad upon labor, skilled or unskilled.

There are undoubtedly many farmers who are members of the Klan. Local Klans have been organized in the agricultural communities in various Southern states and presumably in the North and West. There is every reason to believe, however, that this great reservoir of native Americanism, which has very real affiliations with the Klan, has never been exploited. The explanation lies not in antagonism to the Klan, but rather in the natural difficulties of maintaining effective Klan organization in the country. The Klan is essentially a village and small-town organization. Neither the great city with its hodgepodge of races and

In *The Ku Klux Klan: A Study of the American Mind*, by John M. Mecklin (New York, 1924), pp. 95–109. Copyright 1924 by Harcourt Brace and Company. Reprinted by prmission of Mrs. Hope Mecklin Gordon.

groups nor the country with its isolation lends itself to effective Klan organization.

It would seem, then, that the Klan draws its members chiefly from the descendants of the old American stock living in the villages and small towns of those sections of the country where this old stock has been least disturbed by immigration, on the one hand, and the disruptive effect of industrialism, on the other. As is to be expected, therefore, we find the Klan fairly strong in the South, where the percentage of the old American stock is highest and where it has been left in undisturbed possession of its traditions, in parts of the Middle West, and in states like Oregon.

By far the majority of the native whites of the South are the descendants of the Scotch-Irish who came to America in two great streams during the eighteenth century.

To understand the spread of the Klan in the South one must understand the mental attitudes of this old Scotch-Irish stock in Southern society. They are intensely Protestant. Originally Presbyterians, they are now for the most part members of the Baptist and Methodist communions. The Baptists, the most numerous denomination in the South, with a membership of three and one half millions, are apparently the religious mainstay of the Klan. It is probable that the majority of the Baptist ministers in the small towns and countryside are either secretly or openly sympathetic with the Klan. The Klud, or official chaplain of the Klan, Rev. Caleb Ridley, was a member of the Baptist Association of Atlanta.

It would be a gross injustice to the South to imagine, however, that the prejudices and fears appealed to by Klan leaders are entertained by all members of the community. The intelligentsia of the South, as of other sections, are opposed to the Klan, though they are, of course, a very small minority.

Almost without exception the leaders in the various professions and in business are not in sympathy with the Klan. The strength of the Klan lies in that large, well-meaning, but more or less ignorant and unthinking middle class, whose inflexible loyalty has preserved with uncritical fidelity the traditions of the original American stock. This class is perhaps more in evidence in the South than in any other section of the country. The Klan leaders have been able to play upon their prejudices and unreasoned loyalties with success. The most dangerous weakness in a democracy is the uninformed and unthinking average man.   .

The Klan, however, appeals to other sections as well as to the South. What are the psychological factors, common to the mind of America as a whole, which have paved the way for the national expansion of the Klan? The original Klan was organized by a group of young men in the little village of Pulaski, Tennessee, who had recently returned from the war and found time hanging heavy on their hands. This organization with its mysterious signs, its queer name, its fantastic costume, and its ritual offered some relief from the deadly monotony of small-town life. The same psychological need for escape from the drabness of village and small-town life plays no small part in the appeal of the modern Klan to the average American.

To this large group the appeal of the Klan is almost irresistible. It falls in entirely with their traditional Americanism while offering at the same time through its mystery a means of escape from the wearisome monotony of their daily round. Its cheap moral idealism fills a need not met by business or social and civic life.

It was in this great Southwestern area dominated by orthodox Protestantism that the Klan reached its first peak of success. To understand its remarkable spread we must enter sympathetically into the life of the people. We must realize the appeal of its mystery to imaginations starved by a prosaic and unpoetic environment. We must try to feel as they feel the dramatic interest aroused by the weird costumes, the spectacular initiations beneath the glare of fiery torches, the nightly parades through quiet hamlets where men and women gather from far and near to gaze on this strange apparition. Here was something that broke the deadly monotony of their days, that symbolized the uncharted realm of an Invisible Empire, that fascinated by its appeal to the supernatural. The Klan has learned, as its inveterate enemy, the Roman Catholic Church, learned long ago, the power of the appeal to the spectacular and the mysterious.

The Klan makes a powerful appeal to the petty impotence of the small-town mind. Here we have a curious sidelight upon the psychology of the average man of native American stock who fills the ranks of the Klan. He is tossed about in the hurly-burly of our industrial and so-called democratic society. Under the stress and strain of social competition he is made to realize his essential mediocrity. Here is a large and powerful organization offering to solace his sense of defeat by dubbing him a Knight of the Invisible Empire for the small sum of ten dollars. Surely knighthood was never offered at such a bargain! He joins. He becomes the chosen conservator of American ideals, the keeper of the morals of the community. He receives the label of approved "one hundred percent Americanism." The Klan slogan printed on the outside of its literature is "an urgent call for men." This flatters the pride of the man suffering from the sense of mediocrity and defeat. It stimulates his latent idealism. It offers fantastic possibilities for his dwarfed and starved personality. The appeal is irresistible.

One finds on every page of Klan literature an insistent, imperative, and even intolerant demand for like-mindedness. It is, of course, the beliefs and traditions of the old native American stock that are to provide the basis for this like-mindedness.

VII

The ugliest part of the Klan story was its violence. By 1921 the New York World was able to document one hundred fifty-two cases— and they were certain that this was a small fraction of the whole— where the Klan had whipped, hung, or tarred and feathered its victims. By no means were all the victims black. White women and white businessmen also felt the sadistic hand of the Klan. It is easy to imagine how the Klan became a way of settling private feuds. The cases reprinted below from the exposé of the World *are a sample of these activities, particularly in the Southwest. If the full record could be recovered, it would be even more disgraceful. Ultimately, a rhetoric that pandered to people's fears led, predictably, to shameful and brutal actions.*

KLAN VIOLENCE, 1921

March 13, 1921, Houston, Texas
J. Lafayette Cockrell, Negro dentist, irreparably mutilated by masked men.

March 17, 1921, Houston, Texas
A. V. Hopkins, prominent businessman, kidnapped, taken to point outside city, whipped, and warned to leave city. He left town next day. Hopkins was called from a business meeting by his assailants.

April 2, 1921, Dallas, Texas
Masked men seized Alexander Johnson, Negro, alleged to have been found in a white woman's room. Horsewhipped him, branded symbols of the KKK in his forehead as a warning to other Negroes.

April 10, 1921, Webster, Texas
Gus Beck, stockman, beaten by masked men.

April 10, 1921, Houston, Texas
J. S. Allen, Houston attorney, taken from crowded downtown street into the country and given coat of tar and feathers. He was then returned to the city and dumped from an automobile in the middle of the business section. Nude, except for tar and feathers.

April 15, 1921, Dallas, Texas
Bill Harris, Negro bellboy, kidnapped and taken from town into woods, where he received a severe beating from masked Klansmen and was told to keep quiet, and did so. Harris was accused of insulting a white woman.

June 10, 1921, Shreveport, Louisiana
A number of propaganda spreaders of the National Association for the Advancement of Colored People, fresh from Tulsa, Oklahoma, were run out of Shreveport, Louisiana by the Ku Klux Klan.

June 14, 1921, Houston, Texas
J. W. Boyd, attorney, whipped by masked men.

In *New York World*, September 19, 1921.

June 16, 1921, Dallas, Texas

Well-known citizen whose name was not published received the following notice signed KKK: "It is suggested that the climate of Texas is unhealthy for a man of your character." That was all. After the recipient investigated and learned the letter was genuine he thought it was enough. He departed at once for Arizona.

June 17, 1921, Bolton, Texas

John Colling, Negro, kidnapped and taken into country, severely flogged by masked men and told to leave the city. A placard was fastened on his back which read: "Whipped by KKK." The Negro had been in jail charged with having insulted a white woman. The grand jury failed to indict him.

December 16, 1921, Ocoen, Orange County, Florida

Walter F. White, Associate Secretary of the National Association for the Advancement of Colored People, said that personal investigation of the election riots there convinced him thirty-two to thirty-five Negroes were killed. He charged that the Ku Klux Klan had given warning before the election that if Negroes tried to vote there would be trouble.

June 12, 1921, Daytona, Florida

As a result of the open defiance of the Knights of the Ku Klux Klan, threats were made through the mails to editor H. C. Sparkman of the *Journal* that the Klan would deal with his case and intimating that he was in danger of bodily harm, perhaps death at their hands.

July 8, 1921, Pensacola, Florida

Night of July eighth, white-robed masked men drove up to the restaurant owned by Chris Lochas, a Greek, and in the presence of the Chief of Police of the city handed him this warning: "You are an undesirable citizen, you violate federal Prohibition laws, the laws of decency, and are a running sore of society. Several trains are leaving Pensacola daily. Take your choice, but do not take too much time. Sincerely, in earnest."

July 12, 1921, Enid, Oklahoma

Walter Billings, movie operator, whipped and given coat of cotton and crude oil.

July 14, 1921, Wichita Falls, Texas

D. E. Donnelly brought to this city and placed in jail after threats were made to lynch him at Burkburnett, where he was accused by his two daughters of attacking them. Donnelly said he received a Klan letter warning him.

July 11, 1921, Greenville, Texas

Matt Glisen, Negro, removed from jail before crowd of one hundred masked men gathered and demanded prisoner. He is accused of killing

Orbie Standlee, a white farmer. The attempt to lynch him was not made until the Negro's trial was postponed.

July 16, 1921, Bay City, Texas

W. H. Hoopingarner, former bank cashier, recently tarred and feathered and forced to leave town.

July 16, 1921, Beaumont, Texas

R. F. Scott of Doweyville, who was a marine during the war, was badly beaten, tarred, feathered, and dumped into the business section at ten o'clock at night. (This case was also officially acknowledged by the Beaumont Lodge of the Ku Klux Klan, Inc. as shown yesterday in the *World*.)

July 16, 1921, Tencha, Texas

Mrs. Beulah Johnson was taken from the porch of a hotel, stripped, tarred, and feathered. The attack was said to have been made by masked men wearing white uniforms. They drove up to the hotel in three automobiles, filed out, displaying firearms, and took the young woman into one of the cars. The automobiles proceeded to a point several miles into the country, where Mrs. Johnson's clothing was removed and she received a coat of tar and feathers. She was then placed in the automobile and returned to town. Mrs. Johnson reported she was working at the hotel as a maid. She says she did not know any of the men. The woman was taken to jail the next day and is being held to the next grand jury on a charge of bigamy. Mrs. Johnson was out on bond and was surrendered by bondsmen after the tarring. According to information in the hands of Sheriff Smith, Mrs. Johnson had been married three times. Her first husband being dead, while the two others are living.

Chapter 18

The Urban Family

DURING THE 1920s, a series of changes that had been slowly and often imperceptibly altering the nature of family life became highly visible. Since the 1890s, new styles of child rearing, new expectations about the proper role for women, new definitions of the ideal relationship between husbands and wives had been taking hold. It was only in the 1920s that Americans fully recognized the character of these changes, and proceeded to analyze, debate, and defend them. The ideals and practices that marked family life in this decade persisted right through the World War Two era. The 1920s firmly established the traditions and styles that women's liberation societies would attack so vigorously in the 1960s and 1970s.

The first, and perhaps most important, distinguishing characteristic of the new family style was its focus on affection. A cult of romantic love affected courtship and marriage. The pop songs of the decade spread the message:

> It had to be you,
> It had to be you.
> I wandered around and finally found
> The Somebody who . . .
> It had to be you, wonderful you.

Now, for the first time, the woman's sexuality was not only frankly recognized but celebrated. She became more of a wife-companion than a mother. In magazine and newspaper advertisements in the 1890s, the woman typically appeared in maternal poses, holding her children close. In the 1920s, she appeared, slim and attractive, arm-in-arm with her husband. It is no coincidence that in this decade women put on cosmetics, and the beauty parlor business began to boom.

One implication of this cult of romantic love was to place new demands upon marriage. If the relationship was not fully satisfying and all-encompassing, it should be ended. Thus, during the 1920s, divorce became not only a legal but also a socially acceptable practice. If this one marriage was not all that it should be, both partners ought to have the right to begin another. Another product of the definition of wife as companion was to put a new premium on better education for women. The number attending college rose dramatically—but the goal was not so much to use education for career advancement, but to make wives more intelligent friends for their husbands. Indeed, a curious ambivalence characterized middle-class and upper-class women's attitudes toward work. For some, albeit a minority, the opportunity to pursue a career meant the chance for self-expression. But for most others, the family, not the office, remained the focus of their energies. The household still set the boundaries of their lives.

New ideas about women and the family also encouraged the use of contraception. During this period family size, especially among urban residents, shrank. This change reflected both the availability of effective methods of contraception and its respectability. The crusade that Margaret Sanger had launched in the Progressive period to open birth control clinics, to spread the knowledge and techniques of contraception to a wide audience, triumphed in the 1920s. Clinics in cities withstood legal challenges and kept their doors open. Even more important, middle- and upper-class couples made family limitation a standard feature of their lives.

The cult of affection had clear implications for child-rearing procedures. The traditional emphasis on obedience as the primary task of family training gave way to a new concern for emotional well-being. So intense was this dedication to affection that it bred a vigorous counterattack. Psychologist John Watson charged that mothers were smothering their children by fondling and kissing them. His attack was not ignored. The child-rearing tracts of the period reflect his keen concern for keeping feeding and sleeping habits to a regimented schedule. But the very title of the leading child-rearing tract of the 1920s makes clear just how far family styles had moved from the nineteenth century. No earlier tract ever posed such a question as: "Are You Training Your Child To Be Happy?"

There were basic incongruities and contradictions in the ideals set forward in the 1920s for the family in general and for the woman in particular. Could a college-educated woman really find satisfaction within the confines of the home? Could she rest content in the role of companion? Was the best way to train children for life in an adult bureaucratic society to swaddle them in affection? It is curious that just at the moment when American society became more routinized and disciplined in the economic sector, family life became increasingly affectionate. But the paradox may only be a surface one. Perhaps the very impersonal character of public life made it vital that private life grow intense. But the tensions and ambiguities in the 1920s definition of the family still remained. One cannot begin to fathom the present controversies in this area without understanding the full nature of the legacy we received from this period.

I

*One of the most enlightening analyses of the nature of the family in
the 1920s came from the research of two eminent sociologists,
Robert and Helen Lynd. Borrowing from the techniques of anthro-
pology, they studied life in Middletown, USA (really Muncie,
Indiana). On the basis of their interviews and firsthand observations, they were able to perceive and present an intimate picture
of family styles. The selection below focuses on husband-wife
interactions and child-rearing practices. The Lynds make clear
just how the cult of affection transformed these relationships.*

MIDDLETOWN, 1929

ROBERT AND HELEN LYND

In each of Middletown's homes lives a family, consisting usually of
father, mother, and their unmarried children, with occasionally some
other dependents. These family groups are becoming smaller. According
to the Federal Census, which defines a family as one person living alone
or any number of persons, whether related or not, who live together in
one household, Middletown families shrank from an average of 4.6
persons in 1890 to 4.2 in 1900, to 3.9 in 1910, and 3.8 in 1920. Both
the decrease in the number of children and the decline in the custom of
having other dependents in the home are factors in this change.

The country over, a smaller percentage of the population is unmarried today than a generation ago, and in 1920 the city had a smaller
proportion of both males and females single than had either state or
nation.

Marriage consists in a brief ceremonial exchange of verbal pledges
by a man and woman before a duly sanctioned representative of the
group. This ceremony, very largely religious in the nineties, is becoming
increasingly secularized. In 1890, 85 percent of the local marriages
were performed by a religious representative and 13 percent by a secular
agent, while in 1923 those performed by the religious leaders had fallen
to 63 percent, and the secular group had risen to 34 percent.

Informal demands, made by the fluid sentiments of the group,
have apparently altered little since the nineties. Foremost among these
is the demand for romantic love as the only valid basis for marriage.
Theoretically, it is the mysterious attraction of two young people for
each other and that alone that brings about a marriage, and actually
most of Middletown stumbles upon its partners in marriage guided
chiefly by "romance." Middletown adults appear to regard romance in
marriage as something which, like their religion, must be believed in to

From *Middletown* by Robert S. and Helen Merrell Lynd, pp. 131–33, 137–38,
151–52, 522–27. Copyright 1929 by Harcourt Brace Jovanovich, Inc.; copyright
1957 by Robert S. and Helen M. Lynd. Reprinted by permission of the
publisher.

hold society together. Children are assured by their elders that "love" is an unanalyzable mystery that "just happens"—"You'll know when the right one comes along," they are told with a knowing smile. And so young Middletown grows up singing and hearing its fathers sing lustily in their civic clubs such songs as:

> It had to be you,
> It had to be you.
> I wandered around and finally found
> The Somebody who
> Could make me true, could make me blue,
> And even glad just to be sad
> Thinking of you.
> Some others I've seen might never be mean,
> Might never be cross, or try to be boss,
> But they wouldn't do,
> *For nobody else gave me a thrill.*
> *With all your faults I love you still.*
> It had to be you, wonderful you,
> It had to be you.

And yet, although theoretically this "thrill" is all-sufficient to insure permanent happiness, actually talks with mothers revealed constantly that, particularly among the business group, they were concerned with certain other factors; the exclusive emphasis upon romantic love makes way as adolescence recedes for a pragmatic calculus. Mothers of the business group give much consideration to encouraging in their children friendships with the "right" people of the other sex, membership in the "right" clubs, deftly warding off the attentions of boys whom they regard it as undesirable for their daughters to "see too much of," and in other ways interfering with and directing the course of true love.

Among the chief qualifications sought by these mothers, beyond the mutual attraction of the two young people for each other, are, in a potential husband, the ability to provide a good living, and, in a wife of the business class, the ability, not only to "make a home" for her husband and children, but to set them in a secure social position. In a world dominated by credit this social function of the wife becomes, among the business group, more subtle and important; the emphasis upon it shades down as we descend in the social scale until among the rank and file of the working class the traditional ability to be a good cook and housekeeper ranks first.

"Woman," as Dorothy Dix [writer of an advice column in Middletown's daily newspaper] says,

> makes the family's social status. . . . The old idea used to be that the way for a woman to help her husband was by being thrifty and industrious, by . . . peeling the potatoes a little thinner, and . . . making over her old hats and frocks. . . . But the woman who makes of herself nothing but a domestic drudge . . . is not a help to her husband. She is a hindrance . . . and . . . a man's wife is the show window where he exhibits the measure of his achievement. . . . The biggest deals are put across over luncheon tables; . . . we meet at dinner the people who can push our fortunes. . . . The woman who cultivates a circle of worthwhile people, who belongs to clubs, who makes herself interesting and agreeable . . . is a help to her husband. . . .

Not unrelated to this social skill desired in a wife is the importance of good looks and dress for a woman. In one of Marion Harland's *Talks*, so popular in Middletown in the nineties, one reads, "Who would banish from our midst the matronly figures so suggestive of home, comfort, and motherly love?" Today one cannot pick up a magazine in Middletown without seeing in advertisements of everything from gluten bread to reducing tablets instructions for banishing the matronly figure and restoring "youthful beauty." Beauty parlors were unknown in the county-seat of the nineties; there are seven in Middletown today.

Middletown husbands, when talking frankly among themselves, are likely to speak of women as creatures purer and morally better than men but as relatively impractical, emotional, unstable, given to prejudice, easily hurt, and largely incapable of facing facts or doing hard thinking. A school official, approached regarding the possibility of getting a woman on the school board, replied that "with only three people on the board there isn't much place for a woman."

One of the commonest joint pursuits of husbands and wives is playing cards with friends. A few read aloud together, but this is relatively rare, as literature and art have tended to disappear today as male interests. More usual is the situation described by one prominent woman: "My husband never reads anything but newspapers or the *American Magazine*. He is very busy all day and when he gets home at night he just settles down with the paper and his cigar and the radio and just rests." The automobile appears to be an important agency in bringing husbands and wives together in their leisure, counteracting in part the centrifugal tendency in the family observable in certain other aspects of Middletown's life.

Among the working class, leisure activities and other relations between married couples seem to swing about a somewhat shorter tether than do those of business folk. Not infrequently husband and wife meet each other at the end of a day's work too tired or inert to play or go anywhere together; many of them have few if any close friends.

Traditionally this institution of marriage is indissoluble. But the trend toward secularization noted in the performance of the marriage ceremony appears even more clearly in the increased lifting of the taboo upon the dissolution of marriage. With an increase, between 1890 and 1920, of 87 percent in the population of the county in which Middletown is located, the number of recorded divorces for the four years 1921–24 has increased 622 percent over the number of divorces in the county in the four years 1889–92. There were nine divorces for each one hundred marriage licenses issued in 1889 and eighteen in 1895.

The frequency of divorces and the speed with which they are rushed through have become commonplaces in Middletown. "Anybody with twenty-five dollars can get a divorce" is a commonly heard remark. Or as one recently divorced man phrased it, "Anyone with ten dollars can get a divorce in ten minutes if it isn't contested. All you got to do is to show nonsupport or cruelty and it's a cinch."

Childbearing and child rearing are regarded by Middletown as essential functions of the family. But with increasing regulation of the size of the family, emphasis has shifted somewhat from childbearing to child rearing. The remark of the wife of a prosperous merchant,

"You just can't have so many children now if you want to do for them. We never thought of going to college. Our children never thought of anything else," represents an attitude almost universal today among business-class families and apparently spreading rapidly to the working class.

Child rearing is traditionally conceived by Middletown chiefly in terms of making children conform to the approved ways of the group; a "good" home secures the maximum of conformity; a "bad" home fails to achieve it. But today the swiftly moving environment and multiplied occasion for contacts outside the home are making it more difficult to secure adherence to established group sanctions, and Middletown parents are wont to speak of many of their "problems" as new to this generation, situations for which the formulae of their parents are inadequate. Even from the earliest years of the child's life the former dominance of the home is challenged; the small child spends less time in the home than in the ample days of the nineties. Shrinkage in the size of the yard affords less play space. "Mother, where *can* I play?" wailed a small boy of six, as he was protestingly hauled into a tiny front yard from the enchanting sport of throwing ice at passing autos.

The extensive use of the automobile by the young has enormously extended their mobility and the range of alternatives before them; joining a crowd motoring over to dance in a town twenty miles away may be a matter of a moment's decision, with no one's permission asked. Furthermore, among the high school set, ownership of a car by one's family has become an important criterion of social fitness: a boy almost never takes a girl to a dance except in a car; there are persistent rumors of the buying of a car by local families to help their children's social standing in high school.

The more sophisticated social life of today has brought with it another "problem" much discussed by Middletown parents, the apparently increasing relaxation of some of the traditional prohibitions upon the approaches of boys and girls to each other's persons. Here again new inventions of the last thirty-five years have played a part; in 1890 a "well-brought-up" boy and girl were commonly forbidden to sit together in the dark; but motion pictures and the automobile have lifted this taboo, and, once lifted, it is easy for the practice to become widely extended. Buggy-riding in 1890 allowed only a narrow range of mobility; three to eight were generally accepted hours for riding, and being out after eight-thirty without a chaperon was largely forbidden. In an auto, however, a party may go to a city halfway across the state in an afternoon or evening, and unchaperoned automobile parties as late as midnight, while subject to criticism, are not exceptional. The wide circulation among high school students of magazines of the *True Story* variety and the constant witnessing of "sex films" tend to render familiar postures and episodes taken much less for granted in a period lacking these channels of vivid diffusion.

The following discussion among eighteen high school boys and girls at a young people's meeting in a leading church on the general topic, "What's Wrong with the Home?" reveals the parents perplexity as seen by the children:

Boy: "Parents don't know anything about their children and what they're doing."

Girl: "They don't want to know."

Girl: "We won't let them know."

Boy: "Ours is a speedy world and they're old."

Boy: "Parents ought to get together. Usually one is easy and one is hard. They don't stand together."

Boy: "Parents ought to have a third party to whom they could go for advice." [Chorus of "Yes."]

Boy: "This is the first year I've wanted to dance. Dad wanted me to go to only two this Christmas. [Triumphantly.] I'm going to five and passing up four!"

One shrewd businessman summarized the situation: "These kids aren't pulling the wool over their parents' eyes as much as you may think. The parents are wise to a lot that goes on, but they just don't know what to do, and try to turn their backs on it."

II

The Progressive period witnessed the great triumphs of the feminists. After decades of struggle, they finally did manage to get women the vote. But what happened to the feminist movement after this success? What became of their agitation in the 1920s? In many ways, as the comments by Dorothy Bromley below make clear, women in the 1920s were not especially eager to follow up and extend Progressive styles of agitation into new areas. Rather, they self-consciously differentiated themselves from the older feminists. They were far more comfortable with private, as opposed to public, roles. The legacy of the feminist movement was by no means unimportant to them. But their goals were ultimately different—less political and economic, more personal and individual.

FEMINIST—NEW STYLE, 1927

DOROTHY DUNBAR BROMLEY

Is it not high time that we laid the ghost of the so-called feminist?

"Feminism" has become a term of opprobrium to the modern young woman. For the word suggests the old school of fighting feminists who wore flat heels and had very little feminine charm. Indeed, if a blundering male assumes that a young woman is a feminist simply because she happens to have a job or a profession of her own, she will, be highly— and quite justifiably insulted. Yet she and her kind can hardly be dubbed "old-fashioned" women. What *are* they, then?

In *Harper's Monthly Magazine* 155 (1927): 552–60.

The pioneer feminists were hard-hitting individuals, and the modern young woman admires them for their courage—even while she judges them for their zealotry and their inartistic methods. Furthermore, she pays all honor to them, for they fought her battle. But *she* does not want to wear their mantle, and she has to smile at those women who wear it today.

The constantly increasing group of young women in their twenties and thirties, the truly modern ones, admit that a full life calls for marriage and children as well as a career. These women if they launch upon marriage are keen to make a success of it and an art of child rearing. But *at the same time* they are moved by an inescapable inner compulsion to be individuals in their own right. And in this era of simplified housekeeping they see their opportunity, for it is obvious that a woman who plans intelligently can salvage some time for her own pursuits. Furthermore, they are convinced that they will be better wives and mothers for the breadth they gain from functioning outside the home. In short, they are highly conscious creatures who feel obliged to plumb their own resources to the very depths, despite the fact that they are under no delusions as to the present inferior status of their sex in most fields of endeavor.

Since men must have things pointed out to them in black and white, we beg leave to enunciate the tenets of the modern woman's credo. Let us call her "Feminist—New Style."

First Tenet.   Our modern young woman freely admits that American women have so far achieved but little in the arts, sciences, and professions as compared with men. So far as the arts are concerned, it cannot be stated categorically that women lack creative power, in view of their original work in fiction, poetry, and the plastic arts. As for their status in the professions, it might fairly be claimed that they have scarcely had time to get a running start. And their limited success in business would prove that they have not yet cast off their age-old habit of over-emphasizing detail and, as a consequence, they have not yet learned to grasp the larger issues.

But it remains true that a small percentage of women have proved the capacity, even the creative power of the feminine mind.

Second Tenet.   Why, then, does the modern woman care about a career or a job if she doubts the quality and scope of women's achievement to date? There are three good reasons why she cares immensely: first, she may be of that rare and fortunate breed of persons who find a certain art, science, or profession as inevitable a part of their lives as breathing; second, she may feel the need of a satisfying outlet for her energy whether or no she possesses creative ability; third, she may have no other means of securing her economic independence. And the latter she prizes above all else, for it spells her freedom as an individual, enabling her to marry or not to marry, as she chooses—to terminate a marriage that has become unbearable, and to support and educate her children if necessary.

In brief, Feminist—New Style reasons that if she is economically independent, and if she has, to boot, a vital interest in some work of her own she will have given as few hostages to Fate as it is humanly possible to give. Love may die, and children may grow up, but one's work goes on forever.

Third Tenet. She will not, however, live for her job alone, for she considers that a woman who talks and thinks only shop has just as narrow a horizon as the housewife who talks and thinks only husband and children—perhaps more so, for the latter may have a deeper understanding of human nature. She will therefore refuse to give up all of her personal interests, year in and year out, for the sake of her work. In this respect she no doubt will fall short of the masculine ideal of commercial success, for the simple reason that she has never felt the economic compulsion which drives men on to build up fortunes for the sake of their growing families.

Yet she is not one of the many women who look upon their jobs as tolerable meal tickets or as interesting pastimes to be dropped whenever they may wish. On the contrary, she takes great pride in becoming a vital factor in whatever enterprise she has chosen, and she therefore expects to work long hours when the occasion demands.

Fourth Tenet. Nor has she become hostile to the other sex in the course of her struggle to orient herself. On the contrary, she frankly likes men and is grateful to more than a few for the encouragement and help they have given her.

In the business and professional worlds, for instance, Feminist—New Style has observed that more and more men are coming to accord women as much responsibility as they show themselves able to carry. She and her generation have never found it necessary to bludgeon their way, and she is inclined to think that certain of the pioneers would have got farther if they had relied on their ability rather than on their militant methods. To tell the truth, she enjoys working with men, more than with women, for their methods are more direct and their view larger, and she finds that she can deal with them on a basis of frank comradeship.

Fifth Tenet. By the same corollary, Feminist—New Style professes no loyalty to women *en masse*, although she staunchly believes in individual women. Surveying her sex as a whole, she finds their actions petty, their range of interests narrow, their talk trivial and repetitious. As for those who set themselves up as leaders of the sex, they are either strident creatures of so little ability and balance that they have won no chance to "express themselves" (to use their own hackneyed phrase) in a man-made world; or they are brilliant, restless individuals who too often battle for women's rights for the sake of personal glory.

Sixth Tenet. There is, however, one thing which Feminist—New Style envies Frenchwomen, and that is their sense of "chic." Indeed, she is so far removed from the early feminists that she is altogether baffled by the psychology which led some of them to abjure men in the same voice with which they aped them. Certainly their vanity must have been anaesthetized, she tells herself, as she pictures them with their short hair, so different from her own shingle, and dressed in their unflattering mannish clothes—quite the antithesis of her own boyish effects which are subtly designed to set off feminine charms.

Seventh Tenet.   Empty slogans seem to Feminist—New Style just as bad taste as masculine dress and manners. They serve only to prolong the war between the sexes and to prevent women from learning to think straight. Take these, for instance, "Keep your maiden name." "Come out of the kitchen." "Never darn a sock." After all, what's in a name or in a sock? Madame Curie managed to become one of the world's geniuses even though she suffered the terrible handicap of bearing her husband's name, and it is altogether likely that she darned a sock or two of Monsieur Curie's when there was no servant at hand to do it.

Eighth Tenet.   As for "free love," she thinks that it is impractical rather than immoral. With society organized as it is, the average man and woman cannot carry on a free union with any degree of tranquillity.

Incidentally, she is sick of hearing that modern young women are cheapening themselves by their laxity of morals. As a matter of fact, all those who have done any thinking, and who have any innate refinement, live by an esthetic standard of morals which would make promiscuity inconceivable.

Ninth Tenet.   She readily concedes that a husband and children are necessary to the average woman's fullest development, although she knows well enough that women are endowed with varying degrees of passion and of maternal instinct.

But no matter how much she may desire the sanction of marriage for the sake of having children, she will not take any man who offers. First of all a man must satisfy her as a lover and a companion. And second, he must have the mental and physical traits which she would like her children to inherit.

In fact, it seems to Feminist—New Style that a woman who gratifies her desire to have children without being sure that she can give them a sound heritage and a harminious home environment is unjustifiably selfish. A child should be an end in itself, not merely an extension of the parent's ego, or an object to be loved fiercely and tyrannously; nor should it be a means of keeping a shattered home intact, or of salvaging the health of a woman who is a semi-invalid—even though some doctors are benighted enough to prescribe childbearing as a cure for all ills.

Tenth Tenet.   But even while she admits that a home and children may be necessary to her complete happiness, she will insist upon *more freedom and honesty within the marriage relation.*

She considers that the ordinary middle-class marriage is stifling in that it allows the wife little chance to know other men, and the husband little chance to know other women—except surreptitiously. It seems vital to her that both should have a certain amount of leisure to use exactly as they see fit, without feeling that they have neglected the other.

Finally, Feminist—New Style proclaims that men and children shall no longer circumscribe her world, although they may constitute a large part of it. She is intensely self-conscious whereas the feminists were intensely sex-conscious. Aware of possessing a mind, she takes a keen pleasure in using that mind for some definite purpose; and also in learning to think clearly and cogently against a background of historical and scientific knowledge. She aspires to understand the meaning of the twentieth century as she sees it expressed in the skyscrapers, the rapid pace of city life, the expressionistic drama, the abstract conceptions of art, the new music, the Joycian novel. She knows that it is her American, her twentieth-century birthright to emerge from a creature of instinct into a full-fledged individual who is capable of molding her own life. And in this respect she holds that she is becoming man's equal.

If this be treason, gentlemen, make the most of it.

III

The issue that best exemplified the nature of woman's participation in the wider society was work. Traditionally, it was lower-class women who had to work and who did work—not from any particular desire to advance their own careers, but for the much more mundane and immediate need of keeping family income above subsistence. To a surprising degree, this older pattern had changed by the 1920s. There was now a greater willingness to define work as appropriate for all classes of women. And most dramatically, there was an increase in the number of married women working. The revolution in women's work had begun.

SHALL WE JOIN THE GENTLEMEN? 1926

MARY ROSS

Shall Women Work?

That question is perhaps best answered by the sarcastic laughter which it might well arouse in any but the most dilettante group. Women, by and large, have always worked—as men have—to support themselves and their families. If there is any new consideration on this point, it is the comparative leisure of the middle-class, middle-aged American wives of hard-working husbands.

Perhaps the original query can be more realistically phrased.

Shall Married Women Work for Wages outside Their Homes?

Regardless of the "ought" of the question, married women do, and in growing numbers. Whereas between 1890 and 1920 the proportion of all American women over fifteen "gainfully employed" was increased by 21 percent, the proportion of *married* women working for wages grew 100 percent. Nine married women in every one hundred are now reported by the Census as breadwinners.

In *The Survey,* 57 (December 1, 1926): 263–67.

*Shall We Accept Wage Earning by the Mother as Well as by the
Father as a Normal Condition of Family Life?*

The paid employment of married women is witness of the fact that
the industrial revolution has hit the home.

Farm families, the Department of Agriculture estimates, still produce about a third of the total value of the family's living by their own
labor, and need cash only for the remainder. But the majority of
Americans now are "urban"; they must buy what they need; they must
pay even for sunlight and play space for their children, for the opportunity to live among congenial people in a "nice" neighborhood. It is
this translation of the American family income from one which comes
in terms of the products of the family's own labor, where space and
sunlight and fuel can be taken for granted, to one which must be
measured in cash and what cash will buy, that is driving the women
of the family, who were producing members under the old order, to
adapt themselves to the intricate cogs of the new industrialized society.

A good deal has been said and written of the way in which the
industrial process has undermined the old duties of the housewife,
"robbing" her at once of much productive activity and "freeing" her
from the work which machines can do more surely and accurately.

When you have to *buy* fruit as well as sugar, and pay for the gas
for cooking, why bother to make jam and jelly and preserves? They can
be bought for not a great deal more than the retail cost of ingredients.
Why stew over the spring and fall dressmaking, when for a few dollars
more than the cost of materials and patterns you can get the things
ready-made according to the styles which have been originated by
a specialist? Whichever way you figure it, the greatest part of the outlay
is in cash; the work in the home, by an unspecialized jill-of-all-trades,
brings an almost negligible saving. And so the woman becomes chiefly
a kind of family purchasing agent, with shopping as a major vocation,
saving pennies here and there, adding chiefly in a negative way to the
economic well-being of the family.

An indignant chorus will insist that money is not everything; that
there are intangible values in the constant presence of the "homemaker"
which are not to be measured in cash. Undoubtedly the life of any family
is the richer for the concentration of an interested adult, male or female,
upon the intangibles. But most of us must consider the business of
living before we can afford to think about the art of living. Until money
for essentials, at least, is in sight even the interested homemaker's attention is likely to be concentrated on the petty tangibles of economies
of the cash-and-carry store, dragging the baby along as she shops, rather
than upon the child's recreational needs at that moment.

It is this relentless process of the specialization of modern living,
and its translation into things to be bought, which lies behind the plight
of the would-be middle-class, forcing even married women whose wages
are not essential for mere bread and butter to realize that the family
cannot do without productive work on their part, and that means
specialized work which they can do well enough to be paid for it.

The mounting census statistics of employed married women do not indicate an army of sex-conscious, self-expressing feminists. The woman who knows what she wants to do, and can do it, is as exceptional as the man who has the ability and the opportunity to work in a definite professional field. Most of the women, as most of the men, must muddle along, accepting the best which chance offers, adjusting as best they can to the demands of living and the chances which come.

Such, if I interpret correctly that single comprehensive source of information about working women—the Census—must be the kind of story behind many a woman in that growing army of the gainfully employed. Contrary to popular impression, the large majority (68 percent) of employed women are native-born; almost half of them (43 percent) are of native parentage; the greater number (56 percent) are more than twenty-five years old. While the proportion of employed women has been actually declining among the foreign-born and among Negroes, it proceeds steadily upward among the native-born, particularly in certain occupations, and in many of these the increase of married workers is very much more rapid than that of the women workers as a whole.

During the last decade for which statistics are available, 1910–20, the number of women engaged in agriculture and domestic service decreased by 36 percent and 12 percent while the numbers of married women in these classes declined 46 percent and 3 percent. These are the occupations associated with farm and village life and with the individual home. At the same time, the number of women engaged in manufacturing and mechanical industries increased almost negligibly, .7 percent, but the number of *married* women in this group increased 41 percent; in occupations connected with trade there was an increase of 47 percent for all women and of 88 percent for married women; in professional service the number of all women employed increased 38 percent, and of married women by 62 percent; while in clerical occupations the increase for the whole group was 141 percent; and that for the married women 290 percent.

Analyses by age groups shows that it is to the specialized jobs in the cities, in factories and offices, that the younger women are turning. In clerical work and in professional service women almost equalled the men in numbers in 1920. And it is in just these occupations that the numbers of *married* women are increasing at the most rapid rates. The tendency of American girls in the cities is, apparently, to take specialized jobs and to stay in them, whether by preference or necessity, as they marry, through the years when children or parents must be supported.

In a recent thoughtful paper Dr. Louis I. Dublin points out one factor which is contributing to the increasing entrance of women into outside work. This is education. In 1890 there were 163,000 girls in secondary schools in this country; in 1924, 1,963,000. In 1890 there were 84,00 women in the colleges and normal schools; in 1924, just short of 450,000. Thus during a period in which the population of the United States was not quite doubled, the number of girls in high schools was multiplied by twelve, and the number of girls in colleges and normal schools by more than five. American girls receive as great educational opportunity as do American boys. An increasing number are so trained that a choice is possible between work within and work outside their homes.

Two other factors in the increasing outside occupation of women seem to me at least equally significant: the increasing length of life which the average American, man or woman, has gained during the past half-century, and the declining birthrates and infant and child deathrates. American women have more years of adult life than did their grandmothers, and fewer and healthier children. Taken together, these two facts effect a very material change in the *proportion* of her working life which a woman spends in her unique job of bearing and rearing children.

No "average" experience in the bookkeeping of life can be computed, of course, but it seems fair to suppose that many a grandmother of the present younger American generation spent eight or nine out of twenty adult years in bearing and nursing her children, while her granddaughter is spending perhaps three or four out of forty. Furthermore, there is no such pressing need of a reserve supply of maiden aunts and other useful relatives to bring up other people's motherless children. Indirectly as well as directly, women have been released from this unique task for many years of adult life which may be devoted to other activities.

To the aid of the modern mother there has come also an armament of social resources to help in the upbringing of her children which were unknown a generation ago: the baby health station, the public kindergarten, the public school and its health clinics, the public health nurse, the help of experts in the growth, the behavior, and the needs of children. While in city homes the opportunities for play have been limited, there has passed out of the home into the hands of specialists much responsibility which once was that of the mother alone and unaided.

Hand in hand with the more or less demonstrable increase in the need for women's work away from their families, and their opportunities for it, there is also the force of their changing desires and ideals for their own lives. We have passed, I think, the day of the eager propagandists who chanted the need for "self-expression," the era of the kind of feminists who have been defined as "women who make a fuss about working." In any case, the number of women who were free to choose a type of work for sheer love of it (and the number of men also) has always been negligible. Pounding a typewriter, running a machine, is no less monotonous than the daily dusting and dishwashing. But the office or factory job has the advantage of a social setting, of a touch-and-go companionship with others, a change of scene during the day.

And at the same time, far below any conscious desire for "economic independence" I believe that there is an impulse for partnership in marriage, for the feeling that the man and the woman are working together, both contributing to the support of the family.

The census tides showing the increasing employment of women, and especially of married women, reflect not the results of propaganda or opinion or even, in the large sense, of conscious volition, but the groping of hundreds of thousands of people toward some new alignment of the fundamentals of work, love, and play which will meet the demands which life puts upon them, for themselves and for their families. Such a shift, like all social evolution, is made at the sacrifice of some, at a terrific cost to others. By a process of open-minded inquiry, not in the deceptive light of personal or social prejudice, we must meet one of the most vexing questions of this generation: *Is economic support of the family a normal and continuing part of the lives of women as well as of men?*

IV

Another manifestation of the changing habits of women in the 1920s was the unprecedented attention given to cosmetics and beauty care. Whereas in the nineteenth century the "painted" woman was a disreputable woman, now the use of cosmetics and visits to beauty parlors became commonplace. Some two billion dollars a year was spent on skin care—and cosmetic companies and beauty parlors stood ready to encourage and promote this kind of spending. Some may argue that the new definition of woman as wife-companion was hardly liberating—it simply shifted her responsibility from child care to husband care. More likely, the recognition of the woman as a sexual creature was a crucial step on the road to recognition of woman as a person in her own right.

OUR BOOMING BEAUTY BUSINESS, 1930

PAUL W. WHITE

The average American woman has sixteen square feet of skin. Her dissatisfaction with it—or at least with that portion she exposes to the public gaze—accounts for the expenditure in one year of at least two billion dollars. This enormous cosmetics bill is in excess of the amount spent for millinery, dresses, and jewelry over the same period. Moreover, it surpasses the total budgets of half a dozen states. It represents more than one thousand times the sum spent by the Government on gunpowder and ammunition in a peacetime year. And when editorial writers begin to compare the costs of beauty with the costs of education, they weep public-spirited tears and call on heaven to witness the wretched vanity of Eve's daughters.

Such an attitude is, of course, ridiculous. American women are not yet spending even one-fifth of the amount necessary to improve their appearance. I quote from a public utterance of Elizabeth H. Myers, an accredited member of the Association of Hairdressers and Cosmetologists:

> At least $307 must be spent by every woman every year to keep fit. Women do not realize how important it is to keep fit, nor how much that amount will help them in doing it. Here is an itemized list of the annual beauty needs of every woman: two permanent waves, $20.00; twenty-six shampoos, $26.00; twenty-six special rinses, $13.00; twenty-six haircuts, $13.00; twelve hot oil treatments, $18.00; fifty-two facials, $130.00; twenty-six eyebrow plucks, $13.00; eight eyebrow dyes, $12.00; twenty-six manicures, $19.50; four lipsticks, $4.00; rouge, $10.00; four jars cleansing

In *Outlook and Independent*, 154 (January 22, 1930): 133–35.

cream, $5.00; four jars tissue cream, $5.00; three jars skin food, $3.75; three jars muscle oil, $3.00; four bottles astringent, $6.00; three boxes powder, $6.00—total, $307.25.

The industry is organizing for inevitable growth. Its high priests already are able to toss off statistics with the fluency of a subdivision realtor. In one year, we learn, American women use 4,000 tons of powder and enough lipsticks to reach from Chicago to Los Angeles by way of San Francisco. Likewise there are consumed 52,500 tons of cleansing cream, 26,250 tons of skin lotion, 19,109 tons of complexion soap, 17,500 tons of nourishing cream, 8,750 tons of foundation cream, 6,562 tons of bath powder, and 2,375 tons of rouge.

Let no one think that this urge for beauty is merely a concomitant of the modern era of woman's freedom. It must be admitted, however, that never before in American civilization have the women had as much money to spend as they have today and, accordingly, they are the better able to invest some of their earnings in the beauty shops. For office workers this is due not only to a natural feminine pride but to the realization that youth, or the appearance of it, is a distinct asset and that the grime and dirt encountered in this man's world is not designed to enhance the beauty of that schoolgirl complexion.

So that the industry may expand, those twin gods of contemporary business—advertising and publicity—have been called upon and appropriate financial sacrifices burned before them. Thus the $16,121,297 spent for the national advertising of beauty preparations in 1928 made the cosmetic industry the third largest in volume of magazine advertising.

An important selling point in beauty aids is the use of captivating names. Glancing through one catalogue alone, I find such titles as "Camellia Cream," "Special Texture," "Persian Muscle Oil," "Violet Astringent," "Astringent Cerate," "Vah-Dah Eye Cream," "Mist of Dawn Face Powder," and "Pondre des Perles." Surely here is allure.

One brand of beauty cream, imported from Germany, and exploited as "a triumph in the mysterious realm of the endocrines," is priced at twenty-five dollars for a few ounces. It comes in a fascinating urn which only the most determined woman could resist.

Another kind of advertising is the showroom type best exemplified by a group of the better-known New York beauty specialists who within recent years have moved into sumptuous quarters on or near Fifth Avenue. Movie theaters have been likened in gorgeous verbiage to cathedrals but the display of these salons leaves me wordless. Not so, however, a member of the staff of The Beauty Shop News. In part, he describes the quarters of one of the newer establishments as follows:

> The "Boutique Empire" motif characteristic of the exquisite "Little Shops" of Paris in the days of the First Empire, . . . is retained throughout. The atmosphere of the salon is artistically Gallic in its effect. Touches of rose, blue, green, and gold are used throughout, set off against neutral tones of ivory and gray.

In such surroundings as these women spend hours each week being creamed and patted, oiled and iced. Undergoing a facial massage she relaxes for an hour or two under the expert hands of the operator who smoothes on a cleansing cream; wipes it off with damp pads of cotton; manipulates a nourishing cream or a muscle oil into the skin and, in turn, removes this in the same way. Various astringents and stimulants are used after the cream, and an ice massage often completes the treatment. Completes it, that is, except for the final details of eyebrow shaping, foundation cream, powder, rouge, lipstick, eyeshadow, and mascara.

There are in this country nearly forty thousand beauty shops employing seventy-five thousand men and women, not including those barber shops which cater to women and men. The proprietors of these shops see their customers going to druggists and to toilet goods departments in the larger stores for their supplies and are convinced that something should be done to bring such trade into their own shops. Thus they have organized and created such bodies as The American Master Hairdressers Association, The National Hairdressers and Cosmetologists Association, The National Association of Cosmeticians and Hair Artists, and The American Hairdressers Association.

The aims and ideals of The National Association of Cosmeticians and Hair Artists as set forth in a manifesto are:

> To promote uniform legislation. To bring about a higher standard of skill and education. To educate the public and the members of the profession as to the scope and possibilities of high class service.
>
> We believe that education is necessary if our profession is to win the position it is entitled to. The cosmetician and hair artist of the future must be efficient and thoroughly trained in all branches of the work.
>
> The future will demand greater effort, more self-sacrifice, boundless enthusiasm, and tireless energy if the high standard of our work is to be maintained.

This get-together spirit manifests itself in frequent conventions, exhibitions, and the like. At one of these gatherings, the agenda consisted of contests in permanent, finger, and marcel waving; "educational events"—free lessons in various branches of the art (or shall we cling to "profession?"); exhibits of new machines, new methods, and new ideas, and an entertainment program of music, dancing, and banqueting. Since it is obviously impossible for all the beauty shop employees to attend these conventions, leaving behind a distressed public clamoring at barred doors, there are published such trade journals as *The Western Beauty Shop, The Southern Beauty Shop, The National Beauty Shop, Beauty Culture, The American Hairdresser, The Modern Beauty Shop, The Beautician, Beauty Shop News,* and *The Beauty Journal.* From the pages of these journals, even the stay-at-homes can keep in touch with the latest and most important events in the world of beauty and cosmetics.

The index of one issue of *The Beautician* reveals that the following articles are to be had for the mere turning of the pages: "Coiffure, Complexion, Costume Blend," "Now the Baby Permanent," "The Coiffure Joins the Ensemble," "Beauty Survey Shows Business Trend," "The Sun-Tan Miracle," "The Hair Tells a Story," "Handsome Does as Handsome Is," "This Month's Ten Dollar Idea," "Things New and Noteworthy," and "Match the Mood with Perfume." In addition there is a counter and window display department. There are plentiful illustrations and a full quota of advertising.

V

The affectionate family, as the ideal had it, was a small family, each member intensely involved with the others, parents devoting enormous energy to the emotional well-being of every child. All infants had to be "wanted" infants, otherwise the parents would never be able to make the full and proper investment in their care. Around this argument the proponents of contraception took their stand. Margaret Sanger, the most prominent crusader for birth control, painstakingly detailed the disadvantages of larger families and insisted that all classes, but particularly the poor, ought to heed this message. At first, Sanger met with great opposition—her attack on large families and her support of birth control seemed not only unconventional but immoral. Still, by the 1920s the birth control clinics that she established were flourishing, and the middle classes, at least, had fully accepted the propriety of contraception. A new standard for the family had been established.

WOMEN AND THE NEW RACE, 1920

MARGARET SANGER

The most serious evil of our times is that of encouraging the bringing into the world of large families. The most immoral practice of the day is breeding too many children. The immorality of large families lies not only in their injury to the members of those families but in their injury to society. If one were asked offhand to name the greatest evil of the day one might, in the light of one's education by the newspapers, or by agitators, make any one of a number of replies. One might say prostitution, the oppression of labor, child labor, or war. Yet the poverty and neglect which drives a girl into prostitution usually has its source in a family too large to be properly cared for by the mother, if the girl is not actually subnormal because her mother bore too many children, and, therefore, the more likely to become a prostitute. Labor is oppressed because it is too plentiful; wages go up and conditions improve when labor is scarce. Large families make plentiful labor and they also provide the workers for the child-labor factories as well as the armies of unemployed. That population, swelled by overbreeding, is a basic cause of war. Without the large family, not one of these evils could exist to any considerable extent, much less to the extent that they exist today. The large family—especially the family too large to receive adequate care—is the one thing necessary to the perpetuation of these and other evils and is therefore a greater evil than any one of them.

First of the manifold immoralities involved in the producing of a large family is the outrage upon the womanhood of the mother. If no mother bore children against her will or against her feminine instinct, there would be few large families. The average mother of a baby every year or two has been forced into unwilling motherhood, so far as the later arrivals are concerned. It is not the less immoral when the power which compels enslavement is the church, state, or the propaganda of well-meaning patriots clamoring against "race suicide." The wrong is as great as if the enslaving force were the unbridled passions of her husband. The wrong to the unwilling mother, deprived of her liberty, and all opportunity of self-development, is in itself enough to condemn large families as immoral.

The outrage upon the woman does not end there, however. Excessive childbearing is now recognized by the medical profession as one of the most prolific causes of ill health in women. There are in America hundreds of thousands of women, in good health when they married, who have within a few years become physical wrecks, incapable of mothering their children, incapable of enjoying life.

The effect of the large family upon the father is only less disastrous than it is upon the mother. The spectacle of the young man, happy in health, strength, and the prospect of a joyful love life, makes us smile in sympathy. But this same young man ten years later is likely to present a spectacle as sorry as it is familiar. If he finds that the children come one after another at short intervals—so fast indeed that no matter how hard he works, nor how many hours, he cannot keep pace with their needs—the lover whom all the world loves will have been converted into a disheartened, threadbare incompetent, whom all the world pities or despises. Instead of being the happy, competent father, supporting one or two children as they should be supported, he is the frantic struggler against the burden of five or six, with the tragic prospect of several more. The ranks of the physically weakened, mentally dejected, and spiritually hopeless young fathers of large families attest all too strongly the immorality of the system.

If its effects upon the mother and the wage-earning father were not enough to condemn the large family as an institution, its effects upon the child would make the case against it conclusive. In the United States, some three-hundred thousand children under one year of age die each twelve months. Approximately ninety percent of these deaths are directly or indirectly due to malnutrition, to other diseased conditions resulting from poverty, or to excessive childbearing by the mother.

Many, perhaps, will think it idle to go farther in demonstrating the immorality of large families, but since there is still an abundance of proof at hand, it may be offered for the sake of those who find difficulty in adjusting old-fashioned ideas to the facts. The most merciful thing that the large family does to one of its infant members is to kill it. The same factors which create the terrible infant mortality rate, and which swell the death rate of children between the ages of one and five, operate even more extensively to lower the health rate of the surviving members. Moreover, the overcrowded homes of large families reared in poverty further contribute to this condition. Lack of medical attention is still another factor, so that the child who must struggle for health in competition with other members of a closely packed family has still great difficulties to meet after its poor constitution and malnutrition have been accounted for.

The probability of a child handicapped by a weak constitution, an overcrowded home, inadequate food and care, and possibly a deficient mental equipment, winding up in prison or an almshouse, is too evident for comment. Every jail, hospital for the insane, reformatory, and institution for the feebleminded cries out against the evils of too prolific breeding among wage workers.

We shall see when we come to consider the relation of voluntary motherhood to the rights of labor and to the prevention of war that the large family of the worker makes possible his oppression, and that it also is the chief cause of such human holocausts as the one just closed after the four and a half bloodiest years in history. No such extended consideration is necessary to indicate from what source the young slaves in the child-labor factories come. They come from large impoverished families—from families in which the older children must put their often feeble strength to the task of supporting the younger.

Wage workers and salaried people have a vital interest in the size of the families of those better situated in life. Large families among the rich are immoral not only because they invade the natural right of woman to the control of her own body, to self-development, and to self-expression, but because they are oppressive to the poorer elements of society. If the upper and middle classes of society had kept pace with the poorer elements of society in reproduction during the past fifty years, the working class today would be forced down to the level of the Chinese whose wage standard is said to be a few handfuls of rice a day.

If these considerations are not enough to halt the masculine advocate of large families who reminds us of the days of our mothers and grandmothers, let it be remembered that bearing and rearing six or eight children today is a far different matter from what it was in the generations just preceding. Physically and nervously, the woman of today is not fitted to bear children as frequently as was her mother and her mother's mother. The high tension of modern life and the complicating of woman's everyday existence have doubtless contributed to this result. And who of us can say, until a careful scientific investigation is made, how much the rapid development of tuberculosis and other diseases, even among the well-nurtured, may be due to the depletion of the physical capital of the unborn by the too prolific childbearing of preceding generations of mothers?

Each and every unwanted child is likely to be in some way a social liability. It is only the wanted child who is likely to be a social asset. If we have faith in this intuitive demand of the unfortunate mothers, if we understand both its dire and its hopeful significance, we shall dispose of those social problems which so insistently and menacingly confront us today. For the instinct of maternity to protect its own fruits, the instinct of womanhood to be free to give something besides surplus of children to the world, cannot go astray. The rising generation is always the material of progress, and motherhood is the agency for the improvement and the strengthening and guiding of that generation.

VI

The norms put forward in child-rearing tracts are no sure guide to family practices. One can never be certain that even the best-selling advice book actually caused the reader to adopt its recommendations. Still, our skepticism and caution about the importance of these guidebooks ought not to be complete. For one, it is entirely probable that many families did attempt, with some success, to pattern their child-rearing practices on the advice of the experts. For another, the changing definitions of "right" and "wrong" practices reflect changing priorities among social values. The tract below, published by the Children's Bureau in 1928, summarizes contemporary experts' views on child rearing. Clearly, the ideal of happiness has an importance in twentieth-century tracts that it never had before—and, at the least, one can begin to ponder the causes and implications of these kinds of changes.

ARE YOU TRAINING YOUR CHILD TO BE HAPPY? 1928

Do You Want Your Child To Form Good Habits?

The first time you do something new it is hard.
Next time it is easier.
Next time it is very easy.
Soon you can do it and not think about it at all.
Then we call it a *habit*.
You have learned everything that way.
Your child is learning everything that way.
He is *forming habits*.
He can learn a *good* way to do things.
But he can learn a *bad* way instead.
He learns the way *you* teach him.
Do you want him to form good habits or bad habits?
This lesson will tell you how to teach him good habits.

Begin When He Is Born

Feed him at exactly the same hours every day.
Do not feed him at any other time.
Let him sleep after every feeding.
Do not feed him just because he cries.
Let him wait until the right time.
If you make him wait, his stomach will learn to wait.
His mind will learn that he can not get things by crying.

In *Are You Training Your Child to Be Happy?*, Children's Bureau Publication (Washington, D.C., 1928), pp. 1–3, 11, 13, 23–26.

You do two things for your baby at the same time. You teach his body good habits and you teach his mind good habits.

You Can Teach Him Not To Be a Cross Baby, Too

When he cries, do not pick him up to stop his crying.
See that no pin hurts him.
See that he is warm and dry.
Turn him over.
Then let him alone.
In that way you teach him not to fuss and cry. If mothers pick up their babies when they cry, the babies learn to cry for things. The mothers teach them to cry for things.

Mrs. Guerra and Her Two Babies

Mrs. Guerra had her first baby at home.
A neighbor came in to help her.
The doctor told her to feed the baby every four hours.
The baby cried.
Mrs. Guerra and her friend said, "The baby is hungry; we must feed him."
The baby cried soon again. Mrs. Guerra fed him again.
She fed him many times.
Soon the baby got sick and cross.
His stomach was tired of working.
The mother said, "What is the matter with my baby?"
The baby cried all the time.

Mrs. Guerra had her second baby at the hospital.
The nurses took care of him.
They fed him every four hours.
They bathed him at the same time every day.
They kept him clean and comfortable.
They did not pick him up when he cried.
They knew that babies get exercise when they cry. Babies need exercise.
This baby was well and happy.
The nurses said to Mrs. Guerra, "When you go home, do as we do. Then your baby will be well and happy and good."
Mrs. Guerra went home in two weeks. She did what the nurses told her.
The baby was always good and happy. He was always well.
She said: "I made a mistake before. The nurses are right. Now, I will see what I can do with my big baby to keep him well, too."

Why Do You Punish Your Child?

Do you punish him because *you think* he is naughty and you want to make him good? Are you sure that he is really naughty and not just playing some game or trying to help?

Do you punish him because what he is doing annoys you and you want him to stop?

Do you punish him just to "pay him back" because he has done something naughty?

Do you punish him just because you are tired, and so get angry easily?

These are not good reasons for punishing him.

They are not fair to the child.

They do not make him good.

They do not make him want to be good.

They only teach him to keep out of your way when you are tired or angry.

There is only one good reason to punish a child. That is to make him understand that he must not do the naughty thing again.

But before you punish you must be sure that what he is doing is *really* naughty. It is not naughty for a child to be noisy. It is not naughty for him to want to move about. It is not naughty for him to want to get hold of things.

Children need to move and make a noise. They need to hold things in their hands to find out about them.

Of course they do not need to be *too* noisy. They do not need to be rough. You must stop them if they do these things too much, but you must be very sure they *are* too much before you stop them.

Many times children are punished because their mothers are tired and cross. Is that fair?

When people are tired, little things make them cross. The baby plays with the kitchen pans one day, and his mother is glad. She says, "What a good baby! He plays all alone so nicely!"

Next day mother has done much washing and is very tired. Baby is playing with the pans again; the noise makes her cross. Perhaps she takes the pans away; or perhaps she slaps the baby.

Is that fair? The baby was doing the same today as he was yesterday, when mother said he was good. He was not banging the pans too much.

Did that mother punish because the baby was naughty or because she herself was tired and nervous?

A mother should take time for some rest each day. Then she will not be tired and nervous. Then she will not punish the baby so much.

A mother was whipping her boy very hard. A friend said to her, "Does it do him any good to whip him so hard?"

The mother answered, "Maybe it doesn't do *him* any good, but it does *me* lots of good."

Is that the way we ought to think about punishment?

Children understand that they must be punished when they are naughty. They know when a punishment is fair.

Some punishments are better than others.

Do you spank your child?

Do you scold and scream at him?

Do you shut him in the closet?

Do you keep him from outdoor play?

—*or*—

Do you put him in his room all by himself and shut the door?
Do you send him to bed if he is tired?
Do you pay no attention to him?
Do you refuse to let him have some pleasure or treat?

A wise mother does not need to spank or slap her child very often. She does not shut her child in the closet. She does not scold or scream at him. She does not keep him from outdoor play.

She knows better ways than that.

Perhaps Johnny has not come straight home from school; or perhaps he does not come in when mother calls him. When he does come, she says, "You did not come in on time, so you can not have any dessert tonight."

She does not say, "Tomorrow you cannot go out to play," because she knows Johnny needs to play out in the fresh air. It would be bad for him to go without play, and it would be bad for him to go without fresh air. It will not be bad for him to go without dessert.

Be sure your child is really naughty before you punish him.

Do not expect him to sit still or be quiet all the time. Let him have plenty of outdoor play where he can run and jump and climb.

If you need to punish him, the best way is to take some pleasure or treat away from him, or to leave him in a room by himself and pay no attention to him. He should understand that he must not do the naughty thing again. Do not laugh at him when he is naughty.

Chapter 19

The Relief Office

THE GREAT CRASH of 1929 was unprecedented in the intensity and duration of its effects. No other panic, whether in 1877 or in 1893, persisted for a full decade, and in no other depression were as many as one out of every four workers unemployed. In 1931 and 1932, as the effects of the Depression first became apparent, observers, on the basis of past experience, anticipated rapid improvement—soon the country would return to good times. But by 1933, it was all too clear that this Depression would follow a different course. Over the next six years, every brief improvement in economic conditions was followed by another downturn. Not until the outbreak of World War II did the nation recover from the crash.

The Great Depression made a whole segment of American society poor. The struggle for subsistence suddenly affected lower-middle-class and middle-class families, urban and rural. For the first time, the basic promise of American capitalism seemed broken. Heretofore, middle America could insist that the poor had themselves to blame for their own misery; had they been more hardworking, less addicted to drink, more ambitious and thrifty, they too could have enjoyed abundance and prosperity. The individual, not the system, was at fault. But could such an ideology survive such a cataclysmic event as the Great Depression? Could the assumption that poverty was finally a moral and not an economic failure persist through this decade?

To a surprising degree, the inherited ideology and traditional definition of poverty persisted among the new middle-class victims of economic dislocation. In many ways, they perceived their own fate through the filter of this older perspective. They all too frequently blamed themselves and not the system for their own misfortunes. They retreated into their own private misery, assuming that somehow they had not been equal to the challenge of success. As one result of this outlook, the newly unemployed were loath to apply for public relief.

451

"I would rather die then apply at a relief office," was a refrain common to this decade; and with unrelenting, if ultimately futile, effort, men searched day after day for work, knowing full well in the morning that nothing would turn up by the evening.

To be sure, the federal government during the 1930s for the first time did undertake a massive relief program. Franklin Roosevelt's New Deal included huge expenditures for work relief. Convinced that outright relief, sums simply given to the unemployed, would weaken Americans' moral fiber and corrupt them, Roosevelt successfully urged the administration of work relief programs; these public works projects kept millions of Americans at the job. But invariably, the sums they received were barely enough for subsistence; and given congressional and presidential reluctance to increase federal deficit spending and their desire to keep a balanced budget, the programs could never employ all of the needy. Moreover, those on the WPA rolls were often forced to go off the job after eighteen months, despite the fact that no alternative employment was available to them. In sum, Roosevelt's relief effort was unprecedented in its scope, but it was never able to match the needs of the country.

Still, for all the dislocation, the decade of the 1930s did not witness serious protest on any grand scale, or any real challenges to the capitalist system of the country. Yes, some farmers dumped their milk to protest the lack of financial support, and some of the urban unemployed banded together to picket WPA offices. And a few unions were able to carry out militant strikes and thereby gain recognition. But, on the whole, the 1930s was not a radical decade. For the most part, Americans displayed more lethargy than anger over economic conditions.

Part of this lethargy must be understood in terms of the traditional doctrines about poverty. Despite all kinds of obvious indicators to the contrary, many Americans insisted on faulting themselves for their difficulties. And, to a surprising degree, this sentiment was reinforced both by the media and by the organizations with which they came in contact. Relief offices, for example, typically treated the new poor much as they had treated the old poor: with disdain and little attention to their rights. Social workers, probably all too aware that there was not enough relief money to go round, tried to limit in whatever way they could the benefits that any one family received. And Roosevelt kept insisting that relief at home, as opposed to work relief, was a "dole" and somehow shameful.

Ministers reinforced this attitude. In their view, the Depression was a special challenge to our moral fiber. If Americans turned to the radio or the movies to understand the nature of the Depression, they found escape, not information. Daytime serials told how lust, greed, and envy were responsible for people's misery; they did not mention impersonal economic forces. During this period, the game of *Monopoly* swept the country—what you could not realize in the real world you might find in a fantasy one. Dale Carnegie's *How To Win Friends and Influence People* was a best seller. Its message—the way to success is through a winning personality—had only the most dubious link to the realities of those years.

The materials that follow describe the private misery and the public apathy that was endemic in this decade. They suggest that hard times do not in any simple way provoke or promote radical political action.

I

To men accustomed to working all their adult lives, the effects of unemployment were not only financially but psychologically devastating as well. Their sense of self-esteem, of personal worth, suffered; imagine what it meant in emotional terms for a head of a household to be unable to support his family. Hence, the first and persistent response of the newly unemployed to their plight was to search day after day for a job—any job. That popular image in American minds of the unemployed as a shiftless and lazy lot never really reflected reality. The description below of the response of one of the victims of unemployment to his situation makes clear that the image had no relevance to behavior in the 1930s.

THE UNEMPLOYED WORKER, 1940

E. W. BAKKE

April 19, 1934

Decided to have a go at the State Employment Office. Got there at eight. Fellow I knew sitting on steps. Big sign there "No loitering in the doorway." Janitor or someone came down and asked him to move.

"Are you going upstairs?" he asked. "If you are, go, but don't sit here." The fellow jumped; not looking at the janitor, he began a loud bluster about his father paying taxes to support the place and he could sit on the steps if he wanted to. When the janitor left, he returned to the steps for a moment. Meanwhile a group of people had gathered to see what was going on.

Asked the janitor when the manager would be in. He said, "Nine o'clock." Decided to come back. When I got back, a line had formed clear out into the street. I took my place. Officials and clerks kept coming and had a good cheery word for us as they passed. But after they had gone, many sarcastic remarks followed them like, "Gives you a nice smile, but that's all."

The manager himself drove up before the office a little past nine— appeared sore that there was no parking space in front of the office. The fellows standing outside purposely raised their voices so he could

In *The Unemployed Worker*, by E. W. Bakke (New Haven, 1940), pp. 167–75. Reprinted by permission of the publisher, Yale University Press.

hear and made remarks such as, "Not much use coming here, they never do anything but tell you to come back in sixty days"; "What'd they ever do for me?—Nothing"; "First it was April first, then it was the fifteenth, and now it will be God knows when."

I register, but they say not much chance today; maybe a week from today. I go out. Tony grabs my arm. He says,

> Work?—there is no work. I go to the Employment Office. I stand and wait. Soon—my turn. I give the girl my card. She takes it, turns it over and over in her hand. Bluff—just to take up time. By and by, she gives it back. "Sorry, nothing today." I say, "But I no work in three years, with seven children, what do I eat?" She replied "Come back again, maybe soon there will be something." It is the big bluff.

April 27

Up at seven, cup of coffee, and off to Sargent's. Like to be there when the gang comes to work, the lucky devils. Employment manager not in. Waited in his outer office fitted with six benches and about thirty nearly worn out chairs. Took a bench—looked more likely to stay up. Three others waiting, two reporting for compensation. Other one laid off two weeks ago and said he called at office every day. He inquired what I was doing and when I said "looking for work" he laughed. "You never work here? No? What chance you think you got when four hundred like me who belong here out?" Employment manager showed up at 9:30. I had waited two hours. My time has no value. A pleasant fellow; told me in a kind but snappy way business was very bad. What about the future, would he take my name? Said he referred only to the present. Nothing more for me to say, so left. Two more had drifted into office. Suppose they got the same story. Must be a lot of men in New Haven that have heard it by now.

Down Chestnut Street to Peck Brothers. Thought something might be going there. Since beer bill they have been calling back old employees, might have use for another hand. No real employment office here. From street into a long hall with two offices both with clerks on each side of hall. Picked the wrong one. Smart flapper didn't even speak just tossed her head and thumb in the direction of across the hall. Went across and another girl at an information desk asked if I had ever worked there before. Told her "No." She said no immediate chance then, but I could file an application; but added, "It won't do you no good as there is plenty of our own men to fill the jobs for some time to come." Guess I won't get a job till they've skimmed the cream from their own men. That's proper of course and a good break for them. But if it's like this all over what's the point in applying for jobs? Filled out the application anyway —might as well, didn't have any better way to spend my time. No one else here looking for work.

No heart for any more so dropped into Jake's for a doughnut and a glass of milk and then went home.

April 28

To New Haven Clock Company. Met a company "dick" who said plant was shut down till Monday. Gave me an application blank and said, "You look all right, fill this out in ink. Do it neatly, and they may give you a break. Do you know anybody inside?" I said, "No." Then he shrugs and says, "Well, I don't know if there is much use you sending this in then, but you might try."

In the afternoon went to the park and talked with men, trying to find out what luck they had had. No good news.

May 2

Started out at seven for New Haven Clock Shop. No one in employment office. Lady at information desk asked, "What do you want?" I told her. She wanted to know if I had worked there before and when I said "No," she didn't even ask if I had any experience in clockmaking (which I have). And when I started to tell her so, she cut me off with, "No use—sorry." Suppose she gets tired too.

From Clock Shop to E. Cowells and Co. who make auto equipment. If they want to have old men, well, I worked here in 1916 and 1917. Didn't get to see anyone here because just as you get to the hall there is a big sign "No Help Wanted."

Having heard Seamless Rubber was working quite steady I went down there. Regular employment office furnished with one bench. Another chap, a foreigner, waiting also. In about ten minutes a fellow asked us our business and told us very politely they had no jobs even for skilled men, let alone laborers. No use to tell him I wasn't always a laborer for I never had done the skilled jobs on rubber.

Saw a sign hanging out of one place in gilt letters, "No Help Wanted." In gilt, mind you, as if to make it more permanent.

Then to Bradley-Smith candymakers, where I had also worked before. The first few days I hadn't the heart for more than a couple of tries a morning. I'm getting hardened to the word "No" now, though, and can stick it the most of the morning. Bradley-Smith has no employment office. The telephone switchboard operator is apparently instructed to switch off anyone looking for work, as she made quick work of my question. I notice no one seems to be instructed to find out if we know anything about the business or work. Firms might be passing up some good bets for their force. But apparently that isn't important now.

Walking away, met two friends out going the rounds too. They said it was useless and that they were only looking through force of habit. That's going to be me before long. Even if they hadn't said so, I'm thinking it is useless to run around like this; you just appear ridiculous, and that gets your goat—or would if you kept it up too long. Wish I had some drag with someone on the inside of one of those gates. I expect it's that everyone knows they have to know someone that keeps me from having more company at the employment offices. This is what a former pal of mine who is up at Yale calls "competition in the labor market," I guess. Well, it's a funny competition and with guys you never see.

May 5

Got up at 6:30. Trolleyed to Whitney-Blake Co., makers of telephone wires. Sat on one of six benches for an hour and fifteen minutes to have the employment agent say that he had just laid off some of his own men and that since business was very bad, he could not put me to work. If things get better, it might be different. He told me to keep myself informed by the newspapers, and if I saw that business was picking up to come and see him again. A very pleasant man to talk to, but I have heard his story before.

May 13

Up at 6:30. Walked to Sperry & Barnes, meatpackers. Guard in charge of the gate would not even let me go up to the office because it would be a waste of time.

Down to Schollhorn's, makers of pliers and hardware. Merely a bench in the hall outside the main office. One young man also waiting. After about twenty minutes a young lady walked in and said, "If you are looking for work, there isn't any." When I suggested to the young man that he go along with me to other places, he said there wasn't any use walking around for nothing—that he was going home.

Over to the Ideal Shirt Company. Closed down on account of the strike. Shop not being picketed. Walked into the employment office and asked the clerk for Mr. B. the owner, whom I knew. She said, "Why?" I told her I wanted work. She said I would have to see Mr. B. When I asked her where I could find him she was vague in her answer. Evidently she did not want me to see him.

Walked over to O. B. North's foundry. Found a young man waiting there. Asked him how long he had been waiting, to which he replied, "Long enough, and it looks as though a guy has to wait all morning just to be told there isn't any work." In about ten minutes a very brisk man came in and said there wasn't any help wanted, that he had just laid off some of his own men.

May 21

Interview with sales manager of the Real Silk Hosiery Mills. Had seen their ads for salesmen in the paper. Sales manager approached me with his hand sticking out, the first one who had offered to shake hands with me. I told him my name and inquired about the position. He took me into his private office, well furnished, and asked me if I had had any selling experience. I told him that I hadn't any but I thought I could do the work. He smiled and asked why I thought so. I told him I could learn and that the ad in the paper did not call for experience. He said that experience was not necessary because experienced men thought they knew it all, and he was willing to train me for the job. He asked me if I were Italian, and I said "Yes." "That's very good," he said. "The Italians of New Haven seem to be a better lot than those of other cities. But," he continued, "you don't look like an Italian." To which I answered, "Probably you are wrong in your opinion as to what Italians should look like." That kind of embarrassed him, and he said that that was a hobby of his to try and guess a man's nationality. Asked me to report at 9 A.M. the next morning for further instructions.

II

*When the unemployed had exhausted every other remedy and had no-
where else to turn, they finally applied for public relief. The
experience was as humiliating as they had feared. Relief officials,
undoubtedly burdened with too many applicants for too few funds,
were all too often curt and rude to the clients. Whatever remnants
of self-esteem remained to the unemployed could not survive the
encounter with the relief office. Ann Rivington's account of her
trials was, unfortunately, not a unique one.*

WE LIVED ON RELIEF, 1934

ANN RIVINGTON

When I went to college I studied sociology. I was taught that hunger,
squalor, dirt, and ignorance are the results of environment. Charity,
therefore, is no solution. We must change the environment In order to
do this we have settlement houses, playgrounds, and social workers in
the slums.

In the past year and a half I have again revised my opinion. I am
no longer one of *us*. For all my education, my training in thrift and
cleanliness, I am become one of *them*. My condition is shared by a large
sector of the population. From my new place in society I regard the
problems and misery of the poor with new eyes.

Two years ago I was living in comfort and apparent security. My
husband had a good position in a well-known orchestra and I was
teaching a large and promising class of piano pupils. When the orchestra
was disbanded we started on a rapid downhill path. My husband was
unable to secure another position. My class gradually dwindled away.
We were forced to live on our savings.

In the early summer of 1933 I was eight months pregnant and we
had just spent our last twelve dollars on one month's rent for an apartment. We found that such apartments really exist. They lack the most
elementary comforts. They usually are infested with mice and bedbugs.
Ours was. Quite often the ceilings leak.

What, then, did we do for food when our last money was spent
on rent? In vain we tried to borrow more. So strong was the influence
of our training that my husband kept looking feverishly for work when
there was no work, and blaming himself because he was unable to find
it. An application to the Emergency Home Relief Bureau was the last
act of our desperation.

We were so completely uninformed about the workings of charitable

In *Scribner's Magazine*, 95 (1934): 282–85.

organizations that we thought all we need do was to make clear to the authorities our grave situation in order to receive immediate attention.

My husband came home with an application blank in his pocket. We filled out the application with great care. The next morning my husband started early for the bureau. He returned at about two o'clock, very hungry and weak from the heat. But he was encouraged.

"Well, I got to talk to somebody this time," he said. "She asked me over again all the questions on that paper and more besides. Then she said to go home and wait. An investigator should be around tomorrow or day after. On account of your condition she marked the paper urgent." The next day we waited, and all of two days more. The fourth day, which was Saturday, my husband went back to the bureau. It was closed until Monday.

On Sunday morning the Italian grocer reminded me of our bill. "It get too big," he said. We cut down to one meal a day, and toast.

Monday brought no investigator. Tuesday my husband was at the bureau again. This time he came home angry.

"They said the investigator was here Friday and we were out. I got sore and told them somebody was lying."

"But you shouldn't. Now they won't help us."

"Now they will help us. She'll be here tomorrow."

Late Wednesday afternoon the investigator arrived. She questioned us closely for more than half an hour on our previous and present situation, our personal lives, our relatives. This time we certainly expected the check. But we were told to wait.

"I'm a special investigator. The regular one will be around Friday with the check."

My husband was in a torment of anxiety. "But we can't wait till Friday. We have to eat something."

The investigator looked tired. "I must make my report. And there are other cases ahead of yours."

By Monday morning we had nothing for breakfast but oatmeal, without sugar or milk. We decided we must go together to the bureau and find out what was wrong. Therefore, as soon as we had finished breakfast, we borrowed carfare from our kind neighbors and started out.

We reached the relief station a good fifteen minutes before nine, but the sidewalk was crowded with people. My husband explained to me that they were waiting to waylay the investigators on their way to work, to pour complaints and problems in their ears.

At last the doors were opened. The line crept forward. Three guards stood at the entrance, and every person in the crowd had to tell his business before he was admitted. Many were turned away. For the insistent there was the inevitable answer, "I got my orders," and the policeman within ready call.

By half-past nine we had made our way to the door.

"Room two," the guard said, handing us each a slip of paper.

The place was filled with long brown benches, crowded with our drab companions in hunger. Others were standing along the walls. The air was stifling and rank with the smell of poverty. We sat down at the end of the rear bench. Gradually we were able to slide to the end of our bench, then back along the next bench.

I watched the people around us. There they sat waiting, my fellow indigents. Bodies were gaunt or flabby, faces—some stoical, some sullen—all careworn like my husband's. What had they done, or left undone, to inherit hunger? What was this relief we were asking for? Certainly it was not *charity*. It was dispensed too grudgingly, too harshly, to be that.

When our turn came to talk to one of the women behind the desks we were told that the checks had been held up for lack of funds and that we should go home and wait for an investigator "some time this week." We were not going to be put off in this manner. My husband told her, "We have to have something more than promises. There's no food in the house, and my wife can't live on air."

"Well, that's all I can tell you," said the woman.

"If that's all you can tell me, who knows more than you?" We're not leaving without a better answer. I want the supervisor." At last the supervisor was called.

"The checks will be out tomorrow night. You will get yours Thursday."

Sure enough, early Thursday afternoon the regular investigator arrived. He gave us a check for eight-fifty to cover two weeks' food. We had already spent two dollars at the grocer's. And this amount, of course, was counted off the check. But Pete was not satisfied.

"Gotta take off more. I poor too."

I shook my head. "Wait," I said, "We'll pay you, but not this time."

I looked around the little shop hungrily. I was tortured by a great longing for fresh fruit.

"How much are the grapes?" I asked.

"No grapes," said Pete. "No grapes for you."

"But why not, Pete?"

"Grapes are luxury. You get beans, potatoes, onions. Poor people no eat grapes."

I was bewildered. But Pete meant what he said. He showed me a bulletin he had received from the Relief Bureau, listing the things allowed on the food checks of the jobless. I cannot remember all the regulations. But I do remember that only dried fruit was listed. The quantities of eggs, butter, milk, were strictly limited. No meat except salt pork, unsliced bacon, pig's liver, and other entrails. Rice, beans, potatoes, bread, onions were the main items to be sold. I saw no mention of fresh vegetables. I was highly indignant.

"Listen, Pete, my stomach isn't leather even if I have no money." I picked up a nice juicy cantaloupe and two bunches of carrots.

"These are onions and potatoes," I said, and marched out the door trailing carrot tops.

My baby was born one week later in a public ward where I was taken as an emergency case. The nine days' hospital experience is no part of this history, which deals with my adventures, as one of the city's unemployed, in obtaining food and shelter. But it is necessary to state in this place that I came home after nine days, ill and weak from inadequate care, bad food, and far too short a rest in bed. I came home with a dawning consciousness of my position, not as a unique sufferer, but as one of the mighty and growing mass who had somehow come to be cast aside as useless in the present scheme of things, cast aside in spite of the various skills and talents they may have possessed.

Gradually the more and more deficient diet began to tell on us. We did not lose much weight—the very poor usually eat plenty of starch— but we began to suffer from debility, colds, minor infections.

We began to have other serious worries. Now the landlord was becoming a frequent and insistent visitor.

We admitted that we were on relief, and promised to ask for a rent check. He explained that such a thing was impossible. The relief was not giving out rent checks except after eviction. It would cost him fifteen dollars to evict us, and the check would be for only twelve. He would lose three dollars.

"Try to borrow," he said.

The city elections were approaching. We did not suppose that they would affect us in the least. What, then, was our surprise when the investigator brought us a rent check. It might or might not have been intended as a bribe for our vote. We were too cynical, at that time, to see any connection between economics and politics, and we refrained from voting. However, the check helped us for the time being to stave off the fear of eviction.

The problem of insufficient food was becoming daily more serious. My baby was developing digestive troubles. My husband decided to complain once more at the bureau. He was told in so many words, "You can't expect to eat well. All we're trying to do is to keep you alive."

A few days later, when the investigator came on his regular visit, we found that by complaining we had done the best thing possible. Our food check was for nine dollars and a half.

We had dinner with our friend.

"How much relief did you say you're getting," our host wanted to know. We told him.

"Is that all? It seems pretty small. We have a neighbor over here who's working as an investigator. I'll ask her to come in and give us the dope."

The neighbor was called. She took a pencil and did some figuring.

"You should be getting ten dollars," she said, "ever since early fall." She showed us how the amount was determined: $1.65 a week for a man, $1.55 for a woman, $1.00 for a baby, add 15 percent, then add 15 cents for soap; multiply by two. That should be the check."

"But why don't they give us that, then?"

She laughed. "Either your investigator was too lazy to figure, or, well, he may have been trying to make sure of his job. You see, the investigators are terribly overworked, and always afraid of being fired and having to go back to the relief allowance themselves. We're under pressure to give as little help as possible, to refuse relief on the slightest excuse, to miss some families with the checks occasionally. At the same time, if cases complain, the whole blame is thrown on us. So if we lie to people, or 'put the fear of God into them,' it's all in self-defense. The only ones who get what they're entitled to are those who know what is their quota and demand it, especially if they make their demands in an organized way."

We got our rent check, our ten-dollar food check, letters to turn on our light and gas, a weekly order for salt pork, butter, bread, and eggs, by demanding these things and demanding them fearlessly. My husband applied for work under a musicians' project of the Civil Works Service. As yet he has not been notified of any work, though he takes the long hike across town several times a week, to be sure he is not being forgotten.

Meanwhile we are still living on the relief. We keep wondering, questioning. What if our check does not come next week? What when the relief bureau stops paying rents for the summer? Will we be evicted? Will our family be broken up, our little girl taken away from us? After a time these questions reach out beyond our burning personal needs. What is the cause of our suffering? Whither is it leading us, and the increasing millions like us? What is wrong with the system, the civilization that brings with it such wholesale misery? My own voice is one of many that are asking, more and more insistently.

III

Rural as well as urban families responded to the economic dislocations of the Depression with a bewilderment that frequently turned into resignation and apathy. Farmers unable to meet their debts not only lost their fields to the banks, but their homes as well. Many of them had no choice but to move to a nearby town or city. Thus, to the trauma of unemployment was added the difficulties of adjustment to an alien, urban environment. The experience of the Crumbaugh family, described below, poignantly reveals how one rural family suffered when it had to give up the family farm.

A FARMER'S STORY, 1939

JESSIE A. BLOODWORTH
AND ELIZABETH J. GREENWOOD

Mr. Crumbaugh, with his shaggy snow-white hair, looks older than his fifty-eight years; a network of little broken veins shows through the skin of his cheeks and nose; the pupil of one eye, its vision lost when Mr. Crumbaugh was only seven years old, is slightly smaller than the other, and the eyelid droops. He is a broad and heavy-set man, who moves and talks with a heavy slowness.

In 1930 after he had been forced to sell the last one hundred four-

In *The Personal Side*, by Jessie A. Bloodworth and Elizabeth J. Greenwood (Washington, D.C., 1939), pp. 317-27.

teen acres of his farm—a mortgage on one hundred acres had been foreclosed in 1926—Mr. Crumbaugh came to Dubuque with his wife and the seven children then living at home. Two daughters were married and away from home, and Antony stayed behind to work for a while on a neighbor's farm.

When he came to town, Mr. Crumbaugh had about twelve hundred dollars, the amount realized from the sale of the farm beyond what was necessary to pay off the mortgage; he hoped that this fund would tide him over until he could find work in Dubuque. But he has had no private employment except a few odd jobs, none lasting so long as a week. When this sum and amounts secured by cashing in insurance policies had been exhausted, Mr. Crumbaugh applied for relief. Since 1933 the family has been at least partially dependent on direct relief grants, work relief, and Mr. Crumbaugh's CWA and WPA employment. For more than two years he has been steadily employed on WPA projects.

His acceptance of the present situation has in it something of defeatism; he is not wholly satisfied with his present job or with his present earnings, but he "wouldn't know where to look" for other work. In fact, he has never applied for factory work in Dubuque; it has been his feeling that there were no jobs available. He is handicapped by his age and by his lack of any sort of experience as an industrial wage earner. Perhaps he is still more handicapped by his feeling of helplessness; he does not know how to look for a job, or where. Though he feels that his one sightless eye never lessened his effectiveness as a farmer and does not think of it in terms of a physical handicap, Mrs. Crumbaugh and the oldest son, Antony, believe that it would preclude the possibility of his being employed in any local factory; the factories can find plenty of unhandicapped and experienced men to take over what few jobs are open.

Mrs. Crumbaugh's fatalistic outlook somewhat resembles her husband's, though she is not quite so resigned as he, for her resignation is tinged with bitterness. She is a pleasant, friendly woman, too stout, a little nervous and fidgety, and not very well. Since she has never been satisfied with living in town, she would like now to take the younger children to a farm. Mrs. Crumbaugh is somewhat irritated by her husband's failure even to express any interest in planning to go back to farming, though she states that unless he had some money to invest, Mr. Crumbaugh could not go to a farm except as a hand, in which case no provision could be made for the family to be with him.

No one of the three children of employable age now at home has full-time work. All of the older children have evidently made considerable effort to find jobs, and, for the most part, have not been entirely unemployed. But they have shifted from job to job with some frequency, and their earnings have been consistently meager.

When the Crumbaughs applied for relief in 1933, they had exhausted available resources, and run up grocery and doctor bills. Two of the children were working: Antony had managed to go from one farm job to another, keeping rather steadily employed, and sometimes contributing a little to the family; Marlene, who had gone to country school until she was sixteen but had never attended school in Dubuque, was earning three dollars a week at housework. The younger children were still in school. Mr. and Mrs. Crumbaugh are both anxious to make it clear that they did not apply for relief until it was absolutely necessary to do so. But, having come to this necessity, they applied for assistance without any special reluctance—"there was nothing else to do."

Though Mrs. Crumbaugh found it difficult to manage on the meager food allowance with the seven children in the home, she "didn't complain" about the relief grants. Mr. Crumbaugh inclines to the belief that there was a good deal of "partiality" and "preference" in the distributing of relief; persons with "the most guts" got most in the way of relief; others who were "a little bashful" did not fare so well. Being among the bashful ones, the Crumbaughs made few requests.

Mr. Crumbaugh thinks that he could not have managed so well during the past few years if he had not had "good kids." But he is sorry that none of his children have done very well, or been much interested, in school. He feels that young people nowadays need good educations in order to find jobs. However, the four oldest unmarried children have all helped the family to some extent.

Though the Crumbaughs as a family group do not share in many activities (for they have little recreation of any kind), the children apparently get along well with each other and with the parents. Marlene and Antony are sympathetic with their father in his inability to find work. Marlene thinks that he is discouraged, as "any man would be" when he can't earn enough to support his family. She understands, too, her mother's wish to return to a farm, though Marlene herself would prefer to remain in town.

The Crumbaughs go regularly to church, but Mrs. Crumbaugh says despondently that "people won't even be able to go to church" now that the pastor has asked every adult to contribute ten cents each Sunday. Mrs. Crumbaugh seems to be more discouraged than her husband. If Marlene had only kept her work at Hall's, the family could probably have managed to get along during the winter months; Mr. Crumbaugh's and Patience's earnings combined are not enough to meet minimum expenses. Now the Crumbaughs are getting farther and farther behind with rent and water bills. The water bill, Mr. Crumbaugh may be able to work out, as he has done several times in the past, but no arrangement can be made about the rent.

Mr. Crumbaugh, though not very articulate at any time, shows more interest in a discussion of his farm experience and in the problems of farmers than in any consideration of industrial situations or his own chances of finding private employment. He approves of the present administration because it has "at least tried to help the farmers." He believes that the AAA accomplished its purpose of increasing farm incomes, but does not approve of having lands "lay idle" or "taken out of production." Though he has heard many people "hollering about over-production," Mr. Crumbaugh thinks that if all employable men had jobs paying reasonably good wages, they would be able to buy everything that could be produced. He speaks of the "new depression" which has already seriously affected Dubuque. As far as he can see, times are no better than they were in 1930, when he first came to town. Certainly he has no greater hope now than then of finding a job in Dubuque.

IV

Despite the magnitude of the crisis, the unemployed in particular, and the nation in general, were not very active politically. In part, their definition of their predicament remained private and personal; and the lower-middle and middle classes were simply unaccustomed to operating in the political arena. E. W. Bakke, a sociologist at Yale University during the Depression, conducted extensive interviews with the unemployed. He puzzled over the absence of greater political involvement. On the basis of his investigation, he drew the following conclusions.

CITIZENS WITHOUT WORK, 1939

E. W. BAKKE

Political group action does not rank high among the tactics adopted by the unemployed as a means for solving their problems. In view of the limited part played by politics in the life of employed workers this is not surprising. The worker's conception of government and of his practical relations to it is not such that political action, beyond the regular visit to the polls, appears to be an appropriate method for dealing with the problems raised by the lack of a job.

His customary political practices are limited to voting. No characteristic form of political practice has been developed to meet the recurring problems of working-class life as such. For the great majority of workers, government of the people, by the people, and for the people means primarily a periodic right to kick. He is not very clear about the process by which his vote is interpreted as the "will of the people." He is, in a more or less confused manner, aware that the politicians for whom he casts his vote are employees of a political machine, and he feels a certain contradiction between this reality and the political theory that these men "represent" him. But what he thinks about what the laws should be or the way in which they are administered counts for little until election day when he can register a "kick" or approval about the way these officials have done their job.

This identification of political action with periodic voting for or against employees of a political party is strongly ingrained in the folkways of the workers. It does not suggest to him that he is an integral part of "the government." The government is a thing apart from him. It is not an agency of which all are a part, engaged in a cooperative doing of jobs of common interest to all. The technique of politics for him does not include practical ways other than voting by which he might participate.

In *Citizens Without Work*, by E. W. Bakke (New Haven, 1939), pp. 46–53, 59–65. Reprinted by permission of the publisher, Yale University Press.

Nor is government a fulcrum by which power might be exercised in the interests of his particular class. Even if he understood what certain of the more radical of those who occasionally speak to him from soap-boxes meant by the word "fulcrum," he could not see clearly enough the technique and processes which gave objective meaning to that term to visualize his own place in such political activity. On every day of the year save election day the government tells the worker what to do and what he may not do. He takes orders; he does not give them.

He has enough contact with the game of politics to know that the game is not a free-for-all. He has enough contacts with those who do play the leading roles to know that they are primarily job holders or hangers-on working in self-interest, that their first concern is to keep the machine they serve in power. He does not resent that; "they have their living to make too, you know." But the knowledge does not stimulate confidence that government is "of the people, by the people, and for the people."

It is not difficult for the worker to arrive at such conclusions about politics. Any thinking he does on the subject will have to find a place for such typical comments as the following:

> By doing what the party leader tells you, you are piling up credits for yourself which can be cashed in on good jobs or big favors when the opportunity comes along. The greatest crime for a politician is to become independent of the party once he has been elected to an office. If it takes a lifetime, the party leaders will get you. Why I even know of a boss who gave a police job to a Republican because the Democrat who was in line for the job had crossed him up in a primary election ten years before.
> Laborer.

> There are only two reasons for going into politics—it's either to get something for yourself or to be able to get something for somebody else— usually it's the first. You fellows today are turning to politics more than to anything else just because there's a better chance to get jobs. You have to make a living somehow.
> Carpenter.

From such casually acquired details as these grows the worker's conception of politics and government as a business pursued by the few in the interests of the few. To be sure, those who make a business of politics do favors for humble people like himself in the hope of getting his vote. Yet he is not a real participator in all of this elaborate business which appears to him much more likely to influence the course of events than can his occasional journey to the ballot box.

Moreover, the two-party system does not encourage the practice of reliance upon political action for the solution of the worker's problems as an individual or as a member of the working class. Each political party apparently carries a full stock of goods and services intended to win the support of all economic classes in the community. Aside from the Socialist and Communist parties which are mistrusted on other grounds, the major parties do not pretend to serve the working class alone. The worker assumes that promises to workingmen are placed in the party platforms primarily to catch his votes and not because party

leaders have an understanding of the importance of working-class welfare to community well-being. In this assumption he displays a crude
but realistic political wisdom. The realization of this fact, however, does
not cause him to seek new avenues of political expression. It leads to a
distrust of all politicians rather than to political activity in behalf of a
more consistent working-class party.

It should be remembered also that New Haven is not a strongly
organized town. The political activities of trade unions have not therefore stimulated in any large number of workers the awareness that
such techniques are available as alternative ways of improving their
lot.

The characteristics of *his own* world define for the worker a way of
living which is his conception of the "American way." That radical solutions for his problems would deviate from this American way is enough
to damn them in the minds of many workers, even those whose place
of birth was on foreign soil. Let some of them speak for themselves:

> You know what good American citizens are like. They don't want to
> riot; they want to go straight. They don't carry guns. They don't make
> damn fool speeches. They don't ask advice from foreigners and, by God,
> they *don't take orders* from foreigners. Why should we listen to these
> birds that get their orders from Moscow?
>
> Carpenter.

> Now suppose they could set us up in that kind of a heaven they tell
> about. *Suppose* they could I say, because one look, and you know they
> couldn't. But if they could, would it be America—or would it be Russia?
> And who the hell wants to live in Russia?
>
> Boilermaker.

This identification of all radical ideas with Russia is all but universal. From listening to New Haven workers one would never suspect
that any brand of radicalism could spring, native-born, from American
soil.

I joined a group outside a cigar store at State and Grand Avenue.
For no good reason I asked where the Communist office was. The an-
tagonistic reaction was instantaneous.

In order to draw them out I took up and defended the Communist cause—not one of the men would give ground on the subject.
Two reactions to Communism were constantly reiterated:

1. Anyone who thought that the slavery in Russia was desirable, not
   only was crazy but ought to be shipped back immediately.
2. To be a Communist is similar to being a representative of a foreign
   power attacking our shores. Regardless of how badly one is treated,
   how much he despises his own work and employers, when a Communist is around, it is the American worker's duty to uphold America
   and American conditions. For example, two of the fellows said with
   pride that they were working for anywhere from twelve to eighteen
   hours a day at wages of ten, fifteen, twenty dollars a week. Their

point was that there was work for any decent American who had energy enough to work or get out and look for a job. In the face of Communism the most insecure American workman becomes a hero by defending American conditions.

I assumed the role of one who was out of work and had become a Communist because I couldn't get a job. I was told frankly and with great emotion that I could get work if I wanted it; that I was simply lazy and wanted a handout from people who had energy enough and ambition enough to work for a living, even though it meant twelve to sixteen hours per day.

The "un-American" judgment is emphasized by the fact that many of the radical speakers are members of race and nationality groups which are not trusted and frequently are despised. A reamer in a munitions plant put the matter this way:

> There is a decided swing toward more socialized feeling among factory workers. If capital with all its wealth can't supply men with a living, the workers will demand something else. But the men won't join up with anything that's organized by foreigners. *If the Socialist party had a few honest-to-goodness American leaders, it would be O.K., but you can't put in with something run by fellows with names like Topletsky or some such. They may be American-born and all that, but you can't get away from the name.*

Another former munitions worker stressed the fact that the associations one would have in any radical working-class movement would not be "with our own kind":

> Why don't men riot in this country? I'll tell you why they don't riot. There's no one to start it, and who wants to follow the foreigners that would? And besides that, there are too many languages. We all speak different languages, and you can't feel like joining with men in doing something like that when they don't speak the same language as you do, can you, now? Even if you could trust them what would your own bunch think of you?

He apparently saw no inconsistency in the opposition to "foreign" leaders on the part of Americans who could not understand each other's speech. But the testimony of many of his fellows among the unemployed leaves little doubt that the polyglot character of our population raises solid barriers to any acceptance of working-class solidarity so essential to radical mass action. When workers use the word "foreign" to describe the radical, they mean more than that he was born on a foreign shore. What they mean is that the radical uses ideas which are not customary among their associates, his terms are not in their familiar idiom. They do not know the implications of these terms. Radical speakers and organizers are labeled as "foreign" because that is the handy designation for an out-grouper, one who speaks and acts out of harmony with one's familiar ways of speech and practice.

An almost universal criticism one hears of the Communists is that "they are not constructive." Said a laborer in a clock factory:

They'll give you some mighty perty pictures of what they'd do if
they just could run things. But what have they ever done to show they
could run things? When it comes down to what to do, why it's always a
plan to bust something up.

A major obstacle to the winning of adherents for radical political
action is the fact that such action calls upon men to do more than
political action normally involves, i.e., choosing and checking up on
government officials. Socialism and Communism are not really politics,
thus defined in terms of the workers' folkways. Both involve comprehension of and working for a reorganization of society. That goes beyond
"politics" and involves passing judgment not on an officeholder but
on a change in the social system to which the worker has become accustomed. Even if the blueprints of the new order could be understood,
the habits of political action are not geared to such effort. Being a
Socialist or a Communist involves the adoption of a larger than customary conception of "political action." When supporting Socialism can
be defined as "voting for a Socialist who has demonstrated his ability,"
a larger following can be secured. That is politics as the worker understands the term.

Not only does radical political action involve judgment on a change
of social system, but it requires a greater degree of hope and confidence
in the future than many unemployed can muster. Those qualities among
many workers and particularly among the unemployed have been severely curtailed. Even when hope has not been completely crushed by the
impact of insecurity and misfortune, the goal of that hope is likely to
be not collectivism but individual achievement.

V

*The one bright spot amidst all the gloom of the Depression was the
availability of federal funds for public works programs. First the
Civilian Works Administration (CWA), then the Federal Emergency
Relief Administration (FERA), then the Public Works Administration (PWA), and finally the Works Progress Administration (WPA)
gave federal funds to city governments to employ men and women
on relief. The funds went into the building of such public facilities
as bridges, libraries, airports, and highways. Not only did the opportunity for work keep up the spirits of those lucky enough to be
on the public work rolls, but it also gave to the communities highly
visible evidence that progress in America was not altogether dead,
that there was still some hope for the nation making its way out
of this morass. When Helen and Robert Lynd returned to Middletown in the mid-1930s, they were struck by some of these signs
of optimism. They may well have exaggerated how deep it went.
But, nevertheless, their image of Middletown in the Great Depression does at least highlight the ways in which citizens could
find reasonable grounds for keeping their faith in the future.*

MIDDLETOWN IN TRANSITION, 1937

ROBERT AND HELEN LYND

When, on November 15, 1933, the blessed rain of Federal CWA funds began to fall upon the parched taxpayers, the straining city brought out projects big and little to catch the golden flood. "County Rushes Projects To Place Unemployed Persons on Government Payrolls" shouted the headlines. It was too good to be true! Thirty hours a week at fifty cents an hour would, the press gloated, bring $22,500 of federal money every week in place of that amount of local taxpayers' money. And under the CWA the golden stream was not even confined entirely to persons on relief. Good old Uncle Sam! Nobody was talking then about the unbridled waste of Washington spending in the hands of "brainless bureaucrats." It was manna direct from heaven, and Middletown came back for more, and more, and more.

The first week's shower of $6,700 reached less than 500 workers, but by mid-December of 1933 the workers had increased to 1,750, and by mid-January 1934, $33,500 of Federal funds were pouring in each week to 1,840 workers. The number of workers was forced down to 905 in the spring. Then, after $350,000 of CWA funds had been expended locally, the FERA took up the load, and, operating on a more economical basis and hiring only persons on relief, paid in sums ranging up to $16,000 to $17,000 a week. The peak number of men carried under the FERA funds was 1,100 in January and February 1935, and, with increasing employment, this total had dropped to 900 in mid-June 1935.

In returning to Middletown in 1935 one got an impression of external improvement and sprucing up at a number of points. And, upon inquiry, it developed that many of these changes had actually occurred during the Depression. Here was the paradox of a city's largely standing still from the standpoint of civic improvements during the boom years, and actually going in for extensive improvements in the midst of Depression. The answer was blithely stated in a local editorial comment in June 1935, under the caption, "Good Old Santa Claus Comes to Town": "If [Middletown] is not so improved pretty soon that she will not be able to recognize her 'lifted' face, it will not be the fault of good old Uncle Sam." As another press statement expressed it:

> Thus far the federal government apparently has agreed to finance, in part, about everything the city has suggested. [Middletown] now has, or proposes to put through, a list of improvements that probably would not have been considered if the last five years had been "prosperous." It has been said that, had it not been for the "hard times," the city would not have some of these public works twenty-five years from now.

The local projects began as rather obvious jobs such as redecorating public schools and improving their grounds but quickly spread to such things as the following:

From *Middletown in Transition* by Robert S. and Helen Merrell Lynd, pp. 120–127. Copyright 1937 by Harcourt Brace Jovanovich, Inc.; copyright 1965 by Robert S. and Helen M. Lynd. Reprinted by permission of the publisher.

A riverside boulevard across the city.

The dredging and cleaning of the river, looking toward its use for recreational purposes when the new sewage system is secured.

New bridges across the river.

A park and $90,000 municipal swimming pool replacing an unsightly city dump near the center of town.

Draining and reclaiming of swamp areas.

Widening, repairing, and paving of streets and construction of traffic signs.

A handsome $350,000 arts building (a PWA project for which the X family contributed the necessary local funds), a swimming pool, and other extensive improvements to buildings and campus at the college.

Drainage and grading of the airport.

Construction of sidewalks, gutters, and back-yard privies (the property owners paying cost of materials only).

An extensive supervised recreational program for adults and children in the city parks.

School athletic fields.

An exhaustive local housing inventory.

The making of mattresses and bedding for the needy.

Provision of plowing and watchmen for community vegetable gardens.

Supplementary staff help for health and welfare agencies, public library, etc.

Remodeling, repairing, redecorating, and in some cases building of additions to public buildings.

The city even received a large federal grant for the construction of the long-needed modern sewage plant, but local political bickerings prevented the then mayor, who secured the grant from Washington, from floating the necessary bond issue. As this is being written, in the summer of 1936, other large improvements are going forward with the help of Federal and State funds:

Part of the long-planned new sewer system is actually under construction, with the WPA paying for the labor and the city supplying the materials and equipment.

A three-state highway through the city, direct to the state capital, is under construction, with the city paying only $125,000 of the $675,000 cost of the construction within its city limits.

Favorable action was also expected on a $500,000 project to build five additional modern bridges over the river that crosses the city.

The city was congratulating itself over the prospect: Middletown, the press reported, "will see in progress the most extensive program of public improvements ever seen here at one time." And, sensing the fact that such a Cinderella existence will not go on forever, a press comment on the new bridges stated: "It is unlikely that ever again will there be an opportunity for the county to build new bridges here at a little more than half of their cost to the local taxpayers."

Here, in the experience of this city in achieving undreamed-of things in the midst of paralyzing bad times and under the guise of "relief," one sees a highly significant commentary on the process of social change in this culture. From an engineering point of view, such things as constructing adequate sewers, streets capable of carrying a given volume of traffic without undue congestion and accidents, and the other physical equipment of urban living present no problem. Middletown has engineers eager to do these things and the nation's warehouses contain materials clamoring for use. It is not, therefore, to the engineering area of the culture that one must look for the checks that make the inauguration of avowedly needed social changes so haphazard and turbulent a process. Given adequate technological skills and raw materials, where do the hindrances lie? They may lie in a lack of ideas, of popular demand, of men, of money, or of social organization. Actually, Middletown has long had many of the ideas that are now being embodied in relief projects; the mangy river, the lack of a modern sewage system, antiquated school equipment, were things people talked about and editors wrote about as old, familiar "local problems" ten years ago. Also, there have always been men unemployed and wanting work. Judging from the amount of local graft and mismanagement habitually tolerated in the spending of the city's budget, there has been money enough to finance the luxury of chronic mismanagement. And in the city government, Chamber of Commerce, and civic clubs there has been a paraphernalia of social organization that even in 1925 was noted as searching for things to "boost." But these human and institutional resources operate in a culture; and that culture by long habituation is patterned. Among these patterns are the following:

1. A tradition of approaching and stating problems negatively rather than positively. The outward *slogans* of Middletown's municipal leaders are "Economy," "We will reduce taxes," "We will give the city a cheap administration," and "Harmony."

2. A tradition, generated by the concept of democracy and shaped in civic matters by the tradition immediately preceding, which emphasizes "the average": "We're up to the average," "We're as good as most," "We're no worse than other cities of our size."

3. A tradition of the competence of the untrained common man to direct public affairs effectively. Such training as a Middletown civic official has is training in being a backslapping politician. One is a popular backslapper first and foremost, and only incidentally, and according to the wheel of chance, a city controller or councilman.

4. A distrust of "planners," "idealists," "intellectuals," of all men who let their thoughts and imaginations run beyond immediacies.

5. The tradition of short-term officeholding with the ever-imminent threat of the "next election," which diverts officeholders' attention from all but routine city business, to the crafty business of building personal political fences. Middletown's officeholders are not as a rule engaged in building a city, but in building a personal political organization.

6. A pervasive pride, itself stereotyped, in "how far we've come since ————," whereby the present usually appears good as compared with the past: potholed brick-paved streets are good as compared with the old potholed dusty streets; a dozen dingy grade-school buildings look good as compared with the half-dozen of a generation ago.

7. A long list of traditions as to what is a proper tax rate; how much salary a mayor or city controller or schoolteacher is worth; what a health officer's duties are; the efficiency of public administration; the relation of administrative units to each other; and so on, indefinitely. Proposals for change in any of these popular stereotypes must work against the set brakes of public custom and private habits.

In a culture so patterned, the likelihood of the emergence of forth-right civic social change through the city's elected and appointed administrators is curtailed almost to the vanishing point. In good times things inch along; in bad times the city takes in sail. Everything that comes up for consideration as a possible innovation is weighed as a discrete, short-run absolute. A $100,000 expenditure for a new type of civic service is, *ipso facto* and almost regardless of its nature, thrown heavily on the defensive, for the city is not building a city but keeping down the tax rate, and $100,000 is "an awful lot of money." There is no civic frame of reference, no civic design for living, except such rule-of-thumb traditions as those suggested above. People have no idea of what they "have a right to expect," except the average achievement that other cities of similar size and similarly case-hardened institutions nearby have. Hair shirts under these circumstances become normal, and Middletown wears its institutional hair shirt willingly.

Now to Middletown, so operating and so equipped with its full quota of rationalizations for so operating, its world made sense even in the early years of the Depression; times were hard, but there was no divine Santa Claus to lift the burden off the city, and the only thing to do was to pull in one's belt and meet the civic responsibilities. Then, suddenly, in 1933 the city shifted over, with the interjection of federal planning into the local scene, and began to move in a non-Euclidian world in which the old civic axioms were suspended and the city was asked to state its civic desires positively, to frame a new series of axioms, and to go ahead and act on them. Having no alternative, the city began to play the new game. Some at least of the conventional institutional checks were removed: here was money and here was a cultural weather in which ideas for civic betterment were not blighted but encouraged to grow.

Never before has this sort of chance to be Cinderella come to Middletown. It may conceivably never happen again. But for a brief span of months Middletown has had the experience of pressing the buttons and pulling the levers to "see how it works." The animus of the city leaders is such that, with the flickering dawn of returning good times, they want to rush headlong back to the old ways. But experiences such as Middletown has been going through tend not to disappear entirely. Precedents have been established and bench marks set, to which the culture may return more and more familiarly in the future.

Chapter 20

The Black Ghetto

JUST AS the urban landscape in 1900 was dotted with immigrant ghettos, so in 1960 it was marked with black ghettos. In the aftermath of World War I, Southern blacks, in steadily mounting numbers, sought to escape the economic and social restraints of rural life by moving to Northern and Western cities. Once there, they, like the immigrants before them, clustered together. In part, their poverty left them no choice but to settle in the ghetto; in part, landlords and private home-owners refused to let them occupy quarters elsewhere. And, in part, they preferred to live among their own, to organize their own kind of churches, or to shop in their own kind of stores. By 1960, every major city had its black ghetto: Harlem in New York, the Southside in Chicago, and Watts in Los Angeles were among the better-known enclaves. But ghettos could be found in Newark, Philadelphia, Cleveland, Detroit, and Omaha as well. Residential segregation was the rule, not the exception.

Although ordinary Americans were certainly aware of the black ghettos well before the 1960s, it took the riots of that decade to bring ghetto conditions to national attention. Between 1964 and 1968 almost every black ghetto experienced a riot. In the aftermath, television cameramen and journalists, Senate investigators and newly appointed commissioners descended on the ghetto, interviewed its residents, photographed its streets, examined its economic make-up, and tried to explain to a troubled nation what conditions lay behind the riots.

For some observers, the riots reflected nothing more than the outburst of the riffraff, the triumph of criminal elements within an otherwise stable and peaceful black community. These critics, with some justification, insisted that the decade of the 1960s had been one of unparalleled progress for blacks. Why would the generally law-abiding black want to riot when his income was rising faster than ever before, when public segregation was at an all-time low, when the possibilities for the future progress of the race seemed better than ever before? But many others understood that the riots could not be explained away

473

so easily. For all the progress of the last decade, blacks were still the victims of massive economic and social discrimination—the first to be fired, the first to be frisked on the streets. The ghetto riots, they insisted, could not be understood apart from poverty and prejudice. More was at stake than controlling the riffraff.

Even if one agreed with this broader diagnosis, it was still not clear how American society should respond to the problem. Was the ghetto ultimately a deviant form of social organization, a reflection of prejudice pure and simple? Was it true that the sooner blacks escaped from it the better? Or was the ghetto a base from which blacks could organize to exert economic and political pressures and promote their own interests? This debate, begun in the late 1960s, continues today, and each side has its persuasive advocate. The Kerner Commission, whose investigation into the facts and causes of the 1960s riots was thorough and insightful, recommended the integration approach. Blacks would never escape poverty no matter how much money government poured into the ghetto. Leaders who echoed some if not all of the principles of black power saw it differently: only when blacks acted together would the wider society give blacks their due. In the end, the question comes down to the issue of how one understands the impact of the ghetto on black lives. The materials that follow address this question. Does the ghetto invariably corrupt and degrade its members? Does it trap its citizens in poverty? Or does the ghetto have the potential of giving blacks strength in numbers, offering not only psychological but also economic rewards for self-help?

I

It was often young black novelists who most vividly and insightfully presented the complex character of black ghetto life. Claude Brown is one of those novelists. Raised in Harlem, he had several brushes with the law, and ended up in a training school for delinquent boys. While for most inmates the training schools are little more than preparations for survival in state penitentiaries, Brown was that exceptional case. He returned to Harlem and published a gripping account of life on its streets: Manchild in the Promised Land. *He appeared, together with a close friend, Arthur Dunmeyer, before a 1966 Senate hearing on the role of the federal government in improving urban conditions. Their testimony explains what happens as black ghetto residents learn that the ghetto is not a promised land.*

GHETTO LIFE, 1966

TESTIMONY OF CLAUDE BROWN AND ARTHUR DUNMEYER

Senator Ribicoff: Both of you, I assume, were born in Harlem.

Mr. Dunmeyer: No, I was born in Charleston, South Carolina.

Senator Ribicoff: And how old were you when your parents moved to New York?

Mr. Dunmeyer: I was six months old when my mother came to New York.

Senator Ribicoff: How about you, Mr. Brown?

Mr. Brown: I was born and raised in Harlem.

Senator Ribicoff: And your parents, were they born in Harlem or did they come from the South?

Mr. Brown: They came from the South about two years before I was born in 1935, from South Carolina—not a large city, but the backwoods area of South Carolina.

Senator Ribicoff: What is the impact on the Negro from the rural South who comes up to the slums of New York? What happens to them physically, emotionally, mentally, morally?

Mr. Brown: Once they get there and become disillusioned, they can see the streets aren't paved with gold, and there exist no great economic opportunities for them, they become pressured. Many of the fathers who brought the families can't take the pressure any more, the economic pressure. How can you support a family of five kids on sixty-five dollars a week? So he just leaves. Maybe he just goes out one night and he is so depressed because he missed a day's pay. During the week—he was sick. He couldn't help it. And he wasn't in the union, and this depression leads to a sort of touchiness, I will say—to become more mundane, where in a bar a person can step on his foot and he or the person gets his throat cut.

Somebody is dead. The other is in jail. He is going to the electric chair.

Many of the physical reactions—they took out their frustrations on their kids—they beat the hell out of them. My father used to beat me nearly to death every day. Still they take it out on their wives. They beat their wives. It is just frustration that they feel.

The wives lose respect for their husbands. They can't really support their families. There are many affairs, you know Mama is having sexual relationships with the butcher for an extra piece of pork chop for the kids. She wants to see them well fed—this sort of thing.

Or maybe the number runner on the corner digs Mama or something. She has got a couple of kids. He can give her twenty-five dollars a week. All her husband can make is, say, sixty dollars at most a week, and it isn't enough, and the twenty-five dollars helps because she wants her kids to have the things that TV says that they should have.

In *Federal Role in Urban Affairs*, Hearings Before the Subcommittee on Executive Reorganization, U.S. Senate, 89th Congress, 2nd session, August 29–30, 1966, part 5, pp. 1090–97, 1105–108, 1110–12.

Mr. Dunmeyer: I would like to bring this up also. In some cases this is the way you get your drug dealers and prostitutes and your numbers runners. You get people that come here and it is not that they are disillusioned. They see that these things are the only way they can compete in the society, to get some sort of status. They realize that there aren't any real doors open to them, and so, to commit crime was the only thing to do, they can't go back. There is nothing to go back to.

Society has made this law to protect itself, not to protect this man in any way, just to protect itself so there is a law that he can't do this, and he doesn't recognize this law. Really, he doesn't recognize anything in society, because of this one particular thing. He sees there are no doors really open to him; and until these doors can be open to this man and this woman, there is going to be the same thing over and over again.

My father started when he came, the only thing he knew was what his father had taught him as a trade, considered illegitimate by Internal Revenue Service, of course, but it was making corn liquor in the bathtub—White Light, King Corn, perhaps you heard of it in those terms. And so he did this and ran his parlor parties and his crap games.

When I was coming up I wanted things, too, as a child, that my parents couldn't give me because my father he wanted to be with his family, he wasn't going to jail and had to give up his way of life, and at this time he was making a little more money. Of course, by the age of forty or forty-two he was making, say, seventy-five dollars a week, because he had been working on the job for about fifteen years at that time and this was a big deal to him. But still, he couldn't afford to give me the things, buy the sport jackets and things that the kids were wearing at the time to go along with the fad of the community. Anyway, I took to selling drugs.

Senator Ribicoff: How old were you when you started selling drugs?

Mr. Brown: I was selling drugs at thirteen.

Senator Ribicoff: Thirteen?

Mr. Brown: Yes; heroin. Anyway, it is like, in the community, in the Negro ghettos throughout the country, these things that are considered criminal by society, the solid citizen, aren't considered criminal. It is like a war between them and us, the society which oppresses us, and us, the oppressed. When a guy goes to jail, it is OK. You are looked up to, if you are a successful hustler, you have a big Cadillac and you have always got three hundred dollars in your pocket, you are taking numbers, you are selling drugs, you are a stickup artist, you are anything, you are a prostitute, anything you may be doing, you are a con man, a hustler.

At thirteen I learned how to cut drugs, how much quinine to put in cocaine. At the age of fifteen I learned how to "Murphy" somebody. The "Murphy" is the flimflam. Anyway, had I been in the South, had I been in a better society, I would have been learning. I would have been in school and learning how to make it legitimately, but I wasn't. I was learning how to make it illegitimately, but these were the best possible ways to make it financially, to establish a decent place for yourself in America's greatest metropolis.

The TV's were saying, yes, get this, you know, have a car. Everybody should have a car. Even color TV, how are you going to get it?

You can get it selling drugs. You can get it taking numbers. You know, you can get it playing the Murphy. You can get it if you ran around taking off people, sticking up people, this sort of thing. As long as you were making it, as long as you were a success, that is why in Harlem people respect the guy who is always clean.

You know, he has a two hundred dollar silk suit every day, fifty-five dollar alligator shoes, and this sort of thing. He drives a big Cadillac, and, they know he is winning the war. He is a soldier, he is a real soldier. He is a general in the community. If he gets busted, well, he is just a prisoner of war. That is the way it is looked upon.

I would like to make an interjection at this point, just to avoid any misconstruing of what has been said in the past. You know, there are many solid citizens in Harlem, the nice old people who get up and go to church every Sunday. They pray for their sons. They hope he doesn't go out and get caught on none of that old dope. They work hard every day for fifty dollars a week. But she wants to make an honest living. She believes it. This is the way she believes.

She believes the game that has been run down, the con game of American society, equal opportunity and all that and everybody is supposed to be a solid citizen, like my friend here. You know, work hard every day. Anyway, to most of the younger generation, it is a myth, but even to these people, the good solid citizens, the Christians, the church-going people who want to live righteously, something like numbers is an economic institution in Harlem and it is not a crime for them. They will go to war over it.

You will have a riot if everybody hit the numbers or something, and the police come and they want to make a bust. They want to arrest him, the guy who pays off for the numbers. And these women who go to church every Sunday and scrub floors every day during the week will jump on top of the police. They will have to call out the entire precinct you know to calm this thing down, and, furthermore, with these people, even with them, the solid citizens, it is like they know that they must have—they must have some kind of a dream.

The only way they can possibly make it is, "one day, maybe, I will hit a number." So, if you take the numbers away from them you take away their dream. They know they are not going to make it off their fifty dollars a week.

Senator Kennedy: Do you think, based on that history and background and as you described it before this committee in earlier hearings, do you think it possible in the future to work out these problems?

Mr. Brown: It is. I am going to get to that, yes.

Senator Kennedy: What I would like to also have you discuss is why there hasn't been more violence in the communities up to the last couple of years.

Mr. Brown: Because for a long time Negroes have been more subservient. I started off with the large, great urban generation. We knew what were the things that were in the offing, what was out there to be had. Our past generation didn't have TV, we had it. We came up in school and read the same comic books. They showed us the same magazines even though they didn't include us in them—*Life, Look,* this sort of thing, the *Saturday Evening Post.* But we knew what the good life was supposed to be; and knowing this, these people, they are, let's say, a generation ahead.

Senator Kennedy: If you were in charge of the establishment, whether it is the economic or the political or whatever it might be, whether it is state, city, or federal, if you had control over that, what would you do in the situation—whether it is Harlem, Bedford Stuyvesant, Watts, or whatever it might be?

Mr. Dunmeyer: First of all, I would find enough numbers runners in the neighborhood, all the dope pushers in the neighborhood who are doing this because, like I said, this is a way of life, but who have something more to offer in the way if intelligence. They know how to get around the police. These people I can use to my advantage. They might know how to get around another problem by using the same ideas, and I would use these people. And I wouldn't come out of this neighborhood until these people themselves felt that they were human, again, not until I felt it, because unless I was living there, unless I was a part of this thing, you see I couldn't sit behind a desk and do it. I would have to know it inside and out.

I would have to get Miss Jones, who lives on the top floor who never comes downstairs, who merely sends the kids downstairs, put her in charge of upstairs. She would know more about the upstairs. I wouldn't ask this other fellow, because he is the superintendent, what happens upstairs and over here. He doesn't know these things. He is the superintendent and he has his little wine concession downstairs where he sells and has parties and whatnot. He knows about this, the downstairs, I couldn't ask him about upstairs.

And I would employ each person that I did hire in any capacity, and use them to the extent of what they can offer themselves, not what the books say are right. I couldn't sit down and write any laws, any mandates for anyone to follow. I would have to feel out the block itself. I would have to feel out the people themselves.

Mr. Brown: And you can't take the psychologists and the sociologists who are at least five years behind in their theories to analyze these people and find out what kind of people they are, just what they are made of, and what is the best approach to them.

You have got to take the people from the neighborhood, with whom you can communicate.

Senator Kennedy: Do you think we are doing that at all now?

Mr. Brown: Pardon me?

Senator Kennedy: Do you think we are doing that at all now?

Mr. Brown: I don't know, Senator. I will tell you, I am certain you are familiar with the fiasco of Haryou-ACT last year. You see, implied in their approach, they were going to deal with the kids mainly, and ignore the parents, and this is ridiculous, you know. Like you can take the kid in school. A schoolteacher can only have so much influence. If the child went to school eight hours a day, the greatest influence would still be in the home. He has been in the home five years—all of his ideas, all of his attitudes toward life have come from inside the home, and he spends more time there even if it is just sleeping.

You know he has to come home and eat with the parents, and in the approach of Haryou-ACT, that this "generation is gone but we are going to save the next one and work with the kids," you couldn't do it because if you don't get the cooperation of the parents, everything that Haryou-ACT could have accomplished with the children would have been undone immediately as soon as they got home that night.

Senator Ribicoff: As I listen to both of you, it seems that one of the great problems is that the overall white community sees the Negroes in a lump. They look at a Negro and they do not see Claude Brown, they do not see Arthur Dunmeyer. You look the same to all of them, instead of being treated as individuals. Arthur Dunmeyer is a different man than Claude Brown. Claude Brown has certain problems and has certain attributes, and Arthur Dunmeyer has certain problems and certain attributes. The time has come to look at everybody, no matter who they are, whether they are white or whether they are Negro or Puerto Rican or Mexican-Americans, or American Indians—let's look at each individual as an individual and treat him as an individual.

II

A persuasive analysis of the origins of the riots of the 1964–1968 period demands not just an awareness of the events immediately prior to the outbreak, but an understanding of the long-term causes of the event. The Kerner Commission, appointed by President Lyndon Johnson, was charged to conduct such an analysis and, to their credit, they did it well. They examined the major ghetto riots and in their report presented a vignette of each of them. Their description of events in Newark in the summer of 1967, reprinted below, is typical of their findings. Here and elsewhere, the riots turn out to be the result of a series of totally fortuitous and petty events and the end product of a long tradition of whites exploiting blacks.

KERNER COMMISSION REPORT ON THE NEWARK RIOT, 1968

On Tuesday night, June 20, in Newark, New Jersey, a tumultuous meeting of the Planning Board took place. Until 4 A.M., speaker after speaker from the Negro ghetto arose to denounce the city's intent to turn over a hundred and fifty acres in the heart of the Central Ward as a site for the state's new medical and dental college.

The growing opposition to the city administration by vocal black residents had paralyzed both the Planning Board and the Board of Education. Tension had been rising so steadily throughout the northern New Jersey area that, in the first week of June, Colonel David Kelly, head of the state police, had met with municipal police chiefs to draw

In *U.S. Kerner Commission Report* (Washington, D.C., 1968), pp. 56–69.

up plans for state police support of city police wherever a riot developed. Nowhere was the tension greater than in Newark.

Although in 1967 Newark's population of four-hundred thousand still ranked it thirtieth among American municipalities, for the past twenty years the white middle class had been deserting the city for the suburbs.

In the late 1950s the desertions had become a rout. Between 1960 and 1967, the city lost a net total of more than seventy thousand white residents. Replacing them in vast areas of dilapidated housing where living conditions, according to a prominent member of the County Bar Association, were so bad that "people would be kinder to their pets," were Negro migrants, Cubans, and Puerto Ricans. In six years the city switched from 65 percent white to 52 percent Negro and 10 percent Puerto Rican and Cuban.

The white population, nevertheless, retained political control of the city. In the Central Ward, where the medical college controversy raged, the Negro constituents and their white councilman found themselves on opposite sides of almost every crucial issue.

The municipal administration lacked the ability to respond quickly enough to navigate the swiftly changing currents. Even had it had great astuteness, it would have lacked the financial resources to affect significantly the course of events.

In 1962, seven-term Congressman Hugh Addonizio had forged an Italian-Negro coalition to overthrow long-time Irish control of the City Hall. A liberal in Congress, Addonizio, when he became Mayor, had opened his door to all people. Negroes, who had been excluded from the previous administration, were brought into the government. The police department was integrated.

Nevertheless, progress was slow. As the Negro population increased, more and more of the politically oriented found the progress inadequate.

The Negro-Italian coalition began to develop strains over the issue of the police. The police were largely Italian, the persons they arrested largely Negro. Community leaders agreed that, as in many police forces, there was a small minority of officers who abused their responsibility. This gave credibility to the cries of "Brutality!" voiced periodically by ghetto Negroes.

During the daytime Newark more than doubled its population— and was, therefore, forced to provide services for a large number of people who contributed nothing in property taxes. The city's per capita outlay for police, fire protection and other municipal services continued to increase. By 1967 it was twice that of the surrounding area.

Consequently, there was less money to spend on education. Newark's per capita outlay on schools was considerably less than that of surrounding communities. Yet within the city's school system were seventy-eight thousand children, fourteen thousand more than ten years earlier.

Twenty thousand pupils were on double sessions. The dropout rate was estimated to be as high as 33 percent. Of thirteen thousand six hundred Negroes between the ages of sixteen and nineteen, more than six thousand were not in school. In 1960 over half of the adult Negro population had less than an eighth grade education.

The typical ghetto cycle of high unemployment, family breakup, and crime was present in all its elements. Approximately 12 percent of Negroes were without jobs. An estimated 40 percent of Negro children lived in broken homes. Although Newark maintained proportionately the largest police force of any major city, its crime rate was among the highest in the nation. In narcotics violations it ranked fifth nationally. Almost 80 percent of the crimes were committed within two miles of the core of the city, where the Central Ward is located. A majority of the criminals were Negro.

Under such conditions a major segment of the Negro population became increasingly militant. Largely excluded from positions of traditional political power, Negroes, tutored by a handful of militant social activists who had moved into the city in the early 1960s, made use of the anti-poverty program, in which poor people were guaranteed representation, as a political springboard.

On July 8, Newark and East Orange Police attempted to disperse a group of Black Muslims. In the melee that followed, several police officers and Muslims suffered injuries necessitating medical treatment. The resulting charges and countercharges heightened the tension between police and Negroes.

Early on the evening of July 12, a cab driver named John Smith began, according to police reports, tailgating a Newark police car. Smith was an unlikely candidate to set a riot in motion. Forty years old, a Georgian by birth, he had attended college for a year before entering the Army in 1950. In 1953 he had been honorably discharged with the rank of corporal. A chess-playing trumpet player, he had worked as a musician and a factory hand before, in 1963, becoming a cab driver.

As a cab driver, he appeared to be a hazard. Within a relatively short period of time he had eight or nine accidents. His license was revoked. When, with a woman passenger in his cab, he was stopped by the police, he was in violation of that revocation.

From the high-rise towers of the Reverend William P. Hayes Housing Project, the residents can look down on the orange-red brick facade of the Fourth Precinct Police Station and observe every movement. Shortly after 9:30 P.M., people saw Smith, who either refused or was unable to walk, being dragged out of a police car and into the front door of the station.

Within a few minutes at least two civil rights leaders received calls from a hysterical woman declaring a cab driver was being beaten by the police. When one of the persons at the station notified the cab company of Smith's arrest, cab drivers all over the city began learning of it over their cab radios.

A crowd formed on the grounds of the housing project across the narrow street from the station. As more and more people arrived, the description of the beating purportedly administered to Smith became more and more exaggerated. The descriptions were supported by other complaints of police malpractice that, over the years, had been submitted for investigation—but had never been heard of again.

Several Negro community leaders, telephoned by a civil rights worker and informed of the deteriorating situation, rushed to the scene.

By 10:15 P.M. the atmosphere had become so potentially explosive that Kenneth Melchior, the senior police inspector on the night watch, was called. He arrived at approximately 10:30 P.M.

Met by a delegation of civil rights leaders and militants who requested the right to see and interview Smith, Inspector Melchior acceded to their request.

When the delegation was taken to Smith, Melchior agreed with their observations that, as a result of injuries Smith had suffered, he needed to be examined by a doctor. Arrangements were made to have a police car transport him to the hospital.

Both within and outside of the police station the atmosphere was electric with hostility. Carloads of police officers arriving for the 10:45 P.M. change of shifts were subjected to a gauntlet of catcalls, taunts, and curses. Two of the Negro spokesmen went outside to attempt to pacify the people.

There was little reaction to the spokesmen's appeal that the people go home. The second of the two had just finished speaking from atop a car when several Molotov cocktails smashed against the wall of the police station.

With the call of "Fire!" most of those inside the station, police officers and civilians alike, rushed out of the front door. The Molotov cocktails had splattered to the ground; the fire was quickly extinguished.

From the dark grounds of the housing project came a barrage of rocks. Some of them fell among the crowd. Many smashed the windows of the police station. The rock throwing, it was believed, was the work of youngsters; approximately twenty-five hundred children lived in the housing project.

Almost at the same time, an old car was set afire in a parking lot. The police, their heads protected by World War I-type helmets, sallied forth to disperse the crowd. A fire engine, arriving on the scene, was pelted with rocks. As police drove people away from the station, they scattered in all directions.

A few minutes later a nearby liquor store was broken into. Some persons, seeing a caravan of cabs appear at City Hall to protest Smith's arrest, interpreted this as evidence that the disturbance had been organized, and generated rumors to that effect.

However, only a few stores were looted. Within a short period of time the disorder ran its course.

The next afternoon, Thursday, July 13, the Mayor described it as an isolated incident. At a meeting with Negro leaders to discuss measures to defuse the situation, he agreed to appoint the first Negro police captain, and announced that he would set up a panel of citizens to investigate the Smith arrest. To one civil rights leader this sounded like "the playback of a record," and he walked out. Other observers reported that the Mayor seemed unaware of the seriousness of the tensions.

Reports and rumors, including one that Smith had died, circulated through the Negro community. Tension continued to rise.

On Thursday, inflammatory leaflets were circulated in the neighborhoods of the Fourth Precinct. A "Police Brutality Protest Rally" was announced for early evening in front of the Fourth Precinct Station.

Several television stations and newspapers sent news teams to interview people. Cameras were set up. A crowd gathered. Between 7:00 and 7:30 P.M. James Threatt, Executive Director of the Newark Human Rights Commission, arrived to announce to the people the decision of the Mayor to form a citizens group to investigate the Smith incident, and to elevate a Negro to the rank of captain.

The response from the loosely milling mass of people was derisive. One youngster shouted "Black Power!" Rocks were thrown at Threatt, a Negro. The barrage of missiles that followed placed the police station under siege.

After the barrage had continued for some minutes, police came out to disperse the crowd. According to witnesses, there was little restraint of language or action by either side. A number of police officers and Negroes were injured.

As on the night before, once the people had been dispersed, reports of looting began to come in. Soon the glow of the first fire was seen.

Without enough men to establish control, the police set up a perimeter around a two-mile stretch of Springfield Avenue, one of the principal business districts, where bands of youths roamed up and down smashing windows. Grocery and liquor stores, clothing and furniture stores, drug stores and cleaners, appliance stores and pawnshops were the principal targets. Periodically police officers would appear and fire their weapons over the heads of looters and rioters. Laden with stolen goods, people began returning to the housing projects. As news of the disturbance had spread, however, people had flocked into the streets. As they saw stores being broken into with impunity, many bowed to temptation and joined the looting.

Between 2:00 and 2:30 A.M. on Friday, July 14, the Mayor decided to request Governor Richard J. Hughes to dispatch the state police, and National Guard troops. The first elements of the state police arrived with a sizeable contingent before dawn. Command of antiriot operations was taken over by the governor, who decreed a "hard line" in putting down the riot.

As a result of technical difficulties, such as the fact that the city and state police did not operate on the same radio wavelengths, the three-way command structure—city police, state police, and National Guard—worked poorly.

At 3:30 P.M. that afternoon Horace W. Morris, an associate director of the Washington Urban League who had been visiting relatives in Newark, was about to enter a car for the drive to Newark Airport. With him were his two brothers and his seventy-three-year-old stepfather, Isaac Harrison. About sixty persons had been on the street watching the looting. As the police arrived, three of the looters cut directly in front of the group of spectators. The police fired at the looters. Bullets plowed into the spectators. Everyone began running. As Harrison, followed by the family, headed toward the apartment building in which he lived, a bullet kicked his legs out from under him. Horace Morris lifted him to his feet. Again he fell. Mr. Morris' brother, Virgil, attempted to pick the old man up. As he was doing so, he was hit in the left leg and right forearm. Mr. Morris and his other brother managed to drag the two wounded men into the vestibule of the building, jammed with sixty to seventy frightened, angry Negroes.

Bullets continued to spatter against the walls of the buildings. Finally, as the firing died down, Morris—whose stepfather died that evening—yelled to a sergeant that innocent people were being shot.

"Tell the black bastards to stop shooting at us," the sergeant, according to Morris, replied.

"They don't have guns; no one is shooting at you," Morris said.

"You shut up, there's a sniper on the roof," the sergeant yelled.

A short time later, at approximately 5:00 P.M., in the same vicinity a police detective was killed by a small caliber bullet. The origin of the shot could not be determined. Later during the riot a fireman was killed by a .30 caliber bullet. Snipers were blamed for the deaths of both.

Although, by nightfall, most of the looting and burning had ended, reports of sniper fire increased. The fire was, according to New Jersey National Guard reports, "deliberately or otherwise inaccurate." Major General James F. Cantwell, Chief of Staff of the New Jersey National Guard, testified that "there was too much firing initially against snipers" because of "confusion when we were finally called on for help and our thinking of it as a military action."

"As a matter of fact," Director of Police Spina told the Commission, "down in the Springfield Avenue area it was so bad that, in my opinion, Guardsmen were firing upon police and police were firing back at them. . . . I really don't believe there was as much sniping as we thought. . . . We have since compiled statistics indicating that there were seventy-nine specific instances of sniping."

Several problems contributed to the misconceptions regarding snipers: the lack of communications; the fact that one shot might be reported half a dozen times by half a dozen different persons as it caromed and reverberated a mile or more through the city; the fact that the National Guard troops lacked riot training. They were, said a police official, "Young and very scared," and had had little contact with Negroes.

In order to protect his property, B. W. W., the owner of a Chinese laundry, had placed a sign saying "Soul Brother" in his window. Between 1:00 and 1:30 A.M., on Sunday, July 16, he, his mother, wife, and brother, were watching television in the back room. The neighborhood had been quiet. Suddenly B. W. W. heard the sound of jeeps, then shots.

Going to an upstairs window he was able to look out into the street. There he observed several jeeps, from which soldiers and state troopers were firing into stores that had "Soul Brother" signs in the windows. During the course of three nights, according to dozens of eyewitness reports, law enforcement officers shot into and smashed windows of businesses that contained signs indicating they were Negro owned.

By Monday afternoon, July 17, state police and National Guard forces were withdrawn. That evening, a Catholic priest saw two Negro men walking down the street. They were carrying a case of soda and two bags of groceries. An unmarked car with five police officers pulled up beside them. Two white officers got out of the car. Accusing the Negro men of looting, the officers made them put the groceries on the sidewalk, then kicked the bags open, scattering their contents all over the street.

Telling the men, "Get out of here," the officers drove off. The Catholic priest went across the street to help gather up the groceries. One of the men turned to him: "I've just been back from Vietnam two days," he said, "and this is what I get. I feel like going home and getting a rifle and shooting the cops."

Of the two hundred and fifty fire alarms, many had been false, and thirteen were considered by the city to have been "serious." Of the $10,251,000 damage total, four-fifths was due to stock loss. Damage to buildings and fixtures was less than two million dollars.

Twenty-three persons were killed—a white detective, a white fireman, and twenty-one Negroes. One was seventy-three-year-old Issac Harrison. Six were women. Two were children.

III

One of the most common precipitating events of the ghetto riots involved rumors or instances of police brutality. The 1967 Newark riot, for example, began in just that manner. Ghetto residents have consistently charged that the police forces in their neighborhoods, generally made up of whites, are abusive. Police will stop and frisk a black simply because he is black, address them in the most derogatory tones, and, worse yet, use an unjustifiable amount of violence against them. A federal investigation of the civil rights of black citizens frequently uncovered evidence of the validity of this charge. Below is an interview that the Commission held with one black in Cleveland—and his story, unfortunately, is not unique.

POLICING THE GHETTO, 1970

TESTIMONY OF MR. GLEN MARKS

Mr. Glickstein: Would you please state your name, age, and address?

Mr. Marks: My name is Glen Marks. My address is 7719 Linwood. I work at Ohio Crankshaft. I am a machinist there.

Mr. Glickstein: Where were you born?

Mr. Marks: I was born in Waycross, Georgia.

Mr. Glickstein: How long have you lived in Cleveland?

Mr. Marks: Approximately twenty-one and a half years.

In *Hearings of the Commission on Civil Rights,* United States Commission on Civil Rights, December 14–15 (1970), pp. 542–48.

Mr. Glickstein: How much education have you had?

Mr. Marks: I am a sophomore at Community College.

Mr. Glickstein: What is your major in college?

Mr. Marks: Electrical engineering.

Mr. Glickstein: You said you are employed by the Ohio Crankshaft Company?

Mr. Marks: Right.

Mr. Glickstein: How long have you been employed there?

Mr. Marks: Roughly two and a half years.

Mr. Glickstein: Were you arrested in 1964?

Mr. Marks: Yes, I was.

Mr. Glickstein: Would you tell us when and what happened?

Mr. Marks: It was about two o'clock in the morning. I was waiting on the local bus in the Greyhound Bus Terminal. I was working part time at the time, doing porter work. John Hill was working there with me, also. He was seated on the floor near the rear entrance to the bus terminal. A policeman entered the rear entrance and he saw Hill sitting there on the floor and he walked over to him and asked him what was he doing sitting down there.

Hill said he was waiting on the bus with myself. The policeman asked him for his identification. He showed the policeman his identification and after looking at this, the policeman returned it to Hill and told him to get up. When he told him to get up, he kicked him in the side of the leg.

Hill jumps up and asks the policeman, why did he kick him.

The policeman said "What are you going to do about it!" And Hill repeated his question and the policeman repeated his and Hill said "If you didn't have a gun on, you wouldn't go around kicking people."

So the policeman said "You come over here to the phone with me." He grabbed Hill by the arm and took him over to the public phone and he made a phone call so at this time I told Hill I was going to get the night superintendent to verify that we worked there and we were not loitering there.

So I went to the superintendent's office and I found that he had left earlier that night, so I come back and told Hill that the superintendent had left that night. So I asked the policeman, would he go to the dispatch office and ask the dispatcher about Hill's employment. The policeman said he wasn't interested in whether Hill worked there or not. I started to walk away and the policeman told me to hold it, to wait there, too, so I waited there. About five minutes later, two more policemen arrived in a car and they came in and one police officer asked "What did they have here?" They walked off a few steps and discussed something and then they came back and they told us that we were under arrest.

They searched us briefly and took us out and put us in the car. They walked off from the car and discussed something else for a few minutes. Then they got into the car and proceeded to the police station at 21st and Payne.

Here we were taken to the fourth floor. We were searched thoroughly at this point. The arresting officer took his coat off, his gun and his night stick and he showed me to a room a couple of doors down the hall. He took me in and about two or three more policemen also entered the room.

At this point they just started swinging at me, hitting me any place they pleased. They did this for about two or three minutes. After they were satisfied they brought me back out into the hall and they escorted Hill into the room. This policeman, I could hear him tell Hill, "I don't have my gun, what are you going to do about it?" and they started beating Hill. In the process, he told Hill to bark, bark like a dog, and Hill wouldn't, at first, so I could hear them punching on him harder and harder and pretty soon he started to bark and he said, "That is right, you bark like a black dog." They beat him a little while longer.

Then they brought him out of the room and had him stand up against the wall with me. Then another policeman came in the room and the policemen that were there, they told him that we were to be taken to a cell. This policeman, he took us out of the room and down the hall to a couple of cells and he locked us in. When he was locking us in, I asked him "Could we make a phone call" and the policeman said, "You are being held here as a suspicious person," and he said a suspicious person is not allowed to make a phone call until seventy-two hours are up.

So we were locked up at this time. We waited roughly for about two and a half days, and a policeman came around and told us that we were charged with disorderly conduct and at this time we were allowed to make a phone call to make arrangements to get out of jail if we wanted to. So I called home and had my sister to come down and post bond and get me out and when I arrived home—

Mr. Glickstein: Mr. Marks, did you ask to see a doctor while you were in jail?

Mr. Marks: Yes, I did. But the policemen said I didn't need to see a doctor.

Mr. Glickstein: And after you were released, were you charged with a crime?

Mr. Marks: After we were released?

Mr. Glickstein: You said you went home.

Mr. Marks: Yes.

Mr. Glickstein: Were you charged with a crime at that time?

Mr. Marks: Yes, the policeman came around on Wednesday afternoon, I think it was, and he said we were charged with disorderly conduct and he said we could make a phone call at this time to make some arrangement to get out of jail if we wanted to. I called home and I found my sister there and I had some money at home and I told her where to go get it, where to come and get me out of jail.

She did this. When I arrived home, I called Hill's parents because they did not know where he was at, but his mother was at work. So I borrowed some money from my sister and I went back down and I bonded Hill out and later that evening I called Miss Turner, Director of CORE, because I was a member of a CORE organization. She referred me to Mr. Stanley Tolliver for legal advice and we had to appear in court the following day. The Judge there asked us did we plead guilty or not guilty. We pleaded not guilty. So the trial was continued and we requested for a jury trial. A couple of months later, we received this trial—

Mr. Glickstein: Were you both tried together?

Mr. Marks: No, we were tried separate.

Mr. Glickstein: Who was tried first?

Mr. Marks: John Hill was tried first.

Mr. Glickstein: What happened?

Mr. Marks: The jury could not come to a decision, so the Judge said that we would have to have another trial. While waiting for the next trial, the police prosecutor made us several offers and we refused them all.

Mr. Glickstein: What kind of offers?

Mr. Marks: If we would plead guilty as charged, they guaranteed us that our fines would only be so much, but if we did not plead guilty and we were found guilty, that we could get the maximum sentence. So we refused this offer and later we had to appear in court again. The day before the new trial, the police prosecutor said that if we agreed to sign papers that we would not try to sue the arresting officer, the Police Department would drop the charges. So we agreed to this and signed papers and that was the end of it.

Mr. Glickstein: So the charges were dropped and you were never yourself put on trial?

Mr. Marks: No, I was never put on trial.

Mr. Glickstein: How has this experience affected your view of the Police Department?

Mr. Marks: I don't think too much of the Police Department. It has been proved time and time again that there is a dual law enforcement standard. There is one law enforcement standard for the Negro citizen and there's another for white.

It is not a question of opinion. It has been proven time and time again.

Mr. Glickstein: Thank you, Mr. Marks. I have no further questions.

IV

The recommendations of the Kerner Commission Report well represented the response of liberal Americans to the ghetto riots. The Commission saw two possible policy routes for the nation to follow: one was "enrichment," the other was "integration." The first would encourage massive federal and state funding to improve ghetto conditions; the second would use the funds to break down the ghetto walls and help the black escape ghetto conditions. The Commission threw its weight solidly behind the integration choice. In no other way, they argued, could American citizens live and work according to their capacities and desires, not their color.

THE KERNER COMMISSION'S
CHOICES FOR THE FUTURE, 1968

The complexity of American society offers many choices for the future of relations between central cities and suburbs and patterns of white and Negro settlement in metropolitan areas. For practical purposes, however, we see two fundamental questions:

1. Should future Negro population growth be concentrated in central cities, as in the past twenty years, and should Negro and white populations become even more residentially segregated?
2. Should society provide greatly increased special assistance to Negroes and other relatively disadvantaged population groups?

For purposes of analysis, the Commission has defined three basic choices for the future embodying specific answers to these questions.

The Present Policies Choice

Under this course, the nation would maintain approximately the share of resources now being allocated to programs of assistance for the poor, unemployed, and disadvantaged. These programs are likely to grow, given continuing economic growth and rising federal revenues, but they will not grow fast enough to stop, let alone reverse, the already deteriorating quality of life in central-city ghettos.

This choice carries the highest ultimate price.

The Enrichment Choice

Under this course, the nation would seek to offset the effects of continued Negro segregation and deprivation in large city ghettos. The enrichment choice would aim at creating dramatic improvements in the quality of life in disadvantaged central-city neighborhoods—both white and Negro. It would require marked increases in federal spending for education, housing, employment, job training, and social services.

The enrichment choice would seek to lift poor Negroes and whites above poverty status and thereby give them the capacity to enter the mainstream of American life. But it would not, at least for many years, appreciably affect either the increasing concentration of Negroes in the ghetto or racial segregation in residential areas outside the ghetto.

The Integration Choice

This choice would be aimed at reversing the movement of the country toward two societies, separate and unequal.

The integration choice—like the enrichment choice—would call for large-scale improvement in the quality of ghetto life. But it would also involve both creating strong incentives for Negro movement out

In *U.S. Kerner Commission Report* (Washington, D.C., 1968), pp. 395–409.

of central-city ghettos and enlarging freedom of choice concerning housing, employment, and schools.

The result would fall considerably short of full integration. The experience of other ethnic groups indicates that some Negro households would be scattered in largely white residential areas. Others—probably a larger number—would voluntarily cluster together in largely Negro neighborhoods. The integration choice would thus produce both integration and segregation. But the segregation would be voluntary.

Articulating these three choices plainly oversimplifies the possibilities open to the country. We believe, however, that they encompass the basic issues—issues which the American public must face if it is serious in its concern not only about civil disorder, but the future of our democratic society.

The present policies choice plainly would involve continuation of efforts like Model Cities, manpower programs, and the War on Poverty. These are in fact enrichment programs, designed to improve the quality of life in the ghetto.

Because of their limited scope and funds, however, they constitute only very modest steps toward enrichment—and would continue to do so even if these programs were somewhat enlarged or supplemented.

The premise of the enrichment choice is performance. To adopt this choice would require a substantially greater share of national resources—sufficient to make a dramatic, visible impact on life in the urban Negro ghetto.

The Effect of Enrichment on Civil Disorders

Effective enrichment policies probably would have three immediate effects on civil disorders.

First, announcement of specific large-scale programs and the demonstration of a strong intent to carry them out might persuade ghetto residents that genuine remedies for their problems were forthcoming, thereby allaying tensions.

Second, such announcements would strongly stimulate the aspirations and hopes of members of these communities—possibly well beyond the capabilities of society to deliver and to do so promptly. This might increase frustration and discontent to some extent cancelling the first effect.

Third, if there could be immediate action on meaningful job training and the creation of productive jobs for large numbers of unemployed young people, they would become much less likely to engage in civil disorders.

Such action is difficult now, when there are about 583,000 young Negro men aged sixteen to twenty-four in central cities—of whom 131,000, or 22.5 percent, are unemployed and probably two or three times as many are underemployed. It will not become easier in the future. By 1975, this age group will have grown to nearly 700,000.

Consequently, there is no certainty that the enrichment choice would do much more in the near future to diminish violent incidents in central cities than would the present policies choice. However, if enrichment programs can succeed in meeting the needs of residents of disadvantaged areas for jobs, education, housing, and city services, then over the years this choice is almost certain to reduce both the level and frequency of urban disorder.

The enrichment choice by no means seeks to perpetuate racial segregation. In the end, however, its premise is that disadvantaged Negroes can achieve equality of opportunity with whites while continuing in conditions of nearly complete separation.

This premise has been vigorously advocated by black power proponents. While most Negroes originally desired racial integration, many are losing hope of ever achieving it because of seemingly implacable white resistance. Yet they cannot bring themselves to accept the conclusion that most of the millions of Negroes who are forced to live racially segregated lives must therefore be condemned to inferior lives —to inferior educations, or inferior housing, or inferior status.

Rather, they reason, there must be some way to make the quality of life in the ghetto areas just as good. And if equality cannot be achieved through integration then it is not surprising that some black power advocates are denouncing integration and claiming that, given the hypocrisy and racism that pervade white society, life in a black society is, in fact, morally superior. This argument is understandable, but there is a great deal of evidence that it is false.

The economy of the United States and particularly the sources of employment are preponderantly white. In this circumstance, a policy of separate but equal employment could only relegate Negroes permanently to inferior incomes and economic status.

In the end, whatever its benefits, the enrichment choice might well invite a prospect similar to that of the present policies choice: separate white and black societies.

The Integration Choice

The third and last course open to the nation combines enrichment with programs designed to encourage integration of substantial numbers of Negroes into the society outside the ghetto.

Enrichment must be an important adjunct to any integration course. No matter how ambitious or energetic such a program may be, few Negroes now living in central-city ghettos would be quickly integrated. In the meantime, significant improvement in their present environment is essential.

The enrichment aspect of this third choice should, however, be recognized as interim action, during which time expanded and new programs can work to improve education and earning power. The length of the interim period surely would vary. For some it may be long. But in any event, what should be clearly recognized is that enrichment is only a means toward the goal; it is not the goal.

The goal must be achieving freedom for every citizen to live and work according to his capacities and desires, not his color.

We believe there are four important reasons why American society must give this course the most serious consideration. First, future jobs are being created primarily in the suburbs, but the chronically unemployed population is increasingly concentrated in the ghetto. This separation will make it more and more difficult for Negroes to achieve anything like full employment in decent jobs. But if, over time, these residents began to find housing outside central cities, they would be exposed to more knowledge of job opportunities. They would have to make much shorter trips to reach jobs. They would have a far better chance of securing employment on a self-sustaining basis.

Second, in the judgment of this Commission, racial and social class integration is the most effective way of improving the education of ghetto children.

Third, developing an adequate housing supply for low-income and middle-income families and true freedom of choice of housing for Negroes of all income levels will require substantial out-movement. We do not believe that such an out-movement will occur spontaneously merely as a result of increasing prosperity among Negroes in central cities. A national fair housing law is essential to begin such movement. In many suburban areas, a program combining positive incentives with the building of new housing will be necessary to carry it out.

Fourth, and by far the most important, integration is the only course which explicitly seeks to achieve a single nation other than accepting the present movement toward a dual society. This choice would enable us at least to begin reversing the profoundly divisive trend already so evident in our metropolitan areas—before it becomes irreversible.

V

The response of many black leaders to the riots in particular, and to the persistence of discrimination in the United States in general, differed markedly from that of the Kerner Commission. Particularly those who headed the new and more radical black organizations, such as the Congress of Racial Equality (CORE), insisted that the only way that blacks would ever improve their condition was through the exertion of black power—that is, through the organization of blacks to further their own economic, political, and social aims. Floyd McKissick, national director of CORE, explained the need for unity among blacks and defended this strategy before a Senate committee concerned with urban conditions.

BLACK POWER, 1966

TESTIMONY OF FLOYD MCKISSICK

The central cities of this country are disaster areas—the debris is mounting, the walking wounded everywhere. For weeks you have been

In *Federal Role in Urban Affairs*, Hearings Before the Subcommittee on Executive Reorganization, U.S. Senate, 89th Congress, 2nd session, December 8, 1966, part 2, pp. 2293–300.

listening to the catalogue of this crisis, much as the legislators of the eighteenth century in the plague cities, studied the lists of the dead. It is true: death is everywhere: the death of the body, the death of hope.

I am no longer certain that we can turn the tide. God knows we must try.

There is no time . . . there is no time to talk of half-measures, no time to prosecute wars, no time to lash back at the angry poor, no time to moralize about an integrated utopia . . . there is no time. The seminars must end, the conferences conclude, our wisdom must now be shaped into specific weapons of change.

I will talk about many things—of entire institutions of our society that are crumbling in the central city. I will talk about the black American—the mass of black Americans; paralyzed in poverty; un-motivated, suspicious of the white man's promise, blooded on the streets of Los Angeles and on the streets of Saigon. I will talk of racism through the entire American fabric—a racism that *cannot be changed by law alone.*

And I will talk about black power, its consequence and its meaning.

The tragedy of the recent spasm of reaction and racism in this country is best dramatized in this room . . . for it is in this room for many weeks that you gentlemen have seen in exquisite detail, the frustration, the hopelessness, and the powerlessness of the American urban Negro. There is no better argument for black power—for the mobilization of the black community as a political, social, and economic bloc. Moreover—and this is what we have always meant by black power— it is a rational, militant call from a whole segment of this nation's population to do what *you* have not been able to do—destroy racism in this country, create full employment in the American ghetto, revise the educational system to cope with the twentieth century, and make the American ghetto a place in which it is possible to live with hope.

And once and for all—I am a man of peace, appalled by a society of violence in which I live.

I am tired of violence—not only that which has been inflicted on myself, and my children—but the deeper violence inflicted on the black child in a hopelessly antique system of education; the violence done to the Negro man and the Negro woman, torn apart by the racist employer and defeated by the humiliation of public welfare. *Do not ever forget* . . . 90 percent of the American black community—that immobile 90 percent—which is the main subject of my discussion today—are both the children and the victims of violence.

Gentlemen, I would ask that you keep two basic themes in mind. One: the scope of the problem facing the central city is so large and at the same time the despair and suspicion in the black community so deep that *any* solutions we discuss must be immediate and in large part be financed by the federal budget. Even more important in any such undertaking we must involve and dignify the black man as a fully enfranchised citizen—capable of administering his own recovery. Secondly, I would ask that we regard this problem in crisis terms, and for the moment set side our understandable dreams of integration—set them aside before the "fire next time" is now. As we in CORE have studied the problems facing the mass of American black people, we found over and over again that the great moral struggle for integration has, in fact, barely touched the lives of the people.

Education

In 1954 the Supreme Court ruled that separate or segregated education is, by definition, inferior. We thought that this represented the removal of the major roadblock to full citizenship and real participation in the mainstream of American life for black people.

But the law of the land was not enforced. Twelve and half years later only 13 percent of Negro children in the South attend integrated schools. Today, over 50 percent of the children in N.Y.C. are Negro or Puerto Rican. Ninety percent attend segregated schools.

Most important, however, is the fact that the children left behind are not being taught. A recent survey of the reading levels in the segregated schools of New York shows that almost 87 percent of the children are reading below grade. This is compared to 50 percent below grade in 1954, the year of that great court decision. At this rate, by 1970 all of the children in ghetto schools in that city will be "underachievers."

From the time a black child enters the public schools, he is fighting an uphill battle not to be pushed out of the educational system. Not the best, but the least, experienced teachers are still being assigned to ghetto schools. Teachers rarely teach; they keep order and impose discipline and too often hold their ghetto pupils in low esteem.

The Harlems of this country are public school disaster areas. The continuing failure to educate black and poor children when education is a necessary ingredient for success in this society amounts to genocide. The fact that the "mind-killing" may be unintentional is irrelevant to the victim and of little comfort to the bereaved family.

Integration for all children is not feasible in many large cities today. Yet parents in the black communities of our cities are no longer willing to stand by and watch their children's minds wither and die. Typical are the Negro parents at New York's widely publicized I.S. 201. They demanded of the Board of Education:

1. Black authority figures (e.g., a black principal) with whom their children might [be] able to identify and to whose position they might aspire.
2. They insisted upon sympathetic teachers who represented black children, were supportive and encouraging and who expected black children to learn.
3. They called for a curriculum that reflected the Negro's contribution to world and American history and therefore could rebuild a self damaged by living in a world that ignored them.
4. They pledged themselves to increased participation in their children's lives. By being vigilant and unafraid they knew that they would compel response and respect from the school administration, the teaching staff, and their own children.

In effect, they were saying to educators that if a child with native intelligence is not achieving, the fault does not lie with the child.

Integrated quality education is still a desirable goal and there must be federal action to insure integration wherever feasible . . . in suburban school districts, smaller cities and towns, Southern school systems.

Of all solutions proposed for the ultimate answer to the big city's educational dilemma, CORE would favor the building of centrally located, well-equipped educational complexes offering superior education to all children and the utilization of intelligent curriculums and staffs at all levels.

None of these solutions can really be considered final unless we realize this. Racism is the crux of this nation's problem. Whites must be reeducated if integration is ever to have meaning. It is time for conferences on the White Problem in America. The experts who have been called together so often to discuss the Negro must now turn their attention to white racism and violence in this society.

Housing

Cities do not have the money to survive.

The federal government must develop new concepts of subsidizing people, and free land to be used for human needs.

We must develop programs which do away with the feeling of uselessness of poor people, of black people. They have no property and no chance to own anything. Our society is based on property ownership, our personal identification comes from our jobs, yet black people have few opportunities to participate in either of these critical activities.

We must rebuild our cities to deal with the needs of the people living in them. Rehabilitation programs should be directed toward the elimination of slumlords exploiting the poor and the development of tenant ownership. They should create new jobs for ghetto residents in the rehabilitation work as well as in the management area.

Nearly 80 percent of our citizens living in urban areas, the cities, are being forced to carry the burden of our domestic problems—without any of the resources necessary to do the job.

There is only one answer: the federal government must accept its responsibility. However, history has shown that federal housing programs have never really been used for the benefit of the masses of the people. Only six hundred thousand low-income units have been built since the start of the public housing program thirty years ago. But in less than half that time, nearly seven hundred thousand units, mostly low rental, have been destroyed by federal urban renewal and highway programs. In addition, federal tax incentives and mortgage programs have enabled private builders to take slum land at low costs to build middle and upper income housing. This has resulted in the dislocated being crowded into remaining ghetto areas, where the deterioration of ghetto housing has increased. People who have money already have been getting more: "To him that has, it shall be given."

Gentlemen, the ghetto is a rotten place to live and it is getting worse. We do not think that integration is the way to decent housing. We do think that federal programs, undertaken in cooperation with local communities, should now be directed to the concrete needs of the people, using all mechanisms and resources that have been so cleverly developed to raise tax revenues and sweep the poor under the rug.

We proposed a two-pronged approach:

The first should be massive central-city rebuilding programs to be developed with ghetto residents. This should not be a continuation of token demonstration programs affecting few people, held up by the facade of token community participation. We call for rehabilitation of all existing structures in ghetto areas and the building of new public housing on under-utilized sites. This must include employing and training ghetto people to do the work, and turning the ownership of the buildings over to tenant housing corporations. Let us use the financial devices of urban renewal in the hands of the poor so that ghetto organizations can acquire and improve slum properties and operate them as decent housing.

Let us make money available at low interest rates. Let us create and develop black contracting companies who train and hire black workers. Let us provide sufficient rent supplements so that people can pay rents increased by rehabilitation costs.

The second is the construction of new cities. While many planners have looked to new towns as a solution to many urban problems, we see them as a way of dealing with the increasing migration of black farm workers to the cities. The construction of new cities offers tremendous opportunities for creation of new jobs, for the development of a whole new skilled population, and most importantly, for the creation of a new environment fit for men, black and white, to live in.

Employment

It is appropriate here to cite the following statistics: In August 1965, the white unemployment rate was 4.1 percent and the Negro unemployment rate was 7.7 percent. The traditional level of almost twice as many unemployed blacks as whites. Presently, white unemployment is down to 3.5 percent while at the same time, Negro unemployment has risen to the tragic figure of 8 percent. The gap continues to widen. Among young men of eighteen to twenty-four, the national rate of unemployment is five times as high for Negros as for whites. In addition to the problem of unemployment is the hidden factor of equal pay for equal work. Negroes with Ph.Ds make four thousand dollars less than white Ph.Ds.

The Congress of Racial Equality believes that immediate corrective measures must be instituted. The development of Negro skills is being prevented by racist practices by both government and private industry. Organized labor hasn't cleared its own house yet. The opening up of apprentice programs across the board could be a first step. For example, in New York City, according to a recent article in the *New York Times*, the plumbers and electricians unions continue gross discriminatory practices to the extent that only about twenty-five Negroes are electricians and plumbers in this great American city, the "example" of democracy.

First, we should consider creation of jobs for the poor. We do not have in mind "make work" programs, but programs which would affect the hard-core unemployed.

Secondly, thousands of ghetto dwellers can be employed in

hospitals. There are tasks too numerous to mention which can be performed by unskilled persons, relieving nurses and other hospital personnel to attend to their primary tasks. Such subprofessional jobs inherently have potential for advancement. In addition, libraries are understaffed, city streets are filthy, parks need more employees. All of these and many other needs can be alleviated by giving people employment in their own communities, with the financial support and insistence of the federal government.

Another primary concern of ours is the operation of businesses by black people in their own communities. In this, too, there is much more that must be done by the federal government. It has been almost impossible for black men to obtain financing from the white banking and mortgaging community.

We need many more black-owned businesses in our black communities, employing local residents. Secretarial schools and small business training programs should be supported by government funds. Cooperatives and credit unions should be encouraged.

The Congress of Racial Equality will continue to do its share. If government, private industry, and labor do theirs, full employment and productivity can be a reality for all.

In summary, the urban crisis must come into this room. The anguish of poor people—black people fenced into the squalid ghettos—must actually govern your deliberations. The themes repeat endlessly—the ghettos are here, polluted by racism and cynicism—and the people are here, shattered, humiliated, and vengeful. Nothing short of an immense national commitment spending the nation's resources on life as easily as we spend them on death in battle—nothing short of this can take us out of this dishonorable time of our history.

Chapter 21

The Women's Liberationist Societies

IN THE FIRST DECADE after World War Two, the ideals set forth for women and children in the 1920s seemed to be flourishing. In mounting numbers middle-class families sought refuge in the suburbs. They defended their choice of life styles by insisting that in the suburbs children could be raised in a safe and protective environment, and that women could most pleasantly fulfill the role of wife-companion. If the family in these suburban communities seemed to resemble a nursery hothouse, so much the better for everyone.

It did not take long, however, for cracks to appear in the picture windows. In 1963, Betty Friedan published her best-selling volume, *The Feminine Mystique*, and it struck a responsive chord in many suburban housewives. Friedan insisted that the hothouse environment of the family was suffocating the woman. She had no independent outlet for her energies; she had to seek self-fulfillment through her children and husband. This inherently frustrating position made her into an overprotective mother and an excessively demanding wife. As a result, her children ended up all too frequently on the psychiatrist's couch and she and her husband ended up in a divorce court. Friedan declared that when a woman responded to the question "Who Am I?" by saying "Tom's wife . . . Mary's mother," she had condemned herself to minimal satisfactions and competence. Friedan's message was clear: women had better escape the confines of the family to find satisfaction in a challenging work setting.

The great popularity of Friedan's book lay in the fact that more and more middle-class and married women were making that very choice. They read *The Feminine Mystique* with relief, for here was a book that told them that the cause of their own dissatisfactions did not rest with their own personal inadequacy but with the domestic role that they

498

were forced to play. Friedan urged them to be not just mothers or wives, but to be persons—and that was a message they desperately wanted to hear.

In the decade following 1963, the dedication of more and more women to the ideal of personhood became intense. Women's liberation organizations took this standard for their own, and, through a myriad of political, economic, and social activities, strove to establish it. No sooner did women begin to enter the work force than they discovered a series of obvious and crucial discriminations. They would work at the same jobs as men for the same hours but receive less pay! Oftentimes, routes of advancement into top management posts were blocked because of male biases against them. They discovered that a quota system limited their ability to enter law schools and medical schools. With each discovery came mounting pressures from feminists to end this discrimination, to give women the status of complete persons throughout society. The imminent passage of the Equal Rights Amendment to the Constitution, prohibiting all forms of discrimination against women, is one manifestation of their success.

The position of the woman in the family, as well as in the work force, has also been a target for women's liberation activities. Why should women perform all the tedious household chores, they ask? If husbands have a night out, why not the wives? Why should child rearing be a responsibility only for the woman? Under the press of these questions, traditional definitions of male and female roles have for the first time been successfully challenged.

In many ways, accommodation between adult men and women is most easily accomplished. They can make their agreements before marriage, and newly liberalized divorce codes help to ensure that no one will be trapped in a marital situation against his or her will. But a more complicated issue raised by the women's movement concerns the place of the child in this new state of affairs. With both man and woman committed to their occupational goals, who is left to care for the child? If men and women are determined to be persons, is there room left over for mothering or fathering? One popular answer to this question among newly married couples today is to restrict the number of children in the household. The post-World-War-Two bulge in family size has receded; middle-class families are now experiencing the unprecedented low birthrate of 1.9 children per family. Another popular answer has been to advocate and utilize day-care centers for children. Let public institutions perform the job that private families once did. Both of these responses certainly indicate that the shape of the family in the coming decades will probably depart in significant ways from the traditional family. The structure and functions of the family in the future cannot yet be predicted. But there can be no doubting the magnitude of the changes that we are about to confront.

I

The growth of the suburbs in the post-World-War-Two period was rapid and extensive. Middle-class families, taking advantage of liberal federally financed mortgage opportunities, left their apartments in the city, and moved to new residential developments. The suburbs were properly called "bedroom communities." The men typically commuted to their jobs nearby in cities (there were no industries or offices in the suburbs), the children went off to school, and the women remained home to meet the school bus and the commuter train. Unlike the city streets, the suburban roads were empty for most of the day; only the very old, the very young, and the women used them. But however odd and unusual these conditions may have seemed, residents defended suburban life as healthy, especially for their children. To examine firsthand the character of suburban life, sociologist John Seely and several colleagues interviewed and studied the families of "Crestwood Heights," their pseudonym for a wealthy suburb on the outskirts of Toronto. Seely's account calls into question just how well the families fared in these new communities.

CRESTWOOD HEIGHTS, 1956

JOHN R. SEELY,

R. ALEXANDER SIM,

AND ELIZABETH W. LOOSEY

The ideal Crestwood family, is, therefore, greatly different from the ideal family of previous decades. If we might use an analogy, the Crestwood family now seems a little like a country which, having operated under an authoritarian form of government, has suddenly switched to a democratic form, without too much preparation for the change. The parents, who are still held legally responsible for the rearing of the children, are, at the same time, shorn of the moral sanction they once had for the exercise of absolute power over the subordinate children, an authority then thought to follow "naturally" from age and the dominant economic position of the parents (particularly the father), and further buttressed supernaturally by traditional religious norms. The father, it is true, still holds the economic power, but he is now culturally enjoined from exercising it in "despotic" ways. A central problem of the family now appears to be the allocation of power among its members so that each may participate, not in the earning of the family income, but in the emotional and social life of the family unit.

Reprinted with permission of Basic Books, Inc. from *Crestwood Heights: A Study of the Culture of Suburban Life*, by John R. Seely, R. Alexander Sim, and Elizabeth W. Loosey (New York, 1956), pp. 167–69, 173–75, 194–96, 208–209. Copyright © 1956 by Basic Books, Inc.

One observation report of Father's Day at a Crestwood Heights nursery school is particularly revealing as to paternal attitudes toward current child rearing theories.

> When I [the researcher, a man] arrived at the Nursery School, Mr. X, [a father], whom I had met twice at meetings previously this week, was leading two children out to the playground, where there were already about a dozen children playing.
>
> Mrs. N., the Nursery School supervisor, provided me with an observation form and sent me out to the playground. There a second father was trailing his daughter on the boardwalk. He followed her around solicitously three or four times, then left to come over to Mr. X. and me. Soon his daughter came running to him.
>
> Both fathers tried periodically to participate with the children, but rather unsuccessfully. They very quickly got tired of the teeter and left. Very soon they were beginning to complain of the cold and to look at their watches.
>
> Mrs. N. came out after a while and seemed compelled to keep the fathers informed and observing. At every free moment she would corner a father, telling him what was happening, psychologically, to the children here.
>
> One father expressed concern about the children falling from the jungle gym. Mrs. N. said her theory was that they wouldn't climb farther than they safely could. "Other teachers [and presumably mothers] would agree with me on that."
>
> A third father, Mr. Y., arrived. He joined the ranks of the watching fathers, saying that things were different now. *His* father would never have come to school. He went on about the respect of children for aged parents. His father-in-law had always taken it out on his children because of his own inferiority complex. Now he was complaining that they didn't look after him. Mr. Y. himself said he wasn't going to rely on *his* children. He was buying a wheel chair and a coffin while he could.
>
> The other father, Mr. T., thought that it was silly for people to take vengeance on their children, or to be very strict simply for the sake of discipline.
>
> Mr. X. commented that he didn't see how his son would be playing like this, when he had fallen at home several days previously and broken a collar bone.
>
> Mrs. N. told Mr. Y. that the sandpile was a popular part of their equipment. "In the Fall, that's the first thing the disturbed children head for."
>
> I asked Mr. X. how this compared with his childhood. He replied that nobody made all this fuss over *him*. "My mother had four children, and my old man was always out hustling, so I didn't get much attention." He didn't think it had done any harm, and that maybe they were making too much fuss.
>
> I asked how all this affected the children when they got home. Mr. X. said they were tired out and didn't want to play with kids in the block, but then that was unorganized play. He went on to tell me about his son [seven] playing space war. One tree was the bombs, another tree was a wing of the space ship, and so on. He couldn't understand this, and his son became annoyed.
>
> Back in the Nursery School, the fathers grouped themselves apart from the children. Mr. Y. commented that this was mother's stuff, and the fathers were embarrassed. They were amazed that here the children were little adults, although at home they were just children; and he

showed surprise when one child upset some blocks and spontaneously picked them up.

Mr. X. and I sneaked out for a smoke in the teacher's room. There he expanded his theories and ideas about modern youth. Their trouble was they had no initiative, no drive, no ambition. He saw that every day in his plant. All they wanted was a car. Single men were the worst. When they married and got some responsibilities their production tripled. His theory of character was that it was cyclical. One generation did well, gave their children everything. When they grew up, they saw that material goods weren't everything, and made their kids appreciate things and fend for themselves. He himself was spoiled but his kid was going to learn to earn. When he was old enough, he would get him a paper route. Of course his son wouldn't lack material things, or love either, but he wouldn't get everything automatically.

The same father was later getting the names of all kinds of toys from the teachers for his son: tempera paints, blocks, easel for painting, etc. And all the time during indoor play, his son kept shouting "Hi, Dad!" Once the child broke away, ran over to his father, and kissed his well-manicured hand. Mr. X. said, "That makes it all worthwhile."

After the fathers had left, and most of the children had been picked up by their mothers (five children had not come because their mothers didn't have time to bring them, and older brothers and sisters wouldn't be bothered), Mrs. N. commented "Fathers are less tied up with the children than mothers, but don't quote me on that. If we'd had the fathers earlier in the year, it might be different. When the mothers were here, they were much more involved with the children at play."

The three teachers agreed that the fathers' visit had been a huge success, and that it did the fathers good to see what went on here. The observer added the following pertinent analysis of paternal behavior in this session: It was particularly noticeable that fathers were uncomfortable when they tried to participate in the child's world. They admired and remarked about the teachers' patience, however. Their orientation to the world of reality prevented them from any genuine appreciation of the child's fantasy world, which definitely annoyed them because of its irrational nature. Some fathers markedly distrusted the material benefits which they freely give to their children, emphasizing that only hard work and individual effort would benefit the child in the long run. At the same time, some fathers appeared to pursue the very spoiling policies they deplored, asking the teachers for advice about toys to buy, wanting to give their children the most of the very best possible.

These generalized attitudes of paternal aloofness toward the child in nursery school are evident within the family, particularly where discipline is concerned; in many instances the fathers throw the full weight of responsibility for discipline as well as for child care upon the mother. One woman informant had assumed complete duty in this respect.

Oh, he [her husband] was away a lot. Generally he left on Monday and came back Saturday, but there were times when he'd be away for three or four weeks at a time. Just when we were moving here, he had to go West for six weeks. I was a little worried; I didn't know how we would get moved but everything came out all right. *I was used to managing by myself by then. In fact, I preferred to manage by myself; Mr. C. was just a bother.* He's not much around the house. One time in Lea's Woods, he was alone and a fuse blew. He couldn't find the fuse box and had to call up an electrician. I could have fixed it in a jiffy and so could the kids.

However, Brown's [husband's firm] sent up a truck and a driver and the kids pitched in and we got moved. The furniture movers took the big things, of course. Brown's are very good that way. One time, Mr. C. was in the hospital all winter. He had an operation and nearly died. Those were terrible times. He was away all winter. Then Brown's sent him South for a couple of weeks' rest. I took the children down to the hospital once around Christmas. They say they remember it, but I don't know. *When their father came home, he was a complete stranger to them.*

I don't remember having any problems particularly in those days. I was busy all the time. There were anxious moments but we always got over them. The children weren't hard to manage. They'd be in bed by seven, so I had time to get things straightened up after that.

Often in the middle teens, a new relationship is established between mother and daughter, or father and son. Girls and their mothers more frequently build up strong friendship ties around common interests: shopping, luncheons, teas (sometimes the début), and finally the girl's engagement and marriage. Boys do not find it as easy to form such a relationship with the father, since they can rarely share as yet in the father's business or profession. A few fathers and sons do become "buddies," spending time together at baseball games, hunting or fishing, or in the family car.

[In the following passage a young girl describes her social life and that of her teenage sister.]

Most of my sister's friendships can be traced to the school to which she goes. She participates in a wide range of school activities (modern dance group, choir, etc.) and hence has a wide range of friends. Her two closest friends are not as active as she, and both are in fifth form, while my sister is in fourth form. Both of them live very close to us and they all walk to school together every day. The boys that she goes out with are usually those in their fifth form at Crestwood Heights. They usually met her at fraternity parties when she was with a boy from Crestwood Heights. *Thus both her girlfriends and boyfriends can ultimately be traced to the school.*

Another group from which many of her friendships can be traced is the sorority to which she belongs. This group is composed of about twenty-three girls from different schools, of whom thirteen go to Crestwood Heights. The sorority helps to widen her sphere of friends both in terms of school affiliation and age (since the group is composed of girls from second to fifth forms, and even the "alums" maintain their interest in it, my sister tells me).

As for myself, my closest friends are those I've made at school. One of these I've known since second form High School, and we have gone right through high school and university together. The others I met when I first came to university. Most of them are in the same course as myself, though I have one very good friend in Psychology. I guess we more or less form a clique, sitting together in class, eating lunch together, borrowing notes from one another, etc. When I became engaged, these girls held a party for my fiancé and me, and similarly when another one of the clique became engaged, we held a sleigh-ride party for her. My two closest friends are engaged, and although I do not see as much of them in the evenings as I do of my fiancé's friends, nevertheless, I think I see more of them now than I did when each of us was unattached and going out with a different group of boys.

I find in my university course, not only my close friends (i.e. those that I see also when school is over) but also people whom I consider my friends, but whom I don't see outside of school.

The sorority to which I belong has helped me to cement the friendships formed at school, for many of the latter are also sorority sisters, and hence we have the added bond of working together in a joint effort for a common purpose. Through the sorority, I have not only made friends among my peers, but have formed close relationships with the girls who have graduated, many of whom are now married and have children, and with the girls who have just entered Varsity and with those in their second and third years. The sorority has thus widened my sphere of friends, and by joining the alumni group next year, I intend to lend continuity to these friendships which I have gained as an undergraduate.

Another group that is becoming increasingly significant for me is the family and friendship group of my fiancé. Since he is an only son, I was afraid, at first, that his family might resent me. However, I've been extremely fortunate in that his parents have been wonderful to me and have always made me feel welcome. His mother likes to have me drop in on her some afternoon during the week, and, in fact, is quick to remind me if I skip a week or two. However, she is also quite understanding and takes an interest in my activities. I am usually at their home for dinner every Friday night, and feel very much at home there. With regard to the friends of my fiancé, two of them were friends even before I met my fiancé: one is the son of the family who used to live next door to us and who are still such close friends of my parents, and the other (who is now married) had gone to public school with me and had occasionally taken me out during high school and my first year of university. The other friends I got to know quite well simply from the process of double-dating with them whenever I was with my fiancé. Hence, these boys were not strangers to me when I became engaged, and I have come to look upon them more and more as my own friends.

II

"The problem that has no name" is how Betty Friedan first described the malaise that she found so endemic among middle- and upper-class suburban women in the early 1960s. Friedan came upon her subject rather by accident when she attended a tenth year reunion among the graduates of Smith college—a prestigious all-woman institution. In the course of interviewing these women, she found that they expressed an incredible dissatisfaction with their lives. The complaints, she quickly realized, were not idiosyncratic. Rather, they reflected in clear fashion the emptiness of the roles that these women were fulfilling. Her analysis of this phenomenon, The Feminine Mystique, *quickly became a best seller. It is no exaggeration to say that the American women's liberation movement was born with this tract.*

THE FEMININE MYSTIQUE, 1963

BETTY FRIEDAN

Just what was this problem that has no name? What were the words women used when they tried to express it? Sometimes a woman would say "I feel empty somehow . . . incomplete." Or she would say, "I feel as if I don't exist." Sometimes she blotted out the feeling with a tranquilizer. Sometimes she thought the problem was with her husband, or her children, or that what she really needed was to redecorate her house, or move to a better neighborhood, or have an affair, or another baby. Sometimes, she went to a doctor with symptoms she could hardly describe: "A tired feeling . . . I get so angry with the children it scares me . . . I feel like crying without any reason." (A Cleveland doctor called it "the housewife's syndrome.")

Sometimes a woman would tell me that the feeling gets so strong she runs out of the house and walks through the streets. Or she stays inside her house and cries. Or her children tell her a joke, and she doesn't laugh because she doesn't hear it. I talked to women who had spent years on the analyst's couch, working out their "adjustment to the feminine role," their blocks to "fulfillment as a wife and mother." But the desperate tone in these women's voices, and the look in their eyes, was the same as the tone and the look of other women, who were sure they had no problem, even though they did have a strange feeling of desperation.

A mother of four who left college at nineteen to get married told me:

> I've tried everything women are supposed to do—hobbies, gardening, pickling, canning, being very social with my neighbors, joining committees, running PTA teas. I can do it all, and I like it, but it doesn't leave you anything to think about—any feeling of who you are. I never had any career ambitions. All I wanted was to get married and have four children. I love the kids and Bob and my home. There's no problem you can even put a name to. But I'm desperate. I begin to feel I have no personality. I'm a server of food and putter-on of pants and a bedmaker, somebody who can be called on when you want something. But who am I?

In 1960, the problem that has no name bursts like a boil through the image of the happy American housewife. In the television commercials the pretty housewives still beamed over their foaming dishpans and *Time's* cover story on "The Suburban Wife, an American Phenomenon" protested: "Having too good a time . . . to believe that they should be unhappy." But the actual unhappiness of the American housewife was suddenly being reported—from the *New York Times* and *Newsweek* to *Good Housekeeping* and CBS Television ("The Trapped Housewife"), although almost everybody who talked about it found some superficial reason to dismiss it. It was attributed to incompetent appliance repair-

Selection reprinted from *The Feminine Mystique* by Betty Friedan. By permission of W. W. Norton & Company, Inc. Copyright © 1974, 1963 by Betty Friedan (New York, 1963), pp. 20–22, 26–28, 32, 282, 287–88, 296, 304, 338, 342–45, 378.

men (*New York Times*), or the distances children must be chauffeured in the suburbs (*Time*), or too much PTA (*Redbook*). Some said it was the old problem—education: more and more women had education, which naturally made them unhappy in their role as housewives. "The road from Freud to Frigidaire, from Sophocles to Spock, has turned out to be a bumpy one," reported the *New York Times* (June 28, 1960). "Many young women—certainly not all—whose education plunged them into a world of ideas feel stifled in their homes. They find their routine lives out of joint with their training. Like shut-ins, they feel left out. In the last year, the problem of the educated housewife has provided the meat of dozens of speeches made by troubled presidents of women's colleges who maintain, in the face of complaints, that sixteen years of academic training is realistic preparation for wifehood and motherhood."

It is no longer possible today to blame the problem on loss of femininity: to say that education and independence and equality with men have made American women unfeminine. I have heard so many women try to deny this dissatisfied voice within themselves because it does not fit the pretty picture of femininity the experts have given them. I think, in fact, that this is the first clue to the mystery: the problem cannot be understood in the generally accepted terms by which scientists have studied women, doctors have treated them, counselors have advised them, and writers have written about them. Women who suffer this problem, in whom this voice is stirring, have lived their whole lives in the pursuit of feminine fulfillment. They are not career women (although career women may have other problems); they are women whose greatest ambition has been marriage and children. For the oldest of these women, these daughters of the American middle class, no other dream was possible. The ones in their forties and fifties who once had other dreams gave them up and threw themselves joyously into life as housewives. For the youngest, the new wives and mothers, this was the only dream. They are the ones who quit high school and college to marry, or marked time in some job in which they had no real interest until they married. These women are very "feminine" in the usual sense, and yet they still suffer the problem.

Are the women who finished college, the women who once had dreams beyond housewifery, the ones who suffer the most? According to the experts they are, but listen to these four women:

> My days are all busy, and dull, too. All I ever do is mess around. I get up at eight—I make breakfast, so I do the dishes, have lunch, do some more dishes, and some laundry and cleaning in the afternoon. Then it's supper dishes and I get to sit down a few minutes, before the children have to be sent to bed. That's all there is to my day. It's just like any other wife's day. Humdrum. The biggest time, I am chasing kids.

> Ye Gods, what do I do with my time? Well, I get up at six. I get my son dressed and then give him breakfast. After that I wash dishes and bathe and feed the baby. Then I get lunch and while the children nap, I sew or mend or iron and do all the other things I can't get done before noon. Then I cook supper for the family and my husband watches TV while I do the dishes. After I get the children to bed, I set my hair and then I go to bed.

The problem is always being the children's mommy, or the minister's wife, and never being myself.

A film made of any typical morning in my house would look like an old Marx Brothers' comedy. I wash the dishes, rush the older children off to school, dash out in the yard to cultivate the chrysanthemums, run back in to make a phone call about a committee meeting, help the youngest child build a blockhouse, spend fifteen minutes skimming the newspapers so I can be well-informed, then scamper down to the washing machines where my thrice-weekly laundry includes enough clothes to keep a primitive village going for an entire year. By noon I'm ready for a padded cell. Very little of what I've done has been really necessary or important. Outside pressures lash me through the day. Yet I look upon myself as one of the more relaxed housewives in the neighborhood. Many of my friends are even more frantic. In the past sixty years we have come full circle and the American housewife is once again trapped in a squirrel cage. If the cage is now a modern plate-glass-and-broadloom ranch house or a convenient modern apartment, the situation is no less painful than when her grandmother sat over an embroidery hoop in her gilt-and-plush parlor and muttered angrily about women's rights.

If I am right, the problem that has no name stirring in the minds of so many American women today is not a matter of loss of femininity or too much education, or the demands of domesticity. It is far more important than anyone recognizes. It is the key to these other new and old problems which have been torturing women and their husbands and children, and puzzling their doctors and educators for years. It may well be the key to our future as a nation and a culture. We can no longer ignore that voice within women that says: "I want something more than my husband and my children and my home."

Over the past fifteen years a subtle and devastating change seems to have taken place in the character of American children. Evidence of something similar to the housewife's problem that has no name in a more pathological form has been seen in her sons and daughters by many clinicians, analysts, and social scientists. They have noted, with increasing concern, a new and frightening passivity, softness, boredom in American children. The danger sign is not the competitiveness engendered by the Little League or the race to get into college, but a kind of infantilism that makes the children of the housewife-mothers incapable of the effort, the endurance of pain and frustration, the discipline needed to compete on the baseball field, or get into college. There is also a new vacant sleepwalking, playing-a-part quality of youngsters who do what they are supposed to do, what the other kids do, but do not seem to feel alive or real in doing it.

The boys and girls in whom I saw it were children of mothers who lived within the limits of the feminine mystique. They were fulfilling their roles as women in the accepted, normal way. Some had more than normal ability, and some had more than normal education, but they were alike in the intensity of their preoccupation with their children, who seemed to be their main and only interest.

One mother, who was terribly disturbed that her son could not learn to read, told me that when he came home with his first report card from kindergarten, she was as "excited as a kid myself, waiting for someone to ask me out on a date Saturday night." She was convinced that the teachers were wrong when they said he wandered around the room in a dream, could not pay attention long enough to do the reading-readiness test. Another mother said that she could not bear it when her sons suffered any trouble or distress at all. It was as if they were herself. She told me:

> I used to let them turn over all the furniture and build houses in the living room that would stay up for days, so there was no place for me even to sit and read. I couldn't bear to make them do what they didn't want to do, even take medicine when they were sick. I couldn't bear for them to be unhappy, or fight, or be angry at me. I couldn't separate them from myself somehow. I was always understanding, patient. I felt guilty leaving them even for an afternoon. I worried over every page of their homework; I was always concentrating on being a good mother. I was proud that Steve didn't get in fights with other kids in the neighborhood. I didn't even realize anything was wrong until he started doing so badly in school, and having nightmares about death, and didn't want to go to school because he was afraid of the other boys.

I do not think it is a coincidence that the increasing passivity—and dreamlike unreality—of today's children has become so widespread in the same years that the feminine mystique encouraged the great majority of American women—including the most able, and the growing numbers of the educated—to give up their own dreams, and even their own education, to live through their children.

In a clinic, a therapist spoke of a mother who was panicky because her child could not learn to read at school, though his intelligence tested high. The mother had left college, thrown herself into the role of housewife, and had lived for the time when her son would go to school, and she would fulfill herself in his achievement. Until therapy made the mother "separate" herself from the child, he had no sense of himself as a separate being at all. He could, would, do nothing, even in play, unless someone told him to. He could not even learn to read, which took a self of his own.

It is time to stop exhorting mothers to "love" their children more, and face the paradox between the mystique's demand that women devote themselves completely to their home and their children, and the fact that most of the problems now being treated in child-guidance clinics are solved only when the mothers are helped to develop autonomous interests of their own, and no longer need to fill their emotional needs through their children. It is time to stop exhorting women to be more "feminine" when it breeds a passivity and dependence that depersonalizes sex and imposes an impossible burden on their husbands, a growing passivity in their sons. . . . When society asks so little of women, every woman has to listen to her own inner voice to find her identity in this changing world. She must create, out of her own needs and abilities, a new life plan, fitting in the love and children and home that have defined femininity in the past with the work toward a greater purpose that shapes the future.

It would be quite wrong for me to offer any woman easy how-to answers to this problem. There are no easy answers, in America today; it is difficult, painful, and takes perhaps a long time for each woman to find her own answer. First, she must unequivocally say "no" to the housewife image. This does not mean, of course, that she must divorce her husband, abandon her children, give up her home. She does not have to choose between marriage and career; that was the mistaken choice of the feminine mystique. In actual fact, it is not as difficult as the feminine mystique implies, to combine marriage and motherhood and even the kind of lifelong personal purpose that once was called "career." It merely takes a new life plan—in terms of one's whole life as a woman.

The first step in that plan is to see housework for what it is—not a career, but something that must be done as quickly and efficiently as possible. Once a woman stops trying to make cooking, cleaning, washing, ironing, "something more," she can say "no, I don't want a stove with rounded corners, I don't want four different kinds of soap." She can say "no" to those mass daydreams of the women's magazines and television, "no" to the depth researchers and manipulators who are trying to run her life. Then, she can use the vacuum cleaner and the dishwasher and all the automatic appliances, and even the instant mashed potatoes for what they are truly worth—to save time that can be used in more creative ways.

The second step, and perhaps the most difficult for the products of sex-directed education, is to see marriage as it really is, brushing aside the veil of over-glorification imposed by the feminine mystique. Many women I talked to felt strangely discontented with their husbands, continually irritated with their children, when they saw marriage and motherhood as the final fulfillment of their lives. But when they began to use their various abilities with a purpose of their own in society, they not only spoke of a new feeling of "aliveness" or "completeness" in themselves, but of a new, though hard to define, difference in the way they felt about their husbands and children. Many echoed this woman's words:

> The funny thing is, I enjoy my children more now that I've made room for myself. Before, when I was putting my whole self into the children, it was as if I was always looking for something through them. I couldn't just enjoy them as I do now, as though they were a sunset, something outside me, separate. Before, I felt so tied down by them, I'd try to get away in my mind. Maybe a woman has to be *by herself* to be really *with* her children.

The only way for a woman, as for a man, to find herself, to know herself as a person, is by creative work of her own. There is no other way. But a job, any job, is not the answer—in fact, it can be part of the trap. Women who do not look for jobs equal to their actual capacity, who do not let themselves develop the lifetime interests and goals which require serious education and training, who take a job at twenty or forty to "help out at home" or just to kill extra time, are walking, almost as surely as the ones who stay inside the housewife trap, to a nonexistent future.

If a job is to be the way out of the trap for a woman, it must be a job that she can take seriously as part of a life plan, work in which she can grow as part of society. Suburban communities, particularly the new communities where social, cultural, educational, political, and recreational patterns are not as yet firmly established, offer numerous opportunities for the able, intelligent woman. But such work is not necessarily a "job." In Westchester, on Long Island, in the Philadelphia suburbs, women have started mental-health clinics, art centers, day camps. In big cities and small towns, women all the way from New England to California have pioneered new movements in politics and education. Even if this work was not thought of as "job" or "career," it was often so important to the various communities that professionals are now being paid for doing it.

Who knows what women can be when they are finally free to become themselves? Who knows what women's intelligence will contribute when it can be nourished without denying love? Who knows of the possibilities of love when men and women share not only children, home, and garden, not only the fulfillment of their biological roles, but the responsibilities and passions of the work that creates the human future and the full human knowledge of who they are? It has barely begun, the search of women for themselves. But the time is at hand when the voices of the feminine mystique can no longer drown out the inner voice that is driving women on to become complete.

III

The women who did join the work force did not often find quick and easy acceptance in what had been traditionally a man's world. Rather, they learned firsthand what discrimination meant. They probably had read of how blacks in the 1950s had been denied service in restaurants, admission to clubs, or the right to rent vacant apartments. But still they were unprepared to find themselves confronting similar circumstances. Hence, one major focus of the women's movement was to combat these prejudices; their efforts took the form of securing federal antidiscrimination legislation. Reprinted below is the testimony of two outstanding leaders in the women's liberation movement before congressional committees. Gloria Steinem, a noted writer and critic, and Billie Jean King, the outstanding woman tennis player of her generation, described their own experiences in breaking the sex barriers.

ON SEXISM IN AMERICA, 1970

TESTIMONY OF GLORIA STEINEM

Miss Steinem: My name is Gloria Steinem. I am a writer and editor, and I am currently a member of the policy council of the Democratic committee.

During twelve years of working for a living, I have experienced much of the legal and social discrimination reserved for women in this country. I have been refused service in public restaurants, ordered out of public gathering places, and turned away from apartment rentals; all for the clearly-stated, sole reason that I am a woman. And all without the legal remedies available to blacks and other minorities. I have been excluded from professional groups, writing assignments on so-called unfeminine subjects such as politics, full participation in the Democratic Party, jury duty, and even from such small male privileges as discounts on airline fares. Most important to me, I have been denied a society in which women are encouraged, or even allowed to think of themselves as first-class citizens and responsible human beings.

The truth is that all our problems stem from the same sex-based myths. We may appear before you as white radicals or the middle-aged middleclass or black soul sisters, but we are all sisters in fighting against these outdated myths. Like racial myths, they have been reflected in our laws. Let me list a few.

That women are biologically inferior to men. In fact, an equally good case can be made for the reverse. Women live longer than men, even when the men are not subject to business pressures. Women survived Nazi concentration camps better, keep cooler heads in emergencies currently studied by disaster-researchers, are protected against heart attacks by their female sex hormones, and are so much more durable at every stage of life that nature must conceive 20 to 50 percent more males in order to keep the balance going.

Another myth, that women are already treated equally in this society. I am sure there has been ample testimony to prove that equal pay for equal work, equal chance for advancement, and equal training or encouragement are obscenely scarce in every field, even those—like food and fashion industries—that are supposedly "feminine."

A deeper result of social and legal injustice, however, is what sociologists refer to as "Internalized Aggression." Victims of aggression absorb the myth of their own inferiority, and come to believe that their group is in fact second class. Even when they themselves realize they are not second class, they may still think their group is, thus the tendency to be the only Jew in the club, the only black woman on the block, the only woman in the office.

Women suffer this second-class treatment from the moment they are born. They are expected to be, rather than achieve, to function

In *The Equal Rights Amendment*, Hearings Before the Subcommittee on Constitutional Amendments of the Committee on the Judiciary, U.S. Senate, 91st Congress, 2nd session, May 5, 1970, pp. 102–106.

biologically rather than learn. A brother, whatever his intellect, is more likely to get the family's encouragement and education money, while girls are often pressured to conceal ambition and intelligence, to "Uncle Tom."

Another myth, that American women hold great economic power. Fifty-one percent of all shareholders in this country are women. That is a favorite male-chauvinist statistic. However, the number of shares they hold is so small that the total is only 18 percent of all the shares. Even those holdings are often controlled by men.

Similarly, only 5 percent of all the people in the country who receive ten thousand dollars a year or more, earned or otherwise, are women. And that includes the famous rich widows.

Another myth, that children must have full-time mothers. American mothers spend more time with their homes and children than those of any other society we know about. In the past, joint families, servants, a prevalent system in which grandparents raised the children, or family field work in the agrarian systems—all these factors contributed more to child care than the labor-saving devices of which we are so proud.

The truth is that most American children seem to be suffering from too much mother, and too little father. Part of the program of Women's Liberation is a return of fathers to their children. If laws permit women equal work and pay opportunities, men will then be relieved of their role as sole breadwinner. Fewer ulcers, fewer hours of meaningless work, equal responsibility for his own children: these are a few of the reasons that Women's Liberation is Men's Liberation, too.

As for psychic health of the children, studies show that the quality of time spent by parents is more important than the quantity. The most damaged children were not those whose mothers worked, but those whose mothers preferred to work but stayed home out of the role-playing desire to be a "good mother."

Another myth, that the women's movement is not political, won't last, or is somehow not "serious." When black people leave their nineteenth-century roles, they are feared. When women dare to leave theirs, they are ridiculed. We understand this; we accept the burden of ridicule. It won't keep us quiet anymore.

Similarly, it shouldn't deceive male observers into thinking that this is somehow a joke. We are 51 percent of the population; we are essentially united on these issues across boundaries of class or race or age; and we may well end by changing this society more than the civil rights movement. That is an apt parallel. We, too, have our right wing and left wing, our separatists, gradualists, and Uncle Toms. But we are changing our own consciousness, and that of the country. Engels noted the relationship of the authoritarian, nuclear family to capitalism: the father as capitalist, the mother as means of production, and the children as labor. He said the family would change as the economic system did, and that seems to have happened, whether we want to admit it or not. Women's bodies will no longer be owned by the state for the production of workers and soldiers; birth control and abortion are facts of everyday life. The new family is an egalitarian family.

Gunnar Myrdal noted thirty years ago the parallel between women and Negroes in this country. Both suffered from such restricting social myths as: smaller brains, passive natures, inability to govern them-selves (and certainly not white men), sex objects only, childlike natures, special skills, and the like. When evaluating a general statement about women, it might be valuable to substitute "black people" for "women" —just to test the prejudice at work.

And it might be valuable to do this constitutionally as well. Neither group is going to be content as a cheap labor pool anymore. And neither is going to be content without full constitutional rights.

It seems to me that much of the trouble in this country has to do with the "masculine mystique"; with the myth that masculinity some-how depends on the subjugation of other people. It is a bipartisan prob-lem; both our past and current Presidents seem to be victims of this myth, and to behave accordingly.

Women are not more moral than men. We are only uncorrupted by power. But we do not want to imitate men, to join this country as it is, and I think our very participation will change it. Perhaps women-elected leaders—and there will be many of them—will not be so likely to dominate black people or yellow people or men; anybody who looks different from us.

After all, we won't have our masculinity to prove.

ON SEXISM IN AMERICA, 1973

TESTIMONY OF BILLIE JEAN KING

Ms. King: As you know I think more and more we are realizing how important it is to be in shape. I know when I am not in shape I cannot think as well. All through my childhood it was always stressed that athletics really built character in boys.

My father was a fireman and mom was a housewife, and my dad was a sports nut; my mother does not like sports at all. So this was a good balance for me, but when I became eleven years old my mother said, "You cannot play touch football any more; you must be a lady at all times"—whatever that means. I still have not figured that one out.

All I know is that deep inside of me I have loved sports—all sports— and I was oriented in team sports. I can remember one morning at the breakfast table asking my father what a good sport would be for a woman, and right there now that I reflect back, I realized I was already a product of the conditioning that goes on.

Why should I worry about it? But I did. So I got into tennis, which I had never heard of getting into, and playing at the local level I realized that in the school system there was no tennis available in high school.

As far as local associations helping girls in tennis, we were not helped. I can remember examples of boys in the fifteen-and-under age group receiving one thousand dollars to travel to the East Coast to play. I was No. 1 in southern California, and when I went to the association

In *Women's Educational Equity Act,* Hearings Before the Subcommittee on Education of the Committee on Labor and Public Welfare, U.S. Senate, 93rd Congress, 1st session, October 17 and November 9, 1973, pp. 76–79, 82–83.

and asked for funds, they said, "No." I never could understand why, I was No. 1, and here they were giving a boy who was No. 5 one thousand dollars—and I really needed the money because my parents could not afford it.

I was told when you go on a tennis court and you play against a fellow, make sure that you let him win. I am telling you I used to do this. As I started seeing things happen, I realized how stupid and how ridiculous it really is because I love to hit the ball, and I get just as big a charge out of this as Rod Laver does; it is the esthetics of it. It is a great life, and all I know is there have been too many battles from a personal point of view.

It is tough enough to guts it out on the tennis court than to have to worry about all the other aspects of society accepting you as a human being, and we are just now being accepted. I had to wait this long.

Senator Mondale: Would you say that your experience is a usual one or an unusual one for girls interested in athletics? Have the other girl athletes you talked to had similar experiences, the difficulty in being recognized?

Ms. King: It is very common but because of our lack of acceptance women athletes have a tendency to bend over backward to try to be more feminine—"Don't rock the boat"—they try to be more passive.

There seems to be a difference now. Some women are going out and saying what they really feel, but, privately, yes, they tell me these things, but when it comes to saying it in public, they are afraid because they want to be accepted.

Senator Mondale: Do you see a change in that now?

Ms. King: Very much, but only through those vehicles, because the only way that people appreciate me is through the success I have achieved, because money is a measuring stick. It does not mean that I do not love my tennis—and that is what people in this country have to learn to get rid of, the word "amateur." I think it is the most misleading word ever.

Senator Javits: The question I have to ask you if you had equality of funding, would you not have immediately some real problems? How would you solve them, such as breaking down among girls and women the concept of the unladylikeness and also the matter of jumping from say swimming and tennis to some other sports, and how do we educate society on the social mores that obviously are involved?

Ms. King: I think it starts at home. I know mothers come to me with daughters and now they are very concerned. They hold their daughters on their laps, and all of a sudden they think, I want my little girl to have the same opportunities as my little boy; so she starts thinking, but she does not have those opportunities.

I think that is one of the factors that is starting to change. At least I notice this because more people come to me and tell me what they are thinking.

I got the same shots in 1966 that I made in 1973. Now, why all of a sudden do people know me? I was world champion in 1966. I used to come home and get off the plane, and they did not know anything; right?

It is the vehicle. It is getting the attention of the sports writers as an athlete, and not writing the stories such as "Cute, blue-eyed, petite da-da boo-boo." That is the way they talk about women athletes. They do not start a story about a male athlete the same way.

As an amateur, I was saying the same things I am saying to you today, and nobody could care less. So we have to have examples for young people to look up to, and the better you do something, the more responsibility you have to yourself as well as to others, because young people come up to me and ask me a lot of things about drugs—about everything.

I do not know how to answer all their questions, but at least they have identity. They identify for the first time in their lives. Little boys come up to me and say, I want to be a great tennis player like you. They don't think of me as a woman or man; all they know is I am an athlete.

I think it is at the educational level, it is through our textbooks, it is through sports, whatever field you are talking about, but we have wasted half the potential of this country.

IV

By 1970, it was difficult to remember that birth control had once been a controversial issue. Practically no group in American society stood out against the virtues of family limitation and zero population growth. For feminists, smaller families meant greater freedom of choice for women. For ecologists, smaller families meant less drain on natural resources and less pollution. For those concerned with the plight of the poor, smaller families meant the poor might enjoy a higher standard of living. The 1970 White House Conference on Children echoed this unanimity of views. The Conference's recommendations on the federal role in family planning programs, reprinted below, reflected the general consensus. It is not surprising that that same year Congress passed and the President signed the first appropriation of federal funds for the support of birth-control clinics.

FAMILY PLANNING, 1970

In his July 1969 message to Congress about population growth, President Nixon reaffirmed as national policy the right of all Americans to plan the number and timing of children that they want. He also established as a national goal the provision of adequate voluntary family planning services by 1974 to all who desire such services.

The first White House Conference on Children and Youth to recom-

In *Report to the President*, White House Conference on Children (Washington, D.C., 1970), pp. 260–64.

mend family planning was in 1960. That recommendation (number 106) was by a divided vote and was made shortly after the American Public Health Association had adopted its historic policy statement on population in 1959 and after President Eisenhower had rejected birth control as a proper governmental activity or responsibility. It has taken most of the decade for the nation to complete a remarkable reversal of policy. Meanwhile, the states and cities, with slowly increasing but still inadequate federal financial support, have made a good beginning on implementing the policy by making family planning services a part of health services.

The basic objective of family planning programs in the United States today should be to enable all individuals to have family planning opportunities and services. Each individual has the right to decide for himself on the basis of social norms, and his own family goals and resources, when and how many children to have. Safeguards are essential to protect welfare recipients and members of religious and racial minority groups from any type of coercion. A wide range of services should be provided so that each individual can select a contraceptive method best suited to his beliefs and life style.

National fertility surveys of the United States in 1955, 1960, and 1965 have documented the fact that, despite legal and religious restrictions, the American people use contraception extensively. Excluding the one-tenth of the population of reproductive age who are definitely sterile (largely because of surgical sterilizations, half of which are performed primarily for treatment of a pathological condition) about 85 percent have voluntarily used a method of contraception at some time. Most Americans obtain their family planning services and supplies from private physicians, pharmacists, and other consumer outlets for the various kinds of contraceptives produced by private industry, with quality controlled by the Federal Food and Drug Administration.

Use of different methods of contraception has shifted rapidly as new, more effective methods have become available. In 1955, 27 percent of contraceptors used condoms, 25 percent diaphragms, and about 22 percent rhythm. In 1965, 24 percent used oral pills, 18 percent condoms, 13 percent rhythm, and about 10 percent diaphragms, and a small but increasing proportion of intrauterine devices.

Most women have responded remarkably to the availability of services and improved methodology. Rarely has a health measure, especially so personal a one, been so readily and widely accepted. Studies document that, when family planning services are included in public obstetric services, the number of women who usually return for postpartum checkups increase from one-quarter or one-third to over three-quarters. Nevertheless, publicly supported family planning programs are still too new and inadequate to measure their effect on unwanted births. In 1970, the Family Planning Service and Population Research Act was enacted. This authorizes $352 million over three years to expand research capacity, training facilities, and service activities within the United States. This is much less money than will be needed for future service and research in this field.

We are still a long way from achieving the national goal of providing adequate voluntary family planning services to all by 1974.

Present estimates indicate that adequate family planning services are unavailable to over four million individuals in the United States. In this country, where 97 percent of babies are delivered in hospitals, it would appear a simple matter to add family planning to existing health services. But many problems exist: in much of our country prenatal, postnatal, and infant health services for the poor are inextricably related to the problems of developing and financing comprehensive personal health services for all individuals and families. Even with money and good local planning, essential manpower must be provided in all program phases. Family planning programs offer many opportunities for pioneering use of specially trained workers, not only to achieve the 1974 goal in family planning services but also to provide the base for additional future services. *We recommend that:*

Certified nurse midwives, professional graduate nurses, and paramedical personnel be trained and permitted to assume medical activities, such as performing physical examinations, administering contraceptives, counseling, and program administration.

A systematic network of training resources be established to meet critical shortages.

Career ladders be established for all family planning personnel.

Shocking statistics show that one-third of all deliveries in the United States are to mothers nineteen years of age and under, and increasing numbers of mothers are in the age group fifteen and under, where the risks to the mother and the baby are of the highest order. Unfortunately, in many states, the legal framework and local customs do not allow vital services to be provided to this high-risk group. *We strongly urge the removal of all impediments to the education of school-age parents in family planning.*

Family planning and family economics must also be considered in the broad context of the crisis of population growth facing all mankind. The size, growth, and distribution of the United States population, subjects formerly the esoteric preserve of the scholarly profession of demography, have become in recent years increasingly debated issues of public policy. Not only are the calamitous consequences of rapid population growth generally acknowledged in less developed areas of the world, but concern is also widespread that our own population has been growing, and will continue to grow, at a rate that threatens to produce acute social, educational, economic, and environmental problems.

Wide disagreement exists about population growth in the United States. It begins with the very question of whether there is or will soon be a population problem. Even those who agree that a problem exists cannot unanimously agree on the definition of the problem or on proposed solutions.

The White House Conference on Children considered carefully the effect various possible population problems would have on the quality of life of children in the seventies. *The Conference concludes that the enhanced well-being of children requires the early stabilization of United States population. We recommend a national program to educate all*

citizens in the problems of population growth for the purpose of achiev-
ing early population stability. While it is true that birthrates are much
higher among the poor and among blacks, middle-class whites constitute
the largest number of people in the United States. Birthrates among the
poor and blacks are not high enough to offset the effects of the larger
number of middle-class whites. This means that population growth in the
United States occurs primarily because of reproduction of affluent and
middle-class whites who in 1965 through 1970 produced 70 percent of
our births. Therefore, particular attention should be directed to reducing
their natality.

We urge a national policy of early population stabilization because
United States population growth *must* stabilize eventually. Only a small
fraction of finite earth is ours to inhabit, and the problems facing the
country grow more severe as our population grows.

The achievement of replacement reproduction in the United States
without coercion appears possible. The latest national data indicate that
if perfect contraception and/or induced abortion were available so that
families had only those children they wanted, in 1965 we would have
had an average of 2.5 live births per woman. Changes in education, in
alternative roles for women, and in present economic incentives might
well close the gap to the 2.11 needed for stabilization. Particular attention should be paid to encouraging women to find satisfactions beyond
motherhood and to providing opportunities to achieve those satisfactions.
The process should be speeded by governmental programs and incentives
for employers to provide part-time work opportunities and high quality
child care, plus assurance of equal pay and equal jobs.

V

The keen desire on the part of women, and particularly married women,
to hold full-time jobs poses in acute form the challenge of making
parenthood and child care compatible. How is a woman to fulfill
both tasks? How is she to raise her family and pursue her career?
One simple answer—to divide child-care responsibilities evenly
between husband and wife—is not much of a solution. With both
partners employed, neither has the time to devote to child care.
Another alternative has been to establish federally financed day-
care centers. Professionals would take care of the preschool children
during working hours, enabling both parents to pursue careers. The
centers could serve families of all classes, but especially the poor—
they are the ones least able to afford the cost of child care. To be
sure, day-care institutions are not without their own problems. To
date, they have been segregated places with blacks using some
centers and whites others; and they have not lived up to the
promise of providing first-rate child care. But, as the remarks of
Congressman John Brademas and Congresswoman Bella Abzug
reprinted below make clear, day care remains a very popular
method for furthering women's liberation.

DAY-CARE NEEDS, 1971

TESTIMONY OF BELLA ABZUG

Mr. Brademas: I am especially pleased to begin our hearings today as an appropriate part of this week's observance of "The Week of the Young Child." I view this as a beginning of a commitment on the part of the Government of the United States to the welfare of the young children of this country.

Traditionally it was easy to conceive of a child-care program. The creche and the orphanage are typical of what we used to expect: food, a roof over the head, and a minimum of adult supervision—these basic needs were seen as enough for children whose parents worked.

In recent years psychologists have come to learn more about how children grow. As a result we have gained a deeper understanding of what intelligence, accomplishment, and development are. We have come to see the breadth of the variety of ways in which children can develop, and we have looked for ways of affecting those vital processes.

We have found that the first five years of life are probably the most important in a child's life from the point of view of forming his or her potential for later achievement. And we have come to see the importance of emotional security, stimulating environment, good food, and health care. All contribute to, and all are vital to, the development of intelligence, ability, creativity, initiative, and self-assurance.

The monumental studies made under James S. Coleman's direction have made it clear that children from poor surroundings develop more quickly when they mix with children from homes of higher socio-economic status, no matter what their ethnic heritage.

This should not surprise us, of course. Children learn largely from each other, and tearing down the barriers of social class discrimination can only broaden poor children's horizons beyond what the late Oscar Lewis called "the culture of poverty."

For these reasons the legislation we are to consider today would extend the benefits of Headstart-type programs—including health, educational, nutritional, and family counseling services—not only to poor children, but to millions of other children of preschool age, particularly to the children of working parents. Today there are over five million preschool children both of whose parents must work, and adequate day care is available for only a fraction of them.

This bill would start the process of providing adequate care for them, committing funds to the construction of facilities, the training of personnel, and to the actual operation of comprehensive child development programs. A major provision of the bill calls for establishment of local policy councils composed of parents of children in the neighborhood to be served by each program.

In *Comprehensive Child Development Act of 1971*, Hearings Before the Select Subcommittee on Education of the Committee on Education and Labor, House of Representatives, 92nd Congress, 1st session, May 17, 21, and June 3, 1971, pp. 61–65.

One would hope that at least one significant possible contribution that could be made by a major comprehensive child development bill would be to afford still further opportunities for women who wish to pursue careers and at the same time want to assure that their children will have developmental opportunity.

Mrs. Abzug: I am pleased to be here this morning to testify on the important matter of child care. The bill before you—H.R. 6748, the Subcommittee, or Brademas bill—is a good bill, a bill which takes the basic first steps toward providing comprehensive child-care services in this country for all the women and children who need them. But Representative Chisholm and I believe that the universe of need is so great that this bill is inadequate. We plan to introduce a stronger bill later today, and I would like to describe it to you now.

H.R. 6748 needs more emphasis on the needs of women; it needs coverage for small communities as well as for large urban areas; and above everything else it needs enough money to make it work.

Our bill proposes, first of all, an appropriation of five, eight, and ten billion dollars over a three year period.

Now some will say that in political terms such a figure is totally unrealistic. But I say that a figure that is anything less than that is totally unrealistic in practical terms. There are now in the United States an estimated five million children under five years of age whose mothers work. There are eighteen million children under five in the population as a whole. If the cost of child care is roughly sixteen hundred dollars per year (and estimates have run as high as twenty-three hundred dollars), then we will need eight billion dollars just to meet the needs of those women who are already working. To provide comprehensive educational and health services for every child under five would cost us almost twenty-eight billion dollars annually.

Such figures seem "unrealistic" to us only because we have learned to give human needs low budgetary priority. We spend upward of seventy billion dollars a year on weapons and defense, and no one bats an eye. We pour a billion dollars into a useless white elephant like the SST, and when the plane turns out to be a dud we pour in millions more. Yet we refuse to support a program like this one—an innovative, creative program which enriches our children and liberates our women —at anything like an adequate level of funding.

It's especially ironic because other countries, such as those in Scandinavia, Israel, the Soviet Union, and France, put us to shame when it comes to child care. We're terrorized that they might beat us in building a supersonic transport—but when it comes to child care, that's something else again.

You know and I know that we are the richest nation in the world, that we need these services desperately, and that we have the capacity to pay for them if we only would.

This bill is also a woman's bill, and that is something no one seems to want to mention. Indeed, I find it highly ironic that a bill which talks so much of the potential of growing children fails even to mention the undeveloped potential of over half our adult population.

Yet we can't deny that in our society it is the woman, rather than the man, who normally assumes the burdens of child care. We can't deny that women, not men, lack the opportunity to achieve their full employment potential. We can't deny that women, rather than men, are underpaid in the job market, and yet it's women—particularly the women who are heads of households—who must singlehandedly pay the costs of child care.

Of course I realize that though the general practice is for women to take care of the children in our society, some men assume these responsibilities also. There are many men who are single working parents; and their children should have access to child-care facilities, too.

Yet when we talk about this bill we must recognize that it is primarily a bill for women as well as for children and that our ultimate objective must be to make child-care facilities available to every one of us.

Yes, women's rights is definitely an issue here. For this reason Representative Chisholm and I have added a number of strengthening amendments. As a starter, we've expanded the statement of purpose at the beginning of the bill to recognize that thousands of American women suffer *themselves* through the absence of child care. Isn't it clear yet that if a woman must stay home to mind the kids she won't be able to go to school, take a job, or work harder for a promotion. Isn't it clear that she will be doomed to hold low-paying, low-prestige jobs that no man would hold still for?

Another amendment that will help women is one that will let the Secretary designate a nongovernmental sponsor, not only to meet the needs of economically disadvantaged children, but also to provide services for preschool-age children and children of working mothers regardless of income. Think for a moment what this would mean. It would let local groups of parents and women set up child-care centers for children from all socioeconomic backgrounds. It would let community groups create the models for that universal kind of child care that we are all talking about—a child-care system that would accommodate rich and poor alike, that would let our kids grow up with a chance to know each other and to learn that they can bridge that racial and economic gap that divides their parents. But we can't do it unless the HEW Secretary can authorize private groups to set up centers wherever there is a need, not only for poor kids.

VI

Although the woman's liberation movement has much to recommend in the arena of public policy, it has much to say about the nature of private relationships also. Betty Friedan, for her part, had counseled women to get jobs. But the new leaders of the movement went further, arguing that women must become much more independent people at home. It did not seem farfetched to counsel women to rewrite their marriage contracts. The days of "love, honor, and obey" were long passed. Now it was time to spell out who would do the dishes, on which nights, and who would do the laundry, on which days. The advice offered in this article on how to write your own marriage contract, is not without its own special humor. But the piece reflects in very clear terms that women's liberation is bound to effect changes not just in the marketplace but in the family as well.

HOW TO WRITE YOUR OWN MARRIAGE CONTRACT, 1973

SUSAN EDMISTON

First we thought marriage was when Prince Charming came and took you away with him. Then we thought that marriage was orange blossoms and Alençon lace and silver patterns. Then we thought that marriage—at least—was when you couldn't face signing the lease on the new apartment in two different names.

But most of us never even suspected the truth. Nobody ever so much as mentioned that what marriage is, at its very heart and essence, is a contract. When you say "I do," what you are doing is not, as you thought, vowing your eternal love, but rather subscribing to a whole system of rights, obligations, and responsibilities that may very well be anathema to your most cherished beliefs.

Worst of all, you never even get to read the contract—to say nothing of the fine print. If you did, you probably wouldn't agree to it.

In recent years, many people have taken to writing their own marriage ceremonies in a desperate attempt to make the institution more relevant to their own lives. But ceremonies, they are finding, do not reach the heart of the matter. So some couples are now taking the logical next step of drawing up their own contracts. These agreements may delineate any of the financial or personal aspects of the marriage relationship—from who pays which bills to who uses what birth control. Though many of their provisions may not be legally binding, at the very least they can help us to examine the often inchoate assumptions underlying our relationships, help us to come to honest and equitable terms with one another, and provide guidelines for making our marriages what we truly want them to be.

Before their first child was born, Alix Kates Shulman and her husband had an egalitarian, partnership marriage. Alix worked full time as an editor in New York, and both shared the chores involved in maintaining their small household. After two children, however, the couple found that they had automatically fallen into the traditional sex roles: he went out and worked all day to support his family; she stayed home and worked from 6 A.M. to 9 P.M. taking care of children and house-work. Unthinkingly, they had agreed not only to the legalities of marriage but to the social contract as well.

After six years at home—six years of chronic dissatisfaction—Alix became involved in the Women's Liberation movement and realized that it might be possible to change the contract under which she and her husband lived. The arrangement they worked out, basically a division of household duties and child care, rejected "the notion that the work which brings in more money is more valuable. The ability to earn money is a privilege which must not be compounded by enabling the larger earner to buy out of his/her duties."

Sitting down and writing out a contract may seem a cold and formal way of working out an intimate relationship, but often it is the only way of coping with the ghosts of two thousand years of tradition lurking in our definitions of marriage. After three years, Alix had written six books, and both Shulmans found their agreement a way of life rather than a document to be followed legalistically.

The Shulmans' contract renegotiates husband's and wife's roles as far as the care of children and home are concerned. Psychologists Barbara and Myron Kultov took their agreement one step further.

"We agreed in the beginning that since I didn't care a bit about the house, he would do a lot of cleaning and I would do a lot of cooking," says Barbara.

> He does a lot of the shopping, too, because he likes to buy things and I don't. Whenever either of us feels "I'm doing all the drudge work and you're not doing anything," we switch jobs. Gradually we've eliminated a lot of stuff neither of us wanted to do. In the early days, we'd cook dinner for people because we didn't feel it was hospitable to ask them to go out, but now we often go out instead.
>
> In the beginning we literally opened up separate bank accounts. We split our savings and checking accounts. At the time he made a third more money than I did. I deferred to him all the time, even though it was only a third. I felt that if he didn't spend so much money on the eight dozen book clubs he belongs to, I would only have to work about two hours a day. He said I wasn't realistic, that I didn't know how much we had and was being tight.
>
> Each of us paid the bills alternate months. I thought this was the only way to prove to him I could handle money. After six months, when I figured out how much I was spending and how much of his money I was using, I decided to take on more patients to expand my practice. I found I was spending as much on cabs as he was on book clubs. Since that time we haven't had a single argument about money.

When the Koltuvs' child was born, they reopened negotiations.

> We decided to split the care of our daughter between us equally. We knew there were certain hours we'd both be working so we found a woman to take care of her during these hours. Then I had the mornings and he had the evenings. The person whose time it was had to make all the decisions—whether she could have Pepsi-Cola, whether she could visit a friend, and so forth.
>
> The hardest thing was being willing to give up control. What we call

responsibility is often control, power, being the boss. When I was really able to recognize that my husband's relationship with Hannah is his and mine is mine, everything was all right. He's going to do it differently but he's going to do it all right. We've been teaching her all along that different people are different.

The husband, generally, has had the right to decide where he and his wife live, although recently he has been required to make a reasonable decision taking her wishes into account. The burden of proving she is reasonable, however, still rests with the wife.

To some women the loss of these rights may seem a small price to pay for support. In fact, the arrangement works out differently depending on economic class. The higher up the ladder her husband is, the better a woman is supported and the fewer services she gives in return. For the many millions of women who work outside the home, on the other hand, the bargain is not a terribly good one: in reality all they earn for the services they give their husbands is the responsibility of working outside the home as well as in it to help their families survive. These women learn another price they pay for the illusion of support—the low salaries they receive compared with men's are ironically justified by the argument that the "men have families to feed." This is not the fault of husbands but of an economy structured on the unpaid services of women.

But the heaviest price those women who accept the role of dependent pay is a psychological one. Economic dependency is in itself corrupting, as can be seen in rawest form in country-and-Western songs of the "I-know-he's-being-untrue-but-I-never-confront-him-with-it-because-if-he-left-me-who-would-support-the-children" variety. And economic dependency breeds other kinds of dependency. The woman who has no established legal right in the family income fares better or worse depending on how well she pleases the head of the household. In the attempt to please she may surrender her own tastes, her own opinions, her own thoughts. If she habitually defers to or depends on her husband's decisions she will eventually find herself incapable of making her own.

The solution is not that wives should never work in the home or that husbands should not share their incomes with them. The solution is that we must begin to recognize that the work wives do belongs to them, not their husbands, and should be accorded a legitimate value. If wives make the contribution of full partners in their marriages, they should receive the rights of partners—not only, like slaves, the right to be housed, clothed, and fed, or in other words, supported.

Readers are probably thinking, "But we love each other, so why should we have a contract?" As Barbara Koltuv says, "Part of the reason for thinking out a contract is to find out what your problems are; it forces you to take charge of your life. Once you have the contract, you don't have to refer back to it. The process is what's important."

Whether these contracts are legally enforceable or not, just drawing them up may be of great service to many couples. What we are really doing in thrashing out a contract is finding out where we stand on issues, clearing up all the murky, unexamined areas of conflict, and unflinchingly facing up to our differences.

THE SHULMANS' MARRIAGE AGREEMENT

I. Principles

We reject the notion that the work which brings in more money is more valuable. The ability to earn money is a privilege which must not be compounded by enabling the larger earner to buy out of his/her duties and put the burden on the partner who earns less or on another person hired from outside.

We believe that each partner has an equal right to his/her own time, work, values, choices. As long as all duties are performed, each of us may use his/her extra time any way he/she chooses. If he/she wants to use it making money, fine. If he/she wants to spend it with spouse, fine.

As parents we believe we must share all responsibility for taking care of our children and home—and not only the work but also the responsibility. At least during the first year of this agreement, *sharing responsibility* shall mean dividing the *jobs* and dividing the *time*.

II. Job Breakdown and Schedule

(A) Children

1. Mornings: Waking children; getting their clothes out; making their lunches; seeing that they have notes, homework, money, bus passes, books; brushing their hair; giving them breakfast (making coffee for us). Every other week each parent does all.
2. Transportation: Getting children to and from lessons, doctors, dentists (including making appointments), friends' houses, etc. Parts occurring between 3 and 6 P.M. fall to wife. She must be compensated by extra work from husband. Husband does weekend transportation and pickups after 6.
3. Help: Helping with homework, personal questions; explaining things. Parts occurring between 3 and 6 P.M. fall to wife. After 6 P.M. husband does Tuesday, Thursday, and Sunday; wife does Monday, Wednesday, and Saturday. Friday is free for whoever has done extra work during the week.
4. Nighttime (after 6 P.M.): Getting children to take baths, brush their teeth, put away their toys, and clothes, go to bed; reading with them; tucking them in and having nighttime talks; handling if they wake at night. Husband does Tuesday, Thursday, and Sunday. Wife does Monday, Wednesday, and Saturday. Friday split according to who has done extra work.
5. Baby sitters: Baby sitters must be called by the parent the sitter is to replace. If no sitter turns up, that parent must stay home.
6. Sick care: Calling doctors; checking symptoms; getting prescriptions filled; remembering to give medicine; taking days off to stay home with sick child, providing special activities. This must still be worked out equally, since now wife seems to do it all. In any case, wife must be compensated (see 10 below).
7. Weekends: All usual child care, plus special activities (beach, park, zoo). Split equally. Husband is free all Saturday, wife is free all Sunday.

(B) Housework

8. Cooking: Breakfasts during the week are divided equally; husband does all weekend breakfasts (including shopping for them and dishes). Wife does all dinners except Sunday nights. Husband does Sunday dinner and any other dinners on his nights of responsibility if wife isn't home. Whoever invites guests does shopping, cooking, and dishes; if both invite them, split work.

9. Shopping: Food for all meals, housewares, clothing, and supplies for children. Divide by convenience. Generally, wife does daily food shopping; husband does special shopping.

10. Cleaning: Husband does dishes Tuesday, Thursday, and Sunday. Wife does Monday, Wednesday, and Saturday. Friday is split according to who has done extra work during week. Husband does all the housecleaning in exchange for wife's extra child care (3 to 6 daily), and sick care.

11. Laundry: Home laundry, making beds, dry cleaning (take and pick up). Wife does home laundry. Husband does dry-cleaning delivery and pick-up. Wife strips beds, husband remakes them.

Chapter 22

The Counterculture

EVERY GENERATION tends to exaggerate the uniqueness of its own dilemmas and crisis. We are by no means the first Americans to be concerned about cohesion of our society, or about the role and strength of the family, the school, or the church. The Puritans, as we have seen, were absolutely persuaded that the family was in a state of breakdown; Jacksonians feared the imminent dissolution of society; Progressives were all too nervous that immigration posed an insuperable problem for the integrity and good order of our civilization. In retrospect, we tend to view their concerns with a certain wonderment. Yes, to be sure, we can understand their perspective, and empathize with their issues. Still, they strike us as exaggerated. Surely they should have been able to comprehend that American society would not crumble in the face of the growth of cities or the increase in immigrants. And so, too, future historians may well puzzle over our sense of crisis in the 1960s and 1970s. They may find our fears exaggerated and our concerns inflated.

But such knowledge offers us little comfort. In so far as we perceive the nature of the current challenge to institutions, it appears unprecedented in scope and intensity. Over the past two decades, practically every institution in society has come under strong attack. From feminists, as we have seen, comes a critique of the family in particular, and social institutions in general, for keeping women in subjugation, for denying them personhood. From blacks comes an attack on the police in particular, and on social institutions in general, for keeping them in second-class citizenship. But this is only part of the story. Over the past several years, workers have decried the nature of their working conditions, insisting that their jobs offer them no satisfaction, that they are forced to spend most of their waking hours performing a series of isolated and meaningless tasks. The institutions of work no longer seem to be satisfying human needs. And students have been no less vigorous in their attacks on institutions of learning. They insist that colleges and universities are not fulfilling adequately the job of teaching or their broader social responsibilities to the community. In similar spirit, caretaker and custodial institutions of the state have come under sustained attack. Prisons do not rehabilitate, mental hospitals do not cure, welfare agencies do not relieve poverty—and the list could be easily extended.

These anti-institutional critiques have focused clearly and often persuasively on the inadequacies of present arrangements. But they have been less successful in posing alternatives. Some of the responses to these tough issues has been escapist. One notable, if idiosyncratic, reaction to the perceived crisis of institutions has been the commune—a retreat to a simple form of living, an escape from the city, the machine, the demands of family, and the larger society. Unlike earlier communitarian experiments, the communes do not intend to reform society so much as to avoid it. So, too, the dramatic increase in the use of drugs represents a form of escapism. The reality is too grim and depressing, one hears; the drug experience is liberating, expanding, and pleasurable. Again, the drug culture has no message to the larger culture—it is a way of avoiding the issues, not resolving them.

Not all reactions, however, have been escapist. Many workers and students have rallied around the slogan of participation. Students should have a greater voice in determining university policies; workers should have more say in determining the nature of their jobs and the decisions of the corporations. So, too, government committees have tried to fathom the nature of the crisis and pose solutions. The campus crisis was the focus of one important investigation; the subject of worker alienation, another.

For the moment, the diagnoses of the ills are more powerful than the cures. We have a better understanding of the inadequacies of institutions but no clear programs of how to improve them. It is no exaggeration to suggest that the most important task facing the nation in the next several decades is to respond to these attacks intelligently and imaginatively. The social history of the United States in the 1970s and 1980s will to a large extent be the history of how we reshape our institutions to serve the needs and welfare of all Americans.

I

The traditional concern of labor organizations in this country has been with the size of the paycheck and the length of the working day. Union leaders have focused their efforts on "bread and butter" issues, to increase wages and shorten working hours. But beginning in the 1970s a new issue emerged: the quality of work. For the first time one heard about more fundamental discontent. As one steelworker put it: "It's hard to feel pride in a bridge you're never gonna cross, in a door you're never gonna open. You're mass producing things and you never see the end of it." Indeed, so strong is some workers' dissatisfaction with their roles as cogs in the machinery of mass production that they have started to practice a type of industrial sabotage—leaving this screw unturned, not tightening that bolt on the car they helped to manufacture. To understand the nature of worker alienation, a Senate subcommittee in 1972 held extensive hearings. The testimony they received helps to explain the root cause of the dissatisfactions and to suggest some possible remedies.

WORKER ALIENATION, 1972

TESTIMONY OF GARY BRYNNER AND DAN CLARK

Senator Kennedy: The Secretary of Labor, James Hodgson, was on the "Today Show" this morning. He said that the only two things that workers are interested in are their paychecks and their families.

I think they are also interested in the content of their jobs and about what they do when they go through the plant doors. I think the Secretary has misread what has happened across this land, if he does not understand workers are increasingly dissatisfied by working conditions, even if they are satisfied by their paycheck.

As a nation, we have prided ourselves in the past on the skills and initiative and capacity of the American worker. And we have watched as pay raises and benefits seemed to provide a just recompense for the workers.

Now we have stopped looking again. The nation marvels at the impressive speed of the automotive equipment in the nation's modern plants and assumes that productivity is at an all-time high. Unfortunately, it is as if the nation's institutions were mesmerized by the industrial machine and unable to see the man behind the machine.

For the key element in the productivity equation is the worker and the noneconomic needs of the worker have been forgotten. Too many young workers are finding their jobs a place of confinement and frustration. And we should not be surprised that our lack of concern is producing a class of angry and rebellious workers.

Few people in America have ever heard of Lordstown, where auto workers have tied up the lines more than once to protest the robot-like monotony of a thirty-six-second interval assembly process.

Fewer of us are aware or can understand the causes why a worker recently went beserk in the Eldon axle plant in Detroit and shot three foremen. His defense was insanity, brought about by working in the noise and filth and danger of that plant. The judge and jury visited the plant and their verdict was unanimous. It was a verdict for acquittal.

That is the extreme. But how many men and women unnecessarily

In *Worker Alienation*, Hearings Before the Subcommittee on Employment, Manpower, and Poverty of the Committee on Labor and Public Welfare, U.S. Senate, 92nd Congress, 2nd session, July 25–26, 1972, pp. 8–13.

suffer mental or physical illnesses whose cause is linked to their jobs? What is the extent of use of drugs and alcoholism among young workers? How many men and women could function more effectively as parents and citizens if they did not feel dissatisfied with their jobs?

Equally important for the economic vitality of this nation is the effect that worker discontent has on productivity. The National Commission on Productivity states that in at least one major industry, absenteeism increased by 50 percent, worker turnover by 70 percent, worker grievances by 38 percent, and disciplinary layoffs by 44 percent in a period of five years. How much does that cost the economy in terms of lost time, in terms of retraining new workers, in terms of low productivity?

A steelworker was quoted in an interview recently and his words sum up the kind of discontent that may be endemic to U.S. modern industry. "It's hard to take pride when you work for a large steel company," he said. "It's hard to take pride in a bridge you're never gonna cross, in a door you're never gonna open. You're mass producing things and you never see the end of it."

And at least there is some evidence, in Europe and here at home, that industrialization can be compatible with a sense of self-worth for the workers. And what is equally important, it is becoming clear that management and union leadership will be forced by their workers and their members to address themselves to this issue.

I view these hearings as a challenge, a challenge to business leadership, a challenge to union leadership, and a challenge to political leadership to find what constructive role we can play in halting worker alienation.

Statement of Gary Brynner, President, UAW Local 1112, Lordstown, Ohio, Accompanied by Dan Clark, Member, UAW Local 1112, Lordstown, Ohio

Mr. Brynner: Thank you. I might say it is our pleasure to offer testimony to your committee. We feel it is an avenue that should have been traveled, and we are glad that it has taken place now. There are problems with the workers.

"Alienation" is, I guess, a good term. We offer some suggestions and some criticisms as they be.

There are symptoms of the alienated worker in our plant where we specialize, where I am President, and Dan is an assembler. Absentee rate, as you said, has gone continually higher. Turnover rate is enormous. The use and turning to alcohol and drugs is becoming a bigger and bigger problem, and apathy—apathy within our union movement toward union leaders and to the Government.

I think those lead from the alienation of the worker. In our plant we make 101.6 Vegas an hour, the fastest line speed in the country. A guy has about thirty-six seconds to do an operation. The jobs are so fragmented that he is offered very little as far as input to that product. He cannot associate with it or he does not realize what he is doing to it.

Conveyor lines in our plant, the heights, and every movement of the conveyor line is determined to make the guy a little more efficient, to take movement of the bending and stretching, to make him more efficient.

They believe in discipline. When they do not have the discipline rule to cover a violation, they create one. Drugs has been on the increase in plants as you well know. So our corporation drafts up another shop rule to cover misuse or selling of drugs on company premises, another form or way to discipline the workers. They correct and they deal with the problem, but they never look for the cause. They further alienate the worker by more discipline. You cannot control people with fear. They should have learned that in our fight in just this past year, where they disciplined some one thousand workers who refused to speed up on their lines, and out of that one thousand—and I do not want you to feel sorry for us, because it cost them tens of thousands of dollars in back-pay, because the union was able to establish they were wrong, the workers were not suppressed to that kind of action without regress or redress.

I brought with me a guy who is an assembler in the plant where we make the 101.6 Vegas an hour. His name is Dan Clark. Dan is faced with those problems. I am not because as president I am full-time, and he can tell you how an assembler feels and how he suffers and the inequities that go on.

At this time I would like to have Dan present the assembler's view.

Senator Kennedy: Very good.

Mr. Clark: Senator Kennedy, members of the committee: I have briefly a few problems that face the workers. I work in the body shop, and that is where your car first begins. You start putting certain parts together—

Senator Kennedy: How long have you worked there?

Mr. Clark: I have been there now about five years, which is a year and a half short of the highest seniority there.

The problems that face the workers are monotony of the job, repetition, and boredom. We are constantly doing the same job over and over again. Where you have problems of hours, like right now—I am on sick leave, just had an operation, but before I left, four days ago, we were working ten and one half to eleven hours, which you have no excuse to leave.

Eight hours, a working day, which it should be eight hours, you cannot leave in eight hours unless you have an excuse to go to the doctor's, hospital, or emergency call of one of your kids are sick. That is the only way you are going to leave.

You stay in that plant for ten and one half to eleven hours of their choosing, and it may be maybe 95 degrees outside, but inside you can almost bet in the body shop it is a good 110. But that is not the warmest place in the whole plant. The warmest place in the whole plant is the paint ship. That is on the second level.

When it is 95 outside, it is 120 or so in that paint shop, and your ventilation system, the air you are getting blown in on you, is supposed to be so cooled down—that is that 95-degree temperature outside that is coming on. You have no ventilation really at all. They are situated in such a place, they are not on the job anyhow. Your job may be off to the lefthand side and the ventilation is on the righthand side.

They say there is nothing we can do about it, that is the way it was designed, and that is the way it is. There is nothing we can do.

There is the noise level in the plant. The body shop is worse. One man says, he is a supervisor there, has taken under his control, he says, noise level. I know there are problems there, it is above the noise level that it is supposed to be. He says I will take care of it. That is a year and a half now which has gone by and nothing has been done yet. There has been nothing provided unless you want to provide it yourself.

I know I put cotton in my ears, because I cannot take it too much longer. There is pollution in the plant.

In the body shop that consists of, where you are welding, you are assembling the car together, and you are welding. You will have fumes like smoke or something that come on over, and dust and fumes and smoke coming out, and they do not have anything for that either. You put on your safety glasses and grin and bear it. That is about it.

You are going to find men today, who are younger—most of the men there are my age, I am twenty-five years old, and most of us agree that we do not want to spend all of our life in this plant working under these conditions.

In the 1930s our fathers or forefathers, whatever you want to say, they revolted. They wanted the rights for a union.

In 1970 we revolted and all we want to do is improve on things. That is all we want. Why should we be criticized for something like that? All we want is improvement in working conditions.

II

Between 1965 and 1970, practically every major college campus was the scene of student sit-ins and protests. Classes were disrupted, buildings occupied, presidents and deans confronted. Each campus had its own particular issue—at Columbia it was a gym to be built in the park dividing the college from Harlem, at Harvard it was officer training in ROTC programs, at Cornell it was discrimination against blacks. But uniting all of the student protests was a bitter outrage at America's involvement in Vietnam, and a more low key, but nevertheless common disenchantment with the dominant institutions in American life from the university itself to the massive corporations that ran the economy. One of the most intelligent and persuasive examinations of the causes of student protest emerged from a presidential committee headed by former Pennsylvania Governor William Scranton. The committee understood well that the protest was not the work of a small or embittered minority, but rather that it reflected a broad-based discontent of youth with the nature of the society they were about to enter.

THE REPORT OF THE PRESIDENT'S COMMISSION ON CAMPUS UNREST, 1971

We find that campus unrest has many causes, that several of these are not within the control of individuals or of government, and that some of these causes have worked their influence in obscure or indirect ways. Identifying them all is difficult, but they do exist and must be sought— not in order to justify or condemn, but rather because no rational response to campus unrest is possible until its nature and causes have been fully understood.

Race, the war, and the defects of the modern university have contributed to the development of campus unrest, have given it specific focus, and continue to lend it a special intensity. But they are neither the only nor even the most important causes of campus unrest.

Of far greater moment have been the advance of American society into the postindustrial era, the increasing affluence of American society, and the expansion and intergenerational evolution of liberal idealism. Together, these have prompted the formation of a new youth culture that defines itself through a passionate attachment to principle and an equally passionate opposition to the larger society. At the center of this culture is a romantic celebration of human life, of the unencumbered individual, of the senses, and of nature. It rejects what it sees to be the operational ideals of American society: materialism, competition, rationalism, technology, consumerism, and militarism. This emerging culture is the deeper cause of student protest against war, racial injustice, and the abuses of the multiversity.

During the past decade, this youth culture has developed rapidly. It has become ever more distinct and has acquired an almost religious fervor through a process of advancing personal commitment. This process has been spurred by the emergence within the larger society of opposition both to the youth culture itself and to its demonstrations of political protest. As such opposition became manifest—and occasionally violently manifest—participants in the youth culture felt challenged, and their commitment to that culture and to the political protest it prompts grew stronger and bolder. Over time, more and more students have moved in the direction of an ever deeper and more inclusive sense of opposition to the larger society. As their alienation became more profound, their willingness to use violence increased.

The best place to begin any search for the causes of student protest is to consider the reasons which student protestors themselves offer for their activities. There are many such reasons, and students are not reluctant to articulate them. These reasons—these positions on the major national issues of the day—must be taken seriously.

Both historically and in terms of the relative frequency with which it is the focus of protest, the first great issue is also the central social

In *The Report of the President's Commission on Campus Unrest* (New York, 1971), pp. 51–52, 56–59.

and political problem of American society: the position of racial minorities, and of black people in particular. It was over this issue that student protest began in 1960.

The targets of protest have shifted accordingly. At first, there was protest against local merchants for not serving blacks, against local businesses for not employing them, and against the university for tolerating discrimination in sororities and fraternities. Soon there were protests against discrimination in university admissions, and demands that more be done to recruit blacks and that more be done to assist them once admitted. Black students demanded, too, that the university begin to give assistance to local black communities, that it establish a curriculum in black studies, and that it recruit more black faculty to teach courses in these and other areas. As the target of protest moved from the society at large to the university, it also widened to represent the aspirations of other minority groups, often in a "Third World" coalition.

The second great issue has been the war in Southeast Asia. The war was almost from the beginning a relatively unpopular war, one which college youth on the whole now consider a mistake and which many of them also consider immoral and evil. It has continued now for more than five years, and it has pressed especially on youth. During the last decade, the war issue was less commonly the object of student protest than were questions of race, but as the years went by it became more and more prominent among student concerns.

A third major protest issue has been the university itself. Though at times this issue has been expressed in protests over curriculum and the nonretention of popular teachers, the overwhelming majority of university-related protests have dealt with school regulations affecting students, with the role of students in making those regulations, and more generally with the quality of student life, living facilities, and food services. The same impulse moves students to denounce what they feel to be the general regimentation of American life by large-scale organizations and their byproducts—impersonal bureaucracy and the anonymous IBM card. University regulation of political activity—the issue at Berkeley in 1964—has also been a prominent issue.

These three issues—racism, war, and the denial of personal freedoms—unquestionably were and still are contributing causes of student protest. Students have reacted strongly to these issues, speak about them with eloquence and passion, and act on them with great energy.

Moreover, students feel that government, the university, and other American institutions have not responded to their analysis of what should be done, or at least not responded rapidly enough. This has led many students to turn their attacks on the decision-making process itself. Thus, we hear slogans such as "power to the people."

Of course, students have a deep personal interest in these issues and believe that the outcome will make their own individual lives better or worse. Yet their beliefs and their protest clearly are founded on principle and ideology, not on self-interest. The war and race issues did not arise primarily because they actually and materially affected the day-to-day lives of college youth—black students again excepted. The issues were defined in terms not of interest but of principle, and their emergence was based on what we must infer to have been a fundamental change in the attitudes and principles of American students.

War and racism were not new to American society; and if their horrors and injustices were, over time, marginally diminishing rather than increasing—the emergence on campus of these issues as objects of increasingly widespread student protest could only have been the result of some further cause, a change in some factor that intervened between the *conditions* (racism, war) in the country and their emergence as *issues* that led to student protest. The emergence of these issues was caused by a change in opinions, perceptions, and values—that is, by a change in the culture of students. Students' basic ways of seeing the world became, during the 1960s, less and less tolerant of war, of racism, and of the things these entail. This shift in student culture is a basic—perhaps *the* basic—contributing cause of campus unrest.

In early Western societies, the young were traditionally submissive to adults. Largely because adults retained great authority, the only way for the young to achieve wealth, power, and prestige was through a cooperative apprenticeship of some sort to the adult world. Thus, the young learned the traditional adult ways of living, and in time they grew up to become adults of the same sort as their parents, living in the same sort of world.

Advancing industrialism decisively changed this cooperative relationship between the generations. It produced new forms and new sources of wealth, power, and prestige, and these weakened traditional adult controls over the young. It removed production from the home and made it increasingly specialized; as a result, the young were increasingly removed from adult work places and could not directly observe or participate in adult work. Moreover, industrialism hastened the separation of education from the home, in consequence of which the young were concentrated together in places of formal education that were isolated from most adults. Thus, the young spent an increasing amount of time together, apart from their parents' home and work, in activities that were different from those of adults.

This shared and distinct experience among the young led to shared interests and problems, which led, in turn, to the development of distinct subcultures. As those subcultures developed, they provided support for any youth movement that was distinct from—or even directed against—the adult world.

This subculture took its bearings from the notion of the autonomous, self-determining individual whose goal was to live with "authenticity," or in harmony with his inner penchants and instincts. It also found its identity in a rejection of the work ethic, materialism, and conventional social norms and pieties. Indeed, it rejected all institutional disciplines externally imposed upon the individual, and this set it at odds with much in American society.

Its aim was to liberate human consciousness and to enhance the quality of experience; it sought to replace the materialism, the self-denial, and the striving for achievement that characterized the existing society with a new emphasis on the expressive, the creative, the imaginative. The tools of the workaday institutional world—hierarchy, discipline, rules, self-interest, self-defense, power—it considered mad and tyrannical. It proclaimed instead the liberation of the individual to feel, to experience, to express whatever his unique humanity prompted. And its perceptions of the world grew ever more distant from the perceptions of the existing culture: what most called "justice" or "peace" or "accomplishment," the new culture envisioned as "enslavement" or "hysteria" or "meaninglessness." As this divergence of values and of vision proceeded, the new youth culture became increasingly oppositional.

No one who lives in contemporary America can be unaware of the surface manifestations of this new youth culture. Dress is highly distinctive; emphasis is placed on heightened color and sound; the enjoyment of flowers and nature is given a high priority. The fullest ranges of sense and sensation are to be enjoyed each day through the cultivation of new experiences, through spiritualism, and through drugs. Life is sought to be made as simple, primitive, and "natural" as possible, as ritualized, for example, by nude bathing.

It is not difficult to compose a picture of contemporary America as it looks through the eyes of one whose premises are essentially those just described. Human life is all; but women and children are being killed in Vietnam by American forces. All living things are sacred; but American industry and technology are polluting the air and the streams and killing the birds and the fish. The individual should stand as an individual; but American society is organized into vast structures of unions, corporations, multiversities, and government bureaucracies. Personal regard for each human being and for the absolute equality of every human soul is a categorical imperative; but American society continues to be characterized by racial injustice and discrimination. The senses and the instincts are to be trusted first; but American technology and its consequences are a monument to rationalism. Life should be lived in communion with others, and each day's sunrise and sunset enjoyed to the fullest; American society extols competition, the accumulation of goods, and the work ethic. Each man should be free to lead his own life in his own way; American organizations and statute books are filled with regulations governing dress, sex, consumption, and the accreditation of study and of work, and many of these are enforced by armed police.

An important theme of this new culture is its oppositional relationship to the larger society, as is suggested by the fact that one of its leading theorists has called it a "counterculture." If the rest of the society wears short hair, the member of this youth culture wears his hair long. If others are clean, he is dirty. If others drink alcohol and illegalize marijuana, he denounces alcohol and smokes pot. If others work in large organizations with massively complex technology, he works alone and makes sandals by hand. If others live separated, he lives in a commune. If others are for the police and the judges, he is for the accused and the prisoner. In such ways, he declares himself an alien in a larger society with which he feels himself to be fundamentally at odds.

He will also resist when the forces of the outside society seek to impose its tenets upon him. He is likely to see police as the repressive minions of the outside culture imposing its law on him and on other students by force or death if necessary. He will likely try to urge others to join him in changing the society about him in the conviction that he is seeking to save that society from bringing about its own destruction. He is likely to have apocalyptic visions of impending doom of the whole social structure and the world. He is likely to have lost hope that society can be brought to change through its own procedures. And if his psychological makeup is of a particular kind, he may conclude that the only outlet for his feelings is violence and terrorism.

In recent years, some substantial number of students in the United States and abroad have come to hold views along these lines. It is also true that a very large fraction of American college students, probably a majority, could not be said to be participants in any significant aspect of this cultural posture except for its music. As for the rest of the students, they are distributed over the entire spectrum that ranges from no participation to full participation.

But almost no college student today is unaffected by the new youth culture in some way. If he is not included, his roommate or sister or girlfriend is. If protest breaks out on his campus, he is confronted with a personal decision about his role in it. In the poetry, music, movies, and plays that students encounter, the themes of the new culture are recurrent. Even the student who finds older values more comfortable for himself will nevertheless protect and support vigorously the privilege of other students who prefer the new youth culture.

A vast majority of students are not complete adherents. But *no* significant group of students would join older generations in condemning those who are. And almost *all* students will condemn repressive efforts by the larger community to restrict or limit the life style, the art forms, and the nonviolent political manifestations of the new youth culture.

To most Americans, the development of the new youth culture is an unpleasant and often frightening phenomenon. And there is no doubt that the emergence of this student perspective has led to confrontations, injuries, and death. It is undeniable, too, that a tiny extreme fringe of fanatical devotees of the new culture have crossed the line over into outlawry and terrorism. There is a fearful and terrible irony here as, in the name of the law, the police and National Guard have killed students, and some students, under the new youth culture's banner of love and compassion, have turned to burning and bombing.

But the new youth culture itself is not a "problem" to which there is a "solution"; it is a mass social condition, a shift in basic cultural viewpoint. How long this emerging youth culture will last and what course its future development will take are open questions. But it does exist today, and it is the deeper cause of the emergence of the issues of race and war as objects of intense concern on the American campus.

III

The gap between the generations, the differing outlooks of youth and adults, was nowhere more dramatically or disturbingly evident than in the use of drugs. For many parents, the evils of drug use were so numerous that they could not begin to understand why the younger generation used them. It was illegal—and more than one adolescent would end up in a state or federal penitentiary for several years for smoking marijuana; moreover, it was dangerous—LSD, for example, caused genetic damage. And, no less important, the drug experience itself seemed to be a cop-out, a way of avoiding responsibility and adulthood. To the young, these arguments were wrong-headed or hypocritical. They reminded their parents of that earlier, ill-fated experiment with prohibition; for all the illegality of alcoholic beverages, Americans continued to drink. And they insisted that marihuana was less dangerous to health than either alcohol or nicotine. As for copping out, they either denied the charge, or insisted that there were many good reasons for doing so. On the whole, it was not easy for either side to understand the other. Attempts were made; a Senate hearing on Drug Abuse in 1971 was among them. But these efforts have not often been successful.

YOUTH AND DRUGS, 1971

TESTIMONY OF ROBERT MEINERT AND A
YOUNG DRUG USER

Mr. Meinert: Senator, I appreciate the chance of being here today to testify to the Subcommittee on Alcoholism and Narcotics. I am a policeman in Ross Township, Allegheny County, which has a population of thirty-five thousand. I have been involved in investigating drug abuse problems in Ross Township and surrounding communities for the past two and one half years. In this time several arrests have been made in our area and also communities nearby. The majority of our arrests have been made for the use and possession of marihuana and hashish, although there have been arrests in hard drugs such as heroin.

The drug abuse problem, as I see it, is definitely on the increase in areas such as Ross Township where I live. Our arrest statistics show younger children becoming involved in drug abuse every day. In Ross Township we have made an arrest of a thirteen-year-old junior high girl and she has relayed to us that several of her high school friends are trying and have tried marihuana.

In *Narcotics and Alcoholism*, Hearings Before the Subcommittee on Alcoholism and Narcotics of the Committee on Labor and Public Welfare, U.S. Senate, 92nd Congress, 1st session, January 18–19, 1971, part 1, pp. 750–58.

I also am surprised to find out how knowledgeable junior high school students are about drugs. I am not sure the knowledge they have is all the truth but nevertheless they are hearing more and more about drugs daily.

Our arrests in drug abuse have been in ages as young as thirteen years and as old as twenty-seven years of age. This of course I feel is not the true picture of the range of people involved in drug abuse for many reasons. In talking with those arrested I tried to obtain the knowledge of their problem and I also attempted to find out from them how many people are trying drugs and how many people may be addicted to drugs, and also I attempt to find out their names.

When asked on questionnaires in high school, to find the true picture of how many young people are using drugs, I hear from young people if they are trying drugs they will say no, if they are not trying drugs, they will sometimes say yes. So to have a true picture of the drug abuse problem in high schools, is a very difficult thing to find out.

In Ross Township, which again I say is thirty-five thousand population, approximately eleven thousand people under eighteen years of age, we have had eighty-seven arrests in the last two and one half years. In talking with all those arrested we attempted to find out who and how many are abusing drugs.

An attempt was made by our department and myself after receiving several names of young people who are abusing drugs, to go to the parents, confronted them with their child, daughter or son, right there, and asked them about their abuse of drugs. I do not go with search warrants, I do not go with arrest warrants. I simply say: "Mr. and Mrs. X, I understand that your son or daughter is abusing or involved in drugs."

I attempt, No. 1, to get a communication between myself and the youngster and the parents hoping that I can get at least the youngster to admit to his parents and myself that he is or has been abusing drugs. To obtain a communication between the parent and the youngster I feel is a start in the right direction.

At this time I can also plead with the parents and youngster to attempt some type of a rehabilitation, whether it be soft drugs or hard drugs.

One of the priority aspects of drug abuse, I believe, is education. I feel that first of all parents should be taught drug education so that they can in turn teach their children. As it stands, the majority of families today, the child does know more about drugs than the parent. I think in most cases the parents cannot sit down and have an intelligent conversation with the child about the drug abuse problem.

Only recently are our schools placing drug education programs in the schools. This lack of education over the past several years has naturally been the lack of educated teachers in the drug field. It is a very serious mistake to have a teacher attempt to teach a sixth grader about drugs, especially if the teacher has merely attended a three-day seminar.

In talking with young people today, again I attempt to find out how they are learning about drugs, whether through the news media or in high school or through their parents. I find out that many, many teachers are dabbling in education of drug abuse which I feel can be very damaging to the youth, when we are talking about the teachers not being educated.

Research work being conducted by the Federal Government on the effects of marihuana I feel is very important in the priority project also. The truth about marihuana, whether it proves to be harmful or not, is very important to the education of young people. I can see by a recent study that marihuana is possibly causing genetic defects in newborn babies. If this is in concrete evidence form, it would make a great difference in educating young people about using marihuana. I am saying this when I see in my estimation and in my opinion the use of LSD on the decline in an area such as Ross Township.

I also find it very difficult to answer young people in questions such as, "Why do I receive a felony record for smoking a joint—marihuana cigarette—when a numbers writer receives a hundred dollar fine and part of his organization is responsible for bringing hard narcotics to young people?"

Senator Schweiker: I would like to interrupt to say we have changed the federal law in that regard as of last year. That is not true statewide but federally we did revise the code last year.

Mr. Meinert: And I believe Pennsylvania is looking at the same thing right now. I feel that this is what they are doing.

I feel it is very important to have our laws enforced, especially when it comes to numbers writing, prostitution, and anything that feeds an organized crime syndicate. When young people see organized crime in operation and find little being done, it is very hard to talk to them about obeying laws. I have had this brought to my attention many times by young people. This may be called copping out or passing the buck, so to speak, but I feel they have a lot of good points in this respect.

Hospitals in suburban communities are going to have to start taking drug addicts in for detoxification. It seems in an area such as ours, a middle-class area, that as soon as someone hears "drug addict" or "drug abuser" they feel they themselves will become inflicted by some type of dirt. I have seen hospitals in our area taking in young people and treating them for items other than drug addiction, and when I say this I am talking about yellow jaundice and hepatitis caused by putting needles in your arms.

Senator Schweiker: You might tell us about the situation concerning your friend and let him take it from there.

Mr. Meinert: All right. This young person beside me, Senator, is eighteen years of age; and I have had the occasion to arrest this young person for drug abuse. I first try to talk young people out of using drugs. Of course, I am not in counseling, I am in the enforcement end, although I do take this on as part of my job.

This young person had started using drugs at the age of—I believe he might even tell me younger than what I know—fifteen years of age. He has used, I think, every drug that is on the market and for a short time I believe was addicted to heroin. Now I hope he is not any longer. He has used all the drugs in the soft variety—marihuana, LSD, hashish. He has used amphetamines, barbiturates, heroin, cocaine. I think he may be able to enlighten us about the ideas of young people getting involved in drug abuse at age fifteen in communities such as Ross Township and maybe in communities all across the United States.

Senator Schweiker: For lack of a better name we will call you John. First tell us whatever comes to your mind about this problem and then I will have some questions. You have been pretty patient listening to a lot of us experts who probably don't know the problem at all. You certainly are in a position to give us some help and advice, so go ahead.

John: For one thing I was never addicted to heroin, I used it a couple of times but was not addicted to it.

Another thing, I started a little earlier than fifteen.

The problem of pills around the outlying suburbs really is not in the hard drugs that much although there are a couple people using it. The thing is now with the marihuana and LSD and barbiturates and such like that, but I can fastly see heroin creeping up on everybody, even the younger kids. I think the best thing to do right now is to try to counterattack the heroin. Certainly the marihuana is like in the background. Try to stop the heroin and morphine and the amphetamines and barbiturates, put the pressure on the people that are using the hard drugs. A lot more than you know the people are using soft drugs. Educate the people to the soft drugs and stop the people in the hard drugs is what I think.

Senator Schweiker: John, why do you think the young generation today turns or looks toward drugs as an outlet? In other words, what is the allure, what is the appeal, and what are some of the reasons? We hear a lot of different opinions and I would be glad to get yours.

John: It's fun. It started like, you know, a kick like back when everybody started in San Francisco and the younger generation, the hippies and the flower people, so it just gradually went on like the stone rolling down the hill and it has come to the point where a sixteen-year-old kid does not think anything of putting a needle in his arm where if you mention that to a middle-class kid before he would probably flip out and go crazy or something.

I don't know. I just think it is like the thing to do now. Now instead of going out and getting drunk, you go get stoned.

Senator Schweiker: In terms of your own case, what factor or what developments were instrumental or helpful to you to take a second look at the whole pattern? What triggered it, what was the turning point, and what circumstances changed your outlook, would you say?

John: It sort of got boring dropping LSD, you know. I still smoke weed and hash a lot but it got boring dropping out and stuff, so I thought maybe I will get some hard drugs and see what that is like. I did that and I could see my personality changing and I was getting a mean disposition all the time. I now just don't think I'm that kind of person so I changed, I just quit. Now I just drink a lot of wine and smoke a little bit of weed.

Senator Schweiker: You are probably in a position to offer us some advice concerning one of the questions we are continually asked. How deep a problem is this with our young people today? How would you define it in terms of the people that you know and associate with and those of your age group? Statistically or percentagewise, how widespread a problem is it? That is one thing we don't know or seem to be able to put our finger on. I realize you can only go by your own immediate circle of friends and associates, but that might be helpful to us.

John: Well, there are not too many people I know that don't smoke marihuana and smoke hash. I know a lot of people that don't use hard drugs and a lot of them that don't use psychedelics but just about everybody I know smokes weed all the time. It is just like a social thing, you know.

Senator Schweiker: Would you say that hard drug usage is on the increase, decrease, or about the same with your age bracket?

John: It is really getting on the increase.

Senator Schweiker: It is getting on the increase?

John: Yes.

Senator Schweiker: Is this mainly heroin or LSD?

John: In my area?

Senator Schweiker: Yes.

John: In the North Hills?

Senator Schweiker: Yes.

John: It is a combination of a lot of drug stores, you know. Narcotics like morphine and barbiturates and more amphetamines and stuff. There is a lot of heroin and cocaine around.

Senator Schweiker: Is there anything that you can suggest to our committee that we ought to be doing that we are not doing? What are we doing wrong, and where did we miss the boat in not being tuned in on, so to speak, to the problem? Do you have any advice in that regard?

John: Better educate the officers that are concerned with this. A lot of times the officers that are helping Officer Meinert and other people like him just ruin the whole thing, like they counterattack all the good that is done by being stupid. I would send them to the school so they know what is going on, too, you know. You can't have somebody that is walking the beat and taking care of old age and stuff try to nab somebody that is geared up.

Senator Schweiker: Regarding the school you attended, and I don't want to get into names or anything, what was the attitude of the faculty there? How would you rate what they did or didn't do or try to do? How would you evaluate their role in this thing?

John: Well, I can't really say, I didn't go to school too much. Mostly they didn't care one way or the other from what I noticed. Like we used to smoke joints in the lab. I have even seen people getting off. It is just like a teacher walks in and everybody is smoking cigarettes and the other guys are in the booths kicking off and they just dump everything down the toilet. So the teachers really don't know what is going on.

Senator Schweiker: Taking into account the way our society is set up today, who will young people listen to? For example, one of the approaches used is to elicit the help of someone who has been through the ropes, either an addict or a person like yourself who has had some experience with it. Are they the best people to reach other people? Who is the best rap person or persons to reach and influence young people?

John: I always thought it was a personal thing. You yourself have to get yourself out of it, you know. I really have not met anybody that was really good at talking you out of it unless they had the figures and everything to put in front of you. Like in Boulder, Colo., the whole town, the old people and everybody, the Government, were trying to wipe out all the hard drugs and in turn they said that they don't care if people are smoking weed as long as they are not using hard drugs. All the freaks in the town are smoking weed or trying to get rid of the hard dopers, too, trying to throw them out of town. It is working pretty good from what I hear, I really don't know. What I have read, it sounds like it is working.

IV

In our own times, the most novel anti-institutional institution is the commune. It represents one alternative to the American culture— it is a way of saying no to the city, to industry, to the traditional family, to middle-class values. Precisely what it affirms is less clear. Unlike other communitarian ventures, the communes are not self-sufficient; the turnover in membership is especially rapid, and there is really no sustained ideological base to the movement. Earlier experiments (such as the Puritans' "city on a hill" or Robert Owen's New Harmony colony) were self-consciously attempting to teach the larger society the way it should go; the latest experiments seem more concerned with self-satisfaction than broad social reform. Hence, as the description below of one California commune makes clear, the larger community will not find answers to its problems in the commune experience. But its very popularity at this time does indicate the extent of the dissatisfaction and disillusionment with the organization and structure of American society in the 1970s.

GETTING BACK TO THE
COMMUNAL GARDEN, 1970

SARA DAVIDSON

I had started north from San Francisco in late afternoon, having heard vague descriptions of a commune called Wheeler's that was much beloved by those who had passed through it. At sunset, a storm came up, and rather than turn back, I continued slowly along narrow, unlit country roads. An hour later, the rain let up, and a few feet from the car I found a crude sign with an arrow, "Wheeler's." After six miles, there was a gate and a sign, "Beware of Cattle." I opened it and drove

In *Harper's*, 240 (June 1970): 89–96. Copyright © 1970 by Harper's Magazine, Inc. Reprinted by permission of Curtis Brown, Ltd.

down to a fork. Another fork. To the left the road was impassable—deep ruts and rocks; to the right, a barbed-wire fence. Raining harder, darker. This is enough. Get out of here fast. Try to turn the car around. Struggling to see . . . then the sickening dip.

[The next morning] I walked a mile, then another mile, through rolling green hills, thinking, "If I can just get out of here." At last, around a bend were two tents and a sign, "Welcome, God, love." The first tent had a light burning inside, and turned out to be a greenhouse filled with boxes of seedlings. At the second tent, I pushed open the door and bells tinkled. Someone with streaked brown hair was curled in a real bed on two mattresses. There was linoleum on the floor, a small stove, a table, and books and clothes neatly arranged on shelves. The young man lifted his head and smiled. "Come in."

I was covered with mud, my hair was wild, and my eyes red and twitching. "I tried to drive in last night, my car went down a ravine and got stuck in the mud, and I've been sleeping in it all night."

"Far out," he said.

"I was terrified."

The young man, who had gray eyes set close together and one gold earring, said, "Of what?"

"There were horses."

He laughed. "Far out. One of the horses walked into Nancy's house and made a hole in the floor. Now she just sweeps her dirt and garbage down the hole."

My throat was burning. "Could we make some coffee?"

He looked at me sideways. "I don't have any." He handed me a clump of green weeds. "Here's some yerba buena. You can make tea." I stared at the weeds.

"What's your name?" I asked.

"Shoshone."

"Mine's Sara."

"Far out."

He got dressed, watered the plants in the greenhouse, and started down a path into the bushes, motioning for me to follow. Every few feet, he would stop to pick yerba buena, listen to birds, watch a trio of pheasants take off, and admire trees that were recently planted—almond, Elberta peach, cherry, plum.

The dwellings at Wheeler's are straight out of Dogpatch—old boards nailed unevenly together, odd pieces of plastic strung across poles to make wobbly igloos, with round stovepipes poking out the side. Most have dirt floors, though the better ones have wood. We came to a crooked green shack with a peace sign on the door and the inside papered with paintings of Krishna. Nancy, a blond former social worker, was sleeping on the floor with her children, Gregory, eight, and Michelle, nine. Nancy said, "Sunday's the best day here. You've got to stay for the steam bath and the feast. There'll be lots of visitors."

Shoshone and I walked back to the main road that cuts across the three hundred and twenty-acre ranch. The sun had burned through the fog, highlighting streaks of yellow wild flowers in the fields. Black Angus cows were grazing by the road. People in hillbilly clothes, with funny hats and sashes, were coming out of the bushes carrying musical instruments and sacks of rice and beans. About a mile from the front gate we came to the community garden, with a scarecrow made of rusty metal in the shape of a nude girl. Two children were chasing each other from row to row, shrieking with laughter, as their mother picked cabbage. A sign read, "Permit not required to settle here."

The garden, like a jigsaw puzzle whose pieces have floated together, presents the image of a nineteenth-century tableau: women in long skirts and shawls, men in lace-up boots, coveralls, and patched jeans tied with pieces of rope, sitting on the grass playing banjos, guitars, lyres, wood flutes, dulcimers, and an accordian. In a field to the right are the community animals—chickens, cows, goats, donkeys, and horses. As far as the eye can see, there are no houses, no traffic, nothing but verdant hills, a stream, and the ocean with whitecaps rising in the distance. Nine-year-old Michelle is prancing about in a pink shawl and a floppy hat warbling, "It's time for the feast!" Nancy says, "The pickin's are sort of spare, because tomorrow is welfare day and everybody's broke." She carries from the outdoor wood stove pots of brown rice—plain, she says, "for the purists who are on Georges Ohsawa's ten-day brown-rice diet"—and rice with fruit and nuts for everyone else.

Bill Wheeler was working in his studio, an airy, wood-and-glass building with large skylights, set on a hill. When Bill bought the ranch in 1963, looking for a place to paint and live quietly, he built the studio for his family. Four years later, when he opened the land to anyone who wanted to settle there, the county condemned his studio as living quarters because it lacked the required amount of concrete under one side. Bill moved into a tent and used the studio for his painting and for community meetings.

Bill is a tall, lean man of thirty with an aristocratic forehead, straight nose, deep-set blue eyes, and a full beard and flowing hair streaked yellow by the sun. His voice is gentle with a constant hint of mirth, yet it projects, like his clear gaze, a strength which is understood in this community as divine grace. He lives at the center of the ranch with his third wife, Gay, twenty-two, and their infant daughter, Raspberry. His humor and self-assurance make it easy for those around him to submit to the hippie credo that "God will provide," because they know that what God does not, Bill Wheeler will.

Everyone who lives at Wheeler's ranch is a vegetarian. By some strange inversion, they feel that by eating meat they are hastening their own death. Bill Wheeler says that diet is "very, very central to the revolution. It's a freeing process which people go through, from living on processed foods and eating gluttonous portions of meat and potatoes, to natural foods and a simple diet that is kinder to your body. A lot has to do with economics. It's much cheaper to live on grains and vegetables you can grow in your garden. When Gay and I moved here, we had to decide whether to raise animals to slaughter. Gay said she couldn't do it. Every Thanksgiving, there's a movement to raise money to buy turkeys, because some people think the holiday isn't complete without them. But an amazing thing happens when carrion is consumed. People are really greedy, and it's messy. The stench and the grease stay with us for days."

Gravy, roast beef, mashed potatoes, Parker House rolls, buttered peas—the weekly fare when Bill was growing up in Bridgeport, Connecticut. His father, a lawyer who speculated famously in real estate, told Bill he could do anything with his life as long as he got an education. So Bill, self-reliant, introspective, who loved the outdoors, went to Yale and studied painting. After graduating, he came to San Francisco to find a farmhouse where he could work. When he saw the three hundred and twenty acre ranch which was then a sheep and Christmas tree farm, he felt, "I've got to have it. This is my land." He bought it with his inheritance, and still has enough money to live comfortably the rest of his life. "My parents would be shocked out of their gourds if they saw the land now," Bill says. "They died before I opened it."

The idea of open land, or free land, was introduced to Bill by Lou Gottlieb, a singer with the pop folk group, "The Limelighters," who, in 1962, bought a thirty-two-acre piece of land called Morning Star about ten miles from Wheeler's Ranch. Gottlieb visits Wheeler's every Sunday for the feast.

"From the first, the land selected the people. Those who couldn't work hard didn't survive. When the land got crowded, people split. The vibrations of the land will always protect the community." Gottlieb points to the sky. "With open land, *He* is the casting director." What happens, I ask, if someone behaves violently or destructively? Gottlieb frowns. "There have been a few cases where we've had to ask people to go, but it's at terrible, terrible cost to everyone's soul that this is done. When the land begins to throw off people, everyone suffers." He shakes his body, as if he were the land, rejecting a germ. "Open land has no historical precedent. When you give free land, not free food or money, you pull the carpet out from under the capitalist system. Once a piece of land is freed, 'no trespassing' signs pop up all along the adjoining roads."

Bill Wheeler refers to his ranch as "the land," and talks about people who live on the land, babies that are born on the land, music played on the land.

It was surprising to hear people refer to themselves as "hippies"; I thought the term had been rendered meaningless by overuse. Our culture has absorbed so much of the style of hip—clothes, hair, language, drugs, music—that it has obscured the substance of the movement with which people at Morning Star and Wheeler's still strongly identify. Being a hippie, to them, means dropping out completely, and finding another way to live, to support oneself physically and spiritually. It does not mean being a company freak, working nine to five in a straight job and roaming the East Village on weekends. It means saying no to competition, no to the work ethic, no to consumption of technology's products, no to political systems and games. Lou Gottlieb, who was once a Communist party member, says, "The entire Left is a dead end." The hippie alternative is to turn inward and reach backward for roots, simplicity, and the tribal experience. In the first bloom of the movement, people flowed into slums where housing would be cheap and many things could be obtained free—food scraps from restaurants, second-hand clothes, free clinics and services. But the slums proved inhospitable. The hippies did nothing to improve the dilapidated neighborhoods, and they were preyed upon by criminals, pushers, and the desperate. In late 1967, they began trekking to rural land where there would be few people and life would be hard. They took up what Ramon Sender calls "voluntary primitivism," building houses out of mud and trees, planting and harvesting crops by hand, rolling loose tobacco into cigarettes, grinding their own wheat, baking bread, canning vegetables, delivering their own babies, and educating their own children. They gave up electricity, the telephone, running water, gas stoves, even rock music, which, of all things, is supposed to be the cornerstone of hip culture. They started to sing and play their own music—folksy and quiet.

Getting close to the earth meant conditioning their bodies to cold, discomfort, and strenuous exercise. At Wheeler's, people walk twenty miles a day, carrying water and food, gardening, and visiting each other. Only four-wheel-drive vehicles can cross the ranch, and ultimately Bill wants all cars banned. "We would rather live without machines. And the fact that we have no good roads protects us from tourists. People are car-bound, even police. They would never come in here without their vehicles." Although it rains a good part of the year, most of the huts do not have stoves and are not waterproof. "Houses shouldn't be designed to keep out the weather," Bill says. "We want to get in touch with it." He installed six chemical toilets on the ranch to comply with county sanitation requirements, but, he says, "I wouldn't go in one of those toilets if you paid me. It's very important for us to be able to use the ground, because we are completing a cycle, returning to Mother Earth what she's given us." Garbage is also returned to the ground. Food scraps are buried in a compost pile of sawdust and hay until they decompose and mix with the soil. Paper is burned, and metal buried. But not everyone is conscientious; there are piles of trash on various parts of the ranch.

Because of the haphazard sanitation system, the water at Wheeler's is contaminated, and until people adjust to it, they suffer dysentery, just as tourists do who drink the water in Mexico. There are periodic waves of hepatitis, clap, crabs, scabies, and streptococcic throat infections. No one brushes his teeth more than once a week, and then they often use "organic toothpaste," made from eggplant cooked in tinfoil. They are experimenting with herbs and Indian healing remedies to become free of manufactured medicinal drugs, but see no contradiction in continuing to swallow any mind-altering chemical they are offered. The delivery of babies on the land has become an important ritual. With friends, children, and animals keeping watch, chanting, and getting collectively stoned, women have given birth to babies they have named Morning Star, Psyche Joy, Covelo Vishnu God, Rainbow Canyon King, and Raspberry Sundown Hummingbird Wheeler.

The childbirth ritual and the weekly feasts are conscious attempts at what is called "retribalization." But Wheeler's Ranch, like many hippie settlements, has rejected communal living in favor of a loose community of individuals. People live alone or in monogamous units, cook for themselves, and build their own houses and sometimes gardens. "There should not be a main lodge, because you get too many people trying to live under one roof and it doesn't work," Bill says. As a result, there are cliques who eat together, share resources, and rarely mix with others on the ranch.

Because of the fluidity of the community, it is almost impossible for it to become economically self-sufficient. None of the communes have been able to live entirely off the land. Most are unwilling to go into cash crops or light industry because in an open community with no rules, there are not enough people who can be counted on to work regularly. The women with children receive welfare, some of the men collect unemployment and food stamps, and others get money from home. They spend very little—perhaps six hundred dollars a year per person. "We're not up here to make money," Bill says, "or to live like country squires."

When darkness falls, the ranch becomes eerily quiet and mobility stops. No one uses flashlights. Those who have lived there some time can feel their way along the paths by memory. Others stay in their huts, have dinner, go to sleep, and get up with the sun. Around 7:00 P.M., people gather at the barn with bottles for the late milking. During the week, the night milking is the main social event. Corky says, "It's the only time you know you're going to see people. Otherwise you could wander around for days and not see anyone."

With morning comes a hailstorm, and Bill Wheeler must go to court in Santa Rosa for trial on charges of assaulting a policeman when a squad came to the ranch looking for juvenile runaways and Army deserters. It is a tedious day. Witnesses give conflicting testimony, but all corroborate that one of the officers struck Wheeler first, leading to a shoving, running, tackling, pot-throwing skirmish which also involved Peter. The defendants spend the night in a motel, going over testimony with their lawyer. Bill and Corky go to a supermarket to buy dinner, and wheel down the aisle checking labels for chemicals, opening jars to take a taste with the finger, uhmmmh, laughing at the "obsolete consciousness" of the place. They buy greens, Roquefort dressing, peanut butter, organic honey, and two Sara Lee cakes.

The jury goes out at 3:00 P.M. and deliberates until 9:00. In the courtroom, a mottled group in pioneer clothes, mud-spattered and frizzy-wet, are chanting, "Om." The jury cannot agree on four counts, and finds Bill and Peter not guilty on three counts. The judge declares a mistrial. The county fathers are not finished, though. They are still attempting to close the access road to Wheeler's and to get an injunction to raze all buildings on the ranch as health hazards. Bill Wheeler is not worried, nor are his charges, climbing in the jeep and singing, "Any day now . . ." God will provide.

SUGGESTIONS FOR
FURTHER READING

Kenneth C. Jackson, *The K.K.K. in the Cities: 1915–1930* (New York, 1967) shows the broad base of support for the *Ku Klux Klan*. The power of anti-immigrant sentiments in this country is analyzed by John Higham, *Strangers in the Land* (New Brunswick, N.J., 1955). Joseph Gusfield, *Symbolic Crusade: Status Politics and the American Temperance Movement* (Urbana, Ill., 1963), ably links this subject to the broader issue.

For an exploration of the implications of living conditions for the *Urban Family*, begin with David Kennedy, *Birth Control in America: The Career of Margaret Sanger* (New Haven, 1970). Pertinent too is William O'Neill, *Divorce in the Progressive Era* (New Haven, 1967). A general survey of the material is William Chafe, *The American Woman: 1920–1970* (New York, 1972).

The quality of life in the *Black Ghetto* is portrayed vividly in Robert Coles's *Children of Crisis* (New York, 1967); see also his *The South Goes North* (Boston, 1972) for an intimate reporting of the black urban experience. A relevant collection of documents is August Meier and Elliot Rudwick, eds., *Black Protest in the 1960's* (New York, 1970).

For the views of *Women Liberationists* see Vivian Gornick and Barbara Moran, eds., *Woman in Sexist Society* (New York, 1971) and Mary Jane Sherfy, *The Nature and Evolution of Female Sexuality* (New York, 1973).

One major statement on behalf of the *Counterculture* in Charles Reich *The Greening of America* (New York, 1970). On youth in contemporary American society see Kenneth Keniston, *The Uncommitted* (New York, 1965) and *Young Radicals* (New York, 1968). Testimony on worker alienation runs through the pages of Studs Terkel, *Working* (New York, 1974). For a different view of where our society is heading, see Daniel Bell *The Coming of Post-Industrial Society* (New York, 1973).